Honda CBR125R, CBR250R/RA and CRF250L/M
Service and Repair Manual

by Matthew Coombs

(5919-352)

Models covered
CBR125R. 124.7cc. 2011-on
CBR250R/RA. 249.6cc. 2011 to 2014
CRF250L. 249.6cc. 2013-on
CRF250M. 249.6cc. 2014-on

© Haynes Publishing 2014

A book in the Haynes Service and Repair Manual Series

ABCDE
FGHIJ
KLMNO
PQRST

ISBN: **978 0 85733 919 5**

Library of Congress Control Number 2014944110

Printed in the USA

Haynes Publishing
Sparkford, Yeovil, Somerset BA22 7JJ, England

Haynes North America, Inc
861 Lawrence Drive, Newbury Park, California 91320, USA

Haynes Publishing Nordiska AB
Box 1504, 751 45 Uppsala, Sweden

Printed using 33-lb Resolute Book 65 4.0 from Resolute Forest Products Calhoun, TN mill. Resolute is a member of World Wildlife Fund's Climate Savers programme committed to significantly reducing GHG emissions. This paper uses 50% less wood fibre than traditional offset. The Calhoun Mill is certified to the following sustainable forest management and chain of custody standards: SFI, PEFC and FSC Controlled Wood.

Contents

Contents

REPAIRS AND OVERHAUL

REFERENCE

The Birth of a Dream

by Julian Ryder

There is no better example of the Japanese post-War industrial miracle than Honda. Like other companies which have become household names, it started with one man's vision. In this case the man was the 40-year old Soichiro Honda who had sold his piston-ring manufacturing business to Toyota in 1945 and was happily spending the proceeds on prolonged parties for his friends.

However, the difficulties of getting around in the chaos of post-War Japan irked Honda, so when he came across a job lot of generator engines he realised that here was a way of getting people mobile again at low cost.

A 12 by 18-foot shack in Hamamatsu became his first bike factory, fitting the generator motors into pushbikes. Before long he'd used up all 500 generator motors and started manufacturing his own engine, known as the 'chimney', either because of the elongated cylinder head or the smoky exhaust or perhaps both. The chimney made all of half a horsepower from its 50 cc engine but it was a major success and became the Honda A-type.

Less than two years after he'd set up in Hamamatsu, Soichiro Honda founded the Honda Motor Company in September 1948. By then, the A-type had been developed into the 90 cc B-type engine, which Mr Honda decided deserved its own chassis not a bicycle frame. Honda was about to become Japan's first post-War manufacturer of complete motorcycles. In August 1949 the first prototype was ready. With an output of three horsepower, the 98 cc D-type was still a simple two-stroke but it had a two-speed transmission and most importantly a pressed steel frame with telescopic forks and hard tail rear end. The frame was almost triangular in profile with the top rail going in a straight line from the massively braced steering head to the rear axle. Legend has it that after the D-type's first tests the entire workforce went for a drink to celebrate and try and think of a name for the bike. One man broke one of those silences you get when people are thinking, exclaiming 'This is like a dream!' 'That's it!' shouted Honda, and so the Honda Dream was christened.

'This is like a dream!' 'That's it' shouted Honda

Mr Honda was a brilliant, intuitive engineer and designer but he did not bother himself with the marketing side of his business. With hindsight, it is possible to see that employing Takeo Fujisawa who would both sort out the home market and plan the eventual expansion into overseas markets was a masterstroke. He arrived in October 1949 and in 1950 was made Sales Director. Another vital new name was Kiyoshi Kawashima, who along with Honda himself, designed the company's first four-stroke after Kawashima had told them that the four-stroke opposition to Honda's two-strokes sounded nicer and therefore sold better. The result of that statement was the overhead-valve 148 cc E-type which first ran in July 1951 just two months after the first drawings were made. Kawashima was made a director of the Honda Company at 34 years old.

The E-type was a massive success, over 32,000 were made in 1953 alone, a feat of mass-production that was astounding by the

Honda C70 and C90 OHV-engined models

standards of the day given the relative complexity of the machine. But Honda's lifelong pursuit of technical innovation sometimes distracted him from commercial reality. Fujisawa pointed out that they were in danger of ignoring their core business, the motorised bicycles that still formed Japan's main means of transport. In May 1952 the F-type Cub appeared, another two-stroke despite the top men's reservations. You could buy a complete machine or just the motor to attach to your own bicycle. The result was certainly distinctive, a white fuel tank with a circular profile went just below and behind the saddle on the left of the bike, and the motor with its horizontal cylinder and bright red cover just below the rear axle on the same side of the bike. This was the machine that turned Honda into the biggest bike maker in Japan with 70% of the market for bolt-on bicycle motors, the F-type was also the first Honda to be exported. Next came the machine that would turn Honda into the biggest motorcycle manufacturer in the world.

The C100 Super Cub was a typically audacious piece of Honda engineering and marketing. For the first time, but not the last, Honda invented a completely new type of motorcycle, although the term 'scooterette' was coined to describe the new bike which had many of the characteristics of a scooter but the large wheels, and therefore stability, of a motorcycle. The first one was sold in August 1958, fifteen years later over nine-million of them were on the roads of the world. If ever a machine can be said to have brought mobility to the masses it is the Super Cub. If you add in the electric starter that was added for the C102 model of 1961, the design of the Super Cub has remained substantially unchanged ever since, testament to how right Honda got it first time. The Super Cub made Honda the world's biggest manufacturer after just two years of production.

Honda's export drive started in earnest in 1957 when Britain and Holland got their first bikes, America got just two bikes the next year. By 1962 Honda had half the American market with 65,000 sales. But Soichiro Honda had already travelled abroad to Europe and the USA, making a special point of going to the Isle of Man TT, then the most important race in the GP calendar. He realised that no matter how advanced his products were, only racing success would convince overseas markets for whom 'Made in Japan' still meant cheap and nasty. It took five years from Soichiro Honda's first visit to the Island before his bikes were ready for the TT. In 1959 the factory entered five riders in the 125. They did not have a massive impact on the event being benevolently regarded as a curiosity, but sixth, seventh and eighth were good enough for the team prize. The bikes were off the pace but they were well engineered and very reliable.

The TT was the only time the West saw the Hondas in '59, but they came back for more

The CB250N Super Dream became a favorite with UK learner riders of the late seventies and early eighties

the following year with the first of a generation of bikes which shaped the future of motorcycling - the double-overhead-cam four-cylinder 250. It was fast and reliable - it revved to 14,000 rpm - but didn't handle anywhere near as well as the opposition.

However, Honda had now signed up non-Japanese riders to lead their challenge. The first win didn't come until 1962 (Aussie Tom Phillis in the Spanish 125 GP) and was followed up with a world-shaking performance at the TT. Twenty-one year old Mike

The GL1000 introduced in 1975, was the first in Honda's line of Goldwings

Hailwood won both 125 and 250 cc TTs and Hondas filled the top five positions in both races. Soichiro Honda's master plan was starting to come to fruition, Hailwood and Honda won the 1961 250 cc World Championship. Next year Honda won three titles. The other Japanese factories fought back and inspired Honda to produce some of the most fascinating racers ever seen: the awesome six-cylinder 250, the five-cylinder 125, and the 500 four with which the immortal Hailwood battled Agostini and the MV Agusta. When Honda pulled out of racing in '67 they had won sixteen rider's titles, eighteen manufacturer's titles, and 137 GPs, including 18 TTs, and introduced the concept of the modern works team to motorcycle racing. Sales success followed racing victory as Soichiro Honda had predicted, but only because the products advanced as rapidly as the racing machinery. The Hondas that came to Britain in the early '60s were incredibly sophisticated. They had overhead cams where the British bikes had pushrods, they had electric starters when the Brits relied on the kickstart, they had 12V electrics when even the biggest British bike used a 6V system. There seemed no end to the technical wizardry. It wasn't that the technology itself was so amazing but just like that first E-Type, it was the fact that Honda could mass-produce it more reliably than the

Carl Fogarty in action at the Suzuka 8 hour on the RC45

lower-tech competition that was so astonishing.

When in 1968 the first four-cylinder CB750 road bike arrived the world of motorcycling changed for ever, they even had to invent a

An early CB750 Four

new word for it, 'Superbike'. Honda raced again with the CB750 at Daytona and won the World Endurance title with a prototype DOHC version that became the CB900 roadster. There was the six-cylinder CBX, the CX500T – the world's first turbocharged production bike, they invented the full-dress tourer with the GoldWing, and came back to GPs with the revolutionary oval-pistoned NR500 four-stroke, a much-misunderstood bike that was more a rolling experimental laboratory than a racer. Just to show their versatility Honda also came up with the weird CX500 shaft-drive V-twin, a rugged workhorse that powered a new industry, the courier companies that oiled the wheels of commerce in London and other big cities.

It was true, though, that Mr Honda was not keen on two-strokes – early motocross engines had to be explained away to him as lawnmower motors! However, in 1982 Honda raced the NS500, an agile three-cylinder lightweight against the big four-cylinder opposition in 500 GPs. The bike won in its first year and in '83 took the world title for Freddie Spencer. In four-stroke racing the V4 layout took over from the straight four, dominating TT, F1 and Endurance championships with the RVF750, the nearest thing ever built to a Formula 1 car on wheels. And when Superbike arrived Honda were ready with the RC30. On the roads the VFR V4 became an instant classic while the CBR600 invented another new class of bike on its way to becoming a best-seller. The V4 road bikes had problems to start with but the VFR750 sold world-wide over its lifetime while the VFR400 became a massive commercial success and cult bike in Japan. The original RC30 won the first two World Superbike Championships is 1988 and '89, but Honda had to wait until 1997 to win it again with the RC45, the last of the V4 roadsters. In Grands Prix, the NSR500 V4 two-stroke superseded the NS triple and became the benchmark racing machine of the '90s. Mick Doohan secured his place in history by winning five World Championships in consecutive years on it.

In yet another example of Honda inventing a new class of motorcycle, they came up with the astounding CBR900RR FireBlade, a bike with the punch of a 1000 cc motor in a package the size and weight of a 750. It became a cult bike as well as a best seller, and with judicious redesigns continues to give much more recent designs a run for their money.

When it became apparent that the high-tech V4 motor of the RC45 was too expensive to produce, Honda looked to a V-twin engine to power its flagship for the first time. Typically, the VTR1000 FireStorm was a much more rideable machine than its opposition and once accepted by the market formed the basis of the next generation of Superbike racer, the VTR-SP-1.

One of Mr Honda's mottos was that technology would solve the customers' problems, and no company has embraced cutting-edge technology more firmly than Honda. In fact Honda often developed new technology, especially in the fields of materials science and metallurgy. The embodiment of that was the NR750, a bike that was misunderstood nearly as much as the original NR500 racer. This limited-edition technological tour-de-force embodied many of Soichiro Honda's ideals. It used the latest techniques and materials in every component, from the oval piston, 32-valve V4 motor to the titanium coating on the windscreen, it was – as Mr Honda would have wanted – the best it could possibly be. A fitting memorial to the man who has shaped the motorcycle industry and motorcyles as we know them today.

The CX500 – Honda's first V-Twin and a favorite choice of dispatch riders

The new CBR and CRF

One of the many things Honda is clever at is drawing on their history, seemingly keeping the same design alive for longer than is feasible by subtle updates or by giving new designs the hallmarks of an older model. The first four-stroke Honda, the CB125, appeared in the early 1970s and had a model life of over ten years before the two-stoke NS appeared, swiftly followed by the NSR. The era of the two-stroke race-replica saw a need for another four-stroke 125 Honda.

The globalisation of the industry meant there was one still being made up to 2008, the CG125 produced by factories in Brazil and Turkey. This was a determinedly low-tech bike with an OHV engine rather than the CB's SOHC unit, designed to survive the rigours of use in developing countries. That clearly wouldn't do for the modern world. That meant the water-cooled CBR125, in production in Thailand since 2004 and designed for the Far Eastern market was adapted for other markets. Originally the motor used a carburettor but was upgraded to Honda's PGM-FI fuel injection in 2007 as part of a raft of engine updates. The result was a CBR600 lookalike but rather a small bike by the standards of european riders.

Meanwhile the emerging market of India, with its enormous potential, needed some suitable models. Enter the CBR250R, another fuel-injected water-cooled single, but this time with double overhead cams. It first appeared in

The 2013 CBR125R

The 2013 CBR250RA in Repsol trim

The 2013 CRF250L

The 2014 CRF250M

late 2010 for the Thai market, where the bike was also manufactured, before being launched on the Japanese home market. At the same time in early 2011, an Indian-made CBR250R was launched in India and some South American markets. As it would have been a serious error to try and palm those markets off with a parts-bin special, the 250R got a new engine and an up-to-date styling package derived from the VFR range. The same engine also got a home in the CRF-M and CRF-L models with trailbike and supermoto styling. Despite the nomenclature and engine capacity, they share nothing with the CRF-R and CRF-X, which are genuine competition models.

The CBR250's lines are very much based on the big VFR1300 sports tourer, another subtle change of emphasis away from the sports-bike references that were obligatory for small bikes in the two-stroke era and continued with the first CBR125. For the model's first major revamp for the 2011 model year, the CBR125 shed its CBR600 bodywork and followed the 250's example by adopting the big VFR's look. In fact the only thing common to the two models is the engine, the rest of the motorcycle is significantly different.

The new model feels much more like a big bike. That's not just because it is indeed physically bigger in line with the difference in size of the average European rider compared to the average in Asian markets. The major difference is the increase in section of the rear tyre from 110 to 130, giving a much more secure feel on the road. The look of Honda's four-stroke 125 may have changed over the years, but very little else has. The SOHC motor has kept up with the times and legislation by growing fuel injection and water cooling, but one thing has remained constant. The bikes have been favourites with learner riders and in developing markets alike because they just go on and on. CG, CB, CBR, or CBR-R, they have all been bullet proof against the ham-fisted learner or road conditions in rural India. Generations of riders have started out on them and will continue to do so for as long as Honda make them.

Acknowledgements

Our thanks are due to Bransons Motorcycles of Yeovil who supplied the machines featured in the illustrations throughout this manual. We would also like to thank NGK Spark Plugs (UK) Ltd for supplying the colour spark plug condition photographs, the Avon Rubber Company for supplying information on tyre fitting and Draper Tools Ltd for some of the workshop tools shown.

Thanks are also due to Julian Ryder who wrote the introduction 'The Birth of a Dream' and to Honda (UK) Ltd. for use of model photographs.

About this Manual

The aim of this manual is to help you get the best value from your motorcycle. It can do so in several ways. It can help you decide what work must be done, even if you choose to have it done by a dealer; it provides information and procedures for routine maintenance and servicing; and it offers diagnostic and repair procedures to follow when trouble occurs.

We hope you use the manual to tackle the work yourself. For many simpler jobs, doing it yourself may be quicker than arranging an appointment to get the motorcycle into a dealer and making the trips to leave it and pick it up. More importantly, a lot of money can be saved by avoiding the expense the dealer must pass on to you to cover its labour and overhead costs. An added benefit is the sense of satisfaction and accomplishment that you feel after doing the job yourself.

References to the left or right side of the motorcycle assume you are sitting on the seat, facing forward.

We take great pride in the accuracy of information given in this manual, but motorcycle manufacturers make alterations and design changes during the production run of a particular motorcycle of which they do not inform us. No liability can be accepted by the authors or publishers for loss, damage or injury caused by any errors in, or omissions from, the information given.

Illegal copying

Frame and engine numbers

The frame serial number is stamped into the right-hand side of the steering head. The engine number is stamped into the left-hand side of the crankcase. Both of these numbers should be recorded and kept in a safe place so they can be given to law enforcement officials in the event of a theft. There is also a colour code label on the top of the rear mudguard on CBR models, visible after removing the passenger seat, and on the frame behind the rear brake fluid reservoir on CRF models. The throttle body also has an ID number stamped into it.

The frame serial number, engine serial number, and colour code should also be kept in a handy place (such as with your driver's licence) so they are always available when purchasing or ordering parts for your machine.

The procedures in this manual identify models by their code letters (e.g. CBR or CRF), engine size (e.g. 125 or 250) and by model suffix (e.g. CBR250RA or CRF250L), as required according to procedural differences.

The model suffix is followed by a production year letter as shown in the table below. The full model code, including the production year appears on the colour code label attached to the frame.

Model	Year
CBR125RWB	2011
CBR125RC/RSC/RTC	2012
CBR125RD/RSD/RTD	2013/14
CBR250RB	2011/12
CBR250RAB	2011/12
CBR250RD	2013/14
CBR250RAD	2013/14
CRF250LD	2013
CRF250LE	2014
CRF250M3	2014

The frame number is stamped into the right-hand side of the steering head

Engine number (arrowed) – 125 models

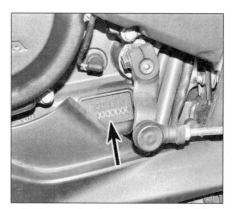

Engine number (arrowed) – 250 models

Colour code label (arrowed) – CBR models

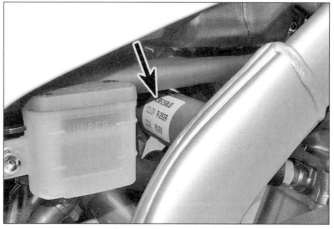

Colour code label (arrowed) – CRF models

Buying spare parts

Once you have found all the identification numbers, record them for reference when buying parts. Since the manufacturers change specifications, parts and vendors (companies that manufacture various components on the machine), providing the ID numbers is the only way to be reasonably sure that you are buying the correct parts.

Whenever possible, take the old part to the dealer so direct comparison with the new component can be made. Along the trail from the manufacturer to the parts shelf, there are numerous places that the part can end up with the wrong number or be listed incorrectly.

The two places to purchase new parts for your motorcycle – the franchised or main dealer and the parts/accessories store – differ in the type of parts they carry. While dealers can obtain every single genuine part for your motorcycle, the accessory store is usually limited to normal high wear items such as chains and sprockets, brake pads, spark plugs and cables, and to tune-up parts and various engine gaskets, etc. Rarely will an accessory outlet have major suspension components, camshafts, transmission gears, or engine cases.

Used parts can be obtained from breakers yards for roughly half the price of new ones, but you can't always be sure of what you're getting. Once again, take your worn part to the breaker for direct comparison, or when ordering by mail order make sure that you can return it if you are not happy.

Whether buying new, used or rebuilt parts, the best course is to deal directly with someone who specialises in your particular make.

Professional mechanics are trained in safe working procedures. However enthusiastic you may be about getting on with the job at hand, take the time to ensure that your safety is not put at risk. A moment's lack of attention can result in an accident, as can failure to observe simple precautions.

There will always be new ways of having accidents, and the following is not a comprehensive list of all dangers; it is intended rather to make you aware of the risks and to encourage a safe approach to all work you carry out on your bike.

Asbestos

● Certain friction, insulating, sealing and other products - such as brake pads, clutch linings, gaskets, etc. - contain asbestos. Extreme care must be taken to avoid inhalation of dust from such products since it is hazardous to health. If in doubt, assume that they do contain asbestos.

Fire

● Remember at all times that petrol is highly flammable. Never smoke or have any kind of naked flame around, when working on the vehicle. But the risk does not end there - a spark caused by an electrical short-circuit, by two metal surfaces contacting each other, by careless use of tools, or even by static electricity built up in your body under certain conditions, can ignite petrol vapour, which in a confined space is highly explosive. Never use petrol as a cleaning solvent. Use an approved safety solvent.

● Always disconnect the battery earth terminal before working on any part of the fuel or electrical system, and never risk spilling fuel on to a hot engine or exhaust.

● It is recommended that a fire extinguisher of a type suitable for fuel and electrical fires is kept handy in the garage or workplace at all times. Never try to extinguish a fuel or electrical fire with water.

Fumes

● Certain fumes are highly toxic and can quickly cause unconsciousness and even death if inhaled to any extent. Petrol vapour comes into this category, as do the vapours from certain solvents such as trichloro-ethylene. Any draining or pouring of such volatile fluids should be done in a well ventilated area.

● When using cleaning fluids and solvents, read the instructions carefully. Never use materials from unmarked containers - they may give off poisonous vapours.

● Never run the engine of a motor vehicle in an enclosed space such as a garage. Exhaust fumes contain carbon monoxide which is extremely poisonous; if you need to run the engine, always do so in the open air or at least have the rear of the vehicle outside the workplace.

The battery

● Never cause a spark, or allow a naked light near the vehicle's battery. It will normally be giving off a certain amount of hydrogen gas, which is highly explosive.

● Always disconnect the battery ground (earth) terminal before working on the fuel or electrical systems (except where noted).

● If possible, loosen the filler plugs or cover when charging the battery from an external source. Do not charge at an excessive rate or the battery may burst.

● Take care when topping up, cleaning or carrying the battery. The acid electrolyte, evenwhen diluted, is very corrosive and should not be allowed to contact the eyes or skin. Always wear rubber gloves and goggles or a face shield. If you ever need to prepare electrolyte yourself, always add the acid slowly to the water; never add the water to the acid.

Electricity

● When using an electric power tool, inspection light etc., always ensure that the appliance is correctly connected to its plug and that, where necessary, it is properly grounded (earthed). Do not use such appliances in damp conditions and, again, beware of creating a spark or applying excessive heat in the vicinity of fuel or fuel vapour. Also ensure that the appliances meet national safety standards.

● A severe electric shock can result from touching certain parts of the electrical system, such as the spark plug wires (HT leads), when the engine is running or being cranked, particularly if components are damp or the insulation is defective. Where an electronic ignition system is used, the secondary (HT) voltage is much higher and could prove fatal.

Remember...

✗ **Don't** start the engine without first ascertaining that the transmission is in neutral.

✗ **Don't** suddenly remove the pressure cap from a hot cooling system - cover it with a cloth and release the pressure gradually first, or you may get scalded by escaping coolant.

✗ **Don't** attempt to drain oil until you are sure it has cooled sufficiently to avoid scalding you.

✗ **Don't** grasp any part of the engine or exhaust system without first ascertaining that it is cool enough not to burn you.

✗ **Don't** allow brake fluid or antifreeze to contact the machine's paintwork or plastic components.

✗ **Don't** siphon toxic liquids such as fuel, hydraulic fluid or antifreeze by mouth, or allow them to remain on your skin.

✗ **Don't** inhale dust - it may be injurious to health (see Asbestos heading).

✗ **Don't** allow any spilled oil or grease to remain on the floor - wipe it up right away, before someone slips on it.

✗ **Don't** use ill-fitting spanners or other tools which may slip and cause injury.

✗ **Don't** lift a heavy component which may be beyond your capability - get assistance.

✗ **Don't** rush to finish a job or take unverified short cuts.

✗ **Don't** allow children or animals in or around an unattended vehicle.

✗ **Don't** inflate a tyre above the recommended pressure. Apart from overstressing the carcass, in extreme cases the tyre may blow off forcibly.

✔ **Do** ensure that the machine is supported securely at all times. This is especially important when the machine is blocked up to aid wheel or fork removal.

✔ **Do** take care when attempting to loosen a stubborn nut or bolt. It is generally better to pull on a spanner, rather than push, so that if you slip, you fall away from the machine rather than onto it.

✔ **Do** wear eye protection when using power tools such as drill, sander, bench grinder etc.

✔ **Do** use a barrier cream on your hands prior to undertaking dirty jobs - it will protect your skin from infection as well as making the dirt easier to remove afterwards; but make sure your hands aren't left slippery. Note that long-term contact with used engine oil can be a health hazard.

✔ **Do** keep loose clothing (cuffs, ties etc. and long hair) well out of the way of moving mechanical parts.

✔ **Do** remove rings, wristwatch etc., before working on the vehicle - especially the electrical system.

✔ **Do** keep your work area tidy - it is only too easy to fall over articles left lying around.

✔ **Do** exercise caution when compressing springs for removal or installation. Ensure that the tension is applied and released in a controlled manner, using suitable tools which preclude the possibility of the spring escaping violently.

✔ **Do** ensure that any lifting tackle used has a safe working load rating adequate for the job.

✔ **Do** get someone to check periodically that all is well, when working alone on the vehicle.

✔ **Do** carry out work in a logical sequence and check that everything is correctly assembled and tightened afterwards.

✔ **Do** remember that your vehicle's safety affects that of yourself and others. If in doubt on any point, get professional advice.

● If in spite of following these precautions, you are unfortunate enough to injure yourself, seek medical attention as soon as possible.

Engine oil level

Before you start:
✔ Make sure the motorcycle is on level ground.
✔ Start the engine and let it idle for 3 to 5 minutes.
Caution: Do not run the engine in an enclosed space such as a garage or workshop.
✔ Stop the engine and allow the oil level to stabilise for 2 to 3 minutes. Support the motorcycle upright using an auxiliary stand or by having an assistant hold it.

Bike care:
● If you have to add oil frequently, check whether you have any oil leaks from the engine joints, oil seals and gaskets. If not, the engine could be burning oil, in which case there will be white smoke coming out of the exhaust (see *Fault Finding*).

The correct oil:
● Modern, high-revving engines place great demands on their oil. It is very important that the correct oil for your bike is used. Do not use oil designed for use in car engines.
● Always top up with a good quality oil of the specified type and viscosity and do not overfill the engine.
Caution: Do not use chemical additives or oils labelled "ENERGY CONSERVING". Such additives or oils could cause clutch slip.

Oil type	API grade: SG or higher motorcycle oil JASO T 903 grade: MA
Oil viscosity	SAE 10W/30 or 10W/40

125 MODELS

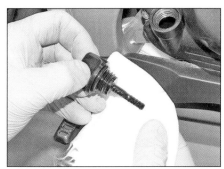

1 The oil level dipstick is incorporated with the filler cap, which is on the right-hand side of the engine. Unscrew the cap and wipe the dipstick clean.

2 Insert the dipstick so that the cap contacts the engine, but do not screw it in.

3 Remove the dipstick and check the oil mark – it should lie between the upper and lower level lines (arrowed).

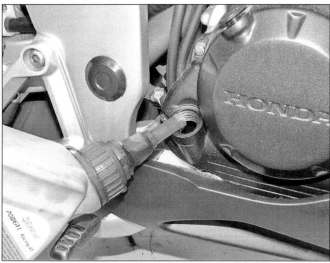

4 If the level is on or below the lower line, top up the engine with the recommended grade and type of oil to bring the level almost up to the upper line. Do not overfill.

5 Make sure the O-ring (arrowed) on the underside of the cap is in good condition and properly seated. Wipe it clean and smear new oil onto it. Fit the cap, making sure it is secure in the cover.

250 MODELS OVERLEAF ▶

Engine oil level (continued)

250 MODELS

1 The oil level inspection window is located on the right-hand side of the engine. If necessary wipe the window so that it is clean. With the motorcycle vertical, the oil level should lie between the upper and lower level lines (arrowed).

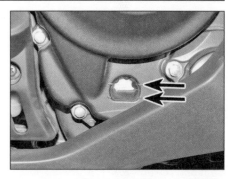

2 If the level is near, on or below the lower line, unscrew the oil filler cap, noting the O-ring.

3 Top up the engine with the recommended grade and type of oil to bring the level almost up to the upper line on the inspection window. Do not overfill.

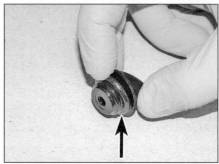

4 Make sure the O-ring (arrowed) on the underside of the cap is in good condition and properly seated. Fit a new one if necessary. Wipe it clean and smear new oil onto it. Fit the cap, making sure it is secure in the cover.

Coolant level

⚠ **Warning: DO NOT remove the radiator pressure cap to add coolant. Topping up is done via the coolant reservoir tank filler. DO NOT leave open containers of coolant about, as it is poisonous.**

Before you start:

✔ Make sure you have a supply of coolant available. A bottle of pre-mixed coolant is best. Alternatively prepare a mixture of 50% distilled water and 50% silicate-free corrosion inhibited ethylene glycol anti-freeze for topping up.
✔ Check the coolant level when the engine is at normal working temperature.
Caution: Do not run the engine in an enclosed space such as a garage or workshop.
✔ Make sure the motorcycle is on level ground. Support it upright using an auxiliary stand or by having an assistant hold it.

Bike care:

● Use only the specified coolant mixture. It is important that anti-freeze is used in the system all year round, and not just in the winter. Do not top the system up using only water, as the system will become too diluted.
● Do not overfill the reservoir tank. If the coolant is significantly above the UPPER level line at any time, the surplus should be siphoned or drained off to prevent the possibility of it being expelled out of the overflow hose.
● If the coolant level falls steadily, check the system for leaks (see Chapter 1). If no leaks are found and the level continues to fall, it is recommended that the machine is taken to a Honda dealer for a pressure test.

CBR125R

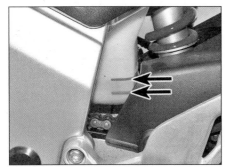

1 The coolant reservoir is in front of the shock absorber. With the motorcycle vertical, the coolant level should lie between the upper and lower level lines (arrowed).

2 If on or below the LOWER line, remove the rider's seat (see Chapter 7). Remove the reservoir filler cap.

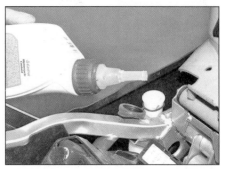

3 Top the reservoir up with the recommended coolant mixture to the UPPER level line, using a suitable funnel if required. Fit the cap and install the seat.

CBR250R

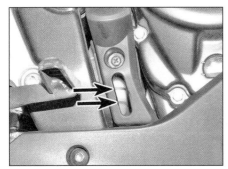

1 The coolant reservoir is on the right-hand side, behind the engine. With the motorcycle vertical, the coolant level should lie between the upper and lower level lines (arrowed) on the reservoir.

2 If on or below the LOWER line, undo the screw and remove the reservoir cover.

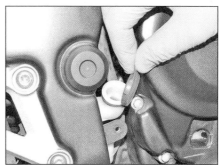

3 Remove the reservoir filler cap.

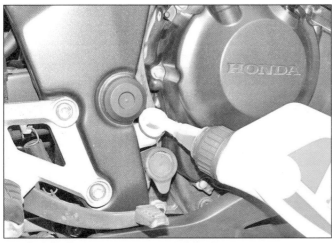

4 Top the reservoir up with the recommended coolant mixture to the UPPER level line, using a suitable funnel if required. Fit the cap.

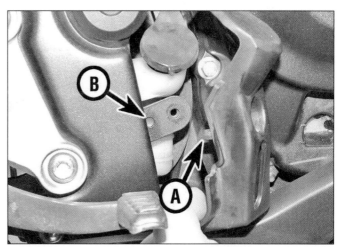

5 Fit the cover, locating the peg (A) in the hole (B).

CRF250L and M

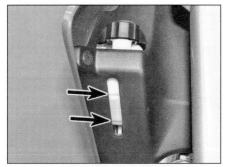

1 The coolant reservoir is on the right-hand side, behind the fuel tank cover. With the motorcycle vertical, the coolant level should lie between the upper and lower level lines (arrowed) marked on the front of the reservoir.

2 If the coolant level is on or below the LOWER line, remove the reservoir filler cap.

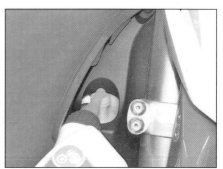

3 Top the reservoir up with the recommended coolant mixture to the UPPER level line, using a suitable funnel if required. Fit the cap.

Brake fluid levels

 Warning: Brake hydraulic fluid can harm your eyes and damage painted surfaces, so use extreme caution when handling and pouring it and cover surrounding surfaces with rag. Do not use fluid that has been standing open for some time, as it is hygroscopic (absorbs moisture from the air) which can cause a dangerous loss of braking effectiveness.

Before you start:

✔ The front brake fluid reservoir is on the right-hand handlebar. The rear brake fluid reservoir is on the right-hand side at the rear.
✔ Make sure you have the correct hydraulic fluid. DOT 4 is recommended.
✔ Wrap a rag around the reservoir being worked on to ensure that any spillage does not come into contact with painted surfaces.

✔ When checking the fluid in the front reservoir turn the handlebars so the reservoir is level.
✔ When checking the fluid in the rear reservoir support the motorcycle upright.

Bike care:

● The fluid in the front and rear brake master cylinder reservoirs will require only occasional topping up as the brake pads wear down.
● If either fluid reservoir requires repeated topping-up there is a leak somewhere in the system. Check for signs of fluid leakage from the hydraulic hoses and/or brake system components – if found, rectify immediately (see Chapter 6).
● Check the operation of both brakes before taking the machine on the road; if there is evidence of air in the system (spongy feel to lever or pedal), it must be bled (see Chapter 6).

FRONT

1 The front brake fluid level is visible through the window in the reservoir body – it must be above the LOWER level line (arrowed).

2 If the level is on or below the LOWER line, undo the cover screws and remove the cover, diaphragm plate and diaphragm.

3 Top up with new clean DOT 4 hydraulic fluid, until the level is up to the UPPER line (arrowed) on the inside of the reservoir. Do not overfill and take care to avoid spills (see **Warning** above).

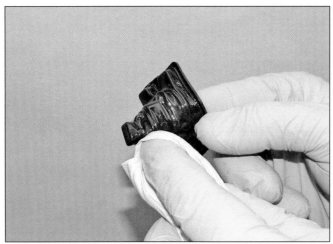

4 Wipe any moisture off the diaphragm with a tissue.

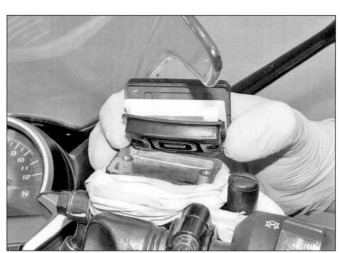

5 Make sure the diaphragm is correctly seated before fitting the plate and cover. Secure the cover with the screws.

REAR

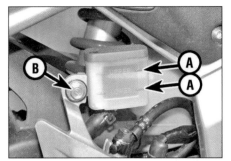

1 CBR125R – fluid level must be between the UPPER and LOWER lines (A). If the level is low undo the bolt (B) securing the reservoir and draw it out.

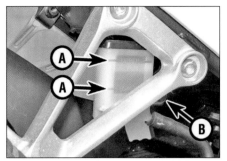

2 CBR250R – fluid level must be between the UPPER and LOWER lines (A). If the level is low undo the bolt (B) securing the reservoir and draw it out.

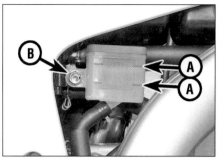

3 CBF250 – fluid level must be between the UPPER and LOWER lines (A). If the level is low undo the bolt (B) securing the reservoir and draw it out.

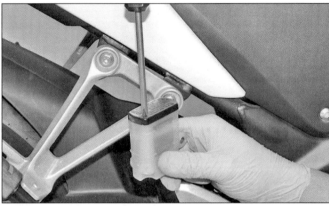

4 Undo the reservoir cover screws and remove the cover, diaphragm plate and diaphragm.

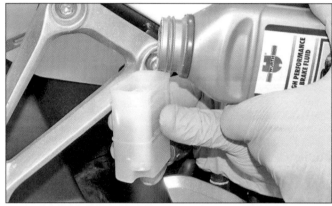

5 Top up with new clean DOT 4 hydraulic fluid, until the level is up to the UPPER line. Do not overfill and take care to avoid spills (see **Warning** on page 0•14).

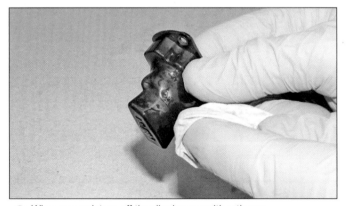

6 Wipe any moisture off the diaphragm with a tissue.

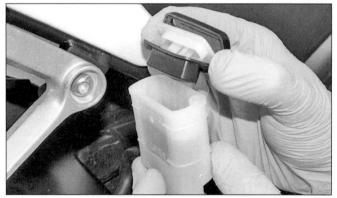

7 Make sure the diaphragm is correctly seated before fitting the plate and cover. Secure the cover with its screws. Fit the reservoir onto its mount and tighten the bolt.

Suspension, steering and drive chain

Suspension and Steering:
● Check that the front and rear suspension operates smoothly without binding (see Chapter 1).
● Check that the suspension is adjusted as required (see Chapter 5).
● Check that the steering moves smoothly from lock-to-lock.

Drive chain:
● Check that the chain isn't too loose or too tight, and adjust it if necessary (see Chapter 1).
● If the chain looks dry, lubricate it (see Chapter 1).

Tyres

The correct pressures:
● The tyres must be checked when **cold**, not immediately after riding. This is because the pressure inside the tyre will increase when the tyre is hot. Note that tyre pressure will also change from one day to the next as air temperature changes.
● Use an accurate pressure gauge. Many forecourt gauges are wildly inaccurate. If you buy your own, spend as much as you can justify on a quality gauge.
● The correct air pressure will increase tyre life and provide maximum stability and ride comfort. Incorrect tyre pressures will cause abnormal tread wear and unsafe handling. Low tyre pressures may cause the tyre to slip on the rim or come off.

Tyre care:
● Check the tyres carefully for cuts, tears, embedded nails or other sharp objects and excessive wear. Operation of the motorcycle with excessively worn tyres is extremely hazardous, as traction and handling are directly affected.
● Check the condition of the tyre valve and ensure the dust cap is in place.
● Pick out any stones or nails which may

Model	Front	Rear
CBR125R	25 psi (1.75 Bar)	29 psi (2.0 Bar) solo 33 psi (2.25 Bar) with passenger
CBR250R	29 psi (2.0 Bar)	29 psi (2.0 Bar) solo 33 psi (2.25 Bar) with passenger
CRF250L	22 psi (1.5 Bar)	22 psi (1.5 Bar)
CRF250M	29 psi (2.0 Bar)	29 psi (2.0 Bar)

have become embedded in the tyre tread. If left, they will eventually penetrate through the casing and cause a puncture.
● If tyre damage is apparent, or unexplained loss of pressure is experienced, seek the advice of a tyre fitting specialist without delay.

Tyre tread depth:
● At the time of writing UK law requires that tread depth must be at least 1 mm over 3/4 of the tread breadth all the way around the tyre, with no bald patches. Many riders, however, consider 2 mm tread depth minimum to be a safer limit. Honda recommend a minimum of 1.5 mm on the front and 2 mm on the rear, but note that German law requires a minimum of 1.6 mm for each tyre.
● Tyres incorporate wear indicators in the tread. Identify the location marking on the

tyre sidewall to locate the indicator bar and replace the tyre if the tread has worn down to the bar.

1 Remove the dust cap from the valve and do not forget to fit the cap after checking the pressure.

2 Check the tyre pressures when the tyres are **cold**.

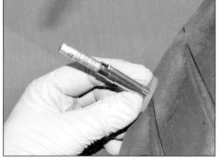

3 Measure tread depth at the centre of the tyre using a depth gauge.

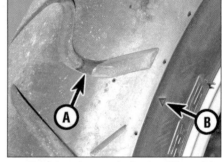

4 Tyre tread wear indicator (A) and its location marking (B) on the edge or sidewall (according to manufacturer).

Legal and safety checks

Lighting and signalling:
● Take a minute to check that the headlight, tail light, brake light, instrument lights and turn signals all work correctly.
● Check that the horn sounds when the button is pressed.
● A working speedometer, graduated in mph, is a statutory requirement in the UK.

Safety:
● Check that the throttle grip rotates smoothly when opened and snaps shut when released, in all steering positions. Also check for the correct amount of freeplay (see Chapter 1).
● Check that the brake lever and pedal, clutch lever and gearchange lever operate smoothly. Lubricate them at the specified intervals or when necessary (see Chapter 1).
● Check that the engine shuts off when the kill switch is operated.
● Check that the stand return springs hold the stand up securely when retracted.

Fuel:
● This may seem obvious, but check that you have enough fuel to complete your journey. If you notice signs of fuel leakage rectify the cause immediately.
● Ensure you use the correct grade fuel – see Chapter 4 Specifications.

CBR125R

Overall length	1985 mm
Overall width	710 mm
Overall height	1135 mm
Wheelbase	1310 mm
Seat height	795 mm
Footrest height	330 mm
Ground clearance	185 mm
Weight (wet)	137 kg
Maximum weight capacity	
UK and Europe models	180 kg
Canada models	166 kg

CBR250R/RA

Overall length	2030 mm
Overall width	720 mm
Overall height	1127 mm
Wheelbase	1369 mm
Seat height	780 mm
Footrest height	328 mm
Ground clearance	145 mm
Weight (wet)	
UK and Europe models	
R models	161 kg
RA models	165 kg
US and Canada models	
R models	162 kg
RA models	166 kg
Maximum weight capacity	
UK and Europe models	180 kg
US models	218 kg

CRF250L

Overall length	2195 mm
Overall width	815 mm
Overall height	1195 mm
Wheelbase	1445 mm
Seat height	875 mm
Footrest height	365 mm
Ground clearance	253 mm
Weight (wet)	
UK and Europe models	143 kg
US and Canada models	145 kg
Maximum weight capacity	159 kg

CRF250M

Overall length	2125 mm
Overall width	815 mm
Overall height	1150 mm
Wheelbase	1445 mm
Seat height	855 mm
Footrest height	339 mm
Ground clearance	225 mm
Weight (wet)	146 kg
Maximum weight capacity	159 kg

CBR125R

This generation of the CBR125R has the same single cylinder liquid-cooled engine as its predecessor, but in a completely new chassis. Drive to the single overhead camshaft, which actuates the two valves via a pair of rocker arms, is by chain from the left-hand end of the crankshaft. A balancer shaft driven directly off the crankshaft keeps things smooth. The clutch is a conventional wet multi-plate unit and the gearbox is 6-speed. Drive to the rear wheel is by chain and sprockets.

The PGM-FI fuel injection system supplies fuel and air to the engine via a single 30 mm throttle body and injector. An electronic ignition system ignites the mixture via a single spark plug. An oxygen sensor and catalytic converter are incorporated in the one-piece exhaust system.

The twin-spar steel frame uses the engine as a stressed member. Front suspension is by oil-damped 31 mm forks. Rear suspension is by a progressively damped single shock absorber. The box-section steel swingarm pivots through the frame.

The front brake system has a twin-piston sliding caliper acting on a conventional disc, and the rear brake system has a single piston sliding caliper acting on a conventional disc.

CBR250R/RA

The CBR250R uses a new 249cc single cylinder liquid-cooled engine. Drive to the double overhead camshafts, which actuate the four valves via rocker a pair of rocker arms, is by chain from the right-hand end of the crankshaft. A balancer shaft driven directly off the crankshaft keeps things smooth. The clutch is a conventional wet multi-plate unit and the gearbox is 6-speed. Drive to the rear wheel is by chain and sprockets.

The PGM-FI fuel injection system supplies fuel and air to the engine via a single 38 mm throttle body and injector. An electronic ignition system ignites the mixture via a single spark plug. An oxygen sensor and catalytic converter are incorporated in the two-piece exhaust system.

The twin-spar steel frame uses the engine as a stressed member. Front suspension is by oil-damped 37 mm forks. Rear suspension is by a progressively damped single shock absorber and Honda Pro-link. The box-section steel swingarm pivots through the frame.

The front brake system has a twin-piston sliding caliper acting on a floating disc, and the rear brake system has a single piston sliding caliper acting on a conventional disc. RA models feature Honda's combined ABS system, which links the front and rear brake systems and incorporates an anti-lock system.

CRF250L and CRF250M

The CRF models use the same engine and fuel injection system as the CBR250R.

The engine sits in a twin-spar steel cradle frame. Front suspension is by oil-damped upside-down forks. Rear suspension is by a progressively damped single shock absorber and Honda Pro-link. The box-section steel swingarm pivots through the frame.

The front brake system has a twin-piston sliding caliper acting on a conventional disc on L models and a floating disc on M models, and the rear brake system has a single piston sliding caliper acting on a conventional disc. Both models have wire-spoke wheels; traditional trail style on the L with 21 inch front and 18 inch rear, and Supermoto style on the M with 17 inch wheels.

Bike spec

Engine

CBR125R

Type	Four-stroke 2-valve single
Capacity	124.7 cc
Bore	58.0 mm
Stroke	47.2 mm
Compression ratio	11.0 to 1
Cooling system	Liquid cooled
Clutch	Wet multi-plate, cable actuation
Transmission	Six-speed constant mesh
Final drive	Chain and sprockets
Camshafts	SOHC, chain-driven
Fuel system	PGM-FI fuel injection, 30mm throttle body
Ignition system	Computer-controlled digital transistorised with electronic advance

CBR250R/RA, CRF250L/M

Type	Four-stroke 4-valve single
Capacity	249.6 cc
Bore	76.0 mm
Stroke	55.0 mm
Compression ratio	10.7 to 1
Cooling system	Liquid cooled
Clutch	Wet multi-plate, cable actuation
Transmission	Six-speed constant mesh
Final drive	Chain and sprockets
Camshafts	DOHC, chain-driven
Fuel system	PGM-FI fuel injection, 38mm throttle body
Ignition system	Computer-controlled digital transistorised with electronic advance

Chassis

CBR125R

Frame type	Steel, twin spar
Rake and Trail	25°00', 90 mm
Fuel tank	13 litres
Front suspension	
Type	31 mm oil-damped Showa telescopic forks
Travel	109 mm
Rear suspension	
Type	Single shock absorber, box section steel swingarm
Travel (at axle)	126 mm
Wheels	17 inch 5-spoke alloys
Tyres	Front 100/80-17M/C (52P); rear 130/70-17M/C (62P)
Front brake	Single 276 mm disc with Nissin twin piston sliding caliper
Rear brake	Single 220 mm disc with Nissin single piston sliding caliper

CBR250R/RA

Frame type	Steel, twin spar
Rake and Trail	25°00', 95 mm
Fuel tank	13 litres
Front suspension	
Type	37 mm oil-damped Showa telescopic forks
Travel	118 mm
Rear suspension	
Type	Honda Pro-Link rising rate linkage, box section steel swingarm, Showa shock absorber
Travel (at axle)	104 mm
Adjustment	Spring pre-load
Wheels	17 inch 5-spoke alloys
Tyres	Front 110/70-17 (54S); rear 190/50-ZR17 (66S)
Brakes	
R models	Single 296 mm disc with Nissin twin piston sliding caliper at the front, single 220 mm disc with single piston Nissin sliding caliper at the rear
RA models	Honda C-ABS, using single 296 mm disc with Nissin triple piston sliding caliper at the front, and single 220 mm disc with single piston Nissin sliding caliper at the rear

CRF250L

Frame type	Steel, twin spar cradle
Rake and Trail	27°35', 113 mm
Fuel tank	7.7 litres
Front suspension	
Type	Showa oil-damped upside-down telescopic forks
Travel	222 mm
Rear suspension	
Type	Honda Pro-Link rising rate linkage, box section aluminium swingarm, Showa shock absorber
Travel (at axle)	240 mm
Wheels	Wire-spoke, 21 inch front, 18 inch rear
Tyres	Front 3.00-21 (51P); rear 120/80-18M/C (62P)
Front brake	Single 256 mm disc with Nissin twin piston sliding caliper
Rear brake	Single 220 mm disc with Nissin single piston sliding caliper

CRF250M

Frame type	Steel, twin spar cradle
Rake and Trail	25°45', 71 mm
Fuel tank	7.7 litres
Front suspension	
Type	Showa oil-damped upside-down telescopic forks
Travel	225 mm
Rear suspension	
Type	Honda Pro-Link rising rate linkage, box section aluminium swingarm, Showa shock absorber
Travel (at axle)	240 mm
Wheels	Wire-spoke, 17 inch
Tyres	Front 110/70-17M/C (54S); rear 130/70-17M/C (62S)
Front brake	Single 296 mm disc with Nissin twin piston sliding caliper
Rear brake	Single 220 mm disc with Nissin single piston sliding caliper

Chapter 1
Routine maintenance and servicing

Contents

Degrees of difficulty

| **Easy,** suitable for novice with little experience | **Fairly easy,** suitable for beginner with some experience | **Fairly difficult,** suitable for competent DIY mechanic | **Difficult,** suitable for experienced DIY mechanic | **Very difficult,** suitable for expert DIY or professional |

Specifications

Engine

Spark plug type
  125 models
    Standard . . . . NGK CR8E or Denso U24ESR-N
    For continuous high speed use . . . . NGK CR9E or Denso U27ESR-N
  250 models . . . . NGK SIMR8A9

Spark plug electrode gap
  125 models . . . . 0.7 to 0.8 mm
  250 models . . . . 0.8 to 0.9 mm

Engine idle speed
  CBR125 . . . . 1450 ± 100 rpm
  CBR250 . . . . 1400 ± 100 rpm
  CRF250 . . . . 1450 ± 100 rpm

Valve clearances (COLD engine)
  125 models
    Intake valve . . . . 0.04 to 0.08 mm
    Exhaust valve . . . . 0.25 to 0.29 mm
  250 models
    Intake valves . . . . 0.13 to 0.19 mm
    Exhaust valves . . . . 0.24 to 0.31 mm

Cycle parts

Drive chain slack
  CBR125 . . . . 30 to 40 mm
  CBR250 . . . . 20 to 30 mm
  CRF250. . . . . 25 to 35 mm
Throttle cable freeplay . . . . 2 to 6 mm at twistgrip flange
Clutch cable freeplay . . . . 10 to 20 mm at lever end
Tyre pressures (cold). . . . . see *Pre-ride checks*
Steering head bearing pre-load (see text)
  CBR250 models . . . . 15.7 to 24.5 N (1.6 to 2.5 kgf)
  CRF250 models . . . . 10.6 to 21.2 N (1.08 to 2.16 kgf)

Lubricants and fluids

Engine oil . . . . SAE 10W/30 or 10W/40 motorcycle oil. API grade: SG or higher; JASO T 903 grade: MA

Engine oil capacity
  125 engines
    Oil change. . . . . 1.0 litre
    Following engine overhaul . . . . 1.3 litres
  250 engines
    Oil change. . . . . 1.4 litres
    Oil and filter change . . . . 1.5 litres
    Following engine overhaul . . . . 1.8 litres
Coolant type. . . . . Pre-mixed coolant or 50% distilled water, 50% silicate-free corrosion inhibited ethylene glycol anti-freeze

Coolant capacity
  CBR125
    Radiator and engine . . . . 0.76 litre
    Reservoir. . . . . 0.24 litre
  CBR250
    Radiator and engine . . . . 1.1 litres
    Reservoir. . . . . 0.25 litre
  CRF250
    Radiator and engine . . . . 1.02 litres
    Reservoir. . . . . 0.16 litre
Brake fluid . . . . DOT 4
Drive chain . . . . Aerosol chain lubricant or SAE 80 or 90 gear oil
Steering head bearings and seals . . . . Urea-based multi-purpose grease with EP2 rating
Swingarm pivot bearings and seal lips. . . . . Multi-purpose grease
Shock absorber pivots . . . . Multi-purpose grease
Suspension linkage bearings and seal lips . . . . Multi-purpose grease
Sidestand pivot . . . . Multi-purpose grease
Wheel bearing seal lips. . . . . Multi-purpose grease
Wheel axles . . . . Multi-purpose grease
Gearchange lever/rear brake pedal/footrest pivots . . . . . Multi-purpose grease
Clutch lever pivot . . . . Multi-purpose grease
Throttle twistgrip. . . . . Multi-purpose grease
Front brake lever pivot and piston tip . . . . Silicone grease
Cables . . . . Aerosol cable lubricant

Torque settings

Crankshaft end cap . . . . 8 Nm
Engine oil drain plug
  125 models. . . . . 25 Nm
  250 models. . . . . 24 Nm
Fork clamp bolts (top yoke)
  CBR125 . . . . 23 Nm
  CBR250 . . . . 22 Nm
  CRF250. . . . . 32 Nm
Handlebar clamp bolts (CBR models) . . . . 27 Nm
Rear axle nut
  CBR125 . . . . 69 Nm
  CBR250 and CRF250. . . . . 88 Nm
Spark plug . . . . 16 Nm
Steering stem nut
  125 models. . . . . 88 Nm
  250 models. . . . . 103 Nm
Timing inspection cap . . . . 6 Nm

Pre-ride
- [ ] See *'Pre-ride checks'* at the beginning of this manual.

After the initial 600 miles (1000 km)
Note: *This check is usually performed by a Honda dealer after the first 600 miles (1000 km) from new. Thereafter, maintenance is carried out according to the following intervals of the schedule.*

Every 600 miles (1000 km)
- [ ] Check, adjust, clean and lubricate the drive chain (Section 1)

Every 2500 miles (4000 km) or 6 months
- [ ] Check the brake pads for wear (Section 2)
- [ ] Check the brake system and brake light switch operation (Section 2)
- [ ] Check and adjust the clutch cable freeplay (Section 3)
- [ ] Check the crankcase breather system (Section 4)
- [ ] Check the idle speed (Section 6)
- [ ] Check the fuel system and hoses (Section 7)
- [ ] Check and adjust the throttle cable (Section 8)
- [ ] Check the spark plug (Section 9)
- [ ] Check and adjust the valve clearances (Section 10)
- [ ] Check the headlight beam aim (Section 11)
- [ ] Check the sidestand and starter interlock circuit (Section 12)
- [ ] Check the front and rear suspension (Section 13)
- [ ] Check the condition of the wheels, wheel bearings and tyres (Section 14)

Every 5000 miles (8000 km) or 12 months
Carry out all the items under the 2500 mile (4000 km) check, plus the following:
- [ ] Fit a new spark plug (Section 9)
- [ ] Change the engine oil (Section 15)
- [ ] Check the cooling system (Section 16)
- [ ] Lubricate the clutch, gearchange and brake levers, brake pedal, sidestand pivot, and the throttle cable (Section 17)
- [ ] Check the tightness of all nuts, bolts and fasteners (Section 18)

Every 7500 miles (12,000 km) or 18 months
Carry out all the items under the 2500 mile (4000 km) check, plus the following:
- [ ] Clean the engine oil filter (Section 15)
- [ ] Check and adjust the steering head bearings (Section 19)

Every 10,000 miles (16,000 km)
Carry out all the items under the 5000 mile (8000 km) check, plus the following:
- [ ] Clean the air filter element (Section 21)

Every two years
- [ ] Change the brake fluid (Section 2)
- [ ] Change the coolant (Section 16)

Non-scheduled maintenance
- [ ] Check the battery (Section 23)
- [ ] Change the front fork oil (Section 13)
- [ ] Re-grease the swingarm pivot (Section 13)
- [ ] Re-grease the steering head bearings (Section 19)

Pre-ride
- ☐ See *'Pre-ride checks'* at the beginning of this manual.

After the initial 600 miles (1000 km)
Note: *This check is usually performed by a Honda dealer after the first 600 miles (1000 km) from new. Thereafter, maintenance is carried out according to the following intervals of the schedule.*

Every 500 miles (800 km)
- ☐ Check, adjust, clean and lubricate the drive chain (Section 1)

Every 4000 miles (6000 km) or 6 months
- ☐ Check the brake pads for wear (Section 2)
- ☐ Check and adjust the clutch cable freeplay (Section 3)
- ☐ Check the crankcase breather system (Section 4)
- ☐ Clean the spark arrester (US CRF models only) (Section 5)
- ☐ Check the idle speed (Section 6)

Every 8000 miles (12,000 km) or 12 months
Carry out all the items under the 4000 mile (6000 km) check, plus the following:
- ☐ Check the brake system and brake light switch operation (Section 2)
- ☐ Check the fuel system and hoses (Section 7)
- ☐ Check and adjust the throttle cables (Section 8)
- ☐ Check the headlight beam aim (Section 11)
- ☐ Check the sidestand and starter interlock circuit (Section 12)
- ☐ Check the front and rear suspension (Section 13)
- ☐ Check the condition of the wheels, wheel bearings and tyres (Section 14)
- ☐ Change the engine oil and fit a new filter (Section 15)
- ☐ Check the cooling system (Section 16)
- ☐ Lubricate the clutch, gearchange and brake levers, brake pedal, sidestand pivot, and the throttle cables (Section 17)
- ☐ Check the tightness of all nuts, bolts and fasteners (Section 18)
- ☐ Check and adjust the steering head bearings (Section 19)
- ☐ Check the pulse secondary air injection (PAIR) system (Section 20)

Every 12,000 miles (18,000 km)
Carry out all the items under the 4000 mile (6000 km) check, plus the following:
- ☐ Fit a new air filter element (US models) (Section 21)
- ☐ Check the EVAP (evaporative emission control) system (US models only) (Section 22)

Every 12,000 miles (18,000 km) or two years
- ☐ Change the brake fluid (Section 2)

Every 16,000 miles (24,000 km)
Carry out all the items under the 8000 mile (12,000 km) check, plus the following:
- ☐ Check the spark plug (Section 9)
- ☐ Fit a new air filter element (UK/Europe models) (Section 21)
- ☐ Check and adjust the valve clearances (Section 10)

Every 24,000 miles (36,000 km) or two years
Carry out all the items under the 12,000 mile (18,000 km) and 8000 mile (12,000 km) checks, plus the following:
- ☐ Change the coolant (Section 16)

Every 32,000 miles (48,000 km)
Carry out all the items under the 16,000 mile (24,000 km) check, plus the following:
- ☐ Fit a new spark plug (Section 9)

Non-scheduled maintenance
- ☐ Check the battery (Section 23)
- ☐ Change the front fork oil (Section 13)
- ☐ Re-grease the swingarm and suspension linkage bearings (Section 13)
- ☐ Re-grease the steering head bearings (Section 19)

CBR125 right side

1 Colour/model code label
2 Rear brake fluid reservoir
3 Throttle cable lower adjuster
4 Spark plug
5 Front brake fluid reservoir
6 Throttle cable upper adjuster
7 Frame number
8 Coolant drain bolt
9 Oil drain bolt
10 Oil strainer
11 Clutch cable lower adjuster
12 Oil filler cap/dipstick
13 Rear brake light switch
14 Rear brake pedal height adjuster
15 Drive chain adjuster

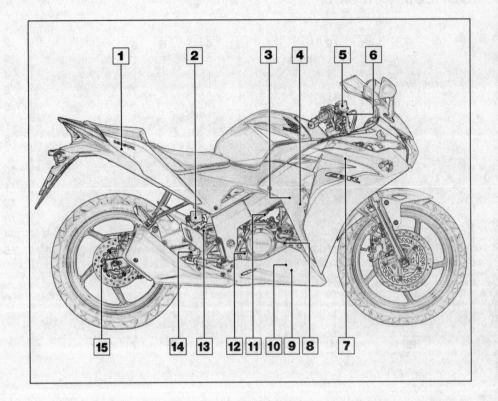

CBR125 left side

1 Clutch cable upper adjuster
2 Steering head bearing adjuster
3 Air filter
4 Coolant filler cap
5 Battery
6 Drive chain adjuster
7 Coolant reservoir level marks
8 Drive chain slider wear check point
9 Crankcase breather drain hose
10 Engine number
11 Crankshaft end cap
12 Timing mark plug

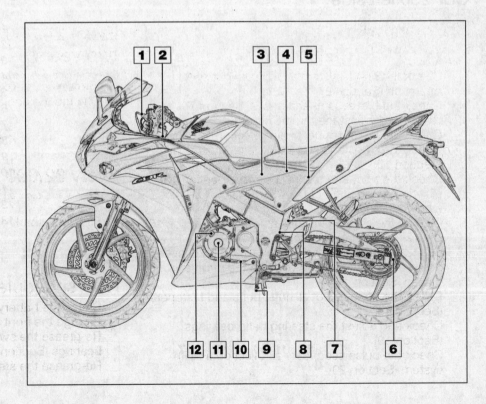

CBR250 right side

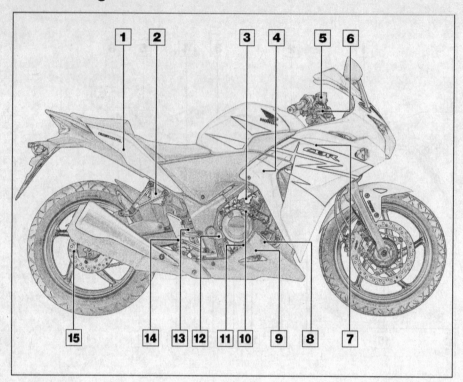

1   Colour/model code label
2   Rear brake fluid reservoir
3   Clutch cable lower adjuster
4   Throttle cable lower adjuster
5   Front brake fluid reservoir
6   Throttle cable upper adjuster
7   Frame number
8   Coolant drain bolt
9   Oil filter
10 Oil filler cap
11 Oil level window
12 Coolant reservoir filler cap
13 Rear brake light switch
14 Rear brake pedal height adjuster
15 Drive chain adjuster

CBR250 left side

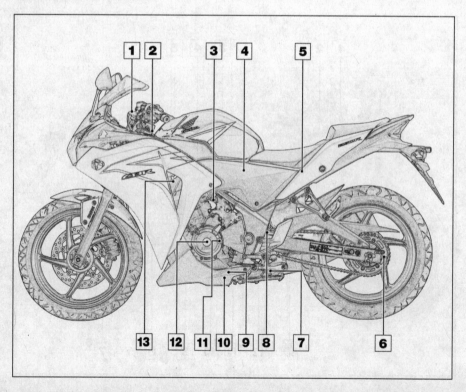

1   Clutch cable upper adjuster
2   Steering head bearing adjuster
3   EVAP canister location (where fitted)
4   Air filter
5   Battery
6   Drive chain adjuster
7   Crankcase breather drain hose
8   Drive chain slider wear check points
9   Engine number
10 Oil drain bolt
11 Timing mark plug
12 Crankshaft end cap
13 Spark plug

CRF250 right side (M shown)

1 Air filter
2 Rear brake fluid reservoir
3 Colour/model code label
4 Throttle cable lower adjuster
5 Front brake fluid reservoir
6 Throttle cable upper adjuster
7 Coolant reservoir filler cap
8 Frame number
9 Coolant drain bolt
10 Oil filter
11 Oil filler cap
12 Oil level window
13 Rear brake light switch
14 Rear brake pedal height adjuster
15 Drive chain adjuster

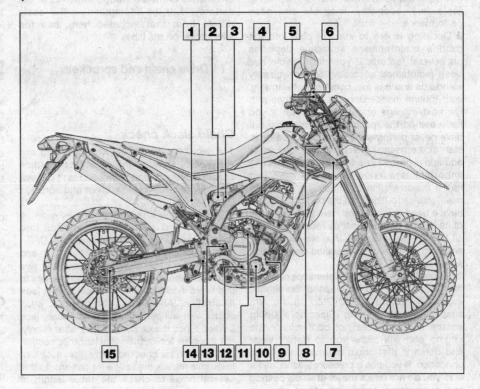

CRF250 left side (M shown)

1 Clutch cable adjusters
2 Steering head bearing adjuster
3 EVAP canister location (where fitted)
4 Battery
5 Crankcase breather drain hose
6 Spark arrester
7 Drive chain adjuster
8 Drive chain slider wear check points
9 Engine number
10 Oil drain bolt
11 Timing mark plug
12 Crankshaft end cap
13 Spark plug

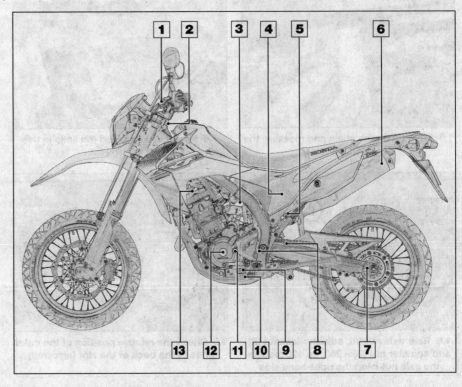

1 This Chapter is designed to help the home mechanic maintain his/her motorcycle for safety, economy, long life and peak performance.

2 Deciding where to start or plug into the routine maintenance schedule depends on several factors. If your motorcycle has been maintained according to the warranty standards and has just come out of warranty, start routine maintenance as it coincides with the next mileage or calendar interval. If you have owned the machine for some time but have never performed any maintenance on it, start at the nearest interval and include some additional procedures to ensure that nothing important is overlooked. If you have just had a major engine overhaul, then start the maintenance routine from the beginning. If you have a used machine and have no knowledge of its history or maintenance record, combine all the checks into one large service initially and then settle into the specified maintenance schedule.

3 Before beginning any maintenance or repair, the machine should be cleaned thoroughly, especially around the oil filter, drive chain, suspension, wheels, etc. Cleaning will help ensure that dirt does not contaminate the engine and will allow you to detect wear and damage that could otherwise easily go unnoticed. If you use a pressure washer make sure you do not direct the jet at wheel bearing and suspension seals and at the steering head, or at any electrical/ignition components and connectors.

4 Certain maintenance information is sometimes printed on labels attached to the motorcycle. If the information on the labels differs from that included here, use the information on the label.

1   Drive chain and sprockets

Chain slack check

1 A neglected drive chain won't last long and will quickly damage the sprockets. Routine chain adjustment and lubrication isn't difficult and will ensure maximum chain and sprocket life.

2 To check the chain, place the bike on its sidestand and shift the transmission into neutral. Make sure the ignition switch is OFF.

3 Push up on the bottom run of the chain and measure the slack midway between the two sprockets, then compare your measurement to that listed in this Chapter's Specifications **(see illustration)**. As the chain stretches with wear, adjustment will periodically be necessary (see below). Since the chain will rarely wear evenly, roll the bike forward so that another section of chain can be checked (having an assistant to do this makes the task a lot easier); do this several times to check the entire length of chain, and mark the tightest spot.

Caution: Riding the bike with excess slack in the chain could lead to damage.

4 If the chain has been neglected, corrosion and dirt may cause the links to bind and kink, which effectively shortens the chain's length and makes it tight **(see illustration)**. Thoroughly clean and work free any such links, then highlight them with a marker pen or paint. Take the bike for a ride.

5 After the bike has been ridden, repeat the measurement for slack in the highlighted area. If the chain has kinked again and is still tight, replace it with a new one (see Chapter 6). A rusty, kinked or worn chain will damage the sprockets and can damage transmission bearings. If in any doubt as to the condition of a chain, it is far better to install a new one than risk damage to other components and possibly yourself.

6 Check the entire length of the chain for damaged rollers, loose links and pins, and missing O-rings and replace it with a new one if necessary. **Note:** *Never fit a new chain onto old sprockets, and never use the old chain if you fit new sprockets – replace the chain and sprockets as a set.*

Chain slack adjustment

7 Move the bike so that the chain is positioned with the tightest point at the centre of its bottom run, then put it on the sidestand.

CBR models

8 Slacken the rear axle nut **(see illustration)**. Slacken the locknut on the adjuster on each side of the swingarm.

9 To reduce chain slack turn the adjuster nut on each side clockwise by the same amount until the amount of freeplay specified at the beginning of the Chapter is obtained at the centre of the bottom run of the chain. Following adjustment, check that the same index line on each chain adjustment marker is in the same position in relation to the back edge of the slot in the swingarm **(see illustration)**. It is important the alignment is the same on each side otherwise the rear wheel will be out of alignment with the front. Also make sure that the front face of each adjuster nut is butted against the end of the swingarm. If there is a difference in the positions, adjust one of them so that its position is exactly the same as the other. Check the chain freeplay again and readjust if necessary.

10 To increase chain slack turn the adjuster nut on each side of the swingarm anti-clockwise by the same amount, then push the wheel forwards in the swingarm until the nut butts the end of the swingarm, then apply the same principles given in Step 9 for checking alignment.

11 Also check the alignment of the double-headed arrow on the adjustment marker with the wear decal on the left-hand side of the swingarm **(see illustration 1.9)**. When the arrow meets the red REPLACE CHAIN zone, the drive chain has stretched excessively and must be replaced with a new one (see Chapter 6).

12 When adjustment is complete,

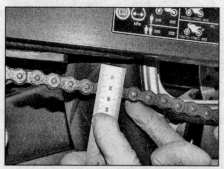

1.3 Push up on the chain and measure the slack

1.4 Neglect has caused the links in this chain to kink

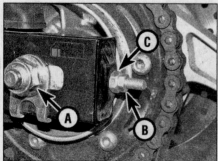

1.8 Rear axle nut (A), adjuster locknut (B) and adjuster nut (C) – 250, on 125 models the axle nut is on the right-hand side

1.9 Check the relative position of the index lines to the back of the slot (arrowed)

1.13a Rear axle nut (arrowed)

1.13b Slacken each locknut (A) and turn each adjuster bolt (B) as required

1.14 Check the relative position of the alignment notches to the punch mark (arrowed)

counter-hold the adjuster nuts to prevent them turning and tighten the locknuts against them. Push the wheel forwards and keep pressure on it, and tighten the axle nut to the torque setting specified at the beginning of the Chapter. Recheck the adjustment and alignment as above, then place the machine on an auxiliary stand and spin the wheel to make sure it runs freely.

CRF models

13 Slacken the rear axle nut **(see illustration)**. Slacken the locknut on each adjuster bolt **(see illustration)**.

14 To reduce chain slack turn the adjuster bolt on each side of the swingarm anti-clockwise by the same amount until the amount of freeplay specified at the beginning of the Chapter is obtained at the centre of the bottom run of the chain. Following adjustment, check that the same notch on the bottom edge of each chain adjustment marker is in the same position in relation to the punch mark in the swingarm **(see illustration)**. It is important the alignment is the same on each side otherwise the rear wheel will be out of alignment with the front. Always make sure that the front edge of each marker is butted against the end of the adjuster bolt. If there is a difference in the positions, adjust one of them so that its position is exactly the same as the other. Check the chain freeplay again and readjust if necessary.

15 To increase chain slack turn the adjuster bolt on each side of the swingarm clockwise by the same amount, then push the wheel forwards in the swingarm until the adjustment marker butts the head of the bolt, then apply the same principles given in Step 14 for checking alignment.

16 Also check the alignment of the notch in the top of the marker on the left-hand side with the wear decal on the swingarm **(see illustration)**. When the mark meets the red REPLACE CHAIN zone, the drive chain has stretched excessively and must be replaced with a new one (see Chapter 6).

17 When adjustment is complete, hold the adjuster bolt and tighten locknut on each side **(see illustration 1.13b)**. Push the wheel forwards and keep pressure on it, and tighten the axle nut to the torque setting specified at the beginning of the Chapter. Recheck the adjustment and alignment as above, then place the machine on an auxiliary stand and spin the wheel to make sure it runs freely.

Chain cleaning and lubrication

18 If required, wash the chain using a dedicated aerosol cleaner, or in paraffin (kerosene) or a suitable non-flammable or high flash-point solvent that will not damage the O-rings, using a soft brush to work any dirt out if necessary **(see illustration)**. Wipe the cleaner off the chain and allow it to dry. If the chain is excessively dirty remove it from

the bike and allow it to soak in the paraffin or solvent (see Chapter 6).

Caution: Don't use petrol (gasoline), an unsuitable solvent or other cleaning fluids which might damage the internal sealing properties of the chain. Don't use high-pressure water to clean the chain. The entire process shouldn't take longer than ten minutes, otherwise the O-rings could be damaged.

19 The best time to lubricate the chain is after the motorcycle has been ridden. When the chain is warm, the lubricant will penetrate the joints between the sideplates better than when cold. **Note:** *Honda specifies SAE 80 to SAE 90 gear oil or an aerosol chain lube that it is suitable for O-ring (sealed) chains; do not use any other chain lubricants – the solvents could damage the chain's sealing rings. Apply the lubricant to the area where the sideplates overlap – not the middle of the rollers* **(see illustration)**.

⚠ **Warning: Take care not to get any lubricant on the tyre or brake components. If any of the lubricant inadvertently contacts them, clean it off thoroughly using a suitable solvent or dedicated brake cleaner before riding the machine.**

Sprocket check

20 Remove the front sprocket cover. Check the teeth on the front sprocket and the rear

1.16 Here the notch (arrowed) is at the beginning of the green zone, showing the chain is new

1.18 Specially shaped chain cleaning brushes are commercially available

1.19 Apply the lubricant to the overlapping sections of the sideplates

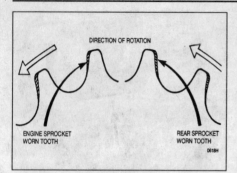

1.20 Check the sprockets in the areas indicated to see if they are worn excessively

2.1 Brake pad material is easily viewed through mouth of caliper

2.8 Check all hoses and unions for cracks and leaks

sprocket for wear **(see illustration)**. If the sprocket teeth are worn excessively, renew the chain and both sprockets as a set.

21 With the sprocket cover removed check for wear and damage on the chain slider around the front of the swingarm – if the rubbing surfaces of the slider have worn to the markers or there is evidence of damage remove the swingarm and replace the slider with a new one (see Chapter 5).

2 Brake system

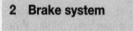

Brake pad wear check

1 Each brake pad has wear indicators – there are grooves in the face of the friction material, or there is a cut-out in the side of the material, depending on model and caliper **(see illustration)**. The wear indicators should be plainly visible, but note that an accumulation of road dirt and brake dust could make them difficult to see. If the indicators aren't visible, then the amount of friction material remaining should be.

2 If the pads are worn to the bottom of the grooves or to the beginning of the cut-outs,

or the friction material thickness is down to 1 mm, they must be replaced with new ones (see Chapter 6).

3 On the front caliper also check for uneven wear in the brake pads, which is indicative of a sticking or seized piston. If found, the calipers must be overhauled (see Chapter 6).

4 If the pads are dirty or if you are in doubt as to the amount of friction material remaining, remove them for inspection (see Chapter 6). If the pads have worn to the backing material check the brake discs for scoring (see Chapter 6). From time to time check the thickness of each disc and replace them with new ones if worn below the service limit specified in Chapter 6 and stamped on the disc centre.

Brake system check

5 A routine general check of the brake system will ensure that any problems are discovered and remedied before the rider's safety is jeopardised.

6 Check the brake pads for wear (see above) and make sure the fluid level in each reservoir is correct (see *Pre-ride checks*).

7 Check the brake lever and pedal pivots for sloppy or rough action, excessive play, bends, and other damage. Replace any damaged parts with new ones (see Chapter 5). Clean and lubricate the lever and pedal pivots if their

action is stiff or rough (see Section 17). If the lever or pedal is spongy, bleed the brakes (see Chapter 6).

8 Look for leaks from the hoses and their connections, plus cracks in the hoses **(see illustration)**. On CBR250RA models similarly check the metal ABS system pipes. If a hose shows signs of deterioration it must be replaced with a new one. Make sure all brake hose and pipe fasteners are tight.

9 Also inspect the master cylinders and calipers for any sign of fluid leakage due to failed seals. Leakage from the master cylinders is unlikely, but the caliper pistons can become corroded over a period of time, especially due to road salt over the winter, and this can lead to seal damage. Seal kits are available for the master cylinders and calipers – refer to Chapter 6.

10 Make sure the brake light comes on when the front brake lever or rear pedal is applied. If it fails to operate properly, check the switch (see Chapter 8).

11 Make sure the brake light comes on just before the rear brake takes effect. If adjustment is necessary, hold the switch and turn the adjuster ring on the switch body until the brake light is activated when required **(see illustrations)**. If the brake light comes on too late or not at all, turn the ring clockwise (when

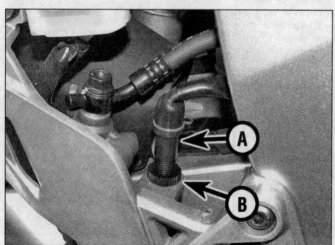

2.11a Hold the rear brake light switch body (A) and turn the adjuster ring (B) as required – CBR shown...

2.11b ...on CRF models the switch (arrowed) is behind the guard – remove the guard for best access

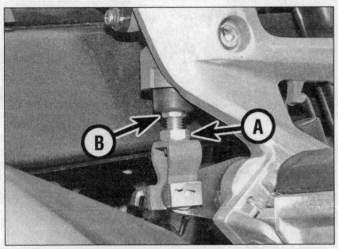

2.12a Slacken the locknut (A) and turn the pushrod using the hex (B) to adjust pedal height

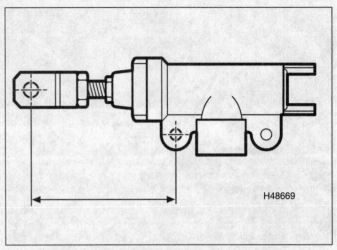

2.12b Standard pedal height measurement points

looked at from the top) so the switch threads up out of the bracket. If the brake light comes on too soon or is permanently on, turn the ring anti-clockwise so the switch threads down into the bracket. If the switch doesn't operate the brake light, check it (see Chapter 8).

12 The height of the rear brake pedal can be adjusted to an extent to suit the rider's preference. Slacken the clevis locknut on the master cylinder pushrod, then turn the pushrod using a spanner on the hex at the top of the rod until the pedal is at the desired height (see illustration). Note that Honda specify that the distance between the bottom mounting bolt for the master cylinder and the clevis pin (measured centre-to-centre parallel to the pushrod) should be 64 to 65 mm on CBR125 and CRF250 models and 66.5 to 68.5 mm on CBR250 models (see illustration). On completion tighten the locknut. Adjust the rear brake light switch after adjusting the pedal height (see Step 11).

Brake fluid change

13 The brake fluid should be changed at the prescribed interval or whenever a master cylinder or caliper overhaul is carried out. Refer to Chapter 6 for details. Ensure that all the old fluid is be pumped from the hydraulic system and that the level in the fluid reservoirs is checked and the brakes tested before riding the motorcycle.

3 Clutch

1 Check that the clutch lever operates smoothly and easily.

2 If the clutch lever operation is heavy or stiff, lubricate both the cable and the lever (see Section 17). If the cable is still stiff, replace it with a new one.

3 With the cable operating smoothly, check that it is correctly adjusted. Periodic adjustment is necessary to compensate for wear in the clutch plates and stretch of the cable. Check that the amount of freeplay at the clutch lever end is within the specifications listed at the beginning of the Chapter (see illustration).

4 If adjustment is required, this can be done first at the lever end of the cable. Pull the boot off the adjuster, then slacken the lockring and turn the adjuster in or out until the required amount of freeplay is obtained (see illustration). To reduce freeplay, thread the adjuster out of the bracket. To increase freeplay, thread the adjuster into the lever bracket.

5 Make sure that the slot in the adjuster is not aligned with the slot in the lever bracket – these slots are to allow removal of the cable, and if they are all aligned while the bike is in use the cable could jump out. Also make sure the adjuster is not threaded too far out of the bracket so is only held by a few threads – this will leave it unstable and the threads could be damaged.

6 On all models, if no more adjustment is available at the lever, thread the adjuster all the way into the bracket to give the maximum amount of freeplay, then back it out one turn, making sure the slots are offset – this resets the adjuster to its start point. Now refer to Step 7, 8 or 9 as applicable.

7 On CBR125 models now set the correct amount of freeplay using the adjuster on the cable bracket on the clutch cover on the right-hand side of the engine. Counter-hold the adjuster nut and slacken the locknut (see illustration). To increase freeplay turn the adjuster nut anti-clockwise as you look down at it until the freeplay is as specified. To reduce freeplay turn the adjuster nut clockwise as you look down at it. Tighten the locknut

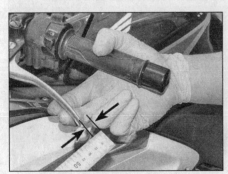

3.3 Measure the amount of freeplay at the clutch lever ball end as shown

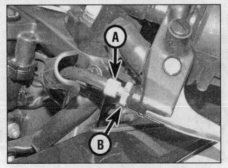

3.4 Slacken the lockring (B) and turn the adjuster (A) as required

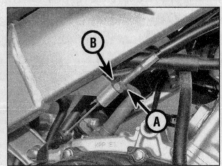

3.7 Slacken the locknut (A) and turn the adjuster nut (B) – CBR125

3.8 Slacken and adjust the nuts (arrowed) – CBR250

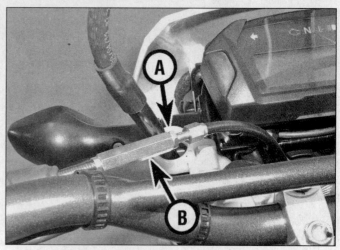

3.9 Slacken the locknut (A) and turn the adjuster (B) – CRF250

on completion. Subsequent adjustments can now be made using the lever adjuster only.

8 On CBR250 models now set the correct amount of freeplay using the adjuster in the cable bracket on the clutch cover on the right-hand side of the engine. Use the nuts on each end of the threaded section of the cable to adjust freeplay **(see illustration)**. To reduce freeplay slacken the rear nut and tighten the front nut until the freeplay is as specified, then tighten the rear nut. To increase freeplay slacken the front nut and tighten the rear

nut, then tighten the front nut. Subsequent adjustments can now be made using the lever adjuster only.

9 On CRF250 models now set the correct amount of freeplay using the adjuster in the cable near the lever bracket. Slacken the adjuster locknut **(see illustration)**. To reduce freeplay turn the adjuster away from the locknut until the freeplay is as specified. To increase freeplay turn the adjuster towards the locknut. Tighten the locknut. Subsequent adjustments can now be made using the lever adjuster only.

4 Crankcase breather

1 Check the crankcase breather hose between the engine and the air filter housing for cracks, splits and damage, make sure it is not pinched, and check it is securely connected and secured by a clamp at each end **(see illustrations)**. Replace the hose with a new one if necessary.
2 Check the air filter housing drain for accumulated deposits. On CBR models remove the plug from the end of the hose and allow any deposits to rain into a rag **(see illustrations)**. On CRF models remove the drain collector from the housing and clean it out **(see illustration)**.

5 Spark arrester (US CRF models)

1 Remove the shield and end cap from the silencer.
2 Unscrew the spark arrester bolts and draw the arrester out of the silencer. Remove the gasket – a new one must be used.

4.1a Crankcase breather hose (arrowed) – 125 models

4.1b Crankcase breather hose (arrowed) – 250 models

4.2a Air filter housing drain hose plug (arrowed) – CBR125

4.2b Air filter housing drain hose plug (arrowed) – CBR250

4.2c Air filter housing drain collector (arrowed) – CRF250

7.2 Check the fuel system hoses

7.4 Check for leakage around the injector holder (arrowed)

3 Clean the screen mesh on the inner end using a soft brush. Check the mesh for splits and holes. Replace the arrester with a new one if damage is found.
4 Fit the arrester using a new gasket and tighten the bolts.
5 Fit the end cap and shield.

6 Idle speed

Note: *If other engine-related service items are to be carried out (i.e. spark plug, air filter, valve clearances), do these before checking the idle speed.*
1 The engine must be at normal operating temperature when the idle speed is checked. Take the machine for a 10 to 15 minute ride, then place it on the sidestand with the engine running and the transmission in neutral. Check the idle speed shown on the tachometer against the figure specified for your model at the beginning of this Chapter.
2 Snap the throttle open and shut a few times, then recheck the idle speed.
3 Turn the handlebars from side-to-side and check the idle speed does not change as you do. If it does, the throttle cables may not be adjusted or routed correctly, or may be worn out. This is a dangerous condition that can cause loss of control of the bike. Be sure to correct this problem before proceeding.
4 At all times, the engine idle speed is controlled by the ECM, and is not adjustable. If the idle speed is incorrect or is not smooth and steady, first check for an intake air leak between the throttle body and the cylinder head, and on 250 models also check the PAIR system (see Section 20). Make sure the crankcase breather hose is not pinched or blocked (Section 4). If all appears good check the idle air control valve (see Chapter 4, Section 6).

7 Fuel system

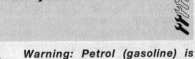

⚠ **Warning: Petrol (gasoline) is extremely flammable, so take extra precautions when you work on any part of the fuel system. Don't smoke or allow open flames or bare light bulbs near the work area, and don't work in a garage where a natural gas-type appliance is present. If you spill any fuel on your skin, rinse it off immediately with soap and water. When you perform any kind of work on the fuel system, wear safety glasses and have a fire extinguisher suitable for a Class B type fire (flammable liquids) on hand.**

1 On CBR models raise the fuel tank (see Chapter 4). On CRF models remove the right-hand fuel tank cover (see Chapter 7).
2 Check the tank, the fuel supply hose, and on CBR models the fuel filter and its hoses, for signs of leaks, deterioration or damage **(see illustration)**. Replace any hose that is cracked or deteriorated with a new one (see Chapter 4).
3 Check for signs of leakage around the fuel pump mounting plate on the underside of the tank **(see illustration 7.2)**. If any is evident, check the mounting nuts are tightened to the specified torque setting (see Chapter 4). If the leak persists, remove the pump and fit new seals (see Chapter 4).
4 Inspect the joints between the fuel injector holder, the injector and the throttle body **(see illustration)**. If there are any leaks, remove the injector and fit a new seal and O-ring (see Chapter 4).
5 Fuel filter replacement is not a service item. If fuel starvation is experienced, and all other possibilities have been checked, a blocked filter could be the cause. Refer to Chapter 4 for filter replacement.

8 Throttle cable(s)

1 Make sure the throttle grip rotates smoothly and freely from fully closed to fully open with the front wheel turned at various angles. The grip should return automatically from fully open to fully closed when released. If the throttle sticks, lubricate the cable as described below.

Checking cable freeplay

2 Check for a small amount of freeplay in the cables, measured in terms of the amount of twistgrip rotation before the throttle opens, and compare the amount to that listed in this Chapter's Specifications **(see illustration)**. If it's incorrect, adjust the cables to correct it as follows.
3 Initially adjust freeplay using the adjuster in the throttle opening cable where it leaves the throttle/switch housing on the handlebar. Slide the boot off the adjuster (CBR models). Loosen the locknut and turn the adjuster in or out as required until the specified amount of freeplay is obtained, then retighten the

8.2 Throttle cable freeplay is measured in terms of twistgrip rotation

8.3a Locknut (A) and adjuster (B) – CBR125

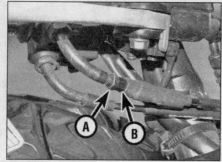

8.3b Locknut (A) and adjuster (B) – CBR250

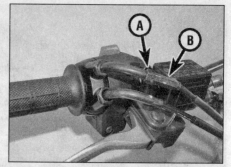

8.3c Locknut (A) and adjuster (B) – CRF250

locknut, and on CBR models fit the boot **(see illustrations)**.

4 If the adjuster has reached its limit of adjustment, reset it to its start point by turning it fully in, so that freeplay is at a maximum. Now adjust the cable at the throttle body end – on CBR125 models remove the right-hand fairing side panel, and on CBR250 models remove the right-hand fuel tank cover (see Chapter 7), then carefully pull the side panel pegs out of the fuel tank.

5 Slacken the adjuster locknut, then turn the adjuster in or out as required, making sure the lower nut remains captive in the bracket, thereby threading itself along the adjuster as you turn it, until the specified amount of freeplay is obtained, then tighten the locknut **(see illustrations)**. Subsequent adjustments can be made at the throttle end when required.

If the cable cannot be adjusted as specified, replace it with a new one (see Chapter 4).

Cable and twistgrip lubrication

6 If the throttle sticks, this is probably due to a cable fault. Remove the cable(s) (see Chapter 4) and lubricate it/them (see Section 17). Check that the inner cable slides freely and easily in the outer cable. If not, replace the cable with a new one.

7 With the cable(s) removed, make sure the throttle twistgrip rotates freely on the handlebar – dirt combined with a lack of lubrication can cause the action to be stiff. If necessary slide the twistgrip off – on CBR models first remove the handlebar end-weight. Clean any old grease from the bar and the inside of the tube. Smear some multi-purpose grease onto the bar, then refit the twistgrip.

On CBR models, when fitting the end-weight, align the boss with the cut-out on the inner weight inside the handlebar. Clean the threads of the end-weight screw, then apply a suitable non-permanent thread locking compound.

8 Install the cable(s), making sure the routing is correct (see Chapter 4). If this fails to improve the operation of the throttle, fit a new cable. Note that in very rare cases the fault could lie in the throttle body – check the action of the throttle pulley and valve.

⚠️ *Warning: Turn the handlebars all the way through their travel with the engine idling. Idle speed should not change. If it does, the cable(s) may be routed incorrectly. Correct this condition before riding the bike.*

9 Spark plug

125 models

Special tool: *A wire gauge or feeler gauge set is necessary for measuring the spark plug gap (see illustrations 9.9a and b).*

1 For best access remove the right-hand fairing side panel (see Chapter 7).
2 Clean the area around the spark plug to prevent any dirt falling into the combustion chamber.
3 Pull the cap off the plug **(see illustration)**.
4 Using either the plug removing tool supplied in the bike's toolkit or a plug socket, unscrew and remove the plug **(see illustration)**.
5 Before cleaning the plug refer to the colour spark plug chart at the end of this manual and compare your plug to those shown, identifying any abnormal condition and assessing its cause if necessary.
6 Clean the electrodes using a wire brush – if you can't remove the deposits fit a new plug. Cleaning the spark plug by sandblasting is fine as long as you blow out any residue and clean the plug with a high flash-point solvent afterwards. Also clean any deposits off the white ceramic body of the plug.
7 Check the condition of the cleaned electrodes. Both the centre and side electrodes should have square edges and the side electrode should be of uniform thickness.

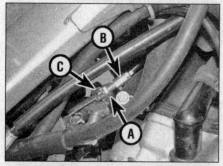

8.5a Throttle cable adjuster locknut (A), adjuster (B) and lower nut (C) – 125 models

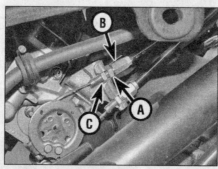

8.5b Throttle cable adjuster locknut (A), adjuster (B) and lower nut (C) – 250 models

9.3 Pull the cap off...

9.4 ...then unscrew the plug

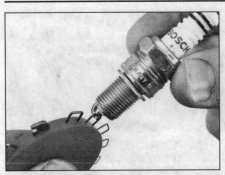

9.9a Using a wire type gauge to measure the spark plug electrode gap

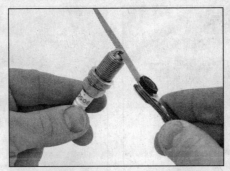

9.9b Using a feeler gauge to measure the spark plug electrode gap

9.9c Adjust the gap by bending the side electrode – a wire gauge is fitted with the correct tool for this

Check for evidence of a cracked or chipped insulator around the centre electrode. Check the plug threads, the washer and the ceramic insulator body for cracks and other damage.

8 If in doubt concerning the condition of the plug, replace it with a new one, as the expense is minimal.

9 If the plug can be re-used check the gap between the electrodes with a wire type gauge or feeler gauge **(see illustrations)**. The gap should be as given in the Specifications at the beginning of this chapter. If the electrodes have worn and the gap is wider than it should be, or for some reason the gap is narrower than it should be (if the plug has been dropped for instance) carefully bend the outer electrode as required to restore the correct gap **(see illustration)**.

10 Thread the plug into the head by hand until finger-tight, making sure it does not cross-thread **(see illustration)**. Once the plug is finger-tight, tighten it using a spanner on the tool supplied or a socket drive **(see illustration 9.4)**. If a torque wrench can be applied, tighten the spark plug to the torque setting specified at the beginning of the Chapter. Otherwise, if a new plug is being used tighten it by 1/2 a turn after the washer has seated, and if the old plug is being reused tighten it by 1/8 to 1/4 turn after it has seated, according to feel. Do not over-tighten it.

9.10 Thread the plug in by hand

11 Fit the cap onto the plug and push it down so it is fully seated **(see illustration 9.3)**.
12 Install the fairing side panel.

> **HAYNES HiNT** *Stripped plug threads in the cylinder head can be repaired with a thread insert – see 'Tools and Workshop Tips' in the Reference section.*

250 models

Special tool: *A wire gauge is necessary– do not use a blade type gauge **(see illustration 9.9a)**.*

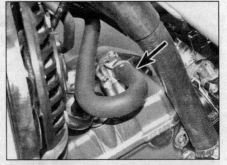

9.14 Release the clamp and detach the hose (arrowed)

13 On CBR models remove the fairing side panels (see Chapter 7). Displace the radiator from its mounts and move it forwards (see Chapter 3) – there is no need to drain the cooling system or detach any hoses.
14 On CRF models remove the left-hand fuel tank cover (see Chapter 7). Detach the PAIR system hose from the reed valve cover **(see illustration)**.
15 Clean the area around the plug cap seal to prevent any dirt falling into the spark plug channel.
16 Pull the cap off the plug **(see illustrations)**.
17 Clean around the base of the spark plug

9.16a Pulling the cap off the plug – CBR models

9.16b Pulling the cap off the plug – CRF models

9.18a Unscrew the plug...

9.18b ...and lift it out with the tool

9.20a If the centre electrode has rounded off the plug is worn

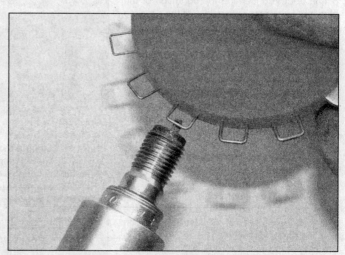

9.20b Check the gap using a wire gauge

using compressed air if available to prevent any dirt falling into the combustion chamber.

18 Using either the plug removing tool supplied in the bike's toolkit or a spark plug socket and extension, unscrew and remove the plug **(see illustrations)**.

19 Check the condition of the electrodes, referring to the spark plug reading chart at the end of this manual if signs of contamination are evident. Note that a contaminated iridium plug should not be cleaned – discard it and fit a new one.

20 Examine the pointed iridium-tipped centre electrode; if the tip has rounded off, the plug is worn **(see illustration)**. Measure the gap between the two electrodes with a 1 mm wire type gauge only **(see illustration)** – do not use blade type feeler gauges because the iridium tip might be damaged. If the wire gauge fits between the electrodes the tip has worn (the gap when new is 0.8 to 0.9 mm) and a new plug must be fitted. Do not bend the outer

electrode to adjust the gap. If for some reason the gap is narrower than it should be (if the plug has been dropped for instance) a new plug must be fitted.

21 Check the threads, the washer and the ceramic insulator body for cracks and other damage.

22 Note that Honda advise that the specified iridium plugs only must be fitted – do not substitute with conventional plugs.

23 Fit the plug into the end of the tool or socket and thread the plug into the head by hand until finger-tight, making sure it does not cross-thread **(see illustration 9.18b)**. Once the plug is finger-tight, tighten it using a spanner on the tool supplied or a socket drive **(see illustration 9.18a)**. If a torque wrench can be applied, tighten the spark plug to the torque setting specified at the beginning of the Chapter. Otherwise, if a new plug is being used tighten it by 1/2 a turn after the washer has seated, and if the old plug is being reused

tighten it by 1/8 to 1/4 turn after it has seated, according to feel. Do not over-tighten it.

24 Fit the cap onto the plug and push it down so it is fully seated **(see illustration 9.16a or b)**.

25 Install all displaced and removed components (see Step 13 or 14).

10 Valve clearances

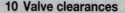

Special tool: *A set of feeler gauges is necessary for this job (see illustration 10.6).*

125 models

1 The engine must be completely cold.

2 Remove the valve cover (see Chapter 2A). Remove the spark plug (see Section 9).

3 Unscrew the timing inspection cap and the crankshaft end cap from the alternator

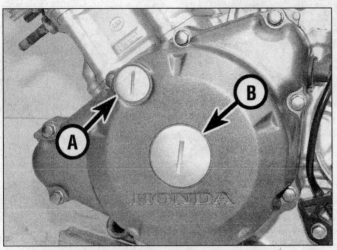

10.3 Remove the timing inspection cap (A) and the crankshaft end cap (B)

10.5a Turn the engine anti-clockwise using the nut...

cover on the left-hand side of the engine **(see illustration)**.

4 To check the valve clearances the crankshaft must be turned to position the piston at top dead centre (TDC) on its compression stroke so that the valves are closed. The engine can be turned using a suitable socket on the alternator rotor nut and must be turned in an anti-clockwise direction only.

5 Turn the crankshaft anti-clockwise until the line next to the T mark on the rotor aligns with the notch in the inspection hole rim, and the index line on the camshaft sprocket is parallel and flush with the cylinder head top surface (the line will be below the sprocket bolts) **(see illustrations)**. There should now be some freeplay in each rocker arm (i.e. they are not contacting the valve stem). If the index line is parallel but not flush with the head, i.e. it is above the sprocket bolts not below them, rotate the engine anti-clockwise one full turn (360°) until the line next to the T mark again aligns with the notch, the index line on the sprocket is flush with the head, and there is some freeplay in the rockers.

6 With the engine in this position, check the clearance of each valve by inserting a feeler gauge of the same thickness as the correct valve clearance (see Specifications and select the mid-point in the range) in the gap between the rocker arm and the valve stem **(see illustration)**. The intake valve is on the back of the cylinder head and the exhaust valve is on the front. The gauge should be a firm sliding fit – you should feel a slight drag when you pull it out.

7 If the gap (clearance) is either too wide or too narrow, slacken the locknut on the adjuster in the rocker arm and turn the adjuster as required using a screwdriver until the gap is as specified and the feeler gauge is a sliding fit, then hold the adjuster still and tighten the locknut **(see illustration)**. Recheck the clearance after tightening the locknut.

8 When the clearances are correct install the

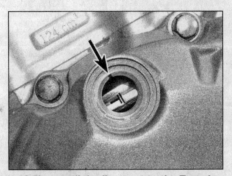

10.5b ...until the line next to the T mark aligns with the notch (arrowed)...

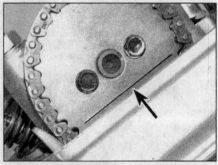

10.5c ...and the camshaft sprocket line (arrowed) is as shown

valve cover (see Chapter 2A) and the spark plug (Section 9).

9 Fit the timing inspection cap and crankshaft end cap using new O-rings if required, and smear the O-rings and the cap threads with clean oil.

10 Check the idle speed (see Section 5).

250 models

11 The engine must be completely cold.

10.6 Insert the feeler gauge between the base of the adjuster on the arm and the top of the valve stem as shown

12 Remove the valve cover (see Chapter 2B). Remove the spark plug (see Section 9).

13 Make a chart or sketch of the valve positions so that a note of each clearance can be made against the relevant valve. The intake valves are on the back of the cylinder head and the exhaust valves are on the front.

14 Unscrew the timing inspection cap and the crankshaft end cap from the alternator

10.7 Slacken the locknut then turn the adjuster using a screwdriver until the gap is correct

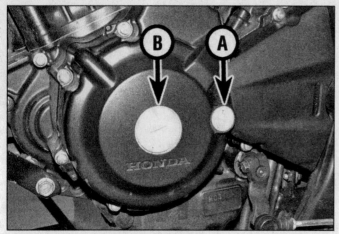

10.14 Remove the timing inspection cap (A) and the crankshaft end cap (B)

10.16a Turn the engine anti-clockwise using the bolt...

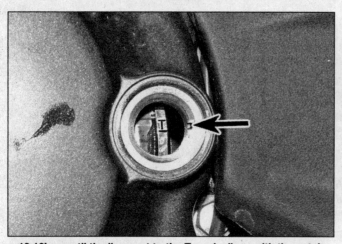

10.16b ...until the line next to the T mark aligns with the notch (arrowed)...

10.16c ...and the camshaft sprocket marks are as shown

cover on the left-hand side of the engine **(see illustration)**.

15 To check the valve clearances the crankshaft must be turned to position the piston at top dead centre (TDC) on its compression stroke so that all four valves are closed. The engine can be turned using a suitable socket on the alternator rotor bolt and must be turned in an anti-clockwise direction.

16 Turn the crankshaft anti-clockwise until the line next to the T mark on the rotor aligns with the notch in the inspection hole rim, and the IN and EX marks on the intake and exhaust camshaft sprockets are the correct way up and flush with the cylinder head top surface so the punch marks are at the top **(see illustrations)**. If the marks are upside down turn the crankshaft anti-clockwise one full turn (360°) until the line next to the T mark again aligns with the notch. The sprocket marks will now be as required.

17 With the engine in this position, check the clearance of each valve by inserting a feeler gauge of the same thickness as the correct valve clearance (see Specifications and select the mid-point in the range) in the gap

between the rocker arm and the valve stem **(see illustration)**. The gauge should be a firm sliding fit – you should feel a slight drag when you pull it out. If the gap (clearance) is either too wide or too narrow use the feeler gauges to measure the exact clearance and record it on the chart.

18 When all four clearances have been measured and charted, identify whether

the clearance on any valve falls outside the specified range. If any do, the shim must be replaced with one of a thickness that will restore the correct clearance.

19 To replace a shim you need to displace the rocker arm. Unscrew the rocker shaft plug and remove the sealing washer **(see illustration)** – a new one must be used. Thread a 6 mm bolt into the end of the shaft and use it to draw the

10.17 Insert the feeler gauge between the base of the adjuster on the arm and the top of the valve stem as shown

10.19a Unscrew the plug...

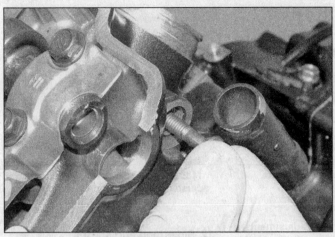

10.19b ...then thread a 6mm bolt in...

10.19c ...and pull the shaft out

10.19d Push the arm off the valve

10.21 Remove the shim

shaft out **(see illustrations)**. Slide the rocker arm off the valves **(see illustration)** – you will need to keep the intake rocker arm held back while removing and fitting a shim.

20 Place a rag over the spark plug hole and the cam chain tunnel to prevent a shim from dropping into the engine on removal. Work on one valve at a time to prevent the possibility of mixing up the shims. If you want to remove more than one shim at a time, store them in a

marked container, denoting which valve the shim is from, so that they do not get mixed up.

21 Remove the shim from the top of the valve using either a magnet, a screwdriver with a dab of grease on it (the shim will stick to the grease), or a very small screwdriver and a pair of pliers or tweezers **(see illustration)**. Do not allow the shim to fall into the engine.

22 Measure and record the thickness of the shim using a micrometer **(see illustration)**.

23 Calculate the required replacement shim by using the formula $a = (b - c) + d$, where a is the required size of the new shim, b is the measured valve clearance, c is the specified valve clearance (select the mid-point of the range), and d is the existing shim thickness. For example:

The measured clearance of an exhaust valve is 0.33 mm, so b = 0.33
The specified clearance range for an exhaust valve is 0.24 to 0.31 mm, the mid-point being 0.27 mm, so c = 0.27
The thickness of the existing shim is 2.00 mm, so d = 2.0
Therefore, the required replacement shim a = 0.33 – 0.27 + 2.0, so a = 2.06 mm.

Note: *If the required replacement shim is greater than 2.900 mm (the largest available), the valve is probably not seating correctly due to a build-up of carbon deposits and should be checked and cleaned or resurfaced as required (see Chapter 2B).*

24 Shims are available in 0.025 mm increments from 1.200 mm to 2.900 mm – the size is marked on the shim **(see illustration)**. Obtain

10.22 Measure the thickness of the shim

10.24 Shim thickness is marked on one face

the correct replacement shim (or the nearest one to the size required), then lubricate it with molybdenum disulphide oil (a 50/50 mixture of molybdenum disulphide grease and engine oil) and fit it into its recess in the top of the valve with the size mark facing up **(see illustration 10.21)**. Check that the shim is correctly seated
25 Repeat the process for any other valves until the clearances are correct.
26 Lubricate the rocker shaft with molybdenum disulphide oil (a 50/50 mixture of molybdenum disulphide grease and engine oil). Position the rocker arm over the valves and hold it there, then slide the shaft through the arm **(see illustration)**. Fit the plug, using a new sealing washer **(see illustration 10.19a)**.
27 Rotate the crankshaft anti-clockwise several turns to seat the new shim(s), then check the clearances again.
28 When the clearances are correct install the valve cover (see Chapter 2B) and the spark plug (Section 9).
29 Fit the timing inspection cap and crankshaft end cap using new O-rings if required, and smear the O-rings and the cap threads with clean oil. Tighten the caps to the torque settings specified at the beginning of the Chapter.
30 Check the idle speed (see Section 6).

11 Headlight aim

Note: *An improperly adjusted headlight may cause problems for oncoming traffic or provide poor, unsafe illumination of the road ahead. Before adjusting the headlight aim, be sure to consult with local traffic laws and regulations – for UK models refer to MOT Test Checks in the Reference section.*
1 The headlight beam can adjusted both horizontally and vertically. Before making any adjustment, check that the tyre pressures are correct and the suspension is adjusted as required. Make any adjustments to the headlight aim with the machine on level ground, with the fuel tank half full and with an assistant sitting on the seat. If the bike is usually ridden with a passenger on the back, have a second assistant to do this.

10.26 Align the bores and insert the shaft

2 On CBR models vertical adjustment is made by turning the adjuster screw on the right-hand side of the headlight using a Phillips screwdriver and accessing it from the underside via the channel **(see illustration)**. Turn it clockwise to move the beam up, and anti-clockwise to move it down. Horizontal adjustment is made by turning the adjuster screw on the left-hand side of the headlight. Turn it clockwise to move the beam to the right, and anti-clockwise to move it to the left. For best access to the adjusters remove the fairing side panel on the relevant side (see Chapter 7).

HAYNES HINT *The adjuster can be turned via the screw head, or by engaging the screwdriver in the toothed edge of the adjuster via the channel.*

3 On CRF models vertical adjustment is made by turning the adjuster screw on the right-hand side of the headlight using a Phillips screwdriver and accessing it from the side via the channel **(see illustration)**. Turn it clockwise to move the beam up, and anti-clockwise to move it down. Horizontal adjustment is made by turning the adjuster screw on the left-hand side of the headlight using a spanner and accessing it from the side **(see illustration)**. Turn it clockwise to move the beam to the right, and anti-clockwise to move it to the left.

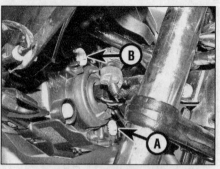
11.2 Vertical adjuster (A), horizontal adjuster (B) – CBR models, fairing side panel removed

12 Sidestand and starter interlock circuit

1 Check the stand springs for damage and distortion **(see illustration)**. The springs must be capable of retracting the stand fully and holding it retracted when the motorcycle is in use. If a spring is sagged or broken it must be replaced with a new one.
2 Lubricate the stand pivot regularly (see Section 17).
3 Check the stand and its mount for bends and cracks. Stands can often be repaired by welding.
4 Check the operation of the starter interlock circuit as follows:
● Make sure the transmission is in neutral, then retract the stand and start the engine. Pull in the clutch lever and select a gear. Keeping the clutch lever pulled in, extend the sidestand. The engine should stop as the sidestand is extended.
● Make sure the engine is in neutral and the sidestand is down, then start the engine. Pull the clutch lever in and select a gear. The engine should cut out.
● Check that when the sidestand is down the engine can only be started if the transmission is in neutral, and when the sidestand is up and the transmission is in gear the engine can only be started if the clutch lever is pulled in.

11.3a Vertical alignment adjuster...

11.3b ...and horizontal adjuster (arrowed) – CRF250

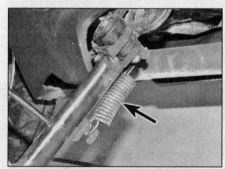
12.1 Check the springs (arrowed) as described

5 If the circuit does not operate as described, check the sidestand switch, neutral switch, clutch switch and diodes, and the circuit between them (see Chapter 8).

13 Suspension

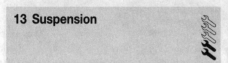

1 The suspension components must be maintained in top operating condition to ensure rider safety. Loose, worn or damaged suspension parts decrease the motorcycle's stability and control.

Front suspension check

2 While standing alongside the motorcycle, apply the front brake and push on the handlebars to compress the forks several times **(see illustration)**. See if they move up-and-down smoothly without binding. If binding is felt, the forks should be disassembled and inspected (see Chapter 5).
3 Inspect each fork inner tube for scratches, corrosion and pitting in the area of travel through the seals, which will cause premature seal failure **(see illustration)** – if the damage is excessive, new inner tubes should be fitted (see Chapter 5), or the inner tubes must be re-chromed using hard chrome.
4 Also check the inner tubes for signs of oil leakage. Carefully lever the dust seal out using a flat-bladed screwdriver and inspect the area around the oil seal. If leakage is evident, the seals must be replaced with new ones (see Chapter 5). If there is evidence of corrosion between the oil seal retaining ring and its groove in the fork tube, spray the area with a penetrative lubricant, otherwise the ring will be difficult to remove if needed. Press the dust seal back into the outer tube on completion.
5 Check the tightness of all suspension nuts and bolts to be sure none have worked loose, referring to the torque settings specified at the beginning of Chapter 5.

Rear suspension check

6 Inspect the rear shock absorber for fluid leakage and tightness of its mountings. If leakage is found, the shock must be replaced with a new one (see Chapter 5).
7 With the aid of an assistant to support the bike, compress the rear suspension several times **(see illustration)**. It should move up-and-down freely without binding. If any binding is felt, the worn or faulty component must be identified and checked (see Chapter 5). The problem could be due to the shock absorber, the swingarm, or on 250 models the suspension linkage.
8 Support the bike on an auxiliary stand (but not a paddock stand under the swingarm!) so that the rear wheel is off the ground. Grab the swingarm and rock it from side-to-side – there

13.2 Compress the forks to check their action

13.3 Check each inner tube (arrowed) for pitting and signs of oil leakage

should be no discernible movement at the rear **(see illustration)**.
9 Next, grasp the top of the rear wheel and pull it upwards – there should be no discernible freeplay before the shock absorber begins to compress.
10 If there's a little movement or a slight clicking can be heard, check the tightness of the swingarm pivot, referring to the procedure in Chapter 5, and re-check for movement. Also check the shock absorber mounting bolts/nut(s), and on 250 models the suspension linkage mounting bolts/nuts. If there is still some noise or freeplay after everything has been correctly tightened then there is a worn bush or bearing(s) in one of the rear suspension components. The worn components must be identified and replaced with new ones (see Chapter 5).
11 You can make a more accurate assessment by isolating the components from each other – remove the rear wheel (see Chapter 6) and on 250 models detach the linkage (see Chapter 5).
12 Grasp the rear of the swingarm with one hand and place your other hand at the junction of the swingarm and the frame. Try to move the rear of the swingarm from side-to-side. Any wear (play) in the bearings should be felt as movement between the swingarm and the frame at the front. If there is any play, the swingarm will be felt to move forward and backward at the front (not from side-to-side). Next, move the swingarm up and down through its full travel. It should move freely,

without any binding or rough spots. If there is any play in the swingarm or if it does not move freely, remove the bearings for inspection (see Chapter 5).
13 With the shock absorber, and on 250 models the linkage, detached check the bearings and bush in each component for corrosion and wear and failure of the seals, referring to Chapter 5 for details according to model, and clean and re-grease or replace components as required.

Front fork oil change

14 Although there is no set interval for changing the fork oil, the oil will degrade over a period of time and lose its damping qualities. Refer to Chapter 5 for details of front fork removal, oil draining and refilling. The forks do not need to be completely disassembled to change the oil.

Rear suspension bearing lubrication

15 Although there is no set interval for re-greasing the suspension bearings, over a considerable mileage the seals are likely to fail and the grease in the bearings will be washed out or will harden allowing the ingress of dirt and water.
16 The swingarm, and on 250 models the suspension linkage, should be removed periodically and the bearings cleaned and re-greased as necessary (see Chapter 5).

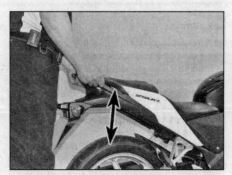

13.7 Compress the rear suspension to check its action

13.8 Checking for play in the swingarm bearings

14.2 Adjusting spoke tension using a spanner

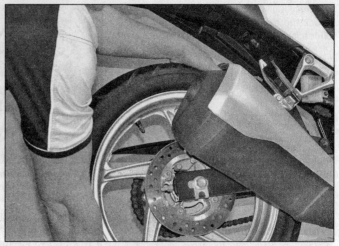

14.6 Checking for play in the wheel bearings

14 Wheels, wheel bearings and tyres

Wheels

CBR models

1 Cast wheels are virtually maintenance free, but they should be kept clean and checked periodically for cracks and other damage. Never attempt to repair cast wheels – if damaged they must be replaced with new ones. Also check wheel run-out and alignment (see Chapter 6). Check that the wheel balance weights are fixed firmly to the wheel rim. If you suspect that a weight has fallen off, have the wheel rebalanced by a motorcycle tyre specialist.

CRF models

2 Visually check the spokes for damage and corrosion. A broken or bent spoke must be replaced with a new one immediately because the load taken by it will be transferred to adjacent spokes which may in turn fail. Check the tension in each spoke by tapping each one lightly with a screwdriver and noting the sound produced – each should make the same sound of the correct pitch. Properly tensioned spokes will make a sharp pinging sound, loose ones will produce a lower pitch dull sound and tight ones will be higher pitched. If a spoke needs adjustment turn the adjuster at the rim using a spoke adjustment tool or an open-ended spanner **(see illustration)**.
3 Unevenly tensioned spokes will promote rim misalignment – refer to information on wheel runout in Chapter 6 and seek the advice of a Honda dealer or wheel building specialist if the wheel needs realigning, which it may well do if many spokes are unevenly tensioned. Check front and rear wheel alignment as described in Chapter 6. Check that any wheel balance weights are fixed firmly to the wheel rim. If you suspect that a weight has fallen off, have

the wheel rebalanced by a motorcycle tyre specialist.

Wheel bearings

4 Wheel bearings will wear over a considerable mileage and should be checked periodically to avoid handling problems.
5 Support the motorcycle upright using an auxiliary stand so that the wheel being examined is off the ground.
6 Check for any play in the bearings by pushing and pulling the wheel against the hub **(see illustration)**. When checking the front wheel turn the handlebars to full lock on one side and hold the wheel against the lock. Also rotate the wheel and check that it turns smoothly and without any grating noises (bearing in mind that the brakes and final drive make some noise – do not confuse them).
7 If any play is detected in the hub, or if the wheel does not rotate smoothly (and this is not due to brake or transmission drag), the wheel should be removed and the bearings inspected for wear or damage (see Chapter 6).

Tyres

8 Check the tyre condition and tread depth thoroughly – see Pre-ride checks.
9 Make sure the valve cap is in place and tight. Check the valve for signs of damage. If tyre deflation occurs and it is not due to a slow puncture the valve core may be loose or it could be leaking past the seal – remove the cap and make sure the core is tight; if it is tight then it could be leaking – unscrew the core from the valve housing using a core removal tool (sometimes incorporated in the valve cap) and thread a new one in its place. A tool can be made quite easily by cutting a slot into the threaded end of a bolt using a hacksaw – the bolt must fit inside the valve housing and the slot must be the correct thickness to fit over the top of the core.

15 Engine oil and filter

1 Consistent routine oil changes are the single most important maintenance procedure you can perform. The oil not only lubricates the internal parts of the engine, transmission and clutch, but it also acts as a coolant, a cleaner, a sealant, and a protector. Because of these demands, the oil takes a terrific amount of abuse and should be replaced as specified with new oil of the recommended grade and type.

> ⚠ **Warning: Be careful when draining the oil, as the exhaust pipe, the engine, and the oil itself can cause severe burns.**

Oil change – 125 models

2 Warm up the engine so the oil will drain easily. Place the bike on its sidestand on level ground. The oil drain plug is on the underside of the engine. For easiest access to the drain plug remove the lower fairing (See Chapter 7).
3 Position a clean drain tray below the engine. Unscrew the oil filler cap/dipstick from the clutch cover to vent the crankcase and to act as a reminder that there is no oil in the engine **(see illustration)**.

15.3 Unscrew the oil filler cap to act as a vent...

15.4a …then unscrew the oil drain plug…

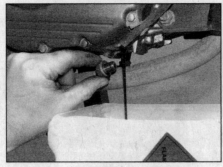

15.4b …and allow the oil to drain

15.4c Some sealing washers need to be cut off

4 Unscrew the oil drain plug and allow the oil to flow into the drain tray **(see illustrations)**. Remove the sealing washer from the drain plug – you may have to cut it off **(see illustration)**. A new washer must be used.

5 When the oil has completely drained clean the drain hole and rim. Fit a new sealing washer onto the drain plug. Fit the plug and tighten it to the torque setting specified at the beginning of the Chapter **(see illustration)**. Do not overtighten it as the threads in the engine are easily damaged.

6 Refer to the Specifications at the beginning of the Chapter and refill the engine using the specified type and amount of oil **(see illustration)**. Wipe the dipstick clean, fit it into the filler hole and allow it to rest on the threads **(see illustration)** – do not screw it in. With the motorcycle vertical the oil level should lie between the upper and lower level lines **(see illustration)**. Check the condition of the O-ring on the filler cap and replace it with new a one if damaged or worn.

7 Start the engine and let it run for two or three minutes. Shut it off, wait a few minutes, then recheck the oil level. If necessary, add more oil to bring the level close to the upper line on the dipstick, but do not go above it.

8 Check that there are no oil leaks from the drain plug.

9 The old oil drained from the engine cannot be re-used and should be disposed of properly. Check with your local refuse disposal company, disposal facility or environmental agency to see whether they will accept the used oil for recycling. Don't pour used oil into drains or onto the ground.

Oil strainer clean – 125 models

10 Drain the engine oil (see Steps 2 to 5).
11 Remove the clutch cover (see Chapter 2A).
12 Withdraw the strainer from its slot in the bottom of the engine, noting which way round it fits **(see illustration)**.
13 Wash the strainer in solvent making sure all debris is removed from the mesh – blow through it using compressed air if available. Check the mesh for holes and damage and replace the strainer with a new one if necessary.
14 Coat the rubber rim of the strainer with clean oil, then slide it into the grooves in its chamber with the thinner edge going in first and the flanged side at the top.
15 Install the clutch cover. Refill the engine with oil (see Steps 6 to 8).

Oil and filter change – 250 models

16 Warm up the engine so the oil will drain easily. Place the bike on its sidestand on level ground. The oil drain plug is on the underside of the engine. For easiest access to the drain plug on CBR models remove the lower fairing (See Chapter 7).
17 Position a large clean drain tray below the engine, so it is under the drain plug and the filter housing. Unscrew the oil filler cap from the clutch cover to vent the crankcase and

15.5 Fit the drain plug using a new sealing washer

15.6a Add the correct type and amount of oil via the filler hole

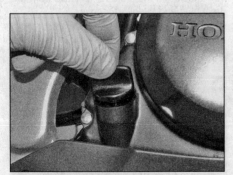

15.6b Check the level with the dipstick resting on its threads

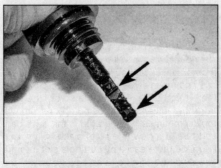

15.6c The level must lie between the lines (arrowed)

15.12 Withdraw the strainer, noting how it locates in the grooves and how the thin edge faces in

15.17 Unscrew the oil filler cap to act as a vent...

15.18a ...then unscrew the oil drain plug (arrowed)...

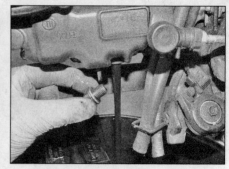

15.18b ...and allow the oil to drain

to act as a reminder that there is no oil in the engine **(see illustration)**.

18 Unscrew the oil drain plug and allow the oil to flow into the drain tray **(see illustrations)**. Remove the sealing washer from the drain plug

– you may have to cut it off **(see illustration 15.4c)**. A new washer must be used.

19 Unscrew the filter cover bolts and remove the cover, noting the spring **(see illustration)**. Remove the filter from the engine and allow

it and the housing to drain **(see illustration)**. Remove the gasket **(see illustration)** – a new one must be used.

20 When the oil has completely drained clean the drain hole and rim. Fit a new sealing washer onto the drain plug **(see illustration)**. Fit the plug and tighten it to the torque setting specified at the beginning of the Chapter. Do not overtighten it as the threads in the sump are easily damaged.

21 Clean the filter housing and cover and the gasket faces. Fit the spring into the cover.

22 Fit the new filter into the housing with the OUTSIDE mark facing out **(see illustration)** – if the mark faces in oil will not flow through the filter and you will severely damage the engine. Make sure the spring is in the cover. Fit the cover using a new gasket and tighten the bolts evenly in a criss-cross sequence.

23 Refer to the Specifications at the beginning of the Chapter and refill the engine using the specified type and amount of oil **(see illustration)**. With the motorcycle vertical the oil level should lie between the upper and lower level lines on the inspection window **(see illustration)**. Check the condition of the O-ring on the filler cap and replace it with a new one if damaged or worn.

24 Start the engine and let it run for two or three minutes. Shut it off, wait a few minutes, then recheck the oil level. If necessary, add more oil to bring the level close to the upper line on the inspection window, but do not go above it.

25 Check that there are no oil leaks from the drain plug and the oil filter cover.

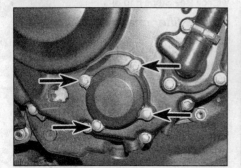

15.19a Unscrew the bolts and remove the cover...

15.19b ...and the filter

15.19c Remove the gasket

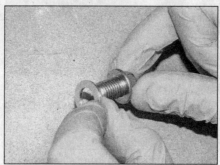

15.20 Fit a new sealing washer

15.22 Fit the filter and the cover with its spring and a new gasket

15.23a Add the correct type and amount of oil via the filler hole

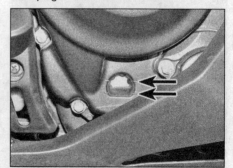

15.23b Check the level is between the lines (arrowed)

16.3 Check all the coolant hoses as described

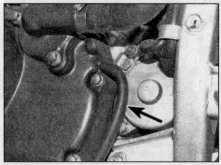

16.5a Pump drain hose (arrowed) – 125 models

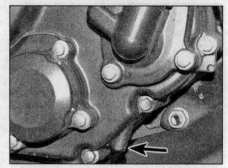

16.5b Pump drain hole (arrowed) – 250 models

26 The old oil drained from the engine cannot be re-used and should be disposed of properly. Check with your local refuse disposal company, disposal facility or environmental agency to see whether they will accept the used oil for recycling. Don't pour used oil into drains or onto the ground.

 HAYNES HiNT *Check the old oil carefully – if it is very metallic coloured, then the engine is experiencing wear from break-in (new engine) or from insufficient lubrication. If there are flakes or chips of metal in the oil, then something is drastically wrong internally and the engine will have to be disassembled for inspection and repair. If there are pieces of fibre-like material in the oil, the clutch is experiencing excessive wear and should be checked.*

 **OIL CARE** *Note: It is illegal and anti-social to dump oil down the drain. To find the location of your local oil recycling bank in the UK, call 08708 506 506 or visit www.oilbankline.org.uk*

16 Cooling system check and coolant change

Check

 Warning: The engine must be cool before beginning this procedure.

1 On CBR models remove the fairing side panels and the lower fairing (see Chapter 7). On CBR125 models raise the fuel tank (see Chapter 4). On CRF models remove the fuel tank covers (see Chapter 7).
2 Check the coolant level in the reservoir (see *Pre-ride checks*).
3 Examine each rubber coolant hose along its entire length. Look for cracks, abrasions and other damage. Squeeze each hose at various points to see whether they are dried out or hard (see illustration). They should feel firm, yet pliable, and return to their original shape when released. If necessary, replace them with new ones (see Chapter 3).
4 Check the entire cooling system for evidence of leaks, particularly at each cooling system joint and around the pump housing on the right-hand side of the engine (see illustration 16.15a or b). Tighten the hose clips carefully to prevent future leaks. If the pump is leaking around the cover, check that the bolts are tight. If they are, remove the cover and replace the O-ring with a new one (see Chapter 3).
5 To prevent leakage of coolant from the cooling system to the lubrication system and vice versa, two seals are fitted on the pump shaft. The coolant seal on the water pump side is of the mechanical type and bears on the rear face of the impeller. The oil seal, mounted behind the mechanical seal, is of the normal feathered lip type. On the front of the pump housing there is a drain hose on 125 engines and a drain hole on 250 engines (see illustrations). If either seal fails, the drain allows the coolant or oil to escape. If on inspection the drain shows signs of leakage, particularly of continuous leakage with the engine running, remove the pump and replace the seals with new ones (see Chapter 3). Honda states that a small amount of coolant weeping is normal, so you may have to decide for yourself the difference between a small amount of weeping and continuous leakage – if in doubt seek the advice of your dealer.

6 Check the radiator for leaks and other damage. Leaks leave tell-tale scale deposits or coolant stains on the outside of the core below the leak. If leaks are noted, remove the radiator (see Chapter 3) and have it repaired or replace it with a new one – do not use a liquid leak stopping compound to try to repair leaks.
7 Check the radiator fins for mud, dirt and insects, which will impede the flow of air through the radiator (see illustration). If the fins are dirty, remove the radiator (see Chapter 3) and clean it using water or low pressure compressed air directed through the fins from the inner side of the radiator. If the fins are bent or distorted, straighten them carefully with a screwdriver. If airflow is restricted by bent or damaged fins over more than 20% of the radiator's surface area, replace the radiator with a new one.

 Warning: Do not remove the pressure cap when the engine is hot. It is good practice to cover the cap with a heavy cloth and turn the cap slowly anti-clockwise. If you hear a hissing sound (indicating that there is still pressure in the system), wait until it stops, then continue turning the cap until it can be removed.

8 Undo the radiator pressure cap screw (see illustration). Remove the cap by turning it anti-clockwise until it reaches the stop. Now

16.7 Check for debris that impedes airflow, and use a small screwdriver to straighten bent fins

16.8a Undo the screw...

16.8b ...and remove the pressure cap as described

16.13 Undo the screw and remove the cover

16.15a Cooling system drain bolt (arrowed) – 125 models

press down on the cap and continue turning it until it can be removed **(see illustration)**.

9 Check the condition of the coolant in the system. If it is rust-coloured or if accumulations of scale are visible, drain, flush and refill the system with new coolant (see below). Check the antifreeze content of the coolant with an antifreeze hydrometer – a 50% content should give a reading of 1.084 at 5°C to 1.074 at 25°C, varying accordingly in between. The system must have the correct coolant mixture (see Specifications) – if the coolant is too weak (i.e. too little anti-freeze giving a low reading – anything below 1.07 when cold and 1.06 when hot) there will not be adequate protection against freezing and corrosion, and if it is too strong the ability to cool the engine is reduced. If the hydrometer indicates an incorrect mixture, drain and refill the system (see below).

10 The function of the pressure cap is crucial to the correct running of the cooling system. Check the cap seal for cracks and other damage. If the coolant level consistently drops and/or the bike overheats, and no evidence of leaks can be found, have the cap pressure checked by a Honda dealer, or just fit a new one. If a new cap does not cure the problem have the entire system pressure checked by a dealer.

11 Fit the cap by turning it clockwise until it reaches the first stop then push down on it and continue turning until it can turn no further. Fit the screw.

12 Start the engine and let it reach normal operating temperature, then check for leaks again. As the coolant temperature increases, the electric fan (mounted on the back of the radiator) should come on automatically and the temperature should begin to drop. If not, refer to Chapter 3 and check the fan and fan circuit.

Change the coolant

⚠️ *Warning: Allow the engine to cool completely before performing this maintenance operation. Also, don't allow anti-freeze to come into contact with your skin or the painted surfaces of the motorcycle. Rinse off spills immediately with plenty of water. Anti-freeze is highly toxic if ingested.*

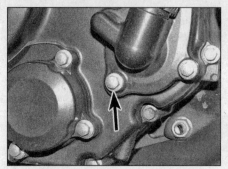

16.15b Cooling system drain bolt (arrowed) – 250 models

Never leave anti-freeze lying around in an open container or in puddles on the floor; children and pets are attracted by its sweet smell and may drink it. Check with local authorities (councils) about disposing of anti-freeze. Many communities have collection centres which will see that anti-freeze is disposed of safely. Anti-freeze is also combustible, so don't store it near open flames.

Draining

13 Make sure the engine is cold. Support the motorcycle upright on a level surface using an auxiliary stand. On CBR models remove the fairing side panels and lower fairing (see Chapter 7). On CBR 125 models remove the rider's seat (see Chapter 7). On CBR250 models undo the reservoir cover screw and remove the cover **(see illustration)**. On CRF

16.16a Coolant reservoir cap – CBR125

16.15c Draining the cooling system

models remove the fuel tank covers (see Chapter 7).

14 Undo the radiator pressure cap screw **(see illustration 16.8a)**. Remove the cap by turning it anti-clockwise until it reaches a stop. Now press down on the cap and continue turning it until it can be removed **(see illustration 16.8b)**.

15 Position a suitable container beneath the water pump housing on the right-hand side of the engine. Unscrew the drain bolt and allow the coolant to completely drain from the system **(see illustrations)**. Remove the sealing washer from the bolt – a new one must be used.

16 On CBR models remove the reservoir cap **(see illustrations)**. Disconnect the siphon hose from the radiator filler neck and release it from the clamps, then lower the hose to the

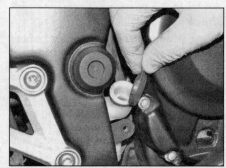

16.16b Coolant reservoir cap – CBR250

16.16c Disconnect the hose (arrowed) and drain the reservoir through it

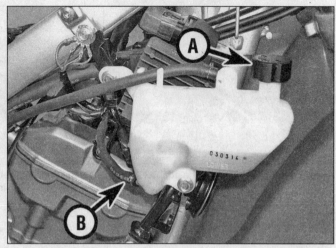

16.17 Unscrew the cap (A), then disconnect the hose (B) – CRF250

container and allow the reservoir to drain **(see illustration)**.

17 On CRF models remove the reservoir cap **(see illustration)**. Hold the container under the reservoir, then disconnect the siphon hose from the bottom of the reservoir and allow the reservoir to drain.

Flushing

18 Flush the system with clean tap water by inserting a hose in the radiator filler neck. Allow the water to run through the system until it is clear and flows out cleanly. If the radiator is extremely corroded, remove it (see Chapter 3) and have it cleaned by a specialist. Also flush the reservoir.

Refilling

19 Fit the drain bolt using a new sealing washer **(see illustration)**. Connect the siphon hose to the radiator or reservoir, according to model **(see illustration 16.16c or 16.17)**.

20 Fill the system to the base of the filler neck with the proper coolant mixture (see this Chapter's Specifications) **(see illustration)**. **Note:** *Pour the coolant in slowly to minimise the amount of air entering the system, and when full carefully waggle the bike from side to side and squeeze the coolant hoses to*

dislodge any trapped air. Fill the reservoir to the UPPER level line.

21 Start the engine and allow it to idle for 2 to 3 minutes. Flick the throttle twistgrip part open 3 or 4 times, so that the engine speed rises to approximately 4000 to 5000 rpm, then stop the engine. Any air trapped in the system should bleed back to and out of the filler neck.

22 If necessary, top up the coolant level to the base of the radiator filler neck, then fit the pressure cap and its screw.

23 Start the engine and allow it to reach normal operating temperature, then shut it off. Let the engine cool then remove the pressure cap as described in Step 14. Check that the coolant level is still up to the base of the radiator filler neck. If it's low, add the specified mixture until it reaches the base of the filler neck. Refit the cap.

24 Check the coolant level in the reservoir and top up to the UPPER level line if necessary.

25 Check the system for leaks. Install all removed components (see Step 13).

26 Do not dispose of the old coolant by pouring it down the drain. Instead pour it into a heavy plastic container, cap it tightly and take it into an authorised disposal site or service station – see **Warning** at the beginning of this Section.

17 Pivot points and cable lubrication

Pivot points

1 Since the controls, cables and various other components of a motorcycle are exposed to the elements, they should be checked and lubricated periodically to ensure safe and trouble-free operation.

2 The footrest pivots, clutch and brake lever pivots, brake pedal and gearchange lever pivots and linkage and sidestand pivot should be lubricated frequently. In order for the lubricant to be applied where it will do the most good, the component should be disassembled (see Chapter 5). The lubricant recommended by Honda for each application is listed at the beginning of the Chapter.

3 If an aerosol lubricant is used, it can be applied to the pivot joint gaps and will usually work its way into the areas where friction occurs, so less disassembly of the component is needed. If however, the area is dirty or the pivot is stiff to operate it is preferable to dismantle it and clean off all corrosion, dirt and old lubricant first.

4 If motor oil or light grease is being used, apply it sparingly as it may attract dirt (which could cause the controls to bind or wear at an accelerated rate). **Note:** *One of the best lubricants for the control lever pivots is a dry-film lubricant (available from many sources by different names).*

Cables

Special tool: *A cable lubricating adapter is necessary for this procedure (see illustration 17.5a).*

5 To lubricate the cables, disconnect the relevant cable at its upper end, then lubricate it with a pressure adapter and aerosol lubricant

16.19 Fit the drain bolt using a new sealing washer

16.20 Fill the system as described

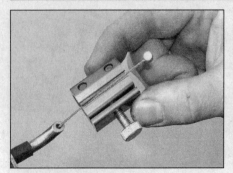

17.5a Fit the cable into the adapter...

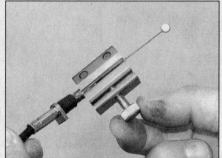

17.5b ...and tighten the screw to seal it in...

17.5c ...then apply the lubricant using the nozzle provided inserted in the hole in the adapter

(see illustrations). See Chapter 4 for throttle cable removal procedures, and Chapter 2 for the clutch cable.

18 Nuts and bolts

1 Since vibration of the machine tends to loosen fasteners, all nuts, bolts, screws, etc. should be periodically checked for proper tightness.

2 Pay particular attention to the following, referring to the relevant Chapter:

Spark plug
Engine oil drain plug
Lever and pedal bolts
Footrest and sidestand bolts
Engine mounting bolts
Shock absorber and suspension linkage bolts
Swingarm pivot bolt nut
Handlebar bolts
Front fork clamp bolts (top and bottom yoke) and fork top bolts

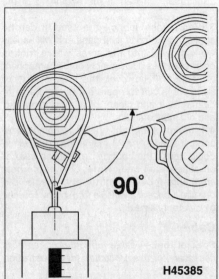

19.4 Steering head bearing pre-load check

Steering stem nut
Front axle
Front axle clamp bolt(s) (250 models)
Rear axle nut
Front sprocket bolts and rear sprocket nuts or bolts
Brake caliper and master cylinder mounting bolts
Brake hose banjo bolts and caliper bleed valves
Brake disc bolts
Exhaust system bolts/nuts

3 If a torque wrench is available, use it along with the torque settings given at the beginning of this and other Chapters.

19 Steering head bearings

1 Steering head bearings can become dented, rough, loose or corroded during normal use of the machine, and in extreme cases worn or loose bearings can cause potentially dangerous handling problems.

Freeplay check

2 Remove the lower fairing on CBR models (see Chapter 7). Raise the front wheel off the ground using an auxiliary stand placed under the engine. Always make sure that the bike is properly supported and secure.

3 Point the front wheel straight-ahead and slowly move the handlebars from lock to lock. Any dents or roughness in the bearing races

19.5 Checking for play in the steering head bearings

will be felt and if the bearings are too tight the bars will not move smoothly and freely. Again point the wheel straight-ahead, and tap the front of the wheel to one side. The wheel should 'fall' under its own weight to the limit of its lock, indicating that the bearings are not too tight (take into account the restriction that cables and wiring may have). Check for similar movement to the other side.

4 On 250 models, if a spring balance (graduated zero to 30 N) is available, attach one end around the top of the fork **(see illustration).** With the steering straight-ahead, pull on the balance and check the reading at which the handlebars start to turn. If the reading is below the minimum value specified in the pre-load range given in the Specifications at the beginning of the Chapter, the steering head is too loose, if the reading is above the maximum value specified the steering head is too tight. If the steering doesn't perform as described, and it's not due to the resistance of cables or hoses, then the bearings should be adjusted as described below.

5 Next, grasp the bottom of the forks and gently pull and push them forward and backward **(see illustration).** Any looseness or freeplay in the steering head bearings will be felt as front-to-rear movement of the forks. If play is felt, adjust the bearings as described below.

> **HAYNES HiNT** *Make sure you are not mistaking any movement between the bike and stand, or between the stand and the ground, for freeplay in the bearings. Do not pull and push the forks too hard – a gentle movement is all that is needed. Freeplay between the fork tubes due to worn bushes can also be misinterpreted as steering head bearing play – do not confuse the two.*

Adjustment

CBR125 and CRF250 models

6 As a precaution, on CBR models remove the fuel tank covers and the fairing, and on CRF models remove the fuel tank covers (see Chapter 7). Though not actually necessary,

19.7a Handlebar clamp bolts (arrowed)...

19.7b ...and fork clamp bolts (arrowed)

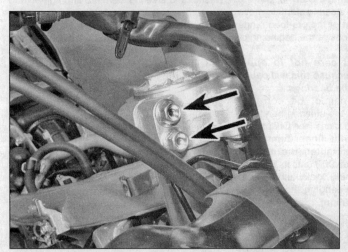

19.8 Slacken the fork clamp bolts (arrowed) on each side

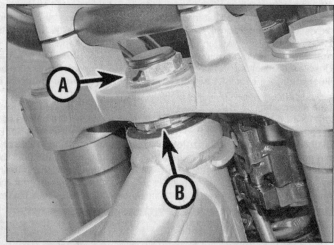

19.9 Steering stem nut (A), bearing adjuster nut (B)

this will prevent the possibility of damage should a tool slip.

7 On CBR models slacken the handlebar clamp bolts and the fork clamp bolts in the top yoke **(see illustrations)**.

8 On CRF models displace the complete handlebar assembly from the top yoke (see Chapter 5). Slacken the fork clamp bolts in the top yoke **(see illustration)**.

9 Slacken the steering stem nut **(see illustration)**.

10 Using a suitable drift located in one of the notches in the adjuster nut under the top yoke, turn the adjuster nut, either clockwise to tighten the head bearings or anti-clockwise to loosen them, and only moving it a small amount at a time **(see illustration 19.9)**. After each small adjustment recheck the freeplay as described above (steps 2 to 5), before making further adjustments. The object is to set the adjuster nut so that the bearings are under a very light loading, just enough to remove any freeplay, but not so much that the steering does not move freely from side-to-side as described in the check procedure above.

Caution: Take great care not to apply excessive pressure because this will cause premature failure of the bearings.

11 If the bearings cannot be correctly adjusted, disassemble the steering head and check the bearings and races (see Chapter 5).

12 With the bearings correctly adjusted, tighten the steering stem nut to the torque setting specified at the beginning of the chapter **(see illustration 19.9)**. Tighten the fork clamp bolts to the specified torque **(see illustration 19.7b or 19.8)**. On CBR models make sure the handlebars are correctly aligned by pulling them back against the stops then tighten the handlebar clamp bolts to the specified torque **(see illustration 19.7a)**. On CRF models fit the handlebars onto the yoke (see Chapter 5).

13 Check the bearing adjustment as described above and re-adjust if necessary.

14 Install the fuel tank covers and on CBR models the fairing (see Chapter 7) if removed.

CBR250

Special tool: *A suitably sized C-spanner to locate in the notches in the adjuster nut* is necessary for this procedure **(see illustration 19.21)**.

15 As a precaution, remove the fuel tank covers and the fairing (see Chapter 7). Though not actually necessary, this will prevent the possibility of damage should a tool slip.

16 Remove the handlebar stopper ring from the groove in the top of each fork, using a small screwdriver to ease them out **(see illustration)**.

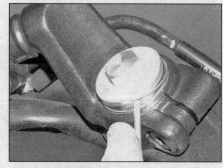

19.16 Remove the stopper ring from each fork

19.17 Slacken the clamp bolts (arrowed) on each side...

19.18 ...then unscrew the steering stem nut

19.19 Ease the handlebars and yoke up

17 Slacken the handlebar clamp bolts and the fork clamp bolts in the top yoke (**see illustration**).
18 Unscrew the steering stem nut and remove the washer (**see illustration**).
19 Gently ease the handlebars and top yoke up the forks so the adjuster locknut is fully exposed (**see illustration**).
20 Bend the lockwasher tabs out of the notches in the locknut (**see illustration**). Unscrew the locknut using your fingers (**see illustration**) – it shouldn't be tight. If it is tight use a C-spanner located in one of the notches (**see illustration 12.21**).
21 To turn the adjuster nut you need a C-spanner, or a suitable drift to locate in one of the notches (**see illustration**). Slacken the adjuster nut slightly until pressure is just released. Tighten the adjuster nut until all freeplay is removed, yet the steering is able to move freely. The object is to set the adjuster

nut so that the bearings are under a very light loading, just enough to remove any freeplay, but not so much that the steering is prevented from moving freely from side-to-side. If you have a spring balance (see Step 4), set the adjuster nut so that the steering starts to move at around the mid-point of the pre-load range given in the Specifications at the beginning of the Chapter.
Caution: Take great care not to apply excessive pressure because this will cause premature failure of the bearings.
22 If the bearings cannot be correctly adjusted, disassemble the steering head and check the bearings and races (see Chapter 5).
23 Tighten the locknut finger-tight (**see illustration 19.20b**). Tighten the locknut further (but no more than 90°) until its notches align with the remaining lockwasher tabs. Secure the locknut by bending the tabs into its notches (**see illustration**).

24 Slide the top yoke and handlebars back down the forks – make sure the lug on each handlebar clamp locates in the gap above the fork clamp bolt (**see illustration 19.17**). Fit the washer and steering stem nut and tighten it to the torque setting specified at the beginning of the Chapter (**see illustration 19.18**).
25 Tighten the fork clamp bolts in the top yoke then the handlebar clamp bolts to the specified torque settings (**see illustration 19.17**). Fit the stopper rings (**see illustration 19.16**).
26 Check the bearing adjustment as described above and re-adjust if necessary.
27 Install the fairing and the fuel tank cover (see Chapter 7).

Lubrication

28 Although there is no set interval for re-greasing the steering head bearings, over a considerable time the grease in the bearings will be dispersed or will harden, or the seal could fail allowing the ingress of dirt and water, leading to corrosion.
29 Refer to Chapter 5 to disassemble the steering head.

19.20a Bend down the tabs securing the locknut...

19.20b ...then unscrew the locknut

19.21 Adjust the bearings as described using a C-spanner

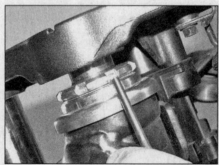

19.23 Bend the tabs up into the notches in the locknut

20 PAIR system (250 models)

1 To reduce the amount of unburned hydrocarbons released in the exhaust gases, a pulse secondary air supply (PAIR) system is fitted. The system consists of the control valve (mounted behind the left-hand side cover on CBR models and behind the right-hand fuel tank cover on CRF models), the reed valve (fitted in the valve cover) and the hoses between the air filter housing, the control valve and the reed valve. The control valve is actuated electronically by the ECM.
2 Under normal operating conditions, the valve allows filtered air to be drawn through the reed valves and cylinder head passages and into the exhaust ports. The air mixes with the exhaust gases, causing any unburned particles of the fuel in the mixture to be burnt in the exhaust port/pipes. This process changes a considerable amount of hydrocarbons and carbon monoxide into relatively harmless

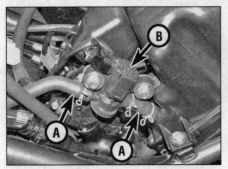

20.3a PAIR hoses (A), control valve (B)...

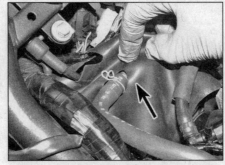

20.3b ...and reed valve (arrowed – under rubber shield) – CBR models

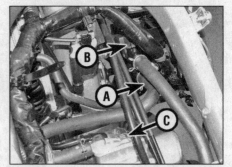

20.3c PAIR hoses (A), control valve (B) and reed valve (C) – CRF models

carbon dioxide and water. The reed valve in the valve cover is fitted to prevent the flow of exhaust gases back up the cylinder head passages and into the air filter housing.

3 The system is not adjustable and requires little more than a visual check of the hoses. To access them remove the fuel tank (see Chapter 4). Check that the hoses are not kinked or pinched, are in good condition and are securely connected at each end **(see illustrations)**. Replace any hoses that are cracked, split or generally deteriorated with new ones.

4 Refer to Chapter 4 for further information on the system and for checks if it is believed to be faulty.

21 Air filter

Caution: If the machine is continually ridden in wet or dusty conditions, the filter should be replaced more frequently.

CBR125

1 Raise the fuel tank (see Chapter 4).

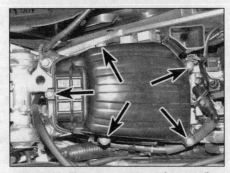

21.2 Air filter cover screws (arrowed)

2 Undo the air filter cover screws and remove the cover **(see illustration)**.
3 Remove the filter from the housing, noting how it fits **(see illustration)**.
4 Clean the filter by tapping it on a hard surface to dislodge any dirt from the folds, then check for anything stuck between them. Use compressed air to blow through it, directing the air in the opposite way to normal flow, i.e. from the underside. Do not use any solvents or cleaning agents on the filter. If the filter is excessively dirty or is damaged replace it with a new one.
5 Check the sealing rings in the housing and

21.3 Remove the filter element – CBR125

cover are in good condition and correctly seated **(see illustration)**. Fit new ones if necessary.
6 Fit the filter into the housing, making sure it locates correctly and is properly seated **(see illustration 21.3)**.
7 Fit the filter cover. Lower the fuel tank (see Chapter 4).

CBR250

8 Remove the seat (see Chapter 7).
9 Undo the air filter cover screws and remove the cover **(see illustration)**.
10 Unclip the filter and withdraw it from the

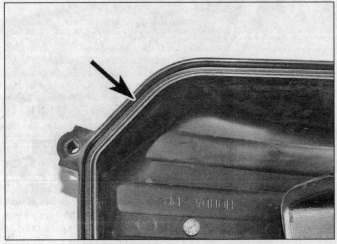

21.5 Check the seals (cover seal shown)

21.9 Air filter cover screws (arrowed)

21.10a Release the clips...

21.10b ...and withdraw the filter – CBR250

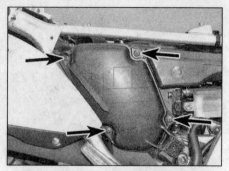

21.15 Air filter cover screws (arrowed)

housing and replace it with a new one, making sure it seats properly (see illustrations).

11 If you need to clean the filter between renewal intervals tap it on a hard surface to dislodge any dirt from between the folds, then use compressed air to blow through it, directing the air in the opposite way to normal flow, i.e. from the outside. Do not use any solvents or cleaning agents on the element. If the element is excessively dirty or is damaged replace it with a new one.

12 Check the cover sealing ring is in good condition and correctly seated. Fit a new one if necessary.

13 Fit the filter cover. Fit the seat.

CRF250

14 Remove the right-hand side cover (see Chapter 7).

15 Undo the air filter cover screws and remove the cover (see illustration).

16 Unclip the filter and withdraw it from the housing and replace it with a new one, making sure it seats properly (see illustrations).

17 If you need to clean the filter between

replacement intervals tap it on a hard surface to dislodge any dirt from between the folds, then use compressed air to blow through it, directing the air in the opposite way to normal flow, i.e. from the outside. Do not use any solvents or cleaning agents on the element. If the element is excessively dirty or is damaged replace it with a new one.

18 Check the cover sealing ring is in good condition and correctly seated. Fit a new one if necessary.

19 Fit the filter cover. Fit the side cover.

22 EVAP system (US 250 models)

1 Visually inspect all the system hoses between the fuel tank, the purge control solenoid valve, and the canister for kinks and splits and any other damage or deterioration. Make sure that the hoses are securely connected with a clamp on each end. Replace any hoses that are damaged or deteriorated.

2 Check the EVAP canister and the valve for cracks or other damage.

3 See Chapter 4 for further information and tests on the system. Note that there is an emission control system information label under the passenger seat on CBR models and on the tail cover to the rear of the seat on CRF models.

23 Battery

1 All models covered in this manual are fitted with a sealed MF (maintenance free) battery. Note: Do not attempt to remove the battery caps to check the electrolyte level or battery specific gravity. Removal will damage the caps, resulting in electrolyte leakage and battery damage. All that should be done is to check that the terminals are clean and tight and that the casing is not damaged or leaking. See Chapter 8 for further details.

2 If the machine is not in regular use, disconnect the battery and give it a refresher charge every month to six weeks (see Chapter 8).

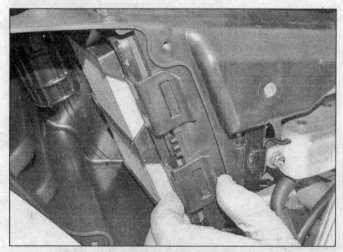

21.16a Release the clips...

21.16b ...and withdraw the filter – CRF250

Chapter 2A
Engine, clutch and transmission – CBR125

Contents

Degrees of difficulty

Easy, suitable for novice with little experience 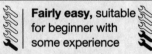 | **Fairly easy,** suitable for beginner with some experience | **Fairly difficult,** suitable for competent DIY mechanic | **Difficult,** suitable for experienced DIY mechanic | **Very difficult,** suitable for expert DIY or professional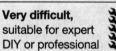

Specifications

General

Type	Four-stroke 2-valve single
Capacity	124.7 cc
Bore	58.0 mm
Stroke	47.2 mm
Compression ratio	11.0 to 1
Cylinder compression	195 psi (13.7 Bar) @ 530 rpm
Cooling system	Liquid cooled
Lubrication	Wet sump, trochoid pump
Clutch	Wet multi-plate
Transmission	Six-speed constant mesh
Final drive	Chain

Cylinder head

Warpage (max)	0.05 mm

Camshaft and rocker arms

Intake lobe height
    Standard . . . . 29.316 to 29.556 mm
    Service limit (min) . . . . 29.05 mm
Exhaust lobe height
    Standard . . . . 29.138 to 29.378 mm
    Service limit (min) . . . . 28.85 mm
Runout (max) . . . . 0.02 mm
Rocker arm bore diameter
    Standard . . . . 10.000 to 10.015 mm
    Service limit (min) . . . . 10.10 mm
Rocker arm shaft diameter
    Standard . . . . 9.972 to 9.987 mm
    Service limit (min) . . . . 9.75 mm
Rocker arm-to-shaft clearance
    Standard . . . . 0.013 to 0.043 mm
    Service limit (min) . . . . 0.10 mm

Valves, guides and springs

Valve clearances . . . . see Chapter 1
Stem diameter
    Intake valve
        Standard . . . . 4.975 to 4.990 mm
        Service limit (min) . . . . 4.863 mm
    Exhaust valve
        Standard . . . . 4.965 to 4.980 mm
        Service limit (min) . . . . 4.853 mm
Guide bore diameter – intake and exhaust valves
    Standard . . . . 5.000 to 5.012 mm
    Service limit (max) . . . . 5.040 mm
Stem-to-guide clearance
    Intake valve
        Standard . . . . 0.010 to 0.037 mm
        Service limit . . . . 0.065 mm
    Exhaust valve
        Standard . . . . 0.020 to 0.047 mm
        Service limit . . . . 0.075 mm
Seat width – intake and exhaust valves
    Standard . . . . 0.90 to 1.10 mm
    Service limit (max) . . . . 1.50 mm
Valve guide height above cylinder head
    Intake valve . . . . 11.5 to 11.7 mm
    Exhaust valve . . . . 12.3 to 12.5 mm
Valve spring free length– intake and exhaust valves
    Inner spring
        Standard . . . . 33.5 mm
        Service limit (min) . . . . 31.0 mm
    Outer spring
        Standard . . . . 35.7 mm
        Service limit (min) . . . . 34.0 mm

Cylinder

Bore diameter
    Standard . . . . 58.000 to 58.010 mm
    Service limit (max) . . . . 58.05 mm
Warpage (max) . . . . 0.05 mm
Ovality (out-of-round) and taper (max) . . . . 0.01 mm

Piston

	Standard	Service limit
Piston diameter (measured 6.5 mm up from skirt, at 90° to piston pin axis)	57.97 to 57.99 mm	56.67 mm
Piston-to-bore clearance	0.01 to 0.04 mm	0.09 mm*
Piston pin diameter	12.994 to 13.000 mm	12.70 mm
Piston pin bore diameter in piston	13.002 to 13.008 mm	13.045 mm
Piston pin-to-piston pin bore clearance	0.002 to 0.014 mm	0.08 mm

*If the piston-to-bore clearance exceeds the service limit, the cylinder can be re-bored – Honda supply +0.25, +0.50, +0.75 and +1.00 oversize pistons and rings. Following a re-bore, the piston-to-bore clearance must be as standard for a normal piston

Piston rings

Ring end gap (installed)
  Top ring
    Standard . . . .   0.10 to 0.25 mm
    Service limit (max) . . . .   0.40 mm
  Second ring
    Standard . . . .   0.35 to 0.50 mm
    Service limit (max) . . . .   0.70 mm
  Oil ring side-rail
    Standard . . . .   0.20 to 0.70 mm
    Service limit (max) . . . .   1.1 mm
Ring-to-groove clearance
  Top ring
    Standard . . . .   0.045 to 0.075 mm
    Service limit (max) . . . .   0.10 mm
  Second ring
    Standard . . . .   0.015 to 0.050 mm
    Service limit (max) . . . .   0.09 mm

Starter clutch

Starter driven gear hub ID
  Standard . . . .   22.010 to 22.031 mm
  Service limit (min) . . . .   22.08 mm
Starter driven gear hub OD
  Standard . . . .   45.660 to 45.673 mm
  Service limit (min) . . . .   45.60 mm

Clutch

Friction plates   5
Plain plates   4
Friction plate thickness
  Standard . . . .   2.92 to 3.08 mm
  Service limit (min) . . . .   2.85 mm
Plain plate warpage (max) . . . .   0.20 mm
Spring free length
  Standard . . . .   40.0 mm
  Service limit (min) . . . .   37.3 mm
Clutch housing ID
  Standard . . . .   23.000 to 23.021 mm
  Service limit (max) . . . .   23.08 mm
Clutch guide OD
  Standard . . . .   22.959 to 22.980 mm
  Service limit (min) . . . .   22.93 mm
Clutch guide ID
  Standard . . . .   16.991 to 17.009 mm
  Service limit (max) . . . .   17.04 mm
Input shaft OD at clutch guide
  Standard . . . .   16.966 to 16.984 mm
  Service limit (min) . . . .   16.586 mm

Oil pump

Inner rotor tip-to-outer rotor clearance (max) . . . .   0.15 mm
Outer rotor-to-body clearance
  Standard . . . .   0.15 to 0.21 mm
  Service limit (max) . . . .   0.26 mm
Rotor end-float
  Standard . . . .   0.05 to 0.10 mm
  Service limit (max) . . . .   0.12 mm

Crankshaft

Runout (max) . . . .   0.03 mm

Connecting rod

Small-end internal diameter
    Standard . . . . 13.016 to 13.034 mm
    Service limit (max) . . . . 13.06 mm
Small-end-to-piston pin clearance
    Standard . . . . 0.016 to 0.040 mm
    Service limit (max) . . . . 0.10 mm
Big-end side clearance
    Standard . . . . 0.40 to 0.60 mm
    Service limit (max) . . . . 0.85 mm
Big-end radial clearance
    Standard . . . . 0.006 to 0.014 mm
    Service limit (max) . . . . 0.05 mm

Selector drum and forks

Selector fork end thickness
    Standard . . . . 4.93 to 5.00 mm
    Service limit (min) . . . . 4.82 mm
Selector fork bore ID
    Standard . . . . 10.000 to 10.018 mm
    Service limit (max) . . . . 10.03 mm
Selector fork shaft OD
    Standard . . . . 9.986 to 9.995 mm
    Service limit (min) . . . . 9.93 mm
Selector drum right-hand journal OD
    Standard . . . . 25.959 to 25.980 mm
    Service limit (min) . . . . 25.90 mm
Selector drum bore ID in right-hand crankcase
    Standard . . . . 26.000 to 26.021 mm
    Service limit (max) . . . . 26.50 mm
Selector drum left-hand journal OD
    Standard . . . . 24.959 to 24.980 mm
    Service limit (min) . . . . 24.90 mm
Selector drum bore ID in left-hand crankcase
    Standard . . . . 25.000 to 25.021 mm
    Service limit (max) . . . . 25.50 mm

Transmission

Gear ratios (no. of teeth)
    Primary reduction . . . . 3.350 to 1 (67/20)
    Final reduction . . . . 2.933 to 1 (44/15)
    1st gear . . . . 3.454 to 1 (38/11)
    2nd gear . . . . 1.941 to 1 (33/17)
    3rd gear . . . . 1.450 to 1 (29/20)
    4th gear . . . . 1.174 to 1 (27/23)
    5th gear . . . . 1.041 to 1 (25/24)
    6th gear . . . . 0.923 to 1 (24/26)

Torque settings

Camshaft holder nuts . . . . 29 Nm
Camshaft sprocket bolts . . . . 9 Nm
Clutch lifter plate bolts . . . . 12 Nm
Clutch nut . . . . 74 Nm
Crankcase bolts
    Large head bolts (right-hand side) . . . . 12 Nm
    Small head bolts (left-hand side) . . . . 10 Nm
Crankshaft end cap . . . . 8 Nm
Engine mounting bolt nuts . . . . 59 Nm
Gearchange mechanism stopper arm bolt . . . . 12 Nm
Oil pump cover bolts . . . . 5 Nm
Primary drive gear nut . . . . 64 Nm
Rocker shaft stopper bolts . . . . 9 Nm
Selector drum cam plate bolt . . . . 12 Nm
Starter clutch bolts . . . . 16 Nm
Timing inspection cap . . . . 6 Nm
Valve cover bolts . . . . 10 Nm

1 General information

The engine/transmission unit is a liquid-cooled single cylinder of unit construction. The two valves are operated by rocker arms actuated by a single overhead camshaft that is chain driven off the left-hand end of the crankshaft. The crankcase divides vertically.

The crankcase incorporates a wet sump, pressure-fed lubrication system that uses a single rotor trochoidal oil pump that is gear-driven off the primary drive gear on the right-hand end of the crankshaft. Oil is filtered by a strainer in the bottom of the crankcase.

The alternator is on the left-hand end of the crankshaft. The ignition timing triggers are on the outside of the alternator rotor, and the crankshaft position (CKP) sensor is mounted in the alternator cover along with the stator.

The water pump is on the right-hand side of the engine, and is gear driven off the primary drive gear on the right-hand end of the crankshaft.

Power from the crankshaft is routed to the transmission via the clutch. The clutch is of the wet, multi-plate type and is gear-driven off the crankshaft. The clutch is operated by cable. The transmission is a six-speed constant-mesh unit. Final drive to the rear wheel is by chain and sprockets.

2 Component access

Operations possible with the engine in the frame

The components and assemblies listed below can be removed without having to remove the engine from the frame. If however, a number of areas require attention at the same time, removal of the engine is recommended.

Valve cover
Camshaft and rockers
Clutch
Gearchange mechanism
Alternator
Starter clutch
Oil pump and oil strainer
Starter motor
Water pump

Operations requiring engine removal

It is necessary to remove the engine from the frame to gain access to the following components.

Cylinder head
Cam chain, tensioner and blades
Cylinder barrel and piston
Crankshaft, connecting rod and bearings
Balancer shaft
Transmission shafts and bearings
Selector drum and forks

3 Compression test

Special tool: *A compression gauge and 10 x 1.0 mm threaded adaptor are required to perform this test.*

1 Poor engine performance may be caused by leaking valves, incorrect valve clearances, a leaking head gasket, a worn piston, worn piston rings or worn cylinder walls. A cylinder compression check will highlight these conditions.

2 Make sure the valve clearances are correctly set (see Chapter 1). Remove the right-hand fairing side panel (see Chapter 7).

3 Run the engine until it is at normal operating temperature. Remove the spark plug (see Chapter 1). Fit the plug back into the plug cap and earth the plug against the engine away from the plug hole – if the plug is not earthed the ignition system could be damaged.

4 Screw the threaded adaptor into the spark plug hole making sure that it seats securely and there are no air leaks **(see illustrations)**. Connect the compression gauge to the adaptor.

5 With the ignition switch ON, the throttle held fully open and the spark plug earthed, turn the engine over on the starter motor until the gauge reading has built up and stabilised **(see illustration)**.

6 Compare the reading on the gauge to the cylinder compression figure specified at the beginning of the Chapter (under General specifications).

7 If the reading is low, it could be due to a worn cylinder bore, piston or rings, failure of the head gasket, or worn valve seats. To determine which is the cause, pour a small quantity of engine oil into the spark plug hole to seal the rings, then repeat the compression test. If the figures are noticeably higher the cause is a worn cylinder, piston or rings. If there is no change the cause is a leaking head gasket or worn valve seats.

8 Although unlikely, if the reading is high there could be a build-up of carbon deposits in the combustion chamber. Remove the cylinder head and scrape all deposits off the piston and the cylinder head.

3.4a Select the correct adapter to match the spark plug threads...

3.4b ...then thread the gauge into the plug hole

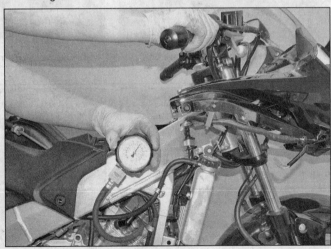

3.5 Hold the throttle fully open and turn the engine using the starter motor

4.7a Detach the hoses (arrowed) from the water pump cover...

4.7b ...thermostat cover...

4.7c ...and cylinder head

4 Engine removal and installation

Caution: The engine is not particularly heavy (around 25 kg), but the aid of an assistant is advised to prevent personal injury or damage if the engine falls or is dropped.

Removal

1 Support the bike either on its sidestand or using an auxiliary stand, making sure it is on level ground. Work can be made easier by raising the machine to a suitable working height on an hydraulic ramp or a suitable platform. Make sure the motorcycle is secure and will not topple over, and tie the front brake lever to the handlebar to prevent it rolling forwards.

2 Remove the fairing side panels and lower fairing (see Chapter 7).

3 If the engine is dirty, particularly around its mountings, wash it thoroughly. This makes work much easier and rules out the possibility of caked on lumps of dirt falling into some vital component.

4 Drain the engine oil and coolant (see Chapter 1).

5 Disconnect the negative (–ve) lead from the battery (see Chapter 8).

6 Remove the fuel tank and the air filter housing (Chapter 4). Either remove the throttle body completely, or fully slacken the clamp screw securing it to the cylinder head intake duct, noting the orientation of the clamp, and ease the throttle body out of the rubber leaving its cables and hoses still connected (see Chapter 4). Either way, plug the engine intake duct with clean rag to prevent contamination.

7 Release the clamps securing the cooling system hoses to the water pump cover, thermostat housing cover and cylinder head and detach them, noting their positions and routing (see illustrations). Remove the radiator along with its hoses, noting their routing (see Chapter 3).

8 Remove the exhaust system (see Chapter 4).

9 Pull the spark plug cap off the plug and secure it clear of the engine (see illustration). Disconnect the oxygen sensor wiring connector (see illustration).

10 If required, remove the starter motor (see Chapter 8). If you leave it on the engine, pull back the rubber cover on its terminal, then unscrew the nut and disconnect the lead (see illustration) – spray it with some penetrating fluid first if it is corroded. Also unscrew the mounting bolt securing the earth lead and detach the lead (see illustration).

11 Make a mark where the slot in the gearchange linkage arm aligns with the shaft (see illustration). Unscrew the linkage arm pinch bolt and slide the arm off the shaft.

12 Remove the front sprocket (see Chapter 6). Lay the drive chain against the front of the swingarm.

13 Draw the rubber boot off the wiring connectors on the inside of the frame on the left-hand side, then disconnect the alternator/ CKP sensor (natural 6-pin) connector, and

4.9a Pull the cap off the spark plug

4.9b Oxygen sensor connector (arrowed)

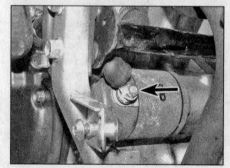

4.10a Detach the lead (arrowed) from the starter motor terminal...

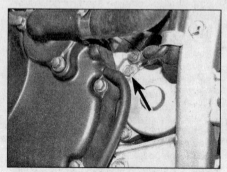

4.10b ...and the mounting bolt (arrowed)

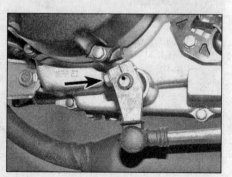

4.11 Make an alignment mark then unscrew the bolt (arrowed) and slide the arm off

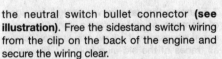

4.13 Disconnect the connectors (arrowed)

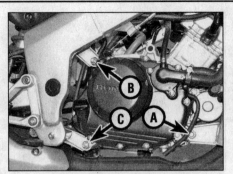

4.16a Front mounting bolt nut (A), upper rear mounting bolt nut (B), lower rear mounting bolt nut (C)

4.16b Unscrew the bolts (arrowed) on each side and remove the two hangers and crossbar

the neutral switch bullet connector **(see illustration)**. Free the sidestand switch wiring from the clip on the back of the engine and secure the wiring clear.

14 Slacken the locknut on the clutch cable adjuster, then thread the locknut and adjuster nut fully up the adjuster **(see illustration 17.3a)**. Free the cable end from the release arm (create more slack if required using the adjuster on the clutch lever bracket – see Chapter 1) then draw the cable out of the bracket **(see illustrations 17.3b and c)**. Position the cable clear of the engine.

15 Position an hydraulic or mechanical jack under the engine with a block of wood between the jack head and sump. Make sure the jack is centrally positioned so the engine will not topple in any direction when the last mounting bolt is removed. Raise the jack to take the weight of the engine, but make sure it is not lifting the bike and taking the weight of that as well. The idea is to support the engine so that there is no pressure on any of the mounting bolts once they have been slackened, so they can be easily withdrawn. Note that it may be necessary to alter the position of the jack as some of the bolts are removed to relieve the stress transferred to the other bolts.

16 Unscrew the nut on the right-hand end of the engine front mounting bolt then withdraw the bolt **(see illustration)**. Unscrew the bolts securing the engine hangers and cross-bar to the frame and remove them, noting how they fit **(see illustration)**.

17 Unscrew the nuts on the right-hand ends of the engine upper and lower rear mounting bolts **(see illustration 4.16a)**.

18 Check that the engine is properly supported by the jack. Withdraw the upper and lower rear mounting bolts from the left-hand side.

19 The engine can now be removed from the frame (see *Caution* above). Check that all wiring, cables and hoses are free and clear, then carefully lower the jack and manoeuvre the engine clear. Fully lower the jack, then with the aid of an assistant remove the jack from under the engine and remove the engine.

Installation

Note: *It is advised to smear copper grease onto the engine mounting bolt shafts, not the threads, to prevent the possibility of them seizing in the engine or frame due to corrosion.*

20 Manoeuvre the engine into position under the frame and lift it onto the jack. Raise the engine to align all the mounting bolt holes, making sure that all cables and wiring are correctly routed and do not get trapped. Note that it may be necessary to adjust the jack as some of the bolts are installed to realign the other bolt holes.

21 Insert the upper and lower rear mounting bolts from the left-hand side, then fit their nuts and tighten them finger-tight **(see illustration 4.16a)**.

22 Fit the engine hangers and cross-bar to the frame and tighten their bolts/nuts finger-tight **(see illustration 4.16b)**. Insert the front mounting bolt from the left-hand side then fit the nut and tighten it finger-tight **(see illustration 4.16a)**.

23 First tighten the upper and lower rear mounting bolt nuts to the torque setting specified at the beginning of the Chapter. Next tighten the engine hanger/cross-bar bolt nuts. Finally tighten the front mounting bolt nut to the specified torque.

24 Remove the jack from under the engine.

25 The remainder of the installation procedure is the reverse of removal, noting the following points:

● When fitting the gearchange linkage arm onto the gearchange shaft, align the slit in the arm with the mark you made on the shaft **(see illustration 4.11)**.
● Use a new gasket on the exhaust pipe.
● Make sure all wires, cables and hoses are correctly routed and connected, and secured by any clips or ties.
● Refill the engine with oil and coolant to the correct levels (see Chapter 1 and *Pre-ride checks*).
● Adjust the throttle and clutch cable freeplay.
● Adjust the drive chain (see Chapter 1).
● Start the engine and check that there are no oil or coolant leaks. Check the idle speed (see Chapter 1).

5 Engine overhaul – general information

1 Before beginning the engine overhaul, read through the related procedures to familiarise yourself with the scope and requirements of the job. Overhauling an engine is not all that difficult, but it is time consuming. Check on the availability of parts and make sure that any necessary special tools are obtained in advance.

2 Most work can be done with a decent set of typical workshop hand tools, although a number of precision measuring tools are required for inspecting parts to determine if they are worn.

3 To ensure maximum life and minimum trouble from a rebuilt engine, everything must be assembled with care in a spotlessly clean environment.

Disassembly

4 Before disassembling the engine, thoroughly clean and degrease its external surfaces. This will prevent contamination of the engine internals, and will also make the job a lot easier and cleaner. A high flash-point solvent, such as paraffin (kerosene) can be used, or better still, a proprietary engine degreaser such as Gunk. Use old paintbrushes and toothbrushes to work the solvent into the various recesses of the casings. Take care to exclude solvent or water from the electrical components and intake and exhaust ports.

 Warning: The use of petrol (gasoline) as a cleaning agent should be avoided because of the risk of fire.

5 When clean and dry, position the engine on the workbench, leaving suitable clear area for working. Gather a selection of small containers, plastic bags and some labels so that parts can be grouped together in an easily identifiable manner. Also get some paper and a pen so that notes can be taken. You will also need a supply of clean rag, which should be as absorbent as possible.

6 Before commencing work, read through the appropriate section so that some idea of the

6.3a Unscrew the bolts (arrowed)...

6.3b ...and remove the cover

6.7 Make sure the gasket locates in the groove and over the dowel (arrowed)

necessary procedure can be gained. When removing components note that great force is seldom required, unless specified (checking the specified torque setting of the particular bolt being removed will indicate how tight it is, and therefore how much force should be needed). In many cases, a component's reluctance to be removed is indicative of an incorrect approach or removal method – if in any doubt, re-check with the text.

7 When disassembling the engine, keep 'mated' parts together that have been in contact with each other during engine operation. These 'mated' parts must be reused or replaced as an assembly.

8 A complete engine stripdown should be done in the following general order with reference to the appropriate Sections.

Remove the valve cover
Remove the camshaft holder
Remove the cylinder head
Remove the alternator and starter clutch (see
 Chapter 8)
Remove the cam chain and blades
Remove the cylinder barrel and piston
Remove the starter motor (see Chapter 8)
Remove the clutch
Remove the gearchange mechanism
Remove the oil pump
Remove the water pump (see Chapter 3)
Separate the crankcase halves
Remove the selector drum and forks
Remove the transmission shafts
Remove the crankshaft and balancer shaft

Reassembly

9 Reassembly is accomplished by reversing the general disassembly sequence.

6 Valve cover

Removal

1 Remove the fairing side panels (see Chapter 7).

2 Displace the radiator from its mounts and move it forwards (see Chapter 3) – there is no need to drain the cooling system or detach any hoses.

3 Unscrew the two valve cover bolts and lift the cover off the cylinder head (see illustrations). If it is stuck, do not try to lever it off with a screwdriver. Tap it gently around the sides with a rubber hammer or block of wood to dislodge it. Note the rubber washers for the bolts and remove them if they are loose (see illustration 6.8).

4 Remove the dowel if loose.

5 The rubber gasket is normally glued into the groove in the cover, and is best left there if it is reusable. If the gasket is in any way damaged, deformed or deteriorated, remove it (see illustration 6.7).

Installation

6 Fit the dowel if removed.

7 Examine the valve cover gasket for signs of damage or deterioration and fit a new one if necessary. If a new one is used, clean all traces of the old glue from the groove in the cover and clean it and the cylinder head mating surface with solvent. Fit the new gasket into the groove and over the dowel, using a suitable glue, sealant or grease to hold it in place (see illustration).

8 Position the valve cover on the cylinder head, making sure the gasket stays in place (see illustration 6.3b). If removed, fit the rubber washers into the cover, using new ones if required, and making sure they are installed with the metal side (marked UP) facing up (see illustration). Fit the cover bolts and tighten them to the specified torque setting.

9 Install the remaining components in the reverse order of removal.

7 Cam chain tensioner

Removal

1 If required for improved access remove the left-hand fairing side panel (see Chapter 7). Note that it is advisable to remove the valve cover (Section 6) and set the engine to TDC compression before removing the tensioner (see Section 8, Step 4).

2 Undo the tensioner cap screw and remove the O-ring (see illustrations).

6.8 Make sure the washers are the correct way up

7.2a Undo the cap screw (arrowed)...

7.2b ...and remove the O-ring

7.3a Slacken the mounting bolts (arrowed) slightly...

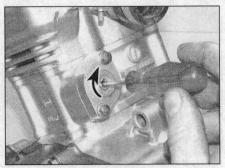

7.3b ...then insert the screwdriver, retract the plunger,..

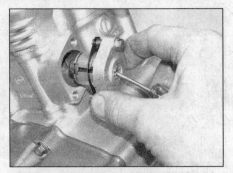

7.3c ...unscrew the mounting bolts and remove the tensioner

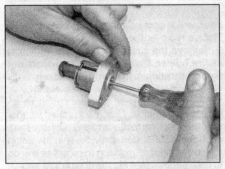

7.5 Check the action of the plunger

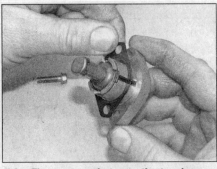

7.6a Fit a new gasket onto the tensioner...

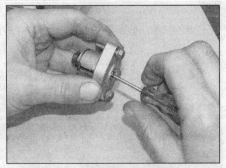

7.6b ...then insert the screwdriver and retract the plunger

3 Slacken the tensioner mounting bolts slightly (see illustration). Insert a small flat-bladed screwdriver in the end of the tensioner so that it engages the slotted plunger and turn it clockwise until the plunger is fully retracted and hold it in this position, then unscrew the tensioner mounting bolts and withdraw the tensioner from the engine (see illustrations). Release the screwdriver – the plunger will spring back out, but can be easily reset on installation.

4 Discard the gasket and O-ring as new ones must be used on installation. Do not attempt to dismantle the tensioner.

Installation

5 Check that the plunger moves smoothly when wound into the tensioner and springs back out freely when released (see illustration). Ensure the tensioner and cylinder barrel surfaces are clean and dry.

6 Fit a new gasket onto the tensioner body (see illustration). Insert a small flat-bladed screwdriver in the end of the tensioner so that it engages the slotted plunger (see illustration). Turn the screwdriver clockwise until the plunger is fully retracted and hold it in this position, then install the tensioner with its mounting bolts and tighten them (see illustration 7.3c). Release and remove the screwdriver.

7 Fit a new O-ring smeared with clean oil onto the tensioner, then fit the cap screw and tighten it (see illustration).

8 Turn the engine anti-clockwise through two

full turns and check again that all the timing marks still align (see Section 8, Step 4)

9 Install the left-hand fairing side panel (see Chapter 7).

8 Camshaft holder, camshaft and rocker arms

Note: *Stuff clean rag into the cam chain tunnel to prevent anything dropping into the engine. When setting the position of the crankshaft for the engine timing (Steps 4 and 22), be sure that you have the correct timing mark on the flywheel – the T mark that denotes top dead centre (TDC) for engine timing is on its side and can be easily confused with the F mark, also on its side, that denotes the firing (ignition timing) point.*

7.7 Fit a new O-ring then the cap screw

Removal

1 Drain the coolant (see Chapter 1). Remove the radiator (See Chapter 3).

2 Remove the spark plug (see Chapter 1). Remove the valve cover (see Section 6).

3 Unscrew the timing inspection cap and the crankshaft end cap from the alternator cover on the left-hand side of the engine (see illustration). Check the condition of the cap O-rings and replace them with new ones if necessary.

4 The crankshaft must be turned so that the piston is at TDC (top dead centre) on its compression stroke. Turn the crankshaft anti-clockwise using a suitable socket on the alternator rotor nut until the line next to the T mark on the rotor aligns with the notch in the inspection hole rim, and the index line on the camshaft sprocket is parallel and flush with

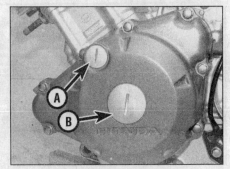

8.3 Remove the timing inspection cap (A) and the crankshaft end cap (B)

8.4a Turn the engine anti-clockwise using the nut...

8.4b ...until the line next to the T mark aligns with the notch (arrowed)...

8.4c ...and the camshaft sprocket line is as shown

8.7a Camshaft holder nuts (A), cylinder head bolts (B)

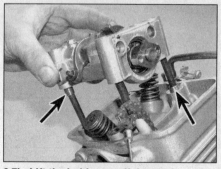

8.7b Lift the holder up off the studs, noting the dowels (arrowed)

the cylinder head top surface (the line will be below the sprocket bolts) **(see illustrations)**. There should now be some freeplay in each rocker arm (i.e. they are not contacting the valve stem). If the index line is parallel but not flush with the head, i.e. it is above the sprocket bolts not below them, rotate the engine anti-clockwise one full turn (360°) until the line next to the T mark again aligns with the notch, the index line on the sprocket is flush with the head, and there is some freeplay in the rockers.

5 Remove the cam chain tensioner (see Section 7).

6 Unscrew the cam chain sprocket bolts, slip the sprocket off its flange on the end of the camshaft and disengage it from the chain

(see illustration 8.26). Prevent the chain from dropping down its tunnel by securing it with a piece of wire.

7 Unscrew the camshaft holder nuts, slackening them evenly and a little at a time in a criss-cross sequence **(see illustration)**. Remove the nuts and their washers, and lift off the holder complete with the camshaft and rockers **(see illustration)**. Remove the two locating dowels from the studs or the underside of the holder if they are loose.

Caution: Make sure the holder lifts up squarely and evenly and does not stick on a dowel.

8 While the camshaft holder is out do not rotate the crankshaft – the chain may drop down and bind between the crankshaft and

case, which could damage these components. Place a rag over the cylinder head.

9 Remove the circlip securing the camshaft in the holder, then draw the camshaft out **(see illustrations)**. Discard the circlip if it has deformed and fit a new one on assembly.

10 Mark each rocker arm according to its location in the holder. Unscrew the shaft stopper bolt, then hold the rocker arm and push the shaft out using a flat-bladed screwdriver in the slot in the end of the shaft, rotating the shaft as you do to ease removal **(see illustrations 8.19b and a)**. Slide the rocker back onto its shaft to prevent mixing up – both shafts and rocker arms are identical and are therefore interchangeable, but mark them according to their location so they can be installed in their original position.

Inspection

11 Check the bearing on each end of the camshaft – they must run smoothly, quietly and freely, and there should be no excessive play between the inner and outer races, or between the inner race and the camshaft, or between the outer race and the holder **(see illustration)**. If not, replace the camshaft with a new one – it comes fitted with bearings, and the bearings are not available separately. Check that the bearing housings in the holder are neither worn nor damaged.

12 Check the camshaft lobes for heat discoloration (blue appearance), score marks, chipped areas, flat spots and spalling **(see illustration 8.14)**. Measure the height of each

8.9a Release the circlip...

8.9b ...and withdraw the camshaft

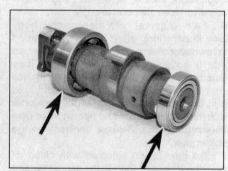

8.11 Check the bearings (arrowed) as described

8.12 Measure the height of the camshaft lobes with a micrometer

8.14 Check the contacting surfaces on the rocker arms and camshaft lobes (arrowed)

8.15a Measure the internal diameter of each bore...

lobe with a micrometer **(see illustration)** and compare the results to the minimum height listed in this Chapter's Specifications. If damage is noted or wear is excessive, the camshaft must be replaced with a new one.

13 Check the amount of camshaft runout by supporting each end on V-blocks, and measuring any runout using a dial gauge. If the runout exceeds the specified limit the camshaft must be replaced with a new one.

14 Check the rocker arms for heat discoloration (blue appearance), score marks, chipped areas, flat spots and spalling where they contact the camshaft lobes **(see illustration)**. Similarly check the bottom of each clearance adjuster and the top of each valve stem. If damage is noted or wear is excessive, the rocker arms, camshaft and valves must be replaced with new ones as required.

15 Check for freeplay between each rocker arm and its shaft. The arms should move freely with a light fit but no appreciable freeplay. Measure the internal diameter of the arm bores and the corresponding diameter of the shaft **(see illustrations)**. Replace the arms and/or shafts with new ones if they are worn beyond their specifications. Check that the fork shaft holes in the holder are neither worn nor damaged.

16 Except in cases of oil starvation, the cam chain should wear very little. If the chain has stretched excessively, which makes it difficult to maintain proper tension, or if it is stiff or the links are binding or kinking, replace it with a new one. Refer to Section 9 for replacement.

17 Check the sprocket for wear, cracks and other damage, and replace it with a new one if necessary. If the sprocket is worn, the cam chain is also worn, and so probably is the sprocket on the crankshaft. If severe wear is apparent, the entire engine should be disassembled further for inspection.

18 Inspect the cam chain guide and tensioner blade (see Section 9).

Installation

19 Lubricate each rocker shaft and arm with molybdenum disulphide oil (a 50/50 mixture of molybdenum disulphide grease and engine oil). Position each rocker arm in its location in the holder, making sure the adjuster is on the outside, and slide its shaft through, again using a flat-bladed screwdriver to rotate the shaft to ease installation and to align the stopper bolt hole with that in the holder **(see illustration)**. Fit the shaft stopper bolts and tighten them to the torque setting specified at the beginning of the Chapter **(see illustration)**.

20 Lubricate the camshaft bearings with clean engine oil and the camshaft lobes with molybdenum disulphide oil. Slide the camshaft into the holder with the tab on the sprocket flange at the top, holding the rocker arms against the valves so they are clear, and secure it with the circlip, using a new one if necessary **(see illustrations 8.9b and a)**.

21 Make sure the mating surfaces on the holder and the cylinder head are clean. If

8.15b ...and the external diameter of each shaft

removed fit the dowels over the studs and push them into the head.

22 Check that the line next to the T mark on the alternator rotor aligns with the notch in the inspection hole rim **(see illustration 8.4b)**.

23 Fit the camshaft holder assembly over the studs and onto the head, making sure the rocker shaft stopper bolts are on the right-hand side, and that the rocker arms locate correctly over the valve stem ends, and locate it onto the dowels, making sure it is correctly seated on all sides **(see illustration 8.7b)**.

24 Smear clean engine oil onto the seating surfaces of the nuts. Fit the nuts with their washers and tighten them evenly in three stages and in a criss-cross sequence to the torque setting specified at the beginning of the Chapter **(see illustration)**.

8.19a Slide the shaft into the holder and through the rocker...

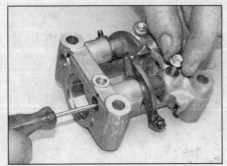

8.19b ...then turn it to align the holes and fit the stopper bolt

8.24 Fit the nuts with their washers and tighten them as described

8.25 With everything correctly aligned fit the sprocket into the chain and onto the camshaft...

8.26 ...then install the bolts

8.30 Fit the caps using new O-rings and smear them and the threads with oil

25 Check again that the line next to the T mark on the alternator rotor aligns with the notch in the inspection hole rim **(see illustration 8.4b)**, and make sure the tab on the camshaft flange is at the top and the bolt holes are parallel with the head. Engage the cam chain sprocket with the chain, making sure the crankshaft does not rotate, that the front run of the chain between the sprockets is tight and that any slack is in the rear run so it will be taken up by the tensioner, that the index line is facing out and is flush with the cylinder head, i.e. below the bolt holes, and that the bolt holes align, and fit the sprocket onto the flange **(see illustration)**.

26 Fit the cam chain sprocket bolts and tighten them to the specified torque setting **(see illustration)**.

27 Use a piece of wooden dowel or other suitable tool to press on the back of the cam

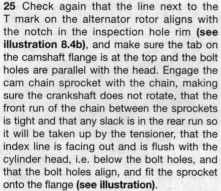

9.3 Removing the cam chain

chain tensioner blade via the tensioner bore in the cylinder barrel to ensure that any slack in the cam chain is taken up and transferred to the rear run of the chain. At this point check that all the timing marks are still in exact alignment as described in Step 4 **(see illustrations 8.4b and c)**. Note that it is easy to be slightly out (one tooth on the sprocket) without the marks appearing drastically out of alignment. If the marks are out unscrew the sprocket's bolts and slide the sprocket off the camshaft, then disengage it from the chain. Move the camshaft and/or crankshaft round as required, then fit the sprocket back into the chain and onto the camshaft, and check the marks again. With everything correctly aligned, tighten the bolts to the torque setting specified at the beginning of the Chapter.

Caution: If the marks are not aligned exactly as described, the valve timing will be incorrect and the valves may strike the piston, causing extensive damage to the engine.

28 Install the cam chain tensioner (see Section 7).

29 Turn the engine anti-clockwise through two full turns and check again that all the timing marks still align (see Step 4) **(see illustrations 8.4a, b and c)**. Check the valve clearances and adjust them if necessary (see Chapter 1).

30 Fit the timing inspection cap and crankshaft end cap using new O-rings if required, and smear the O-rings and the cap threads with clean oil **(see illustration)**. Tighten the caps to

the torque settings specified at the beginning of the Chapter.

31 Install the valve cover (see Section 6). Install the spark plug (see Chapter 1). Install the radiator (see Chapter 3).

9 Cam chain, tensioner blade and guide blade

Removal

Cam chain

1 Remove the cylinder head (see Section 10).

2 Remove the alternator rotor and starter clutch (see Chapter 8). Remove the tensioner and guide blades.

3 Draw the cam chain off the crankshaft sprocket and out of the engine **(see illustration)**.

Tensioner blade

4 Remove the cylinder head (see Section 10).

5 Remove the alternator rotor and starter clutch (see Chapter 8).

6 Unscrew the tensioner blade retainer bolt and remove the retainer and the washer, then slide the blade off its pivot and draw it out of the top of the cylinder barrel **(see illustrations)**.

Guide blade

7 Remove the cylinder head (see Section 10).

8 Draw the guide blade out of the top of the

9.6a Unscrew the bolt and remove the retainer...

9.6b ...the washer...

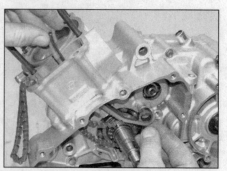

9.6c ...and the blade

cylinder barrel, noting how it locates **(see illustration)**.

Inspection

Cam chain

9 Check the chain for binding, kinks and any obvious damage and replace it with a new one if necessary. Check the camshaft and crankshaft sprocket teeth for wear and replace the cam chain, camshaft sprocket and crankshaft sprocket with a new set if necessary – the drive sprocket on the crankshaft is pressed on, so the crankshaft will have to be taken to an engineering workshop or dealer equipped with an hydraulic press to remove it and to fit a new one.

Tensioner and guide blades

10 Check the sliding surface and edges of the blades for excessive wear, deep grooves, cracking and other obvious damage, and replace them with new ones if necessary.

Installation

11 Installation of the sprocket, chain and blades is the reverse of removal. Make sure the bottom of the guide blade sits in its seat and the lugs near its top locate in the cut-outs in the cylinder barrel **(see illustrations)**. Lubricate the tensioner blade pivot with clean oil, and make sure the retainer plate locates over the end of the pivot **(see illustration)**.

10 Cylinder head removal and installation

Removal

1 Remove the engine from the frame (Section 4). If required remove the oxygen sensor (see Chapter 4).
2 Remove the camshaft holder (Section 8).
3 Slacken the clamp screw securing the coolant hose and detach it, being prepared with a rag to catch any residual coolant **(see illustration 4.7c)**.
4 If required slacken the clamp screw securing the intake duct and slip it off the head **(see illustration 4.7c)**.
5 Unscrew and remove the two bolts in the cam chain tunnel **(see illustration 8.7a)**.

9.8 Draw the guide blade out, noting how it locates

9.11b ...and the lugs locate in the cut-outs

9.11a Make sure the bottom locates in its seat...

9.11c Make sure the hole in the retainer locates over the pivot

6 Hold the cam chain up and pull the cylinder head up off the barrel, then pass the cam chain down through the tunnel **(see illustration)**. Do not let the chain fall into the engine – lay it over the front of the barrel and secure it with a piece of wire. If the head is stuck, tap around the joint faces with a soft-faced mallet. Do not attempt to free it by inserting a screwdriver between the head and barrel mating surfaces – you'll damage them.
7 Remove the cylinder head gasket and discard it - a new one must be used **(see illustration 10.11)**. If they are loose, remove the dowels from the cylinder barrel or the underside of the cylinder head **(see illustration 10.10)**.
8 Check the cylinder head gasket and the mating surfaces on the cylinder head and cylinder barrel for signs of leakage, which could indicate warpage. Refer to Section 11 and check the cylinder head gasket surface for warpage.

9 Clean all traces of old gasket material from the cylinder head and cylinder barrel. If a scraper is used, take care not to scratch or gouge the soft aluminium. Be careful not to let any of the gasket material fall into the cylinder bore or the oil and coolant passages.

Installation

10 If removed, fit the dowels into the cylinder barrel **(see illustration)**. Make sure the cam chain guide blade is correctly seated (Section 9).
11 Ensure both cylinder head and cylinder barrel mating surfaces are clean. Lay the **new** head gasket over the studs, the cam chain and blades and onto the barrel, locating it over the dowels and making sure all the holes are correctly aligned **(see illustration)**. Never reuse the old gasket.
12 Carefully fit the cylinder head over the

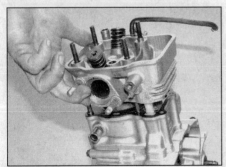

10.6 Carefully lift the head up off the block

10.10 Fit the dowels (arrowed)...

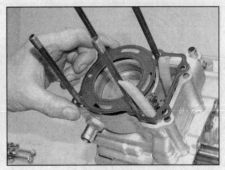

10.11 ...then lay the new gasket on the block

studs and blades and onto the barrel, feeding the cam chain up through the tunnel as you do, and making sure it locates correctly onto the dowels **(see illustration 10.6)**. Secure the chain in place with a piece of wire to prevent it from falling back down.

13 Install the camshaft holder and tighten its nuts (Section 8), then before fitting the cam chain sprocket onto the camshaft fit the two cylinder head bolts and tighten them **(see illustration)**. Finish the installation of the camshaft holder components.

14 If removed fit the intake duct, aligning it so the ribs locate on each side of the tab, and tighten its clamp screw **(see illustration 4.7c)**. Connect the coolant hose.

15 If removed install the oxygen sensor (see Chapter 4). Install the engine (Section 4).

11 Cylinder head and valve overhaul

Special tool: *A valve spring compressor (suitable for motorcycle engines) is essential for this operation.*

1 Valve overhaul involves removing the valves and associated components from the cylinder head, cleaning them and checking them for wear. Valve seat re-cutting or valve guide replacement, if necessary, is a job for an engineer.

Disassembly

2 Label and store the valves along with their

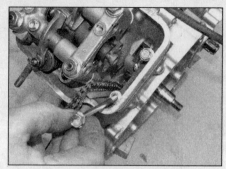

10.13 Fit the cylinder head bolts after the camshaft holder

related components in such a way that they can be returned to their original locations without getting mixed up **(see illustration)**. Labelled plastic bags or a plastic container with compartments is ideal.

3 Compress the valve spring on the first valve with a spring compressor, making sure it is correctly located onto each end of the valve assembly **(see illustration)**. On the top of the valve the adaptor needs to be about the same size as the spring retainer – if it is too small it will be difficult to remove and install the collets **(see illustration)**. On the underside of the head make sure the plate on the compressor only contacts the valve and not the soft aluminium of the head **(see illustration)** – if the plate is too big for the valve, use a spacer between them. Do not compress the springs any more than is absolutely necessary.

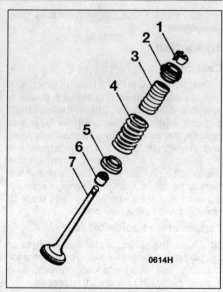

0614H

11.2 Valve components

1 Collets
2 Spring retainer
3 Inner valve spring
4 Outer valve spring
5 Spring seat
6 Valve stem oil seal
7 Valve

4 Remove the collets, using a magnet or a screwdriver with a dab of grease on it **(see illustration)**. Carefully release the valve spring compressor and remove the spring retainer, noting which way up it fits, the springs and the valve **(see illustrations)**. If the valve binds in

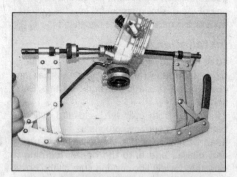

11.3a Compressing the valve springs using a valve spring compressor

11.3b Make sure the compressor locates correctly both on the top of the spring retainer...

11.3c ...and on the bottom of the valve

11.4a Remove the collets...

11.4b ...the spring retainer...

11.4c ...the springs...

11.4d ...and the valve

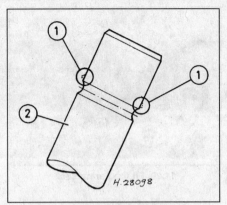

11.4e If the valve stem (2) won't pull through the guide, deburr the area above the collet groove (1)

the guide and won't pull through, push it back into the head and deburr the area around the collet groove with a very fine file or whetstone (see illustration).

5 Pull the valve stem seal off the top of the valve guide with pliers and discard it (the old seals should never be reused), then remove the spring seat noting which way up it fits (see illustrations).

6 Repeat the procedure for the other valve. Remember to keep the parts for each valve together so they can be reinstalled in the same location.

7 Clean the cylinder head with solvent and dry it thoroughly. Compressed air will speed the drying process and ensure that all holes and recessed areas are clean. Note: Do not use a wire brush mounted in a drill motor to clean the combustion chamber as the head material

is soft and may be scratched or eroded away by the wire brush.

8 Clean all of the valve springs, collets, retainers and spring seats with solvent and dry them thoroughly. Do the parts from one valve at a time so that no mixing of parts between valves occurs.

9 Scrape off any deposits that may have formed on the valve, then use a motorised wire brush to remove deposits from the valve heads and stems. Again, make sure the valves do not get mixed up.

Inspection

10 Inspect the head very carefully for cracks

and other damage. If cracks are found, a new head is required.

11 Using a precision straight-edge and a feeler gauge set to the warpage limit listed in the specifications at the beginning of the Chapter, check the head gasket mating surface for warpage. Take six measurements, one along each side and two diagonally across. If the head is warped beyond the limit specified at the beginning of this Chapter, consult a Honda dealer or take it to a specialist repair shop for advice on having the surface skimmed.

12 Examine the valve seats in the combustion chamber. If they are pitted, cracked or burned, the head will require work beyond the scope of the home mechanic. Measure the valve seat width and compare it to this Chapter's Specifications (see illustration). If it exceeds the service limit, or if it varies around its circumference, overhaul is required.

13 Working on one valve and guide at a time, measure the valve stem diameter (see illustration). Clean the valve's guide using a guide reamer to remove any carbon build-up – insert the reamer from the underside of the head and turn it clockwise only. Now measure the inside diameter of the guide (at both ends and in the centre of the guide) with a small bore gauge, then measure the gauge with a micrometer (see illustration). Measure the guide at the ends and at the centre to determine if they are worn in a bell-mouth pattern (more wear at the ends). Subtract the stem diameter from the valve guide diameter to obtain the valve stem-to-guide clearance. If the stem-to-guide clearance is greater than listed in this Chapter's Specifications, replace whichever component is beyond its service limit with a new one – take the head to an engineer for valve guide replacement – note the guide fitting details given in the Specifications.

14 Carefully inspect each valve face, stem and collet groove area for cracks, pits and burned spots.

15 Rotate the valve and check for any obvious indication that it is bent, in which case it must be replaced with a new one. Check the end of the stem for pitting and excessive wear.

16 Check the end of each valve spring

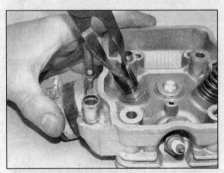

11.5a Pull the seal off the valve stem...

11.5b ...then remove the spring seat

11.12 Measure the valve seat width

11.13a Measure the valve stem diameter with a micrometer

11.13b Measure the valve guide with a small bore gauge, then measure the bore gauge with a micrometer

11.16 Measure the free length of the valve springs and check them for bend

11.20 Fit the spring seat

11.21a Fit a new valve stem seal...

11.21b ...and press it squarely into place

11.23 Locate each collet in its groove in the top of the valve stem

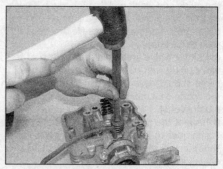

11.25 Seat the collets as described

for wear and pitting. Measure the spring free lengths and compare them to the specifications (see illustration). If any spring is shorter than specified it has sagged and must be replaced with a new one. Also place the spring upright on a flat surface and check it for bend by placing a ruler against it, or alternatively lay it against a set square. If the bend in any spring is excessive, it must be replaced with a new one.

17 Check the spring seats, retainers and collets for obvious wear and cracks. Any questionable parts should not be reused, as extensive damage will occur in the event of failure during engine operation.

18 If the inspection indicates that no overhaul work is required, the valve components can be reinstalled in the head.

Reassembly

19 Coat the valve stem with molybdenum disulphide oil (a 50/50 mixture of molybdenum disulphide grease and engine oil), then install it into its guide, rotating it slowly to avoid damaging the seal (see illustration 11.4d). Check that the valve moves up-and-down freely in the guide.

20 Working on one valve at a time, lay the spring seat in place in the cylinder head with its shouldered side facing up (see illustration).

21 Fit a new valve stem seal onto the guide, using finger pressure, a stem seal fitting tool

or an appropriate size deep socket, to push the seal squarely onto the end of the valve guide until it is felt to clip into place (see illustrations).

22 Next, install the springs, with their closer-wound coils facing down into the cylinder head (see illustration 11.4c). Fit the spring retainer, with its shouldered side facing down so that it fits into the top of the springs (see illustration 11.4b).

23 Apply a small amount of grease to the collets to help hold them in place. Compress the valve springs with a spring compressor, making sure it is correctly located onto each end of the valve assembly (see illustrations 11.3a, 11.3b and 11.3c). Do not compress the springs any more than is necessary to slip the collets into place. Locate each collet in turn into the groove in the valve stem using a screwdriver with a dab of grease on it (see illustration). Carefully release the compressor, making sure the collets seat and lock in the retaining groove.

24 Repeat the procedure for the other valve.

25 Support the cylinder head on wood blocks so the valves can't contact the work surface, then tap the end of each valve stem lightly to seat the collets in their grooves (see illustration).

26 After the cylinder head and camshaft holder have been installed, check the valve clearances and adjust as required (see Chapter 1).

12 Cylinder barrel

Removal

1 Remove the cylinder head (see Section 10).

2 Draw the cam chain guide blade out of the top of the barrel, noting how it locates (see illustration 9.8).

3 Slacken the clamp screw securing the coolant hose and detach it, being prepared with a rag to catch any residual coolant (see illustration).

4 Hold the cam chain up and pull the cylinder barrel up off the crankcase, supporting the piston so the connecting rod does not knock

12.3 Slacken the clamp (arrowed) and detach the hose

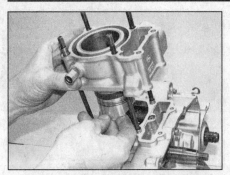

12.4 Carefully lift the block up off the crankcase

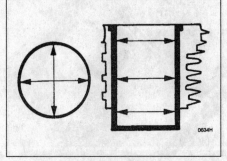

12.10a Measure the cylinder bore in the directions shown...

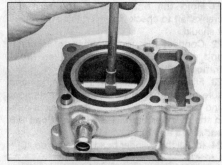

12.10b ...using a telescoping gauge, then measure the gauge with a micrometer

against the engine, then pass the cam chain down through the tunnel **(see illustration)**. Do not let the chain fall into the engine – lay it over the front and secure it with a piece of wire. If the barrel is stuck, tap around the joint faces with a soft-faced mallet. Do not attempt to free it by inserting a screwdriver between the barrel and crankcase mating surfaces – you'll damage them.

5 Remove the base gasket and discard it - a new one must be used. If they are loose, remove the dowels from the crankcase or the underside of the barrel **(see illustration 12.15)**.

6 Stuff clean rag into the cam chain tunnel and around the connecting rod to protect and support it and the piston and to prevent anything falling into the engine.

7 Clean all traces of old gasket material from the cylinder barrel and crankcase. If a scraper is used, take care not to scratch or gouge the soft aluminium. Be careful not to let any of the gasket material fall into the engine.

Inspection

Note: *Do not attempt to separate the cylinder liner from the cylinder barrel.*

8 Check the cylinder walls carefully for scratches and score marks.

9 Using a precision straight-edge and a feeler gauge set to the warpage limit listed in the specifications at the beginning of the Chapter, check the barrel top surface for warpage. Take six measurements, one along each side and two diagonally across. If the barrel is warped beyond the limit specified at the beginning of this Chapter, consult a Honda dealer or take it to an engineer for an opinion, though be prepared to have to buy a new one.

10 Using a telescoping bore gauge and a micrometer, check the dimensions of the cylinder to assess the amount of wear, taper and ovality. Measure near the top (but below the level of the top piston ring at TDC), centre and bottom (but above the level of the oil ring at BDC) of the bore, both parallel to and across the crankshaft axis **(see illustrations)**. Compare the results to the specifications at the beginning of the Chapter. If the cylinder is worn, oval or tapered beyond the service limit it can be re-bored – oversize (+0.25,

+0.50, +0.75 and +1.00) piston and ring sets are available. Note that the engineer carrying out the re-bore must be aware of the piston-to-bore clearance (see Specifications).

11 If the precision measuring tools are not available, take the cylinder barrel to a Honda dealer or engineer for assessment and advice.

Installation

12 Check that the mating surfaces of the cylinder barrel and crankcase are free from oil or pieces of old gasket.

13 Check that all the studs are tight in the crankcase. If any are loose, or need to be replaced with new ones, remove them. Clean their threads and smear them with clean engine oil. Fit them into the crankcase with the marked end at the top, and tighten them using a stud tool, or by threading two of the camshaft holder nuts onto the top of the stud and tightening them together so they are locked on the stud, then tighten the stud by turning the upper of the two nuts. The distance between the top of each stud and the crankcase surface should be 168.5 ± 1 mm.

14 If removed, fit the dowels over the studs and into the crankcase and push them firmly home **(see illustration 12.15)**.

15 Remove the rags from around the piston and the cam chain tunnel, taking care not to let the connecting rod fall against the rim of the crankcase, and lay the **new** base gasket in place, locating it over the dowels **(see illustration)**. The gasket can only fit one way, so if all the holes do not line up properly it is the wrong way round. Never re-use the old gasket.

16 Ensure the piston ring end gaps are positioned correctly before fitting the cylinder barrel (see Section 14) **(see illustration 14.10)**. If possible, have an assistant to support the cylinder barrel while the piston rings are fed into the bore.

17 Rotate the crankshaft so that the piston is at its highest point (top dead centre). It is useful to place a support under the piston so that it remains at TDC while the barrel is fitted, otherwise the downward pressure will turn the crankshaft and the piston will drop. Lubricate the cylinder bore, piston and piston rings with clean engine oil.

18 Carefully lower the barrel over the studs and onto the piston until the crown fits into the bore, holding the underside of the piston if you are not using a support to prevent it dropping, and making sure it enters the bore squarely and does not get cocked sideways **(see illustration 12.4)**. Feed the cam chain up the tunnel and slip a piece of wire through it to prevent it falling back into the engine. Keep the chain taut to prevent it becoming disengaged from the crankshaft sprocket.

19 Carefully compress and feed each ring into the bore as the cylinder is lowered **(see illustration)**. If necessary, use a soft mallet to gently tap the cylinder down, but do not use force if it appears to be stuck as the piston and/or rings will be damaged.

20 When the piston and rings are correctly located in the bore, remove the support if used then press the cylinder barrel down onto the base gasket, making sure the dowels locate.

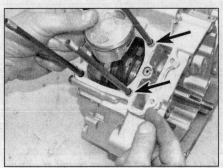

12.15 Lay the new gasket over the dowels (arrowed) and onto the crankcase

12.19 Carefully feed each ring into the bore as you lower the block

21 Hold the barrel down and turn the crankshaft to check that everything moves as it should.

22 Connect the coolant hose to its union and secure it with its clamp **(see illustration 12.3)**.

23 Fit the cam chain guide blade, making sure the bottom of the blade sits in its seat and the lugs near its top locate in the cut-outs in the cylinder barrel **(see illustrations 9.8 and 9.11a and b)**.

24 Install the cylinder head (see Section 10).

13 Piston

Removal

1 Remove the cylinder barrel (see Section 12). Check that the holes into the crankcase and the cam chain tunnel are completely blocked with rag.

2 Note that the piston crown is marked IN (though the mark is likely to be invisible until the piston is cleaned) and this mark faces the intake side of the cylinder.

3 Carefully prise out the circlip on one side of the piston using needle-nose pliers or a small flat-bladed screwdriver inserted into the notch **(see illustration)**. Push the piston pin out from the other side to free the piston from the connecting rod **(see illustration)**. Remove the other circlip and discard them as new ones must be used.

If the piston pin is a tight fit in the piston bosses, heat the piston using a heat gun – this will expand the alloy piston sufficiently to release its grip on the pin. If the piston pin is particularly stubborn, extract it using a drawbolt tool, but be careful to protect the piston's working surfaces.

4 Using your thumbs or a piston ring removal and installation tool, carefully remove the rings from the piston **(see illustrations 14.9, 14.8a and b, 14.6c, b and a)**. Do not nick or gouge

13.3a Prise out the circlip using a suitable tool in the notch...

the piston in the process. Carefully note which way up each ring fits and in which groove as they must be installed in their original positions if being re-used. Look for identification marks on the upper surfaces of the two compression rings, such as R on the top ring and RN on the second ring **(see illustration 14.8a)**.

5 Scrape all traces of carbon from the top of the piston. A hand-held wire brush or a piece of fine emery cloth can be used once most of the deposits have been scraped away. Do not, under any circumstances, use a wire brush mounted in a drill motor to remove carbon deposits; the piston material is soft and will be eroded away by the wire brush.

6 Use a piston ring groove cleaning tool to remove any carbon deposits from the ring grooves. If a tool is not available, a piece broken off an old ring will do the job. Be very careful to remove only the carbon deposits. Do not remove any metal and do not nick or gouge the sides of the ring grooves.

7 Once the deposits have been removed, clean the piston with solvent and dry it thoroughly. Make sure the oil return holes below the oil ring groove are clear.

Inspection

8 Carefully inspect the piston for cracks around the skirt, at the pin bosses and at the ring lands. Normal piston wear appears as even, vertical wear on the thrust surfaces. If the skirt is scored or scuffed, the engine may have been suffering from overheating and/or abnormal combustion, which caused excessively high operating temperatures.

13.3b ...then push out the pin and separate the piston from the rod

Also check that the circlip grooves are not damaged.

9 A hole in the top of the piston, in one extreme, or burned areas around the edge of the piston crown, indicate that pre-ignition or knocking under load have occurred. If you find evidence of any problems the cause must be corrected or the damage will occur again (see *Fault Finding* in the Reference section).

10 Measure the piston ring-to-groove clearance by laying each piston ring in its groove and slipping a feeler gauge in beside it **(see illustration)**. Make sure you have the correct ring for the groove (see Step 4). Check the clearance at three or four locations around the groove. If the clearance is greater than specified, replace both the piston and rings as a set. If new rings are being used, measure the clearance using the new rings. If the clearance is greater than that specified, the piston is worn and must be replaced with a new one.

11 Check the piston-to-bore clearance by measuring the bore (see Section 12), then measure the piston 6.5 mm up from the bottom of the skirt and at 90° to the piston pin axis **(see illustration)**. Refer to the Specifications at the beginning of the Chapter and subtract the piston diameter from the bore diameter to obtain the clearance. If it is greater than the specified figure, the piston must be replaced with a new one (assuming the bore itself is within limits).

12 Apply clean engine oil to the piston pin, insert it into the piston and check for any freeplay between the two **(see illustration)**. Measure

13.10 Measure the piston ring-to-groove clearance with a feeler gauge

13.11 Measure the piston diameter with a micrometer at the specified distance from the bottom of the skirt

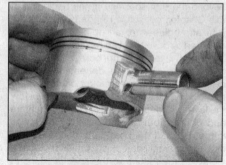

13.12a Fit the pin into the piston and check for any freeplay

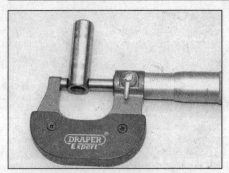

13.12b Measure the external diameter of each end of the pin...

13.12c ...and the internal diameter of the bore in the piston on each side

13.12d Measure the external diameter of the middle of the pin...

the pin external diameter at each end **(see illustration)**, and the pin bores in the piston **(see illustration)**. Calculate the difference to obtain the piston pin-to-piston pin bore clearance. Compare the result to the specifications at the beginning of the Chapter. If the clearance is greater than specified, replace the components that are worn beyond their specified limits. Repeat the check and measurements between the middle of the pin and the connecting rod small-end **(see illustrations)**.

Installation

13 Inspect and install the piston rings (see Section 14).

14 Lubricate the piston pin, the piston pin bore and the connecting rod small-end bore with molybdenum disulphide oil (a 50/50 mixture of molybdenum disulphide grease and clean engine oil).

15 When fitting the piston onto the connecting rod make sure the IN mark on the piston crown faces the intake side (back) of the engine.

16 Fit a **new** circlip into one side of the piston (do not reuse old circlips). Line up the piston on the connecting rod and insert the piston pin from the other side **(see illustration 13.3b)**. Secure the pin with the other **new** circlip **(see illustration)**. When fitting the circlips, compress them only just enough to fit them in the piston, and make sure they are properly seated in their grooves with the open end away from the removal notch.

17 Install the cylinder barrel (see Section 12).

13.12e ...and the internal diameter of the small-end of the connecting rod

13.16 Use new circlips and make sure they locate correctly

14 Piston rings

Inspection

1 It is good practice to replace the piston rings with new ones when an engine is being overhauled. Before installing the new rings, check the end gaps with the rings installed in the bore, as follows.

2 Insert the top ring into the top of the bore and square it up with the bore walls by pushing it in with the top of the piston **(see illustrations)**. The ring should be about 20 mm below the top edge of the bore. Slip a feeler gauge between the ends of the ring and compare the measurement to the

specifications at the beginning of the Chapter **(see illustration)**.

3 If the gap is larger or smaller than specified, double check to make sure that you have the correct ring before proceeding; excess end gap is not critical unless it exceeds the service limit.

4 If the service limit is exceeded with new rings, check the bore for wear (see Section 12). If the gap is too small, the ring ends may come in contact with each other during engine operation, which can cause serious damage.

5 Repeat the procedure for the middle ring and the oil control ring side-rails, but not the expander ring.

Installation

6 Fit the oil control ring (lowest on the piston) first. It is composed of three separate components, namely the expander and the

14.2a Fit the ring in its bore...

14.2b ...and set it square using the piston...

14.2c ...then measure the end gap using a feeler gauge

14.6a Fit the oil ring expander in its groove...

14.6b ...then fit the lower side rail...

14.6c ...and the upper side rail on each side of it

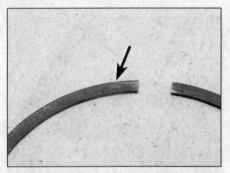

14.8a Note the marking on the ring and make sure it faces up

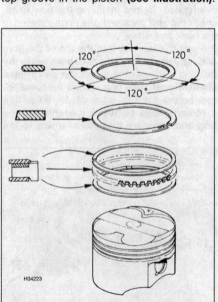

14.8b Install the middle ring...

Make sure the identification letter (where present) near the end gap is facing up.
10 Once the rings are correctly installed, check they move freely without snagging and stagger their end gaps as shown **(see illustration)**.

15 Starter clutch and gears

Check

1 The operation of the starter clutch can be checked while it is in situ. Remove the starter motor (see Chapter 8). Check that the idle/reduction gear is able to rotate freely clockwise as you look at it via the starter motor aperture, but locks when rotated anti-clockwise. If not, the starter clutch is faulty and should be removed for inspection.

Removal

2 Remove the alternator rotor (see Chapter 8) – the starter clutch is bolted to the back of it.
3 Remove the collar from the idle/reduction gear shaft, then remove the gear and the shaft **(see illustrations)**.

Inspection

4 With the alternator face down on a workbench, check that the starter driven gear rotates freely anti-clockwise and locks against the rotor in a clockwise direction **(see**

upper and lower side-rails. Slip the expander into the groove, making sure the ends don't overlap, then fit the lower side-rail **(see illustrations)**. Do not use a piston ring installation tool on the side-rails as they may be damaged. Instead, place one end of the side-rail into the groove between the expander and the ring land. Hold it firmly in place and slide a finger around the piston while pushing the rail into the groove. Next, fit the upper side-rail in the same manner **(see illustration)**. Check that the ends of the expander have not overlapped.
7 After the three oil ring components have been installed, check to make sure that both the upper and lower side-rails can be turned smoothly in the ring groove.
8 The upper surface of the two compression rings should be marked at one end, the top ring

R and the middle ring RN **(see illustration)**. Fit the second (middle) ring next. Make sure that its identification letters are facing up. Fit the ring into the middle groove in the piston **(see illustration)**. Do not expand the ring any more than is necessary to slide it into place. To avoid breaking the ring, use a piston ring installation tool.
9 Fit the top ring in the same manner into the top groove in the piston **(see illustration)**.

14.9 ...and the top ring as described

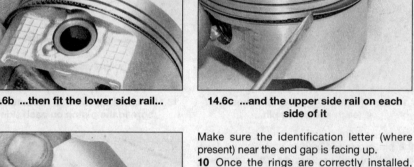

14.10 Piston ring installation details – stagger the ring end gaps as shown

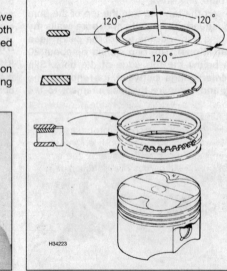

15.3a Remove the collar...

15.3b ...the idle/reduction gear...

15.3c ...and the shaft

15.4 Check the operation of the clutch as described

15.5 Withdraw the driven gear

15.6 Measure the diameter of the hub

15.7 Check the bush (arrowed) for wear

illustration). If it doesn't, the starter clutch should be dismantled for further investigation.

5 Withdraw the starter driven gear from the starter clutch, rotating it anti-clockwise as you do (see illustration).

6 Check the condition of the rollers inside the clutch body and the corresponding surface on the driven gear hub. If they are damaged, marked or flattened at any point, the starter clutch should be replaced with a new one. Measure the outside diameter of the hub and check that it has not worn beyond the service limit specified (see illustration). To remove the starter clutch assembly, hold the alternator rotor using a holding strap and unscrew the bolts inside the rotor. The clutch is supplied as an assembly. Fit the new assembly in a reverse sequence. Apply clean engine oil to the rollers. Apply a suitable non-permanent thread locking compound to the bolts and tighten them to the torque setting specified at the beginning of the Chapter.

7 Check the bush in the starter driven gear hub and its bearing surface on the crankshaft (see illustration). If the bush shows signs of excessive wear (the groove in the surface of the bush for holding the oil will be barely visible) replace the driven gear with a new one.

8 Check the teeth of the reduction and idle gears and the corresponding teeth of the starter driven gear and starter motor drive shaft. Replace the gears and/or starter motor if worn or chipped teeth are discovered on

related gears. Also check the idle gear shaft for damage, and check that the gear is not a loose fit on it. Check the reduction gear shaft ends and the bores they run in for wear.

Installation

9 Lubricate the idle/reduction gear shaft with clean engine oil and insert it into its bore in the crankcase (see illustration 15.3c). Slide the gear onto the shaft, meshing the teeth of the larger inner gear with those of the starter motor shaft (see illustration 15.3b). Slide the collar over the shaft (see illustration 15.3a).

10 Lubricate the outside of the starter driven gear hub and the bush in its centre with clean engine oil, then fit the gear into the clutch, rotating it anti-clockwise as you do so to spread the rollers and allow the hub to enter (see illustration 15.5).

11 Install the alternator rotor (see Chapter 8), making sure the teeth on the starter driven gear mesh with those on the smaller outer gear teeth on the idle/reduction gear.

16 Clutch

Removal

1 Remove the fairing side panels and the lower fairing (see Chapter 7).

2 Drain the engine oil and the coolant (see Chapter 1).

3 Release the clamps securing the coolant hoses to the water pump and detach the hoses, noting which fits where (see illustration).

4 Slacken the locknut on the clutch cable adjuster, then thread the locknut and adjuster nut fully up the adjuster (see illustration 17.3a). Free the cable end from the release arm (create more slack if required using the adjuster on the clutch lever bracket – see Chapter 1) then draw the cable out of the bracket (see illustrations 17.3b and c). Position the cable clear of the engine.

5 Working evenly in a criss-cross pattern, unscrew the clutch cover bolts, noting the guide for the water pump drain hose (see

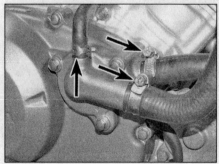

16.3 Release the clamps (arrowed) and detach the hoses

16.5 Unscrew the bolts (arrowed) and remove the cover – note the hose guide (A)

16.6 Unscrew the bolts (arrowed) and remove the pressure plate and springs

16.7 A peg spanner is needed to unscrew the nut and the clutch must be held – this shows a commercially available holding tool

16.8 Draw the complete clutch assembly off the shaft

illustration). Remove the cover, being prepared to catch any residual oil. Remove the gasket and discard it (see illustration 16.26a). Remove the two dowels from either the cover or the crankcase if they are loose. Note the clutch lifter piece in the cover – make sure it does not drop out (see illustration 16.25).

6 Working in a criss-cross pattern, gradually slacken the clutch spring bolts until pressure is released (see illustration). To prevent the assembly from turning, cover it with a rag and hold it securely – the bolts are not very tight. If available, have an assistant hold the clutch while you unscrew the bolts. Remove the bolts, lifter plate and springs (see illustrations 16.24b and a). Remove the bearing from the lifter plate if it is loose (see illustration 16.16a).

7 To remove the clutch nut, a peg spanner (Honda tool Pt. No. 07716-0020100) is required (see illustration 18.2a), or alternatively one can be made by cutting castellations into an old socket. Also the input shaft must be locked – this can be done in several ways: if the engine is in the frame, engage 6th gear and have an assistant hold the rear brake on hard with the rear tyre in firm contact with the ground; alternatively, and if the engine has been removed, the Honda service tool (Pt. No. 07GMB-KT7010) or a commercially available clutch holding tool (as shown) can be used to stop the clutch centre from turning (see illustration). Unscrew the nut and remove the washer (see illustration 16.23a).

8 Grasp the complete clutch assembly and draw it off the shaft (see illustration). Unless the plates are being replaced with new ones, keep the assembly together.

9 Slide the guide and the inner washer off the shaft (see illustrations).

10 If required, grab hold of the pressure plate posts and draw the clutch plate assembly out of the clutch housing, noting how the friction

16.9a Slide the guide off the shaft...

16.9b ...followed by the washer

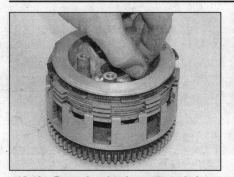

16.10a Draw the clutch centre and plate assembly out of the housing

16.10b Lift the pressure plate off the back of the assembly

16.11 Measuring clutch friction plate thickness

plate tabs locate **(see illustration)**. Remove the outer washer that sits between the pressure plate and the clutch housing. Place the clutch centre face down and remove the pressure plate from the back **(see illustration)**. Remove the clutch friction and plain plates, noting how they fit and keeping them in order **(see illustrations 16.20b and a)**.

Inspection

11 After an extended period of service the clutch friction plates will wear and promote clutch slip. Measure the thickness of each friction plate using a Vernier caliper **(see illustration)**. If any plate has worn to or beyond the service limits given in the Specifications at the beginning of the Chapter, or if any of the plates smell burnt or are glazed, the friction plates must be replaced with a new set.

12 The plain plates should not show any signs of excess heating (bluing). Check for warpage using a flat surface and feeler gauges **(see illustration)**. If any plate exceeds the maximum permissible amount of warpage, or shows signs of bluing, all plain plates must be replaced with a new set.

13 Measure the free length of each clutch spring using a Vernier caliper **(see illustration)**. Place each spring upright on a flat surface and check it for bend by placing a ruler against it, or alternatively lay it against a set square. If any spring is below the minimum free length specified or if the bend in any spring is excessive, replace all the springs as a set.

14 Inspect the friction plates and the clutch housing for burrs and indentations on the edges of the protruding tabs on the plates and/or the slots in the housing **(see illustration)**. Similarly check for wear between the inner teeth of the plain plates and the slots in the clutch centre **(see illustration)**. Wear of this nature will cause clutch drag and slow

disengagement during gear changes as the plates will snag when the pressure plate is lifted. With care a small amount of wear can be corrected by dressing with a fine file, but if this is excessive the worn components should be renewed.

15 Inspect the bearing surfaces of the clutch housing bush and on the clutch guide and input shaft **(see illustration)**. Measure the internal diameter of the housing bush, the external and internal diameters of the guide and the external diameter of the input shaft where the guide sits, and compare the results to the specifications at the beginning of the Chapter. If there are any signs of wear, pitting or other damage the affected parts must be replaced with new ones.

16 Check the lifter plate and its bearing for signs of wear or damage and roughness **(see illustration)**. Check that the bearing outer race is a good fit in the centre of the

16.12 Check the plain plates for warpage

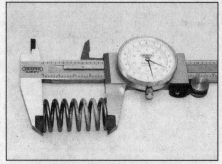

16.13 Measure the free length of the clutch springs and check them for bend

16.14a Check the friction plate tabs and housing slots...

16.14b ...and the plain plate teeth and centre slots as described

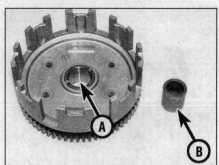

16.15 Check the bearing surfaces on the bush (A), the guide (B) and the shaft

16.16a Check the lifter plate and its bearing

16.16b Check the lifter piece and its cut-out in the shaft for wear

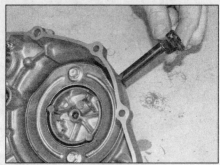

16.17a Withdraw the shaft from the cover

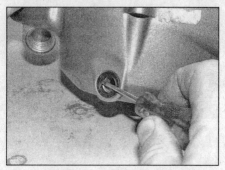

16.17b Lever out the seal...

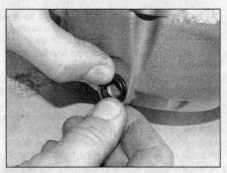

16.17c ...and press a new one into place

16.17d Make sure the spring is fitted so the top end locates in the hole in the shaft

lifter, and that the inner race rotates freely without any rough spots. Check the lifter piece and the corresponding cut-out in the release mechanism shaft for signs of wear or damage (see illustration). Replace any parts necessary with new ones.

17 Check the release mechanism in the clutch cover for a smooth action. If the action is stiff or rough, withdraw the shaft and remove the spring, noting how its ends locate (see illustration). Clean and check the oil seal and the shaft bore in the cover. The seal can be replaced by levering the old one out with a seal hook or screwdriver and pressing the new one in (see illustrations). Lubricate the shaft with molybdenum disulphide oil (a 50/50 mixture of molybdenum disulphide grease and engine oil) and the seal lips with grease before installing the shaft and fitting the spring. Make sure the return spring ends locate correctly (see illustration).

18 Check the teeth of the primary driven gear on the back of the clutch housing and the corresponding teeth of the primary drive gear on the crankshaft. Replace the clutch housing and/or primary drive gear with a new one if worn or chipped teeth are discovered – refer to Section 18 for the primary drive gear. Check the condition of the crankshaft oil seal in the cover and replace it with a new one if necessary – release the circlip, then lever the old one out with a seal hook or screwdriver and press the new one in (see illustrations). Fit the circlip, using a new one if necessary, making sure it locates in its groove.

Installation

19 Remove all traces of old gasket from the crankcase and clutch cover surfaces.

20 If the clutch plate assembly was disassembled, coat each clutch plate with engine oil, then build up the plates, starting with a friction plate, then a plain plate, then alternating friction and plain plates until all are installed (see illustrations). Fit the pressure

16.18a Release the circlip...

16.18b ...then lever out the seal

16.18c Press the new seal in using a suitable socket

16.20a Fit a friction plate...

16.20b ...then a plain plate and so on...

16.20c ...then fit the pressure plate, aligning the marks...

16.20d ...and making sure the castellations engage

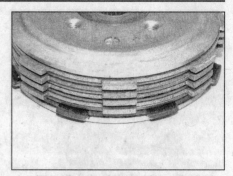

16.22 Align the friction plate tabs as shown

plate into the back of the pack, aligning the mark on the plate with that on the clutch centre, and making sure its castellations locate in the teeth of the inner plain plate **(see illustrations)**. Grasp the pack and turn it on its side, then pull on the pressure plate posts and check for any freeplay between the clutch plates – there should be none; if there is, it means the pressure plate has not located properly.

21 Slide the inner washer onto the shaft **(see illustration 16.9b)**. Smear the clutch guide inside and out with clean engine oil, then slide

it onto the shaft **(see illustration 16.9a)**. Slide the clutch housing onto the guide, engaging the primary drive and driven gear teeth. Slide the outer washer on.

22 Align the tabs of the friction plates as shown **(see illustration)**. Turn the clutch plate assembly over, grab hold of the pressure plate posts and fit the clutch plate assembly into the clutch housing, locating the friction plate tabs in the slots, making sure the tabs of the outermost plate locate in the shallow slots **(see illustration 16.10a)**.

23 Fit the clutch nut washer, then apply oil to

the seating face of the clutch nut and thread it onto the shaft **(see illustration)**. Using the method employed on removal to lock the input shaft and the tool to fit the nut (see Step 7), tighten the nut to the torque setting specified at the beginning of the Chapter **(see illustration)**.

24 Fit the bearing into the lifter plate if removed, and lubricate it with oil **(see illustration 16.16a)**. Fit the clutch springs, lifter plate and bolts and tighten them evenly and a little at a time in a criss-cross sequence to the specified torque **(see illustrations)**.

16.23a Fit the washer and clutch nut...

16.23b ...and tighten it to the specified torque

16.24a Fit the springs...

16.24b ...and the lifter plate, and tighten the bolts as described

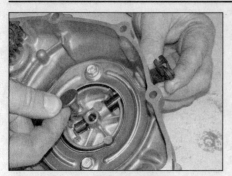

16.25 Turn the shaft to align the cut-out then fit the lifter piece

16.26a Locate the new gasket over the dowels (arrowed)...

16.26b ...then fit the cover

25 Apply some oil to the lifter piece, then turn the release mechanism shaft in the cover until the cut-out is aligned and insert the lifter piece **(see illustration)**.

26 Fit the two dowels into the crankcase if removed, then fit a **new** gasket, locating it over the dowels **(see illustration)**. Lubricate the crankshaft end with oil. Make sure the oil strainer is installed. Fit the cover, turning the water pump impeller as required to ease engagement of its gear with the primary drive gear **(see illustration)**. Install all the bolts finger-tight, not forgetting the hose guide, then tighten them evenly and a little at a time in a criss-cross pattern **(see illustration 16.5)**.

27 Engage the clutch cable end in the release lever arm, then locate the cable in its bracket and adjust freeplay (see Chapter 1) **(see illustrations 17.3c, b and a)**.

28 Fit the coolant hoses onto their unions on the water pump and secure them with the clamps – the hose from the bottom of the radiator fits onto the outer union on the front **(see illustration 16.3)**.

29 Fill the engine with the correct amount and type of oil and coolant (see Chapter 1). Install the fairing panels (See Chapter 7).

17 Clutch cable

1 Pull the rubber boot off the adjuster at the handlebar end of the cable. Fully slacken the lockring then thread the adjuster fully in **(see illustration)**. This provides freeplay in the cable and resets the adjuster to the beginning of its span.

2 Remove the right-hand fairing side panel (see Chapter 7).

3 Slacken the locknut on the clutch cable adjuster, then thread the locknut and adjuster nut fully up the adjuster **(see illustration)**. Free the cable end from the release arm then draw the cable out of the bracket **(see illustrations)**.

4 Align the slots in the adjuster and lockring at the handlebar end of the cable with that in the lever bracket, then pull the outer cable end from the socket in the adjuster and release the inner cable from the lever **(see illustrations)**. Remove the cable from the machine, noting its routing through the guides.

> **HAYNES HiNT**
> *Before removing the cable from the bike, tape the lower end of the new cable to the upper end of the old cable. Slowly pull the lower end of the old cable out, guiding the new cable down into position. Using this method will ensure the cable is routed correctly.*

17.1 Slacken the lockring and turn the adjuster in

17.3a Counter-hold the adjuster nut and slacken the locknut, then thread both nuts up the adjuster...

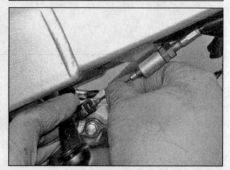

17.3b ...then detach the cable end...

17.3c ...and draw the cable out

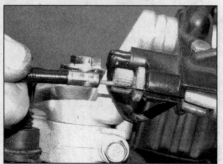

17.4a Free the outer cable from the adjuster...

17.4b ...and the inner cable from the lever

18.2a A peg spanner is needed to unscrew the nut

18.2b Using a piece of rolled strap (arrowed) to jam the gears while unscrewing the nut

18.3a Unscrew the nut and remove the washer...

5 Installation is the reverse of removal. Apply grease to the cable ends. Make sure the cable is correctly routed through its guides. Adjust the amount of clutch lever freeplay (see Chapter 1).

18 Primary drive gear

Removal

1 Remove the clutch, then remove the plate assembly from the clutch housing (see Section 16, Steps 1 to 8 and 10). Slide the housing back onto its guide on the shaft.
2 To unscrew the primary drive gear nut, the peg spanner used to undo the clutch nut is

required again (Honda Pt. No. 07716-0020100) or home-made equivalent (see illustration). Wedge a stout piece of rag or rolled up strap between the teeth of the primary drive and driven gears where they mesh at the top – this will lock them together to prevent them turning (see illustration). Slacken the primary drive gear nut. Remove the rag.
3 Slide the clutch housing, guide and inner washer off the shaft (see illustrations 16.9a and b). Unscrew the primary drive gear nut and remove the washer, then slide the gear off the end of the crankshaft, noting how it locates on the Woodruff key (see illustrations). Remove the key from its slot (see illustration 18.7).
4 If you want to remove the inner washer first remove the oil pump (Section 20). Slide the inner washer off the shaft (see illustration).

Installation

5 If a new primary drive gear is being installed it must be selected so that its colour code matches that of the one being replaced – either yellow, blue or white (see illustration).
6 If removed slide the inner washer onto the shaft (see illustration 18.4). Install the oil pump (Section 20).
7 Fit the Woodruff key into its slot in the crankshaft (see illustration). Align the cut-out in the gear with the key, then slide the gear onto the shaft so it locates over the key (see illustration 18.3b). Fit the washer and the nut and tighten it finger-tight (see illustration 18.3a).
8 Install the clutch (see Section 16).
9 Wedge the stout piece of rag where the gear teeth mesh at the bottom (see illustration). Tighten the nut to the torque setting specified at the beginning of the Chapter (see illustration).

18.3b ...and the gear

18.4 The oil pump must be removed before the washer can be slid off

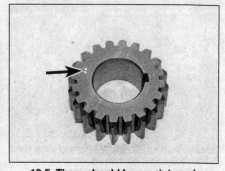

18.5 There should be a paint mark (arrowed) on the gear

18.7 Fit the key into its slot

18.9a Wedge the rag or strap as shown...

18.9b ...and tighten the nut to the specified torque

19.4 Note how the spring ends and roller locate, then unscrew the bolt and remove the arm

19.5 Lower the arm and withdraw the shaft/arm assembly, noting how it fits

19.6a Hold the camplate to prevent it turning and unscrew the bolt (arrowed)

19 Gearchange mechanism

Removal

1 Make sure the transmission is in neutral. Remove the clutch (see Section 16).
2 Make a mark where the slot in the gearchange linkage arm aligns with the shaft (see illustration 4.11). Unscrew the linkage arm pinch bolt and slide the arm off the shaft.
3 Wrap a single layer of thin insulating tape around the gearchange shaft splines to protect the oil seal lips as the shaft is removed.
4 Note how the stopper arm spring ends locate and how the roller on the arm locates

in the neutral detent on the selector drum cam, then unscrew the stopper arm bolt and remove the arm, the washer and the spring, noting how they fit (see illustration).
5 Note how the gearchange shaft centralising spring ends fit on each side of the locating pin in the casing, and how the pawls on the selector arm locate onto the pins on the end of the selector drum behind the cam plate. Grasp the end of the shaft, then push the selector arm down until it clears the cam plate and withdraw the shaft/arm assembly (see illustration).
6 If the crankcases are being separated, unscrew the cam plate bolt, locking the selector drum with a holding tool as shown or using a suitable tool wedged between the plate and the crankcase, and remove the washer (see illustration). Remove the plate, noting that

there are six small pins pressed into the back of it – they should not be loose but take care just in case (see illustration 19.10a). There are also two pins that locate the plate on the end of the selector drum – they should stay in the end of the drum, but again take care as they could drop out. Remove them from the drum for safekeeping (see illustration).

Inspection

7 Check the selector arm for cracks, distortion and wear of its pawls, and check for any corresponding wear on the pins on the selector drum cam plate (see illustration). Also check the stopper arm roller and the detents in the cam plate for any wear or damage, and make sure the roller turns freely (see illustration). Replace any components that are worn or damaged with new ones.
8 Inspect the shaft centralising spring, the selector arm spring and the stopper arm return spring for fatigue, wear or damage. If any is found, they must be replaced with new ones. To replace the shaft spring, slide it off the end of the shaft, noting how its ends locate (see illustration). Fit the new spring, locating the ends on each side of the tab. To replace the selector arm spring simply unhook its ends. Also check that the centralising spring locating pin in the crankcase is securely tightened. If it is loose, remove it and apply a non-permanent thread locking compound to its threads, then tighten it.

19.6b Remove the plate locating pins from the drum

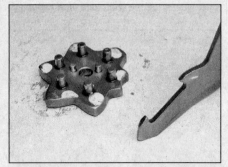

19.7a Check the selector arm pawls and camplate pins...

19.7b ...and the stopper arm roller and camplate detents

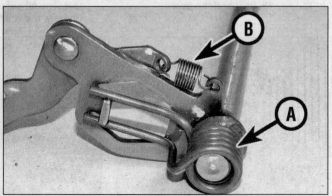

19.8 Centralising spring (A), selector arm spring (B)

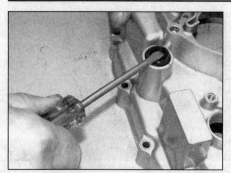

19.9a Lever out the seal...

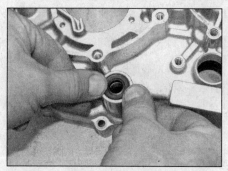

19.9b ...and press a new one into place

19.10a Fit the camplate onto the pins...

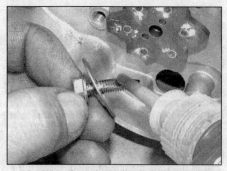

19.10b ...then threadlock the bolt and tighten it to the specified torque

19.12 Stopper arm components

19.13 Gearchange mechanism correctly installed

9 Check the gearchange shaft is straight and look for damage to the splines. If the shaft is bent you can attempt to straighten it, but if the splines are damaged the shaft must be replaced with a new one. Also check the condition of the shaft oil seal in the left-hand side of the crankcase. If it is damaged, deteriorated or shows signs of leakage it must be replaced with a new one – lever out the old seal with a seal hook or screwdriver **(see illustration)**. Press or drive the new seal squarely into place using your fingers, a seal driver or suitable socket **(see illustration)**.

Installation

10 If removed, fit the cam plate locating pins into the end of the selector drum **(see illustration 19.6b)**. Locate the cam plate onto the pins **(see illustration)**. Apply a suitable non-permanent thread locking compound to the cam plate bolt and tighten it to the torque setting specified at the beginning of the Chapter **(see illustration)** – lock the drum with a holding tool as on removal **(see illustration 19.6a)**.
11 Check that the shaft centralising spring is properly positioned **(see illustration 19.8)**. Apply some grease to the lips of the gearchange shaft oil seal in the left-hand side of the crankcase. Slide the shaft into place and push it all the way through the case until the splined end comes out the other side, and push the selector arm down so it fits behind the cam plate **(see illustration 19.5)**. Locate the selector arm pawls onto the pins on the selector drum and the centralising spring

ends onto each side of the locating pin in the crankcase.
12 Fit the stopper arm spring onto its post with the ends facing back and the curved end outermost. Fit the bolt through the stopper arm, then fit the washer **(see illustration)**. Apply a suitable non-permanent thread locking compound to the bolt. Install the arm, locating the roller onto the neutral detent on the selector drum and making sure the spring ends are positioned correctly **(see illustration 19.4)**. Tighten the bolt to the torque setting specified at the beginning of the Chapter.
13 Check that all components are correctly positioned **(see illustration)**. Install the clutch (see Section 16).
14 Remove the insulating tape from around the gearchange shaft splines. Slide the gearchange linkage arm onto the shaft,

aligning its slit with the punch mark on the shaft **(see illustrations 4.11)**. Fit the pinch bolt and tighten it.

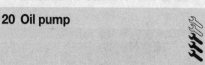

20 Oil pump

Removal

1 Remove the clutch cover (see Section 16, Steps 1 to 5).
2 Unscrew the three bolts and remove the pump from the crankcase **(see illustration)**.

Inspection

3 Remove the E-clip from the outer end of the shaft **(see illustration)**. Lift the gear off the cover on the inner face of the pump

20.2 Unscrew the bolts (arrowed) and remove the pump

20.3a Remove the E-clip...

20.3b ...then remove the gear/shaft assembly

20.3c Slide the gear down off the shaft and remove the drive pin

20.4a Unscrew the bolts...

and withdraw the shaft from the pump (see illustration). Slide the gear off the shaft and remove the drive pin (see illustration).

4 Unscrew the bolts securing the cover to the pump body, then remove the dowels and the cover (see illustrations). Remove the inner and outer rotors, noting which way round they fit (see illustration).

5 Clean all the components in solvent.

6 Inspect the pump body and rotors for scoring and wear. If any damage, scoring or uneven or excessive wear is evident, replace the components with new ones.

7 Fit the inner and outer rotors into the pump body with the punch marks facing out and aligned (see illustration 20.12). Fit the shaft into the inner rotor (see illustration). Measure the clearance between the inner rotor tip and the outer rotor with a feeler gauge and compare it to the service limit listed in the specifications at the beginning of the Chapter (see illustration). If the clearance measured is greater than the maximum listed, replace the rotors with new ones.

8 Measure the clearance between the outer rotor and the pump body with a feeler gauge and compare it to the maximum clearance listed in the specifications at the beginning of the Chapter (see illustration). If the clearance measured is greater than the maximum listed, replace the outer rotor and pump body with new ones.

9 Lay a straight-edge across the rotors and the pump body and, using a feeler gauge, measure the rotor end-float (the gap between the rotors and the straight-edge (see illustration). If the clearance measured is greater than the maximum listed, replace the rotors and pump body with new ones.

10 Check the pump drive gear, shaft and drive pin for wear or damage, and replace them with new ones if necessary. If wear and/or broken teeth are found on the gear check the primary drive gear teeth as well (Section 18).

11 If the pump is good, make sure all the

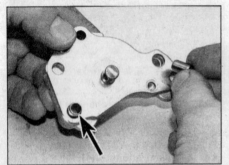

20.4b ...then remove the dowels...

20.4c ...the cover...

20.4d ...and the rotors

20.7a Fit the shaft to align the rotors...

20.7b ...then measure the inner rotor tip-to-outer rotor clearance as shown

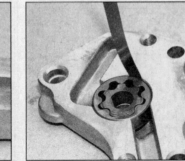

20.8 Measure the outer rotor-to-body clearance as shown

20.9 Measure rotor end-float as shown

20.12 Fit the inner rotor into the outer rotor

20.14 Make sure the E-clips locates correctly in its groove

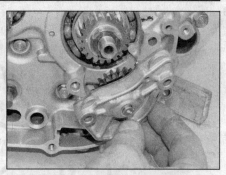

20.16 Make sure the dowels locate and the gears engage

components are clean, then lubricate them with new engine oil.

12 Fit the outer rotor into the pump body with the punch mark facing outwards **(see illustration 20.4d)**. Fit the inner rotor into the outer rotor with the punch mark facing outwards **(see illustration)**. Fill the pump with oil.

13 Fit the cover onto the pump body, then fit the locating dowels **(see illustrations 20.4c and b)**. Fit the bolts and tighten them to the torque setting specified at the beginning of the Chapter **(see illustration 20.4a)**.

14 Fit the drive pin and gear onto the shaft, locating the pin ends into the cut-outs in the gear **(see illustration 20.3c)**. Slide the drive shaft through the pump, aligning the flats between the shaft and inner rotor **(see illustration 20.3b)**. Fit the E-clip into its groove in the outer end of the shaft **(see illustration)**.

15 Rotate the pump shaft by hand and check it turns the rotors smoothly and freely.

Installation

16 Fit the pump, making sure the dowels locate in the crankcase, and the gears engage correctly, then fit and tighten the bolts **(see illustration)**.

17 Install the clutch cover (see Section 16, Steps 25 to 29).

21 Crankcase separation and reassembly

Separation

1 To access the crankshaft and connecting rod assembly, balancer shaft, transmission shafts, selector drum and forks, and their bearings, the crankcase halves must be separated. Remove the engine from the frame (see Section 4).

2 Before the crankcases can be separated the following components must be removed:
Starter motor (Chapter 8)
Neutral switch (Chapter 8)
Valve cover (Section 6)
Camshaft holder (Section 8)
Cylinder head (Section 10)
Cam chain and blades (Section 9)
Cylinder barrel (Section 12)
Piston (Section 13)
Alternator (Chapter 8)
Starter clutch gears (Section 15)
Clutch (Section 16)
Primary drive gear (Section 18)
Gearchange mechanism (Section 19)
Oil pump (Section 20)
Oil strainer (Chapter 1)

3 Fit a suitable 3 mm screw that is 34 mm long through the washer and spring in the inner edge of the cam chain tunnel, and thread it into the hole in the bearing stopper pin below the spring to compress the spring until the pressure is off the circlip **(see illustration)**. Remove the circlip, then pull the washer/spring/pin out using the head of the screw to pull them **(see illustrations)**. Keep the screw in place for installation. Replace the circlip with a new one if it has deformed.

4 Remove the oil jet from its orifice in the top of the right-hand crankcase half **(see illustration)**.

5 Unscrew the four right-hand crankcase bolts evenly, a little at a time and in a criss-cross sequence until they are finger-tight, then remove them, noting the one fitted with a sealing washer **(see illustration)**. Note that

21.3a Thread the screw into the pin to compress the spring...

21.3b ...then remove the circlip...

21.3c ...and withdraw the pin by pulling the screw head

21.4 Remove the oil jet

21.5 Right-hand crankcase bolts (arrowed)

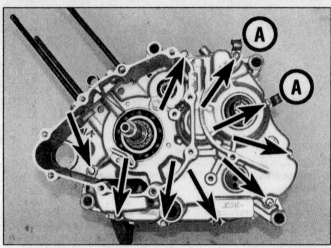

21.6 Left-hand crankcase bolts (arrowed) – note the wiring guides (A)

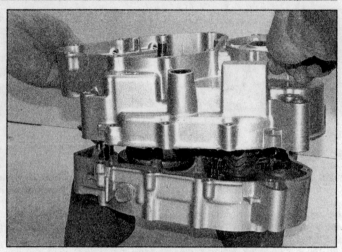

21.7 Carefully separate the crankcase halves

a new sealing washer should be used on assembly.

As each bolt is removed, store it in its relative position in a cardboard template of the crankcase halves. This will ensure all bolts and any washers/guides with them are returned to their original locations on reassembly.

6 Unscrew the nine left-hand crankcase bolts evenly, a little at a time and in a criss-cross sequence until they are finger-tight, then remove them, noting the wiring guides secured by the upper rear bolts, and noting which bolts fit where as there are four different lengths (see illustration).

7 Place the engine on its right-hand side, laying it on wooden blocks so that the shaft ends are clear of the bench. Carefully lift the left crankcase half off the right half, using a soft-faced hammer to tap around the joint to initially separate the halves if necessary (see illustration). Note: If the halves do not separate easily, make sure all fasteners have been removed. Do not try and separate the halves by levering against the crankcase mating surfaces as they are easily scored and will leak oil in the future if damaged. The left-hand crankcase half will come away leaving the crankshaft, balancer shaft, transmission shafts and selector drum and forks in the right-hand half.

8 Note the thrust washer on the left-hand end of the transmission output shaft – if it is not there it is stuck to the bearing in the crankcase, in which case retrieve it and fit it back onto the shaft. Remove the two locating dowels from the crankcase if they are loose (they could be in either half) (see illustration 21.13).

9 Refer to Sections 22 to 27 for the removal and installation of the components housed within the crankcases.

Reassembly

10 Remove all traces of sealant from the crankcase mating surfaces.

11 Ensure that all components and their bearings are in place in the right-hand crankcase half, and that all bearings and new oil seals are in the left-hand half (see Section 19 for the gearchange shaft oil seal and Section 25 for the transmission output shaft seal).

12 Generously lubricate the crankshaft and transmission shaft bearings and gears and the selector fork shafts and fork ends and the tracks in the selector drum with clean engine oil, then use a rag soaked in high flash-point solvent to wipe over the mating surfaces of both crankcase halves to remove all traces of oil.

13 If removed, fit the two locating dowels into the right-hand crankcase half (see illustration). Make sure the thrust washer is in place on the left-hand end of the transmission output shaft.

14 Apply a small amount of suitable sealant (Three-Bond 1207B or equivalent RTV sealant – ask your dealer) to the mating surface of the left-hand crankcase half as shown, avoiding the oil passage in the top of the crankcase (see illustration).

21.13 Make sure the dowels (A) and the thrust washer (B) are fitted

21.14 Apply the sealant as shown, avoiding the oil passage (arrowed)

21.17 Fit a new sealing washer onto the upper bolt

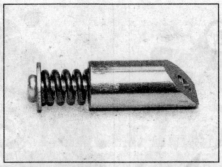

21.21a Assemble the components and use the screw to compress the spring

21.21b The tip of the pin (arrowed) should be visible against the rim of the bearing

Caution: Apply the sealant only to the mating surfaces. Do not apply an excessive amount as it will ooze out when the case halves are assembled and may obstruct oil passages. Do not apply the sealant close to any of the oil passages.

15 Check again that all components are in position (see illustration 21.13). Carefully fit the left-hand crankcase half down onto the right-hand crankcase half, making sure the shaft ends and dowels all locate correctly (see illustration 21.7).

16 Check that the left-hand crankcase half is correctly seated. Clean the threads of all the crankcase bolts. Turn the engine over.

Caution: The crankcase halves should fit together without being forced. If the casings are not correctly seated, remove the left-hand crankcase half and investigate the problem. Do not attempt to pull them together using the crankcase bolts as the casing will crack and be ruined.

17 Install the four right-hand crankcase bolts, fitting the two longer bolts in the upper holes, and fitting a new sealing washer with the uppermost bolt (see illustration and 21.5). Secure the bolts finger-tight at first, then tighten them evenly and a little at a time in a criss-cross sequence – no torque setting is specified, but bolts of that size should be tightened to 12 Nm.

18 Turn the engine over. Install the nine left-hand crankcase bolts, making sure they are fitted in their correct positions as noted on removal, and not forgetting to fit the wiring guides with the upper rear bolts (see illustration 21.6). Secure the bolts finger-tight at first, then tighten them evenly and a little at a time in a criss-cross sequence – no torque setting is specified, but bolts of that size should be tightened to 10 Nm.

19 With all crankcase fasteners tightened, check that the crankshaft, balancer shaft and transmission shafts rotate smoothly and easily. Check that the transmission shafts rotate freely and independently in neutral, then rotate the selector drum by hand and select each gear in turn whilst rotating the input shaft. If there are any signs of undue stiffness, tight or rough spots, or of any other problem, the fault must be rectified before proceeding further.

20 Fit the oil jet into its orifice in the top of the right-hand crankcase half (see illustration 21.4).

21 If the bearing stopper pin assembly was taken apart after removal (Step 3), fit the spring into the pin and fit the washer, then fit the 3 mm screw used earlier through the washer and spring and thread it into the pin to compress the spring (see illustration). Fit the bearing stopper pin into its hole (see illustration 21.3c), locating the tip against the outer edge of the bearing (see illustration). Fit the circlip, making sure it locates correctly, then undo the screw, allowing the spring and washer to settle against the circlip (see illustrations 21.3b and a).

22 Install all other removed assemblies in a reverse of the sequence given in Step 2.

22 Crankcases and bearings

Crankcases

1 After the crankcases have been separated, remove the crankshaft and balancer shaft, the selector drum and forks and the transmission shafts, referring to the relevant Sections of this Chapter.

2 Clean the crankcases thoroughly with new solvent and dry them with compressed air. Blow out all oil passages with compressed air.

3 Remove all traces of old sealant from the mating surfaces. Clean up minor damage to the surfaces with a fine sharpening stone or grindstone.

Caution: Be very careful not to nick or gouge the crankcase mating surfaces or oil leaks will result. Check both crankcase halves very carefully for cracks and other damage.

4 Small cracks or holes in aluminium castings can be repaired with an epoxy resin adhesive as a temporary measure or with one of the low temperature welding kits. Permanent repairs can only be done by TIG (tungsten inert gas or heli-arc) welding, and only a specialist in this process is in a position to advise on the economy or practical aspect of such a repair.

If any damage is found that can't be repaired, replace the crankcase halves as a set.

5 Damaged threads can be economically reclaimed using a diamond section wire insert, for example of the Heli-Coil type (though there are other makes), which are easily fitted after drilling and re-tapping the affected thread.

6 Sheared studs or screws can usually be removed with extractors, which consist of a tapered, left-hand thread screw of very hard steel. These are inserted into a pre-drilled hole in the stud, and usually succeed in dislodging the most stubborn stud or screw. If a stud has sheared above its bore line, it can be removed using a conventional stud extractor which avoids the need for drilling.

7 Install all components and assemblies, referring to the relevant Sections of this and the other Chapters, before reassembling the crankcase halves.

Bearing information

8 The crankshaft, balancer shaft, and transmission shaft bearings should all be replaced with new ones as part of a complete engine overhaul, or individually as required due to wear or failure.

9 Bearing failure occurs mainly because of lack of lubrication, the presence of dirt or other foreign particles, overloading the engine, break-up of one or more of the bearing components due to fatigue, or corrosion. Regardless of the cause of bearing failure, it must be corrected before the engine is reassembled to prevent it from happening again.

10 The bearings should rotate smoothly, freely and quietly, there should be no rough spots or excessive play between the inner and outer races, or between the inner race and the shaft it fits on, or between the outer race and its housing in the crankcase.

11 Dirt and other foreign particles get into the engine in a variety of ways. They may be left in the engine during assembly or they may pass through filters or breathers, then get into the oil and from there into the bearings. Metal chips from machining operations and normal engine wear are often present. Abrasives are sometimes left in engine components after reconditioning operations, especially when parts are not thoroughly cleaned afterwards.

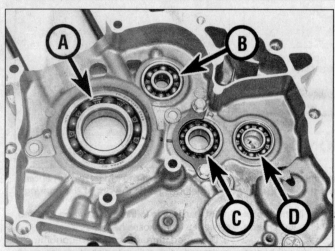

22.15a Main bearing (A), balancer shaft bearing (B), input shaft bearing (C) and output shaft bearing (D) – right-hand crankcase half

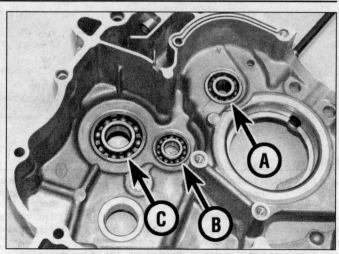

22.15b Balancer shaft bearing (A), input shaft bearing (B) and output shaft bearing (C) – left-hand crankcase half

The best prevention for this cause of bearing failure is to clean all parts thoroughly and keep everything spotlessly clean during engine reassembly. Regular oil changes are also recommended.

12 Lack of lubrication or lubrication breakdown has a number of interrelated causes. Excessive heat (which thins the oil), overloading and oil leakage all contribute to lubrication breakdown. Blocked oil passages will starve a bearing of lubrication and destroy it.

13 Riding habits can have a definite effect on bearing life. Full throttle low speed operation, or labouring the engine, puts very high loads on bearings. Short trip riding leads to corrosion of bearings, as insufficient engine heat is produced to drive off the condensed water and corrosive gases produced. These products collect in the engine oil, forming acid and sludge. As the oil is carried to the engine bearings, the acid attacks and corrodes the bearing material.

14 Incorrect bearing installation during engine assembly will lead to bearing failure as well. To avoid bearing problems, clean all parts thoroughly before reassembly, and lubricate the new bearings with clean engine oil during installation.

Bearing removal and installation

Note: *If the correct bearing removal and installation tools are not available take the crankcases and crankshaft to a Honda dealer for removal and installation of the bearings ñ do not risk damaging either the cases or the crankshaft.*

Crankshaft (main) bearings

15 If the crankshaft (main) bearings have failed, excessive rumbling and vibration will be felt when the engine is running **(see illustrations)**.

16 Separate the crankcase halves (Section 21) and remove the crankshaft (Section 23).

17 To remove the right-hand main bearing from the crankcase, heat the bearing housing with a hot air gun, then tap the bearing out from the outside of the crankcase using a bearing driver or a suitable socket **(see illustration)**.

18 Smear the outside of the new bearing with clean oil. Note that it should be fitted with its marked side towards the inside of the engine. Heat the housing again and drive the bearing squarely in until it seats using a driver or socket that bears only on the bearing's outer race **(see illustration)**.

19 To remove the left-hand main bearing from the crankshaft, use an external bearing puller as shown to draw it off **(see illustration)**.

20 Smear the inside of the new bearing with clean oil. Note that it should be fitted with its marked side towards the crankshaft. Heat the bearing inner race and drive the bearing squarely on until it seats using a tubular driver that bears only on the bearing's inner race.

Connecting rod (big-end) bearing

21 If the connecting rod (big-end) bearing has failed, there will be a pronounced knocking noise when the engine is running, particularly under load and increasing with engine speed. Refer to Section 23, Step 6 for checks that can be made.

22 The connecting rod and its bearing are an integral part of the crankshaft assembly, which comes as a pressed-up unit – individual components are not available. If the big-end bearing fails replace the crankshaft/connecting rod assembly with a new one (see Section 23).

Balancer shaft bearings

23 If the balancer bearings have failed, excessive rumbling and vibration will be

22.17 Drive the bearing out from the outside...

22.18 ...and drive it in from the inside until it seats

22.19 Using a puller to remove the bearing from the crankshaft

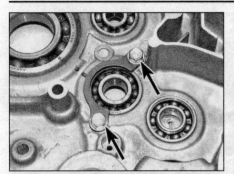

22.29 Unscrew the bolts (arrowed) and remove the plate

22.32a Locate the end of the puller behind the bearing...

22.32b ...and use the slide-hammer to jar it out

felt when the engine is running (see illustrations 22.15a and b).
24 Separate the crankcase halves (Section 21) and remove the balancer shaft (Section 24).
25 To remove the bearings from the crankcase, heat the bearing housing with a hot air gun, then tap the bearing out from the outside of the crankcase using a bearing driver or a suitable socket.
26 Smear the outside of the new bearing with clean oil and fit it with its marked side towards the inside of the engine, then heat the housing again and drive the bearing squarely in until it seats using a driver or socket that bears only on the bearing's outer race.

Transmission shaft bearings

27 If the transmission bearings have failed, excessive rumbling and vibration will be felt when the engine is running (see illustrations 22.15a and b).
28 Separate the crankcase halves (Section 21) and remove the transmission shafts and the output shaft oil seal (Section 25).
29 Unscrew the two bolts securing the input shaft bearing retainer plate on the inside of the right-hand crankcase (see illustration).
30 To remove the input shaft bearing from the right-hand crankcase and the output shaft bearing from the left-hand crankcase, heat the bearing housing with a hot air gun, then tap the bearing out from the outside of the crankcase using a bearing driver or a suitable socket.
31 Smear the outside of the new bearing with clean oil. Note that it should be fitted with its marked side towards the inside of the engine. Heat the housing again and drive the bearing

squarely in until it seats using a driver or socket that bears only on the bearing's outer race.
32 To remove the input shaft bearing from the left-hand crankcase and the output shaft bearing from the right-hand crankcase, an expanding knife-edge bearing puller with slide-hammer attachment is required. Heat the bearing housing with a hot air gun, then fit the expanding end of the puller behind the bearing, then turn the puller to expand it and lock it in position (see illustration). Attach the slide-hammer to the puller, then hold the crankcase firmly down and operate the slide-hammer to jar the bearing out (see illustration).
33 Smear the outside of the new bearing with clean oil. Note that it should be fitted with its marked side towards the inside of the engine. Heat the housing again and drive the bearing squarely in until it seats using a driver or socket that bears only on the bearing's outer race.
34 Apply a suitable non-permanent thread locking compound to the bearing retainer plate bolts, then fit the plate and tighten the bolts (see illustration 22.29).

23 Crankshaft and connecting rod

Note: *The connecting rod is an integral part of the crankshaft assembly, which comes as a pressed-up unit – individual components are not available.*

Removal

1 Remove the engine from the frame (see Section 4) and separate the crankcase halves (see Section 21).
2 Grasp the crankshaft and balancer shaft together and lift them both out of the crankcase (see illustration). If the shafts are stuck, use a soft-faced hammer and gently tap on their right-hand ends.

Inspection

3 Clean the crankshaft with solvent. If available, blow the crank dry with compressed air. Check the balancer drive gear for wear or damage (see illustration). If any of the gear teeth are excessively worn, chipped or broken, the crankshaft must be replaced with a new one. If wear or damage is found, also inspect the driven gear on the balancer shaft (see illustration 24.3).
4 Place the crankshaft on V-blocks and check for runout using a dial gauge. Compare the reading to the maximum specified at the beginning of the Chapter. If the runout exceeds the limit, the crankshaft must be replaced with a new one.
5 Measure the connecting rod side clearance (the gap between the connecting rod big-end and the crankshaft web) with a feeler gauge (see illustration 22.5 in Chapter 2B). If the clearance is greater than the service limit listed in this Chapter's Specifications, replace the crankshaft with a new one.
6 Hold the crankshaft still and check for any radial (up and down) play in the big-end bearing by pushing and pulling the rod against the crank (see illustration). If a dial

23.2 Lift the crankshaft and balancer shaft out together

23.3 Balancer drive gear (arrowed)

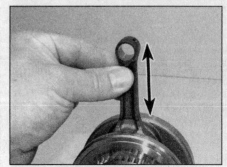

23.6 Check for any radial play in the big-end bearing

23.10a Align the lower punch marks (arrowed), then engage the gears...

23.10b ...so that the upper punch marks (arrowed) then align

gauge is available measure the amount of radial play and compare the reading to the maximum specified at the beginning of the Chapter. If the play exceeds the limit, the crankshaft must be replaced with a new one.

7 Refer to Section 13 and check the connecting rod small-end and piston pin for wear.

8 Have the rod checked for twist and bend by a Honda dealer if you are in doubt about its straightness.

9 Refer to Section 22 and check the crankshaft (main) bearings.

Installation

10 Engage the crankshaft with the balancer shaft, aligning the punch marks on the gear teeth and web as shown **(see illustrations)**. Carefully lower them into the right-hand crankcase, locating the shaft ends in the bearings **(see illustration 23.2)**.

11 Reassemble the crankcase halves (see Section 21).

24 Balancer shaft

Removal

1 Remove the engine from the frame (see Section 4) and separate the crankcase halves (see Section 21).

2 Grasp the crankshaft and balancer shaft together and lift them both out of the crankcase **(see illustration 23.2)**. If the shafts are stuck, use a soft-faced hammer and gently tap on their right-hand ends.

Inspection

3 Clean the balancer shaft with solvent. If available, blow it dry with compressed air. Check the balancer driven gear for wear or damage **(see illustration)**. If any of the gear teeth are excessively worn, chipped or broken, the gear must be replaced with a new one. If wear or damage is found, also inspect the drive gear on the crankshaft **(see illustration 23.3)**.

4 If required remove the circlip, spring washer and plain washer, then draw the gear off the shaft, noting its alignment and how the rubber dampers and the springs fit **(see illustrations)**. Replace them with new ones if necessary. Make sure the circlip has not deformed.

24.3 Balancer driven gear (arrowed)

24.4a Remove the circlip...

24.4b ...the spring washer...

24.4c ...and the plain washer...

24.4d ...then draw off the gear and remove the springs and dampers

24.6a Align the gear on the shaft...

24.6b ...then fit the dampers...

24.6c ...and the springs

5 If a new gear is being installed it must be selected so that its colour code, identified by a paint mark on the gear **(see illustration 24.3)**, matches that of the gear being replaced – either yellow, blue or white.

6 Slide the gear onto the shaft with the shaped side facing out, making sure the holes for the springs and dampers are correctly aligned, and the pins locate in the small cut-outs, then fit the rubber dampers and springs **(see illustrations)**. Fit the plain washer and the spring washer, making sure the raised inner rim faces out, and secure them with the circlip, using a new one if necessary and making sure it locates correctly in its groove **(see illustrations 24.4c, b and a)** – you'll need to push the circlip hard against the spring washer to compress it so the circlip can locate in its groove.

7 Refer to Section 22 and check the balancer shaft bearings.

Installation

8 Engage the crankshaft with the balancer shaft, aligning the punch marks on the gear teeth and web as shown **(see illustrations 23.10a and b)**. Carefully lower them into the right-hand crankcase, locating the shaft ends in the bearings **(see illustration 23.2)**.

9 Reassemble the crankcase halves (see Section 21).

25 Transmission shaft removal and installation

Removal

1 Remove the engine from the frame (see Section 4) and separate the crankcase halves (see Section 21).

2 Remove the selector drum and forks (see Section 27).

3 Grasp the input shaft and output shaft together and lift both shafts out of the crankcase – hold the bottom pinion on the output shaft to prevent it dropping off **(see illustration)**. If the shafts are stuck, use a soft-faced hammer and gently tap on their ends. Note that there is a thrust washer on the right-hand end of the output shaft that may stick to the bearing or fall off as you remove the shafts – if so retrieve the washer and fit it back onto the shaft.

4 Prise the output shaft oil seal out of the left-hand crankcase using a seal hook or screwdriver **(see illustration)**. Discard the seal as a new one must be used.

5 If necessary, the transmission shafts can be disassembled and inspected for wear or damage (see Section 26).

6 Refer to Section 22 and check the transmission shaft bearings.

Installation

7 Press or drive a new output shaft oil seal into the left-hand crankcase and lubricate its lips with grease **(see illustration)**.

8 Make sure the thrust washer is on the right-hand end of the output shaft and that it stays in place when installing the shafts – stick it in place with some oil or grease if it is likely to fall off **(see illustration)**.

9 Join the shafts together on the bench so their related gears are engaged **(see illustration)**. Grasp the shafts together, holding the pinion and washer on the right-hand end of the

25.3 Lift the transmission shafts out together

25.4 Remove and discard the oil seal

25.7 Drive the new seal into place – using a piece of wood as shown sets the seal flush with the rim

25.8 Use grease to stick the washer in place

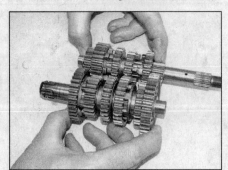

25.9 Join the shafts so all related gears are engaged

26.2a Note how the out-of-round section (arrowed) locates in the groove

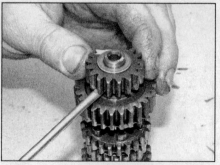

26.2b Use a screwdriver behind the 2nd gear pinion to lever the washer out of the groove

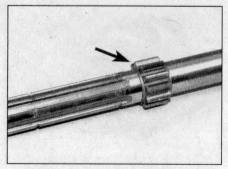

26.6 1st gear pinion (arrowed) is part of the shaft

output shaft to prevent them dropping off. Fit the shafts into their bearings in the right-hand crankcase **(see illustration 25.3)**. Make sure both transmission shafts are fully seated and their related pinions are correctly engaged.

10 Install the selector drum and forks (see Section 27).

11 Make sure the thrust washer is in place on the left-hand end of the transmission output shaft.

12 Reassemble the crankcase halves (see Section 21).

26 Transmission shaft overhaul

1 Remove the transmission shafts from the crankcase (see Section 25). Always disassemble the transmission shafts separately to avoid mixing up the components.

 HAYNES HiNT | *When disassembling the transmission shafts, place the parts on a long rod or thread a wire through them to keep them in order and facing the proper direction.*

Input shaft

Disassembly

2 The thrust washer on the left-hand end of the shaft has a slightly out-of round section on its inner rim that locates in a groove in the shaft **(see illustration)**. To remove the washer slip

one or two flat-bladed screwdrivers behind the 2nd gear pinion and lever it up so the washer is forced out of the groove and towards the end of the shaft **(see illustration)**. Slide the thrust washer and the 2nd gear pinion off the left-hand end of the shaft – note which way around the pinion is fitted; there should be a paint mark on the outer face but if one is not visible make your own **(see illustrations 26.18b and a)**.

3 Slide the 6th gear pinion and its bush off the shaft, followed by the splined washer **(see illustrations 26.17b and a)**.

4 Remove the circlip securing the combined 3rd/4th gear pinion, then slide the pinion off the shaft **(see illustrations 26.16b and a)**.

5 Remove the circlip securing the 5th gear pinion, then slide the splined washer, the pinion and its bush, and the thrust washer off the shaft **(see illustrations 26.15b and a)**.

6 The 1st gear pinion is integral with the shaft **(see illustration)**.

Inspection

7 Wash all of the components in clean solvent and dry them off.

8 Check the gear teeth for cracking, chipping, pitting and other obvious wear or damage. Any pinion that is damaged as such must be replaced with a new one.

9 Inspect the dogs and the dog holes in the gears for cracks, chips, and excessive wear especially in the form of rounded edges. Make sure mating gears engage properly. Replace the paired gears as a set if necessary.

10 Check for signs of scoring or bluing on the pinions, bushes and shaft. This could be caused by overheating due to inadequate lubrication.

Check that all the oil holes and passages are clear. Replace any damaged pinions or bushes.

11 Check that each pinion moves freely on the shaft or its bush but without undue freeplay. Check that each bush moves freely on the shaft but without undue freeplay.

12 The shaft is unlikely to sustain damage unless the engine has seized, placing an unusually high loading on the transmission, or the machine has covered a very high mileage. Check the surface of the shaft, especially where a pinion turns on it, and replace the shaft if it has scored or picked up, or if there are any cracks. Damage of any kind can only be cured by replacement.

13 Check the washers and circlips and replace any that are bent or appear weakened or worn. Use new ones if in any doubt. Note that it is good practice to renew all circlips when overhauling gearshafts.

Reassembly

14 During reassembly, apply molybdenum disulphide oil (a 50/50 mixture of molybdenum disulphide grease and clean engine oil) to the mating surfaces of the shaft, pinions and bushes. When installing the circlips, do not expand their ends any further than is necessary. Install the stamped circlips and washers so that their chamfered side faces away from the thrust side.

15 Slide the thrust washer onto the shaft, followed by the 5th gear pinion bush, then slide the 5th gear pinion onto the bush with its dogs facing away from the integral 1st gear. Slide the splined washer onto the shaft, then fit the circlip, making sure that it locates correctly in the groove in the shaft **(see illustrations)**.

26.15a Slide the splined washer onto the shaft...

26.15b ...and fit the circlip...

26.15c ...making sure it locates properly in its groove

26.16a Slide the combined 3rd/4th gear pinion onto the shaft...

26.16b ...and secure it with the circlip...

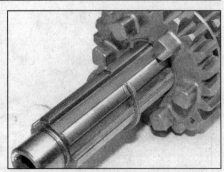

26.16c ...making sure it locates properly in its groove

16 Slide the combined 3rd/4th gear pinion onto the shaft with the smaller 3rd gear pinion facing the 5th gear pinion **(see illustration)**. Fit the circlip, making sure it is locates correctly in its groove in the shaft **(see illustrations)**.
17 Slide the splined washer onto the shaft, followed by the 6th gear pinion bush, then slide the 6th gear pinion onto the bush with its dogs facing the 3rd/4th gear pinion **(see illustrations)**.
18 Slide the 2nd gear pinion onto the end of the shaft – the side with the paint mark faces out **(see illustration)**. Fit the shaped thrust washer onto the end of the shaft and press it down to the groove using a suitable socket until the out-of-round section on its inner rim locates in the groove **(see illustrations and 26.2a)**.
19 Check that all components have been correctly installed **(see illustration)**.

Output shaft

Disassembly

20 Slide the thrust washer off the left-hand end of the shaft, followed by the 2nd gear pinion, its bush and the thrust washer **(see illustrations 26.34d, c, b and a)**.
21 Slide the thrust washer off the right-hand end of the shaft, followed by the 1st gear pinion, its bush, the thrust washer and the 5th gear pinion **(see illustrations 26.33c, b and a, and 26.32b and a)**.
22 Release the circlip securing the 3rd gear pinion – the circlip does not have shaped ends to accommodate circlip pliers, so it is easier

26.17a Slide the splined washer...

26.17b ...and the 6th gear pinion bush and pinion onto the shaft

26.18a Slide the 2nd gear pinion onto the shaft...

26.18b ...then fit the thrust washer...

to remove it using two small screwdrivers to spread it clear of the groove then to pull the pinion behind it against it so it slides up the shaft **(see illustration)**. Slide the circlip,

splined washer and the pinion off the shaft **(see illustrations 26.31c, b and a)**.
23 Slide the tabbed lockwasher off the shaft, then turn the splined washer to offset the

26.18c ...and use a socket to drive it into the groove

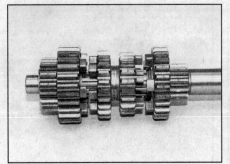

26.19 The complete input shaft

26.22 Spread the circlip using a screwdriver then push the pinion behind it to move the circlip up the shaft

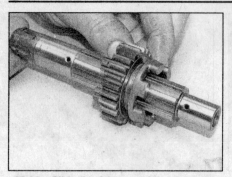

26.28a Slide the 6th gear pinion onto the shaft...

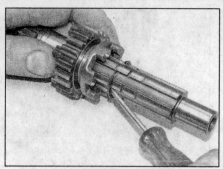

26.28b ...and secure it with the circlip...

26.28c ...making sure it locates in the groove

splines and slide it off the shaft, noting how they fit together (see illustrations 26.30c, b and a).
24 Slide the 4th gear pinion and the splined

washer off the shaft (see illustrations 26.29b and a).
25 Release the circlip securing the 6th gear pinion (see Step 22), then slide the circlip and

pinion off the shaft (see illustrations 26.28b and a).

Inspection

26 Refer to Steps 7 to 13 above.

Reassembly

27 During reassembly, apply molybdenum disulphide oil (a 50/50 mixture of molybdenum disulphide grease and clean engine oil) to the mating surfaces of the shaft, pinions and bushes. When installing the circlips, do not expand the ends any further than is necessary. Install the stamped circlips and washers so that their chamfered side faces away from the thrust side.
28 Slide the 6th gear pinion onto the right-hand end of the shaft, with its selector fork groove facing the right, then fit the circlip, using small screwdrivers as on removal to spread it, making sure it is locates correctly in its groove in the shaft (see illustrations).
29 Slide the splined washer and the 4th gear pinion onto the shaft, with its dog holes facing the 6th gear pinion (see illustrations).
30 Slide the splined washer onto the shaft and locate it in its groove, then turn it in the groove so that the splines on the washer align with the splines on the shaft and secure the washer in the groove (see illustrations). Slide the tabbed lockwasher onto the shaft, so that the tabs locate under the inner rim of the splined washer (see illustration).
31 Slide the 3rd gear pinion onto the shaft, with its dog holes facing away from the 4th gear pinion (see illustration). Slide the splined washer on, then fit the circlip, using

26.29a Slide the splined washer...

26.29b ...and the 4th gear pinion onto the shaft

26.30a Slide the splined washer onto the shaft...

26.30b ...and locate it as shown

26.30c Slide the lockwasher onto the shaft and locate its tabs under the inner rim of the slotted washer

26.31a Slide the 3rd gear pinion...

26.31b ...and the splined washer onto the shaft...

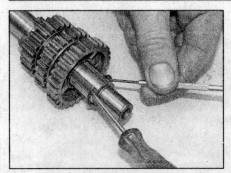

26.31c ...and secure them with the circlip...

26.31d ...making sure it locates in the groove

26.32a Slide the 5th gear pinion...

small screwdrivers as on removal to spread it, making sure it is locates correctly in its groove in the shaft **(see illustrations)**.

32 Slide the 5th gear pinion onto the shaft with its selector fork groove facing the 3rd gear pinion, followed by the thrust washer **(see illustrations)**.

33 Slide the 1st gear pinion bush onto the shaft, then slide the 1st gear pinion onto the bush with its shaped side facing the 5th gear pinion **(see illustrations)**. Fit the thrust washer onto the end of the shaft **(see illustration)**.

34 Slide the thrust washer onto the left-hand end of the shaft, followed by the 2nd gear

pinion bush, then slide the 2nd gear pinion onto the bush with its shaped side facing the 6th gear pinion **(see illustrations)**. Fit the thrust washer onto the end of the shaft **(see illustration)**.

35 Check that all components have been correctly installed **(see illustration)**.

26.32b ...and the thrust washer onto the shaft

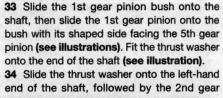

26.33a Slide the bush...

26.33b ...the 1st gear pinion...

26.33c ...and the thrust washer onto the shaft

26.34a Slide the thrust washer onto the left-hand end...

26.34b ...followed by the 2nd gear pinion bush...

26.34c ...the 2nd gear pinion...

26.34d ...and the thrust washer

26.35 The complete output shaft

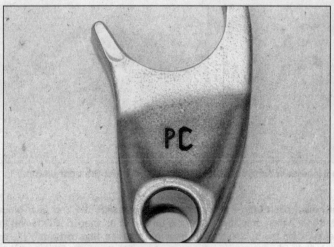

27.2 Note the identification letters on the forks

27.3 Withdraw the shaft and move the forks aside...

27 Selector drum and forks

Removal

1 Remove the engine (see Section 4) and separate the crankcase halves (see Section 21).
2 Before removing the selector forks, note that each fork carries an identification letter (see illustration). The right-hand fork has PR, the centre fork PC, and the left-hand fork PL, with all marks facing the right-hand side of the engine.

27.4 ...then remove the selector drum

If no letters are visible, mark them yourself using a felt pen. The R and L forks fit into the output shaft and the C fork fits into the input shaft.
3 Support the selector forks and withdraw the shaft from the casing (see illustration). Pivot each fork out of its groove in the selector drum.
4 Remove the selector drum (see illustration). Slide each fork out of its pinion and remove them (see illustrations 27.11c, b and a). Once removed, slide the forks back onto the shaft to keep them in the correct order and way round.

Inspection

5 Inspect the selector forks for any signs of

27.5 Check the fit of each fork in its pinion...

wear or damage, especially around the fork ends where they engage with the groove in the pinion. Check that each fork fits correctly in its pinion groove (see illustration). Check closely to see if the forks are bent. If the forks are in any way damaged they must be replaced with new ones.
6 Measure the thickness of the fork ends and compare the readings to the specifications (see illustration). Replace the forks with new ones if they are worn beyond their specifications.
7 Check that the forks fit correctly on the shaft. They should move freely with a light fit but no appreciable freeplay. Measure the internal diameter of the fork bores and the corresponding diameter of the fork shaft (see illustration). Replace the forks and/or shaft with new ones if they are worn beyond their specifications. Check that the fork shaft holes in the casing are neither worn nor damaged.
8 Check the selector fork shaft is straight by rolling it along a flat surface. A bent rod will cause difficulty in selecting gears and make the gearchange action heavy. Replace the shaft with a new one if it is bent.
9 Inspect the selector drum grooves and selector fork guide pins for signs of wear or damage (see illustration). If either component shows signs of wear or damage the fork(s) and drum must be replaced with new ones.

27.6 ...and measure the fork end thickness

27.7 Measure the fork shaft OD and the fork bore ID

27.9 Check the guide pins and their grooves in the drum

27.10 Measure the diameters of the journal and its bore in the crankcase

27.11a Locate the PR fork...

27.11b ...the PC fork...

10 Check that the selector drum rotates freely in each crankcase half and has no sign of freeplay between it and the casing. Measure the diameter of each journal and the corresponding internal diameter of the bore in each crankcase **(see illustration)**. Replace the drum and/or crankcases with new ones if they are worn beyond their specifications.

Installation

11 Lubricate each fork with oil. Locate each fork in turn in its pinion groove, making sure they are correctly positioned – see Step 2 **(see illustrations)**.

12 Lubricate the selector drum ends and tracks with clean engine oil. Slide the selector drum into position in the crankcase **(see illustration 27.4)**. Rotate it so that the hole for the neutral switch contact pin points to the bottom of the crankcase.

13 Pivot each fork round to locate its guide pin in its groove in the selector drum **(see illustration)**.

14 Lubricate the selector fork shaft with oil. With all three forks installed and aligned slide the shaft through each and into its bore in the crankcase **(see illustration 27.3)**.

15 Reassemble the crankcase halves (see Section 21).

28 Running-in procedure

1 Make sure the engine oil and coolant levels are correct (see *Pre-ride checks*). Make sure there is fuel in the tank.

2 Turn the engine kill switch to the ON position and shift the gearbox into neutral. Turn the ignition ON.

3 Start the engine and allow it to run until it reaches operating temperature.

⚠️ *Warning: If the oil pressure warning light doesn't go off, or it comes on while the engine is running, stop the engine immediately. If an engine is run without oil, even for a short period of time, severe damage will occur.*

4 Check carefully that there are no oil, coolant or fuel leaks and make sure the transmission and controls, especially the brakes, function properly before road testing the machine.

5 Treat the machine gently for the first few miles to make sure oil has circulated throughout the engine and any new parts installed have started to seat.

6 Even greater care is necessary if a new piston and rings have been fitted and the cylinder rebored; the bike will have to be run in as when new. This means greater use of the transmission and a restraining hand on the throttle until at least 300 miles (500 km) have been covered. There's no point in keeping to any set speed limit – but don't labour the engine and gradually increase performance up to the 300 miles (500 km) mark. Experience is the best guide, since it's easy to tell when an engine is running freely.

7 Upon completion of the road test, and after the engine has cooled down completely, recheck the valve clearances (see Chapter 1) and check the engine oil and coolant levels (see *Pre-ride checks*).

27.11c ...and the PL fork

27.13 Locate each fork guide pin in its groove in the drum

Chapter 2B
Engine, clutch and transmission – CBR250 and CRF250

Contents

Degrees of difficulty

Easy, suitable for novice with little experience		**Fairly easy,** suitable for beginner with some experience		**Fairly difficult,** suitable for competent DIY mechanic		**Difficult,** suitable for experienced DIY mechanic		**Very difficult,** suitable for expert DIY or professional	

Specifications

General

Type	Four-stroke 4-valve single
Capacity	249.6 cc
Bore	76.0 mm
Stroke	55.0 mm
Compression ratio	10.7 to 1
Cylinder compression	188 psi (13.2 Bar) @ 490 rpm
Cooling system	Liquid cooled
Lubrication	Wet sump, trochoid pump
Clutch	Wet multi-plate
Transmission	Six-speed constant mesh
Final drive	Chain

Cylinder head

Warpage (max)	0.05 mm

Camshafts and rocker arms

Intake lobe height
    Standard.. 30.931 to 31.171 mm
    Service limit (min)................................. 30.911 mm
Exhaust lobe height
    Standard.. 30.839 to 31.079 mm
    Service limit (min)................................. 30.819 mm
Camshaft bearing oil clearance
    Standard.. 0.020 to 0.062 mm
    Service limit.................................... 0.10 mm
Rocker arm bore diameter
    Standard.. 10.000 to 10.015 mm
    Service limit (max)............................... 10.10 mm
Rocker arm shaft diameter
    Standard.. 9.972 to 9.987 mm
    Service limit (min)................................. 9.75 mm
Rocker arm-to-shaft clearance
    Standard.. 0.013 to 0.043 mm
    Service limit (max)............................... 0.10 mm

Valves, guides and springs

Valve clearances................................... see Chapter 1
Stem diameter
    Intake valve
        Standard.................................... 4.470 to 4.495 mm
        Service limit (min)............................ 4.46 mm
    Exhaust valve
        Standard.................................... 4.460 to 4.485 mm
        Service limit (min)............................ 4.45 mm
Guide bore diameter – intake and exhaust valves
    Standard.. 4.500 to 4.512 mm
    Service limit (max)............................... 4.540 mm
Stem-to-guide clearance
    Intake valve
        Standard.................................... 0.005 to 0.042 mm
        Service limit................................ 0.07 mm
    Exhaust valve
        Standard.................................... 0.015 to 0.052 mm
        Service limit................................ 0.08 mm
Seat width – intake and exhaust valves
    Standard.. 0.90 to 1.10 mm
    Service limit (max)............................... 1.50 mm
Valve guide height above cylinder head................ 13.8 to 14.0 mm
Valve spring free length – intake and exhaust valves
    Inner spring
        Standard.................................... 34.58 mm
        Service limit (min)............................ 32.85 mm
    Outer spring
        Standard.................................... 40.37 mm
        Service limit (min)............................ 38.35 mm

Cylinder

Bore diameter
    Standard.. 76.000 to 76.010 mm
    Service limit (max)............................... 76.04 mm
Warpage (max)...................................... 0.05 mm
Ovality (out-of-round) and taper (max)................ 0.01 mm

Piston

	Standard	Service limit
Piston diameter (measured 11 mm up from skirt, at 90° to piston pin axis)	75.96 to 75.98 mm	75.89 mm
Piston-to-bore clearance	0.02 to 0.05 mm	0.09 mm
Piston pin diameter	16.994 to 17.000 mm	16.98 mm
Piston pin bore diameter in piston	17.002 to 17.008 mm	17.03 mm
Piston pin-to-piston pin bore clearance	0.002 to 0.014 mm	0.08 mm

Piston rings

Ring end gap (installed)

Top ring

Standard . . . .   0.22 to 0.38 mm

Service limit (max) . . . .   0.40 mm

Second ring

Standard . . . .   0.40 to 0.55 mm

Service limit (max) . . . .   0.70 mm

Oil ring side-rail

Standard . . . .   0.20 to 0.70 mm

Service limit (max) . . . .   1.1 mm

Ring-to-groove clearance

Top ring

Standard . . . .   0.040 to 0.080 mm

Service limit (max) . . . .   0.10 mm

Second ring

Standard . . . .   0.015 to 0.050 mm

Service limit (max) . . . .   0.09 mm

Starter clutch

Starter driven gear hub ID

Standard . . . .   34.000 to 34.013 mm

Service limit (max) . . . .   34.033 mm

Starter driven gear hub OD

Standard . . . .   51.705 to 51.718 mm

Service limit (min) . . . .   51.685 mm

Clutch

Friction plates   5

Plain plates   4

Friction plate thickness

Standard . . . .   2.3 to 2.5 mm

Service limit (min) . . . .   2.27 mm

Plain plate warpage (max) . . . .   0.30 mm

Spring free length

Standard . . . .   41.5 mm

Service limit (min) . . . .   37.5 mm

Clutch guide ID

Standard . . . .   20.000 to 20.021 mm

Service limit (max) . . . .   20.04 mm

Input shaft OD at clutch guide

Standard . . . .   19.967 to 19.980 mm

Service limit (min) . . . .   19.947 mm

Oil pump

Inner rotor tip-to-outer rotor clearance

Standard . . . .   0.15 mm

Service limit (max) . . . .   0.20 mm

Outer rotor-to-body clearance

Standard . . . .   0.15 to 0.22 mm

Service limit (max) . . . .   0.35 mm

Rotor end-float

Standard . . . .   0.02 to 0.09 mm

Service limit (max) . . . .   0.10 mm

Crankshaft

Runout (max) . . . .   0.03 mm

Connecting rod

Small-end internal diameter

Standard . . . .   17.016 to 17.034 mm

Service limit (max) . . . .   17.06 mm

Small-end-to-piston pin clearance

Standard . . . .   0.016 to 0.040 mm

Service limit (max) . . . .   0.10 mm

Big-end side clearance

Standard . . . .   0.05 to 0.50 mm

Service limit (max) . . . .   0.85 mm

Big-end radial clearance

Standard . . . .   0.004 to 0.016 mm

Service limit (max) . . . .   0.05 mm

Selector drum and forks

Selector fork end thickness
    Standard... 4.93 to 5.00 mm
    Service limit (min).. 4.82 mm
Selector fork bore ID
    Standard... 12.000 to 12.018 mm
    Service limit (max)... 12.05 mm
Selector fork shaft OD
    Standard... 11.957 to 11.968 mm
    Service limit (min).. 11.95 mm
Selector drum left-hand journal OD
    Standard... 13.966 to 13.984 mm
    Service limit (min).. 13.94 mm
Selector drum bore ID in left-hand crankcase
    Standard... 14.000 to 14.027 mm
    Service limit (max)... 14.06 mm
Selector drum left-hand journal clearance
    Standard... 0.016 to 0.061 mm
    Service limit (max)... 0.08 mm

Transmission

Gear ratios (no. of teeth)
    Primary reduction... 2.808 to 1 (73/26)
    Final reduction
        CBR models.. 2.714 to 1 (38/14)
        CRF models.. 2.857 to 1 (40/14)
    1st gear... 3.333 to 1 (40/12)
    2nd gear.. 2.117 to 1 (36/17)
    3rd gear... 1.571 to 1 (33/21)
    4th gear... 1.304 to 1 (30/23)
    5th gear... 1.115 to 1 (29/26)
    6th gear... 0.962 to 1 (26/27)

Torque settings

Balancer driven gear nut .... 44 Nm
Cam chain tensioner blade pivot bolt .... 10 Nm
Camshaft holder bolts .... 12 Nm
Clutch nut... 108 Nm
Clutch spring bolts.. 12 Nm
Crankcase bolts .... 10 Nm
Crankshaft end cap .... 8 Nm
Cylinder head nuts .... 45 Nm
Engine mounting bolts
    CBR models
        Engine hanger-to-frame bolts.......................... 45 Nm
        Engine mounting bolt nuts .... 45 Nm
    CRF models
        Engine hanger-to-frame bolts.......................... 27 Nm
        Upper and lower front mounting bolt nuts .... 55 Nm
        Upper and lower rear mounting bolt nuts.................... 45 Nm
Gearchange mechanism stopper arm bolt............. 10 Nm
Primary drive gear nut .... 108 Nm
Selector drum camplate bolt .... 10 Nm
Starter clutch bolts... 30 Nm
Timing inspection cap .... 6 Nm
Valve cover bolts .... 10 Nm

1 General information

The engine/transmission unit is a liquid-cooled single cylinder of unit construction. The four valves are operated by rocker arms actuated by double overhead camshafts that are chain driven off the right-hand end of the crankshaft. The crankcase divides vertically.

The crankcase incorporates a wet sump, pressure-fed lubrication system that uses a single rotor trochoidal oil pump that is gear-driven off the primary drive gear on the right-hand end of the crankshaft. Oil passes through a filter in the clutch cover and a strainer in the bottom of the crankcase.

The alternator is on the left-hand end of the crankshaft. The ignition timing triggers are on the outside of the alternator rotor, and the crankshaft position (CKP) sensor is mounted in the alternator cover along with the stator.

The water pump is on the right-hand side of the engine, and is driven off the balancer shaft.

Power from the crankshaft is routed to the transmission via the clutch. The clutch is of the wet, multi-plate type and is gear-driven off the crankshaft. The clutch is operated by cable. The transmission is a six-speed constant-mesh unit. Final drive to the rear wheel is by chain and sprockets.

2 Component access

Operations possible with the engine in the frame

The components and assemblies listed below can be removed without having to remove the engine from the frame. If however, a number of areas require attention at the same time, removal of the engine is recommended.

Valve cover
Camshafts and rockers
Clutch
Gearchange mechanism
Alternator
Starter clutch
Oil pump and oil strainer
Starter motor
Water pump

Operations requiring engine removal

It is necessary to remove the engine from the frame to gain access to the following components.

Cylinder head
Cam chain, tensioner and blades
Cylinder barrel and piston
Crankshaft, connecting rod and bearings

Balancer shaft
Transmission shafts and bearings
Selector drum and forks

3 Compression test

Refer to Chapter 2A, Section 3. The compression figure is given in the Specifications at the beginning of this Chapter under the 'General' heading.

4 Engine removal and installation

Caution: The engine is not particularly heavy (around 35 kg), but the aid of an assistant is advised to prevent personal injury or damage if the engine falls or is dropped.

CBR models

Removal

1 Support the bike either on its sidestand or using an auxiliary stand, making sure it is on level ground. Work can be made easier by raising the machine to a suitable working height on an hydraulic ramp or a suitable platform. Make sure the motorcycle is secure and will not topple over, and tie the front brake lever to the handlebar to prevent it rolling forwards.

2 Remove the fairing side panels and lower fairing (see Chapter 7).

3 If the engine is dirty, particularly around its mountings, wash it thoroughly. This makes work much easier and rules out the possibility of caked on lumps of dirt falling into some vital component.

4 Drain the engine oil and coolant (see Chapter 1).

5 Disconnect the negative (–ve) lead from the battery (see Chapter 8).

6 Remove the fuel tank and the air filter housing (Chapter 4).

7 Either remove the throttle body completely, or fully slacken the clamp screws securing it to the cylinder head intake duct, noting the orientation of the clamp, and ease the throttle body out of the duct leaving its cables and hoses still connected (see Chapter 4). Plug the engine intake duct with clean rag to prevent contamination.

8 Release the clamps securing the cooling system hoses to the water pump cover and thermostat housing (see illustrations). Remove the radiator along with its hoses, noting their routing (see Chapter 3).

9 Remove the exhaust system (see Chapter 4).

10 Pull the spark plug cap off the plug and secure it clear of the engine (see illustration). Disconnect the oxygen sensor wiring connector and release the wiring from the guide (see illustration).

11 Unscrew the clutch cable bracket bolts

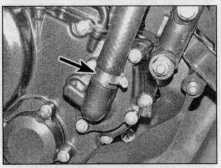

4.8a Detach the hoses (arrowed) from the water pump cover...

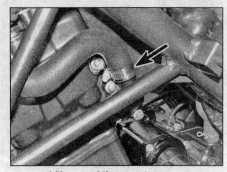

4.8b ...and thermostat cover

4.10a Pull the cap off the spark plug

4.10b Oxygen sensor connector (arrowed)

4.11a Unscrew the bolts (arrowed)…

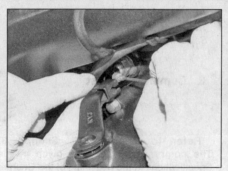

4.11b …and disconnect the clutch cable

4.12 Detach the leads (arrowed) from the starter motor terminal and mounting bolt

(see illustration). Free the cable end from the release arm and position it clear of the engine (see illustration). Thread the bracket bolts back into the clutch cover.

12 If required, remove the starter motor (see Chapter 8). If you leave it on the engine, pull back the rubber cover on its terminal, then unscrew the nut and disconnect the lead (see illustration) – spray it with some penetrating fluid first if it is corroded. Also unscrew the mounting bolt securing the earth lead and detach the lead.

13 Note the alignment of the slot in the gearchange linkage arm with the punch mark on the shaft (see illustration). Unscrew the linkage arm pinch bolt and slide the arm off the shaft.

14 Remove the front sprocket (see Chapter 6). Lay the drive chain against the front of the swingarm.

15 Draw the rubber boot off the wiring connectors on the left-hand side, then disconnect the alternator wiring connector, the CKP sensor/neutral switch wiring connector, and the speed sensor wiring connector (see illustration). Free the speed sensor wiring from its guides. Disconnect the ECT sensor wiring connector (see illustration).

16 Position an hydraulic or mechanical jack under the engine with a block of wood between the jack head and sump. Make sure the jack is centrally positioned so the engine will not topple in any direction when the last mounting bolt is removed. Raise the jack to take the

weight of the engine, but make sure it is not lifting the bike and taking the weight of that as well. The idea is to support the engine so that there is no pressure on any of the mounting bolts once they have been slackened, so they can be easily withdrawn. Note that it may be necessary to alter the position of the jack as some of the bolts are removed to relieve the stress transferred to the other bolts.

17 Unscrew the nuts on the right-hand ends of the engine upper and lower front mounting bolts (see illustration). Unscrew the bolts securing the engine hangers to the frame (see illustration). Withdraw the front mounting bolts and remove the engine hangers (see illustration).

18 Unscrew the nuts on the right-hand ends

4.13 Note the alignment then unscrew the bolt (arrowed) and slide the arm off

4.15a Disconnect the connectors (arrowed)

4.15b ECT sensor connector (arrowed)

4.17a Unscrew the nuts (arrowed)

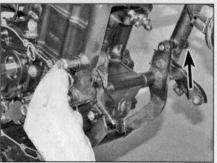

4.17b Unscrew the hanger bolt on each side

4.17c Withdraw the mounting bolts and remove the hangers

4.18 Unscrew the nuts (arrowed)

4.19 Withdraw the rear bolts and remove the engine

4.28 Unscrew the bolts (arrowed) and remove the guard

of the upper and lower rear mounting bolts **(see illustration)**.

19 Check that the engine is properly supported by the jack. Check that all wiring, cables and hoses are free and clear. Withdraw the upper and lower rear mounting bolts from the left-hand side **(see illustration)**.

20 The engine can now be removed from the frame (see *Caution* above). Carefully lower the jack and manoeuvre the engine clear. Fully lower the jack, then with the aid of an assistant remove the jack from under the engine and remove the engine.

Installation

21 Manoeuvre the engine into position under the frame and lift it onto the jack. Raise the engine to align all the mounting bolt holes, making sure that all cables and wiring are correctly routed and do not get trapped. Note that it may be necessary to adjust the jack as some of the bolts are installed to realign the other bolt holes.

22 Insert the upper and lower rear mounting bolts from the left-hand side, then fit their nuts and tighten them finger-tight **(see illustrations 4.19 and 4.18)**.

23 Fit the engine hangers and insert the front mounting bolts from the left-hand side **(see illustration 4.17c)**. Fit the hanger bolts and tighten them finger-tight **(see illustration 4.17b)**. Fit the front mounting bolt nuts and tighten them finger-tight **(see illustration 4.17a)**.

24 First tighten the engine hanger-to-frame

bolts to the torque setting specified at the beginning of the Chapter. Next tighten the upper and then the lower front mounting bolt nuts to the specified torque setting. Finally tighten the upper and then the lower rear mounting bolt nuts to the specified torque.

25 Remove the jack from under the engine.

26 The remainder of the installation procedure is the reverse of removal, noting the following points:

● When fitting the gearchange linkage arm onto the shaft, align the slit in the arm with the punch mark on the shaft **(see illustration 4.13)**.
● Use a new gasket on the exhaust pipe.
● Make sure all wires, cables and hoses are correctly routed and connected, and secured by any clips or ties.
● Refill the engine with oil and coolant to the correct levels (see Chapter 1 and *Pre-ride checks*).
● Adjust the throttle and clutch cable freeplay.
● Adjust the drive chain (see Chapter 1).
● Start the engine and check that there are no oil or coolant leaks. Check the idle speed (see Chapter 1).

CRF models

Removal

27 Support the bike either on its sidestand or using an auxiliary stand, making sure it is on level ground. Work can be made easier by raising the machine to a suitable working

height on an hydraulic ramp or a suitable platform. Make sure the motorcycle is secure and will not topple over, and tie the front brake lever to the handlebar to prevent it rolling forwards.

28 Remove the fuel tank covers and the sump guard (see Chapter 7). Remove the heel guard **(see illustration)**.

29 If the engine is dirty, particularly around its mountings, wash it thoroughly. This makes work much easier and rules out the possibility of caked on lumps of dirt falling into some vital component.

30 Drain the engine oil and coolant (see Chapter 1).

31 Disconnect the negative (–ve) lead from the battery (see Chapter 8).

32 Remove the fuel tank (Chapter 4).

33 Remove the throttle body (see Chapter 4). Plug the engine intake duct with clean rag to prevent contamination. On US models remove the EVAP system control valve and canister along with all hoses, noting their routing (see Chapter 4).

34 Release the clamps securing the cooling system hoses to the water pump cover and thermostat housing **(see illustrations 4.8a and b)**. Remove the radiator along with its hoses, noting their routing (see Chapter 3).

35 Remove the exhaust system (see Chapter 4).

36 Detach the PAIR system hose **(see illustration)**. Pull the spark plug cap off the plug and secure it clear of the engine **(see illustration)**. Disconnect the oxygen sensor wiring connector **(see illustration)**.

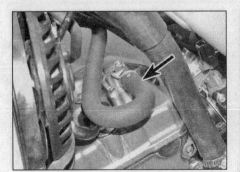

4.36a Detach the hose (arrowed)...

4.36b ...then pull the cap off the spark plug

4.36c Oxygen sensor connector (arrowed)

4.39 Release the clamp and detach the hose (arrowed)

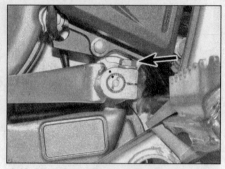

4.40 Note the alignment then unscrew the bolt (arrowed) and slide the arm off

4.42 Unscrew the bolt (arrowed)

37 Unscrew the clutch cable bracket bolts (see illustration 4.11a). Free the cable end from the release arm and position it clear of the engine (see illustration 4.11b). Thread the bracket bolts back into the clutch cover.

38 If required, remove the starter motor (see Chapter 8). If you leave it on the engine, pull back the rubber cover on its terminal, then unscrew the nut and disconnect the lead (see illustration 4.12) – spray it with some penetrating fluid first if it is corroded. Also unscrew the mounting bolt securing the earth lead and detach the lead.

39 Detach the crankcase breather hose (see illustration).

40 Note the alignment of the punch marks on the gearchange lever and shaft (see illustration). Unscrew the lever pinch bolt and slide the arm off the shaft.

41 Remove the front sprocket (see Chapter 6). Lay the drive chain against the front of the swingarm.

42 Remove the rear brake pedal (see Chapter 5). Unscrew the brake light switch bracket bolt and secure the switch clear of the engine (see illustration).

43 Draw the rubber boot off the wiring connectors on the left-hand side of the frame, then disconnect the alternator wiring connector, the CKP sensor/neutral switch wiring connector, and the speed sensor wiring connector (see illustration). Free the wiring from its clamps. Disconnect the ECT sensor wiring connector (see illustration 4.15b).

44 Position an hydraulic or mechanical jack under the engine with a block of wood between the jack head and sump. Make sure the jack is centrally positioned so the engine will not

topple in any direction when the last mounting bolt is removed. Raise the jack to take the weight of the engine, but make sure it is not lifting the bike and taking the weight of that as well. The idea is to support the engine so that there is no pressure on any of the mounting bolts once they have been slackened, so they can be easily withdrawn. Note that it may be necessary to alter the position of the jack as some of the bolts are removed to relieve the stress transferred to the other bolts.

45 Unscrew the nut on the right-hand end of the engine upper rear mounting bolt then withdraw the bolt (see illustration). Unscrew the bolts securing the engine hanger to the frame and remove it, noting how it fits (see illustration).

46 Unscrew the nut on the right-hand end of the upper front mounting bolt and remove the washer (see illustration). Withdraw the bolt and remove the spacers from between the engine and frame on each side.

47 Unscrew the nut on the right-hand end of the lower front mounting bolt and remove the washer (see illustration 4.46). Withdraw the bolt and remove the spacer from between the engine and frame on the left-hand side.

48 Unscrew the nut on the right-hand end of the lower rear mounting bolt and remove the washer (see illustration). Check that the engine is properly supported by the jack. Check that all wiring, cables and hoses are free and clear. Place some rag over the right-hand side of the frame to protect it. Withdraw the lower rear mounting bolt from the left-hand side.

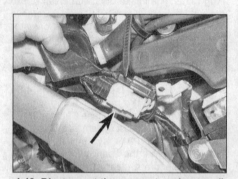

4.43 Disconnect the connectors (arrowed)

4.45a Unscrew the nut (arrowed) then withdraw the bolt

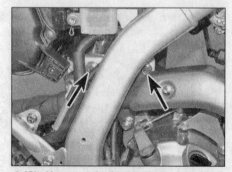

4.45b Unscrew the hanger bolts (arrowed)

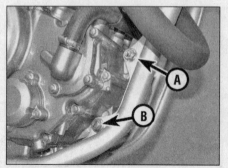

4.46 Upper front mounting bolt nut (A), lower front mounting bolt nut (B)

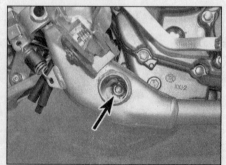

4.48 Access the nut (arrowed) via the hole in the frame

49 The engine can now be removed from the frame (see *Caution* above). Carefully raise the jack a bit, then with help from an assistant manoeuvre engine out from the right-hand side of the frame.

Installation

50 Manoeuvre the engine into position in the frame and rest it on the jack. Use the jack to align all the mounting bolt holes, making sure that all cables and wiring are correctly routed and do not get trapped. Note that it may be necessary to adjust the jack as some of the bolts are installed to realign the other bolt holes.
51 Insert the lower rear mounting bolt from the left-hand side, then fit the nut and tighten it finger-tight **(see illustrations 4.48)**.
52 Insert the lower front mounting bolt from the left-hand side, locating the spacer between the engine and frame on the left, then fit the washer and tighten the nut finger-tight **(see illustrations 4.46)**.
53 Insert the upper front mounting bolt from the left-hand side, locating the spacers between the engine and frame on each side, then fit the washer and tighten the nut finger-tight **(see illustrations 4.46)**.
54 Fit the engine hanger to the frame and tighten the bolts finger-tight **(see illustration 4.45b)**. Insert the upper rear mounting bolt from the left-hand side then fit the nut and tighten it finger-tight **(see illustrations 4.45a)**.
55 First tighten the lower rear mounting bolt nut to the torque setting specified at the beginning of the Chapter. Next tighten the lower then the upper front mounting bolt nuts to the specified torque setting.
56 Next tighten the engine hanger bolts to the specified torque. Finally tighten the upper rear mounting bolt nut to the specified torque.
57 Remove the jack from under the engine.
58 The remainder of the installation procedure is the reverse of removal, noting the following points:
● When fitting the gearchange lever onto the shaft, align the punch marks **(see illustration 4.40)**.
● Use a new gasket on the exhaust pipe.
● Make sure all wires, cables and hoses

6.4a Unscrew the bolts (arrowed)...

6.2a Unscrew the reservoir bolts (arrowed)...

are correctly routed and connected, and secured by any clips or ties.
● Refill the engine with oil and coolant to the correct levels (see Chapter 1 and *Pre-ride checks*).
● Adjust the throttle and clutch cable freeplay.
● Adjust the drive chain (see Chapter 1).
● Start the engine and check that there are no oil or coolant leaks. Check the idle speed (see Chapter 1).

5   Engine overhaul – general information

Refer to Chapter 2A, Section 5, noting the stripdown order given below.
Remove the valve cover
Remove the camshafts
Remove the cylinder head
Remove the cylinder barrel and piston
Remove the alternator and starter clutch (see Chapter 8)
Remove the starter motor (see Chapter 8)
Remove the clutch and water pump
Remove the primary drive gear
Remove the gearchange mechanism
Remove the oil pump
Remove the cam chain and blades
Remove the balancer shaft gears
Separate the crankcase halves
Remove the selector drum and forks
Remove the transmission shafts
Remove the crankshaft and balancer shaft

6.4b ...and remove the valve cover

6.2b ...and the earth point bolt (arrowed)

6   Valve cover

Removal

1 On CBR models remove the fairing side panels (see Chapter 7). Displace the radiator from its mounts and move it forwards (see Chapter 3) – there is no need to drain the cooling system or detach any hoses. For best access, particularly when checking/adjusting valve clearances, remove the fuel tank (see Chapter 4), then move the rubber cover out of the way – this enables you to work from the top.
2 On CRF models remove the fuel tank and the ignition coil (see Chapter 4). Unscrew the coolant reservoir bracket bolts, noting the earth terminal secured by the upper bolt **(see illustrations)**.
3 Detach the PAIR system hose **(see illustration 4.36a)**. Pull the spark plug cap off the plug **(see illustration 4.10a or 4.36b)**.
4 Unscrew the two valve cover bolts and lift the cover off the cylinder head **(see illustrations)**. If it is stuck, do not try to lever it off with a screwdriver. Tap it gently around the sides with a rubber hammer or block of wood to dislodge it. Note the rubber washers for the bolts and remove them if they are loose **(see illustration 6.11)**.
5 Remove the dowel if loose **(see illustration 6.9)**.
6 The rubber gasket is normally glued into the groove in the cover, and is best left there if it is reusable. If the gasket is in any way damaged, deformed or deteriorated, remove it **(see illustration 6.9)**.

Installation

7 Clean any old sealant from the gasket cut-outs in the cylinder head.
8 Fit the dowel if removed **(see illustration 6.9)**.
9 Examine the valve cover gasket for signs of damage or deterioration and fit a new one if necessary. If a new one is used, clean all traces of the old glue from the groove in the cover and clean it and the cylinder head mating surface with solvent. Fit the new

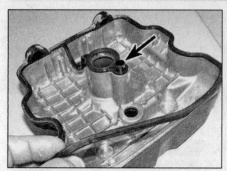

6.9 Make sure the gasket locates in the groove and over the dowel (arrowed)

6.11 Make sure the washers are the correct way up

gasket into the groove and over the dowel, using a suitable glue, sealant or grease to hold it in place **(see illustration)**.
10 Smear some sealant into the gasket cut-outs in the cylinder head.

11 If removed, fit the rubber washers into the cover, using new ones if required, and making sure they are fitted with the metal side (marked UP) facing up **(see illustration)**. Position the valve cover on the cylinder head, making sure

the gasket stays in place **(see illustration 6.4b)**. Fit the cover bolts and tighten them to the specified torque setting.
12 Install the remaining components in the reverse order of removal.

7 Cam chain tensioner

Removal

1 Unscrew the clutch cable bracket bolts, detach the cable from the release arm, and position it clear **(see illustrations 4.11a and b)**. On US CRF models remove the EVAP control valve and canister (see Chapter 4).
2 It is advisable to set the engine at TDC on compression before removing the tensioner. Remove the valve cover (Section 6) and position the engine as described in Section 8, Step 4.
3 Undo the tensioner cap screw and remove the O-ring **(see illustrations)**.
4 Slacken the tensioner mounting bolts slightly **(see illustration)**. Insert a small flat-bladed screwdriver in the end of the tensioner so that it engages the slotted plunger **(see illustration)**. Turn the screwdriver clockwise until the plunger is fully retracted and hold it in this position, then unscrew the tensioner mounting bolts and withdraw the tensioner from the engine **(see illustration)**. Release the screwdriver – the plunger will spring back out, but can be easily reset on installation.
5 Discard the gasket and O-ring as new ones must be used on installation. Do not attempt to dismantle the tensioner.

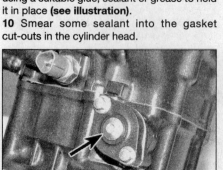

7.3a Undo the cap screw (arrowed)...

7.3b ...and remove the O-ring

7.4a Slacken the mounting bolts (arrowed) slightly...

7.4b ...then insert the screwdriver, retract the plunger,...

Installation

6 Check that the plunger moves smoothly when wound into the tensioner and springs back out freely when released **(see illustration)**. Ensure the tensioner and cylinder barrel surfaces are clean and dry.
7 Retract the plunger as before and hold the screwdriver **(see illustration 7.6)**. Fit a new gasket onto the tensioner body **(see illustration)**. Fit the tensioner with

7.4c ...unscrew the mounting bolts and remove the tensioner

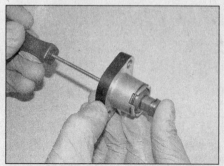

7.6 Check the action of the plunger

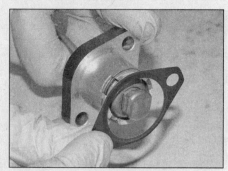

7.7a Fit a new gasket onto the tensioner...

7.7b ...then fit the tensioner, keeping the plunger retracted by holding the screwdriver

its mounting bolts and tighten them **(see illustration)**. Release and remove the screwdriver.

8 Fit a new O-ring smeared with clean oil onto the tensioner, then fit the cap screw and tighten it **(see illustration 7.3b)**.

9 Check that all the timing marks are in

exact alignment as described in Section 8, Step 4

10 On US CRF models install the EVAP control valve and canister (see Chapter 4).

11 Connect the clutch cable and fit the bracket bolts.

---

8   Camshafts and rocker arms

Note: *Stuff clean rag into the cam chain tunnel to prevent anything dropping into the engine. When setting the position of the crankshaft for the engine timing (Step 4), be sure that you have the correct timing mark on the flywheel – the T mark that denotes top dead centre (TDC) for engine timing is on its side and can be easily confused with the F mark, also on its side, that denotes the firing (ignition timing) point.*

Removal

1 Remove the valve cover (see Section 6).

2 Remove the spark plug (see Chapter 1).

3 Unscrew the timing inspection cap and the crankshaft end cap from the alternator cover on the left-hand side of the engine **(see illustration)**. Check the condition of the cap O-rings and replace them with new ones if necessary.

4 The crankshaft must be turned so that the piston is at TDC (top dead centre) on its compression stroke. Turn the crankshaft anti-clockwise using a suitable socket on the alternator rotor bolt until the line next to the T mark on the rotor aligns with the notch in the inspection hole rim, and the IN and EX marks on the intake and exhaust camshaft sprockets are the correct way up and flush with the cylinder head top surface so the punch marks are at the top **(see illustrations)**. If the marks are upside down turn the crankshaft anti-clockwise one full turn (360°) until the line next

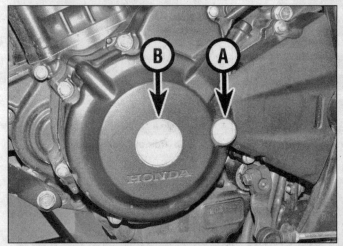

8.3 Remove the timing inspection cap (A) and the crankshaft end cap (B)

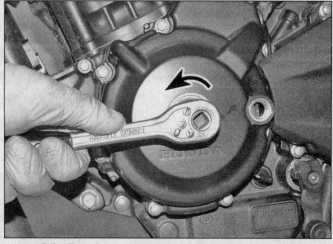

8.4a Turn the engine anti-clockwise using the nut...

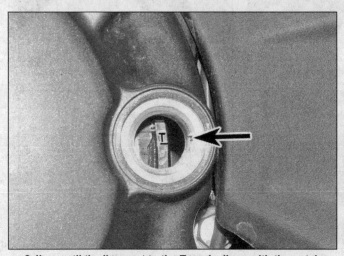

8.4b ...until the line next to the T mark aligns with the notch (arrowed)...

8.4c ...and the camshaft sprocket marks are as shown

to the T mark again aligns with the notch. The sprocket marks will now be as required.

5 Remove the cam chain tensioner (see Section 7).

6 Remove the top cam chain guide **(see illustration)**.

7 Unscrew the camshaft holder bolts, slackening them evenly and a little at a time in a criss-cross sequence **(see illustration)**. Remove the holders **(see illustration)**. Remove the two locating dowels from the underside of each holder if they are loose.

8 Lift the intake camshaft off the head and disengage the chain, then repeat for the exhaust camshaft **(see illustrations 8.28a and 8.27a)**. Lay the chain over the front of the head and secure it with some wire to prevent it dropping down the tunnel. While the camshafts are out do not rotate the crankshaft unless you are holding the chain taut, otherwise it could bind between the crankshaft and case.

9 Unscrew the intake rocker shaft plug and remove the sealing washer **(see illustration)** – a new one must be used. Thread a 6mm bolt into the end of the shaft and use it to draw the shaft out **(see illustrations)**. Remove the rocker arm **(see illustration)**. Slide the rocker back onto its shaft to prevent mixing up – both shafts are identical and are therefore interchangeable, but each arm is marked IN or EX according to its location. Repeat for the exhaust rocker arm/shaft.

10 If the shims are being removed from the cylinder head, obtain a container which is divided into four compartments, and label each compartment with the location of a valve, i.e. intake or exhaust camshaft, left or right valve. If a container is not available, use labelled plastic bags (an egg carton also does very well!). Remove each shim from the top of its valve using either a magnet, a screwdriver with a dab of grease on it (the shim will stick

to the grease), or a very small screwdriver and a pair of pliers or tweezers **(see illustration)**. Do not allow the shim to fall into the engine.

11 Place rag over the spark plug hole and the cam chain tunnel to prevent anything from dropping into the engine.

Inspection

12 Inspect the bearing surfaces of the camshaft holders and cylinder head and the corresponding journals on the camshafts. Look for score marks, deep scratches and evidence of spalling (a pitted appearance). Check the oil passages for clogging.

13 Check the camshaft lobes for heat discoloration (blue appearance), score marks, chipped areas, flat spots and spalling. Measure the height of each lobe with a micrometer **(see illustration)** and compare the results to the minimum height listed in this Chapter's Specifications. If damage is noted

8.6 Unscrew the bolts (arrowed) and remove the guide

8.7a Camshaft holder bolts (arrowed)

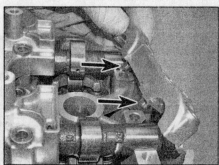

8.7b Remove each holder…

8.7c …noting the dowels (arrowed)

8.9a Unscrew the plug…

8.9b …then thread a 6mm bolt in…

8.9c …pull the shaft out and remove the rocker arm

8.10 Removing a shim using a magnet

8.13 Measure the height of the camshaft lobes with a micrometer

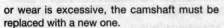

8.17 Measuring the crushed Plastigauge strip

8.18 Check the rocker arm as described

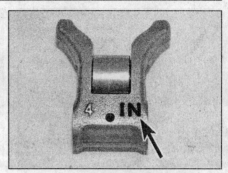

8.24 Each arm is marked IN or EX according to side

or wear is excessive, the camshaft must be replaced with a new one.

14 Next, check the camshaft journal oil clearances using Plastigauge, following the instructions supplied. Clean the camshafts and the bearing surfaces in the cylinder head and camshaft holders with a clean lint-free cloth, then lay each camshaft in its correct location in the head **(see illustrations 8.28a and 8.27a)** – the intake camshaft is marked IN, the exhaust is marked EX **(see illustration 8.25)**. There is no need to fit the chain around the sprockets.

15 Cut four strips of Plastigauge and lay one piece on each journal, parallel with the camshaft centreline. Make sure the camshaft holder dowels are installed. Fit the holders and tighten the bolts as described in Step 30, making sure the holders are pulled down squarely onto the dowels. While doing this, don't let the camshafts rotate, or the Plastigauge will be disturbed and you will have to start again.

16 Now unscrew the camshaft holder bolts evenly and a little at a time in a criss-cross sequence, and remove the holders.

17 To determine the oil clearance, compare the crushed Plastigauge (at its widest point) on each journal to the scale provided **(see illustration)**. Compare the results to this Chapter's Specifications. If the oil clearance is greater than specified, replace the camshaft with a new one and recheck the clearance. If the clearance is still too great, also replace the cylinder head and holders with new ones.

18 Check the rocker arms for heat discoloration (blue appearance), score marks, chipped areas,

flat spots and spalling where they contact the camshaft lobes and shims **(see illustration)**. Make sure the roller rotates freely and smoothly. If damage is noted or wear is excessive, the rocker arms and camshafts must be replaced with new ones as required.

19 Check for freeplay between each rocker arm and its shaft. The arms should move freely with a light fit but no appreciable freeplay. Measure the internal diameter of the arm bores and the corresponding diameter of the shaft. Replace the arms and/or shafts with new ones if they are worn beyond their specifications. Check that the fork shaft holes in the head are neither worn nor damaged.

20 Except in cases of oil starvation, the cam chain should wear very little. If the chain has stretched excessively, which makes it difficult to maintain proper tension, or if it is stiff or the links are binding or kinking, replace it with a new one. Refer to Section 9 for replacement.

21 Check the sprockets for wear, cracks and other damage, and replace the camshafts with new ones if necessary. If the sprocket is worn, the cam chain is also worn, and so probably is the sprocket on the crankshaft. If severe wear is apparent, the entire engine should be disassembled further for inspection.

22 Inspect the cam chain guide and tensioner blade (see Section 9).

Installation

23 If removed, lubricate each shim and its follower with molybdenum disulphide oil (a 50/50 mixture of molybdenum disulphide grease and engine oil). Fit each shim into its recess in the top of the valve with the size

mark facing up, making sure it is correctly seated **(see illustration 8.10)**. **Note:** *It is most important that the shims are returned to their original valves otherwise the valve clearances will be inaccurate.*

24 Lubricate each rocker shaft and arm with molybdenum disulphide oil (a 50/50 mixture of molybdenum disulphide grease and engine oil). Position each rocker arm in its location in the head – the arm marked IN goes on the intake side, the arm marked EX goes on the exhaust side **(see illustration)**. Slide each shaft through, then remove the bolt **(see illustrations 8.9c and b)**. Fit the plugs, using new sealing washers **(see illustration 8.9a)**.

25 Make sure the bearing surfaces on the camshafts and in the cylinder head are clean, then apply molybdenum disulphide oil (a 50/50 mixture of molybdenum disulphide grease and engine oil) to each of them. Also apply it to the camshaft lobes. Make sure that none gets on the mating surfaces between the holders and the head, or in the bolt holes. Identify which camshaft fits where – they are marked IN or EX accordingly **(see illustration)**.

26 Check that the line next to the T mark on the alternator rotor aligns with the notch in the inspection hole rim **(see illustration 8.4b)**.

27 Lift the cam chain and lay the exhaust camshaft (marked EX) onto the head with the EX mark on the sprocket facing forwards and parallel with the head, pulling up on the chain to remove all slack in the front run between the crankshaft and the camshaft, and engaging the chain around the sprocket **(see illustrations)**.

8.25 Each camshaft is marked IN or EX according to side

8.27a Fit the exhaust camshaft...

8.27b ...aligning the EX mark as shown

8.28a Fit the intake camshaft...

8.28b ...aligning the IN mark as shown

9 Cam chain, tensioner blade and guide blade

Removal

Cam chain

1 Remove the cylinder head (see Section 10).
2 Remove the primary drive gear (see Section 17). Remove the tensioner and guide blades.
3 Draw the cam chain sprocket towards the end of the crankshaft, disengage the chain, remove the sprocket and chain **(see illustration)**.

Tensioner blade

4 Remove the intake camshaft (see Section 8).
5 Remove the clutch (see Section 16).
6 Unscrew the tensioner blade pivot bolt and remove the collar, then draw the blade out of the engine **(see illustration)**.

Guide blade

7 Remove the cylinder head (see Section 10).
8 Draw the guide blade out, noting how it locates **(see illustration)**.

Inspection

Cam chain

9 Check the chain for binding, kinks and any obvious damage and replace it with a new one if necessary. Check the camshaft and crankshaft sprocket teeth for wear and replace the cam chain, camshafts and crankshaft sprocket with a new set if necessary.

Tensioner and guide blades

10 Check the sliding surface and edges of the blades for excessive wear, deep grooves, cracking and other obvious damage, and replace them with new ones if necessary.

Installation

11 Installation of the sprocket, chain and blades is the reverse of removal, noting the following:
● Lubricate the cam chain with clean oil.
● Align the wide spline on the cam chain sprocket centrally with the punch mark

28 Lift the cam chain and lay the intake camshaft (marked IN) onto the head with the IN mark on the sprocket facing back and parallel with the head, fitting the cam chain around the sprocket, pulling on it to remove all slack from between the two camshaft sprockets **(see illustrations)**. Any slack in the chain must lie in the rear run of the chain between the intake camshaft and the crankshaft so that it is later taken up by the tensioner.

29 Press on the back of the tensioner blade to take up any slack in the chain and check that all the timing marks are in **exact** alignment as described in Step 4 **(see illustrations 8.4b and c)**. Note that it is easy to be slightly out (one tooth on the sprocket) without the marks appearing drastically out of alignment. If the marks are out, you will have to work out what is misaligned with what then make the necessary adjustment(s) to the relative position(s) of the camshaft(s) and/or crankshaft.

30 Make sure the bearing surfaces in the camshaft holders are clean. If removed fit the dowels into the holders. Apply molybdenum disulphide oil (a 50/50 mixture of molybdenum disulphide grease and engine oil) to the bearing surfaces. Lay the holders in the head making sure they are correctly positioned **(see illustrations 8.7c and b)** – each holder is marked R or L to denote on which side of the head it fits, and the L holder is marked IN and EX to denote which way round **(see illustration 8.7a)**. Apply clean engine oil to the threads and under the heads of all the camshaft holder bolts. Fit the bolts, with the longer ones where the dowels are fitted, and

tighten them finger-tight. Now gradually and evenly tighten the bolts in a criss-cross pattern starting with the inner bolts and working to the outer ones until the holders contact the head, making sure they are drawn down squarely and the dowels all locate. Now tighten all the bolts in the same way to the torque setting specified at the beginning of the Chapter. Recheck the timing marks (Step 4).

Caution: Whilst tightening the bolts, make sure the holders are being pulled evenly and squarely down and are not binding on the dowels or tilting to one side – if they do, adjust the relevant bolts until the holders are again square to the head. A holder or camshaft is likely to break if they are not tightened down evenly and squarely.

31 Fit the top cam chain guide **(see illustration 8.6)**.
32 Install the cam chain tensioner (see Section 7).
33 Turn the engine anti-clockwise through two full turns and check again that all the timing marks still align (see Step 4) **(see illustrations 8.4a, b and c)**. Check the valve clearances and adjust them if necessary (see Chapter 1).
34 Fit the timing inspection cap and crankshaft end cap using new O-rings if required, and smear the O-rings and the cap threads with clean oil. Tighten the caps to the torque settings specified at the beginning of the Chapter.
35 Install the spark plug (see Chapter 1). Install the valve cover (see Section 6).

9.3 Removing the cam chain

9.6 Unscrew the bolt and remove the collar

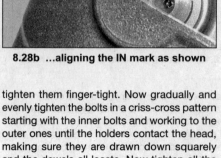

9.8 Draw the guide blade out, noting how it locates

on the end of the crankshaft **(see illustration 9.11a).**

● Clean the threads of the tensioner blade pivot bolt, apply some fresh threadlock and tighten the bolt to the torque setting specified at the beginning of the Chapter.

● Make sure the bottom of the guide blade sits in its seat and the lugs near its top locate in the cut-outs in the cylinder barrel **(see illustration 9.11b).**

10 Cylinder head removal and installation

9.11a Align the wide spline with the punch mark

9.11b Make sure the lower end locates correctly

Removal

1 Remove the engine from the frame (Section 4). If required remove the oxygen sensor (see Chapter 4).

2 Remove the camshafts (Section 8).

3 Unscrew and remove the two bolts in the cam chain tunnel **(see illustration).**

4 Slacken the cylinder head nuts evenly and a little at a time in a criss-cross sequence, then unscrew them and remove the washers **(see illustration 10.3).** Honda specify to use new nuts and washers on installation

5 Hold the cam chain up and pull the cylinder head up off the barrel, then pass the cam chain down through the tunnel **(see illustration).** Do not let the chain fall into the engine – lay it over the front of the barrel and secure it with a piece of wire. If the head is stuck, tap around the joint faces with a soft-faced mallet. Do not attempt to free it by inserting a screwdriver between the head and barrel mating surfaces – you'll damage them.

6 Remove the cylinder head gasket and discard it – a new one must be used **(see illustration 10.10).** If they are loose, remove the dowels from the cylinder barrel or the underside of the cylinder head.

7 Check the cylinder head gasket and the mating surfaces on the cylinder head and cylinder barrel for signs of leakage, which could indicate warpage. Refer to Section 11 and check the cylinder head gasket surface for warpage.

8 Clean all traces of old gasket material from

the cylinder head and cylinder barrel. If a scraper is used, take care not to scratch or gouge the soft aluminium. Be careful not to let any of the gasket material fall into the cylinder bore or the oil and coolant passages.

Installation

9 If removed, fit the dowels into the cylinder barrel **(see illustration 10.10).** Make sure the cam chain guide blade is correctly seated (Section 9).

10 Ensure both cylinder head and cylinder barrel mating surfaces are clean. Lay the **new** head gasket over the studs, the cam chain and blades and onto the barrel, locating it over the dowels and making sure all the holes are correctly aligned **(see illustration).** Never reuse the old gasket.

11 Carefully fit the cylinder head over the

studs and blades and onto the barrel, feeding the cam chain up through the tunnel as you do, and making sure it locates correctly onto the dowels and the cam chain guide blade lugs **(see illustration 10.5).** Secure the chain in place with a piece of wire to prevent it from falling back down.

12 Fit new washers onto the studs **(see illustration).** Lubricate the threads and seats of the new nuts with oil then thread them on and tighten them finger-tight. Now tighten them evenly and a little at a time in a criss-cross sequence to the torque setting specified at the beginning of the Chapter.

13 Fit the two bolts and tighten them **(see illustration).**

14 Install the camshafts (Section 8).

15 If removed install the oxygen sensor (see Chapter 4). Install the engine (Section 4).

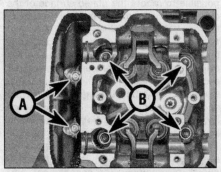

10.3 Cylinder head bolts (A) and nuts (B)

10.5 Carefully lift the head up off the block

10.10 Fit the dowels (arrowed) then lay the new gasket on the block

10.12 Use a screwdriver to guide the washers over the studs

10.13 Fit the two bolts into the chain tunnel

11 Cylinder head and valve overhaul

Refer to the procedure in Chapter 2A, Section 11 – the procedure is the same, with the exception that there are four valves, not two. Specifications are given at the beginning of this Chapter.

12 Cylinder barrel

12.3 Unscrew the bolts (arrowed) and remove the pipe

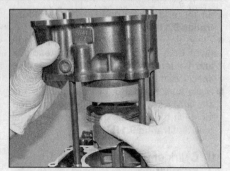

12.4 Carefully lift the block up off the crankcase

Removal

1 Remove the cylinder head (see Section 10).
2 Draw the cam chain guide blade out of the top of the barrel, noting how it locates **(see illustration 9.8)**.
3 Unscrew the water pipe bolts and remove the pipe, being prepared with a rag to catch any residual coolant **(see illustration)**. Remove the O-rings – new ones must be used.
4 Hold the cam chain up and pull the cylinder barrel up off the crankcase, supporting the piston so the connecting rod does not knock against the engine, then pass the cam chain down through the tunnel **(see illustration)**. Do not let the chain fall into the engine – lay it over the front and secure it with a piece of wire. If the barrel is stuck, tap around the joint faces with a soft-faced mallet. Do not attempt to free it by inserting a screwdriver between the barrel and crankcase mating surfaces – you'll damage them.
5 Remove the base gasket and discard it – a new one must be used. If they are loose, remove the dowels from the crankcase or the underside of the barrel **(see illustration 12.15)**.
6 Stuff clean rag into the cam chain tunnel and around the connecting rod to protect and support it and the piston and to prevent anything falling into the engine.
7 Clean all traces of old gasket material from the cylinder barrel and crankcase. If

a scraper is used, take care not to scratch or gouge the soft aluminium. Be careful not to let any of the gasket material fall into the engine.

Inspection

Note: *Do not attempt to separate the cylinder liner from the cylinder barrel.*
8 Check the cylinder walls carefully for scratches and score marks.
9 Using a precision straight-edge and a feeler gauge set to the warpage limit listed in the specifications at the beginning of the Chapter, check the barrel top surface for warpage. Take six measurements, one along each side and two diagonally across. If the barrel is warped beyond the limit specified at the beginning of this Chapter, consult a Honda dealer or take it to an engineer for an opinion, though be prepared to have to buy a new one. It is not possible to rebore the plated surface of the cylinder and accordingly no oversize piston and ring sets are available.
10 Using a telescoping bore gauge and a micrometer, check the dimensions of the cylinder to assess the amount of wear, taper and ovality. Measure near the top (but below the level of the top piston ring at TDC), centre and bottom (but above the level of the oil ring at BDC) of the bore, both parallel to and across the crankshaft axis **(see illustrations)**.
11 If the precision measuring tools are not available, take the cylinder barrel to a Honda dealer or engineer for assessment and advice.

Installation

12 Check that the mating surfaces of the cylinder barrel and crankcase are free from oil or pieces of old gasket.
13 Check that all the studs are tight in the crankcase. If any are loose, or need to be replaced with new ones, remove them. Clean their threads and smear them with clean engine oil. Fit them into the crankcase with the marked end at the top, and tighten them using a stud tool, or by threading two of the old cylinder head nuts onto the top of the stud and tightening them together so they are locked on the stud, then tighten the stud by turning the upper of the two nuts. The distance between the top of each stud and the crankcase surface should be 142 ± 1 mm.
14 If removed, fit the dowels over the studs and into the crankcase and push them firmly home **(see illustration 12.15)**.
15 Remove the rags from around the piston and the cam chain tunnel, taking care not to let the connecting rod fall against the rim of the crankcase, and lay the **new** base gasket in place, locating it over the dowels **(see illustration)**. The gasket can only fit one way, so if all the holes do not line up properly it is the wrong way round. Never re-use the old gasket.
16 Ensure the piston ring end gaps are positioned correctly before fitting the cylinder barrel (see Chapter 2A, Section 14). If possible, have an assistant to support the cylinder barrel while the piston rings are fed into the bore.
17 Rotate the crankshaft so that the piston is at its highest point (top dead centre). It is

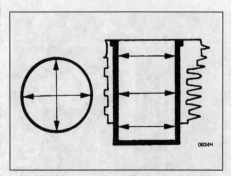

12.10a Measure the cylinder bore in the directions shown...

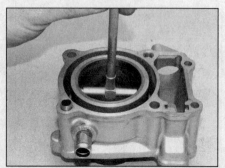

12.10b ...using a telescoping gauge, then measure the gauge with a micrometer

12.15 Lay the new gasket over the dowels (arrowed) and onto the crankcase

12.19 Carefully feed each ring into the bore as you lower the block

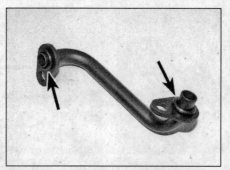

12.22 Fit a new O-ring (arrowed) onto each end of the pipe

useful to place a support under the piston so that it remains at TDC while the barrel is fitted, otherwise the downward pressure will turn the crankshaft and the piston will drop. Lubricate the cylinder bore, piston and piston rings with clean engine oil.

18 Carefully lower the barrel over the studs and onto the piston until the crown fits into the bore, holding the underside of the piston if you are not using a support to prevent it dropping, and making sure it enters the bore squarely and does not get cocked sideways **(see illustration 12.4)**. Feed the cam chain up the tunnel and slip a piece of wire through it to prevent it falling back into the engine. Keep the chain taut to prevent it becoming disengaged from the crankshaft sprocket.

19 Carefully compress and feed each ring into the bore as the cylinder is lowered **(see illustration)**. If necessary, use a soft mallet to gently tap the cylinder down, but do not use force if it appears to be stuck as the piston and/or rings will be damaged.

20 When the piston and rings are correctly located in the bore, remove the support if used then press the cylinder barrel down onto the base gasket, making sure the dowels locate.

21 Hold the barrel down and turn the crankshaft to check that everything moves as it should.

22 Fit the water pipe using new O-rings and tighten the bolts **(see illustration)**.

23 Fit the cam chain guide blade, making sure the bottom of the blade sits in its seat **(see illustrations 9.8 and 9.11b)**.

24 Install the cylinder head (see Section 10).

13 Piston and piston rings

1 Refer to Sections 13 and 14 of Chapter 2A – the procedure is the same, but refer to the Specifications at the beginning of this Chapter.

14 Starter clutch and gears

Check

1 The operation of the starter clutch can be checked while it is in situ. Remove the starter motor (see Chapter 8). Check that the idle/

reduction gear is able to rotate freely clockwise as you look at it via the starter motor aperture, but locks when rotated anti-clockwise. If not, the starter clutch is faulty and should be removed for inspection.

Removal

2 Remove the alternator rotor (see Chapter 8) – the starter clutch is bolted to the back of it.

3 Remove the needle bearing **(see illustrations)**.

Inspection

4 With the alternator rotor face down on a workbench, check that the starter driven gear rotates freely in an anti-clockwise direction and locks against the rotor in a clockwise direction **(see illustration)**. If it doesn't, the starter clutch should be dismantled for further investigation.

5 Withdraw the starter driven gear from the starter clutch **(see illustration)** – if it appears stuck, rotate it anti-clockwise as you withdraw it to free it from the starter clutch.

6 Check the condition of the sprags inside the clutch body and the corresponding surface on the driven gear hub **(see illustration)**. If they are damaged, marked or flattened at any point, they should be replaced with new ones. Measure the outside diameter of the hub and check that it has not worn beyond the service limits specified. To remove the sprag assembly, hold the rotor using a holding strap and unscrew the bolts inside it **(see illustration)**. Remove the sprag housing from the rotor and the sprag assembly from

14.3 Slide the bearing off

14.4 Check the operation of the clutch as described

14.5 Withdraw the driven gear

14.6a Check the related surfaces for damage and wear

14.6b Starter clutch bolts (arrowed)

15.5 Unscrew the bolts (arrowed) and remove the cover

15.6 Unscrew the bolts (arrowed) and remove the pressure plate and springs

the housing, noting how it fits. Install the sprag assembly in a reverse sequence – the flanged side of the sprag assembly seats in the rim in the back of the housing and faces into the rotor. Apply clean engine oil to the sprags. Clean the bolts and apply a suitable non-permanent thread locking compound and tighten them to the torque setting specified at the beginning of the Chapter.

7 Check the bearing and its corresponding surfaces in the starter driven gear hub and on the crankshaft. If the bearing surfaces show signs of excessive wear or the bearing itself is worn or damaged, they should be replaced with new ones. Measure the inside diameter of the hub and check that it has not worn beyond the service limit specified.

8 Check the teeth of the starter motor drive shaft, idle/reduction gear and starter driven gear. Replace the gears and/or starter motor if worn or chipped teeth are discovered on related gears. Also check the starter drive gear and idle/reduction gear shafts for damage, and check that the gears are not a loose fit on the shaft. Replace the shafts with new ones if necessary.

Installation

9 Lubricate the needle roller bearing with

clean engine oil and slide it on the crankshaft **(see illustration 14.3)**.

10 Lubricate the outside of the starter driven gear hub with clean engine oil, then fit the gear into the clutch, rotating it anti-clockwise as you do so to spread the sprags and allow the hub to enter **(see illustration 14.5)**.

11 Install the alternator rotor (see Chapter 8).

15 Clutch

Removal

1 Drain the engine oil and the coolant (see Chapter 1).

2 On CRF models remove the heel guard **(see illustration 4.28)**. Remove the brake pedal (see Chapter 5). Unscrew the brake light switch bracket bolt and secure the switch clear of the engine **(see illustration 4.42)**.

3 Unscrew the clutch cable bracket bolts **(see illustration 4.11a)**. Free the cable end from the release arm and position it clear of the engine **(see illustration 4.11b)**.

4 Slacken the coolant hose clamp and detach

the hose, being prepared with a rag to catch any residual coolant **(see illustration 4.8a)**. Unscrew the water pipe bolts and remove the pipe, again being prepared for residual coolant **(see illustration 12.3)**. Remove the O-rings – new ones must be used.

5 Working evenly in a criss-cross pattern, unscrew the clutch cover bolts, noting the position of the longer bolt **(see illustration)**. Remove the cover, turning the release lever arm back (anti-clockwise) as you do to disengage the shaft from the pull-rod **(see illustration 15.28c)**. Be prepared to catch any residual oil. Remove the two locating dowels from either the cover or the crankcase if they are loose, noting which fits where **(see illustration 15.28a)**. Remove the three oil passage collars and O-rings **(see illustration 15.27)** – new O-rings must be used.

6 Working in a criss-cross pattern, gradually slacken the clutch spring bolts until pressure is released **(see illustration)**. To prevent the assembly from turning, cover it with a rag and hold it securely – the bolts are not very tight. If available, have an assistant to hold the clutch while you unscrew the bolts. Remove the bolts and springs, then remove the pressure plate **(see illustration 15.26b)**. Remove the pull-rod from either the back of the pressure plate or the end of the shaft **(see illustration 15.26a)**.

7 Remove the clutch friction and plain plates as a pack, noting how they fit and keeping them in order **(see illustration)**. On CRF models remove the anti-judder spring and spring seat, noting which way round they fit. Also on CRF models note that the inner plain and friction plates are different to the rest – the inner plain plate has a white paint mark, and the inner friction plate has a larger internal diameter so that it fits over the anti-judder spring and spring seat.

8 The rim of the clutch nut is staked against the input shaft. Unstake the nut using a hammer and punch – take care not to damage the threads on the end of the shaft **(see illustration)**. To remove the clutch nut,

15.7 Slide all the plates out together

15.8a Unstake the rim of the nut

15.8b To unscrew the nut the clutch must be held – this shows a commercially available holding tool

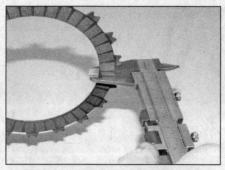

15.11 Measuring clutch friction plate thickness

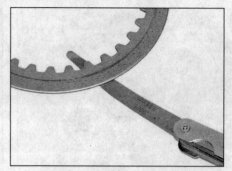

15.12 Check the plain plates for warpage

the input shaft must be locked. This can be done in several ways. If the engine is in the frame, engage 6th gear and have an assistant hold the rear brake on hard with the rear tyre in firm contact with the ground. Alternatively, the Honda service tool (Pt. No. 07724-0050002), or a similar commercially available tool can be used to stop the clutch centre from turning whilst the nut is slackened **(see illustration)**. Unscrew the nut and remove the washer. Discard the nut – a new one must be used on installation.

9 Remove the clutch centre and the thrust washer from the shaft **(see illustrations 15.22b and a)**.

10 Remove the clutch housing **(see illustration 15.21c)**. Slide the clutch guide, needle bearing and washer off the shaft **(see illustrations 15.21b and a)**.

Inspection

11 After an extended period of service the clutch friction plates will wear and promote clutch slip. Measure the thickness of each friction plate using a Vernier caliper **(see illustration)**. If any plate has worn to or beyond the service limits given in the Specifications at the beginning of the Chapter, or if any of the plates smell burnt or are glazed, replace all the friction plates with a new set.

12 The plain plates should not show any signs of excess heating (bluing). Check for warpage using a flat surface and feeler gauges **(see illustration)**. If any plate exceeds the maximum permissible amount of warpage, or shows signs of bluing, replace all the plain plates with a new set.

13 Measure the free length of each clutch spring using a Vernier caliper **(see illustration)**. Place each spring upright on a flat surface and check it for bend by placing a ruler against it, or alternatively lay it against a set square. If any spring is below the minimum free length specified or if the bend in any spring is excessive, replace all the springs with a new set. Also check the anti-judder spring and spring seat for damage or

distortion and replace them with new ones if necessary.

14 Inspect the friction plates and the clutch housing for burrs and indentations on the edges of the protruding tabs on the plates and/or the slots in the housing **(see illustration)**. Similarly check for wear between the inner teeth of the plain plates and the slots in the clutch centre **(see illustration)**. Wear of this nature will cause clutch drag and slow disengagement during gear changes as the plates will snag when the pressure plate is lifted. With care a small amount of wear can be corrected by dressing with a fine file, but if this is excessive the worn components should be renewed.

15 Inspect the needle roller bearing and the bearing surfaces in the clutch housing and on the clutch guide **(see illustration)**. If there are any signs of wear, pitting or other damage the affected parts must be replaced with new ones.

16 Using a Vernier caliper, measure the internal diameter of the clutch guide and the external diameter of the input shaft where the guide sits. Compare the measurements to the specifications at the beginning of the Chapter and renew any part that is worn beyond its service limit.

17 Check the pressure plate and its bearing and the pull-rod for signs of wear or damage

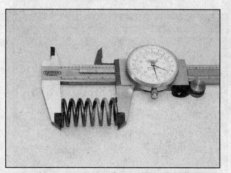

15.13 Measure the free length of the clutch springs and check them for bend

15.14a Check the friction plate tabs and housing slots...

15.14b ...and the plain plate teeth and centre slots as described

15.15 Check the bearing surfaces

15.17a Check the pressure plate and its bearing…

15.17b …and the pull-rod and its cut-out in the shaft

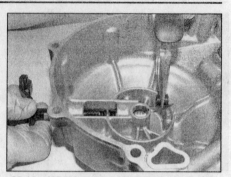

15.18a Withdraw the shaft from the cover and remove the spring

and roughness **(see illustrations)**. Check that the bearing outer race is a good fit in the centre of the lifter, and that the inner race rotates freely without any rough spots. Check the pull-rod end and the corresponding

cut-out in the release lever shaft (in the cover) for signs of wear or damage. Replace any parts necessary with new ones.

18 Check the release mechanism shaft for a smooth action. If the action is stiff or rough,

withdraw the shaft and remove the return spring, noting how its ends locate **(see illustration)**. Check the oil seal in the top of the cover – it can be removed by levering it out with a seal hook or screwdriver **(see illustration)**. Clean and check the two needle bearings in the cover **(see illustration)**. Press the new seal in. Lubricate the bearings with oil before and the seal lips with grease before installing the shaft. Make sure the return spring ends locate correctly **(see illustration)**. Check the crankshaft end bearing in the clutch cover **(see illustration)** – replace it with a new one if necessary (see Section 21).

19 Check the teeth of the primary driven gear on the back of the clutch housing and the corresponding teeth of the primary drive gear on the crankshaft. Replace the clutch housing and/or crankshaft with a new one if worn or chipped teeth are discovered.

Installation

20 Remove all traces of old gasket from the crankcase and clutch cover surfaces.

21 Smear the inside and outside of the clutch guide, the inside of the clutch housing and the needle bearing with molybdenum disulphide oil (a 50/50 mixture of molybdenum disulphide grease and engine oil) **(see illustration 15.15)**. Slide the washer, guide and bearing onto the shaft **(see illustrations)**. Slide the clutch housing onto the bearing, engaging the primary drive and driven gear teeth **(see illustration)**.

22 Slide the thrust washer onto the shaft (see

15.18b Check the seal (arrowed)…

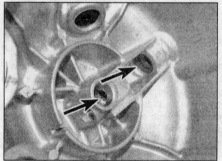

15.18c …and the bearings (arrowed)

15.18d Make sure the spring is fitted so the top end locates in the hole in the shaft (arrowed)

15.18e Crankshaft end bearing (arrowed)

15.21a Fit the thrust washer

15.21b Slide the guide onto the shaft, the bearing onto the guide…

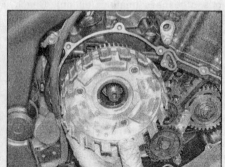

15.21c …and the housing onto the bearing

15.22a Fit the thrust washer...

15.22b ...and the clutch centre

15.23a Fit the washer and nut...

illustration). Slide the clutch centre onto the shaft splines (see illustration).

23 Smear the new clutch nut threads and seat with oil, then fit the washer and thread the nut onto the shaft and, using the method employed on removal to lock the shaft (see Step 8), tighten the nut to the torque setting specified at the beginning of the Chapter (see illustrations). Stake the rim of the nut into the indent on the end of the shaft (see illustration).

24 On CBR models coat each clutch plate with engine oil, then build up the plates, starting with a friction plate, then a plain plate, then alternating friction and plain plates until all are installed (see illustrations).

25 On CRF models fit the anti-judder spring seat into the clutch centre, then fit the spring so that its outer edge is raised off the seat and facing outwards (see illustration). Coat each clutch plate with engine oil prior to installation, then build up the plates as follows. Fit the friction plate with the larger internal diameter

over the spring and spring seat, then fit the plain plate with the white paint mark, then alternate the remaining friction plates and plain plates (see illustrations 15.24a and b).

26 Lubricate the bearing in the pressure plate. Fit the pull-rod into the shaft (see illustration). Fit the pressure plate onto the clutch, engaging

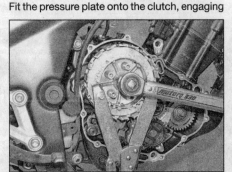

15.23b ...and tighten the nut to the specified torque

the protrusions on its inner rim in the slots in the clutch centre (see illustration). Fit the springs and the bolts and tighten them evenly in a criss-cross sequence to the specified torque setting (see illustration). Counter-hold the clutch housing to prevent it turning when tightening the spring bolts.

15.23c Stake the rim into the detent

15.24a Fit a friction plate...

15.24b ...then a plain plate and so on

15.25 The outer rim of the spring must be raised off the seat

15.26a Insert the pull-rod...

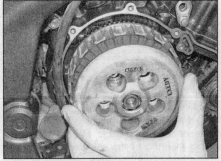

15.26b ...then fit the pressure plate, making sure the castellations engage

15.26c Fit the springs and tighten the bolts as described

15.27 Fit the collars and new O-rings (arrowed)

15.28a Locate the new gasket over the dowels (arrowed)

15.28b Turn the shaft to align the slot (A) with the tab (B)…

15.28c …then fit the cover

27 Fit the three oil passage collars and new O-rings **(see illustration)**.

28 Fit the two dowels into the crankcase if removed – the longer one goes into the rear hole **(see illustration)**. Fit a new gasket, seating it over the dowels. Align the water pump shaft so it will engage with the end of the balancer shaft. Fit the cover, pulling the release lever arm back (anti-clockwise) as you do then moving it forward so that it engages behind the pull-rod end as you push the cover home on the dowels, collars and shaft ends **(see illustrations)**. Make sure the cover is seated all round, then fit the bolts (except the clutch cable bracket bolts) finger tight – the longer bolt goes in the top front corner. Tighten the bolts evenly and a little at a time in a criss-cross pattern **(see illustration 15.5)**.

29 Fit the water pipe using new O-rings and tighten the bolts **(see illustration 12.22)**. Connect the coolant hose and tighten the clamp **(see illustration 4.8a)**.

30 Connect the clutch cable end to the release lever arm, then locate the bracket on the cover and tighten the bolts **(see illustrations 4.11b and a)**.

31 On CRF models fit the brake light switch bracket **(see illustration 4.42)**, the brake pedal (see Chapter 5), and the heel guard **(see illustration 4.28)**.

32 Fill the engine with oil and coolant (see Chapter 1).

16 Clutch cable

1 Pull the rubber boot off the adjuster at the handlebar end of the cable. Fully slacken the lockring then thread the adjuster fully in **(see illustration)**. This provides freeplay in the cable and resets the adjuster to the beginning of its span.

2 On CBR models remove the right-hand fairing side panel (see Chapter 7).

3 Slacken the nuts securing the cable in the bracket on the engine, then thread the front nut fully up the adjuster and the rear nut off

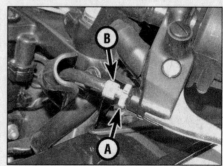

16.1 Slacken the lockring (A) and turn the adjuster (B) in

16.3a Slacken the nuts (arrowed)…

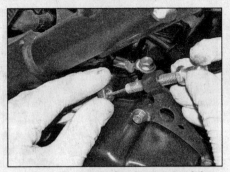

16.3b …thread the front nut up and the rear nut off…

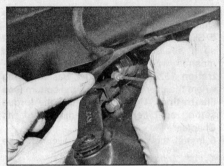

16.3c …then detach the cable end…

16.3d …and draw the cable out

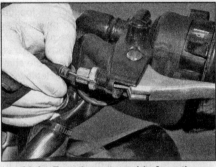

16.4a Free the outer cable from the adjuster…

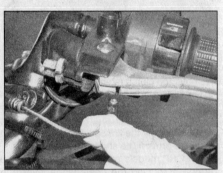

16.4b …and the inner cable from the lever

it **(see illustrations)**. Free the cable end from the release arm then draw the cable out of the bracket **(see illustrations)**.

4 Align the slots in the adjuster and lockring at the handlebar end of the cable with that in the lever bracket, then pull the outer cable end from the socket in the adjuster and release the inner cable from the lever **(see illustrations)**. Remove the cable from the machine, noting its routing through the guides.

HAYNES HINT *Before removing the cable from the bike, tape the lower end of the new cable to the upper end of the old cable. Slowly pull the lower end of the old cable out, guiding the new cable down into position. Using this method will ensure the cable is routed correctly.*

5 Installation is the reverse of removal. Apply grease to the cable ends. Make sure the cable is correctly routed through its guides. Adjust the amount of clutch lever freeplay (see Chapter 1).

17 Primary drive gear

Removal

1 Remove the clutch plates and clutch centre from the clutch housing (see Section 15, Steps 1 to 9).
2 Wedge an aluminium or copper washer (DO NOT use a steel one) or a thick piece of rag or similar between the teeth of the primary

drive and driven gears where they mesh at the top – this will lock them together to prevent them turning **(see illustration)**. Slacken the primary drive gear nut **(see illustration)**. Remove the item used to wedge the gears.
3 Slide the clutch housing off the shaft **(see illustration 15.21c)**. Unscrew the primary drive gear nut and remove the washer, then slide the gear off the end of the crankshaft **(see illustrations 17.4b and a)**.

Installation

4 Slide the gear onto the crankshaft with the raised section facing in, aligning the punch mark and wide spline centrally with the punch mark on the end of the shaft **(see illustration)**. Check the punch marks align. Lubricate the threads and seating surface of the nut with oil,

17.2a Using a copper washer (arrowed) to jam the gears…

17.2b …while unscrewing the nut

17.4a Align the wide spline with the punch mark

then fit the washer and thread the nut onto the shaft **(see illustration)**.

5 Slide the clutch housing onto its shaft so it seats on the needle bearing and meshes with the drive gear **(see illustration 15.21c)**. Wedge the washer or rag where the gear teeth mesh at the bottom **(see illustration)**. Tighten the nut to the torque setting specified at the beginning of the Chapter.

6 Install the remainder of the clutch (see Section 15).

18 Gearchange mechanism

Removal

1 Make sure the transmission is in neutral. Remove the clutch (see Section 15).

2 On CBR models note the alignment of the slot in the gearchange linkage arm with the punch mark on the shaft **(see illustration 4.13)**. Unscrew the linkage arm pinch bolt and slide the arm off the shaft.

3 On CRF models note the alignment of the punch marks on the gearchange lever and shaft **(see illustration 4.40)**. Unscrew the lever pinch bolt and slide the arm off the shaft.

4 Wrap a single layer of thin insulating tape around the gearchange shaft splines to protect the oil seal lips as the shaft is removed.

5 Note how the gearchange shaft centralising

17.4b Fit the washer and the nut

17.5 Wedge the washer or rag as shown and tighten the nut

spring ends fit on each side of the locating pin in the casing, and how the pawls on the selector arm locate onto the pins on the end of the selector drum camplate. Grasp the end of the shaft and withdraw the shaft/arm assembly **(see illustration)**. Retrieve the washer from the crankcase if it didn't come with the shaft.

6 Note how the stopper arm spring ends locate and how the roller on the arm locates in the neutral detent on the selector drum camplate, then unscrew the stopper arm bolt and remove the arm, the washer and the spring, noting how they fit **(see illustration)**.

7 If the crankcases are being separated, unscrew the camplate bolt and remove the plate, noting that there are two pins that locate the plate on the end of the selector drum **(see illustration)** – they should stay in

the end of the drum, but take care as they could drop out. Remove them from the drum for safekeeping **(see illustration)**.

Inspection

8 Check the selector arm for cracks, distortion and wear of its pawls, and check for any corresponding wear on the pins on the selector drum cam **(see illustration)**. Check the arm moves up smoothly and freely and returns under pressure of its spring. Also check the stopper arm roller and the detents in the selector drum cam for any wear or damage, and make sure the roller turns freely **(see illustration)**. Replace any components that are worn or damaged with new ones.

9 Inspect the shaft centralising spring, selector arm return spring and the stopper arm return spring for fatigue, wear or damage

18.5 Withdraw the shaft/arm assembly, noting the washer (arrowed)

18.6 Note how the spring ends and roller locate, then unscrew the bolt (arrowed) and remove the arm

18.7a Hold the camplate to prevent it turning and unscrew the bolt (arrowed)

18.7b Remove the locating pins from the drum

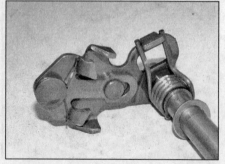

18.8a Check the selector arm pawls...

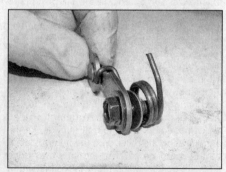

18.8b ...and the stopper arm roller

18.10a Lever out the oil seal

18.10b Check the bearing (arrowed)

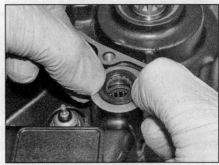

18.10c Press a new oil seal into place

(see illustrations 18.8a and b). If any is found, they must be replaced with new ones. To replace the shaft spring, slide the washer off the shaft, then remove the circlip and slide the spring off the shaft, noting how its ends locate. Fit the new spring, locating the ends on each side of the tab, and secure it with the circlip, making sure it locates in its groove. Slide the washer against the circlip. Also check that the centralising spring locating pin in the crankcase is securely tightened. If it is loose, remove it, clean the threads and apply a non-permanent thread locking compound, then tighten it.

10 Check the gearchange shaft is straight and look for damage to the splines. If the shaft is bent you can attempt to straighten it, but if the splines are damaged the shaft must be replaced with a new one. Also check the condition of the shaft oil seal in the left-hand side of the crankcase. If it is damaged, deteriorated or shows signs of leakage it must be replaced with a new one – lever out the old seal with a seal hook or screwdriver (see illustration). With the seal removed, check the condition of the needle bearing, and replace that with a new one as well if necessary (see illustration) – refer to *Tools and Workshop Tips* in the Reference Section. Drive the new bearing in until it seats. Press the new seal squarely into place using your fingers, a seal driver or suitable socket (see illustration).

Installation

11 If removed, fit the camplate locating pins into the end of the selector drum (see illustration 18.7b). Locate the camplate onto the pins (see illustration). Clean the threads of the bolt and apply a suitable non-permanent thread locking compound, and tighten it to the torque setting specified at the beginning of the Chapter.

12 Clean the threads of the stopper arm bolt. Fit the bolt into the arm then fit the washer and the spring as shown (see illustration 18.8b). Apply a suitable non-permanent thread locking compound to the bolt threads. Fit the arm, locating the roller onto the neutral detent on the camplate and making sure the spring ends are positioned correctly (see illustration 18.6). Tighten the bolt to the torque setting specified at the beginning of the Chapter.

18.11 Fit the camplate onto the pins

13 Check that the shaft centralising spring is properly positioned and slide the washer onto the shaft if removed (see illustration 18.8a). Apply some grease to the lips of the gearchange shaft oil seal in the left-hand side of the crankcase. Slide the shaft into place and push it all the way through the case until the splined end comes out the other side (see illustration 18.5). Locate the selector arm pawls onto the pins on the camplate and the centralising spring ends onto each side of the locating pin in the crankcase.

14 Check that all components are correctly positioned (see illustration). Install the clutch (see Section 15).

15 Remove the insulating tape from around the gearchange shaft splines. On CBR models slide the gearchange linkage arm onto the shaft, aligning its slit with the punch mark on the shaft (see illustration 4.13). On CRF

19.2 Remove the oil pump gear

18.14 Gearchange mechanism fully assembled

models slide the gearchange lever onto the shaft, aligning the punch marks (see illustrations 4.40). Fit the pinch bolt and tighten it.

19 Oil pump, strainer and pressure relief valve

Removal

1 Remove the clutch cover (see Section 15, Steps 1 to 5).

2 Remove the oil pump gear (see illustration).

3 Unscrew the three bolts and remove the pump (see illustration). Remove the O-ring, and the dowels if loose (see illustrations 19.21a and b) – a new O-ring must be used.

19.3 Unscrew the bolts (arrowed) and remove the pump

19.4 Draw the strainer out using pliers

19.5 Pull the valve out of the pump

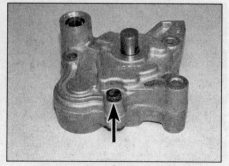

19.6a Unscrew the bolt (arrowed)...

19.6b ...and open the pump, noting the dowels (arrowed)

19.9 Measure the inner rotor tip-to-outer rotor clearance

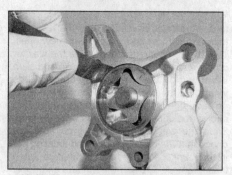

19.10 Measure the outer rotor-to-body clearance

4 Withdraw the strainer from its slot in the bottom of the engine, noting which way round it fits (see illustration).
5 Pull the pressure relief valve out of the pump (see illustration). Remove the O-rings – new ones must be used.

Inspection

Note: *When removing the outer rotor from the oil pump, note whether the T mark faces into or out of the pump body. The mark serves as a guide to which way round to fit the rotor on installation. Refitting the rotor the same way round ensures that mated surfaces continue to run together.*
6 Unscrew the bolt and detach the pump housing from the body (see illustrations). Remove the dowels if loose. Remove the rotors and withdraw the shaft, noting the drive pin and washer (see illustrations 19.14c, b and a).
7 Clean all the components in solvent.

8 Inspect the pump and rotors for scoring and wear. If any damage, scoring or uneven or excessive wear is evident, replace the components with new ones.
9 Fit the shaft and the inner and outer rotors into the pump housing (see illustrations 19.14a, b and c). Measure the clearance between the inner rotor tip and the outer rotor with a feeler gauge and compare it to the service limit listed in the specifications at the beginning of the Chapter (see illustration). Turn the rotors and take several measurements in different places. If the clearance measured at any point is greater than the maximum listed, replace the pump with a new one.
10 Measure the clearance between the outer rotor and the pump body with a feeler gauge and compare it to the maximum clearance listed in the specifications at the beginning of the Chapter (see illustration). If the clearance measured is greater than the maximum listed, replace the pump with a new one.

11 Lay a straight-edge across the rotors and the pump body and, using a feeler gauge, measure the rotor end-float (the gap between the rotors and the straight-edge (see illustration). If the clearance measured is greater than the maximum listed, replace the pump with a new one.
12 Check the pump gear, shaft and drive pin for wear or damage – the gear is available separately, but the shaft and drive pin are part of the pump assembly. If wear and/or broken teeth are found on the gear check the primary drive gear teeth as well (Section 17).
13 If the pump is good, make sure all the components are clean, then lubricate them with new engine oil.
14 Fit the washer and drive pin onto the shaft then slide the shaft into the pump (see illustration). Fit the inner rotor, seating the cut-outs in its inner face over the drive pin ends (see illustration). Fit the outer rotor into the pump body with the T mark facing

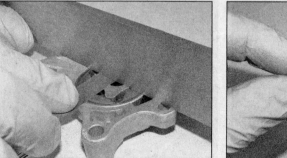

19.11 Measure rotor end-float

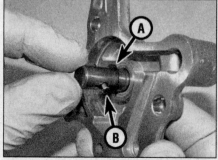

19.14a Fit the washer (A) and drive pin (B) and insert the shaft

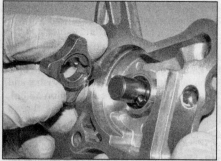

19.14b Fit the inner rotor onto the drive pin...

19.14c ...then fit the outer rotor

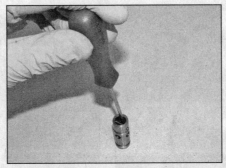

19.17 Check the relief valve plunger

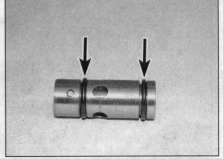

19.19 Fit new O-rings onto the valve

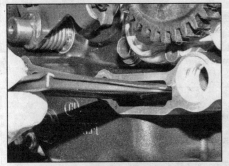

19.20 Fit the strainer as shown

19.21a Fit a new O-ring

19.21b Oil pump locating dowels (arrowed)

the same way as noted on removal (see illustration).

15 Fit the dowels into the body and fit the pump body onto the housing, locating it on the dowels (see illustration 19.6b). Fit the bolt (see illustration 19.6a).

16 Rotate the pump shaft by hand and check it turns the rotors smoothly and freely.

17 Push the relief valve plunger into the valve body and check that it moves smoothly and freely against spring pressure (see illustration). If not, remove the circlip, noting that it is under spring pressure, then remove the washer, spring and plunger. Clean all components in solvent, then check the plunger and the valve body for evidence of scoring, wear and any other damage. If any is found, replace the relief valve with a new one – individual components are not available. Otherwise, coat the plunger with oil and fit it closed end first back into the valve and recheck the movement. If it is good, fit the spring and washer and secure them with the circlip, with its chamfered side facing the washer.

18 Wash the strainer in solvent making sure all debris is removed from the mesh – blow through it using compressed air if available. Check the mesh for holes and damage and replace the strainer with a new one if necessary.

Installation

19 Fit a new O-ring smeared with oil into the groove in each end of the relief valve (see illustration). Push the valve into its bore with the circlip end facing in (see illustration 19.5).

20 Coat the rubber rim of the strainer with clean oil, then slide it into the grooves in its chamber with the thinner edge going in first and the flanged side at the top (see illustration).

21 Fit a new O-ring into the groove in the back of the pump body (see illustration). Fit the dowels if removed (see illustration). Fit the pump, locating the bottom of the cam chain guide blade in the slot (see illustration 9.11b), and making sure the dowels locate, then fit and tighten the bolts. Fit the gear onto the shaft, aligning the flats (see illustration 19.2).

22 Install the clutch cover (see Section 15, Steps 27 to 32).

20 Crankcase separation and reassembly

Separation

1 To access the crankshaft and connecting rod assembly, balancer shaft, transmission shafts, selector drum and forks, and their bearings, the crankcase halves must be separated. Remove the engine from the frame (see Section 4).

2 Before the crankcases can be separated the following components must be removed:

Starter motor (Chapter 8)
Neutral switch (Chapter 8)
Speed sensor (Chapter 8)
Valve cover (Section 6)
Camshafts (Section 8)
Cylinder head (Section 10)
Cylinder barrel (Section 12)
Piston (Chapter 2A, Section 13)
Alternator rotor (Chapter 8)
Starter clutch bearing (Section 14)
Clutch (Section 15)
Primary drive gear (Section 17)
Cam chain, sprocket and blades (Section 9)
Gearchange mechanism (Section 18)
Oil pump, strainer and relief valve (Section 19)

3 Fit a suitable 3 mm pin through the holes in the balancer driven gear to keep the sprung outer sub-gear teeth in line with the main gear teeth (see illustration). Wedge a copper or aluminium washer (DO NOT use a steel one) or a stout piece of rag between the teeth of the balancer drive and driven gears where

20.3a Fit the pin into the holes

20.3b Using a washer (arrowed) to lock the gears while unscrewing the nut

20.3c Remove the key (arrowed) if it is loose

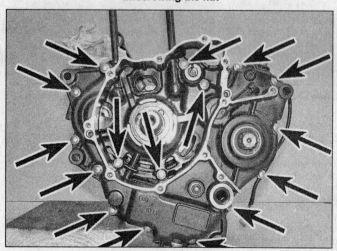

20.4 Crankcase bolts (arrowed)

20.5 Carefully separate the crankcase halves

they mesh at the top (see illustration) – this will lock them together to prevent them turning while slackening the balancer driven gear nut. Remove the washer or rag. Slide the drive gear off (see illustration 20.18c). Unscrew the driven gear nut and remove the washer, then slide the gear off the end of the shaft (see illustrations 20.18b and a). Remove the Woodruff key (see illustration).

4 Place the engine on its right-hand side, laying it on wooden blocks so the shaft ends are clear of the bench. Unscrew the crankcase bolts evenly, a little at a time and in a criss-cross sequence until they are finger-tight, then remove them, noting which bolts fit where as there are two different lengths (see illustration).

HAYNES HINT *As each bolt is removed, store it in its relative position in a cardboard template of the crankcase halves. This will ensure all bolts are returned to their original locations on reassembly.*

5 Carefully lift the left crankcase half off the right half, using a soft-faced hammer to tap around the joint to initially separate the halves if necessary (see illustration). Note: *If the halves do not separate easily, make sure all fasteners have been removed. Do not try and separate the halves by levering against the crankcase mating surfaces as they are easily scored and will leak oil in the future if damaged.* The left-hand crankcase half will come away leaving the crankshaft, balancer shaft, transmission shafts and selector drum and forks in the right-hand half.

6 Note the thrust washer on the left-hand end of each transmission shaft (see illustration 20.11c) – if either is not there it is stuck to the bearing in the crankcase, in which case retrieve it and fit it back onto the shaft. Remove the two locating dowels and the oil passage collar and O-ring from the crankcase if they are loose (they could be in either half) (see illustrations 20.11a and b). A new O-ring must be used.

7 Refer to Sections 21 to 26 for the removal

and installation of the components housed within the crankcases.

Reassembly

8 Remove all traces of sealant from the crankcase mating surfaces.

9 Ensure that all components and their bearings are in place in the right-hand crankcase half, and that all bearings and new oil seals are in the left-hand half (see Section 18 for the gearchange shaft oil seal and Section 24 for the transmission output shaft seal).

10 Generously lubricate the crankshaft, transmission shaft and selector drum bearings, and the gears and the selector fork shafts and fork ends and the tracks in the selector drum and the left-hand journal with clean engine oil, then use a rag soaked in high flash-point solvent to wipe over the mating surfaces of both crankcase halves to remove all traces of oil.

11 If removed, fit the two locating dowels into the right-hand crankcase half (see

20.11a Make sure the dowels (arrowed) are fitted

20.11b Fit a new O-ring (arrowed) with the collar

20.11c Make sure the thrust washers (arrowed) are on the shafts

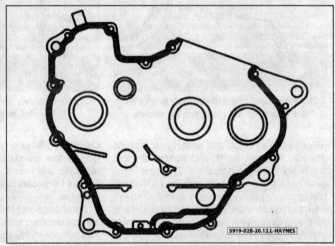

20.12 Apply the sealant in the areas denoted by the heavy black line

illustration). Fit the oil passage collar and a new O-ring smeared with oil (see illustration). Make sure the thrust washer is in place on the left-hand end of each transmission shaft (see illustration).

12 Apply a small amount of suitable sealant (Three-Bond 1207B or equivalent RTV sealant – ask your dealer) to the mating surface of the left-hand crankcase half (see illustration).

Caution: Apply the sealant only to the mating surfaces. Do not apply an excessive amount as it will ooze out when the case halves are assembled and may obstruct oil passages. Do not apply the sealant close to any of the oil passages.

13 Check again that all components are in position (see illustration 20.11a). Carefully fit the left-hand crankcase half down onto the right-hand crankcase half, making sure the shaft ends and dowels all locate correctly (see illustration 20.5).

14 Check that the left-hand crankcase half is correctly seated all round.

Caution: The crankcase halves should

fit together without being forced. If the casings are not correctly seated, remove the left-hand crankcase half and investigate the problem. Do not attempt to pull them together using the crankcase bolts as the casing will crack and be ruined.

15 Clean the threads of all crankcase bolts.

16 Fit the crankcase bolts, making sure they are in their correct positions as noted on removal (see illustration 20.4). Secure the bolts finger-tight at first, then tighten them evenly and a little at a time in a criss-cross sequence to the specified torque setting.

17 With all crankcase fasteners tightened, check that the crankshaft, balancer shaft and transmission shafts rotate smoothly and easily. Check that the transmission shafts rotate freely and independently in neutral, then rotate the selector drum by hand and select each gear in turn whilst rotating the input shaft. If there are any signs of undue stiffness, tight or rough spots, or of any other problem, the fault must be rectified before proceeding further.

18 Turn the balancer shaft so the slot for the Woodruff key is at the top, and turn the crankshaft so the punch mark on its end is at the top. Fit the key into its slot in the balancer shaft (see illustration 20.3c). Slide the driven gear onto the shaft with the circlip facing out, seating the slot in the gear over the key (see illustration). Smear some

20.18a Slide the gear onto the shaft...

20.18b ...and fit the washer and nut

20.18c Align the wide spline (arrowed) with the punch mark on the crankshaft...

20.18d ...and align the punch marks on the gears so they engage as shown

20.18e Washer (arrowed) positioned for tightening the nut

oil onto the threads and seating surface of the nut. Fit the washer and tighten the nut finger-tight (see illustration). Slide the drive gear onto the crankshaft with its OUT mark facing out, aligning the wide spline centrally with the punch mark on the end of the shaft, and engaging the gears with the punch marks aligned (see illustrations). Wedge the washer or rag where the gear teeth mesh at the bottom and tighten the driven gear nut to the torque setting specified at the beginning of the Chapter (see illustration). Remove the pin from the hole (see illustration 20.3a).

19 Install all other removed assemblies in a reverse of the sequence given in Step 2.

21 Crankcases and bearings

Crankcases

1 After the crankcases have been separated, remove the crankshaft and balancer shaft, the selector drum and forks and the transmission shafts, referring to the relevant Sections of this Chapter.

2 Clean the crankcases thoroughly with new solvent and dry them with compressed air. Blow out all oil passages with compressed air.

3 Remove all traces of old sealant from the mating surfaces. Clean up minor damage to the surfaces with a fine sharpening stone or grindstone.

Caution: Be very careful not to nick or gouge the crankcase mating surfaces or oil leaks will result. Check both crankcase halves very carefully for cracks and other damage.

4 Small cracks or holes in aluminium castings can be repaired with an epoxy resin adhesive as a temporary measure or with one of the low temperature welding kits. Permanent repairs can only be done by TIG (tungsten inert gas or heli-arc) welding, and only a specialist in this process is in a position to advise on the economy or practical aspect of such a repair. If any damage is found that can't be repaired, replace the crankcase halves as a set.

5 Damaged threads can be economically reclaimed using a diamond section wire insert, for example of the Heli-Coil type (though there are other makes), which are easily fitted after drilling and re-tapping the affected thread.

6 Sheared studs or screws can usually be removed with extractors, which consist of a tapered, left-hand thread screw of very hard steel. These are inserted into a pre-drilled hole in the stud, and usually succeed in dislodging the most stubborn stud or screw. If a stud has sheared above its bore line, it can be removed using a conventional stud extractor which avoids the need for drilling.

7 Install all components and assemblies, referring to the relevant Sections of this and the other Chapters, before reassembling the crankcase halves.

Bearing information

8 The crankshaft, balancer shaft, and transmission shaft bearings should all be replaced with new ones as part of a complete engine overhaul, or individually as required due to wear or failure.

9 Bearing failure occurs mainly because of lack of lubrication, the presence of dirt or other foreign particles, overloading the engine, break-up of one or more of the bearing components due to fatigue, or corrosion. Regardless of the cause of bearing failure, it must be corrected before the engine is reassembled to prevent it from happening again.

10 The bearing shells for the crankshaft should appear smooth and without signs of excessive wear. The ball bearings for the balancer and transmission shafts should rotate smoothly, freely and quietly, there should be no rough spots or excessive play between the inner and outer races, or between the inner race and the shaft it fits on, or between the outer race and its housing in the crankcase.

11 Dirt and other foreign particles get into the engine in a variety of ways. They may be left in the engine during assembly or they may pass through filters or breathers, then get into the oil and from there into the bearings. Metal chips from machining operations and normal engine wear are often present. Abrasives are sometimes left in engine components after reconditioning operations, especially when parts are not thoroughly cleaned afterwards. The best prevention for this cause of bearing failure is to clean all parts thoroughly and keep everything spotlessly clean during engine reassembly. Regular oil changes are also recommended.

12 Lack of lubrication or lubrication breakdown has a number of interrelated causes. Excessive heat (which thins the oil), overloading and oil leakage all contribute to lubrication breakdown. Blocked oil passages will starve a bearing of lubrication and destroy it.

13 Riding habits can have a definite effect on bearing life. Full throttle low speed operation, or labouring the engine, puts very high loads on bearings. Short trip riding leads to corrosion of bearings, as insufficient engine heat is produced to drive off the condensed water and corrosive gases produced. These products collect in the engine oil, forming acid and sludge. As the oil is carried to the engine bearings, the acid attacks and corrodes the bearing material.

14 Incorrect bearing installation during engine assembly will lead to bearing failure as well. To avoid bearing problems, clean all parts thoroughly before reassembly, and lubricate the new bearings with clean engine oil during installation.

Bearing removal and installation

Note: *If the correct bearing removal and installation tools are not available take the crankcases to a Honda dealer for removal and installation of the bearings – do not risk damaging either the cases or the crankshaft.*

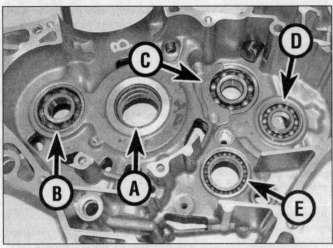

21.16a Bearings in right half – main (A), balancer (B), transmission input (C) and output (D), selector drum (E)

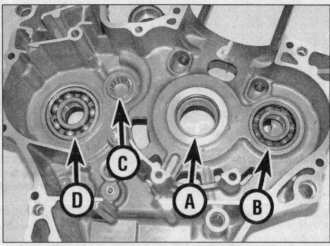

21.16b Bearings in left half – main (A), balancer (B), transmission input (C) and output (D)

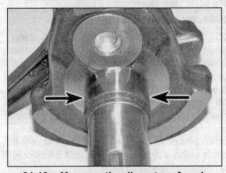

21.18a Measure the diameter of each journal...

21.18b ...and its corresponding bearing

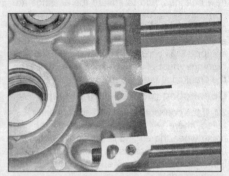

21.19 Bearing housing ID letter (arrowed)

15 Separate the crankcase halves, and remove all components within (Section 20).

Crankshaft (main) bearings

16 If the crankshaft (main) bearings have failed, excessive rumbling and vibration will be felt when the engine is running (**see illustrations**).

Oil clearance check

17 Whether new bearing shells are being fitted or the original ones are being re-used, the main bearing oil clearance should be checked. Clean all oil off the bearings in the crankcase and the journals on the crankshaft.

21.20 Bearing colour code (arrowed)

18 Measure the diameter of each main bearing journal using a micrometer (**see illustration**). Using a bore gauge and micrometer, measure the internal diameter of each main bearing at right angles to the index mark on the crankcase, and measuring the diameter between the raised edge surface on the outer side of the crankcase, not the centre groove (**see illustration**). Calculate the difference between the two to determine the main bearing oil clearance for each journal – make sure you do not mix up which journal runs in which bearing. Compare the results to the specifications at the beginning of the Chapter. If the oil clearance exceeds the service limit proceed to Step 19.

Main bearing selection

19 Remove the old bearings from the crankcases (see Step 21). Using a bore gauge and micrometer, measure the internal diameter of the bearing housing in each crankcase half, measuring at right angles to the index mark on the crankcase. Also locate and note the bearing housing ID code letter (A, B or C) marked adjacent to the housing in each crankcase half (**see illustration**).

20 Replacement main bearings are supplied on a selected fit basis according to the measurements taken – see the table below. If in doubt as to the bearings required or the accuracy of measurements taken, ask your dealer to take the measurements and select the bearings. The bearing colour code is marked on the edge (**see illustration**).

Main bearing housing code	Main bearing housing size	Main bearing journal size (mm)	
		33.985 to 34.000	33.975 to 33.985
A	38.000 to 38.006	C – Brown	B – Black
B	38.006 to 38.012	B – Black	A – Blue
C	38.012 to 38.018	A – Blue	G – Pink
-	38.018 to 38.024	G – Pink	F – Yellow
-	38.024 to 38.030	F – Yellow	E – Green
-	38.030 to 38.036	E – Green	D – Red

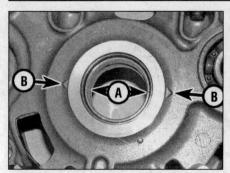

21.21 Align the joints (A) with the marks (B)

21.29 Unscrew the bolts (arrowed) and remove the plate

Main bearing removal and installation

21 Removal and installation of the main bearings requires the use of specially made Honda tools and a hydraulic press in order to avoid damaging either the crankcase or the new bearings, and to ensure the bearings are correctly set in the crankcases. It is therefore necessary to have the bearings removed and installed by a Honda dealer or a suitably equipped specialist. Note that the joints of the bearings must align with the index marks on the crankcase **(see illustration)**.

Connecting rod (big-end) bearing

22 If the connecting rod (big-end) bearing has failed, there will be a pronounced knocking noise when the engine is running, particularly under load and increasing with engine speed. Refer to Section 22, Step 6 for checks that can be made.

23 The connecting rod and its bearing are an integral part of the crankshaft assembly, which comes as a pressed-up unit – individual components are not available. If the big-end bearing fails replace the crankshaft/connecting rod assembly with a new one (see Section 22).

Balancer shaft bearings

24 If the balancer bearings have failed, excessive rumbling and vibration will be felt when the engine is running **(see illustrations 21.16a and b)**.

25 To remove the right-hand bearing from the crankcase, heat the bearing housing with a hot air gun, then tap the bearing out from the outside of the crankcase using a bearing driver or a suitable socket.

26 To remove the left-hand bearing an expanding knife-edge bearing puller with slide-hammer attachment is required – refer to Step 32.

27 Smear the outside of the new bearing with clean oil and fit it with its marked side towards the inside of the engine, then heat the housing again and drive the bearing squarely in until it seats using a driver or socket that bears only on the bearing's outer race.

Transmission shaft bearings

28 If the transmission bearings have failed, excessive rumbling and vibration will be felt when the engine is running **(see illustrations 21.16a and b)**.

29 Unscrew the two bolts securing the input shaft bearing retainer plate on the inside of the right-hand crankcase **(see illustration)**.

30 To remove the input shaft bearing from the right-hand crankcase and the output shaft bearing from the left-hand crankcase, heat the bearing housing with a hot air gun, then tap the bearing out from the outside of the crankcase using a bearing driver or a suitable socket.

31 Smear the outside of the new bearing with clean oil. Note that it should be fitted with its marked side towards the inside of the engine. Heat the housing again and drive the bearing squarely in until it seats using a driver or socket that bears only on the bearing's outer race.

32 To remove the input shaft bearing from the left-hand crankcase and the output shaft bearing from the right-hand crankcase, an expanding knife-edge bearing puller with slide-hammer attachment is required. Heat the bearing housing with a hot air gun, then fit the expanding end of the puller behind the bearing, then turn the puller to expand it and lock it in position **(see illustration)**. Attach the slide-hammer to the puller, then hold the crankcase firmly down and operate the slide-hammer to jar the bearing out **(see illustration)**.

33 Smear the outside of the new bearing with clean oil. Note that the output shaft bearing must be fitted with its sealed side towards the outside of the engine. Heat the housing again and drive the bearing squarely in until it seats using a driver or socket that bears only on the bearing's outer race.

34 Clean the threads of the bearing retainer plate bolts and apply a suitable non-permanent thread locking compound, then fit the plate with the OUTSIDE mark facing up and tighten the bolts **(see illustration 21.29)**.

Selector drum bearing

35 To remove the bearing, heat the bearing housing with a hot air gun, then tap the bearing out from the outside of the crankcase using a bearing driver or a suitable socket **(see illustration 21.16a)**.

36 Smear the outside of the new bearing with clean oil and fit it with its marked side towards the inside of the engine, then heat the housing again and drive the bearing squarely in until it seats using a driver or socket that bears only on the bearing's outer race.

22 Crankshaft and connecting rod

Note: *The connecting rod is an integral part of the crankshaft assembly, which comes as a pressed-up unit ñ individual components are not available.*

Removal

1 Remove the engine from the frame (see Section 4) and separate the crankcase halves (see Section 20).

2 Lift the crankshaft out of the crankcase **(see illustration)**.

21.32a Locate the end of the puller behind the bearing...

21.32b ...and use the slide-hammer to jar it out

22.2 Lift the crankshaft out

22.5 Measuring big-end side clearance

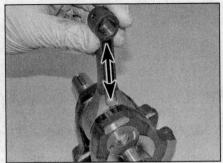

22.6 Check for any radial play in the big-end bearing

23.2 Lift the balancer shaft out

Inspection

3 Clean the crankshaft with solvent. If available, blow the crank dry with compressed air.

4 Place the crankshaft on V-blocks and check for runout using a dial gauge – take a reading at each end, 6 mm in from the right-hand end, and 3 mm in from the left-hand end. Compare the reading to the maximum specified at the beginning of the Chapter. If the runout exceeds the limit, the crankshaft must be replaced with a new one.

5 Measure the connecting rod side clearance (the gap between the connecting rod big-end and the crankshaft web) with a feeler gauge (see illustration). If the clearance is greater than the service limit listed in this Chapter's Specifications, replace the crankshaft with a new one.

6 Hold the crankshaft still and check for any radial (up and down) play in the big-end bearing by pushing and pulling the rod against the crank (see illustration). If a dial gauge is available measure the amount of radial play and compare the reading to the maximum specified at the beginning of the Chapter. If the play exceeds the limit, the crankshaft must be replaced with a new one.

7 Refer to Chapter 2A, Section 13 (and the Specifications at the beginning of this Chapter) and check the connecting rod small-end and piston pin for wear.

8 Have the rod checked for twist and bend by a Honda dealer if you are in doubt about its straightness.

9 Refer to Section 21 and check the crankshaft (main) bearings.

Installation

10 Carefully lower the crankshaft into the right-hand crankcase (see illustration 22.2).

11 Reassemble the crankcase halves (see Section 20).

23 Balancer shaft

Removal

1 Remove the engine from the frame (see Section 4) and separate the crankcase halves (see Section 20).

2 Lift the balancer shaft out of the crankcase (see illustration). If the shaft is stuck, use a soft-faced hammer and gently tap on its right-hand end.

Inspection

3 Clean the balancer shaft with solvent. If available, blow it dry with compressed air.

4 Check the balancer drive and driven gears for wear or damage. If any of the gear teeth are excessively worn, chipped or broken, the gear must be replaced with a new one.

5 Refer to Section 21 and check the balancer shaft bearings.

Installation

6 Carefully lower the balancer shaft into the right-hand crankcase (see illustration 23.2).

7 Reassemble the crankcase halves (see Section 20).

24 Transmission shaft removal and installation

Removal

Note: The output shaft oil seal can be removed and a new one fitted without having to remove the engine and separate the crankcases – refer to Chapter 6 and remove the front sprocket, then follow Steps 4 and 7 below.

1 Remove the engine from the frame (see Section 4) and separate the crankcase halves (see Section 20).

2 Remove the selector drum and forks (see Section 26).

3 Grasp the input shaft and output shaft together and lift both shafts out of the crankcase – hold the bottom pinion on the output shaft to prevent it dropping off (see illustration). If the shafts are stuck, use a soft-faced hammer and gently tap on their ends. Note that there is a thrust washer on the right-hand end of the output shaft that may stick to the bearing or fall off as you remove the shafts – if so retrieve the washer and fit it back onto the shaft.

4 Remove the output shaft oil seal circlip from the left-hand crankcase, then prise the seal out using a seal hook (see illustrations). Discard the seal – a new one must be used. Replace the circlip with a new one if it deformed on removal.

5 If necessary, the transmission shafts can be disassembled and inspected for wear or damage (see Section 25).

6 Refer to Section 21 and check the transmission shaft bearings.

24.3 Lift the transmission shafts out together

24.4a Release the circlip...

24.4b ...then prise the oil seal out

24.7 Press the new oil seal into place using a socket

24.8 Use grease to stick the washer in place

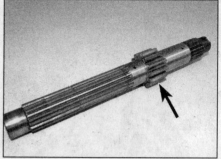

25.6 1st gear pinion (arrowed) is part of the input shaft

Installation

7 Press or drive a new output shaft oil seal into the left-hand crankcase with the marked side facing out, then lubricate its lips with grease (see illustration). Secure it with the circlip (see illustration 24.4a).
8 Make sure the thrust washer is on the right-hand end of the output shaft and that it stays in place when installing the shafts – stick it in place with some oil or grease if it is likely to fall off (see illustration).
9 Join the shafts together on the bench so their related gears are engaged. Grasp the shafts together, holding the pinion and washer on the right-hand end of the output shaft to prevent them dropping off. Fit the shafts into their bearings in the right-hand crankcase (see illustration 24.3). Make sure both transmission shafts are fully seated and their related pinions are correctly engaged.
10 Install the selector drum and forks (see Section 26).
11 Make sure the thrust washer is in place on the left-hand end of each transmission shaft (see illustration 20.11c).
12 Reassemble the crankcase halves (see Section 20).

25 Transmission shaft overhaul

1 Remove the transmission shafts from the crankcase (see Section 24). Always disassemble the transmission shafts separately to avoid mixing up the components.

HAYNES HiNT When disassembling the transmission shafts, place the parts on a long rod or thread a wire through them to keep them in order and facing the proper direction.

Input shaft

Disassembly

2 Slide the thrust washer off the left-hand end of the shaft. Mark the outer face of the 2nd gear pinion so you know which way round it fits, then slide it off the shaft (see illustrations 25.18b and a).
3 Slide the washer, 6th gear pinion and its bush off the shaft, followed by the splined washer (see illustrations 25.17d, c b and a).
4 Remove the circlip securing the combined 3rd/4th gear pinion, then slide the pinion off the shaft (see illustrations 25.16b and a).
5 Remove the circlip securing the 5th gear pinion, then slide the splined washer, the pinion and its bush, and the thrust washer off the shaft (see illustrations 25.15e, d, c, b and a).
6 The 1st gear pinion is integral with the shaft (see illustration).

Inspection

7 Wash all of the components in clean solvent and dry them off.
8 Check the gear teeth for cracking, chipping, pitting and other obvious wear or damage. Any pinion that is damaged as such must be replaced with a new one.
9 Inspect the dogs and the dog holes in the gears for cracks, chips, and excessive wear especially in the form of rounded edges. Make sure mating gears engage properly. Replace the paired gears as a set if necessary.
10 Check for signs of scoring or bluing on the pinions, bushes and shaft. This could be caused by overheating due to inadequate lubrication. Check that all the oil holes and passages are clear. Replace any damaged pinions or bushes.

11 Check that each pinion moves freely on the shaft or its bush but without undue freeplay. Check that each bush moves freely on the shaft but without undue freeplay.
12 The shaft is unlikely to sustain damage unless the engine has seized, placing an unusually high loading on the transmission, or the machine has covered a very high mileage. Check the surface of the shaft, especially where a pinion turns on it, and replace the shaft if it has scored or picked up, or if there are any cracks. Damage of any kind can only be cured by replacement.
13 Check the washers and circlips and replace any that are bent or appear weakened or worn. Use new ones if in any doubt. Note that it is good practice to renew all circlips when overhauling gearshafts.

Reassembly

14 During reassembly, apply molybdenum disulphide oil (a 50/50 mixture of molybdenum disulphide grease and clean engine oil) to the mating surfaces of the shaft, pinions and bushes. When installing the circlips, do not expand their ends any further than is necessary. Install the stamped circlips and washers so that their chamfered side faces away from the thrust side.
15 Slide the thrust washer onto the shaft, followed by the 5th gear pinion bush, then slide the 5th gear pinion onto the bush with its dogs facing away from the integral 1st gear (see illustrations). Slide the splined washer onto the shaft, then fit the circlip, making sure

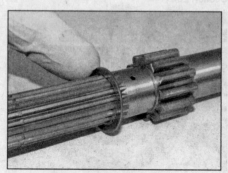

25.15a Slide the washer...

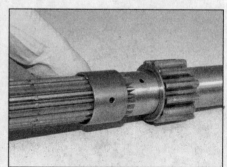

25.15b ...and the bush onto the shaft...

25.15c …then slide the 5th gear onto the bush

25.15d Slide the splined washer on…

25.15e …and fit the circlip in its groove

that it locates correctly in the groove in the shaft (see illustrations).

16 Slide the combined 3rd/4th gear pinion onto the shaft with the larger 4th gear pinion facing the 5th gear pinion (see illustration). Fit the circlip, making sure it is locates

correctly in its groove in the shaft (see illustrations).

17 Slide the splined washer onto the shaft, followed by the 6th gear pinion bush, then slide the 6th gear pinion onto the bush with its dogs facing the 3rd/4th gear pinion (see

illustrations). Slide the washer onto the shaft (see illustration).

18 Slide the 2nd gear pinion onto the end of the shaft with the side you marked facing out (see illustration). Fit the thrust washer onto the end of the shaft (see illustration).

25.16a Slide the combined 3rd/4th gear onto the shaft…

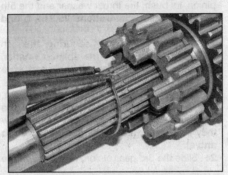

25.16b …and secure it with the circlip…

25.16c …making sure it locates properly in its groove

25.17a Slide the splined washer…

25.17b …and the 6th gear bush onto the shaft…

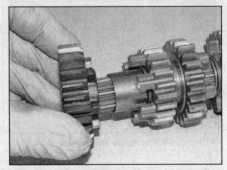

25.17c …then slide the 6th gear onto the bush…

25.17d …and slide the washer on

25.18a Slide the 2nd gear onto the shaft…

25.18b …then fit the thrust washer

25.19 The complete input shaft assembly

19 Check that all components have been correctly installed (see illustration).

Output shaft

Disassembly

20 Slide the thrust washer off the left-hand end of the shaft, followed by the 2nd gear pinion, its bush, the thrust washer, and the 6th gear pinion (see illustrations 25.32e, d, c, b and a).

21 Slide the thrust washer off the right-hand end of the shaft, followed by the 1st gear pinion, its bush, the thrust washer and the 5th gear pinion (see illustrations 25.31c, b and a, and 25.30b and a).

22 Remove the circlip securing the 4th gear pinion, then slide the splined washer, the pinion and its bush off the shaft (see illustrations 25.29d, c, b and a).

23 Slide the tabbed lockwasher off the shaft, then turn the splined washer to offset the splines and slide it off the shaft, noting how they fit together (see illustrations 25.28c, b and a).

24 Slide the 3rd gear pinion, its bush and the

washer off the shaft (see illustrations 25.27c, b and a).

Inspection

25 Refer to Steps 7 to 13 above.

Reassembly

26 During reassembly, apply molybdenum disulphide oil (a 50/50 mixture of molybdenum disulphide grease and clean engine oil) to the mating surfaces of the shaft, pinions and bushes. When installing the circlips, do not expand the ends any further than is necessary. Install the stamped circlips and washers so that their chamfered side faces away from the thrust side.

27 Slide the washer onto the shaft, followed by the 3rd gear pinion bush, then slide the 3rd gear pinion onto the bush with its dog holes facing inwards; towards the 6th gear pinion when later fitted (see illustrations).

28 Slide the splined washer onto the shaft and locate it in its groove, then turn it in the groove so that the splines on the washer align with the splines on the shaft and secure the washer in the groove (see illustrations). Slide the tabbed lockwasher onto the shaft, so that the tabs locate under the inner rim of the splined washer (see illustration).

29 Slide the 4th gear pinion splined bush onto the shaft, then slide the 4th gear pinion onto the bush with its dog holes facing away

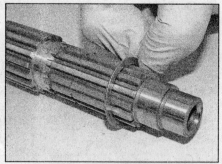

25.27a Slide the washer...

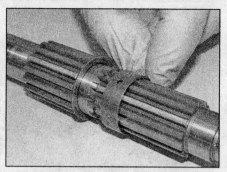

25.27b ...and the bush onto the output shaft...

25.27c ...then slide the 3rd gear onto the bush

25.28a Slide the slotted washer onto the shaft...

25.28b ...and locate it as shown

25.28c Slide the lockwasher onto the shaft and locate its tabs under the inner rim of the slotted washer

25.29a Slide the splined bush onto the shaft...

25.29b ...then slide the 4th gear onto the bush

25.29c Slide the splined washer on...

25.29d ...and fit the circlip...

25.29e ...making sure it locates properly in its groove

25.30a Slide the 5th gear...

25.30b ...and the thrust washer onto the shaft

25.31a Slide the bush...

25.31b ...the 1st gear...

from the 3rd gear pinion (see illustrations). Slide the splined washer on, then fit the circlip, making sure it is locates correctly in its groove in the shaft (see illustrations).

30 Slide the 5th gear pinion onto the shaft with its selector fork groove facing the 4th gear pinion, followed by the thrust washer (see illustrations).

31 Slide the 1st gear pinion bush onto the shaft, then slide the 1st gear pinion onto the bush with its shaped side facing the 5th gear pinion (see illustrations). Fit the thrust washer onto the end of the shaft (see illustration).

32 Slide the 6th gear pinion onto the left-hand end of the shaft, with its selector fork groove facing the 3rd gear pinion (see illustration).

25.31c ...and the thrust washer onto the shaft

25.32a Slide the 6th gear onto the left-hand end of the shaft

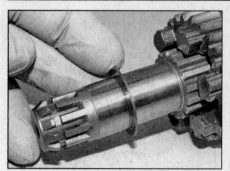

25.32b Slide the thrust washer on...

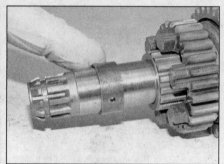

25.32c ...followed by the 2nd gear bush...

25.32d ...the 2nd gear...

25.32e ...and the thrust washer

25.33 The complete output shaft

Slide the thrust washer onto the left-hand end of the shaft, followed by the 2nd gear pinion bush, then slide the 2nd gear pinion onto the bush with its shaped side facing the 6th gear pinion **(see illustrations)**. Fit the thrust washer onto the end of the shaft **(see illustrations)**.
33 Check that all components have been correctly installed **(see illustration)**.

26 Selector drum and forks

Removal

1 Remove the engine (see Section 4) and separate the crankcase halves (see Section 20).
2 Before removing the selector forks, note that

each fork carries an identification letter **(see illustration)**. The right-hand fork has R, the centre fork C, and the left-hand fork L, with all marks facing the left-hand side of the engine. If no letters are visible, mark them yourself using a felt pen. The R and L forks fit into the output shaft and the C fork fits into the input shaft.
3 Support the selector forks and withdraw the shaft from the casing **(see illustration)**. Pivot each fork out of its groove in the selector drum.
4 Remove the selector drum **(see illustration)**.

Slide each fork out of its pinion and remove them **(see illustrations 26.11c, b and a)**. Once removed, slide the forks back onto the shaft to keep them in the correct order and way round.

Inspection

5 Inspect the selector forks for any signs of wear or damage, especially around the fork ends where they engage with the groove in the pinion. Check that each fork fits correctly in its

26.2 Note the identification letters on the forks

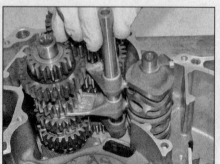

26.3 Withdraw the shaft and move the forks aside...

26.4 ...then remove the selector drum

26.5 Check the fit of each fork in its gear pinion...

26.6 ...and measure the fork end thickness

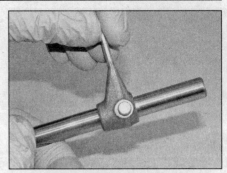

26.7a Check the fit of each fork in its working area of the shaft

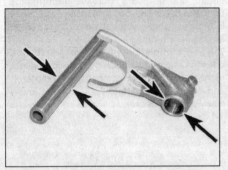

26.7b Measure the fork shaft OD and the fork bore ID

26.9 Check the guide pins and their grooves in the drum

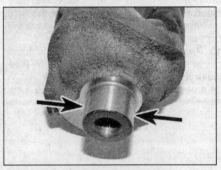

26.10 Measure the diameter of the journal and its bore in the crankcase

pinion groove (see illustration). Check closely to see if the forks are bent. If the forks are in any way damaged they must be replaced with new ones.

6 Measure the thickness of the fork ends and compare the readings to the specifications (see illustration). Replace the forks with new ones if they are worn beyond their specifications.

7 Check that the forks fit correctly on the shaft (see illustration). They should move freely with a light fit but no appreciable freeplay. Measure the internal diameter of the fork bores and the corresponding diameter of the fork shaft (see illustration). Replace the forks and/or shaft with new ones if they are

worn beyond their specifications. Check that the fork shaft holes in the casing are neither worn nor damaged.

8 Check the selector fork shaft is straight by rolling it along a flat surface. A bent rod will cause difficulty in selecting gears and make the gearchange action heavy. Replace the shaft with a new one if it is bent.

9 Inspect the selector drum grooves and selector fork guide pins for signs of wear or damage (see illustration). If either component shows signs of wear or damage the fork(s) and drum must be replaced with new ones.

10 Check that the selector drum rotates freely in each crankcase half and has no sign of freeplay between it and the bearing or casing.

Check the bearing (see Section 21). Measure the diameter of the left-hand journal and the corresponding internal diameter of the bore in the crankcase (see illustration). Replace the drum and/or crankcases with new ones if they are worn beyond their specifications.

Installation

11 Lubricate each fork with molybdenum disulphide oil (a 50/50 mixture of molybdenum disulphide grease and clean engine oil). Locate each fork in turn in its pinion groove, making sure they are correctly positioned – see Step 2 (see illustrations).

12 Lubricate the selector drum tracks with molybdenum disulphide oil. Slide the selector

26.11a Locate the R fork...

26.11b ...the C fork...

26.11c ...and the L fork

26.13 Locate each fork guide pin in its groove in the drum

drum into position in the crankcase **(see illustration 26.4)**. Rotate it so that the hole for the neutral switch contact pin points to the bottom of the crankcase.

13 Pivot each fork round to locate its guide pin in its groove in the selector drum **(see illustration)**.

14 Lubricate the selector fork shaft with molybdenum disulphide oil. With all three forks installed and aligned slide the shaft through each and into its bore in the crankcase **(see illustration 26.3)**.

15 Reassemble the crankcase halves (see Section 20).

27 Running-in procedure

1 Make sure the engine oil and coolant levels are correct (see *Pre-ride checks*). Make sure there is fuel in the tank.

2 Turn the engine kill switch to the ON position and shift the gearbox into neutral. Turn the ignition ON.

3 Start the engine and allow it to run until it reaches operating temperature.

⚠️ *Warning: If the oil pressure warning light doesn't go off, or it comes on while the engine is running, stop the engine immediately. If an engine is run without oil, even for a short period of time, severe damage will occur.*

4 Check carefully that there are no oil, coolant or fuel leaks and make sure the transmission and controls, especially the brakes, function properly before road testing the machine.

5 Treat the machine gently for the first few miles to make sure oil has circulated throughout the engine and any new parts installed have started to seat.

6 Even greater care is necessary if a new piston and rings or a new cylinder have been fitted, and the bike will have to be run in as when new. This means greater use of the transmission and a restraining hand on the throttle until at least 300 miles (500 km) have been covered. There's no point in keeping to any set speed limit – but don't labour the engine and gradually increase performance up to the 300 miles (500 km) mark. Experience is the best guide, since it's easy to tell when an engine is running freely.

7 Upon completion of the road test, and after the engine has cooled down completely, recheck the valve clearances (see Chapter 1) and check the engine oil and coolant levels (see *Pre-ride checks*).

Chapter 3
Cooling system

Contents

Degrees of difficulty

Easy, suitable for novice with little experience	Fairly easy, suitable for beginner with some experience	Fairly difficult, suitable for competent DIY mechanic	Difficult, suitable for experienced DIY mechanic	Very difficult, suitable for expert DIY or professional

Specifications

Coolant
Mixture type and capacity . . . . see Chapter 1

ECT sensor
CBR models
  Resistance @ 50°C. . . . . 6.8 to 7.4 K-ohms
  Resistance @ 80°C. . . . . 2.1 to 2.7 K-ohms
CRF models
  Resistance @ 20°C. . . . . 2.3 to 2.6 K-ohms
  Resistance @ 80°C. . . . . 0.31 to 0.33 K-ohms

Thermostat
125 models
  Opening temperature . . . . 74 to 78°C
  Fully open. . . . . 85°C
  Valve lift . . . . 3.5 to 4.5 mm (min)
250 models
  Opening temperature . . . . 81 to 84°C
  Fully open. . . . . 95°C
  Valve lift . . . . 4.5 mm (min)

Radiator
Cap valve opening pressure. . . . . 13.5 to 17.8 psi (0.95 to 1.25 Bar)

Torque settings
Cooling fan assembly
  Fan blade nut . . . . 1.0 Nm
  Fan bracket bolts . . . . 8.4 Nm
  Fan motor screws. . . . . 2.7 Nm
ECT sensor. . . . . 25 Nm
Thermostat cover bolts (125 models). . . . . 13 Nm
Water pump impeller . . . . 10 Nm

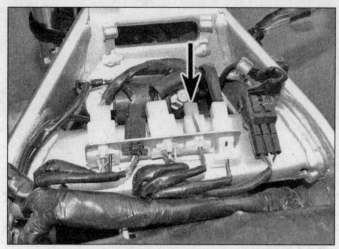

2.2 Cooling fan wiring connector (arrowed) – CBR125

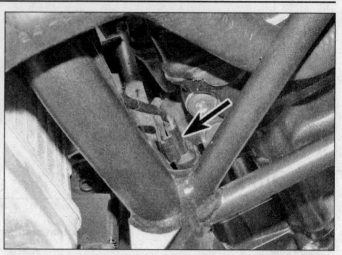

2.3 Cooling fan wiring connector (arrowed) – CBR250

1 General information

The cooling system uses a water/anti-freeze coolant to carry away excess heat from the engine and maintain as constant a temperature as possible. The cylinder is surrounded by a water jacket from which the heated coolant is circulated by thermo-syphonic action in conjunction with a water pump, which is driven by the primary drive gear on 125 engines, and by the balancer shaft on 250 engines. The hot coolant passes upwards to the thermostat and through to the radiator. The coolant then flows across the core of the radiator, then to the water pump and back to the engine where the cycle is repeated.

A thermostat is fitted in the system to prevent the coolant flowing through the radiator when the engine is cold, therefore accelerating the speed at which the engine reaches normal operating temperature. The engine coolant temperature (ECT) sensor mounted in the thermostat housing transmits information to the temperature readout on the instrument panel, and to the engine control module (ECM). A cooling fan on the back of the radiator aids cooling in extreme conditions by drawing extra air through. The fan motor is controlled by a relay that receives a signal from the ECM that in turn receives information from the ECT sensor.

The complete cooling system is partially sealed and pressurised, the pressure being controlled by a valve contained in the spring-loaded radiator cap. By pressurising the coolant the boiling point is raised, preventing premature boiling in adverse conditions. The overflow pipe from the system is connected to a reservoir into which excess coolant is expelled under pressure. The discharged coolant automatically returns to the radiator by the vacuum created when the engine cools.

⚠ *Warning: Do not remove the pressure cap from the radiator when the engine is hot. Scalding hot coolant and steam may be blown out under pressure, which could cause serious injury. When the engine has cooled, place a thick rag, like a towel, over the pressure cap; slowly rotate the cap anti-clockwise to the first stop. This procedure allows any residual pressure to escape. When the steam has stopped escaping, press down on the cap while turning it anti-clockwise and remove it.*
Caution: Do not allow anti-freeze to come in contact with your skin or painted surfaces of the motorcycle. Rinse off any spills immediately with plenty of water. Anti-freeze is highly toxic if ingested. Never leave anti-freeze lying around in an open container or in puddles on the floor; children and pets are attracted by its sweet smell and may drink it. Check with the local authorities about disposing of used anti-freeze. Many communities will have collection centres that will see that anti-freeze is disposed of safely.
Caution: At all times use the specified type of anti-freeze, and always mix it with distilled water in the correct proportion. The anti-freeze contains corrosion inhibitors, which are essential to avoid damage to the cooling system. A lack of these inhibitors could lead to a build-up of corrosion, which would block the coolant passages, resulting in overheating and severe engine damage. Distilled water must be used as opposed to tap water to avoid a build-up of scale, which would also block the passages.

2 Cooling fan and relay

1 The cooling fan is on the back of the radiator. If the engine is overheating and the fan isn't coming on, check the cooling fan fuse (see Chapter 8). If the fuse is good, check the relay as described below.

Cooling fan

Check

2 On CBR125 models raise the fuel tank (see Chapter 4). Displace the rubber shield. Disconnect the cooling fan wiring connector (see illustration).
3 On CBR250 models remove the left-hand fairing side panel (see Chapter 7). Disconnect the cooling fan wiring connector (see illustration).
4 On CRF models remove the fuel tank left-hand cover (see Chapter 7). Disconnect the cooling fan wiring connector (see illustration).
5 To test the cooling fan motor, obtain a 12 volt battery (the bike's battery will do) and two jumper wires with suitable connectors, and connect the battery positive (+) lead to the black/blue (CBR125 models) or blue (all other models) wire terminal on the fan side of the wiring connector, and the battery negative (–) lead to the black wire terminal on the connector. Once connected the fan should operate. If it does not, and the connector and wiring between it and the motor is good, then the fan motor is faulty.

2.4 Cooling fan wiring connector (arrowed) – CRF250

2.7a Fan bracket bolts (arrowed) – CBR

2.7b Fan bracket bolts (arrowed) – CRF

Replacement

 Warning: The engine must be completely cool before carrying out this procedure.

6 On CBR models remove the radiator (see Section 5). Access is possible on CRF models with the radiator in situ.

7 Unscrew the bolts securing the fan bracket to the radiator and remove the fan assembly **(see illustrations)**.

8 To disassemble the fan free the wiring from its guide, where fitted. Unscrew the fan blade nut and remove the blade. Undo the three screws and separate the motor from its bracket.

9 Installation is the reverse of removal. Tighten the fan motor screws to the torque setting specified at the beginning of the Chapter. Clean the threads of the motor shaft. Align the flat on the shaft with that in the fan blade. Apply a suitable non-permanent thread locking compound to the fan blade nut and tighten it to the specified torque. Tighten the bracket bolts to the specified torque.

10 Install the radiator on CBR models (see Section 5).

Cooling fan relay

Check

11 Remove the relay as described below.

12 Set a multimeter to the ohms x 1 scale and connect it across the relay's A and B terminals **(see illustration)**. There should be no continuity (infinite resistance). Using a fully-charged 12 volt battery and two insulated jumper wires, connect the positive (+) terminal of the battery to the C terminal on the relay, and the negative (–) terminal to the D terminal on the relay. At this point the relay should be heard to click and the multimeter read 0 ohms (continuity). If this is the case the relay is proved good. If the relay does not click when battery voltage is applied and still indicates no continuity (infinite resistance) across its terminals, it is faulty and must be replaced with a new one.

13 If the relay is good, check the wiring and connectors in the cooling fan and fan relay circuit, referring to Section 2 at the beginning of Chapter 8 and the Wiring Diagrams at the end of it.

14 If the fan works but is suspected of cutting in at the wrong temperature, check the ECT sensor (see Section 3).

Replacement

15 On CBR125 models remove the fuel tank left-hand cover (see Chapter 7). Carefully pull the side panel away from the tank to release the pegs from the grommets. Remove the relay **(see illustration)**.

16 On CBR250 models remove the fairing

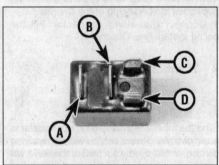

2.12 Fan relay test terminal ID

2.16 Cooling fan relay (arrowed) – CBR250

left-hand side panel (see Chapter 7). Remove the relay **(see illustration)**.

17 On CRF models remove the left-hand side cover (see Chapter 7). Remove the relay **(see illustration)**.

18 Installation is the reverse of removal.

3 Temperature display and ECT sensor

Temperature display

1 The circuit consists of the ECT (engine coolant temperature) sensor and the digital

2.15 Cooling fan relay (arrowed) – CBR125

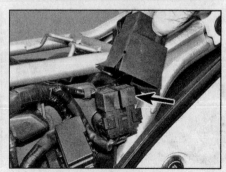

2.17 Cooling fan relay (arrowed) – CRF250

3.4a ECT sensor wiring connector (arrowed) – 125 models

3.4b ECT sensor wiring connector (arrowed) – 250 models

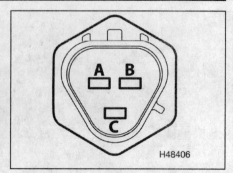

3.6 ECT sensor terminal identification

display (CBR models) or warning light (CRF models) in the instrument cluster. When the ignition is first switched on all the segments in the LCD display or the warning light should come on temporarily – this serves as an indication that the display is functioning correctly (if not, refer to Chapter 8).

2 If there is a problem check the sensor (see below). If the sensor is good check the wiring and connectors in the instrument and ECT sensor circuit, referring to Section 2 at the beginning of Chapter 8 and the Wiring Diagrams at the end of it. If the wiring is good the display is faulty.

ECT sensor

Check

3 On CBR125 models raise the fuel tank (see Chapter 4). On CBR 250 models remove the left-hand fairing side panel (see Chapter 7). The sensor is accessible on CRF models.

4 First make sure the connector is secure on the sensor and the wires are intact **(see illustrations)**.

5 The resistance of the sensor changes with changes in temperature – see the Specifications at the beginning of the chapter. While in theory it is possible to bench test the sensor at those temperatures, in practice the test is difficult to set up and perform.

6 However you can test the resistance of the sensor in the bike with the engine cold, warm and hot. Disconnect the ECT sensor wiring connector **(see illustration 3.5a or b)**. On CBR models connect the positive probe of a multimeter set to read resistance to terminal C on the sensor and the negative probe to

the body of the sensor **(see illustration)**. On CRF models connect the positive probe of a multimeter set to read resistance to terminal A on the sensor and the negative probe to terminal B **(see illustration 3.6)**. Check that the resistance decreases as the sensor gets warmer, with the values being as specified at the given temperatures for your model. If the sensor fails it is most likely to give a zero, constant value, or infinite resistance reading at all temperatures.

Replacement

⚠️ *Warning: The engine must be completely cool before carrying out this procedure.*

7 Drain the cooling system (see Chapter 1).

8 On CBR125 models raise the fuel tank (see Chapter 4).

9 Disconnect the wiring connector **(see illustration 3.4a or b)**. Unscrew and remove the sensor.

10 Fit a new sealing washer onto the sensor. Fit the sensor and tighten it to the torque setting specified at the beginning of the Chapter.

11 Connect the wiring connector. Fill the cooling system (see Chapter 1).

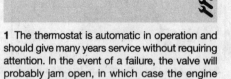

4 Thermostat

1 The thermostat is automatic in operation and should give many years service without requiring attention. In the event of a failure, the valve will probably jam open, in which case the engine will take much longer than normal to warm up.

Conversely, if the valve jams shut, the coolant will be unable to circulate and the engine will overheat. Neither condition is acceptable, and the fault must be investigated promptly.

Removal

⚠️ *Warning: The engine must be completely cool before carrying out this procedure.*

125 models

2 Drain the cooling system (see Chapter 1).

3 Raise the fuel tank (see Chapter 4).

4 Unscrew the thermostat cover bolts and detach it from the housing **(see illustration)**.

5 Withdraw the thermostat, noting how it fits.

250 models

6 Drain the cooling system (see Chapter 1).

7 Unscrew the thermostat cover bolts and detach it from the engine **(see illustration)**.

8 Remove the thermostat either from the cover or the housing as appropriate, noting how it fits **(see illustration 4.17)**.

Check

9 Examine the thermostat visually before carrying out the test. If it remains in the open position at room temperature, it should be replaced with a new one. Also check the condition of the seal – if it is damaged or deformed replace the thermostat with a new one.

10 Suspend the thermostat by a piece of wire in a container of cold water. Place a thermometer capable of reading temperatures up to 110°C in the water so that the bulb is

4.4 Thermostat cover bolts (arrowed) – 125 models

4.7 Thermostat cover bolts (arrowed) – 250 models

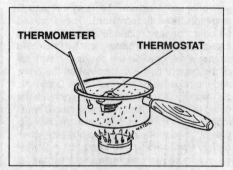

4.10 Thermostat testing set-up

4.16 Check the seal (arrowed)

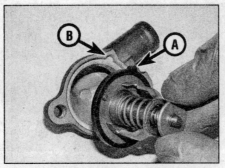

4.17 Locate the tab (A) in the cut-out (B)

4.18 Align the bolt holes as you fit the cover

close to the thermostat **(see illustration)**. Heat the water, noting the temperature when the thermostat opens, and compare the result with the specifications given at the beginning of the Chapter. Also check the amount the valve opens after it has been heated for a few minutes and compare the measurement to the specifications. If the readings obtained differ from those given, the thermostat is faulty and must be replaced with a new one.

11 In the event of thermostat failure, if the thermostat is permanently closed, as an emergency measure only it can be removed and the machine used without it (this is better than leaving it in as the engine will overheat). If it is permanently open you are better to leave it in. In both cases take care when starting the engine from cold as it will take much longer than usual to warm up. Ensure that a new unit is installed as soon as possible.

Installation
125 models
12 Make sure the seal is in good condition and correctly seated around the rim of the thermostat **(see illustration 4.16)**. If the seal is perished fit a new thermostat.
13 Fit the thermostat into the housing with the bleed hole at the top.
14 Fit the cover and tighten the bolts to the torque setting specified at the beginning of the Chapter **(see illustration 4.4)**.
15 Fill the cooling system (see Chapter 1).
250 models
16 Make sure the seal is in good condition and correctly seated around the rim of the thermostat **(see illustration)**. If the seal is perished fit a new thermostat.
17 Fit the thermostat into the cover, aligning the tab on the seal with the cut-out **(see illustration)**.

18 Fit the thermostat and cover and tighten the bolts **(see illustration)**.
19 Fill the cooling system (see Chapter 1).

5 Radiator

Note: *If the radiator is being removed as part of the engine removal procedure, detach the hoses from their unions on the engine rather than on the radiator and remove the radiator with the hoses attached to it. Note the routing of the hoses.*

Removal

⚠ *Warning: The engine must be completely cool before carrying out this procedure.*

CBR models
1 Drain the cooling system (see Chapter 1).
2 On 125 models raise the fuel tank (see Chapter 4). Displace the rubber shield.
3 Disconnect the fan wiring connector **(see illustration 2.2 or 2.3)**.
4 Slacken the clamps securing the hoses to the radiator and detach the hoses **(see illustrations)**.
5 On 125 models unscrew the upper and lower mounting bolts **(see illustration)**. Ease the radiator to the right to free the grommet from its mounting lug, then unhook the rubber shield and remove the radiator, taking care not to knock the fins against anything **(see illustration)**.
6 On 250 models unscrew the mounting bolt **(see illustration)**. Ease the radiator to the left

5.4a Release the clamps (arrowed), and detach the hoses from the right-hand side...

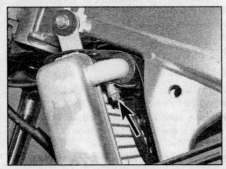

5.4b ...and the left-hand side (125 model shown)

5.5a Unscrew the bolts (arrowed)...

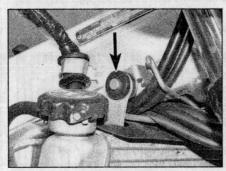

5.5b ...then release the radiator from the peg (arrowed)

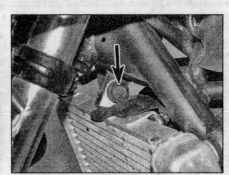

5.6a Unscrew the bolt (arrowed)...

5.6b ...then release the radiator from the pegs

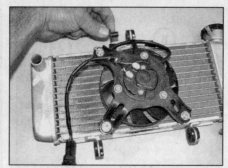

5.7 Note the collar(s) and check the condition of the grommets (250 type shown)

5.9 Release the lead and hose from the guides (arrowed)

5.11 Release the clamps (arrowed) and detach the hoses

5.12 Release and remove the guard

5.13 Unscrew the bolts (arrowed)

to free the grommets from their mounting lugs, then unhook the rubber shield and remove the radiator, taking care not to knock the fins against anything **(see illustration)**.

7 Note the arrangement of the collar(s) and rubber grommets in the radiator mounts. Replace the grommets with new ones if they are damaged, deformed or deteriorated **(see illustration)**. If necessary, remove the cooling fan from the radiator (see Section 2). Check the radiator for signs of damage and clear any dirt or debris that might obstruct air flow and inhibit cooling. If the radiator fins are badly damaged or broken the radiator must be replaced with a new one.

CRF models

8 Drain the cooling system (see Chapter 1).
9 Release the HT lead and overflow hose from the guides **(see illustration)**.
10 Disconnect the fan wiring connector **(see illustration 2.4)**.
11 Slacken the clamps securing the hoses to the radiator and detach the hoses **(see illustration)**.
12 Release and remove the guard from the radiator **(see illustration)**.
13 Unscrew the mounting bolts and remove the radiator, taking care not to knock the fins against anything **(see illustration)**. Note the arrangement of the collars and rubber grommets in the radiator mounts. Replace the grommets with new ones if they are damaged, deformed or deteriorated.

14 If necessary, remove the cooling fan from the radiator (see Section 2). Check the radiator for signs of damage and clear any dirt or debris that might obstruct air flow and inhibit cooling. If the radiator fins are badly damaged or broken the radiator must be replaced with a new one.

Installation

15 Installation is the reverse of removal, noting the following.
● Make sure the coolant hoses and their clamps are in good condition (see Chapter 1).
● Make sure the rubber grommets are in place and the collars for the mounting bolts are fitted **(see illustration 5.7)**.
● Push the hoses fully onto their unions and tighten the clamps.
● Make sure that the fan wiring is connected.
● On completion refill the cooling system as described in Chapter 1.

Pressure cap check

16 If problems such as overheating or loss of coolant occur, check the entire system as described in Chapter 1. The radiator cap opening pressure should be checked by a Honda dealer with the special tester required to do the job. If the cap is defective, replace it with a new one.

6 Water pump

Check

1 Refer to Chapter 1, Section 16.

125 models

Removal

2 Drain the coolant (see Chapter 1).
3 Refer to Chapter 2A, Section 16, Steps 1 to 5, and remove the clutch cover.
4 Unscrew the remaining pump cover bolt and remove the cover **(see illustration)**. A new O-ring must be used.

6.4 Remove the pump cover...

6.5 ...and check the impeller

6.6a Counter-hold the shaft and unscrew the impeller

6.6b Remove the washer...

6.6c ...then withdraw the shaft

6.6d Remove the washer...

6.6e ...the gear...

5 Wiggle the water pump impeller back-and-forth and in-and-out (see illustration). If there is excessive movement, remove and disassemble the pump. Also check for corrosion or a build-up of scale in the pump body.

6 Counter-hold the inner end of the pump shaft using a spanner on the flats, then unscrew the impeller and remove the washer (see illustrations). Draw the shaft out of the cover and remove the washer (see illustrations). Remove the gear and the drive pin from the shaft, noting how they fit (see illustrations).

Seal replacement

Note: *Do not remove the seals unless they need to be replaced with new ones – once removed they cannot be re-used.*

7 To remove the mechanical seal, an expanding knife-edge bearing puller with

slide-hammer attachment is useful, if available. Fit the expanding end of the puller behind the seal, then turn the puller to expand it and lock it (see illustration 6.20a). Attach the slide-hammer to the puller, then hold the cover down and operate the slide-hammer to jar the seal out (see illustrations 6.20b and c). Alternatively prise the seal out using a suitable tool (see illustration 6.20d).

8 Prise the oil seal out using a seal hook or screwdriver (see illustration 6.21). Fit the new oil seal into the cover with the marked side facing out and drive it in until it seats using a 14 mm socket (see illustration 6.23).

9 Fit the new mechanical seal into the cover and drive it in until it seats using a 27 mm socket that bears only on the outer flange (see illustrations 6.25a and b).

10 Remove the seal seat from the inner face

of the impeller and replace it with the new one that should come with the new mechanical seal (see illustrations 6.26a and b).

Installation

11 Fit the drive pin into its hole in the shaft (see illustration 6.6f). Slide the gear onto the shaft with the cut-outs facing the drive pin and locate the gear onto it (see illustration). Slide the washer against the gear (see illustration 6.6d). Fit the shaft through the cover, rotating it to ease its passage through the seals (see illustration 6.6c). Fit the washer onto the outer end of the shaft (see illustration 6.6b). Thread the impeller on and tighten it to the torque setting specified at the beginning of the Chapter, counter-holding the shaft end as before (see illustration). Rotate the pump by hand to make sure it turns freely (but take into account the grip of the seals).

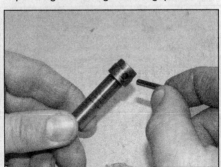

6.6f ...and the drive pin

6.11a Locate the gear onto the drive pin as shown

6.11b Thread the impeller onto the shaft and tighten it

6.12a Fit the O-ring into the groove

6.12b Use a new sealing washer on the bottom bolt

6.17 Unscrew the bolts (arrowed) and remove the cover

12 Smear the new cover O-ring with grease and fit it into its groove in the cover **(see illustration)**. Fit the cover onto the pump **(see illustration 6.4)**. Fit the bolts using a new

sealing washer on the bottom one and tighten them **(see illustration)**.

13 Refer to Chapter 2A, Section 16, Steps 25 to 28, and install the clutch cover.

14 Fill the engine with the correct amount and type of oil and coolant (see Chapter 1).

250 models

Removal

15 Drain the coolant (see Chapter 1).

16 Refer to Chapter 2B, Section 15, Steps 1 to 5, and remove the clutch cover.

17 Unscrew the remaining pump cover bolts and remove the cover **(see illustration)**. A new O-ring must be used.

18 Wiggle the water pump impeller back-and-forth and in-and-out **(see illustration 6.5)**. If there is excessive movement, remove and disassemble the pump. Also check for corrosion or a build-up of scale in the pump body.

19 Counter-hold the inner end of the pump shaft using a spanner on the flats, then unscrew the impeller and remove the washer **(see illustrations)**. Draw the shaft out of the cover.

Seal and bearing replacement

Note: *Do not remove the bearings and seals unless they need to be replaced with new ones – once removed they cannot be re-used.*

20 To remove the mechanical seal, an expanding knife-edge bearing puller with slide-hammer attachment is useful, if available. Fit the expanding end of the puller behind the seal, then turn the puller to expand it and lock it **(see illustration)**. Attach the slide-hammer to the puller, then operate the slide-hammer to jar the seal out **(see illustrations)**. Alternatively prise the seal out using a suitable tool **(see illustration)**.

6.19a Counter-hold the shaft and slacken the impeller

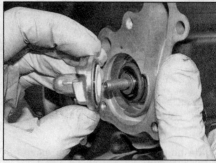

6.19b Unscrew the impeller...

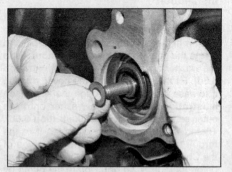

6.19c ...and remove the washer

6.20a Fit the puller behind the seal...

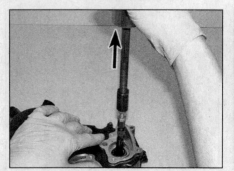

6.20b ...and use the slide-hammer...

6.20c ...to jar the seal out

6.20d The seal can also be prised out

6.21 Lever the oil seal out

6.22 Drive the bearings out using a socket

6.23 Drive the bearings in until they seat

6.24 Fit the oil seal with the marked side facing out

6.25a Position the mechanical seal...

6.25b ...and drive it in until the rim seats using a 27mm socket

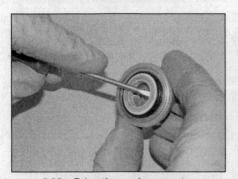

6.26a Prise the seal seat out...

6.26b ...and press the new one in

6.28 Fit the O-ring into the groove

21 Prise the oil seal out using a seal hook or flat-bladed screwdriver (see illustration).
22 Drive the bearings out from the outer side of the cover using a socket on the inner race (see illustration).
23 Heat the bearing housing and drive the bearings in with the marked side facing out using a 20 mm socket on the outer race until they seat (see illustration). Lubricate the bearings with oil.
24 Fit the new oil seal into the cover with the marked side facing out and drive it in until it seats using a 14 mm socket (see illustration).
25 Fit the new mechanical seal into the cover and drive it in until it seats using a 27 mm socket that bears only on the outer flange (see illustrations).
26 Remove the seal seat from the inner face

of the impeller and replace it with the new one that should come with the new mechanical seal (see illustrations).

Installation

27 Fit the shaft through the cover, rotating it to ease its passage through the seals. Fit the washer onto the outer end of the shaft (see illustration 6.19c). Thread the impeller on and tighten it to the torque setting specified at the beginning of the Chapter, counter-holding the shaft end as before (see illustrations 6.19b and a). Rotate the pump by hand to make sure it turns freely (but take into account the grip of the seals).
28 Smear the new cover O-ring with grease and fit it into its groove in the cover (see illustration). Fit the cover onto the pump (see illustration 6.17). Fit the bolts using a new

sealing washer on the bottom one and tighten them.
29 Refer to Chapter 2B, Section 15, Steps 27 to 31, and install the clutch cover.
30 Fill the engine with the correct amount and type of oil and coolant (see Chapter 1). Install the fairing panels (See Chapter 8).

7 Coolant reservoir

Removal

CBR125 models

1 Remove the side panels (see Chapter 7).
2 Remove the air filter housing (see Chapter 4).

7.3 Remove the cap

7.4a Unscrew the bolt (arrowed)…

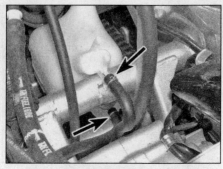

7.4b …then disconnect the hoses (arrowed)

7.6a Undo the screw and remove the cover…

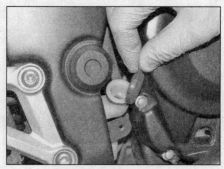

7.6b …for access to the cap

7.6c Disconnect the hose (arrowed) and drain the reservoir through it

3 Remove the reservoir cap **(see illustration)**. Disconnect the siphon hose from the radiator filler neck and release it from the clamps, then lower the hose to the container and allow the reservoir to drain.

4 Unscrew the reservoir bolt, displace the reservoir and disconnect the hoses **(see illustrations)**.

CBR250 models

5 Remove the rear suspension linkage (see Chapter 5).

6 Remove the reservoir cover, then remove the cap **(see illustrations)**. Disconnect the siphon hose from the radiator filler neck and release it from the clamps, then lower the hose to the container and allow the reservoir to drain **(see illustration)**.

7 Unscrew the reservoir bolts, displace the reservoir and disconnect the hoses **(see illustration)**.

CRF250 models

8 Remove the fuel tank right-hand cover (see Chapter 7).

9 Remove the reservoir cap **(see illustration)**.

Disconnect the siphon hose from the bottom of the reservoir and allow the reservoir to drain. Disconnect the overflow hose from the top of the reservoir.

10 Unscrew the bolts and remove the reservoir **(see illustration 7.9)**.

Installation

11 Installation is the reverse of removal. On completion refill the reservoir to the UPPER level line with the specified coolant mixture (see Chapter 1 and *Pre-ride checks*).

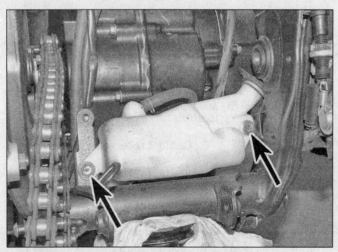

7.7 Reservoir bolts (arrowed)

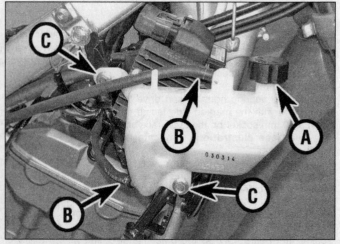

7.9 Reservoir cap (A), hoses (B) and mounting bolts (C)

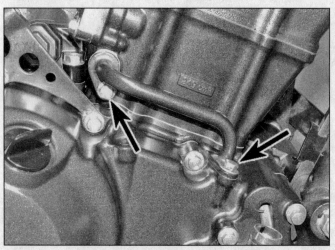

8.4a Coolant inlet pipe bolts (arrowed)

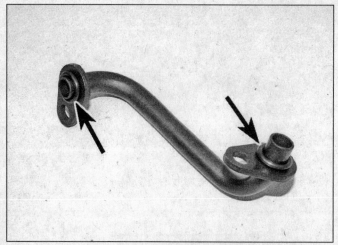

8.4b New O-rings (arrowed) must be used

8 Coolant hoses, pipes and unions

Removal

1 Before removing a hose or pipe, drain the coolant (see Chapter 1).
2 Use a screwdriver to slacken the larger-bore hose clamps, then slide them clear. The smaller-bore hoses are secured by spring clamps that can be expanded by squeezing their ears together with pliers.
Caution: The radiator unions are fragile. Do not use excessive force when attempting to remove the hoses.

3 If a hose proves stubborn, release it by rotating it on its union before working it off. If all else fails, cut the hose with a sharp knife. Whilst this means replacing the hose with a new one, it is preferable to buying a new radiator.
4 On 250 models the inlet pipe to the cylinder barrel can be removed by unscrewing its bolts **(see illustration)**. If the pipe is removed, the O-rings must be replaced with new ones **(see illustration)**.

Installation

5 Slide the clamps onto the hose and then work the hose on to its union.
6 Rotate the hose on its unions to settle it in

HAYNES HiNT

If the hose is difficult to push on its union, soften it by soaking it in very hot water, or alternatively a little soapy water on the union can be used as a lubricant

position before sliding the clamps into place and tightening them securely.
7 On 250 models, if the inlet pipe to the cylinder block has been removed, fit new O-rings, then fit the pipe and tighten the bolts **(see illustrations 8.4b and a)**.
8 Refill the cooling system with fresh coolant (see Chapter 1).

Chapter 4
Engine management system

Contents

Degrees of difficulty

Easy, suitable for novice with little experience	**Fairly easy,** suitable for beginner with some experience	**Fairly difficult,** suitable for competent DIY mechanic	**Difficult,** suitable for experienced DIY mechanic	**Very difficult,** suitable for expert DIY or professional

Specifications

Fuel
Grade . . . . Unleaded. Minimum 91 RON (Research Octane Number) for Europe, 86 PON (Pump Octane Number) for USA.

Fuel tank capacity (including reserve)
  CBR models . . . . 13.0 litres
  CRF models . . . . 7.7 litres
Reserve volume (last segment of display flashes)
  CBR models . . . . approx. 1.4 litres
  CRF models . . . . approx. 1.5 litres

Fuel injection system
Engine idle speed
  CBR125 and CRF250. . . . . 1450 ± 100 rpm
  CBR250. . . . . 1400 ± 100 rpm
Fuel pressure at specified idle speed
  CBR models . . . . 43 psi (3.0 Bar)
  CRF models . . . . 50 psi (3.5 Bar)

Fuel injection system test data

Note: *All values given are only accurate at 20°C (68°F)*

Crankshaft position (CKP) sensor

Resistance

125 models	approx. 115 ohms
250 models	approx. 230 ohms
Minimum peak voltage output	0.7 volt
Engine coolant temperature (ECT) sensor resistance	2.3 to 2.6 K-ohms

Fuel injector resistance

125 models	10.0 to 12.0 ohms
250 models	11.0 to 13.0 ohms
Idle air control valve (IACV) resistance	110 to 150 ohms @ 25°C (77°F)

Fuel level sensor

Resistance

CBR125 and CRF250

Full position	6 to 10 ohms
Empty position	180 to 186 ohms

CBR250

Full position	9 to 11 ohms
Empty position	213 to 219 ohms

Emission control systems

PAIR system control valve resistance (250 models)

CBR250	24 to 28 ohms
CRF250.	20 to 24 ohms

EVAP system control valve resistance (US models)

CBR250	30 to 34 ohms
CRF250.	22 to 26 ohms

Ignition system

Timing

125 models.	8° BTDC (F mark) at idle
250 models.	10° BTDC (F mark) at idle
Coil primary winding resistance	approx. 2.5 ohms

Coil secondary winding resistance

CBR125	approx. 15 K-ohms
CBR250	27 to 30 K-ohms
CRF250.	approx. 15 K-ohms
Spark plug cap resistance	approx. 5 K-ohms
Coil initial voltage (see text)	Battery voltage (approximately 12 volts)
Coil minimum peak voltage (see text)	100 volts

Torque settings

Exhaust system – CBR125

Heat shield screws	10 Nm

Exhaust system – CBR250

Downpipe-to-cylinder head nuts	18 Nm
Silencer clamp bolt.	22.5 Nm

Exhaust system – CRF250

Downpipe-to-cylinder head nuts	18 Nm
Heatshield bolts	12 Nm
Silencer clamp bolt.	22.5 Nm
Silencer front mounting bolt	32 Nm
Fuel injector holder bolts	5 Nm
Fuel pump nuts	12 Nm
Idle air control valve (IACV) screws	2 Nm
Oxygen sensor	25 Nm
Throttle body sensor unit screws	3.5 Nm
Timing inspection cap	6 Nm

1 General information and precautions

General information

Fuel system

The fuel supply system consists of the fuel tank with internal level sensor/pump unit, the fuel hose, the injector, the throttle body, the throttle cable(s), and the fuel filter, which on CBR models is fitted in the fuel hose outside the tank, and on CRF models is inside the tank and part of the fuel pump assembly. Note that the idle speed and fast idle speed for cold starting is set automatically by the Engine Control Module (ECM). The fuel pump is switched on and off with the engine via a relay. The injection system, known as PGM-FI, supplies fuel and air to the engine via the throttle body using the information obtained from the various sensors it monitors.

Many of the fuel system service procedures are considered routine maintenance items and for that reason are covered in Chapter 1.

Ignition system

The transistorised electronic ignition system is combined with the fuel injection system, both being controlled by the ECM. The ignition system comprises a rotor, crankshaft position sensor (CKP sensor), engine control module (ECM) and ignition coil.

The ignition triggers are on the alternator rotor, which is on the left-hand end of the crankshaft, and generate a signal in the CKP sensor as the crankshaft rotates. The CKP sensor sends that signal to the ECM which, in conjunction with information received from the other sensor, calculates the ignition timing and supplies the ignition coil with the power necessary to produce a spark at the plug. There is no provision for adjusting the ignition timing.

The system incorporates a safety interlock circuit that cuts the ignition if the sidestand is extended whilst the engine is running and in gear, or if a gear is selected whilst the engine is running and the sidestand is down. It also prevents the engine from being started if the sidestand is down and the engine is in gear.

The engine can be started with the sidestand up when it is in gear as long as the clutch lever is pulled in.

Note: *Individual engine management system components can be checked but not repaired. If system troubles occur, and the faulty component can be isolated, the only cure for the problem in most cases is to replace the part with a new one. Keep in mind that most electronic parts, once purchased, cannot be returned. To avoid unnecessary expense, make very sure the faulty component has been positively identified before buying a new part.*

Precautions

⚠️ *Warning: Petrol (gasoline) is extremely flammable, so take extra precautions when you work on any part of the fuel system. Always remove the battery (see Chapter 8). Don't smoke or allow open flames or bare light bulbs near the work area, and don't work in a garage where a natural gas-type appliance is present. If you spill any fuel on your skin, rinse it off immediately with soap and water. When you perform any kind of work on the fuel system, wear safety glasses and have a fire extinguisher suitable for a class B type fire (flammable liquids) on hand.*

Some residual pressure will remain in the fuel feed hose after the motorcycle has been used. Before disconnecting any fuel hose, ensure the ignition is switched OFF and make sure you have plenty of clean rag and a suitable container for catching and storing the fuel. It is vital that no dirt or debris is allowed to enter any part of the system while a fuel hose is disconnected. Any foreign matter in the fuel system components could result in injector damage or malfunction. Ensure the ignition is switched OFF before disconnecting or reconnecting any fuel injection system wiring connector. If a connector is disconnected or reconnected with the ignition switched ON, the engine control module (ECM) may be damaged.

Always perform service procedures in a well-ventilated area to prevent a build-up of fumes.

Never work in a building containing a gas appliance with a pilot light, or any other form of naked flame. Ensure that there are no naked light bulbs or any sources of flame or sparks nearby.

Do not smoke (or allow anyone else to smoke) while in the vicinity of petrol (gasoline) or of components containing it. Remember the possible presence of vapour from these sources and move well clear before smoking.

Check all electrical equipment belonging to the house, garage or workshop where work is being undertaken (see the Safety first! section of this manual). Remember that certain electrical appliances such as drills, cutters etc, create sparks in the normal course of operation and must not be used near petrol (gasoline) or any component containing it. Again, remember the possible presence of fumes before using electrical equipment.

Always mop up any spilt fuel and safely dispose of the rag used.

Any stored fuel that is drained off during servicing work must be kept in sealed containers that are suitable for holding petrol (gasoline), and clearly marked as such; the containers themselves should be kept in a safe place. Note that this last point applies equally to the fuel tank if it is removed from the machine; also remember to keep its filler cap closed at all times.

Read the Safety first! section of this manual carefully before starting work.

2 Fuel tank

⚠️ *Warning: Refer to the precautions given in Section 1 before starting work.*

CBR models

Raise

1 Make sure the fuel cap is secure. Remove the seat sections and the fairing side panels, and the fuel tank side and front covers (see Chapter 7).

2 Unscrew the bolt at the front of the tank, noting the collar **(see illustration)**. On 125 models slacken the rear mounting bolt **(see illustration)**. On 250 models unscrew the rear mounting bolts, noting the washers **(see illustration)**.

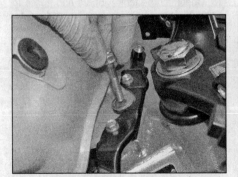

2.2a Unscrew the front bolt

2.2b On 125 models slacken the bolt (arrowed)

2.2c On 250 models unscrew the bolt (arrowed) on each side

2.3 Carefully pull the side panel pegs from the grommets in the tank

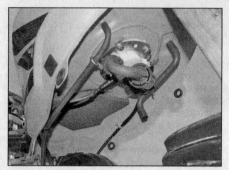

2.4a Tank in raised position with block of wood to support it

2.4b On 250 models disconnect the hoses to allow the tank to be fully raised

2.4c Remove the block

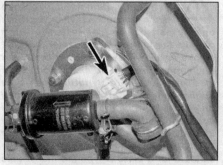

2.7 Fuel pump connector (arrowed) – 125 shown

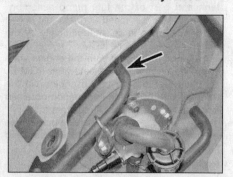

2.9 Disconnect the breather hose (arrowed)

3 Carefully pull the front of each side panel away from the tank to free the pegs from the grommets **(see illustration)**.
4 Lift the front of the tank, on 250 models disconnect the breather and overflow hoses, and support the tank with a suitable piece of wood as shown **(see illustrations)**. On 125 models remove the front mounting block **(see illustration)**.

Lower

5 On 125 models fit the front mounting block. Remove the prop and pivot the tank down onto the frame, connecting the drain and breather hoses on 250 models, and making sure the hoses and wiring do not get squashed or kinked and the side panels are held clear. Make sure the front mounting rubber and collar are in place before fitting the front bolt. On 250 models fit the rear bolts and washers and on 125 models retighten the rear mounting bolt.

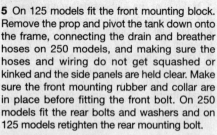

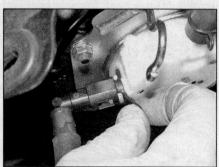

2.10a Pull the retainer out...

Removal

Note: *Removing the tank may involve a small amount of unavoidable fuel spillage, which is obviously dangerous. Refer to the precautions given in Section 1 before starting work, and have plenty of rag to hand. Try to time the removal procedure with a near empty tank, which makes it much easier to lift. Once the tank has been removed, support it so the pump base and filter arrangement are not taking the weight and use soft rag to prevent damaging the paintwork.*

6 Raise the tank as described above.
7 Disconnect the fuel pump wiring connector, then start the engine and let it idle until it stalls **(see illustration)**. Turn the ignition off.
8 Disconnect the battery negative lead (see Chapter 8).
9 On 125 models disconnect the breather hose **(see illustration)**.

2.10b ...then press the tabs in and pull the connector off

10 Clean any dirt from the fuel hose connector. Place a wad of rag for catching any residual fuel in the hose under the connector. Pull the rubber restrictor out of the connector retainer, noting how it seats, and move it clear of the retainer **(see illustration)**. Press the retainer tabs in then pull the connector off the union **(see illustration)**. Remove the retainer – note that Honda specify to replace it with a new one whenever the fuel hose is disconnected. Seal the union and the connector with a piece from a plastic bag or the finger from a latex glove, secured with an elastic band, to prevent dirt getting in.
11 Release the detached hose(s) and pump wiring from the underside of the fuel tank as required according to model.
12 Remove the support and lower the tank.
13 On 125 models unscrew and withdraw the rear mounting bolt **(see illustration 2.2b)**.
14 Carefully remove the tank.
15 Check all the tank rubbers and hoses for signs of damage or deterioration and replace them with new ones if necessary.

Installation

16 Fit the mounting rubbers if removed.
17 Depending on how the tank has been stood and how full it is there is the possibility of fuel having made its way into the breather pipe which could spurt out of the hose when the tank is moved – be prepared with some rag for this. Once the tank is upright the pipe will fill itself with air.
18 Position the tank on the frame. On 125 models fit the rear bolt **(see illustration 2.2b)**. Raise and support the tank as before **(see illustration 2.4a)**.

19 If removed fit the rubber restrictor onto the union and smear the rim with oil, then fit a new retainer, seating it over the restrictor, as shown **(see illustration)**. Fit the connector onto the union and push it until both retainer tabs click into place, then try to pull the connector off to make sure it has locked **(see illustration 2.10b)**. Route and secure the hoses.

20 On 125 models connect the breather hose **(see illustration 2.9)**.

21 Connect the fuel pump wiring connector **(see illustration 2.7)**. Secure the wiring and hoses according to model.

22 Connect the battery (see Chapter 8). Make sure the kill switch is set to RUN, then turn the ignition ON to allow the fuel pump to pressurise the system, then turn it off. Repeat a couple of times and each time check for leaks at the hose connector.

23 Lower the tank as described above.

CRF models

Removal

Note: *Removing the tank may involve a small amount of unavoidable fuel spillage, which is obviously dangerous. Refer to the precautions given in Section 1 before starting work, and have plenty of rag to hand. Try to time the removal procedure with a near empty tank, which makes it much easier to lift. Once the tank has been removed, support it so the pump base is not taking the weight and use soft rag to prevent damaging the paintwork.*

24 Make sure the fuel cap is secure. Remove the seat and the fuel tank covers (see Chapter 7).

25 Release the fuel pump wiring clip from the frame and disconnect it **(see illustration)**. Start the engine and let it idle until it stalls. Turn the ignition off.

26 Disconnect the battery negative lead (see Chapter 8).

27 Disconnect the breather hose **(see illustration)**. Release the fuel hose from its guide **(see illustration)**.

28 Unscrew the bolt on each side at the front and the bolt at the back **(see illustrations)**.

29 Displace and support the tank so you have access to the underside. Clean any dirt from the fuel hose connector. Place a wad of rag for catching any residual fuel in the hose under the connector. Pull the rubber restrictor out of the connector retainer, noting how it

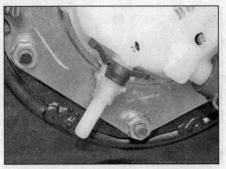

2.19 Fit the restrictor and retainer as shown

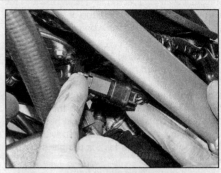

2.25 Release and disconnect the pump wiring connector

2.27a Disconnect the breather hose (arrowed)…

2.27b …and release the fuel hose

2.28a Unscrew the bolt (arrowed) on each side…

2.28b …and the bolt (arrowed) at the back

seats **(see illustration)**. Press the retainer tabs in then pull the connector off the union **(see illustration)**. Remove the retainer – note that Honda specify to replace it with a new one whenever the fuel hose is disconnected. Seal the union and the connector with a piece from

a plastic bag or the finger from a latex glove, secured with an elastic band, to prevent dirt getting in. Release the hose from its guide.

30 Remove the collars from the front mounting rubbers and the sleeve from the rear if required **(see illustration)**. Check all the tank rubbers

2.29a Pull the retainer out…

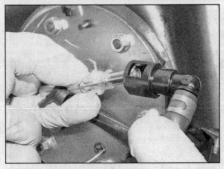

2.29b …then press the tabs in and pull the connector off

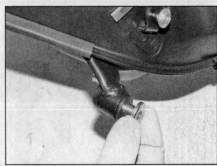

2.30 Remove the collars and check the grommets

and hoses for signs of damage or deterioration and replace them with new ones if necessary.

Installation

31 Fit the mounting rubbers, collars and sleeve if removed **(see illustration 2.30)**.

32 Depending on how the tank has been stood and how full it is there is the possibility of fuel having made its way into the breather pipe which could spurt out of the hose when the tank is moved – be prepared with some rag for this. Once the tank is upright the pipe will fill itself with air.

33 Position the tank on the frame.

34 If removed fit the rubber restrictor and a new retainer onto the union, and smear the restrictor rim with oil. Fit the connector onto the union and push it until both retainer tabs click into place, then try to pull the connector off to make sure it has locked **(see illustration)**. Fit the rubber restrictor into the retainer, so the tabs cannot be pushed in **(see illustration)**.

35 Seat the fuel tank and fit the bolts **(see illustrations 2.28a and b)**. Connect the breather hose and fit the fuel hose in its guide **(see illustrations 2.27a and b)**.

36 Connect the fuel pump wiring connector **(see illustration 2.25)**.

37 Connect the battery (see Chapter 8). Make sure the kill switch is set to RUN, then turn the ignition ON to allow the fuel pump to pressurise the system, then turn it off. Repeat a couple of times and each time check for leaks at the hose connector.

38 Fit the tank covers and seat.

2.34a Fit the restrictor and retainer and push the connector on

2.34b Fit the restrictor into the retainer

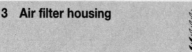

3 Air filter housing

CBR125

1 Remove the fuel tank (see Section 2).

2 Release the clamp and disconnect the crankcase breather hose **(see illustration)**.

3 Slacken the clamp securing the air intake duct to the rear of the throttle body **(see illustration)**.

4 If required release the clamp and disconnect the fuel tank drain hose from the base of the collector on the front left corner of the housing **(see illustration)** – if preferred you can leave the hose connected and remove it with the housing, but note its routing down to the guide on the left-hand side of the bike **(see illustration)**.

5 Release the fuel hose and fuel pump wiring from the guides on the air filter housing **(see illustration)**. Unscrew the bolts and manoeuvre the housing up, and either disconnect the drain hose from the base of the housing **(see illustration 3.4a)** or remove the housing with the hose connected, noting its routing **(see illustration)**.

6 Cover the throttle body with a clean rag.

7 Installation is the reversal of removal. Ensure all fasteners are securely tightened, and any wiring loom/hoses are correctly routed.

CBR250

8 Remove the fuel tank (see Section 2).

9 On US models disconnect the EVAP system vacuum hose at the joint, and disconnect the control valve wiring connector.

10 Disconnect the wiring connector and

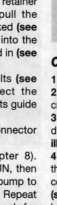

3.2 Disconnect the hose (arrowed)

3.3 Slacken the clamp screw (arrowed)

3.4a Fuel tank drain hose (A), air filter housing drain hose (B)

3.4b Note the routing of the hoses down to the left-hand side

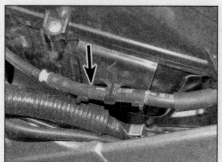

3.5a Release the hose (arrowed)…

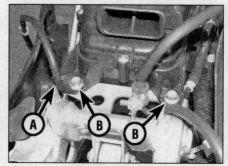

3.5b …and the wiring (A), then unscrew the bolts (B)

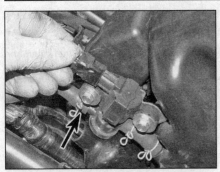

3.10 Disconnect the wiring and the hose (arrowed)

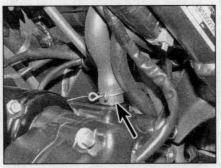

3.11 Disconnect the hose (arrowed)

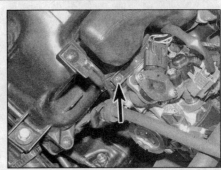

3.12 Slacken the clamp screw (arrowed)

hose from the PAIR system control valve **(see illustration)**.

11 Release the clamp and disconnect the crankcase breather hose **(see illustration)**.

12 Slacken the clamp securing the air intake duct to the rear of the throttle body **(see illustration)**.

13 Unscrew the bolts and manoeuvre the housing up, bringing the drain hose with it and noting its routing **(see illustration)**.

14 Cover the throttle body with a clean rag.

15 Installation is the reversal of removal. Ensure all fasteners are securely tightened, and any wiring loom/hoses are correctly routed.

CRF250

16 Remove the seat and the side panels (see Chapter 7).

17 Remove the fuel tank (see Section 2) and the silencer (see Chapter 4).

18 Remove the battery (see Chapter 8).

19 Displace the rear brake fluid reservoir **(see illustration)**. Release the clamps and detach the PAIR and crankcase breather hoses from the air filter housing **(see illustration)**.

20 Release the cable-ties on the rear sub-frame. Displace the relay holder, the fusebox and the starter relay **(see illustration)**.

21 Release the wiring tie on the left-hand side. Detach the drain hose from the battery holder.

22 Disconnect the tail light wiring connector and release the wiring ties.

23 Slacken the clamp screw securing the air intake duct to the throttle body **(see illustration)**.

24 Check that all wiring and hoses are free from

3.13 Unscrew the two bolts (arrowed) on each side

3.19b ...then release the clamps (arrowed) and detach the hoses

the rear sub-frame. Unscrew the sub-frame lower bolts **(see illustration)**. Unscrew the nuts on the upper bolts, then hold the sub-frame, withdraw the bolts and draw the sub-frame assembly back, detaching the air duct from the throttle body **(see illustration)**.

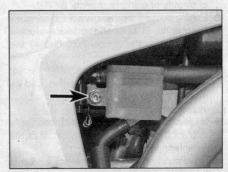

3.19a Unscrew the bolt (arrowed)...

3.20 Displace the relay holder, fusebox and starter relay (arrowed)

25 Unscrew the air filter housing bolts and remove the housing.

26 Installation is the reversal of removal. Ensure all fasteners are securely tightened, and any wiring loom/hoses are correctly routed.

3.23 Slacken the clamp screw (arrowed)

3.24a Unscrew the bolt (arrowed) on each side

3.24b Unscrew the nuts (arrowed), withdraw the bolts and remove the sub-frame

4 Fuel injection system description

1 All models are equipped with Honda's programmed fuel injection (PGM-FI) system. It is controlled by a management system with an engine control module (ECM) that operates both the injection and ignition systems.

2 The engine control module (ECM) monitors signals from the following sensors.

- Throttle position (TP) sensor – informs the ECM of the throttle position, and the rate of throttle opening or closing.
- Engine coolant temperature (ECT) sensor – informs the ECM of engine temperature. It also actuates the temperature display and fan (see Chapter 3).
- Manifold absolute pressure (MAP) sensor – informs the ECM of the engine load by monitoring the pressure in the throttle body intake tract.
- Intake air temperature (IAT) sensor – informs the ECM of the temperature of the air entering the throttle body.
- Crankshaft position (CKP) sensor – informs the ECM of engine speed and crankshaft position.
- Lean angle sensor – stops the engine if the bike falls over.
- Oxygen sensor – informs the ECM of the oxygen content of the exhaust gases.

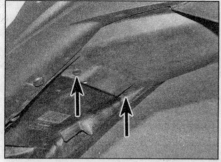

5.3a On CBR models release the trim clips (arrowed) and remove the panel...

3 All the information from the sensors is analysed by the ECM, and from that it determines the appropriate ignition and fuelling requirements of the engine. The ECM controls the fuel injector by varying its pulse width – the length of time the injector is held open – to provide more or less fuel, as appropriate for cold starting, warm up, idle, cruising, and acceleration.

4 At all times, the engine idle speed is controlled by the ECM, and is not adjustable.

5 If there is an abnormality in any of the readings obtained from any sensor, the ECM enters its back-up mode. In this event, the ECM ignores the abnormal sensor signal, and assumes a pre-programmed value that will allow the engine to continue running (albeit at reduced efficiency). If the ECM enters this back-up mode, or when any faults occur, the fuel injection system (FI) warning light in the instrument cluster will come on or flash (depending on the situation), and the relevant fault code will be stored in the ECM memory. The fault can be identified using the fault codes, which can be accessed using the self-diagnosis function (see Section 5). However if there are certain faults detected in the injector or ignition pulse generator, the back-up mode becomes ineffective and the ECM will not allow the engine to run at all.

5 Fuel injection system fault diagnosis

1 If the fuel injection system (FI) warning light on the instrument cluster comes on when the motorcycle is running, a fault has occurred in the fuel injection/ignition system. The engine control module (ECM) will store the relevant fault code in its memory and this code can be read as follows using the self-diagnostic mode of the ECM. While the engine is running above 5000 rpm (CBR125), 1900 rpm (CBR250), or 2100 rpm (CRF models), and the motorcycle is being ridden, the light will come on and stay on. When the motorcycle is on its sidestand and the engine is off or running below the rpm given, the light will flash, the pattern of

the flashes indicating the code for the fault the ECM has identified.

2 If the engine can be started, place the motorcycle on its sidestand then start the engine and allow it to idle. Whilst the engine is idling, observe the FI warning light on the instrument cluster.

3 If the engine cannot be started, and to check for any stored fault codes even though the warning lights have not illuminated, locate the fuel injection system data link connector (DLC), which is a capped 4-pin connector coming out of the wiring loom, located under the tail light on CBR models (remove the access panel from the underside), and above the valve cover on the right-hand side on CRF models (for best access remove the fuel tank right-hand cover – see Chapter 7) **(see illustrations)**. Ensure the ignition is switched OFF then remove the cap and fit the Honda DLC short connector (Part No. 070PZ-ZY30100). Make sure the kill switch is in the RUN position then turn the ignition ON and observe the warning light. If there are no stored fault codes, the light will come on and stay on. If there are stored fault codes, the light will flash.

4 The light emits long (1.3 second) and short (0.3 second) flashes to give out the fault code. A long flash is used to indicate the first digit of a double digit fault code (i.e. 10 and above). If a single digit fault code is being displayed (i.e. 0 – 9), there will be a number of short flashes equivalent to the code being displayed. For example, two long (1.3 sec) flashes followed by three short (0.3 sec) flashes indicates the fault code number 23. If there is more than one fault code, there will be a gap before the other codes are revealed (the codes will be revealed in order, starting with the lowest and finishing with the highest). Once all codes have been revealed, the ECM will continuously run through the code(s) stored in its memory, revealing each one in turn with a short gap between them. The fault codes are shown in the accompanying table. Switch off the ignition and (where necessary) remove the tool from the data link connector. Identify the fault using the table above, then refer below for checking procedures.

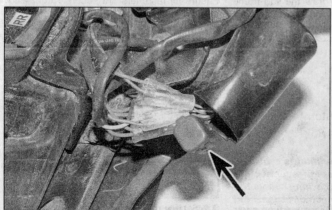

5.3b ...to access the DLC connector (arrowed)

5.3c Fault diagnosis DLC (arrowed) – CRF models

Fault code (No. of flashes)	Symptoms	Possible causes
0 – no code (warning light off)	Engine does not start	● Blown fuse (main or circuit) ● Faulty power supply to ECM ● Short circuit in ECM output voltage wire ● Faulty main relay or wiring (CBR125 only) ● Faulty engine stop switch/open circuit on switch earth (ground) wire ● Faulty ignition switch ● Faulty lean angle sensor or wiring ● Faulty ECM ● No fuel to injector: ● Clogged fuel pipe ● Blocked fuel filter ● Faulty fuel pump
0 – no code (warning light off)	Engine runs normally	● Open or short circuit in warning light wiring ● Faulty ECM
0 – no code (warning light constantly on)	Engine runs normally	● Short circuit in data link connector or wiring ● Faulty ECM
1	Engine runs normally	● Faulty manifold absolute pressure (MAP) sensor or wiring
7	Engine difficult to start at low temperatures	● Faulty engine coolant temperature (ECT) sensor or wiring
8	Poor throttle response	● Faulty throttle position (TP) sensor or wiring
9	Engine runs normally	● Faulty intake air temperature (IAT) sensor or wiring
12	Engine does not start	● Faulty injector or wiring
21	Engine operates normally	● Faulty oxygen sensor (O2) or wiring
29	Engine hard to start, stalls or idles roughly	● Faulty idle air control valve (IACV) or wiring
54	Engine does not start	● Faulty lean angle sensor or wiring

5 Once the fault has been identified and corrected, it will be necessary to reset the system by removing the fault code from the ECM memory. To do this, ensure the ignition is switched OFF then fit the Honda DLC short connector (see Step 3). Make sure the kill switch is in the RUN position, then turn the ignition switch ON. Disconnect the tool from the DLC. When the tool is disconnected the light should come on for about five seconds, during which time the tool must be reconnected. The light should start to flash when it is reconnected, indicating that all fault codes have been erased. Turn off the ignition then remove the tool. Check the FI warning light (in some cases it may be necessary to repeat the erasing procedure more than once) then refit the cap over the DLC.

6 While some of the sensors can be checked using home equipment, there are others that can only be tested using the Honda diagnostic system (HDS) tester, which can be plugged into the system. If a fault appears, use the diagnostic function and fault code system described above to work out which component is faulty. First ensure that the relevant system wiring connectors are securely connected and free of corrosion – poor connections are the cause of the majority of problems. Also check the wiring itself for any obvious faults or breaks, and use a continuity tester to check the wiring between the component, its

connectors and the ECM, referring to Section 2 at the beginning of Chapter 8 and to the correct wiring diagram for your model at the end of Chapter 8. Next refer to Section 6 to see if there are any other specific checks that can be made on that particular component. If this fails to reveal the cause of the problem, the motorcycle should be taken to a suitably-equipped Honda dealer for testing. They will have the tester which should locate the fault quickly and simply.

7 Also ensure that the fault is not due to poor maintenance – i.e. check that the air filter element is clean, that the spark plug is in good condition, that the valve clearances are correctly adjusted, and the cylinder compression pressure is correct (refer to Chapters 1 and 2). It is also worth removing the sensor(s) in question (see Section 6) and checking that the sensing tip or head is clean and not obstructed by anything.

6 Fuel injection and engine management system components

Caution: Ensure the ignition is switched OFF before disconnecting/reconnecting any fuel injection system wiring connector. If a connector is disconnected/reconnected with the ignition switched ON the ECM could be damaged.

MAP sensor, TP sensor and IAT sensor

Check

1 The sensors are all part of the sensor unit attached to the throttle body. The sensor unit can only be checked using the Honda diagnostic system tester, however, the sensor power supply can be checked as follows.

Removal and installation

2 On CBR models remove the throttle body (see Section 7). On CRF models disconnect the sensor unit wiring connector (see illustration).
3 Undo the 3 Torx screws, and remove the

6.2 Sensor unit wiring connector (arrowed)

6.3a Undo the 3 Torx screws (arrowed)...

6.3b ...and pull the sensor unit from the side of the throttle body

6.5a Renew the sealing ring...

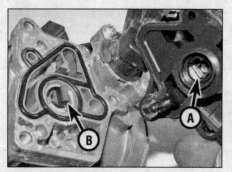

6.5b ...and align the sensor slot (A) with the end of the spindle (B)

6.13a ECT sensor wiring connector (arrowed) – 125 models

6.13b ECT sensor wiring connector (arrowed) – 250 models

sensor unit, complete with sealing ring **(see illustrations)**.

4 If available, use compressed air to clean the various passages in the throttle body.

5 Using a new sealing ring, fit the sensor unit, aligning the slot of the throttle position sensor with the end of the spindle in the throttle body **(see illustrations)**. Tighten the Torx screws to the torque setting specified at the beginning of the Chapter.

6 On CBR models install the throttle body (see Section 6). On CRF models connect the sensor unit wiring connector **(see illustration 6.2)**.

7 It's now necessary to reset the throttle position sensor fully closed position as follows:

8 Remove any stored fault codes from the ECM memory as described in Step 5 of Section 5.

9 Turn the ignition switch off, and fit the Honda short connector to the DLC as described in Step 3 of Section 5.

10 Disconnect the engine coolant temperature sensor (ECT) wiring connector **(see illustration 6.13a or b)**, then use a length of wire to bridge the yellow/blue and green/orange (125 models) or yellow/blue and green/white (250 models) wire terminals on the loom side of the connector.

11 Turn the ignition switch on, and within 10 seconds (while the FI light is blinking), disconnect the bridging wire. If the FI warning light now starts to rapidly blink (0.3 seconds duration and intervals) the throttle position sensor reset procedure has been successful.

If the FI light doesn't blink as stated, repeat the procedure from step 10 onwards.

Engine coolant temperature (ECT) sensor

Check

12 On CBR125 models raise the fuel tank (see Section 2). On CBR 250 models remove the fairing left-hand side panel (see Chapter 7).

13 First make sure the connector is secure on the sensor and the wires are intact **(see illustrations)**.

H48406

6.14 ECT sensor terminal identification

14 Disconnect the wiring connector from the sensor. With the engine cold, connect an ohmmeter between terminals A and B on the sensor and measure the resistance **(see illustration)**. Compare the reading obtained to that given in the Specifications, noting that the specified value is valid at 20°C (68°F). If the resistance reading differs greatly from that specified, the sensor is probably faulty.

Removal and installation

15 Refer to Section 3 of Chapter 3.

Fuel injector

⚠️ *Warning: Refer to the precautions given in Section 1 before starting work.*

Check

16 Remove the fuel tank (Section 2). Disconnect the wiring connector from the injector **(see illustration)**. Connect

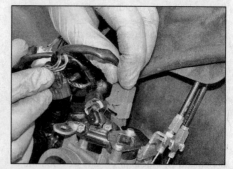

6.16a Disconnect the injector wiring connector...

6.16b ...and measure the resistance between the terminals (arrowed)

6.20a Injector holder bolts (arrowed) and alignment – CBR125

6.20b Injector holder bolts (arrowed) and alignment – CBR250

6.20c Injector holder bolts (arrowed) and alignment – CRF models

6.20d Remove the seal...

6.20e ...and the O-ring (arrowed)

an ohmmeter between the terminals and measure the resistance **(see illustration)**. Compare the reading to that given in the Specifications. Also check that there is no continuity to earth on the black/white (125 models) or black/blue (250 models) wire terminal on the injector. If the resistance of the injector differs greatly from that specified, or there is continuity to earth, a new injector should be installed. Also check for battery voltage at the black/white (125 models) or black/blue (250 models) wire terminal in the wiring connector with the ignition ON and the kill switch set to RUN. If there is no voltage, check the FI fuse (see Chapter 8) and the wiring and connectors in the injector circuit. Check for continuity in the pink/green (125 models) or pink/white (250 models) wire in the connector – there should be no continuity to earth, and there should be continuity to the wire terminal in the ECM wiring connector.

Removal

17 Remove the fuel tank (Section 2). On CBR250 models remove the IACV (see Step 48).
18 Disconnect the wiring connector from the injector **(see illustration 6.16a)**.
19 On CBR models, if required disconnect the fuel hose from the injector holder (see Section 2, Step 10). Plug/cover the openings to prevent contamination.
20 Unscrew the injector holder bolts **(see illustrations)**. Carefully remove the injector

holder then remove the injector from it. Remove the seal from the bottom of the injector or from the throttle body and the O-ring from the top of the injector **(see illustrations)**. Discard them as new ones must be used. On 250 models also remove the cushion ring and replace with a new one if required.

Installation

21 On 250 models fit the cushion ring if removed. Lubricate the new seal and O-ring with clean engine oil, then fit them to the injector.
22 Align the injector with the holder as shown, then carefully press the assembly into the throttle body **(see illustration 6.20a, b or c)**. Tighten the injector holder bolts to the

torque setting specified at the beginning of the Chapter.
23 On CBR models, if removed reconnect the fuel hose (see Section 2, Step 19). Reconnect the wiring connector. Install the fuel tank (Section 2).

Crankshaft position sensor (CKP)

Check

24 On CBR models remove the fuel tank (see Section 2), then on 125 models release the loom clips and displace the relays **(see illustrations)**. On CRF models remove the left-hand side panel (see Chapter 7) and the fuel tank (see Section 2).
25 Draw the rubber boot off the wiring connectors and disconnect the CKP sensor

6.24a Release the loom from the clips (arrowed)...

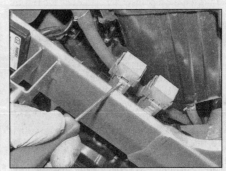

6.24b ...and displace the relays

6.25a Alternator/CKP sensor wiring connector (arrowed) – CBR125

6.25b CKP sensor wiring connector (arrowed) – CBR250

6.25c CKP sensor wiring connector location – CRF models

6.25d Testing CKP sensor resistance...

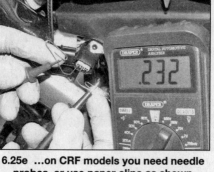

6.25e ...on CRF models you need needle probes, or use paper clips as shown

26 Honda specify their own Imrie diagnostic tester (model 625), or the peak voltage adapter (Pt. No. 07HGJ-0020100) with an aftermarket digital multimeter having an impedance of 10 M-ohm/DCV minimum, for a complete test. If this equipment is available, connect the positive (+) lead of the voltmeter and peak voltage adapter arrangement to the blue/yellow wire terminal on the engine side of the wiring connector, and connect the negative (–) lead to the white/yellow wire terminal.

27 Check that the transmission is in neutral, then turn the ignition switch ON, turn the engine over on the starter motor and note the peak voltage reading on the meter. If the peak voltage reading is lower than the specified minimum, the sensor is faulty.

28 If the sensor functions correctly then the fault must be in the wiring to the ECM. Check the wiring for continuity, referring to the wiring diagrams at the end of Chapter 8. If the wiring is good, the ECM could be faulty.

Removal and installation

29 Remove the alternator stator and replace it with a new one (see Chapter 8) – the CKP sensor and stator come as a complete unit.

Oxygen sensor

Check

30 Apart from the wiring checks that are outlined in Section 5, the operation of the oxygen sensor can only be checked using the Honda diagnostic system tester.

Removal and installation

Note: *The oxygen sensor is delicate and will not work if it is dropped or knocked, or if any cleaning materials are used on it. Ensure the exhaust system is cold before proceeding.*

31 On CBR125 models remove the fairing right-hand side panel (see Chapter 7). On CBR250 models remove the fairing left-hand side panel (See Chapter 7).

32 On 125 models unclip the metal cover, then pull the wiring connector cap off, turning it slightly anti-clockwise (no more than a half turn) as you do (see illustrations).

33 On 250 models pull the wiring connector cap off (see illustration).

34 Unscrew the sensor from the cylinder head (see illustration).

connector (see illustrations). Using a multimeter set to the ohms x 100 scale, measure the resistance between the blue/yellow and white/yellow wire terminals on the engine side of the connector (see illustration) On CRF models you will either need needle probes to connect to the

terminals, or you can use paper clips as shown (see illustration). If the reading obtained is not within the range shown in the Specifications, it is possible that the coil is defective. To confirm this, it must be tested as described below using the specified equipment, or by a Honda dealer.

6.32a Unclip the metal cover...

6.32b ...and pull the connector (arrowed) off the sensor as described

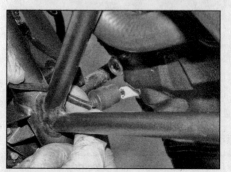

6.33 Pull the connector off the sensor

6.34 Oxygen sensor (arrowed)

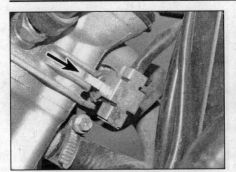

6.37 Seat the tab (arrowed) between the fins on the cylinder head

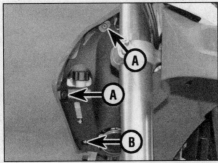

6.40a Release the trim clips (A) and undo the screw (B)...

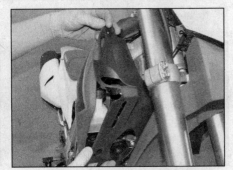

6.40b ...and remove the cover

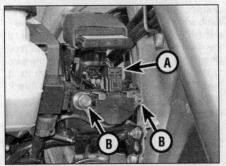
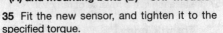

6.40c Lean angle sensor wiring connector (A) and mounting bolts (B) – CRF models

6.42 Lean angle sensor mounting nuts (arrowed) – CBR models

6.45a IACV wiring connector (arrowed) – CBR125

35 Fit the new sensor, and tighten it to the specified torque.
36 On all models press the wiring connector cap squarely onto the sensor without rotating it.
37 On 125 models refit the metal cover (see illustration).
38 On CBR models fit the fairing panel.

Lean angle sensor

Check

39 On CBR models remove the fairing (see Chapter 7).
40 On CRF models remove the coolant reservoir cover (see illustrations) – refer to Chapter 7 for details of trim clip release. Disconnect the lean angle sensor wiring connector (see illustration).
41 With the ignition switch ON and the kill switch set to run, connect the positive (+) lead of a voltmeter to the white/red (CBR125), yellow/red (CBR250) or black/blue (CRF models) wire terminal on the loom side of the connector. Connect the voltmeter negative lead to earth. Check that a voltage of 4.75 to 5.25 volts is present on CBR models, and battery voltage is present on CRF models. If it isn't, check the wire to its source for continuity. Next check the other wire(s) for continuity to the ECM. No further testing of the lean angle sensor is possible without access to the Honda diagnostic system tester.

Removal and installation

42 On CBR models remove the fairing (see Chapter 7). Undo the nuts and remove the sensor (see illustration).
43 On CRF models remove the coolant reservoir cover (see illustrations 6.40a and b)

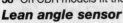

6.45b IACV wiring connector (arrowed) – CBR250

– refer to Chapter 7 for details of trim clip release. Disconnect the lean angle sensor wiring connector (see illustration 6.40c). Undo the nuts, withdraw the bolts and remove the sensor and its mounting plate. Note the collars in the grommets.
44 Installation is the reverse of removal. Make sure the collars are in place and the sensor is fitted with its UP mark facing upwards.

Idle air control valve (IACV)

Check

45 The idle air control valve (IACV) is fitted to the throttle body. On CBR models raise the fuel tank, and on CRF models remove the fuel tank (see Section 2). Disconnect the valve wiring connector (see illustrations). Connect an ohmmeter across the valve's inner terminals and measure the resistance, then repeat the test between the outer terminals (see illustration). Compare the readings obtained

6.45c IACV wiring connector (arrowed) – CRF250

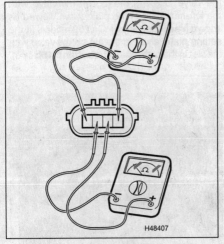

6.45d IACV resistance test connections

6.50a Align the slot (arrowed) in the valve sleeve...

6.50b ...with the pin (arrowed) in the throttle body

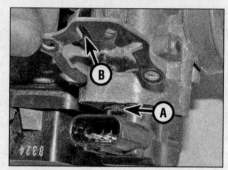

6.51 Align the lug (A) on the valve with the right-hand slot (B) in the setting plate

to that given in the Specifications noting that the specified value is valid at 25°C (77°F). If either resistance reading differs greatly from that specified the valve is probably faulty.

46 Check the operation of the valve by removing it (as described below), then reconnecting the wiring plug and turning the ignition (and KILL switch) to ON. The valve should briefly operate and emit a 'beep'.

47 If the valve appears to be functioning correctly, check for continuity in each wire between the connector and the ECM, and check there is no continuity in any wire to earth. If all the wiring is good the ECM could be faulty.

Removal and installation

48 On CBR models raise the fuel tank, and on CRF models remove the fuel tank (see Section 2). Disconnect the IACV wiring connector **(see illustration 6.45a, b or c)**. Undo the 2 security Torx screws, then remove the setting plate and valve from the throttle body. On CBR125 models, if better access is required, remove the throttle body (see Section 7).

49 Gently turn the valve clockwise until it rests against the stop.

50 Align the slot in the valve sleeve with the pin in the throttle body, and fit the valve **(see illustrations)**.

51 On 125 models fit the setting plate onto the valve, aligning the lug on the valve with the left-hand slot in the plate when viewed as shown **(see illustration)**. On 250 models fit the setting plate, aligning the lug on the valve with the slot in the plate **(see illustration 6.45b or c)**.

Tighten the screws to the torque setting specified at the beginning of the Chapter. Reconnect the wiring.

Engine control module (ECM)
Check

52 The ECM itself cannot be checked, but a process of elimination of other possible faulty components can point to it being faulty. The best action, if possible, is to substitute it with one known to be good and see whether the problem is solved. Otherwise the only thing you can do is to check all the wiring and connectors between all components in the system and the ECM – refer to Section 2 in Chapter 8 and to the Wiring Diagram for your model at the end of it. Alternatively take the bike to a Honda dealer equipped with the test harness.

53 To check the power supply to the ECM and its earth connections, on CBR125 models remove the fairing left-hand side panel (see Chapter 7), on CBR250 models remove the right-hand side panel (see Chapter 7), on CRF models remove the coolant reservoir cover **(see illustrations 6.40a and b)**, and if required for best access remove the fuel tank right-hand cover (see Chapter 7). Make sure the ignition is OFF, then displace the ECM and disconnect the wiring connector **(see illustration 6.56a or b)**. With the ignition switch ON and the kill switch set to run, connect the positive (+) lead of a voltmeter to the black white (125 models, except in Canada and Australia where it is black/green) or black/blue (250 models) wire terminal on the loom side of the connector.

Connect the voltmeter negative (-) lead to earth and check that battery voltage is shown. If it isn't, on 125 models check the wire to the main relay then check the relay itself (see Chapter 8), and on 250 models check the wire to the kill switch then check the switch itself (see Chapter 8). Next check the green/black and green wires for continuity to earth.

Removal and installation

54 Make sure the ignition is OFF.

55 Access the ECM as described in Step 53.

56 Lift the ECM holder from its mounting and disconnect the wiring connector **(see illustrations)**.

57 Installation is the reverse of removal.

7 Throttle body

 Warning: Refer to the precautions given in Section 1 before starting work.

Removal

1 On CBR models remove the air filter housing (Section 3). On CRF models remove the fuel tank (see Section 2).

2 Disconnect the sensor unit, injector and IACV wiring connectors **(see illustrations 6.2, 6.16a and 6.45a, b or c)**. On 250 models release the wiring clamp **(see illustration)**.

3 On CBR models, if required disconnect

6.56a ECM (arrowed) – CBR250

6.56b ECM (arrowed) – CRF250

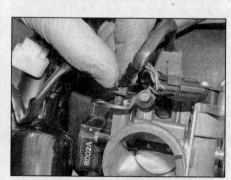

7.2 Release the clamp from the bracket

7.5a Throttle body clamp screw (arrowed) – 125 models

7.5b Throttle body clamp screws (arrowed) – 250 models

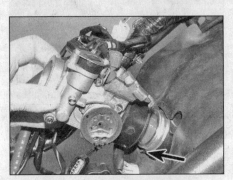

7.10 Seat the ribs around the lug (arrowed)

the fuel hose from the injector holder (see Section 2, Step 10). Plug/cover the openings to prevent contamination.

4 On 250 models disconnect the throttle cables from the throttle body (see Section 8).

5 Slacken the clamp screw(s) securing the throttle body to the intake duct, then pull the throttle body out of the duct (see illustrations).

6 On 125 models disconnect the throttle cable from the throttle body (see Section 8).

7 Tape over or stuff clean rag into the cylinder head intake after removing the throttle body assembly to prevent anything from falling in.

Caution: The throttle body assembly must be treated as a sealed unit. NEVER loosen any of the white-painted nuts/bolts/screws on the assembly as these are pre-set at the factory. The only components on the assembly that are serviceable are described in Section 6.

Caution: NEVER use a solvent-based cleaner to clean the throttle body components. The throttle bores are covered with a molybdenum coating which could be removed by the cleaner.

Installation

8 Remove the tape/plugs from the intake. On 125 models make sure the hole in the clamp is seated over the peg on the intake duct. On 250 models make sure the intake duct is correctly seated on the throttle body with the letters facing away, the ribs located on each side of the lug, and the hole in the clamp seated over the peg. Lubricate the inside of the duct with a light smear of engine oil.

9 On 125 models connect the throttle cable before fitting the throttle body (see Section 8). Push the throttle body fully into the duct, seating the lug in between the ribs, and tighten the clamp screw so the gap between the ends is 6 to 8 mm.

10 On 250 models push the throttle body fully

onto the head, seating the ribs on each side of the lug on the underside, and tighten the clamp screws so there is no gap between the ends (see illustration). Connect the throttle cables (see Section 8).

11 Reconnect the wiring (see Step 2). On CBR models, if removed reconnect the fuel hose (see Section 2, Step 19).

12 Fit the air cleaner housing or fuel tank. Adjust the throttle cable(s) (see Chapter 1).

8 Throttle cable(s)

125 models

Removal

1 Remove the air filter housing (see Section 3). Displace the throttle body (see Section 7).

2 Slacken the locknut on the cable adjuster at the throttle body end and free the cable from the bracket, noting how it locates (see illustration). Free the cable end from the pulley on the throttle body (see illustration).

3 Draw the cable out, noting its routing.

4 Unscrew the cable elbow nut from the throttle pulley housing (see illustration). Undo the housing screws and separate the halves

8.2a Slacken the locknut (arrowed) and free the cable from the bracket...

8.2b ...then detach the cable end

8.4a Unscrew the nut (arrowed)

8.4b Undo the screws (arrowed) and detach the housing

8.4c Detach the cable end...

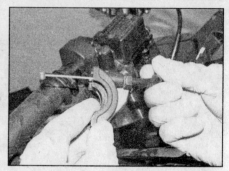

8.4d ...then thread the housing off the cable

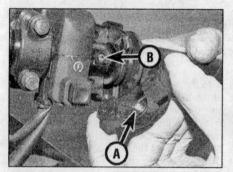

8.5 Locate the pin (A) in the hole (B)

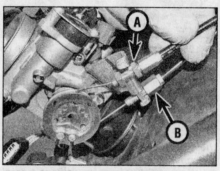

8.13a Slacken the locknut (A) and the hex (B) and free the cables from the bracket...

8.13b ...then detach the opening cable end...

(see illustration). Detach the cable end from the pulley, then thread the housing off the cable (see illustrations).

Installation

5 Thread the throttle cable elbow into the throttle pulley housing without it becoming tight (see illustration 8.4d) – the elbow must stay loose so that it aligns itself. Lubricate the cable end with multi-purpose grease and fit it into the throttle pulley (see illustration 8.4c). Assemble the housing onto the handlebar, making sure the pin locates in the hole, then fit the screws and tighten them (see illustration).
6 Feed the cable through to the throttle body, making sure it is correctly routed. The cable must not interfere with any other component and should not be kinked or bent sharply. Now

tighten the cable elbow nut on the housing (see illustration 8.4a).
7 Lubricate the cable end with multi-purpose grease and fit it into the pulley (see illustration 8.2b). Locate the adjuster in the bracket, leaving the nuts loose (see illustration 8.2a). Refer to Chapter 1, Section 8 and reset the cable adjuster at the handlebar end so freeplay is at a maximum, then set the adjuster in the throttle body so the freeplay is as specified.
8 Operate the throttle to check that it opens and closes freely.
9 Turn the handlebars back-and-forth to make sure the cable doesn't cause the steering to bind.
10 Install the fuel tank (see Section 2).
11 Start the engine and check that the idle speed does not rise as the handlebars are turned. If it does, the throttle cable is routed

incorrectly. Correct the problem before riding the motorcycle.

250 models
Removal

12 Remove the fuel tank (see Section 2). Mark each cable according to its location.
13 Slacken the locknut on the opening (rear) cable at the throttle body end and turn the adjuster until the captive nut is free, then slacken the closing (front) cable hex and slip the cables out of the bracket (see illustration). Detach the ends from the pulley (see illustrations). Withdraw the cables from the frame noting their correct routing.
14 Unscrew the cable elbow nuts at the throttle pulley housing, then remove the switch housing screws and separate the halves (see illustrations). On CRF models then undo the

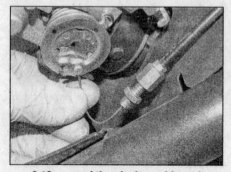

8.13c ...and the closing cable end

8.14a Unscrew the nuts...

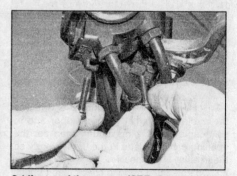

8.14b ...and the screws (CBR shown, screws are on front of housing on CRF models)

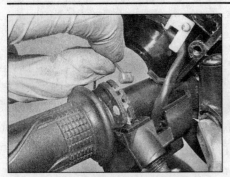

8.14c Detach the closing cable end...

8.14d ...and draw the cable out

8.14e Detach the opening cable end...

pulley housing screws. Detach the closing cable end from the pulley, then withdraw the cable from the housing (see illustrations). Detach the opening cable end from the pulley, then thread the cable elbow out of the housing and withdraw the cable (see illustrations). Mark each cable to ensure it is connected correctly on installation.

Installation

15 Lubricate the cable ends with grease.
16 Thread the throttle opening cable elbow into the front (CBR models) or upper (CRF models) socket of the throttle pulley housing without it becoming tight on the bottom of the threads (see illustration 8.14f) – the elbow must stay loose so that it aligns itself – then thread the nut onto the elbow, again not so that it is tight. Lubricate the cable end with multi-purpose grease and fit it into the pulley (see illustration 8.14e). Fit the closing cable into the rear or lower socket and tighten the nut finger-tight (see illustration 8.14d). Lubricate the cable end with multi-purpose grease and fit it into the pulley (see illustration 8.14c). Assemble the housing(s) onto the handlebar, making sure the pin(s) locate(s) in the hole(s), then fit the screws and tighten them, front or upper screw first (see illustration).
17 Feed the cables through to the throttle bodies, making sure they are correctly routed. The cables must not interfere with any other component and should not be kinked or bent sharply. With the cables correctly aligned at the throttle housing tighten both nuts (see illustration 8.14a).
18 Fit the closing cable end into the front socket in the pulley and the opening cable end in the rear (see illustration 8.13c and b). Seat the cables in the bracket (see illustration 8.13a). Pull the closing cable up so the lower nut is captive, and tighten the hex down onto the bracket, making sure the nut remains captive.
19 Refer to Chapter 1, Section 8 and thread the cable adjuster at the handlebar end in so freeplay is at a maximum, then set the opening cable adjuster in the throttle body so the freeplay is as specified.
20 Operate the throttle to check that it opens and closes freely.
21 Re-check and if necessary adjust the

8.14f ...then thread the cable off the housing

throttle cable freeplay. Turn the handlebars back-and-forth to make sure the cable doesn't cause the steering to bind.
22 Install the fuel tank (see Section 2).
23 Start the engine and check that the idle speed does not rise as the handlebars are turned. If it does, the throttle cables are routed incorrectly. Correct the problem before riding the motorcycle.

9 Fuel pressure check

 Warning: Refer to the precautions given in Section 1 before starting work.

Note: *A pressure gauge is required for this check. Honda specifies the use of their gauge (Pt. No. 07406-0040004) along with a pressure gauge manifold (Pt. No. 07ZAJ-S5A0111) and pipe/ fittings (Pt. No. 07ZAJ-S5A0120 for all models, 0130 and 0150 for CBR models, and 0100 and 0200 for CRF models). If a different gauge is used suitable pipes and fittings will be needed to 'T' into the fuel supply pipe from the tank.*
1 Refer to Section 2 and disconnect the fuel hose from the pump on the underside of the tank, then connect the pressure gauge and pipes between the pump outlet and the hose.
2 Temporarily reconnect the pump wiring and the battery negative lead.
3 Start the engine, and allow it to idle. Note the pressure present in the fuel system by reading the gauge, then turn the engine off.

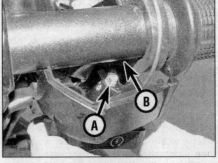

8.16 Locate the pin (A) in the hole (B)

Compare the reading obtained to that given in the Specifications.
4 If the fuel pressure is higher than specified, the fuel pump is faulty and must be replaced with a new one.
5 If the fuel pressure is lower than specified, likely causes are:
● Leaking fuel hose union.
● Blocked fuel filter.
● Blocked or pinched fuel hose
● Blocked or pinched fuel tank breather
● Faulty fuel pump.
If necessary, replace the filter with a new one (Section 11). If the pump's internal pressure regulator is faulty a new pump assembly must be installed (Section 10).
6 On completion, disconnect the battery negative (–) lead again. Remove the pressure gauge assembly, being prepared to catch the residual fuel.
7 Refer to Section 2 and connect the fuel hose to the pump.

10 Fuel pump and relay

 Warning: Refer to the precautions given in Section 1 before starting work.

Fuel pump

Check

1 The fuel pump is located on the underside of the fuel tank, and incorporates the fuel level

10.7 Displace the filter from its bracket

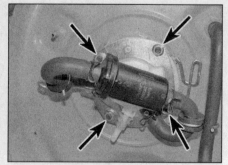

10.8a Fuel pump nuts (arrowed) – CBR125

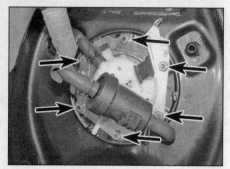

10.8b Fuel pump nuts (arrowed) – CBR250

sensor. The fuel pump runs for a few seconds when the ignition is switched ON to pressurise the fuel system, and then cuts out until the engine is started. Check that it does this. If the pump is thought to be faulty, first check the main and fuel pump fuses (see Chapter 8). If they are OK proceed as follows.

2 On CBR models raise the fuel tank (see Section 2). On CRF models remove the fuel tank left-hand cover (see Chapter 7).

3 Ensure the ignition is switched OFF then disconnect the fuel pump wiring connector **(see illustration 2.7)**. Connect the positive (+) lead of a voltmeter to the black/white (125 models) or brown/red (250 models) wire terminal on the loom side of the connector and the negative (–) lead to the brown/white (125 models) or green (250 models) wire terminal. Switch the ignition ON whilst noting the reading obtained on the meter.

4 If battery voltage is present for a few seconds, the fuel pump circuit is operating correctly and the fuel pump itself is faulty and must be replaced with a new one.

5 If no reading is obtained, check the fuel pump circuit wiring for continuity and make sure all the connectors are free from corrosion and are securely connected. Repair/replace the wiring as necessary and clean the connectors using electrical contact cleaner. If this fails to reveal the fault, check the following components.

● Fuel pump relay (250 models only - see below).
● Engine stop switch (see Chapter 8).
● Lean angle sensor (see Section 6).
● Engine control unit (ECM) (see Section 6).

Removal

6 Remove the fuel tank (see Section 2).

7 If required on CBR models remove the fuel filter assembly (see Section 11). If you don't, on 250 models free the filter from its bracket **(see illustration)**.

8 Clean the area around the pump, then gradually and evenly, working in a 'criss-cross' pattern, undo the pump nuts **(see illustrations)**.

9 Lift the pump/sensor unit from the tank **(see illustration)**. Take care not to damage the sensor float arm as it is withdrawn. Remove the seal – a new one must be used. On CBR models, if the filter assembly has been removed, remove the setting plate.

10 Examine the pump for any signs of damage.

Installation

11 Make sure all wires and connectors are secure **(see illustration)**.

12 Make sure the mounting plate and tank surfaces are clean and dry.

13 Fit a new sealing ring onto the pump, on 250 models making sure the ribs are aligned with the cut-outs and the seal is pressed into its seat **(see illustration)**. Fit the pump into the tank **(see illustration 10.9)**.

14 On CBR models, align the holes (125 models) or slots (250 models) on the setting plate with the tabs on the pump unit flange **(see illustration)**.

15 Fit the pump nuts and tighten them gradually and evenly in a criss-cross sequence to the torque setting specified at the beginning of the Chapter **(see illustration 10.8a, b or c)**.

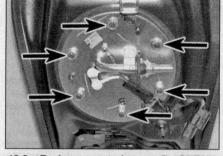

10.8c Fuel pump nuts (arrowed) – CRF250

10.9 Carefully lift the pump/sensor unit from the tank

10.11 Check the wiring and connectors

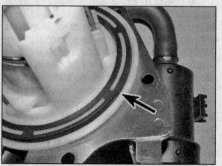

10.13 Fit a new sealing ring (arrowed)

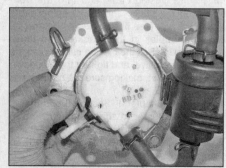

10.14 Make sure the plate is correctly aligned

10.18 Fuel pump relay (arrowed) – CBR models

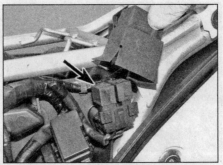

10.19 Fuel pump relay (arrowed) – CRF models

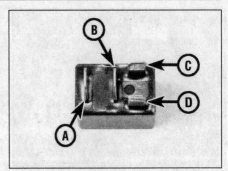

10.20 Relay terminal identification

16 On CBR models fit the fuel filter assembly if removed (see Section 11).
17 Install the tank.

Fuel pump relay (250 models)

18 On CBR models remove the fairing left-hand side panel (see Chapter 7). Remove the relay **(see illustration)**.
19 On CRF models remove the left-hand side panel (see Chapter 7). Remove the relay cover, then remove the relay**(see illustration)**.
20 Set a multimeter to the ohms x 1 scale and connect it across the relay's A and B terminals **(see illustration)**. There should be no continuity (infinite resistance). Using a fully-charged 12 volt battery and two insulated jumper wires, connect the positive (+) terminal of the battery to the C terminal on the relay, and the negative (–) terminal to the D terminal on the relay. At this point the relay should be heard to click and the multimeter read 0 ohms (continuity). If this is the case the relay is proved good. If the relay does not click when battery voltage is applied and still indicates no continuity (infinite resistance) across its terminals, it is faulty and must be replaced with a new one.
21 If the relay is good refer to the wiring diagrams at the end of Chapter 8 and check the wiring and connectors in the circuit to and from the relay.

11 Fuel filter

> **Warning: Refer to the precautions given in Section 1 before starting work.**

CBR models

Removal

1 Remove the fuel tank (see Section 2).
2 Have some rag to hand to catch residual fuel, then release the clamps and detach the fuel filter hoses from the pump and remove the filter assembly, on 250 models releasing the holder from its bracket **(see illustrations)** – the new filter comes with new hoses, but on 250 models remove the filter holder and fit it onto the new filter.

Installation

3 Make sure the hose unions on the pump are clean.
4 Connect the fuel filter hoses to the pump – make sure the filter is the correct way round, and on 250 models fit the holder onto the bracket. Make sure the hose clamps are secure.
5 Install the tank. Check for leakage after starting the engine.

CRF models

Note: *Honda specify not to disassemble the pump, but list a filter kit as a spare part. Before disassembling the pump check with a dealer as to the availability of the filter kit.*
6 Remove the fuel pump (see Section 10).
7 If a new filter unit is being fitted, disassemble the pump, paying close attention to how the components fit together. Fit the new filter using all the new parts that come in the kit.
8 Install the fuel pump.

12 Fuel display and level sensor

Check

1 The circuit consists of the level sensor in the fuel tank and the fuel level display, which is part of the instrument cluster LCD display. Under normal circumstances with the tank full all segments of the display will show, and when there are only about 1.5 litres left the

11.2a Fuel filter assembly – CBR125

final segment flashes. The system performs its own self-diagnosis when the ignition is turned ON. If a fault is detected in the wiring the display will operate as follows – on CBR models all segments of the display will flash; on CRF models the centre segment comes on, then the adjacent two segments also come on, followed by the outer segments, then the segments will go out in that order, and this pattern will repeat until the fault is repaired.
2 If a fault is indicated, on CBR models raise the fuel tank (see Section 2), and on CRF models remove the fuel tank left-hand cover (see Chapter 7). Disconnect the fuel pump wiring connector **(see illustration 2.7)**. Refer to Chapter 8 and disconnect the instrument wiring connector. Check for continuity in the yellow/white wire between the pump wiring connector and the instrument connector, and make sure there is no continuity to earth. Also check there is continuity to earth in the green wire. If the wiring is good check the sensor as follows.
3 To check the sensor connect an ohmmeter or multimeter set to the ohms scale to the yellow/white and green (CBR models) or red/black and black/white (CRF models) wire terminals in the sensor side of the wiring connector and measure the resistance. Compare the reading obtained to those given for a full and empty tank at the beginning of the Chapter, adjusting for the amount of fuel you estimate is there.
4 To accurately check the sensor, remove the pump from the tank (see Section 10). Check the float arm for damage and look for

11.2b Fuel filter assembly – CBR250

12.4a Check the resistance of the sensor with the float in the full position...

12.4b ...and in the empty position

fuel inside the float, and check that the arm moves up and down smoothly and freely. Also check the wiring and connectors. Connect the meter to the sensor connector as above, then manually move the float up and down to simulate movement between the full and empty positions, and compare the resistance readings to those given **(see illustrations)**. If they are not as specified, on 125 models replace the sensor with a new one, and on 250 models replace the pump assembly with a new one.

5 If the sensor is good the instrument PCB is faulty (see Chapter 8).

Removal and installation

6 If the display is faulty refer to Chapter 8.
7 If the sensor is faulty remove the fuel pump (see Section 10).
8 On 125 models disconnect the level sensor

wiring, then remove the sensor and replace it with a new one.
9 On 250 models replace the pump with a new one – the level sensor is an integral component and not available separately.

---

13 Exhaust system

⚠ **Warning: If the engine has been running the exhaust system will be very hot. Allow the system to cool before carrying out any work.**

CBR125

1 Remove the fairing side panels and lower fairing (see Chapter 7).
2 Unscrew the nuts securing the downpipe to

the cylinder head and draw the flange off the studs **(see illustration)**.
3 Unscrew the centre mounting bolt, noting the washer **(see illustration)**.
4 Unscrew the nut on the silencer mounting bolt **(see illustration)**.
5 Support the system, then withdraw the silencer bolt **(see illustration 13.4)** and manoeuvre the system off the bike.
6 Remove the sealing ring from the port in the cylinder head and discard it **(see illustration 13.19)**.
7 If required remove the heat shield – undo the two screws, then slide the shield back to release the hook from the bracket, noting the rubber sleeve.
8 Check the condition of the mounting bolts and nut, washers, collars and rubbers and replace them with new ones if necessary.

> **HAYNES HiNT** *Exhaust system clamp bolts tend to become corroded and seized. It is advisable to spray them with WD40 or a similar product before attempting to slacken them.*

CBR250

Silencer

9 Slacken the clamp bolt securing the silencer in the downpipe.
10 Unscrew the nut on the silencer mounting bolt, then withdraw the bolt and remove the silencer **(see illustration)**.
11 Check the condition of the downpipe-to-silencer sealing ring and replace it with a new one if it is damaged or deformed or no longer sealing correctly – note that Honda specify to always use a new one. If fitting a new sealing ring, slide the clamp off and expand the tangs on the front of the silencer slightly to make it easier to fit.
12 If required remove the heat shields – undo the two screws, then slide each shield back to release the hooks from the brackets, noting the rubber sleeves.
13 Check the condition of the mounting bolt and nut, washer, collar and rubber and replace them with new ones if necessary **(see illustration)**.

13.2 Unscrew the nuts (arrowed) and slide the flange off – CBR125

13.3 Centre mounting bolt (arrowed) – CBR125

13.4 Silencer mounting bolt/nut– CBR125

13.10 Silencer mounting bolt/nut – CBR250

13.13 Remove the collar and check the mounting rubbers – CBR250

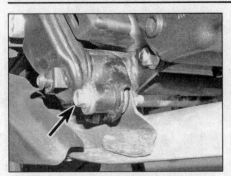

13.16 Downpipe mounting bolt/nut – CBR250

13.17 Unscrew the nuts (arrowed) and slide the flange off – CBR250

13.19 Remove the old sealing ring – CBR250

Downpipe

14 Remove the fairing side panels and lower fairing (see Chapter 7).

15 Remove the silencer as described above.

16 Unscrew the nut on the downpipe mounting bolt **(see illustration)**.

17 Unscrew the nuts securing the downpipe to the cylinder head and draw the flange off the studs **(see illustration)**.

18 Support the downpipe, then withdraw the bolt **(see illustration 10.16)** and manoeuvre the pipe off the bike.

19 Remove the sealing ring from the port in the cylinder head and discard it **(see illustration)**.

20 Check the condition of the mounting bolts and nuts, washers, collars and rubbers and replace them with new ones if necessary.

CRF250

Silencer

21 Remove the seat and right-hand side panel (see Chapter 7).

22 Remove the silencer cover **(see illustration)**.

23 Slacken the clamp bolt securing the silencer in the downpipe **(see illustration)**.

24 Unscrew the front mounting bolt **(see illustration 13.23)**.

25 Unscrew the nut on the rear mounting bolt, then withdraw the bolt and remove the silencer **(see illustration)**.

26 Check the condition of the downpipe-to-silencer sealing ring and replace it with a new one if it is damaged or deformed or no longer sealing correctly – note that Honda specify to always use a new one. If fitting a new sealing ring, slide the clamp off and expand the tangs on the front of the silencer slightly to make it easier to fit.

27 Check the condition of the mounting bolts and nut and replace them with new ones if necessary.

Downpipe

28 If required undo the two screws and remove the heat shield **(see illustration)**.

29 Remove the silencer as described above.

30 Unscrew the nuts securing the downpipe to the cylinder head, draw the flange off the studs and manoeuvre the pipe off the bike **(see illustration)**. Remove the sealing ring from the port in the cylinder head and discard it **(see illustration 13.19)**.

Installation – all models

31 If the studs in the cylinder head are damaged, refer to the stud extractor methods in Section 2 of *Tools and Workshop Tips* in the Reference Section at the end of the manual. Note that on 250 models when installing new studs they should be fitted so that 22 mm of thread extends from the cylinder head casting. On 125 models install the studs until they are fully seated.

32 Installation is the reverse of removal, noting the following:

● Replace any damaged, deformed or deteriorated mounting rubbers with new ones.

13.22 Undo the screws (arrowed) and remove the cover – CRF250

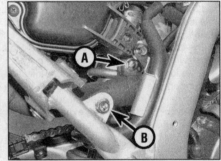

13.23 Clamp bolt (A), front mounting bolt (B) – CRF250

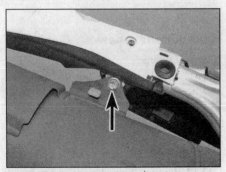

13.25 Rear mounting bolt/nut – CRF250

13.28 Heat shield screws (arrowed) – CRF250

13.30 Unscrew the nuts (arrowed) and slide the flange off – CRF250

- Use a new sealing ring in the cylinder head port, and dab it with grease to stick it in place (see illustration).
- On 250 models use a new sealing ring between the pipe and the silencer if required.
- Apply a smear of copper grease to all nuts and bolts to prevent them from seizing up.
- Leave all fasteners loose until the entire system has been installed, making alignment easier.
- Tighten the downpipe nuts first, then the mounting bolts/nuts. Torque settings are given in the Specifications at the beginning of the Chapter.
- Run the engine and check the system for leaks.

14 Catalytic converter

General information

1 A catalytic converter is incorporated in the exhaust system to minimise the level of exhaust pollutants released into the atmosphere.

2 The catalytic converter consists of a canister containing a fine mesh impregnated with a catalyst material, over which the hot exhaust gases pass. The catalyst speeds up the oxidation of harmful carbon monoxide, unburned hydrocarbons and soot, effectively reducing the quantity of harmful products released into the atmosphere via the exhaust gases.

3 The catalytic converter is of the closed-loop type with exhaust gas oxygen content information being fed back to the fuel injection system engine control module (ECM) by the oxygen sensor in the cylinder head.

4 Refer to Section 13 for exhaust system removal and installation, and Section 6 for oxygen sensor removal and installation information.

Precautions

5 The catalytic converter is a reliable and simple device which needs no maintenance in itself, but there are some facts of which an owner should be aware if the converter is to function properly for its full service life.

- DO NOT use leaded or lead replacement petrol (gasoline) – the additives will coat the precious metals, reducing their converting efficiency and will eventually destroy the catalytic converter.
- Always keep the ignition and fuel systems well-maintained in accordance with the manufacturer's schedule – if the fuel/air mixture is suspected of being incorrect have it checked on an exhaust gas analyser.

13.32 Use a new sealing ring

- If the engine develops a misfire, do not ride the bike at all (or at least as little as possible) until the fault is cured.
- DO NOT use fuel or engine oil additives – these may contain substances harmful to the catalytic converter.
- DO NOT continue to use the bike if the engine burns oil to the extent of leaving a visible trail of blue smoke.
- Remember that the catalytic converter and oxygen sensor are FRAGILE – do not strike them with tools during servicing work.

15 Pulse secondary air (PAIR) system (250 models)

General information

1 To reduce the amount of unburned hydrocarbons released in the exhaust gases, a pulse secondary air (PAIR) system is fitted. The system consists of the control valve, the reed valve and the hoses linking them. The control valve is actuated electronically by the ECM.

2 Under normal operating conditions the control valve is open allowing filtered air to be drawn through the reed valve and cylinder head passage and into the exhaust port. The air mixes with the exhaust gases, causing any unburned particles of the fuel in the mixture to be burnt in the exhaust port/pipe. This process changes a considerable amount of hydrocarbons and carbon monoxide into relatively harmless carbon dioxide and water. The reed valve in the valve cover prevents the flow of exhaust gases back up the cylinder head passage and into the air filter housing.

Testing

3 Start the engine and warm it up to normal temperature. Stop the engine. On CBR models raise the fuel tank (see Section 2), then unscrew the control valve bolts (see illustration 15.8). On CRF models remove the right-hand side panel (see Chapter 7), then

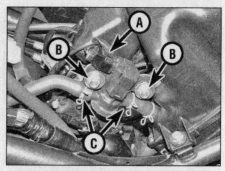
15.8 Control valve wiring connector (A), mounting bolts (B) and hoses (C) – CBR250

displace the rear brake fluid reservoir (see illustration 3.19a).

4 Disconnect the PAIR hose from the air filter housing (see illustration 15.8 or 3.19b). Check that the port in the housing is clean – the presence or carbon deposits indicates a faulty system. Start the engine again and open the throttle slightly, and check the air is being sucked into the hose. If not, stop the engine, then perform the following checks – on CRF models first remove the fuel tank right-hand cover (see Chapter 7).

5 Disconnect the control valve wiring connector (see illustration 15.8 or 15.9a). Clean the end of the air filter housing hose. Manually check the operation of the system by blowing through the hose – air should flow through the control valve and reed valves. Apply battery voltage (12 volts) across the control valve terminals and repeat the check – no air should flow through the control valve. Disconnect the battery. If the valve does not behave as described check its resistance (Step 7).

6 Now suck on the air filter hose union; you should not be able to suck air back up the hose, indicating the reed valve is closing and sealing correctly. If you can suck air through, remove the valve for cleaning, then test it again. Replace the valve with a new one if necessary.

7 Check the resistance of the control valve solenoid by connecting an ohmmeter between its connector terminals and compare the reading obtained to that given in the Specifications. Replace the valve with a new one if faulty.

Component renewal

Control valve

8 On CBR models raise the fuel tank (see Section 2). Detach the front hose from the valve (see illustration). Disconnect the control valve wiring connector. Unscrew the bolts, displace the valve and detach it from the rear hose.

9 On CRF models remove the fuel tank (see Section 2). Displace the ECM (see illustration 6.56b). Disconnect the control valve wiring connector (see illustration). Detach the hoses

15.9a Control valve wiring connector (arrowed)...

15.9b ...and hoses (arrowed) – CRF250

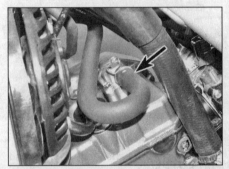

15.12a Detach the hose (arrowed – CRF shown)

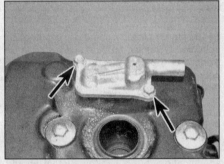

15.12b Reed valve cover bolts (arrowed)

15.12c Remove the valve from the housing

from the valve (see illustration). Unscrew the bolts and remove the valve.

10 Installation is the reverse of removal.

Reed valve

11 On CBR models remove the fairing right-hand side panel (see Chapter 7). On CRF models remove the fuel tank covers (see Chapter 7).

12 Release the clamp and detach the air hose from the reed valve cover (see illustration). Unscrew the bolts and remove the cover (see illustration). Remove the reed valve and the

baseplate, noting which way around they fit (see illustration).

13 Gently push the reed off its seat from the underside to check it is not stuck (see illustration). Release it and make sure there is no gap between it and its seat (see illustration). Check the condition of the rubber around the valve. Replace the valve with a new one if necessary.

14 Installation is the reverse of removal. Make sure the reed valve components and housing are clean and free of carbon deposits, and that the base plate and valve seat correctly.

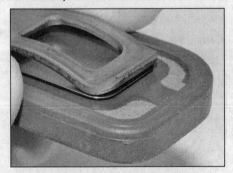

15.13a Make sure the reed is not stuck when pushed from the underside...

15.13b ...and check there is no gap when released

16 Evaporative emission control (EVAP) system

Note: *This system is fitted to US models only.*

General information

1 The evaporative emission control system (EVAP) is fitted to minimise the escape of fuel vapour into the atmosphere. The fuel tank is sealed and a charcoal canister collects the fuel vapours generated when the motorcycle is parked and stores them until they can be cleared from the canister, via the control valve, into the throttle body intake tract to be burned by the engine during normal combustion. The purge control valve for the fuel tank vapour is opened and closed by the ECM.

2 The valve should be tested if there is a problem starting the engine when it is hot.

Testing

Purge control valve

3 Remove the valve (see below).

4 Check the operation of the control valve by blowing through the inlet (canister hose) union – air should not flow through the valve and out the outlet hose union. Connect battery

voltage (12 volts) across the valve terminals and repeat the check – air should flow through the valve if it is functioning correctly.

5 If an ohmmeter is available, check the resistance of the control valve windings and compare the reading obtained to that given in the Specifications. Replace the valve with a new one if the reading differs.

Charcoal canister

6 No testing of the canister is possible, if it is thought to be faulty a new one must be installed.

Component renewal

Purge control valve

7 On CBR models raise the fuel tank (see Section 2) – the valve is on the left-hand side of the air filter housing. Disconnect the wiring connector and hoses from the valve, noting which fits where. Undo the screw and remove the valve. If required unscrew the bolts and remove the valve from the bracket.

8 On CRF models remove the canister (see below). Unscrew the nut and remove the valve.

9 Installation is the reverse of removal.

Charcoal canister

10 On CBR models remove the air filter housing (see Section 3) – the canister is on the front. Disconnect the hoses, noting which fits where. Remove the canister.

11 On CRF models the canister is behind the engine. Disconnect the hoses, noting which fits where. Unscrew the canister bracket bolts, displace the canister and disconnect the control valve wiring connector.

12 Installation is the reverse of removal. On CRF models make sure the hole in each bracket locates over the pin on the frame.

17 Ignition system check

⚠️ *Warning: The energy levels in electronic systems can be very high. On no account should the ignition be switched on whilst the plug or plug cap is being held. Shocks from the HT circuit can be most unpleasant. Secondly, it is vital that the engine is not turned over or run with the plug cap removed, and that the plug is soundly earthed (grounded) when the system is checked for a spark. The ignition system components can be seriously damaged if the HT circuit becomes isolated.*

1 As no means of adjustment is available, any failure of the system can be traced to failure of a system component or a simple wiring fault. Of the two possibilities, the latter is by far the most likely. In the event of failure, check the system in a logical fashion, as described below.

2 On CBR125 models remove the fairing right-hand side panel (see Chapter 7). On CBR250 models remove the fairing side panels (see Chapter 7), then displace the radiator from its mounts and move it forwards

(see Chapter 3) – there is no need to drain the cooling system or detach any hoses. On CRF models remove the fuel tank left-hand cover (see Chapter 7), then detach the PAIR system hose from the reed valve cover **(see illustration 15.12a)**. On 250 models clean the area around the plug cap seal to prevent any dirt falling into the spark plug channel.

3 Pull the cap off the spark plug **(see illustration 18.9b or 18.10a or 18.11a)**. Fit a spare spark plug that is known to be good into the cap and lay the plug against the cylinder head with the threads contacting it. If necessary, hold the spark plug with an insulated tool.

⚠️ *Warning: Do not remove the spark plug from the engine to perform this check – atomised fuel being pumped out of the open spark plug hole could ignite, causing severe injury! Make sure the plug is securely held against the engine – if it is not earthed when the engine is turned over, the ECM could be damaged.*

Check that the transmission is in neutral, then set the kill switch to RUN turn the ignition switch ON, and turn the engine over on the starter motor. If the system is in good condition a regular, fat blue spark should be evident at the plug electrodes. If the spark appears thin or yellowish, or is non-existent, further investigation will be necessary. Turn the ignition off and repeat the test for the other spark plugs.

4 The ignition system must be able to produce a spark that is capable of jumping a particular size gap – Honda do not give a specification, but a healthy system should produce a spark capable of jumping at least 6 mm. Simple ignition spark gap testing tools are commercially available – follow the manufacturer's instructions, and check each spark plug **(see illustration)**.

5 If the test results are good the entire ignition system can be considered good. If the spark appears thin or yellowish, or is non-existent, further investigation is necessary.

6 Ignition faults can be divided into two categories, namely those where the ignition system has failed completely, and those that are due to a partial failure. The likely faults are listed below, starting with the most probable source of failure. Work through the list systematically, referring to the relevant

section or to Chapter 1 or 8 for full details of the necessary checks and tests, and to the *Wiring Diagrams* at the end of Chapter 8. **Note:** *Before checking the following items ensure that the battery is fully charged and that all fuses are in good condition.*

  a) Loose, corroded or damaged wiring connections, broken or shorted wiring between any of the component parts of the ignition system (Chapter 8).
  b) Loose or faulty HT lead or spark plug cap (Section 18).
  c) Faulty spark plug, dirty, worn or corroded plug electrodes, or incorrect gap between electrodes (Chapter 1).
  d) Faulty ignition switch (Chapter 8).
  e) Faulty neutral, clutch or sidestand switch, or safety circuit diodes (Chapter 8).
  f) Faulty CKP sensor or damaged trigger (Section 6).
  g) Faulty ignition coil (Section 18).
  h) Faulty engine control module (ECM) (Section 6).

7 If the above checks don't reveal the cause of the problem, have the ignition system tested by a Honda dealer.

18 Ignition coil

Coil resistance check

1 Disconnect the battery negative (–) lead (see Chapter 8).

2 Remove the coil (see below).

3 Check the coil and its wiring visually for loose or damaged connectors and terminals, cracks and other damage.

4 To check the condition of the primary windings, set a multimeter to the ohms x 1 scale. Connect the meter probes to the primary terminals on the coil and measure the resistance **(see illustration)**. If the reading obtained is not as given in the Specifications, it is likely that the coil is defective.

5 To check the resistance of the secondary windings, set the meter to the K-ohm scale. Connect one meter probe to the contact in the spark plug cap and the other to one of the primary circuit terminals and measure the

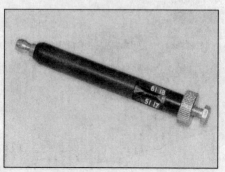

17.4 Ignition spark gap testing tool

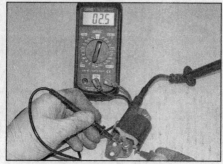

18.4 Primary winding test

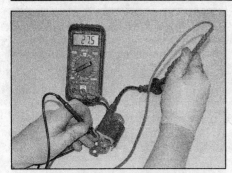

18.5a Secondary winding test

18.5b Unscrew the cap from the lead and test the coil again

18.5c Testing the plug cap

resistance (see illustration). If the reading obtained is not as given in the Specifications, unscrew the plug cap and test the coil again, this time inserting the probe into the end of the HT lead (see illustration). If the reading obtained is not as given in the Specifications (resistance with no cap) it is likely the coil is defective. If the reading is good check the resistance of the plug cap, and if that is as specified replace the coil with a new one, if not replace the plug cap with a new one (see illustration).

Coil peak voltage check

Special tool: Honda specify a peak voltage adapter (Honda pt. no. 07HGJ-0020100) plus an aftermarket digital multimeter having an impedance of 10 M-ohm/DCV minimum for a complete test of the coil (see Step 7).

6 If a peak voltage adapter is available the coil's primary peak voltage can be checked.

Disconnect the plug cap, fit a spare plug into it and earth the plug against the cylinder head. Leaving the primary wires connected, connect the peak voltage adaptor positive probe to the pink/blue (CBR125), light green (CBR250) or green/red (CRF models) primary terminal of the coil, and connect the negative probe to earth. Make sure the engine is in neutral. Crank the engine over on the starter motor and note the peak voltage registered on the meter – it should be above the minimum given in the Specifications at the beginning of this Chapter.

Removal and installation

7 Disconnect the battery negative (–) lead (see Chapter 8).

8 On CBR125 models remove the fairing right-hand side panel (see Chapter 7) and raise or remove the fuel tank as preferred (see Section 2). Disconnect the primary circuit wiring connectors from the coil, making a note

of which fits where (see illustration). Pull the cap off the spark plug (see illustration). Unscrew the coil mounting bolts and remove the coil, noting the shaped double-washers.

9 On CBR250 models remove the fairing side panels (see Chapter 7) and the fuel tank (see Section 2), then displace the radiator from its mounts and move it forwards (see Chapter 3) – there is no need to drain the cooling system or detach any hoses. Clean the area around the plug cap seal to prevent any dirt falling into the spark plug channel. Pull the cap off the spark plug (see illustration). Release the wiring clips from the coil bracket (see illustration). Unscrew the coil bracket bolts and displace the coil assembly, then disconnect the primary circuit wiring connectors, making a note of which fits where. If required unscrew the coil mounting bolts and remove the coil from the bracket, noting the shaped double-washers (see illustration).

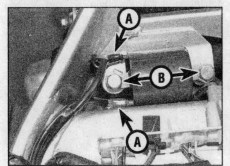

18.8a Primary circuit connectors (A), coil mounting bolts (B) – CBR125

18.8b Pull the cap off the plug – CBR125

18.9a Pull the cap off the plug – CBR250

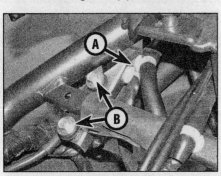

18.9b Release the clips (A), then unscrew the bolts (B)...

18.9c ...and disconnect the wiring – CBR250

18.9d Coil mounting bolts (arrowed) – CBR250

18.10a Pull the cap off the plug – CRF250

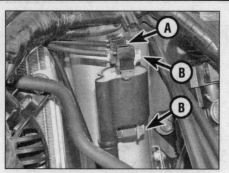

18.10b Primary circuit connectors (A), coil mounting bolts (B) – CRF250

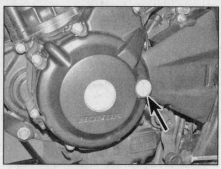

19.4 Timing inspection cap (arrowed) – 250 shown

10 On CRF models remove the fuel tank left-hand cover (see Chapter 7). Detach the PAIR system hose from the reed valve cover **(see illustration 15.12a)**. Clean the area around the plug cap seal to prevent any dirt falling into the spark plug channel. Pull the cap off the spark plug **(see illustration)**. Disconnect the primary circuit wiring connectors from the coil, making a note of which fits where **(see illustration)**. Release the HT lead from the guide. Unscrew the coil mounting bolts and remove the coil, noting the shaped double-washers.

11 Installation is the reverse of removal.

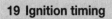
19 Ignition timing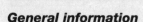

General information

1 Since no provision exists for adjusting the ignition timing and since no component is subject to mechanical wear, there is no need for regular checks: only if investigating a fault such as a loss of power or a misfire, should the ignition timing be checked.

2 The ignition timing is checked dynamically (engine running) using a stroboscopic lamp. The inexpensive neon lamps should be adequate in theory, but in practice may produce a pulse of such low intensity that the timing mark remains indistinct. If possible, one of the more precise xenon tube lamps should be used, powered by an external source of the appropriate voltage. **Note:** *Do not use the machine's own battery, as an incorrect reading may result from stray impulses within the machine's electrical system.*

Check

3 Warm the engine up to normal operating temperature, then stop it.
4 Unscrew the timing inspection cap from the alternator cover on the left-hand side of the engine **(see illustration)**.
5 The mark on the timing rotor that indicates the firing point at idle speed is an 'F'. The static timing mark with which this should align is the notch in the inspection hole.

 HAYNES HiNT *The timing marks can be highlighted with white paint to make them more visible under the stroboscope light.*

6 Connect the timing light to the spark plug lead as described in the manufacturer's instructions.
7 Start the engine and aim the light at the inspection hole.
8 With the machine idling at the specified speed, the 'F' mark should align with the static timing mark.
9 Slowly increase the engine speed whilst observing the 'F' mark. The mark should appear to move, increasing in relation to the engine speed until it reaches full advance (no identification mark).
10 As already stated, there is no means of adjustment of the ignition timing on these machines. If the ignition timing is incorrect, or suspected of being incorrect, one of the ignition system components is at fault, and the system must be tested as described in the preceding Sections of this Chapter.
11 Fit the timing inspection cap using a new O-ring if required, and smear the O-ring and the cap threads with clean oil. Tighten the cap to the torque setting specified at the beginning of the Chapter.

Chapter 5
Frame and suspension

Contents

Degrees of difficulty

Easy, suitable for novice with little experience	**Fairly easy,** suitable for beginner with some experience	**Fairly difficult,** suitable for competent DIY mechanic	**Difficult,** suitable for experienced DIY mechanic	**Very difficult,** suitable for expert DIY or professional

Specifications

Front forks

Fork oil type	Honda Ultra 10W suspension fluid or equivalent 10W fork oil
Fork oil capacity	
CBR125	221 ± 2.5 cc
CBR250	331 ± 2.5 cc
CRF250L	
Right fork	658 ± 2.5 cc
Left fork.	683 ± 2.5 cc
CRF250M	
Right fork	633 ± 2.5 cc
Left fork.	683 ± 2.5 cc
Fork oil level	
CBR125	121 mm
CBR250	150 mm
CRF250L	
Right fork	122 mm
Left fork.	38 mm
CRF250M	
Right fork	142 mm
Left fork.	38 mm
Fork spring free length (min)	
CBR125	
Standard	422.4 mm
Service limit	414.0 mm
CBR250	
Standard.	421.8 mm
CRF250L/M	
Standard	575.0 mm
Fork tube runout limit	0.2 mm

Steering head bearings

Bearing pre-load (see text)
CBR250 . . . . 15.7 to 24.5 N
CRF250. . . . . 10.6 to 21.2 N

Torque settings

Brake/clutch lever pivot or screw bolt . . . . 1 Nm
Brake/clutch lever pivot nut . . . . 6 Nm
Fork damper rod bolt (CBR models) . . . . 20 Nm
Fork damper cartridge bolt (CRF models) . . . . 20 Nm
Fork top bolt
CBR125 . . . . 23 Nm
CBR250 . . . . 22 Nm
CRF250. . . . . 35 Nm
Fork clamp bolts
Top yoke bolts
CBR125 . . . . 23 Nm
CBR250 . . . . 22 Nm
CRF250. . . . . 32 Nm
Bottom yoke bolts
CBR125 . . . . 27 Nm
CBR250 and CRF250 . . . . 32 Nm
Front brake caliper mounting bolts . . . . 30 Nm
Handlebar clamp bolts
CBR125 . . . . 26 Nm
CBR250 . . . . 27 Nm
Rider's footrest bracket bolts
CBR125 . . . . 26 Nm
CBR250 . . . . 27 Nm
Shock absorber bolts/nuts
CBR125
Top bolt. . . . . 39 Nm
Bottom bolt/nut. . . . . 44 Nm
CBR250 . . . . 36 Nm
CRF250
Top bolt/nut. . . . . 54 Nm
Bottom bolt/nut. . . . . 44 Nm
Rear sub-frame bolts/nuts . . . . 27 Nm
Sidestand pivot bolt . . . . 10 Nm
Sidestand pivot bolt nut . . . . 30 Nm
Steering head bearing adjuster nut
CBR125
Initial setting . . . . 27 Nm
Final setting . . . . 1 Nm
CBR250
Initial setting . . . . 39 Nm
Final setting . . . . 29 Nm
CRF250
Initial setting . . . . 29.5 Nm
Final setting . . . . 6.5 Nm
Steering stem nut
CBR125 . . . . 88 Nm
CBR250 and CRF250 . . . . 103 Nm
Suspension linkage bolt nuts
CBR250
Linkage rod-to-frame . . . . 75 Nm
Linkage rod-to-linkage arm . . . . 75 Nm
Linkage arm-to-shock absorber. . . . . 36 Nm
Linkage arm-to-swingarm. . . . . 75 Nm
CRF250
Linkage rod-to-frame . . . . 44 Nm
Linkage rod-to-linkage arm . . . . 44 Nm
Linkage arm-to-shock absorber. . . . . 44 Nm
Linkage arm-to-swingarm. . . . . 74 Nm
Swingarm pivot bolt nut
CBR125 . . . . 80 Nm
CBR250 and CRF250 . . . . 88 Nm

1 General information

CBR models have a twin-spar steel frame that uses the engine as a stressed member. CRF models have a twin-spar steel cradle frame.

On CBR models front suspension is by a pair of conventional oil-damped telescopic forks. CRF models have upside-down forks, with a cartridge damper and no spring in the left-hand fork, and a damper rod and spring in the right-hand fork.

At the rear, a box-section swingarm acts on a single shock absorber, on 250 models via a three-way linkage. The swingarm pivots through the frame. The shock absorber is adjustable for spring pre-load on 250 models.

2 Frame inspection and repair

1 The frame should not require attention unless accident damage has occurred. In most cases, fitting a new frame is the only satisfactory remedy for such damage. A few frame specialists have the jigs and other equipment necessary for straightening frames to the required standard of accuracy, but even then there is no simple way of assessing to what extent the frame may have been over stressed.

2 After a high mileage, the frame should be examined closely for signs of cracking or splitting at the welded joints, and for signs of penetrating rust. Loose engine mounting bolts can cause ovaling or fracturing of the mounting points. Minor damage can often be repaired by welding, depending on the extent and nature of the damage.

3 Remember that a frame that is out of alignment will cause handling problems. If, as the result of an accident, misalignment is suspected, it will be necessary to strip the machine completely so the frame can be thoroughly checked.

3 Footrests, brake pedal and gearchange lever

Footrests

1 On CBR125 models remove the split pin and washer from the bottom of the footrest pivot pin, then withdraw the pivot pin and remove the footrest (see illustration). Note the washer against the inner end of the rubber.

2 On CBR250 models remove the split pin and washer from the bottom of the footrest pivot pin, then withdraw the pivot pin and remove the footrest. On the rider's footrests, note the fitting of the return spring (see illustration). On the passenger footrests note the washer against the inner end of the rubber (see illustration).

3 On CRF250 models remove the split pin and washer from the bottom of the footrest pivot pin, then withdraw the pivot pin and remove the footrest. On the rider's footrests, note the fitting of the return spring (see illustration). On the passenger footrests note the plastic retaining clip (see illustration).

4 On CBR models you can renew the footrest rubbers – for the rider's footrests unscrew the bolt(s) on the underside to release the rubber, and note the fitting of the baseplate on 125 models and the setting plate on 250 models (see illustration 3.1). The passenger footrest rubbers are a sliding fit on the peg, with the outer end locating around the plate (see illustration 3.2b).

5 Installation is the reverse of removal. Apply a small amount of grease to the pivot pin. Use new split pins.

Brake pedal

CBR models

6 Unscrew the footrest bracket mounting bolts and displace the bracket so that you can access the back (see illustration).

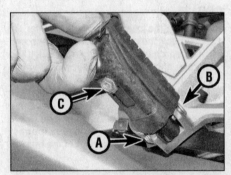

3.1 Split pin and washer (A), pivot pin (B), footrest rubber bolt (C)

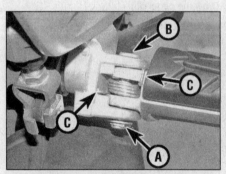

3.2a Split pin and washer (A), pivot pin (B), return spring ends (C) – rider's footrests

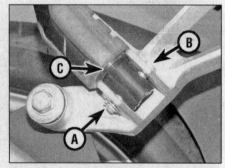

3.2b Split pin and washer (A), pivot pin (B), washer (C) – passenger footrests

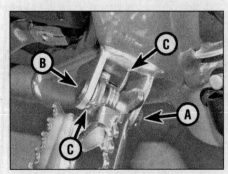

3.3a Split pin and washer (A), pivot pin (B), return spring ends (C) – rider's footrests

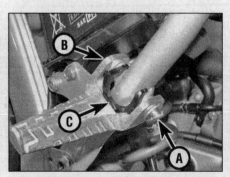

3.3b Split pin and washer (A), pivot pin (B), washer (C) – passenger footrests

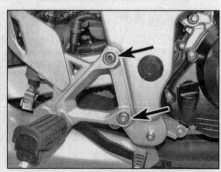

3.6 Footrest bracket bolts (arrowed)

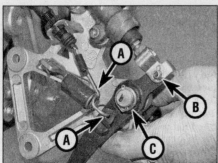

3.7a Springs (A), split pin (B) and clevis pin, pedal split pin (C) – 125 models

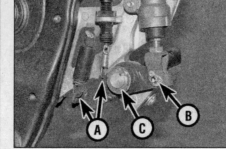

3.7b Springs (A), split pin (B) and clevis pin, pedal circlip (C) – 250 models

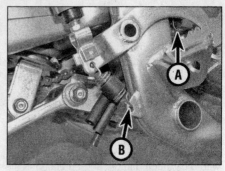

3.11 Brake light switch spring (A), pedal return spring (B)

7 Unhook the brake light switch spring and the pedal return spring **(see illustrations)**.

8 Remove the split pin from the clevis pin securing the brake pedal to the master cylinder pushrod, then withdraw the clevis pin and detach the pushrod from the pedal.

9 Release the split pin or circlip securing the brake pedal and remove the thrust washer. Slide the pedal off its pivot.

10 Installation is the reverse of removal, noting the following:

● Clean any old grease off the pedal and pivot, then apply fresh grease.

● On 125 models use a new split pin to secure the pedal on the pivot.

● On 250 models make sure the circlip locates correctly in the groove, and use a new one if the old one deformed when removed.

● Use a new split pin on the master cylinder pushrod clevis pin.

● Make sure the springs are correctly fitted.

● Tighten the footrest bracket bolts to the torque setting specified at the beginning of the Chapter.

● Check the operation of the rear brake light switch (see Chapter 1).

CRF models

11 Unhook the brake light switch spring and the pedal return spring **(see illustration)**.

12 Remove the split pin from the clevis pin securing the brake pedal to the master cylinder pushrod, then withdraw the clevis pin and detach the pushrod from the pedal **(see illustration)**.

13 Withdraw the stopper pin securing the brake pedal and remove the thrust washer. Draw the pedal out.

14 Check the condition of the seals in the pedal pivot bore – Honda specify to replace them with new ones.

15 Installation is the reverse of removal, noting the following:

● If removed fit new seals into the pivot bore with the marked side on each facing out. Smear the seal lips with grease.

● Clean any old grease off the pedal and pivot, then apply fresh grease.

● If required use a new stopper pin to secure the pedal.

● Use a new split pin on the master cylinder pushrod clevis pin.

● Make sure the springs are correctly fitted.

● Check the operation of the rear brake light switch (see Chapter 1).

Gearchange lever and linkage

CBR125

16 Remove the lower fairing (see Chapter 7).

17 Pull back the rubber boot from each end of the gearchange lever linkage rod, then straighten and remove the split pins, remove the washers, and detach the rod from the lever and the arm **(see illustration)**. New split pins should be used.

18 Remove the circlip, washer and wave washer securing the lever in the footrest bracket, then slide the lever out of the bracket **(see illustrations)**.

19 Make a mark where the slot in the gearchange linkage arm aligns with the shaft **(see illustration)**. Unscrew the linkage arm pinch bolt and slide the arm off the shaft.

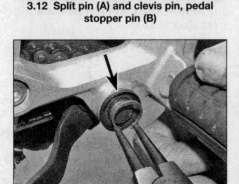

3.12 Split pin (A) and clevis pin, pedal stopper pin (B)

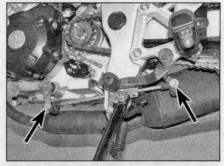

3.17 Remove the split pin and washer (arrowed) from each end of the rod

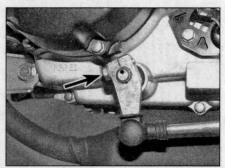

3.19 Mark the alignment then unscrew the bolt (arrowed)

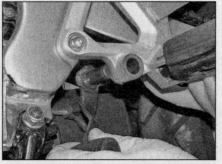

3.18a Release the circlip and remove the washers (arrowed)...

3.18b ...and draw the pedal out

3.21 Slacken the locknuts (arrowed) and unscrew the rod

3.22 Note the alignment then unscrew the bolt (arrowed)

3.23 Gearchange lever bolt (arrowed)

20 Installation is the reverse of removal, noting the following:
● Make sure the rubber boots for each end of the linkage are in good condition and replace them with new ones if necessary.
● Apply grease to the pivot section on the lever.
● Slide the lever into the bracket, then slide the wave washer onto the end of the pivot section, then the thrust washer, then fit the circlip, making sure it locates in the its groove (see illustration 3.18b and a).
● Align the slit in the linkage arm clamp with the mark made on the shaft (see illustration 3.19).
● Use new split pins to secure the linkage rod to the lever and arm and bend their ends round (see illustration 3.17).

CBR250

21 Counter-hold the gearchange lever linkage rod using a spanner on its flats and slacken the locknuts (see illustration). Unscrew the rod and separate it from the lever and the arm – the rod is reverse-threaded on one end and so will simultaneously unscrew from both lever and arm when turned in the one direction. Note how far the rod is threaded onto the lever and arm as this determines the height of the lever relative to the footrest.
22 Note the alignment of the slot in the gearchange linkage arm with the punch mark on the shaft (see illustration). Unscrew the linkage arm pinch bolt and slide the arm off the shaft.
23 Unscrew the gearchange lever bolt and

3.24 Lever pivot nut (arrowed)

remove the washer, then slide the lever off its pivot (see illustration).
24 If required unscrew the nut on the inside of the footrest bracket and remove the pivot (see illustration).
25 Installation is the reverse of removal, noting the following:
● Align the flat on the pivot with that in the footrest bracket.
● Apply grease to the pivot.
● Align the slit in the linkage arm clamp with the mark on the shaft (see illustration 3.22).
● Adjust the gear lever height as required by screwing the linkage rod in or out of the lever and arm. Tighten the locknuts securely (see illustration 3.21).

CRF250

26 On CRF models note the alignment of the

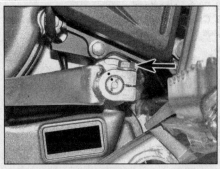

3.26 Note the alignment then unscrew the bolt (arrowed)

punch marks on the gearchange lever and shaft (see illustration). Unscrew the lever pinch bolt and slide the arm off the shaft.
27 Installation is the reverse of removal. Make sure the punch marks align.

4 Sidestand

Removal

1 Support the bike using an auxiliary stand.
2 Displace the sidestand switch (see Chapter 8) – there is no need to disconnect its wiring or remove it completely, just let it hang from its wiring.
3 Carefully unhook and remove the stand springs (see illustration).

4.3a Sidestand springs (A) and pivot bolt nut (B) – CBR125

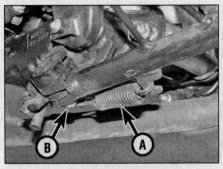

4.3b Sidestand springs (A) and pivot bolt nut (B) – CBR250

4.3c Sidestand springs (A) and pivot bolt nut (B) – CRF250

4 Unscrew the nut from the pivot bolt **(see illustration 4.3a, b or c)**. Unscrew the pivot bolt and remove the stand.

Installation

5 Apply grease to the pivot bolt shank and tighten the bolt to the torque setting specified at the beginning of the Chapter. On CRF models now unscrew the bolt a quarter turn.
6 Fit the nut, then counter-hold the bolt and tighten the nut to the specified torque.
7 Reconnect the springs and check that they hold the stand securely up when not in use – an accident is almost certain to occur if the stand extends while the machine is in motion.
8 Fit the sidestand switch.
9 Check the operation of the stand and switch (see Chapter 1).

5 Handlebars and levers

Note: *If required, for example if the top yoke is being removed to access the steering head bearings, the handlebars can be displaced without detaching any of the assemblies from them – just release the cables, hose and wiring from any ties and guides that restrict freedom of movement as required according to model* **(see illustration 9.15b).**
1 As a precaution, cover the fuel tank and body panels with protective rag – this will prevent the possibility of damage should a tool slip.

5.2a Disconnect the wiring connectors (arrowed)

Handlebars – CBR models

Right handlebar removal

2 Disconnect the wires from the brake light switch **(see illustration)**. Unscrew the two master cylinder assembly clamp bolts and position the assembly clear of the handlebar, wrapping it in some rag, and making sure no strain is placed on the hydraulic hose **(see illustration)**. Keep the master cylinder reservoir upright to prevent possible fluid leakage.
3 Undo the handlebar end-weight retaining screw, then remove the weight from the end of the handlebar **(see illustration)**.
4 On 125 models undo the two handlebar switch housing screws and separate the halves **(see illustration)**. Undo the two throttle housing screws and separate the halves. Release the cable end from the pulley, then slide the twistgrip off **(see illustration)**.

5.2b Master cylinder clamp bolts (arrowed)

5 On 250 models undo the two handlebar switch/throttle housing screws and separate the halves **(see illustration)**. The throttle pulley can be slid off the end of the handlebar with the cable still attached to it and the housing after the handlebar has been lifted off the fork.
6 Remove the handlebar stopper ring from the groove in the top of the fork, using a small screwdriver to ease it out **(see illustration 5.10a)**. Slacken the handlebar clamp bolt, then ease the handlebar up and off the fork **(see illustrations 5.10b and c)**. On 250 models slide the throttle twistgrip and switch housing assembly off the handlebar.

Left handlebar removal

7 Disconnect the wires from the clutch switch **(see illustration)**. Unscrew the two clutch lever bracket clamp bolts and position the assembly clear of the handlebar, wrapping it in some rag **(see illustration)**.

5.3 Handlebar end-weight screw (arrowed)

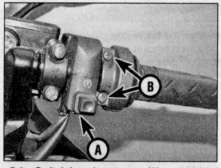

5.4a Switch housing screws (A) are on the underside, throttle pulley housing screws (B)

5.4b Detach the cable end and slide the twistgrip off

5.5 The front screw is shorter than the rear

5.7a Disconnect the wiring connectors (arrowed)

5.7b Clutch lever bracket clamp bolts (arrowed)

5.8 Switch housing screws (arrowed)

5.10a Remove the stopper ring...

5.10b ...unscrew the clamp bolt (arrowed)...

8 Undo the two handlebar switch housing screws and separate the halves **(see illustration)**. On 250 models note how the housing locates around the cap.

9 Undo the handlebar end-weight retaining screw, then remove the weight from the end of the handlebar **(see illustration 5.3)**. If required remove the grip from the left-hand end – you may need to insert a suitable tool (that won't scratch the handlebar) between the grip and the top of the handlebar from the inner end, then squirt some lubricant (such as WD40) in the gap and allow it to work its way round by moving the tool around. If the grip has been glued on, you will probably have to slit it with a knife to remove it, which means replacing it with a new one. On 250 models slide the switch housing cap off after removing the grip.

10 Remove the handlebar stopper ring from the groove in the top of the fork, using a small screwdriver to ease it out **(see illustration)**. Slacken the handlebar clamp bolt, then ease the handlebar up and off the fork **(see illustrations)**. If required, slide the throttle twistgrip and switch housing assembly off the handlebar.

Handlebar weights

11 If a new handlebar is being installed, you need to transfer the inner weight to the new bar – to do this, reinstall the end-weight and tighten its screw. Squirt some lubricant (such as WD40) into the inner weight retainer tab hole, then press down on the tab using a screwdriver and twist and pull the end-weight, drawing the inner weight assembly out **(see illustration)**. Remove the end-weight and discard the retainer as a new one should be used. Check the condition of the rubbers on the inner weight and fit new ones if they are damaged, deformed or deteriorated.

Installation

12 Installation is the reverse of removal, noting the following.
● On 250 models slide the throttle twistgrip and cable housing assembly onto the right handlebar before fitting the handlebar onto the fork. Slide the switch housing cap onto the left handlebar before fitting the grip.
● When fitting the handlebar onto the fork, slide it down and seat it on the top yoke,

5.10c ... and ease the handlebar up and off the fork

locating the lug on the underside in the gap between the clamping sections of the top yoke **(see illustration 5.12a)** – the lug is not a close fit, so pull the bar back so the rear face of the lug butts against the rear section of the yoke, ensuring each side is positioned exactly the same. Tighten the handlebar clamp bolts to the torque setting specified at the beginning of the Chapter. Fit the stopper rings into their grooves **(see illustration 5.10a)**.
● When installing the handlebar inner weights, locate the tab on the retainer in the hole in the handlebar.
● When installing the handlebar end-weights, align the boss with the cut-out on the inner weight inside the handlebar. Clean the threads of the end-weight retaining screws and apply a suitable non-permanent thread locking compound. If new grips are

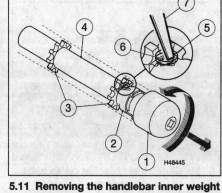

5.11 Removing the handlebar inner weight
1 End-weight
2 Retainer
3 Rubbers
4 Inner weight
5 Hole in handlebar
6 Retainer tab
7 Screwdriver

being fitted, secure them using a suitable adhesive.
● Make sure the front brake master cylinder and clutch lever bracket clamps are installed with the UP mark facing up **(see illustration 5.2b and 5.7b)**, and with the clamp mating surfaces aligned with the punch mark on the top of the handlebar **(see illustration 5.12b)**. Tighten the top clamp bolt first.
● Make sure the pin in one half of each switch/throttle housing locates in its hole in the handlebar. On 250 models make sure the left switch housing locates correctly

5.12a Locate the lug in the gap to align the handlebar

5.12b Align the clamp mating surfaces with the punch mark (arrowed)

5.15a Disconnect the wiring connectors (arrowed)

5.15b Master cylinder clamp bolts (arrowed)

5.16a Disconnect the wiring connectors (arrowed)

5.16b Clutch lever bracket clamp bolts (arrowed)

5.17 Switch housing screws (arrowed)

around the end cap. Tighten the upper or front screw first, then the lower or rear screw.

● Do not forget to reconnect the front brake light switch and clutch switch wiring connectors (see illustrations 5.2a and 5.7a).

● Check the operation of the throttle and clutch, and adjust cable freeplay as required (see Chapter 1).

Handlebar – CRF models

Removal

13 Remove the mirrors (see Chapter 7).
14 Release the cable-ties securing the wiring to the handlebar.

15 Disconnect the wires from the brake light switch (see illustration). Unscrew the two master cylinder assembly clamp bolts and position the assembly clear of the handlebar, making sure no strain is placed on the hydraulic hose (see illustration). Keep the master cylinder reservoir upright to prevent possible fluid leakage.
16 Disconnect the wires from the clutch switch (see illustrations). Unscrew the two clutch lever assembly clamp bolts and position the assembly clear of the handlebar (see illustration).
17 Undo the right- and left-hand switch housing screws and detach the housings (see illustration).
18 Undo the throttle pulley housing screws

and detach the housing, leaving the cables connected.
19 If required remove the grip from the left-hand end – you may need to insert a suitable tool (that won't scratch the handlebar) between the grip and the top of the handlebar from the inner end, then squirt some lubricant (such as WD40) in the gap and allow it to work its way round by moving the tool around. If the grip has been glued on, you will probably have to slit it with a knife to remove it, which means replacing it with a new one.
20 Unscrew the handlebar clamp bolts, remove the clamps, and slide the bar out of the throttle pulley (see illustration).

Installation

21 Installation is the reverse of removal, noting the following.
● Smear some grease onto the throttle twistgrip sliding surface. Slide the throttle pulley housing onto the handlebar before fitting the handlebar onto the yoke.
● Align the punch mark on the back of the handlebar with the surface of the holder, and make sure the handlebar is central (see illustration 5.21a). Fit the handlebar clamps with the punch marks to the front (see illustration 5.21b). Tighten the front bolts first, then the rear.
● To fit new grips onto the throttle twistgrip and left handlebar, apply a suitable glue to each, making sure they are clean, then rotate the grip when in place to evenly

5.20 Handlebar clamp bolts (arrowed)

5.21a Align the punch mark (arrowed) as shown...

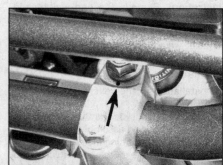

5.21b ...and make sure the mark (arrowed) on the clamp is to the front

5.21c Align the punch mark (arrowed) – clutch side

5.21d Align the punch mark (arrowed) – brake side

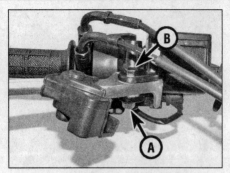

5.22 Front brake lever locknut (A) and pivot screw (B) – CRF250

distribute the glue. Allow the glue to fully dry before riding the bike.

● Fit the clutch lever bracket clamp mating surfaces aligned with the punch mark on the top of the handlebar (see illustration 5.21c). Tighten the top bolt first.
● Fit the front brake master cylinder clamp with the UP mark facing up (see illustration 5.15b) and with the clamp mating surfaces aligned with the punch mark on the top of the handlebar (see illustration 5.21d). Tighten the top bolt first.
● Make sure the pin in one half of each switch/throttle housing locates in its hole in the handlebar. Tighten the upper or front housing screw first, then the lower or rear.
● Do not forget to reconnect the front brake light switch and clutch switch wiring connectors (see illustrations 5.15a and 5.16a). Secure the wiring to the handlebars with cable-ties.
● Check the operation of the throttle and clutch, and adjust cable freeplay as required (see Chapter 1).

Levers – all models

22 To remove the front brake lever, undo the lever pivot bolt locknut, then unscrew the pivot bolt and remove the lever (see illustration).
23 To remove the clutch lever pull the rubber boot off the cable adjuster. Loosen the adjuster lockring then thread the adjuster into the bracket to provide freeplay in the cable (see illustration). Undo the lever pivot bolt

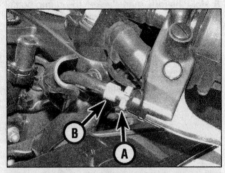

5.23a Slacken the lockring (A) and turn the adjuster (B) in

locknut, then undo the pivot screw or bolt (according to model) and remove the lever, detaching the cable nipple as you do (see illustration).
24 Installation is the reverse of removal. Apply silicone grease to the contact area between the front brake master cylinder pushrod tip and the brake lever. Apply lithium or molybdenum grease to the pivot shafts and the contact areas between the lever and its bracket. Tighten the pivot screw or bolt lightly (to the torque setting specified at the beginning of the Chapter if the correct tools are available), then hold it and tighten the locknut to the specified torque. Adjust clutch cable freeplay (see Chapter 1).

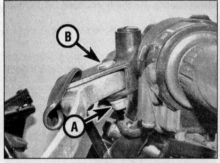

5.23b Clutch lever locknut (A) and pivot screw (B) – CBR models shown

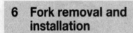

6 Fork removal and installation

Removal

1 On CBR models remove the fairing side panels (see Chapter 7). Displace the handlebars (See Section 5).
2 Remove the front wheel (see Chapter 6).
3 On CRF models displace the brake hose guides from the left-hand fork (see illustration). Remove the fork covers (see illustrations).
4 Unscrew the caliper mounting bolts and slide the caliper assembly off the disc (see

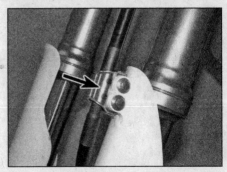

6.3a Displace the lower guide (arrowed)...

6.3b ...and the upper guides

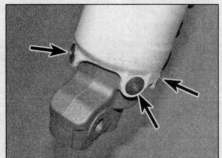

6.3c Fork cover bolts (arrowed)

**6.4a Caliper mounting bolts (arrowed) –
CBR models**

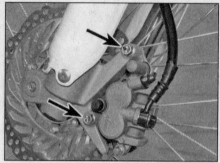

**6.4b Caliper mounting bolts (arrowed) –
CRF models**

**6.7a Fork clamp bolt (arrowed), top yoke –
CBR models**

illustrations). Tie the front brake caliper back
so it is out of the way.

5 On CBR models remove the front mudguard
(see Chapter 7).

6 Note the routing of all cables, hoses and
wiring around the forks, and on CBR models
release the cable-ties from them.

7 Working on one fork at a time, slacken
the fork clamp bolt(s) in the top yoke **(see
illustrations)**. If the fork is to be disassembled,
or if the fork oil is being changed, slacken the
fork top bolt now **(see illustration)**.

8 Hold the fork, then slacken the clamp bolt(s)
in the bottom yoke, and remove the fork by
twisting it and pulling it downwards **(see
illustrations)**.

> **HAYNES
> HINT** *If the fork legs are seized
> in the yokes, spray the area
> with penetrating oil and
> allow time for it to soak in
> before trying again.*

Installation

9 Remove all traces of dirt and corrosion from
the fork tube and in the yokes. Slide the fork
up through the bottom yoke and into the top
yoke, making sure all cables, hoses and wiring
are routed on the correct side of the fork **(see
illustration 6.8c)**.

10 On CBR125 models set the fork so the
joint between the inner tube and the top bolt
is 32 mm above the upper surface of the top
yoke **(see illustration)**. On CBR250 models

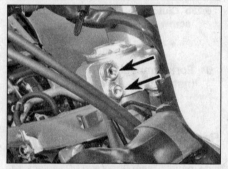

**6.7b Fork clamp bolts (arrowed), top yoke
– CRF models**

**6.7c Slacken the top bolt while the fork is
still held in the bottom yoke**

**6.8a Fork clamp bolt (arrowed), bottom
yoke – CBR models**

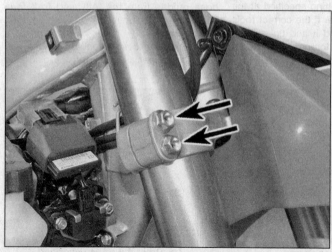

6.8b Fork clamp bolts (arrowed), bottom yoke – CRF models

6.8c Draw the fork down and out of the yokes

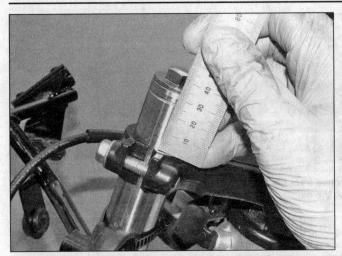

6.10a On CBR125 models set the fork at the correct height

6.10b On CBR250 models align the index line (arrowed) with the yoke

set the fork so the index line on the inner tube aligns with the upper surface of the top yoke **(see illustration)**. On CRF models set the fork so the joint between the outer tube and the top bolt is flush with the upper surface of the top yoke. On all models tighten the fork clamp bolt(s) in the bottom yoke to the torque setting specified at the beginning of the Chapter **(see illustration 6.8a or b)**.

11 If the fork has been dismantled or if the fork oil was changed, tighten the fork top bolt to the specified torque setting **(see illustration 6.7c)**.

12 Tighten the fork clamp bolt(s) in the top yoke to the specified torque setting **(see illustration 6.7a or b)**.

13 Slide the caliper assembly onto the disc making sure the pads locate correctly on each side **(see illustration 6.4a or b)**. Either fit the new caliper mounting bolts, or clean the threads of the original bolts and apply fresh thread locking compound, then tighten them to the torque setting specified at the beginning of the Chapter.

14 Install all remaining components in a reverse of removal. Check the operation of the front forks and brakes before taking the machine out on the road.

7 Fork oil change

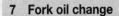

1 After a high mileage the fork oil will deteriorate and its damping and lubrication qualities will be impaired, there is however, no specific time or mileage interval for this. Always change the oil in both fork legs.

2 Remove the fork – make sure you loosen the top bolt while the leg is still clamped in the bottom yoke (see Section 6).

CBR models

3 Unscrew the fork top bolt from the top of

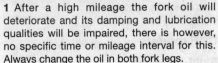

the inner tube – the bolt is under pressure from the fork spring, so use a ratchet tool so it does not need to be removed from the bolt as you unscrew it, and maintain some downward pressure on it, particularly as you come to the end of the threads, or alternatively hold the tool still and twist the fork tube to unthread it from the bolt **(see illustration)**.

4 Slide the inner tube down and remove the spacer, the spacer seat and the spring **(see illustrations)**.

5 Invert the fork leg over a suitable container and pump it several times to expel as much oil as possible **(see illustration)**. Support the fork upside down in the container for a while

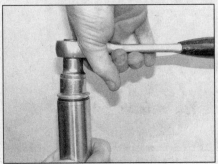

7.3 Thread the top bolt out of the tube

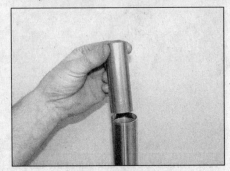

7.4a Remove the spacer...

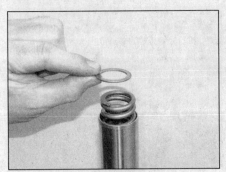

7.4b ...the spacer seat...

7.4c ...and the spring

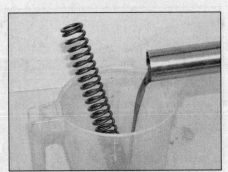

7.5 Drain the oil as described

7.6a Fill the fork slowly to prevent air bubbles and overfilling

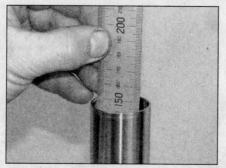

7.6b Measure the distance from the top of the tube to the oil

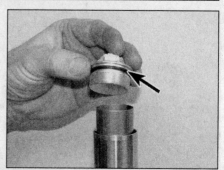

7.8 Check the O-ring (arrowed)

to allow it to drain, then pump the fork again. If the oil contains metal particles inspect the fork bushes for wear (see Section 8). Wipe any excess oil off the spring and spacer.

6 Stand the fork upright. Slowly pour in the specified quantity of the specified grade of fork oil **(see illustration)**. Now pump the fork slowly at least ten times to distribute the oil evenly and expel all air. Slide the inner tube down gently until it seats on the bottom. Measure the oil level from the top of the tube **(see illustration)**. Add or subtract oil until it is at the level specified at the beginning of this Chapter.

7 Pull the inner tube out, then fit the spring with the closer wound coils at the bottom, then fit the spacer seat and spacer **(see illustrations 7.4c, b and a)**.

8 If the top bolt O-ring is damaged or deteriorated fit a new one **(see illustration)**. Smear some fork oil onto the O-ring. Extend

the inner tube and fit the top bolt into it, compressing the spring as you do, and thread it in, making sure it does not cross-thread, keeping downward pressure on the spring, using a ratchet tool or by turning the tube while holding the bolt still, and tighten it as much as possible holding the inner tube by hand **(see illustration 7.3)**. **Note:** *Tighten the top bolt to the specified torque setting when the fork has been installed in the bike and is held in the bottom yoke, but before the top yoke clamp bolt is tightened.*

9 Install the fork (see Section 6).

CRF models

Right-hand fork

10 Unscrew the fork top bolt from the top of the outer tube – the bolt is under pressure from the fork spring, so use a ratchet tool so it does not need to be removed from the bolt as

you unscrew it, and maintain some downward pressure on it, particularly as you come to the end of the threads, or alternatively hold the tool still and twist the fork tube to unthread it from the bolt **(see illustration)**.

11 Invert the fork leg over a suitable container and pump it several times to expel as much oil as possible **(see illustration 7.21)**. Support the fork upside down in the container for a while to allow it to drain, then pump the fork again. If the oil contains metal particles inspect the fork bushes for wear (see Section 8). Wipe any excess oil off the spring and spacer.

12 Slide the outer tube down. Push down on the top bolt to compress the spring and hold it down while releasing the snap-ring from the groove in the top of the tube – due to the shape of the ring and its groove releasing it is tricky, and the best way is to slip a 0.15 to 0.18 mm feeler gauge blade behind the ring, then slowly release the spring so the spring seat pushes on the underside of the ring which will then ride up the feeler blade, then use a pointed tool to help release it all round and remove the top bolt/rod assembly **(see illustrations)**.

13 Remove the spring **(see illustration)**.

14 Stand the fork upright. Slowly pour in the specified quantity of the specified grade of fork oil **(see illustration)**. Now pump the fork slowly at least ten times to distribute the oil evenly and expel all air. Slide the outer tube down gently until it seats on the bottom, then leave it to stand for five minutes.

15 Measure the oil level from the top of the

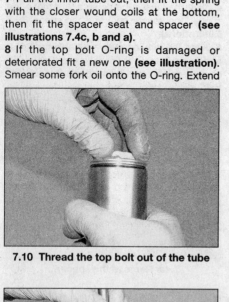

7.10 Thread the top bolt out of the tube

7.12a Release the snap-ring as described...

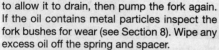

7.12b ...and remove the top bolt and rod assembly...

7.13 ...and the spring

7.14 Fill the fork slowly to prevent air bubbles and overfilling

7.15 Measure the distance from the top of the tube to the oil

7.17 Compress the spring and fit the snap-ring

7.20a Thread the top bolt out of the tube

7.20b Slacken the locknut and thread the top bolt off

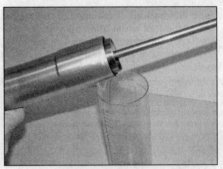

7.21 Drain the oil as described

tube **(see illustration)**. Add or subtract oil until it is at the level specified at the beginning of this Chapter.

16 Fit the spring with its tapered end at the top **(see illustration 7.13)**.

17 Insert the top bolt/rod assembly **(see illustration 7.12b)**. Push down on the top bolt to compress the spring and hold it down while fitting the snap-ring into its groove in the top of the tube, then slowly release the pressure **(see illustration)**.

18 If the top bolt O-ring is damaged or deteriorated fit a new one. Smear some fork oil onto the O-ring. Extend the outer tube and fit the top bolt into it, compressing the spring as you do, and thread it in, making sure it does not cross-thread, keeping downward pressure on the spring, using a ratchet tool or by turning the tube while holding the bolt still, and tighten it as much as possible holding the outer tube by hand **(see illustration 7.10)**. **Note:** *Tighten the top bolt to the specified torque setting when the fork has been installed in the bike and is held in the bottom yoke, but before the top yoke clamp bolt is tightened.*

19 Install the fork (see Section 6).

Left-hand fork

20 Unscrew the fork top bolt from the top of the outer tube **(see illustration)**. Counter-hold the fork top bolt and slacken the locknut underneath it, then thread the top bolt off the rod **(see illustration)**.

21 Invert the fork leg over a suitable container and pump it several times to expel as much

oil as possible **(see illustration)**. Support the fork upside down in the container for a while to allow it to drain, then pump the fork again. If the oil contains metal particles inspect the fork bushes for wear (see Section 8). Wipe any excess oil off the spring and spacer.

22 Stand the fork upright. Slowly pour in the specified quantity of the specified grade of fork oil **(see illustration)**. Now pump the fork slowly at least ten times to distribute the oil evenly and expel all air from the damper. Slide the outer tube down gently until it seats on the bottom, then leave it to stand for five minutes.

23 Measure the oil level from the top of the tube **(see illustration 7.15)**. Add or subtract oil until it is at the level specified at the beginning of this Chapter.

24 If the top bolt O-ring is damaged or

deteriorated fit a new one. Smear some fork oil onto the O-ring. Thread the locknut down to the bottom of the threads then screw the top bolt onto the rod until it seats **(see illustration)**. Counter-hold the top bolt and tighten the locknut up against it **(see illustration 7.20b)**. Fully extend the outer tube and thread the top bolt into it, making sure it does not cross-thread, and tighten it as much as possible holding the outer tube by hand **(see illustration 7.20a)**. **Note:** *Tighten the top bolt to the specified torque setting when the fork has been installed in the bike and is held in the bottom yoke, but before the top yoke clamp bolt is tightened.*

25 Install the fork (see Section 6).

8 Fork overhaul

1 Remove the fork – make sure you loosen the top bolt while the leg is still clamped in the bottom yoke (see Section 6). Always dismantle the fork legs separately to avoid interchanging parts and thus causing an accelerated rate of wear. Store all components in separate, clearly marked containers.

CBR125

Disassembly

2 Lay the fork flat on the bench. Hold the fork down and slacken then lightly retighten the damper rod bolt in the base of the fork

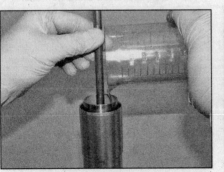

7.22 Fill the fork slowly to prevent air bubbles and overfilling

7.24 Fit the top bolt onto the rod

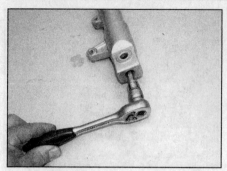

8.2 Slacken the damper rod bolt

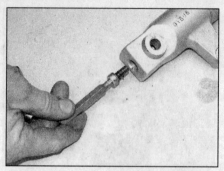

8.4a Unscrew and remove the damper rod bolt...

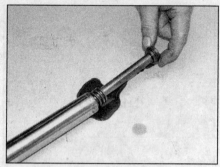

8.4b ...then tip the damper out

(see illustration). If the damper rod rotates inside the fork whilst attempting to unscrew the bolt, compress the fork so that the spring exerts pressure on the rod whilst the bolt is unscrewed. Alternatively, if available use an air wrench.

3 Refer to Section 7, Steps 3 to 5 and drain the oil form the fork.

4 Remove the damper rod bolt and its sealing washer from the bottom of the fork (see illustration). A new sealing washer must be used on reassembly. Tip the damper rod out of the fork tube (see illustration).

5 Carefully prise out the dust seal from the top of the outer tube (see illustration). Withdraw the inner tube from the outer tube, then tip the damper rod oil lock piece out (see illustrations). A new dust seal must be used – it comes with the oil seal as a set.

6 Carefully remove the retaining clip, taking care not to scratch the surface of the inner tube (see illustration).

7 Carefully prise the oil seal from the outer tube using either a seal hook or an internal puller with slide-hammer attachment (see illustrations). If a seal hook is used take great care not to damage the rim of the tube.

Inspection

8 Check the fork inner tube for score marks, dents, pitting, scratches, flaking of its surface and excessive or abnormal wear. Fit a new tube if any are found.

9 Examine the working surface of the bush (see illustration); if the grey Teflon outer surface has been worn away to reveal the copper inner surface over more than 75% of the surface area, or if the bush is scored or badly scuffed, the outer tube must be replaced with a new one – the bush is not available separately.

10 Check the inner tube for runout using V-blocks and a dial gauge. If the amount of runout exceeds the service limit specified, the tube should be replaced with a new one.

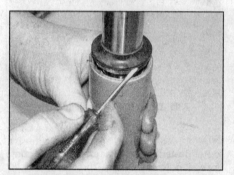

8.5a Prise out the dust seal using a flat-bladed screwdriver

8.5b Draw the inner tube out...

8.5c ...then tip the oil lock piece out

8.6 Prise out the retaining clip using a flat-bladed screwdriver

8.7a Locate the puller under the oil seal then expand the puller...

8.7b ...and jar the seal out using the slide-hammer attachment

8.9 Check the bush (arrowed) for wear

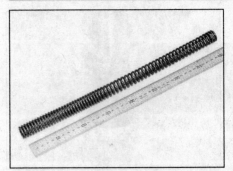

8.12 Measure the free length of the spring

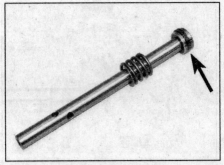

8.13 Check the rod for damage and the ring (arrowed) for wear

8.14a Fit the oil seal...

 Warning: If the tube is bent or exceeds the runout limit, it should not be straightened; replace it with a new one.

11 Check the outer tube for cracks. Check the fork seal seat and housing for nicks, gouges and scratches. If damage is evident, leaks will occur. Also check the oil seal washer for damage or distortion and fit a new one if necessary.

12 Check the spring for cracks and other damage. Measure the spring free length and compare the measurement to the specifications at the beginning of the Chapter **(see illustration)**. If it is defective or sagged below the service limit, replace the main springs in both forks with new ones. Never replace only one spring.

13 Check the damper rod, the rebound spring

fitted on it, and the piston ring in the head for damage and wear **(see illustration)**. Note that it is a good idea to replace the piston ring with a new one as a matter of course as part of a fork overhaul.

Reassembly

14 Smear the lips of the new oil seal with fork oil and press it squarely into its recess in the top of the outer tube, with its markings face upwards, then use a seal driver or a suitable socket and drive it in until it seats and the retaining clip groove is visible above it **(see illustrations)**.

 HAYNES HINT *Place the old oil seal on top of the new one to protect it when driving the seal into place.*

15 Once the seal is correctly seated, fit the retaining clip, making sure it is correctly located in its groove **(see illustration)**.

16 If removed, fit the rebound spring onto the damper rod, and fit the ring into its groove in the head **(see illustration 8.13)**. Slide the damper rod into the top of the inner tube and all the way down so it protrudes from the bottom **(see illustration)**. Fit the oil lock piece onto the bottom of the rod, then push the rod back into the tube so the oil lock piece fits into the bottom **(see illustrations)**.

17 Oil the fork inner tube and bush with the specified fork oil. Insert the inner tube into the outer tube, twisting it as you do and making sure the lips of the seal do not turn inside, and push it fully down until it contacts the bottom **(see illustration)**.

18 Lay the fork flat on the bench. Clean the

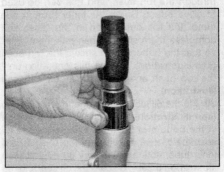

8.14b ...and drive it into place

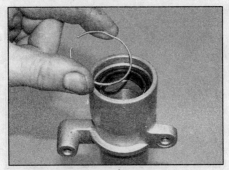

8.15 Fit the seal retaining clip into its groove

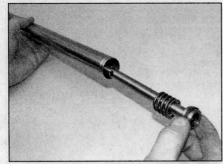

8.16a Fit the damper rod into the tube...

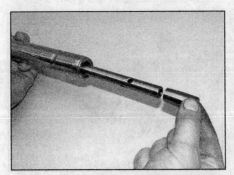

8.16b ...so it protrudes from the bottom, then fit the oil lock piece...

8.16c ...and locate it in the bottom of the tube

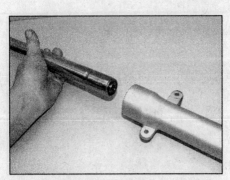

8.17 Fit the inner tube into the outer tube

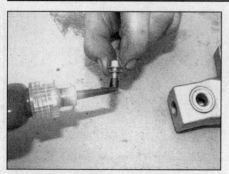

8.18a Fit the bolt using threadlock and a new sealing washer...

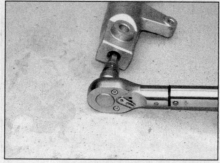

8.18b ...and tighten it to the specified torque

8.19 Fit the dust seal into the top of the slider

threads of the damper rod bolt. Fit a new copper sealing washer onto the bolt and apply a few drops of a suitable non-permanent thread locking compound (see illustration). Fit the bolt into the bottom of the outer tube and thread it into the damper rod, and tighten it to the torque setting specified at the beginning of the Chapter (see illustration). If the damper cartridge rotates inside the tube as you tighten the bolt, wait until the fork is fully reassembled and tighten it then (the pressure of the spring on the cartridge should prevent it from turning, especially if you compress the fork).

19 Lubricate the lips of the new dust seal then slide it down the fork tube and press it into place (see illustration).

20 Refer to Section 7, Steps 6 to 8 and fill the fork with oil and finish reassembly.

21 If the damper rod bolt requires tightening, place the fork upside down on the floor, using a rag to protect it, then have an assistant compress the fork so that maximum spring pressure is placed on the damper rod head while tightening the bolt to the specified torque setting.

22 Install the fork (see Section 6).

CBR250

Disassembly

23 Lay the fork flat on the bench. Hold the fork down and slacken then lightly retighten the damper rod bolt in the base of the fork (see illustration 8.2). If the damper rod rotates inside the fork whilst attempting to unscrew the bolt, compress the fork so that the spring exerts pressure on the rod whilst the bolt is

unscrewed. Alternatively, if available use an air wrench.

24 Refer to Section 7, Steps 3 to 5 and drain the oil from the fork.

25 Remove the damper rod bolt and its sealing washer from the bottom of the fork (see illustration 8.4a). A new sealing washer must be used on reassembly.

26 Tip the damper rod out of the fork (see illustration 8.4b).

27 Carefully prise out the dust seal from the top of the outer tube (see illustration).

28 Carefully prise out the oil seal retaining clip, taking care not to scratch the surface of the inner tube (see illustration).

29 To separate the inner and outer tubes it is necessary to displace the top bush and oil seal from the top of the outer tube. The bottom bush on the inner tube will not pass through the top bush, and this can be used to good effect. Grasp the inner tube in one hand and the outer tube in the other and compress them slightly, then pull them apart so that the bottom bush strikes the top bush (see illustration). Repeat this operation until the top bush and seal are tapped out (see illustration).

30 Tip the oil lock piece out of the outer tube (see illustration) – if it is not there it will be in the bottom of the inner tube. Slide the oil seal, the oil seal washer and top bush off the inner tube, noting which way up they fit (see illustration 8.29b). Discard the oil seal and the dust seal as new ones must be used. Do not remove the bottom bush from the inner tube

8.27 Prise out the dust seal using a flat-bladed screwdriver

8.28 Prise out the retaining clip using a flat-bladed screwdriver

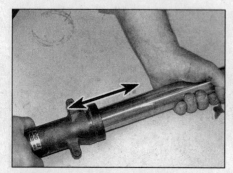

8.29a To separate the tubes pull them apart firmly several times...

8.29b ...the slide-hammer effect will displace the oil seal, washer and top bush

8.30a Tip the oil lock piece out

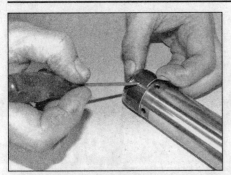

8.30b Carefully lever the bush ends apart to expand it

8.34 Check the working surface (arrowed) of each bush for wear

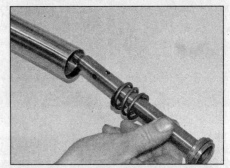

8.37a Fit the damper rod into the tube...

unless it is being replaced with a new one – to remove it carefully lever its ends apart using a screwdriver and slide it out of its recess **(see illustration)**.

Inspection

31 Clean all parts in solvent and blow them dry with compressed air, if available.

32 Check the fork inner tube for score marks, dents, pitting, scratches, flaking of its surface and excessive or abnormal wear. Fit a new tube if any are found. Check the inner tube for runout using V-blocks and a dial gauge. If the amount of runout exceeds the service limit specified, a new tube should be fitted.

 Warning: If the inner tube is bent or exceeds the runout limit, it should not be straightened; replace it with a new one.

33 Check the spring for cracks and other damage. Measure the spring free length and compare the measurement to the specifications at the beginning of the Chapter **(see illustration 8.12)**. If it is defective or sagged below the service limit, replace the springs in both forks with new ones. Never renew only one spring.

34 Examine the working surfaces of the two bushes (i.e. the outer surface of the bottom bush and the inner surface of the top bush) **(see illustration)**; if the grey Teflon outer surface has been worn away to reveal the copper inner surface over more than 75% of the surface area, or if the bushes are scored or badly scuffed, they must be replaced with new ones. Note that it is a good idea to replace the

8.37b ...then fit the oil lock piece onto the protruding end...

bushes with new ones as a matter of course as part of a fork overhaul.

35 Check the damper rod, the rebound spring fitted on it, and the piston ring in the head for damage and wear **(see illustration 8.13)**. Note that it is a good idea to replace the piston ring with a new one as a matter of course as part of a fork overhaul.

Reassembly

36 If necessary, fit a new bottom bush into its recess in the bottom of the inner tube **(see illustration 8.30b)**.

37 If removed, fit a new piston ring into the groove in the head of the damper rod **(see illustration 8.13)**. Fit the rebound spring onto the rod. Slide the damper rod into the top of the inner tube and all the way down so it protrudes from the bottom **(see illustration)**. Fit the oil lock piece onto the bottom of the

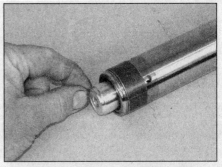

8.37c ...and push it into the tube

rod, then push the rod back into the tube so the oil lock piece fits into the bottom **(see illustrations)**.

38 Apply a smear of the specified clean fork oil to the surface of the bottom bush. Slide the inner tube fully into the outer tube **(see illustration)**.

39 Clean the threads of the damper rod bolt. Lay the fork flat on the bench. Fit a new sealing washer onto the bolt and apply a few drops of a suitable non-permanent thread locking compound **(see illustration)**. Fit the bolt into the bottom of the outer tube and thread it into the damper rod, tightening it to the torque setting specified at the beginning of the Chapter **(see illustration)**. If the rod rotates inside the tube as you tighten the bolt, wait until the fork is fully reassembled and tighten it then (the pressure of the spring on the rod will prevent it from turning).

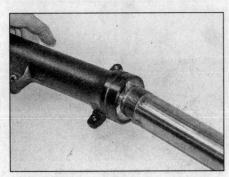

8.38 Slide the inner tube into the outer tube

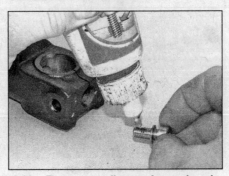

8.39a Fit a new sealing washer and apply threadlock...

8.39b ...and tighten the bolt to the specified torque

8.40a Slide the top bush down and into the outer tube...

8.40b ...then seat the washer on the bush...

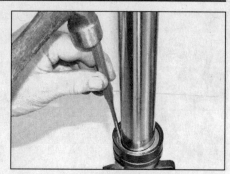

8.41 ...and drive the bush in and onto its seat

40 Apply a smear of the specified clean fork oil to the inner surface of the top bush. Slide the bush down the inner tube and seat it in the top of the outer tube **(see illustration)**. Slide the oil seal washer onto the bush **(see illustration)**.

41 Support the fork upright. Using either the special service tools (Pt. Nos. 07747-0010100 and 07747-0010600) or a suitable drift, carefully drive the top bush fully into its recess – the oil seal washer prevents damaging the edges of the bush **(see illustration)**. If using a drift, wrap tape around it to prevent scratching the inner tube. Make sure the bush

enters the recess squarely. It is best to make sure that the inner tube is withdrawn as much as possible from the outer tube so that any accidental scratching is confined to the area that does not affect the oil seal.

42 Lift the washer to check the bush is seated fully and squarely in its recess in the outer tube, then wipe the recess clean and re-seat the washer **(see illustration)**.

43 Apply a smear of the clean fork oil to the lips of the new oil seal. Slide the seal onto the tube with its marked side facing up **(see illustration)**. Drive the seal into place as described in Step 41 until the retaining clip

groove is visible – to avoid damaging the seal, fit the old seal above it and use it as an interface between the drift and the new seal **(see illustration)**. The new seal is seated when the old seal is just about flush with the rim of the outer tube – at this point lift it and check that the retaining clip groove is fully exposed **(see illustration)**. Remove the old seal.

44 Fit the retaining clip, making sure it is correctly located in its groove **(see illustration)**.

45 Press the dust seal into the top of the outer tube **(see illustration)**.

8.42 Make sure the bush (arrowed) has been fully driven in

8.43a Slide the seal down and into the outer tube

8.43b Drive the new seal in and onto its seat using the old seal as an interface

8.43c Lift the old seal and make sure the retaining clip groove (arrowed) is fully exposed

8.44 Fit the retaining clip in its groove...

8.45 ...then press the dust seal in

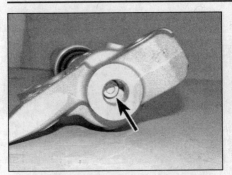

8.49 Slacken the damper cartridge bolt (arrowed)

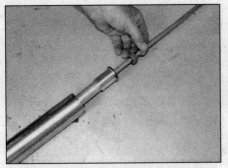

8.51 Remove the bolt then withdraw the damper cartridge

8.52 Prise out the dust seal using a flat-bladed screwdriver

46 Refer to Section 7, Steps 6 to 8 and fill the fork with oil and finish reassembly.

47 If the damper rod bolt requires tightening (see Step 39), place the fork upside down on the floor, using a rag to protect it, then have an assistant compress the fork so that maximum spring pressure is placed on the damper rod head while tightening the bolt to the specified torque setting.

48 Install the fork (see Section 6).

CRF250

Disassembly

49 If working on the left-hand fork, lay the fork flat on the bench with the caliper mounting lugs to the left. Hold the fork down and slacken then lightly retighten the damper cartridge bolt in the base of the fork (see illustration). If the damper cartridge rotates inside the fork whilst attempting to unscrew the bolt, use an air wrench.

50 Refer to Section 7, Steps 10 to 13 or 20 and 21 (according to side) and drain the oil form the fork.

51 On the left-hand fork remove the damper cartridge bolt and its sealing washer from the bottom of the fork. Discard the sealing washer as a new one must be used on reassembly. Withdraw the damper cartridge from the fork (see illustration). Pump the rod a few times over the oil drain tray to expel any residual oil.

52 Carefully prise out the dust seal from the bottom of the outer tube (see illustration).

53 Carefully prise out the oil seal retaining ring, taking care not to scratch the surface of the inner tube (see illustration).

54 To separate the inner and outer tubes it is necessary to displace the bottom bush and oil seal from the bottom of the outer tube. The top bush on the inner tube will not pass through the bottom bush, and this can be used to good effect. Grasp the inner tube in one hand and the outer tube in the other and compress them slightly, then pull them apart so that the top bush strikes the bottom bush (see illustration). Repeat this operation until the bottom bush and seal are tapped out (see illustration).

55 Carefully lever the ends of the top bush

apart using a screwdriver and slide it off. Slide the bottom bush, oil seal washer, oil seal, retaining ring and dust seal off the inner tube, noting which way up they fit (see illustration 8.54b). Discard the oil seal and the dust seal as new ones must be used.

56 On the right-hand fork, if required, counter-hold the fork top bolt and slacken the locknut underneath it, then thread the top bolt off the rod (see illustration). Remove the spring seat and rebound spring.

Inspection

57 Clean all parts in solvent and blow them dry with compressed air, if available.

58 Check the fork inner tube for score marks, dents, pitting, scratches, flaking of its surface and excessive or abnormal wear. Fit a new

tube if any are found. Check the inner tube for runout using V-blocks and a dial gauge. If the amount of runout exceeds the service limit specified, a new tube should be fitted.

⚠ *Warning: If the inner tube is bent or exceeds the runout limit, it should not be straightened; replace it with a new one.*

59 Check the fork outer tube for cracks. Check the fork seal seat and housing for nicks, gouges and scratches. If damage is evident, leaks will occur. Also check the oil seal washer for damage or distortion and fit a new one if necessary.

60 On the right-hand fork check the main spring and rebound spring for cracks and other damage. Measure the main spring free length and compare the measurement to the

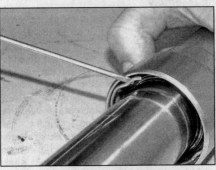

8.53 Prise out the retaining clip using a flat-bladed screwdriver

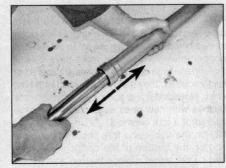

8.54a To separate the tubes pull them apart firmly several times...

8.54b ...the slide-hammer effect will displace the oil seal, washer and bottom bush

8.56 Slacken the locknut (arrowed) as described to release the top bolt

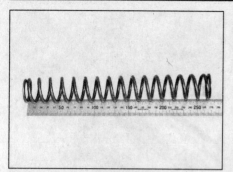

8.60 Measure the free length of the spring

8.65a Use insulating tape to cover sharp edges...

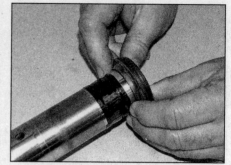

8.65b ...then slide the dust seal...

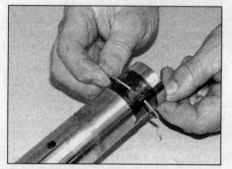

8.65c ...retaining clip...

8.65d ...oil seal...

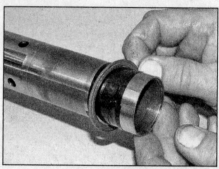

8.65e ...and oil seal washer on

specifications at the beginning of the Chapter **(see illustration)**. If it is defective or sagged below the service limit, replace the spring.

61 Examine the working surfaces of the two bushes (i.e. the inner surface of the bottom bush and the outer surface of the top bush) **(see illustration 8.34)**; if the grey Teflon outer surface has been worn away to reveal the copper inner surface over more than 75% of the surface area, or if the bushes are scored or badly scuffed, they must be replaced with new ones. Note that it is a good idea to replace the bushes with new ones as a matter of course as part of a fork overhaul.

62 On the right-hand fork check the damper ring on the bottom of the cartridge for wear and damage and replace the rod with a new one if necessary.

63 On the left-hand fork check the damper cartridge and rod for damage and wear. Hold the body of the cartridge and pump the rod

in and out. If any wear or damage is found, or if the rod does not move smoothly in the damper, a new damper must be installed.

Reassembly

64 If removed fit the rebound spring onto the right-hand fork rod, then fit the spring seat with the narrower section facing up **(see illustration 8.56)**. Thread the locknut down to the bottom of the threads. Thread the top bolt onto the rod until it seats, then counter-hold it and tighten the locknut up against it.

65 Wrap some thin insulating tape over the edges of the recess for the top bush in the inner tube to protect the seal lips **(see illustration)**. Smear some oil over the tape, and also over the oil seal lips. Slide the new dust seal, retaining ring, new oil seal, and oil seal washer onto the inner tube, making sure they are the correct way round **(see illustrations)**. Remove the tape, then lubricate the surfaces of the

bottom bush and slide it on **(see illustration)**. Fit the top bush into its recess, then lubricate its surface **(see illustration)**.

66 Slide the inner tube fully into the outer tube **(see illustration)**. Support the fork upside down, and have an assistant hold the inner tube and the components on it up. Slide the bottom bush into the bottom of the outer tube, then squeeze the ends together using two suitable plastic or wooden tools to close the gap to allow the bush the drop in (if you are lucky), or at least to start to go in.

67 To get the bush fully in slide the oil seal washer onto it **(see illustration 8.68)**. Using either the special service tool (part No. 07YMD-MCF0100 in the UK and Europe, and 07NMD-KZ3010A in the US) or a suitable drift, carefully drive the bottom bush fully into its recess until the bush and washer seat – the washer prevents damaging the edges of the

8.65f Slide the bottom bush on...

8.65g ...then fit the top bush into its recess

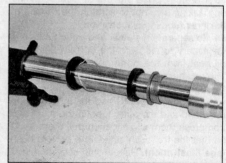

8.66 Slide the inner tube into the outer tube

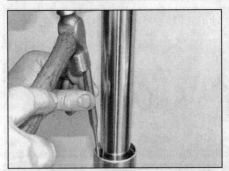

8.67a Use a drift to drive the bush in, with
the washer as an interface...

8.67b ...until the bush is fully seated

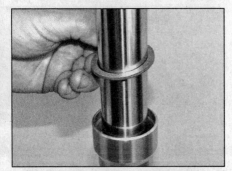

8.68 Fit the washer onto the bush

8.69a Slide the seal down and into the
outer tube

8.69b Cut the old seal in half...

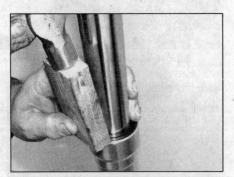

8.69c ...and use it to protect the new seal
while driving it in

bush **(see illustration)**. If using a drift, wrap
tape around it to prevent scratching the inner
tube. Make sure the bush enters the recess
squarely. It is best to make sure that the inner
tube is withdrawn as much as possible from the
outer tube so that any accidental scratching is
confined to the area that does not affect the
oil seal. Lift the washer to check the bush is
seated fully and squarely in its recess in the
slider, then wipe the recess clean.

68 Slide the oil seal washer onto the bush
(see illustration).

69 Slide the new oil seal down and into the
outer tube **(see illustration)**. Push the seal
into place, driving it in as in Step 67 if you
have the Honda tool, until the retaining clip
groove is visible. If you don't have the tool cut
the old seal in half and use it as an interface
between the drift and the new seal, and then
push the seal in or use a piece of wood as a

drift **(see illustrations)**. When the old seal is
flush with the rim of the fork tube the new seal
is seated – remove the pieces of old seal and
check the retaining clip groove is visible.

70 Fit the retaining ring, making sure it is
correctly located in its groove **(see illustration)**.

71 Press the dust seal into the top of the
outer tube **(see illustration)**.

72 On the left-hand fork clean the threads
of the damper cartridge bolt. Lay the fork flat
on the bench with the caliper mounting lugs
to the right. Slide the damper cartridge fully
into the fork tube **(see illustration)**. Fit a new
sealing washer onto the cartridge bolt and
apply a few drops of a suitable non-permanent
thread locking compound **(see illustration
8.39a)**. Fit the bolt into the bottom of the fork
and thread it into the cartridge, tightening it to
the torque setting specified at the beginning
of the Chapter **(see illustration 8.39b)**.

8.69d Make sure the retaining clip groove
(arrowed) is fully exposed

73 Refer to Section 7, Steps 14 to 18 or 22
to 24 (according to side) and fill the fork with
oil and finish reassembly.

74 Install the fork (see Section 6).

8.70 Fit the retaining clip in its groove...

8.71 ...then press the dust seal in

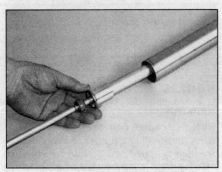

8.72 Insert the damper cartridge

9.2a Release the connector and move the wiring aside

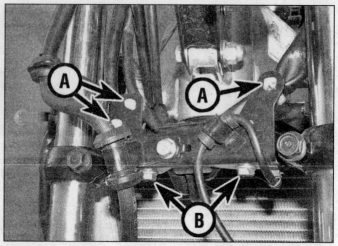

9.2b Release the clips (A) then unscrew the bolts (B)

9.2c Free the cables and wiring (arrowed) from the guide...

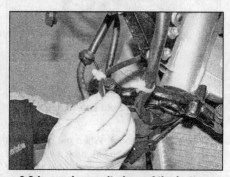

9.2d ...and move it clear of the bottom yoke

9.3a Steering stem nut (arrowed)

9.3b Lift the yoke off

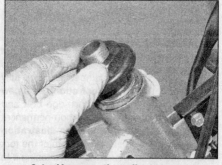

9.4a Unscrew the adjuster nut...

9.4b ...and remove the inner race

9 Steering stem

CBR125

Removal

Note: *Uncaged ball bearings are fitted, which means that the ones in the bottom of the steering head could drop out when the steering stem is lowered out of the head. To avoid this remove the balls as described using a magnet or get a container and hold it below* the head to catch the balls as you lower the stem.

Special tool: *Either the Honda special tool (part No. 07916-3710101), equivalent peg spanner, or a suitably sized C-spanner is necessary for this procedure.*

1 Remove the instruments (see Chapter 8). Remove the front forks (see Section 6).

2 Disconnect the turn signal relay wiring connector and move the front wiring loom out of the way **(see illustration)**. Release the wiring clips from the bracket on the bottom yoke, then unscrew the bolts on the underside and displace the bracket, leaving the brake hose and speed sensor wiring attached **(see** illustration). Release the cables and speed sensor wiring from the guide on the top yoke **(see illustration)**. Move the wiring clear of bottom yoke **(see illustration)**.

3 Unscrew the steering stem nut and remove the washer **(see illustration)**. Lift the top yoke up off the steering stem and position it clear, using a rag to protect other components **(see illustration)**.

4 Support the bottom yoke and unscrew the bearing adjuster nut using your fingers (it shouldn't be tight), or a C-spanner or a suitable drift located in one of the notches if necessary **(see illustration)**. Remove the inner race **(see illustration)**.

5 With the bottom yoke held in place remove the balls from the upper race using a magnet **(see illustration)**.

6 Lower the steering stem slightly and remove the lower balls in the same way **(see illustration)**. Lower the bottom yoke and steering stem out of the frame **(see illustration)**. There should be 18 balls for each bearing.

7 Wash all traces of old grease from the bearing balls and races using solvent or paraffin, then check them for wear or damage as described in Section 10. **Note:** *Do not* *attempt to remove the races from the steering head or the stem unless they are to be replaced with new ones (see Section 10).*

Installation

8 Smear a liberal quantity of Urea-based multi-purpose grease with EP2 rating onto the bearing races, then stick the lower bearing balls to the grease on the inner race on the base of the steering stem and the upper bearing balls to the grease on the outer race in the top of the steering head **(see illustrations)**. There should be 18 balls for each race. Make sure all the balls are pressed against the race to prevent them being dislodged by the opposite race when fitted. Fit the inner race into the upper bearing **(see illustration)**.

9 Carefully lift the steering stem/bottom yoke up through the steering head, holding the upper bearing inner race in place and making sure all balls stay in place, and when it has located turn it a few times to spread and seat the bearing balls, then support it **(see illustration)**. Thread the adjuster nut onto the steering stem and tighten it finger-tight **(see illustration)**.

10 If the Honda service tool described above

9.5 Remove the balls using a magnet

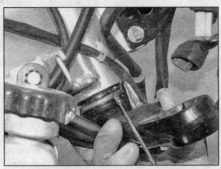

9.6a Lower the yoke and remove the balls...

9.6b ...then remove the yoke/steering stem

9.8a Stick the balls to the lower inner race...

9.8b ...and to the upper outer race...

9.8c ...then fit the upper inner race

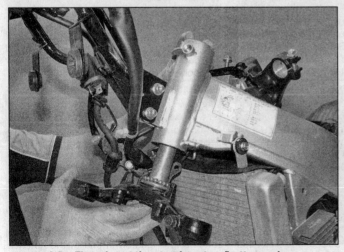

9.9a Fit and seat the steering stem/bottom yoke...

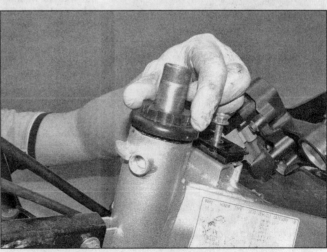

9.9b ...then thread the adjuster nut on finger-tight

9.15a Release the cable and hose and any wiring not already released…

9.15b …and support the handlebars as shown

or a suitable peg spanner (which can be made by cutting castellations into an old socket **(see illustration 9.25))** and a torque wrench are available, tighten the adjuster nut to the initial torque setting specified at the beginning of the Chapter, then turn the steering stem through its full lock at least five times, then slacken the nut so that it is loose, and then tighten it to the final torque setting specified. Check that that the steering stem is able to move freely from lock-to-lock following adjustment. Now install the top yoke, forks, wheel and all remaining components so that their leverage and inertia can be taken into account (Steps 12 and 13),

9.16 Unscrew the bolt (arrowed)

then refer to the check and adjustment procedures in Chapter 1 to set the bearings.
11 If the correct tools are not available, tighten the nut fairly tight using a C-spanner or drift so that bearing play is eliminated, but the steering stem is able to move freely from lock-to-lock, then slacken the nut so that it is loose, and then tighten it finger-tight only – the nut must be literally on the point of being loose, do not put effort into tightening it finger-tight (when the top yoke is fitted and the steering stem nut is tightened these act to lock the adjuster nut in place). Now install the top yoke, forks, wheel and all remaining components so that their leverage and inertia can be taken into account (Steps 12 and 13), then refer to the check and adjustment procedures in Chapter 1 to set the bearings.
Caution: Take great care not to apply excessive pressure because this will cause premature failure of the bearings.
12 Fit the top yoke onto the steering stem **(see illustration 9.3b)**. Fit the steering stem nut with its washer and tighten it finger-tight **(see illustration 9.3a)**. Temporarily install one of the forks to align the top and bottom yokes, and secure it by tightening the bottom yoke clamp bolts only (see Section 6). Now tighten the steering stem nut to the torque setting specified at the beginning of the Chapter.

13 Install the remaining components in a reverse of the removal procedure, referring to the relevant Sections or Chapters, and to the torque settings specified at the beginning of the Chapter. Make sure the wiring, cables and hose are correctly routed and secured **(see illustrations 9.2d, c, b and a)**.
14 Carry out a final check of the steering head bearing freeplay as described in Chapter 1, and if necessary re-adjust.

CBR250

Removal

Special tool: *Either the Honda special tool (part No. 07916-3710101), equivalent peg spanner, or a suitably sized C-spanner is necessary for this procedure.*
15 Remove the instruments (see Chapter 8). Remove the front forks (see Section 6). Release the brake hose and cables from the top yoke and support the handlebars as shown **(see illustrations)**.
16 Displace the brake hose from bottom yoke **(see illustration)**.
17 Remove the cap from the steering stem nut **(see illustration)**. Unscrew the nut and remove the washer **(see illustration)**. Lift the top yoke up off the steering stem and position it clear, using a rag to protect other components **(see illustration)**.

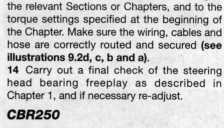

9.17a Remove the cap

9.17b Unscrew the nut and remove the washer…

9.17c …and lift the top yoke off

9.18 Release the tabs then unscrew the locknut and remove the lockwasher

9.20a Unscrew the adjuster nut...

9.20b ...then draw the bottom yoke/ steering stem out of the steering head

18 Bend the lockwasher tabs out of the notches in the locknut. Unscrew the locknut using your fingers **(see illustration)** – it shouldn't be tight. If it is tight use a C-spanner located in one of the notches. Remove the lockwasher. Inspect the tabs for cracks or signs of fatigue. If there is any sign of damage, use a new one – Honda recommend using a new one as a matter of course.

19 If the peg spanner mentioned above is not available, make an alignment mark between the adjuster nut and the frame – this can serve as a rough guide for the tightness of the adjuster nut on installation. As you unscrew the nut count the number of turns.

20 Support the bottom yoke then unscrew the adjuster nut using either a C-spanner or a peg-spanner **(see illustration)**. Gently lower the bottom yoke and steering stem out of the frame **(see illustration)**.

21 Remove the grease seal, inner race and bearing from the top of the steering head **(see illustration)**. Remove the bearing from the base of the steering stem **(see illustration)**.

22 Wash all traces of old grease from the bearings and races using solvent or paraffin and check them for wear or damage as described in Section 10. **Note:** *Do not attempt to remove the races from the steering head or the steering stem unless they are to be replaced with new ones.*

Installation

23 Smear a liberal quantity of Urea-based multi-purpose grease with EP2 rating onto the bearing races, and work some grease well into both the upper and lower bearings. Also smear the grease seal lip, using a new seal if necessary. Fit the lower bearing onto the steering stem **(see illustration 9.21b)**.

24 Carefully lift the steering stem/bottom yoke up through the steering head and support it there **(see illustration 9.20b)**. Fit the upper bearing and its inner race into the top of the steering head, then **(see illustrations)**. Fit the grease seal **(see illustration)**. Apply some oil to the adjuster nut threads and thread the nut onto the steering stem **(see illustration)**.

9.21a Remove the grease seal, inner race and upper bearing...

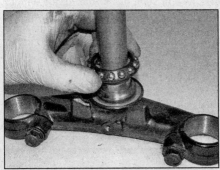

9.21b ...and the lower bearing

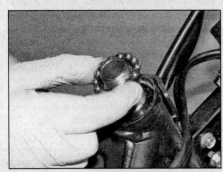

9.24a Fit the upper bearing...

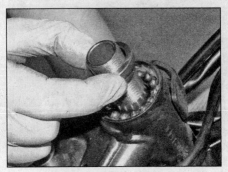

9.24b ...the inner race...

9.24c ...and the grease seal...

9.24d ...and thread the adjuster nut on

9.25 Example of a home-made peg spanner

9.26 Tighten the adjuster nut as described

9.28 Fit the lockwasher

25 Using the Honda service tool described above, or a suitable peg spanner, which can be made by cutting castellations into an old socket or a piece of steel tube **(see illustration)**, tighten the adjuster nut to the initial torque setting specified at the beginning of the Chapter, then turn the steering from lock-to-lock five times, then slacken the nut so that it is loose, and then tighten it to the final torque setting specified.

26 If the correct tools are not available, tighten the nut the number of turns recorded on removal using a C-spanner until the marks align, then tighten it a little bit more **(see illustration)**. Turn the steering from lock-to-lock five times, then slacken the nut so it is loose, and tighten it again until the marks align.

Caution: Take great care not to apply excessive pressure because this will cause premature failure of the bearings.

27 Note that the bearings may feel a bit tight at this stage, but this is normal as the weight of the forks and wheel is not influencing the feel – check and if necessary reset the bearing adjustment as described in Chapter 1 after the forks and front wheel and all other components have been installed.

28 Fit the lockwasher, with the short bent tabs facing down, locating them in the slots in the adjuster nut **(see illustration)**.

29 Fit the locknut and tighten it finger-tight **(see illustration)**. Tighten the locknut further (but no more than 90°) until its notches align with the remaining lockwasher tabs, making sure the adjuster nut does not turn as well (though that is unlikely). Secure the locknut in position by bending up the long lock washer tabs into its notches.

30 Fit the top yoke onto the steering stem **(see illustration 9.17c)**. Fit the washer and the steering stem nut and tighten it finger-tight **(see illustration 9.17b)**. Temporarily install one of the forks to align the top and bottom yokes, and secure it by tightening the bottom yoke clamp bolts only (see Section 6). Now tighten the steering stem nut to the torque setting specified at the beginning of the Chapter.

31 Install the remaining components in a reverse of the removal procedure, referring to the relevant Sections or Chapters, and to the torque settings specified at the beginning of the Chapter.

32 Carry out a final check of the steering head bearing freeplay as described in Chapter 1, and if necessary re-adjust.

CRF250

Removal

Special tool: *Either the Honda special tool (part No. 07916-KA50100), equivalent peg spanner, or a suitably sized C-spanner is necessary for this procedure.*

33 Remove the front forks (see Section 6).

34 Remove the front mudguard and the headlight cowl (see Chapter 7).

35 Disconnect the ignition switch wiring connector then displace the instrument bracket and support it **(see illustration)**.

36 Remove the cap from the steering stem nut **(see illustration 9.17a)**. Unscrew the nut and remove the washer **(see illustration 9.17b)**. Lift the top yoke up off the steering stem and position it clear, using a rag to protect other components **(see illustration 9.17c)**.

37 If the peg spanner mentioned above is not available, make an alignment mark between the adjuster nut and the frame – this can serve as a rough guide for the tightness of the adjuster nut on installation. As you unscrew the nut count the number of turns.

38 Support the bottom yoke then unscrew the adjuster nut using either a C-spanner or a

9.29 Thread the locknut on and tighten as described

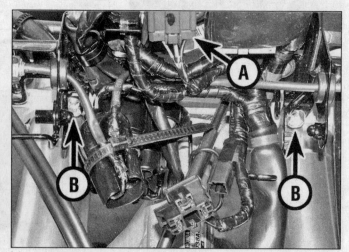
9.35 Disconnect the brown connector (A) then unscrew the bolts (B)

peg-spanner **(see illustration 9.20a)**. Gently lower the bottom yoke and steering stem out of the frame **(see illustration 9.20b)**.

39 Remove the grease seal and bearing from the top of the steering head. Refer to Section 10 for removal of the lower bearing from the stem – only remove it if a new one is being fitted as removal will ruin the old bearing.

40 Wash all traces of old grease from the bearings and races using solvent or paraffin and check them for wear or damage as described in Section 10. **Note:** *Do not attempt to remove the races from the steering head unless they are to be replaced with new ones (see Section 10).*

Installation

41 Smear a liberal quantity of Urea-based multi-purpose grease with EP2 rating onto the bearing races and bearings. Also smear the grease seal lip, using a new seal if necessary.

42 Carefully lift the steering stem/bottom yoke up through the steering head and support it there **(see illustration 9.20b)**. Fit the upper bearing into the top of the steering head. Fit the grease seal. Apply some oil to the adjuster nut threads and thread the nut onto the steering stem.

43 Using the Honda service tool described above, or a suitable peg spanner, which can be made by cutting castellations into an old socket or a piece of steel tube **(see illustration 9.25)**, tighten the adjuster nut to the initial torque setting specified at the beginning of the Chapter, then turn the steering from lock-to-lock five times, then slacken the nut so that it is loose, and then tighten it to the final torque setting specified.

44 If the correct tools are not available, tighten the nut the number of turns recorded on removal using a C-spanner until the marks align, then tighten it a little bit more **(see illustration 9.26)**. Turn the steering from lock-to-lock five times, then slacken the nut so it is loose, and tighten it again until the marks align.

Caution: Take great care not to apply excessive pressure because this will cause premature failure of the bearings.

45 Note that the bearings may feel a bit tight at this stage, but this is normal as the weight of the forks and wheel is not influencing the feel – check and if necessary reset the bearing adjustment as described in Chapter 1 after the forks and front wheel and all other components have been installed.

46 Fit the top yoke onto the steering stem. Fit the washer and the steering stem nut and tighten it finger-tight. Temporarily install one of the forks to align the top and bottom yokes, and secure it by tightening the bottom yoke clamp bolts only (see Section 6). Now tighten the steering stem nut to the torque setting specified at the beginning of the Chapter.

47 Install the remaining components in a reverse of the removal procedure, referring to the relevant Sections or Chapters, and to the torque settings specified at the beginning of the Chapter.

48 Carry out a final check of the steering head bearing freeplay as described in Chapter 1, and if necessary re-adjust.

10 Steering head bearings

Inspection

1 Remove the steering stem (see Section 9).

2 Wash all traces of old grease from the bearings and races using paraffin or solvent, and check them for wear or damage.

3 The races should be polished and free from indentations **(see illustration)**. Inspect the bearings for signs of wear, damage or discoloration. If there are any signs of wear or damage on any of the components both upper and lower bearing assemblies must be renewed as a set. Only remove the outer races in the steering head and the inner race or lower bearing (according to model) on the steering stem if they need to be replaced with new ones – do not re-use them once they have been removed.

Replacement

4 The outer races are an interference fit in the steering head – tap them from position using a suitable drift, with a curved end if necessary, located on the exposed inner lip of the race **(see illustration)**. Tap firmly and evenly swopping from one cut-out to the other to ensure that the race is driven out squarely.

5 Alternatively, remove the races using a slide-hammer type bearing extractor – these can often be hired from tool shops.

6 Press the new outer races into the head using a drawbolt arrangement **(see illustration)**, or drive them in using a large diameter tubular drift (to do this the bike must be solidly supported as all the force needs to be transmitted to the race). Make sure that the drawbolt washer or drift (as applicable) bears only on the outer edge of the race and does not contact the working surface. Alternatively, have the races installed by a dealer equipped with bearing race installation tools.

> **HAYNES HiNT** *Installation of new bearing outer races is made much easier if the races are left overnight in the freezer. This causes them to contract slightly making them a looser fit. Alternatively, use a freeze spray. You can also heat the race seat in the steering stem using a hot air gun.*

7 On CBR models only remove the lower bearing inner race from the steering stem if a new one is being fitted. To remove the race, first thread the steering stem nut onto the top then position the yoke on its front for stability – the nut will protect the threads. If you can get sufficient purchase without damaging anything

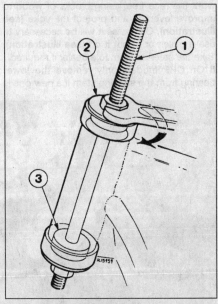

10.6 Drawbolt arrangement for fitting steering stem bearing races

1 Long bolt or threaded bar
2 Thick washer
3 Guide for lower race

10.3 Check the outer races in the top and bottom of the steering head

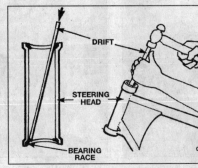

DRIFT

STEERING HEAD

BEARING RACE

10.4 Drive the bearing races out with a brass drift located as shown

10.7a Dislodge the lower bearing using a cold chisel...

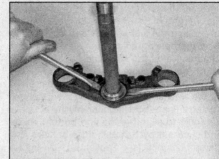

10.7b ...and/or screwdrivers...

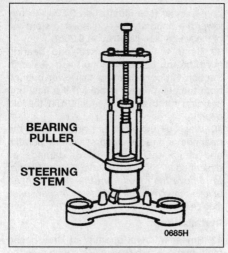

10.7c ...or using a puller if necessary

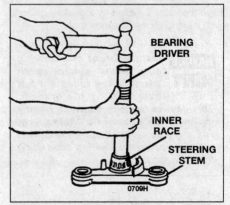

10.10 Drive the new inner race on using a suitable bearing driver or a length of pipe that bears only against the inner rim and not the bearing surface

tap under the race using a cold chisel, or use two screwdrivers placed on opposite sides to work the race free, using blocks of wood to improve leverage and protect the yoke **(see illustration)**. Otherwise it will be necessary to use a puller, or to cut it off **(see illustration)**. Take the steering stem to a dealer if required.
8 On CRF models only remove the lower bearing from the steering stem if a new one is

being fitted. First you need to destroy the cage and remove the rollers to expose the inner race – use a flat-bladed screwdriver to initially open a gap between the top of the cage and the inner race, then use a bigger one to work the cage free. Alternatively cut through the cage using a cold chisel or a Dremel or similar tool. Now refer to Step 7 to remove the race.
9 Remove the dust seal from the bottom of the stem and replace it with a new one. Smear the new one with grease then fit it onto the stem.
10 Fit the new lower race (CBR models) or bearing (CRF models) onto the steering stem. Drive the new race/bearing into position using a length of tubing with an internal diameter slightly larger than the steering stem so it bears only on the top rim of the race **(see illustration)** – heating the race and cooling the steering stem will make installation easier, or use an hydraulic press if necessary.
11 Install the steering stem (see Section 9).

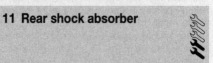

11 Rear shock absorber

⚠️ *Warning: Do not attempt to disassemble this shock absorber. It is nitrogen-charged under high*

pressure. *Improper disassembly could result in serious injury. No individual components are available for it.*
1 Support the motorcycle using axle stands so that no weight is transmitted through any part of the rear suspension **(see illustrations)** – remove any bodywork as required to prevent damage. Tie the front brake lever to the handlebar so the bike can't roll forward. Position a support under the rear wheel or swingarm so that it does not drop when the shock absorber is removed, but also making sure that the weight of the machine is off the rear suspension so that the shock is not compressed.

CBR125

Removal

2 Remove the right-hand side panel (see Chapter 7). Remove the chainguard/ hugger, noting the collars with the bolts **(see illustration 13.24)**.
3 Unscrew the nut and withdraw the bolt

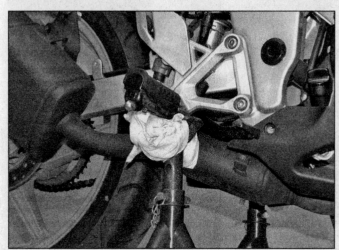

11.1a CBR125 shown supported by axle stands under the footrest brackets – silencer cover removed

11.1b CRF shown supported under the frame using a trolley lift – sump guard removed

11.3 Unscrew the nut and remove the bottom bolt

11.4a Unscrew the bolt (arrowed)...

11.4b ...and remove the shock absorber

securing the bottom of the shock absorber to the swingarm **(see illustration)**.

4 Support the shock absorber and unscrew the bolt securing the top, accessing it via the hole in the frame, then remove the shock absorber **(see illustrations)**.

Inspection

5 Check for obvious physical damage and oil leakage, and the coil spring for looseness, cracks or signs of fatigue.

6 Inspect the bushes in the shock absorber mounts and the mounts themselves for wear or damage **(see illustration)**. If necessary replace the shock absorber with a new one.

Installation

7 Installation is the reverse of removal, noting the following:
● Apply multi-purpose grease to the shock absorber bolt shanks.
● Insert the bolts from the right-hand side.
● Tighten the bolts/nut to the torque settings specified at the beginning of the Chapter.

CBR250

Removal

Note: *If you are removing the suspension linkage as well, do so first (see Section 12).*
8 Remove the air filter housing (see Chapter 4).

9 Unscrew the nut and withdraw the bolt securing the linkage rod to the linkage arm, then pivot it down **(see illustration)**.

10 Unscrew the nut and withdraw the bolt securing the shock absorber to the linkage arm **(see illustration)**.

11 Support the shock absorber and unscrew the nut on the top, then lower the shock absorber and remove it **(see illustrations)**.

12 If required unscrew the nut, withdraw the bolt and remove the bracket from the top **(see illustration)**.

Inspection

13 Check for obvious physical damage and oil leakage, and the coil spring for looseness, cracks or signs of fatigue.

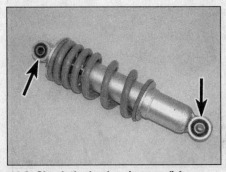

11.6 Check the bushes (arrowed) for wear

11.9 Detach the linkage rods from the arm and swing them down

11.10 Detach the shock absorber from the linkage arm and swing the arm down

11.11a Unscrew the nut...

11.11b ...and remove the shock absorber

11.12 Detach the top bracket if required

11.14 Check the bush (arrowed) for wear

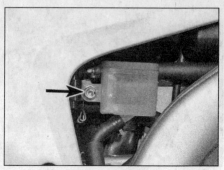

11.17 Unscrew the bolt (arrowed)

11.18 Detach the linkage rods from the arm and swing them down

14 Inspect the bush in the shock absorber top mount and the mounts themselves for wear or damage **(see illustration)**. If necessary, replace the shock absorber with a new one.

Installation

15 Installation is the reverse of removal, noting the following:
● If the top bracket was removed, make sure it remains parallel to the shock absorber as you tighten the nut/bolt.
● Apply multi-purpose grease to the shock absorber bolt shanks.
● Insert all bolts from the right-hand side.
● Tighten the shock absorber bolt/nut before fitting the linkage rods onto the arm, and tighten the bolts/nuts to the torque settings specified at the beginning of the Chapter.

CRF250

Removal

Note: *If you are removing the suspension linkage as well, do so first (see Section 12).*
16 Remove the seat and the side panels (see Chapter 7).
17 Displace the rear brake fluid reservoir **(see illustration)**.
18 Unscrew the nut and withdraw the bolt securing the linkage rods to the linkage arm and pivot the rods down **(see illustration)**.
19 Unscrew the nut and withdraw the bolt securing the shock absorber to the linkage arm **(see illustration)**.
20 Lift the rear wheel and place some blocks of wood under it **(see illustration)**.
21 Hold the nut and unscrew the bolt securing the top of the shock absorber to

the frame **(see illustrations)**. Remove the nut and washer, withdraw the bolt, then remove the shock absorber from the bottom **(see illustration)**.

Inspection

22 Check for obvious physical damage and oil leakage, and the coil spring for looseness, cracks or signs of fatigue.
23 Inspect the bush in the shock absorber top mount and the mounts themselves for wear or damage **(see illustration)**. If necessary, replace the shock absorber with a new one.

Installation

24 Installation is the reverse of removal, noting the following:
● Apply multi-purpose grease to the shock absorber bolt shanks.

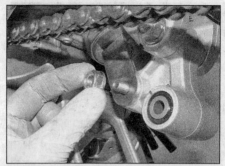

11.19 Detach the shock absorber from the linkage arm and swing the arm down

11.20 Raise and support the rear wheel

11.21a Hold the nut (arrowed)...

11.21b ...unscrew the bolt (arrowed)...

11.21c ...and remove the shock absorber

11.23 Check the bush (arrowed) for wear

12.4 Detach the linkage arm from the swingarm…

12.5 …then detach the linkage rods from the frame – CBR shown

12.6 Withdraw the sleeves – CBR shown

● Insert all bolts from the right-hand side.
● Tighten the shock absorber bolt/nut before fitting the linkage rods onto the arm, and tighten the bolts/nuts to the torque settings specified at the beginning of the Chapter.

12 Rear suspension linkage (250 models)

Removal

1 Support the motorcycle using axle stands so that no weight is transmitted through any part of the rear suspension **(see illustrations 11.1a and b)**. Tie the front brake lever to the handlebar so the bike can't roll forward. Position a support under the rear wheel or swingarm so that it does not drop when the shock absorber is detached, but also making sure that the weight of the machine is off the rear suspension so that the shock is not compressed.
2 Unscrew the nut, on CRF models remove the washer, and withdraw the bolt securing the linkage rods to the linkage arm and pivot the rods down **(see illustration 11.9 or 11.18)**.
3 Unscrew the nut and withdraw the bolt securing the shock absorber to the linkage arm **(see illustration 11.10 or 11.19)**.
4 Unscrew the nut, on CRF models remove the washer, and withdraw the bolt securing the linkage arm to the swingarm and remove the arm **(see illustration)**.

5 Unscrew the nut and withdraw bolt securing the linkage rods to the frame and remove the rod **(see illustration)**.

Inspection

6 Withdraw the sleeves from the linkage arm and rod **(see illustrations)**.
7 Thoroughly clean all components, removing all traces of dirt, corrosion and grease.
8 Check the linkage arm and rods and their mounts, looking for obvious signs of wear such as heavy scoring, or for damage such as cracks or distortion. Replace worn or damaged components with new ones as required.
9 Check the condition of the grease seals and bearings. Fit the sleeves back in and check for play between them and the bearings. Refer to *Tools and Workshop Tips* (Section 5) in the Reference section for more information on bearings. Inspect all components closely, looking for corrosion and obvious signs of wear such as heavy scoring, or for damage such as cracks or distortion. Replace worn or damaged components with new ones as required.
10 If required, lever out the grease seals using a seal hook or screwdriver **(see illustration)**. Discard them – new ones must be used.
11 Worn bearings can be driven or drawn out of their bores, but note that removal will destroy them; new bearings should be obtained before work commences **(see illustration)**. The new bearings should be pressed or drawn into their bores rather than driven into position. In the absence of a press, a suitable drawbolt

tool can be made up as described in *Tools and Workshop Tips* in the Reference section. When fitting the single bearings into the shock absorber and swingarm mounts in the linkage arm make sure they are as central as possible in their bores. When fitting the two bearings into the linkage rod mounts in the linkage arm set each one until it seats so the gap between the outer end and the rim is 6.3 to 6.7 mm on CBR models and 5.8 to 6.2 mm on CRF models. When fitting the two bearings into the linkage rod set each one until it seats so the gap between the outer end and the rim is 5.0 to 5.5 mm on CBR models and 5.8 to 6.2 mm on CRF models.
12 Lubricate the needle bearings, sleeves and seals with grease.
13 Press the new seals squarely into place, with the marked side facing out **(see illustration)**. Fit the sleeves **(see illustration 12.6)**.

Installation

14 Installation is the reverse of removal, noting the following:
● Apply grease to the bearings, seals and sleeves.
● Insert all bolts from the right-hand side.
● On CRF models smear the threads of the linkage arm-to-swingarm bolt with oil.
● Tighten the nuts/bolts to the torque settings specified at the beginning of the Chapter for your model.

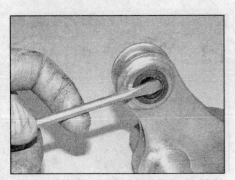

12.10 Lever the seals out…

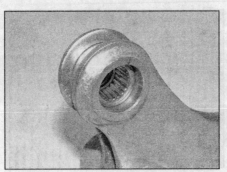

12.11 …to access the bearings

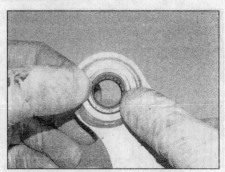

12.13 Press the new seals in

13.4 Undo the guide screws (arrowed)

13.11 Check the bush in each side

13.14 Make sure the chain slider locates correctly

13 Swingarm

1 Support the motorcycle so that no weight is transmitted through any part of the rear suspension (see illustrations 11.1a and b). Tie the front brake lever to the handlebar to ensure the bike can't roll forward.

CBR125

Removal

2 Remove the rear wheel (see Chapter 6). Remove the drive chain adjusters (see illustration 13.23).
3 Remove the chainguard/hugger, noting the collars with the bolts (see illustration 13.24).
4 Undo the brake hose guide screws (see illustration). Displace the rear brake caliper assembly from the swingarm, noting how it locates, and tie it to the passenger footrest bracket, making sure no strain is placed on the hose.
5 Unscrew the nut and withdraw the bolt securing the bottom of the shock absorber to the swingarm (see illustration 11.3).
6 Lever the swingarm pivot blanking caps out of the frame using a small screwdriver (see illustration 13.29a). Unscrew the nut on the right-hand end of the swingarm pivot bolt (see illustration 13.29b).
7 Withdraw the pivot bolt then manoeuvre the swingarm out (see illustration 13.30).
8 Remove the chain slider from the swingarm

if necessary, noting the collar with the screw (see illustration 13.14). If the slider is badly worn or damaged, it should be replaced with a new one.

Inspection

9 Thoroughly clean the swingarm, removing all traces of dirt, corrosion and grease.
10 Inspect the swingarm closely, looking for obvious signs of wear such as heavy scoring, and cracks or distortion due to accident damage.
11 Inspect the bushes in the swingarm pivots for wear or damage (see illustration). If necessary replace the swingarm with a new one – the bushes are not available separately.
12 Check the swingarm pivot bolt is straight by rolling it on a flat surface (first wipe off all old grease and remove any corrosion using wire wool). Replace the pivot bolt with a new one if it is bent.
13 Inspect all pivot components for wear or damage.

Installation

14 If removed, fit the chain slider, making sure it locates correctly over the lug at the front (see illustration). Do not forget to fit the collar with the screw.
15 Lubricate the bushes and the pivot bolt with multi-purpose grease.
16 Offer up the swingarm and have an assistant hold it in place. Make sure the drive chain is looped over the front of the swingarm. Slide the pivot bolt through from the left-hand side (see illustration 13.30).
17 Thread the nut onto the pivot bolt and

tighten it to the torque setting specified at the beginning of the Chapter (see illustration 13.29b). Check the swingarm moves up and down freely. Fit the blanking caps into the frame (see illustration 13.29a).
18 Align the shock absorber with the swingarm then fit the bolt from the right and tighten the nut to the specified torque setting (see illustration 11.3).
19 Locate the brake caliper assembly on the swingarm. Fit the brake hose guides (see illustration 13.4).
20 Fit the chainguard/hugger, not forgetting the collars with the bolts (see illustration 13.24).
21 Fit the drive chain adjusters into the swingarm (see illustration 13.23). Install the rear wheel (see Chapter 6).
22 Check and adjust the drive chain slack (see Chapter 1). Check the operation of the rear suspension and brake before taking the machine on the road.

CBR250

Removal

23 Remove the rear wheel (see Chapter 6). Remove the drive chain adjusters (see illustration).
24 Remove the chainguard/hugger, noting the collars with the bolts (see illustration).
25 Disconnect the drain hose from the air filter housing.
26 Undo the brake hose/wheel sensor wiring (RA models) guide screw and free the hose and wire from the hook (see illustration). Displace the rear brake caliper assembly from

13.23 Remove the adjuster from each end of the swingarm

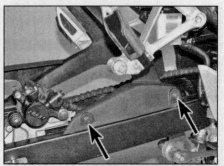

13.24 Unscrew the two bolts (arrowed) on each side to release the chainguard

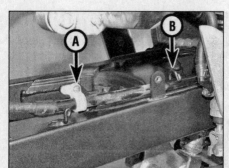

13.26 Undo the screw (A) and release the hose/wire from the hook (B)

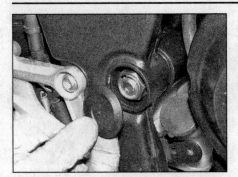

13.29a Remove the blanking cap from each side...

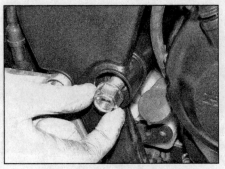

13.29b ...then unscrew the nut...

13.30 ...withdraw the bolt and remove the swingarm

the swingarm, noting how it locates, and tie it to the passenger footrest bracket, making sure no strain is placed on the hose.

27 Unscrew the nut and withdraw the bolt securing the linkage arm to the swingarm **(see illustration 12.4)**.

28 Unscrew the nut and withdraw the bolt securing the shock absorber to the linkage arm **(see illustration 11.10)**.

29 Lever the swingarm pivot blanking caps out of the frame using a small screwdriver **(see illustration)**. Unscrew the nut on the right-hand end of the swingarm pivot bolt **(see illustration)**.

30 Withdraw the pivot bolt then manoeuvre the swingarm out **(see illustration)**.

31 Remove the chain slider from the

swingarm if necessary, noting how it locates **(see illustration)**. If the slider is badly worn or damaged, it should be replaced with a new one – there is a wear limit groove and arrow on the side **(see illustration)**.

32 Remove the spacer from each side **(see illustrations)**. Inspect all pivot components for wear or damage.

Inspection

33 Thoroughly clean the swingarm, removing all traces of dirt, corrosion and grease.

34 Inspect the swingarm closely, looking for obvious signs of wear such as heavy scoring, and cracks or distortion due to accident damage.

35 Check the swingarm pivot bolt is straight

by rolling it on a flat surface such (first wipe off all old grease and remove any corrosion using steel wool). Replace the pivot bolt with a new one if it is bent.

Bearing check and replacement

36 Lever the grease seal out from each side, noting which size fits where **(see illustration)**. New seals must be used, but keep the old ones laid out in order so the new seals can be matched for position. Withdraw the long central spacer from the left **(see illustration)**.

37 Refer to *Tools and Workshop Tips* in the Reference section and check the bearings – there are two caged ball bearings held by a circlip in the right-hand pivot, and a needle bearing in the left-hand pivot **(see**

13.31a Chain slider pegs locate in holes in the swingarm

13.31b Chain slider wear limit mark is denoted by the moulded arrow

13.32a Remove the long spacer from the left-hand side...

13.32b ...and the short one from the right

13.36a Lever the seal out from each side of each pivot

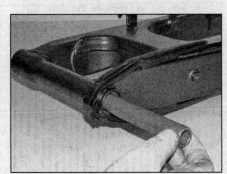

13.36b Withdraw the spacer

13.37a A circlip (arrowed) secures the right-hand bearings

13.37b Left-hand pivot needle bearing (arrowed)

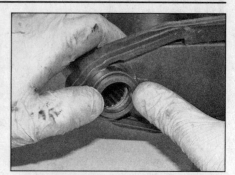

13.39 Make sure you select the correct seal for each pivot

illustrations). Clean them and inspect them for corrosion, wear and damage. If the bearings do not run smoothly and freely or if there is excessive freeplay between them and the collars, they must be replaced with new ones – refer to the Reference Section for removal and installation methods, noting that Honda specify the need for an hydraulic press. The bearings must be replaced with new ones if removed – they cannot be reused.

38 Pack the new bearings with grease. On the right-hand side press or drive the caged ball bearings in with their marked sides facing out using a socket or driver located on the outer race until they seat. Fit the circlip into the groove, using a new one if the old one deformed on removal **(see illustration 13.37a)**. Press the needle bearing into the left-hand side with its marked end facing out until it seats, at which point the seating ledge for the seal will be visible **(see illustration 13.37b)**.

39 Lubricate the spacers and grease seal lips with grease. Slide the central spacer into the left-hand side of the swingarm so it sits between the bearings **(see illustration 13.36b)**. Press the new seals into place – the right-hand seal is larger **(see illustration)**.

Installation

40 If removed, fit the chain slider, making sure it locates correctly over the lug at the front and the pegs locate in the holes **(see illustration 13.31a)**.

41 Fit the short spacer into the right-hand seal and the longer one into the left **(see illustrations 13.32b and a)**. Lubricate the pivot bolt with multi-purpose grease.

42 Offer up the swingarm and have an assistant hold it in place. Make sure the drive chain is looped over the front of the swingarm. Slide the pivot bolt through from the left-hand side **(see illustration 13.30)**.

43 Thread the nut onto the pivot bolt and tighten it to the torque setting specified at the beginning of the Chapter **(see illustration 13.29b)**. Check the swingarm moves up and down freely. Fit the blanking caps into the frame **(see illustration 13.29a)**.

44 Align the shock absorber with the linkage arm then fit the bolt from the right and tighten the nut to the specified torque setting **(see illustration 11.10)**.

45 Align the linkage arm with the swingarm then fit the bolt from the right and tighten the nut to the specified torque setting **(see illustration 12.4)**.

46 Locate the brake calliper assembly on the swingarm. Route the hose, and on RA models the sensor wire, under the hook and fit the guide **(see illustration 13.26)**.

47 Connect the drain hose to the air filter housing.

48 Fit the chainguard/hugger, not forgetting the collars with the bolts **(see illustration 13.24)**.

49 Fit the drive chain adjusters into the swingarm **(see illustration 13.23)**. Install the rear wheel (see Chapter 6).

50 Check and adjust the drive chain slack (see Chapter 1). Check the operation of the rear suspension and brake before taking the machine on the road.

CRF250

Removal

51 Remove the rear wheel (see Chapter 6).

52 Remove the chain slider from the chain guide, then remove the guide from the swingarm **(see illustrations)**. Remove the chainguard, noting how it locates at the front **(see illustration)**.

53 Undo the brake hose guide screws **(see illustration)**. Displace the rear brake caliper assembly from the swingarm, noting how it locates, and tie it to the passenger footrest bracket, making sure no strain is placed on the hose.

54 Unscrew the nut, remove the washer, and withdraw the bolt securing the linkage arm to the swingarm **(see illustration 12.4)**.

55 Unscrew the nut and withdraw the bolt securing the shock absorber to the linkage arm **(see illustration 11.19)**.

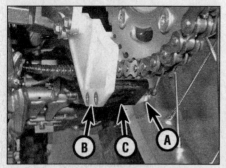

13.52a Undo the nuts (A), withdraw the screws (B) and remove the slider (C)

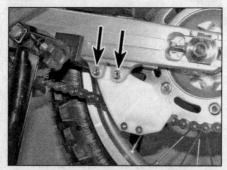

13.52b Unscrew the bolts (arrowed) and remove the guide

13.52c Chainguard bolts (arrowed)

13.53 Undo the guide screws (arrowed)

56 Unscrew the nut on the right-hand end of the swingarm pivot bolt **(see illustration)**.

57 Withdraw the pivot bolt then manoeuvre the swingarm out.

58 Remove the chain slider from the swingarm if necessary, noting the washer and collar locations. If the slider is badly worn or damaged, it should be replaced with a new one – there is a wear limit groove and arrow on the side **(see illustration 13.31b)**.

59 Remove the pivot cap from each side. Inspect all pivot components for wear or damage.

Inspection

60 Thoroughly clean the swingarm, removing all traces of dirt, corrosion and grease.

61 Inspect the swingarm closely, looking for obvious signs of wear such as heavy scoring, and cracks or distortion due to accident damage.

62 Check the swingarm pivot bolt is straight by rolling it on a flat surface such (first wipe off all old grease and remove any corrosion using steel wool). Replace the pivot bolt with a new one if it is bent.

Bearing check and replacement

63 Withdraw the long central spacer from the left **(see illustration 13.36b)**.

64 Refer to *Tools and Workshop Tips* in the Reference section and check the bearings – there is a needle bearing in each side pivot with a seal behind it. Clean them and inspect them for corrosion, wear and damage. If the bearings do not run smoothly and freely or if there is excessive freeplay between them and the spacer, they must be replaced with new ones – refer to the Reference Section for removal and installation methods, noting that Honda specify the need for an hydraulic press. The bearings must be replaced with new ones if removed – they cannot be reused.

65 When installing the new seals and bearings, pack them with grease. Press each seal in with its marked side facing out until it seats. Press each needle bearing in with its marked end facing out until it seats against the seal, then check the set depth from the outer rim – it should be 12 to 12.5 mm on the right pivot and 7 to 7.5 mm on the left pivot.

66 Lubricate the spacer with grease and slide it into the bearings.

13.56 Unscrew the nut (arrowed)

Installation

67 If removed, fit the chain slider, making sure it locates correctly over the lug at the front. The plain washer goes with the upper front screw, the round collar with the lower front screw, and the oblong collars with the rear screws.

68 Lubricate the pivot bolt and the pivot cap seals with multi-purpose grease, and pack grease into the space between each end of the spacer and the swingarm. Fit the caps.

69 Offer up the swingarm and have an assistant hold it in place. Make sure the drive chain is looped over the front of the swingarm. Slide the pivot bolt through from the left-hand side.

70 Thread the nut onto the pivot bolt and tighten it to the torque setting specified at the beginning of the Chapter. Check the swingarm moves up and down freely.

71 Align the shock absorber with the linkage arm then fit the bolt from the right and tighten the nut to the specified torque setting **(see illustration 11.19)**.

72 Align the linkage arm with the swingarm then fit the bolt from the right. Smear the bolt threads with oil, fit the washer and tighten the nut to the specified torque setting.

73 Locate the brake caliper assembly on the swingarm. Fit the hose guides **(see illustration 13.53)**.

74 Fit the chainguard, guide and slider **(see illustrations 13.52c, b and a)** – make sure the guard locates correctly over the bracket at the front **(see illustration)**.

75 Install the rear wheel (see Chapter 6).

13.74 Locate the front of the guard over the bracket

76 Check and adjust the drive chain slack (see Chapter 1). Check the operation of the rear suspension and brake before taking the machine on the road.

14 Rear shock absorber adjustment (250 models)

CBR250

1 Spring pre-load is adjusted using a suitable C-spanner (one is provided in the toolkit) to turn the spring seat on the bottom of the shock absorber **(see illustrations)**.

2 There are three positions. Position 1 is the lowest setting for light loads, position 2 the standard, and position 3 the highest, for heavy loads. Align the setting required with the adjustment stopper.

CRF250

3 Spring pre-load can be adjusted using a suitable C-spanner or a drift to slacken the locknut and turn the adjuster on the top of the spring **(see illustration)**.

4 For access remove the shock absorber (see Section 11). Turn the adjuster clockwise to increase pre-load and anti-clockwise to reduce it. The amount of pre-load is determined by the length of the spring – the longer the spring the less pre-load. No maximum and minimum lengths are provided by Honda, and it is best to make only minor adjustments from the factory set length, if necessary.

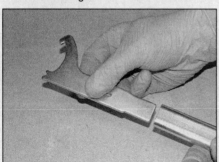

14.1a Fit the C-spanner into the handle...

14.1b ...and turn the spring seat as required

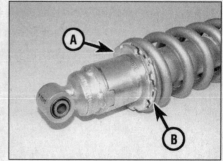

14.3 Slacken the locknut (A) and turn the adjuster (B)

Chapter 6
Brakes, wheels and final drive

Contents

Degrees of difficulty

| **Easy,** suitable for novice with little experience | 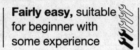 | **Fairly easy,** suitable for beginner with some experience | | **Fairly difficult,** suitable for competent DIY mechanic | | **Difficult,** suitable for experienced DIY mechanic | | **Very difficult,** suitable for expert DIY or professional | |

Specifications

Brake fluid
Brake fluid type . . . . DOT 4

Front brake caliper
Caliper bore ID
  CBR125 and CBR250R
    Standard . . . . 25.400 to 25.450 mm
    Service limit . . . . 25.460 mm
  CBR250RA
    Centre piston
      Standard . . . . 22.650 to 22.700 mm
      Service limit . . . . 22.710 mm
    Outer pistons
      Standard . . . . 27.000 to 27.050 mm
      Service limit . . . . 27.060 mm
  CRF250
    Standard . . . . 27.000 to 27.050 mm
    Service limit . . . . 27.060 mm
Caliper piston OD
  CBR125 and CBR250R
    Standard . . . . 25.318 to 25.368 mm
    Service limit . . . . 25.310 mm
  CBR250RA
    Centre piston
      Standard . . . . 22.585 to 22.618 mm
      Service limit . . . . 22.560 mm
    Outer pistons
      Standard . . . . 26.918 to 26.968 mm
      Service limit . . . . 26.910 mm
  CRF250
    Standard . . . . 26.935 to 26.968 mm
    Service limit . . . . 26.890 mm

Front brake master cylinder

Master cylinder bore ID
  CBR125, CBR250RA and CRF250
    Standard . . . . 12.700 to 12.743 mm
    Service limit . . . . 12.755 mm
  CBR250R
    Standard . . . . 11.000 to 11.043 mm
    Service limit . . . . 11.055 mm
Master cylinder piston OD
  CBR125, CBR250RA and CRF250
    Standard . . . . 12.657 to 12.684 mm
    Service limit . . . . 12.645 mm
  CBR250R
    Standard . . . . 10.957 to 10.984 mm
    Service limit . . . . 10.945 mm

Front brake disc

Disc thickness
  CBR125
    Standard . . . . 3.8 to 4.2 mm
    Service limit . . . . 3.5 mm
  CBR250R/RA
    Standard . . . . 4.3 to 4.7 mm
    Service limit . . . . 3.5 mm
  CRF250
    Standard . . . . 3.3 to 3.7 mm
    Service limit . . . . 3.0 mm
Disc maximum runout . . . . 0.3 mm

Rear brake caliper

Caliper bore ID
  CBR125
    Standard . . . . 32.030 to 32.080 mm
    Service limit . . . . 32.090 mm
  CBR250R/RA
    Standard . . . . 38.180 to 38.230 mm
    Service limit . . . . 38.240 mm
  CRF250
    Standard . . . . 27.000 to 27.050 mm
    Service limit . . . . 27.060 mm
Caliper piston OD
  CBR125
    Standard . . . . 31.948 to 31.998 mm
    Service limit . . . . 31.940 mm
  CBR250R/RA
    Standard . . . . 38.098 to 38.148 mm
    Service limit . . . . 38.090 mm
  CRF250
    Standard . . . . 26.935 to 26.968 mm
    Service limit . . . . 26.890 mm

Rear brake master cylinder

Master cylinder bore ID
  CBR125 and CRF250
    Standard . . . . 12.700 to 12.743 mm
    Service limit . . . . 12.755 mm
  CBR250R/RA
    Standard . . . . 14.000 to 14.043 mm
    Service limit . . . . 14.055 mm
Master cylinder piston OD
  CBR125 and CRF250
    Standard . . . . 12.657 to 12.684 mm
    Service limit . . . . 12.645 mm
  CBR250R/RA
    Standard . . . . 13.957 to 13.984 mm
    Service limit . . . . 13.945 mm

Rear brake disc

Disc thickness
  CBR125
    Standard . . . .   3.8 to 4.2 mm
    Service limit . . . .   3.5 mm
  CBR250R/RA
    Standard . . . .   4.8 to 5.2 mm
    Service limit . . . .   4.0 mm
  CRF250
    Standard . . . .   4.3 to 4.7 mm
    Service limit . . . .   3.5 mm
Disc maximum runout . . . .   0.3 mm

ABS system (CBR250RA)

Wheel speed sensor air gap. . . . .   0.2 to 1.2 mm

Wheels

Maximum wheel runout (front and rear)
  Axial (side-to-side) . . . .   2.0 mm
  Radial (out-of-round) . . . .   2.0 mm
Maximum axle runout (front and rear) . . . .   0.2 mm

Tyres

Tyre pressures . . . .   see *Pre-ride* checks
Tyre sizes*
  CBR125
    Front 100/80-17M/C (52P)
    Rear 130/70-17M/C (62P)
  CBR250R/RA
    Front 110/70-17 (54S)
    Rear 190/50-ZR17 (66S)
  CRF250L
    Front 3.00-21 (51P)
    Rear 120/80-18M/C (62P)
  CRF250M
    Front 110/70-17M/C (54S)
    Rear 130/70-17M/C (62S)

Refer to the owner's handbook or the tyre information label on the swingarm for approved tyre brands.

Final drive

Drive chain slack and lubricant . . . .   see Chapter 1
Drive chain type/links
  CBR125 . . . .   DID428V13/128
  CBR250R/RA . . . .   DID520VF/108LE or RK520KLO/108LE
  CRF250. . . . .   DID520VF/106LE
Joining link pin projection from side plate (unstaked) . . . .   1.1 mm
Joining link staked ends diameter
  CBR125 . . . .   4.75 to 4.95 mm
  CBR250R/RA
    DID . . . .   5.50 to 5.80 mm
    RK . . . .   5.25 to 5.65 mm
  CRF250. . . . .   5.50 to 5.80 mm
Sprocket sizes (No. of teeth)
  CBR125
    Front (engine) sprocket.   15
    Rear (wheel) sprocket.   44
  CBR250R/RA
    Front (engine) sprocket.   14
    Rear (wheel) sprocket.   38
  CRF250
    Front (engine) sprocket.   14
    Rear (wheel) sprocket.   40

Torque settings

Brake caliper bleed valves	5.5 Nm
Brake disc bolts	
Front	
CBR125	43 Nm
CBR250R/RA and CRF250	20 Nm
Rear	42 Nm
Brake hose banjo bolts	34 Nm
Brake pipe nuts (CBR250RA)	14 Nm
Footrest bracket bolts	
CBR125	26 Nm
CBR250R/RA	27 Nm
Front axle nut (CBR125 and CBR250R/RA)	59 Nm
Front axle (CRF250)	74 Nm
Front axle clamp bolt (CBR250R/RA)	22 Nm
Front axle clamp bolts (CRF250)	20 Nm
Front brake caliper mounting bolts	30 Nm
Front brake master cylinder clamp bolts	11 Nm
Front brake pad retaining pin	
CBR125 and CRF250	17 Nm
CBR250R/RA	18 Nm
Front sprocket bolts	10 Nm
Front wheel pulse ring screws (CBR250RA)	7 Nm
Rear axle nut	
CBR125	69 Nm
CBR250R/RA	88 Nm
CRF250	88 Nm
Rear brake pad retaining pin	17 Nm
Rear brake master cylinder mounting bolts	
CBR125 and CBR250R/RA	12 Nm
CRF250	14 Nm
Rear sprocket nuts/bolts	
CBR125	65 Nm
CBR250R/RA	75 Nm
CRF250	50 Nm
Rear wheel pulse ring screws (CBR250RA)	7 Nm

1 General information

CBR models are fitted with 17 inch 5-spoke cast alloy wheels which carry tubeless tyres. Both CRF models have wire-spoked wheels; the L model uses 21 inch front and 18 inch rear knobbly tyres, and the M uses 17 inch wheels with supermotorad style tyres. The tyres on both CRF models are fitted with inner tubes.

Braking components are all hydraulic and manufactured by Nissin. Exact fitments are detailed below:

CBR125R models have a twin piston sliding caliper acting on a 276 mm disc at the front, and a single piston sliding caliper acting on a 220 mm disc at the rear.

CBR250R models have a twin piston sliding caliper acting on a 296 mm disc at the front, and a single piston sliding caliper acting on a 220 mm disc at the rear.

CBR250RA models have Honda's combined anti-lock braking system (ABS), with a triple piston sliding caliper acting on a 296 mm disc at the front, and a single piston sliding caliper acting on a 220 mm disc at the rear. When the front brake lever is applied the system actuates the outer pistons in the front caliper. When the rear brake pedal is applied the system actuates the piston in the rear caliper and the centre piston in the front caliper via a proportional control and a delay valve.

CRF250L/M models have a twin piston sliding caliper acting on a 296 mm disc at the front, and a single piston sliding caliper acting on a 220 mm disc at the rear.

Caution: Disc brake components rarely require disassembly. Do not disassemble components unless absolutely necessary. If an hydraulic brake hose is loosened or disconnected, the banjo union sealing washers must be replaced with new ones and the system must be bled upon reassembly. Do not use solvents on internal brake components. Solvents will cause the seals to swell and distort. Use only clean DOT 4 brake fluid for cleaning. Use care when working with brake fluid as it can injure your eyes and it will damage painted surfaces and plastic parts.

2 Front brake pads

Note: Honda recommend using new caliper mounting bolts. This is because the bolts are pre-treated with a locking compound. If they are not available it is possible, however, to clean up the old bolts and reinstall them using a suitable non-permanent thread locking compound that is commercially available.

⚠ *Warning: The dust created by the brake system is harmful to your health. Never blow it out with compressed air and don't inhale any of it. An approved filtering mask should be worn when working on the brakes.*

Note: Do not operate the brake lever, or the pedal on CBR250RA models, while the caliper is off the disc.

1 For greater freedom of movement displace the brake hose(s) and on CBR250RA models the wheel sensor wire from the mudguard and/or fork as required according to model. Lay some rag over the mudguard to prevent the loose guides scratching it.

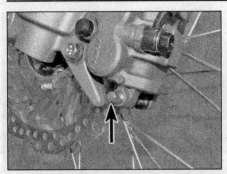

2.2a Slacken the pin (arrowed)

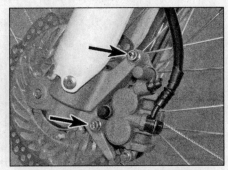

2.2b Unscrew the bolts (arrowed) and slide the caliper off the disc

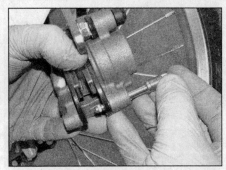

2.2c Unscrew the pin and remove the pads

2.3a Remove the plug then slacken the pin (arrowed)

2.3b Unscrew the bolts (arrowed) and slide the caliper off the disc

2.3c Unscrew the pin and remove the pads

2 On CBR125 and CRF250 models slacken the pad retaining pin **(see illustration)**. Unscrew the caliper mounting bolts and slide the caliper assembly off the disc **(see illustration)**. Unscrew and remove the pad pin, then remove the pads, noting how they locate **(see illustration)**.

3 On CBR250R models unscrew the pad retaining pin plug, then slacken the pad pin **(see illustration)**. Unscrew the caliper mounting bolts and slide the caliper assembly off the disc **(see illustration)**. Unscrew and remove the pad pin, then remove the pads, noting how they locate **(see illustration)**.

4 On CBR250RA models unscrew the speed sensor bolts and displace the sensor. Slacken the pad retaining pin. Unscrew the caliper mounting bolts and slide the caliper assembly off the disc. Unscrew and remove the pad pin, then remove the pads, noting how they locate.

5 Slide the caliper and bracket apart **(see illustration)**.

6 Where fitted and if required remove the shim from the back of each pad, noting how it fits – note that new pads should come with new shims where applicable, but make sure they do, especially if fitting after-market pads, before discarding the old ones.

7 Inspect the surface of each pad for contamination and check that the friction material has not worn to or beyond its service limit (see Chapter 1, Section 2). If any pad is worn, fouled with oil or grease, or heavily

scored or damaged, fit a complete set of new pads. Also check that wear is even across each pad – uneven wear is indicative of a sticking or seized piston (see Steps 9 and 10). **Note:** *It is not possible to degrease the friction material; if the pads are contaminated in any way they must be replaced with new ones.*

8 If the pads are in good condition clean them carefully, using a fine wire brush that is completely free of oil and grease to remove all traces of road dirt and corrosion. Using a pointed instrument, dig out any embedded particles of foreign matter. Spray with a dedicated brake cleaner.

9 Remove the pad spring from the caliper if required, noting which way round it fits **(see**

illustration 2.14a or b). Clean around the exposed section of each piston to remove any dirt or debris that could cause the seals to be damaged. If new pads are being fitted, now push the pistons all the way back into the caliper to create room for them; if the old pads are still serviceable push the pistons in a little way. To push the pistons back use finger pressure or a piece of wood or metal as leverage, or place the old pads back in the caliper and use a metal bar or a screwdriver inserted between them (do not use this method if the pads are being re-used), or use grips or a G-clamp and a piece of wood, with rag or card to protect the caliper body **(see illustration)**. Alternatively obtain a proper piston-pushing tool from a good tool supplier

2.5 Slide the caliper off the bracket

2.9a Press the pistons in as described to make clearance for new pads

2.9b This is a commercially available piston pushing tool

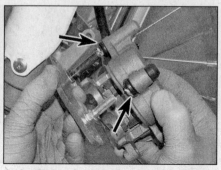

2.13a Slider pin boots (arrowed) – CBR125 and CRF250

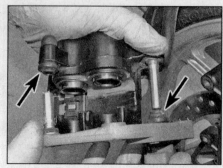

2.13b Slider pin boots (arrowed) – CBR250

(see illustration). It may be necessary to remove the master cylinder reservoir cover, plate and diaphragm and siphon out some fluid (see *Pre-ride checks*). If the pistons are difficult to push back, remove the bleed valve cap, then attach a length of clear hose to the bleed valve and place the open end in a suitable container, then open the valve and try again (see Section 11). Take great care not to draw any air into the system. If in doubt, bleed the brakes afterwards.

10 If a piston appears seized, first block or hold the other piston(s) using wood or cable-ties, then apply the brake lever and check whether the piston in question moves at all. If it moves out but can't be pushed back in the chances are there is some hidden corrosion stopping it. If it doesn't move at all, or to fully clean and inspect the pistons, disassemble the caliper and overhaul it (see Section 3).

11 Check the condition of the brake disc (see Section 4).
12 Remove all traces of corrosion from the pad pin and check for wear and damage. On all except CBR250R models check the condition of the stopper ring on the pin and replace it with a new one if it is damaged or deformed **(see illustration 6.8)**.
13 Clean off all traces of corrosion and hardened grease from the slider pins on the bracket and the rubber boots in the caliper. Replace the boots with new ones if they are damaged, deformed or deteriorated **(see illustrations)**. Make sure the slider pins are tight.
14 Clean the pad spring and fit it into the caliper if removed, making sure it locates correctly **(see illustrations)**. Clean the pad guide on the bracket and check it is correctly fitted **(see illustrations)**. Clean all old grease off the slider pins. Check the condition of the rubber boots and replace them with new ones if necessary.

15 Smear the slider pins and inside the rubber boots with silicone grease. Slide the caliper and bracket together, making sure each boot lip locates correctly in the groove in the pin **(see illustration 2.13a or b)**.
16 Where fitted and if removed fit the shim onto the back of each pad, making sure it locates correctly. Clean the outer face of each shim so it is shiny.
17 On pads without shims lightly smear the back of the pad backing material with copper-based grease, making sure that none gets on the friction material. Also smear the pad pin. On all except CBR250R models apply a smear of silicone grease to the stopper ring on the pad pin **(see illustration 6.8)**.
18 On CBR125 and CRF250 models fit the pads into the caliper, seating the outer pad against the guide on the bracket and the upper hooked end of the inner pad around the post **(see illustrations)**. Press them up against the

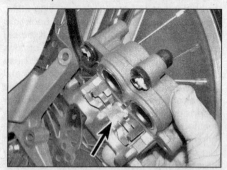

2.14a Pad spring (arrowed) – CBR125 and CRF250

2.14b Pad spring (arrowed) – CBR250

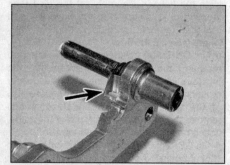

2.14c Pad guide (arrowed) – CBR125 and CRF250

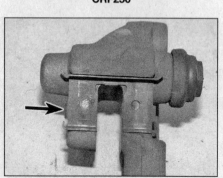

2.14d Pad guide (arrowed) – CBR250

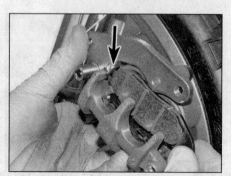

2.18a Fit the outer pad end against the guide…

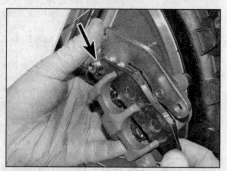

2.18b …and the inner pad end around the post

2.18c Slide the caliper onto the disc and fit the bolts

2.19a Seat the pads against the guide (arrowed)

2.19b Slide the caliper onto the disc and fit the bolts

spring to align the holes, then insert the pad pin and tighten it finger-tight (see illustration 2.2c). Slide the caliper assembly onto the disc making sure the pads locate correctly on each side (see illustration). Either fit new caliper mounting bolts, or clean the threads of the original bolts and apply fresh thread locking compound, then tighten them and the pad pin to the torque settings specified at the beginning of the Chapter.

19 On CBR250R models fit the pads into the caliper, seating them against the guide on the bracket (see illustration). Press them up against the spring to align the holes, then insert the pad pin and tighten it finger-tight (see illustration 2.3c). Slide the caliper assembly onto the disc making sure the pads locate correctly on each side (see illustration). Either fit new caliper mounting bolts, or clean the threads of the original bolts and apply fresh thread locking compound, then tighten them and the pad pin to the torque settings specified at the beginning of the Chapter. Fit the pad pin plug.

20 On CBR250RA models fit the pads into the caliper so the friction material on each pad faces the other, and seat the pads against the guide on the bracket. Press them up against the spring to align the holes, then insert the pad

pin and tighten it finger-tight. Slide the caliper assembly onto the disc making sure the pads locate correctly on each side. Either fit new caliper mounting bolts, or clean the threads of the original bolts and apply fresh thread locking compound, then tighten them and the pad pin to the torque settings specified at the beginning of the Chapter. Make sure the speed sensor head is clean then fit it into the bracket.

21 Fit the brake hose/wiring guide(s) onto the mudguard or fork as required according to model.

22 Pump the brake lever until the pads contact the disc. On CBR250RA models also operate the brake pedal until the centre piston contacts the pads. Check the level of fluid in the reservoir (front and rear on CBR250RA models) and top-up if necessary (see *Pre-ride checks*).

23 Test the brake before riding the motorcycle.

3 Front brake caliper

⚠️ **Warning: Overhaul must be done in a spotlessly clean work area to avoid contamination and**

possible failure of the brake hydraulic system components. Do not, under any circumstances, use petroleum-based solvents to clean brake parts. Use clean DOT 4 brake fluid, dedicated brake cleaner or denatured alcohol only, as described. To prevent damage from spilled brake fluid, always cover paintwork when working on the braking system, and have plenty of absorbent rag to hand to catch and wipe off any spilled fluid.

Removal

Caution: Do not operate the brakes while the caliper is off the disc.

1 Drain the brake fluid from the system (see Section 11).

2 Unscrew the brake hose banjo bolt(s) and detach the hose(s), noting the alignment with the caliper (see illustration). Seal the banjo union to prevent any dirt getting in (see illustration). Note that new sealing washers will be required later.

3 Refer to Section 2, Steps 1 to 5, and remove the brake pads – this involves removing the caliper from the disc.

Overhaul

4 Clean the exterior of the caliper and the bracket with denatured alcohol or brake

3.2a Brake hose banjo bolt (arrowed)

3.2b Seal the banjo using a nut and bolt and the sealing washers

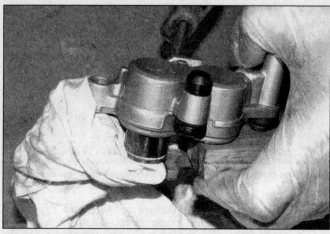

3.6a Apply compressed air to the fluid passage...

3.6b ...until the piston is displaced

system cleaner. Have some clean rag ready to catch any spilled brake fluid.

5 To remove the pistons you need either a supply of compressed air, or a piston removal tool, or if neither are available a good pair of external circlip removal pliers.

6 If you are using compressed air make sure the bleed valve is tight. Cover the pistons and the caliper with rag and apply compressed air gradually and progressively, starting with a fairly low pressure, to the fluid inlet in the caliper and allow the pistons to ease out of the bores (see illustrations). If one piston is being pushed out before the other(s), block that one so more pressure is applied to the sticking one(s), but do not use your fingers. Always make sure the caliper is

covered, with the pistons pointing down onto the bench so they cannot fly out and hit something.

7 If you are using a dedicated tool or the circlip pliers, grip the inner wall of the piston then twist and pull the piston out, keeping it square to the bore wall until it is free (see illustration 7.11). Do not try to remove a piston by levering it out or by using pliers or other grips that may scratch the outer wall, unless you are prepared to fit a new piston, and possibly a new caliper.

8 If a piston is stuck in its bore due to corrosion replace the caliper with a new one.

9 Mark each piston and the caliper body to ensure that the pistons can be matched to their original bores on reassembly.

10 Remove the dust seals and the piston seals from the bores using a plastic tool to avoid scratching the bores (see illustrations). Discard the seals – new ones must be fitted on reassembly.

11 Clean the pistons and bores with clean brake fluid. If compressed air is available, blow it through the fluid passages to ensure they are clear (make sure it is filtered and unlubricated).

Caution: Do not, under any circumstances, use a petroleum-based solvent to clean brake parts.

12 Inspect the caliper bores and pistons for signs of corrosion, nicks and burrs and loss of plating (see illustration). If surface defects are present, the pistons and/or the caliper assembly must be replaced with new ones. If the caliper is in poor condition, the master cylinder should also be checked.

13 Lubricate the new piston seals with clean brake fluid and fit them into the inner grooves in the caliper bores (see illustrations). On CBR250RA models note that there are two sizes of bore (see Specifications) and care must therefore be taken to ensure that the correct size seals are fitted to the correct bores. The same applies when fitting the new dust seals and pistons.

14 Lubricate the new dust seals with silicone grease if available or new brake fluid if not,

3.10a Remove the dust seals...

3.10b ...and the piston seals

3.12 Check the surfaces of the pistons and bores – the plating on this piston is lifting off

3.13a Lubricate the new piston seal with brake fluid...

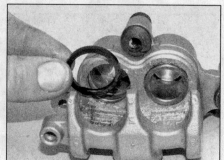

3.13b ...then fit it into its groove...

3.14 ...followed by the new dust seal

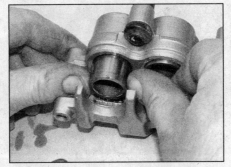

3.15 Fit the piston and push it all the way in

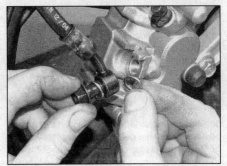

3.17 Always use new sealing washers

and fit them into the outer grooves in the caliper bores **(see illustrations)**.

15 Lubricate the pistons with clean brake fluid and fit them, closed-end first, into the caliper bores, taking care not to displace the seals **(see illustration)**. Using your thumbs, push the pistons all the way in, making sure they enter the bore squarely.

Installation

16 Fit the brake pads into the caliper and the caliper onto the disc (see Section 2, Steps 12 to 21).

17 Connect the brake hose to the caliper, using new sealing washers on each side of the banjo fitting **(see illustration)**. Align the hose as noted on removal. Tighten the banjo bolt to the specified torque.

18 Refer to Section 11 to fill and bleed the system.

19 Pump the brake lever until the pads contact the disc. On CBR250RA models also operate the brake pedal until the centre piston contacts the pads. Check the level of fluid in the reservoir (front and rear on CBR250RA models) and top-up if necessary (see *Pre-ride checks*).

20 Check that there are no fluid leaks and test the brake before riding the motorcycle.

4   Front brake disc

Inspection

1 Inspect the surface of the disc for score marks and other damage. Light scratches are normal after use and won't affect brake operation, but deep grooves and heavy score marks will reduce braking efficiency and accelerate pad wear. If a disc is badly grooved it must be replaced with a new one.

2 The disc must not be allowed to wear down to a thickness less than the service limit listed in this Chapter's Specifications. The minimum thickness is also stamped on the disc. Check the thickness of the disc in the middle of the pad contact area using a micrometer **(see illustration)** – do not measure across the rim of the disc with a ruler. Replace the disc with a new one if necessary.

3 To check if the disc is warped, position the bike on an auxiliary stand so the front wheel is off the ground. Mount a dial gauge to the fork leg, with the gauge plunger touching the surface of the disc about 10 mm from its outer edge **(see illustration)**. Rotate the wheel and watch the gauge needle, comparing the reading with the limit listed in the Specifications at the beginning of this Chapter. If the runout is greater than the service limit, check the wheel bearings for play (see Chapter 1). If the bearings are worn, fit new ones (see Section 19) and repeat this check. If the disc runout is still excessive, remove the disc (see below) and check for corrosion where it seats on the hub and clean it up if necessary. You can also try moving the disc around the wheel one bolt hole at a time and after each movement rechecking for runout. In most cases a new disc will have to be fitted.

Removal

Note: *Honda recommend using new disc mounting bolts. This is because the bolts are pre-treated with a locking compound. If they are not available it is possible, however, to clean up the old bolts and reinstall them using a suitable non-permanent thread locking compound that is commercially available.*

4 Remove the wheel (see Section 17).

5 On CBR250RA models remove the pulse ring from the wheel (see Section 14).

6 If you are not replacing the disc with a new one, mark the relationship of the disc to the wheel, so it can be installed in the same position and on the same side as originally fitted. Unscrew the disc bolts, loosening them evenly and a little at a time in a criss-cross pattern to avoid distorting the disc, then remove the disc **(see illustration)**.

Installation

7 Before fitting the disc, make sure there is no dirt or corrosion where the disc seats on the hub. If the disc does not sit flat when it is bolted down, it will appear to be warped when checked or when the front brake is used.

8 Fit the disc on the wheel with its marked side facing out, aligning the previously applied matchmarks (if you're reinstalling the original disc), and making sure the arrow points in the direction of normal rotation.

9 Either fit the new bolts, or clean the threads of the original bolts and apply fresh thread locking compound, and tighten them evenly and a little at a time in a criss-cross pattern to

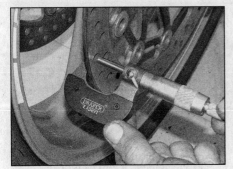

4.2 Measuring disc thickness using a micrometer

4.3 Checking disc runout with a dial gauge

4.6 Brake disc bolts (arrowed)

the torque setting specified at the beginning of this Chapter. Clean the disc using acetone or brake system cleaner. If a new disc has been installed, remove any protective coating from its working surfaces and fit new brake pads.

10 On CBR250RA models fit the pulse ring (see Section 14).

11 Install the front wheel (see Section 17).

12 Operate the brake lever until the pads contact the disc. On CBR250RA models also operate the brake pedal until the centre piston contacts the pads. Check the level of fluid in the reservoir (front and rear on CBR250RA models) and top-up if necessary (see *Pre-ride checks*).

13 Test the brake before riding the motorcycle.

5 Front brake master cylinder

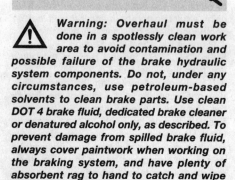

> ⚠ *Warning: Overhaul must be done in a spotlessly clean work area to avoid contamination and possible failure of the brake hydraulic system components. Do not, under any circumstances, use petroleum-based solvents to clean brake parts. Use clean DOT 4 brake fluid, dedicated brake cleaner or denatured alcohol only, as described. To prevent damage from spilled brake fluid, always cover paintwork when working on the braking system, and have plenty of absorbent rag to hand to catch and wipe off any spilled fluid.*

5.6 Unscrew the clamp bolts (arrowed)

5.8 Release the circlip and draw out the piston assembly and the spring

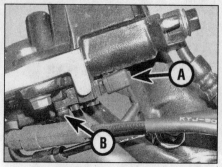

5.4 Brake light switch wires (A), switch mounting screw (B)

Removal

1 On CRF models remove the right-hand mirror (see Chapter 7).

2 Drain the brake fluid from the system (see Section 11).

3 Remove the brake lever (see Chapter 5).

4 Disconnect the brake light switch wiring connectors, and if required remove the switch **(see illustration)**.

5 Unscrew the brake hose banjo bolt and detach the hose, noting its alignment with the master cylinder **(see illustration)**. Seal the banjo union to prevent any dirt getting in **(see illustration 3.2b)**. Note that new sealing washers will be required later.

6 Unscrew the two clamp bolts and remove the master cylinder **(see illustrations)**.

Overhaul

7 Remove the rubber boot from the master cylinder **(see illustration)**.

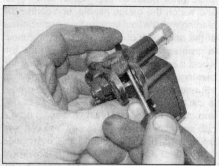

5.7 Remove the boot

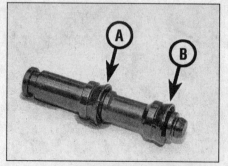

5.12 Fit the seal (A) and the cup (B) onto the piston as shown

5.5 Brake hose banjo bolt (arrowed)

8 Push the piston in and use circlip pliers to remove the circlip, then slide out the piston assembly and spring, noting how they fit **(see illustration)**. Lay the parts out in the proper order to prevent confusion during reassembly.

9 Clean the master cylinder and reservoir with clean brake fluid. If compressed air is available, blow it through the fluid galleries to ensure they are clear (make sure the air is filtered and unlubricated).

Caution: Do not, under any circumstances, use a petroleum-based solvent to clean brake parts.

10 Check the master cylinder bore for corrosion, scratches, nicks and score marks. If damage or wear is evident, the master cylinder must be replaced with a new one. If the master cylinder is in poor condition, then the caliper should be checked as well.

11 The dust boot, circlip, piston and its cup and seal, and the spring are all included in a master cylinder rebuild kit, and all other components are available individually. Use all of the new parts, regardless of the apparent condition of the old ones. Lubricate the master cylinder bore with new brake fluid.

12 Smear the cup and seal with new brake fluid and if not already in place fit them into their grooves in the piston so their wider ends will fit into the master cylinder first **(see illustration)**.

13 Fit the spring onto the piston **(see illustration)**. Lubricate the piston, cup and seal with clean brake fluid and slide the spring

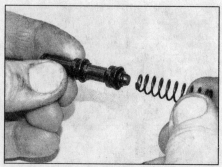

5.13a Fit the spring onto the end of the piston...

5.13b ...then fit them into the cylinder

5.14 Fit the rubber boot and press it into place

5.16 Align the mating surfaces with the punch mark (arrowed)

and piston assembly into the master cylinder **(see illustration)**. Make sure the lips on the cup and seal do not turn inside out. Push the piston in to compress the spring and fit the new circlip, making sure it locates in the groove **(see illustration 5.8)**.

14 Smear the outer end of the piston and the inside of the boot with silicone grease. Carefully push the wide rim of the boot onto its seat in the master cylinder and locate the narrow end lips in the groove in the piston **(see illustration)**.

15 Inspect the reservoir diaphragm and fit a new one it if it is damaged or deteriorated.

Installation

16 Fit the master cylinder onto the handlebar, aligning the clamp joint with the punch mark on the top of the handlebar, then fit the back of the clamp with its UP mark facing up **(see illustration)**. Tighten the upper bolt to the torque setting specified at the beginning of this Chapter, followed by the lower bolt.

17 Connect the brake hose to the master cylinder, using new sealing washers on each side of the banjo fitting **(see illustration 3.17)**. Align the hose as shown and tighten the banjo bolt to the specified torque **(see illustration 5.5)**.

18 Fit the brake light switch if removed, and connect the wiring connectors **(see illustration 5.4)**.

19 Install the brake lever (see Chapter 5). On CRF models install the mirror (see Chapter 7).

20 Refer to Section 11 to fill and bleed the system.

21 Check that there are no fluid leaks and test the brake before riding the motorcycle.

6 Rear brake pads

⚠️ *Warning: The dust created by the brake system is harmful to your health. Never blow it out with compressed air and don't inhale any of it. An approved filtering mask should be worn when working on the brakes.*

Note: *Do not operate the brake pedal while the pads are out.*

1 Push the caliper against the disc, as far as it will go if new pads are being fitted so the piston is pushed all the way back into the caliper to create room for them. It may be necessary to remove the master cylinder reservoir cover, plate and diaphragm and siphon out some fluid (see *Pre-ride checks*). If the piston is difficult to push back, remove the bleed valve cap, then attach a length of clear hose to the bleed valve and place the open end in a suitable container, then open the valve and try again (see Section 11). Take great care not to draw any air into the system. If in doubt, bleed the brake afterwards.

2 If the caliper is difficult to push in the chances are there is some hidden corrosion stopping it. If it doesn't move at all, or to fully clean and inspect the piston, remove the caliper and overhaul it (see Section 7).

3 On CBR125 and CRF250 models remove the pad retaining pin plug then unscrew and remove the pad pin and draw the pads out **(see illustrations)**.

4 On CBR250R/RA models unscrew the pad retaining pin and the caliper rear mounting bolt/slider pin **(see illustration)**. Pivot the back of the caliper up off the disc and remove the pads, noting how they fit.

5 Where fitted and if required remove the shim from the back of each pad, noting how it fits – note that new pads should come with new shims where applicable, but make sure they do, especially if fitting after-market pads, before discarding the old ones.

6 Inspect the surface of each pad for contamination and check that the friction material has not worn beyond its service limit (see Chapter 1, Section 2). If either pad is worn, is fouled with oil or grease, or heavily scored or damaged, fit a set of new pads. **Note:** *It is not possible to degrease the friction material; if the pads are contaminated in any way they must be replaced with new ones.*

7 If the pads are in good condition clean them carefully, using a fine wire brush that is completely free of oil and grease to remove all traces of road dirt and corrosion. Using a pointed instrument, dig out any embedded particles of foreign matter. Spray with a dedicated brake cleaner to remove any dust.

8 Remove all traces of corrosion from the pad pin and check it for wear and damage. Check the condition of the stopper ring on the pin

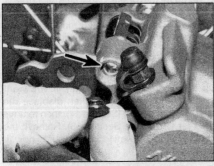

6.3a Remove the plug then unscrew the pin (arrowed)...

6.3b ...and remove the pads

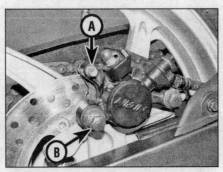

6.4 Unscrew the pin (A) and the bolt (B)

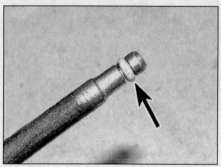

6.8 Fit a new ring (arrowed) if necessary

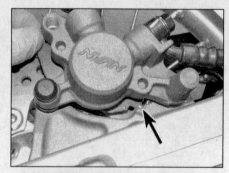

6.13a Make sure the inner end locates correctly against the guide...

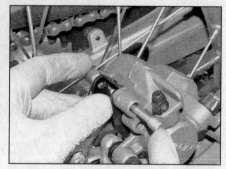

6.13b ... then press the pads up against the spring and insert the pin

6.14a Fit and tighten the rear bolt...

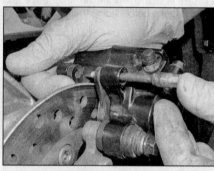

6.14b ...then press the pads up against the spring and insert the pin

and replace it with a new one if it is damaged or deformed **(see illustration)**.

9 Check the condition of the brake disc (see Section 8).

10 Where fitted and if removed fit the shim onto the back of each pad, making sure it locates correctly. Clean the outer face of each shim so it is shiny.

11 On pads without shims lightly smear the back of the pad backing material with copper-based grease, making sure that none gets on the friction material. Also smear the pad pin, including the threads but not the stopper ring.

12 Apply a smear of silicone grease to the stopper ring on the pad pin **(see illustration 6.8)**.

13 On CBR125 and CRF250 models fit the

pads into the caliper and seat them against the guide on the bracket **(see illustration)**. Press them up against the spring to align the holes, then insert the pad pin and tighten it to the torque setting specified at the beginning of this Chapter **(see illustration)**. Fit the pad pin plug **(see illustration 6.3a)**.

14 On CBR250R/RA models fit the pads into the caliper and seat them against the guide on the bracket **(see illustration 6.13a)**. Pivot the caliper down and fit the rear mounting bolt/ slider pin **(see illustration)**. Press the pads up against the spring to align the holes, insert the pad pin and tighten it to the torque setting specified at the beginning of this Chapter **(see illustration)**.

15 Operate the brake pedal until the pads contact the disc. Check the level of fluid in

each reservoir and top-up if necessary (see *Pre-ride checks*).

16 Test the brake before riding the motorcycle.

7 Rear brake caliper

 Warning: Overhaul of the brake caliper must be done in a spotlessly clean work area to avoid contamination and possible failure of the brake hydraulic system components. Do not, under any circumstances, use petroleum-based solvents to clean brake parts. Use clean DOT 4 brake fluid, dedicated brake cleaner or denatured alcohol only, as described. To prevent damage from spilled brake fluid, always cover paintwork when working on the braking system, and have plenty of absorbent rag to hand to catch and wipe off any spilled fluid.

Removal

1 Drain the brake fluid from the system (see Section 11).

2 Unscrew the brake hose banjo bolt and detach the banjo union, noting its alignment with the caliper **(see illustration)**. Seal the banjo union to prevent any dirt getting in **(see illustration 3.2b)**. Note that new sealing washers will be required later.

3 Remove the brake pads (see Section 6, Steps 3 or 4 as applicable).

4 On CBR125 and CRF250 models remove the rear wheel (see Section 18). Slide the caliper and bracket apart **(see illustration)**.

5 On CBR250R/RA models pivot the caliper up and slide it off the bracket. If you want to remove the caliper bracket, displace the wheel speed sensor (Section 14), then remove the rear wheel (see Section 18). Remove the bracket from the swingarm, noting how it locates.

Overhaul

6 Remove the pad spring from the caliper and

7.2 Brake hose banjo bolt (arrowed)

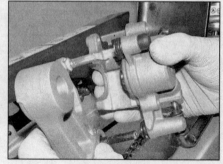

7.4 Slide the caliper and bracket apart

7.6a Pad spring (arrowed)...

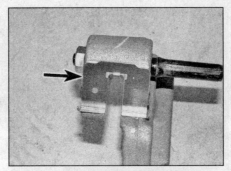

7.6b ...and pad guide – CBR125 and CRF250

7.6c Pad spring (arrowed)...

7.6d ...and pad guide – CBR250

7.8 Note the sleeve (arrowed) in the boot

7.10a Use compressed air to force the piston out...

the guide from the bracket if required (see illustrations).

7 Clean the exterior of the caliper with denatured alcohol or brake system cleaner. Have some clean rag ready to catch any spilled brake fluid.

8 Clean all old grease off the slider pins and rubber boots (see illustration 7.4). Check the condition of the rubber boots and replace them with new ones if necessary. Note the sleeve in the caliper boot on CBR250R/RA models (see illustration).

9 To remove the piston you need either a supply of compressed air, or a piston removal tool, or if neither are available a good pair of external circlip removal pliers.

10 If you are using compressed air make sure the bleed valve is tight. Cover the piston and

the caliper with rag and apply compressed air gradually and progressively, starting with a fairly low pressure, to the fluid inlet in the caliper and allow the piston to ease out of the bore (see illustrations). Always make sure the caliper is covered, with the piston pointing down onto the bench so it cannot fly out and hit something.

11 If you are using a dedicated tool or the circlip pliers, grip the inner wall of the piston then twist and pull the piston out, keeping it square to the bore wall until it is free (see illustration). Do not try to remove the piston by levering it out or by using pliers or other grips that may scratch the outer wall, unless you are prepared to fit a new piston, and possibly a new caliper.

12 If the piston is stuck in its bore due to

corrosion replace the caliper with a new one.

13 Remove the dust seal and the piston seal from the bore using a plastic tool to avoid scratching the bore (see illustration). Discard the seals – new ones must be fitted.

14 Clean the piston and bore with clean brake fluid. If compressed air is available, blow it through the fluid passages to ensure they are clear (make sure it is filtered and unlubricated).

Caution: Do not, under any circumstances, use a petroleum-based solvent to clean brake parts.

15 Inspect the caliper bore and piston for signs of corrosion, nicks and burrs and loss of plating (see illustration 3.12). If surface defects are present, the piston and/or the

7.10b ...and remove it

7.11 Using circlip pliers to remove a piston

7.13 Remove the dust seal and piston seal

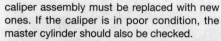

7.16a Lubricate the new piston seal with brake fluid...

7.16b ...then fit it into the lower groove

7.17 Lubricate the new dust seal with silicone grease and fit it into the upper groove

caliper assembly must be replaced with new ones. If the caliper is in poor condition, the master cylinder should also be checked.

16 Lubricate the new piston seal with new brake fluid and fit it into the inner groove in the bore **(see illustrations)**.

17 Lubricate the new dust seal with silicone grease if available or new brake fluid if not, and fit it into the outer groove in the bore **(see illustration)**.

18 Lubricate the piston with new brake fluid and fit it, closed-end first, into the caliper bore, taking care not to displace the seals **(see illustration)**. Using your thumbs, push the piston squarely all the way in **(see illustration)**.

19 If the pad spring was removed, make sure it is clean then fit it into the caliper, making sure it locates correctly **(see illustration 7.6a or c)**. Make sure the pad guide on the bracket is clean and correctly fitted **(see illustration 7.6b or d)**. Make sure the slider pins are tight. Smear the slider pins and inside the rubber boots with silicone grease. On CBR250R/RA models make sure the sleeve is in the caliper boot

Installation

20 On CBR125 and CRF250 models slide the caliper and bracket together, making sure each boot lip locates correctly in the groove in the pin **(see illustration 7.4)**. Install the wheel (see Section 18).

21 On CBR250R/RA models, locate the bracket on the swingarm, then install the wheel (see Section 18) and the wheel sensor

(see Section 14). Slide the caliper onto the bracket.

22 Fit the brake pads into the caliper (see Section 6, Steps 7 to 14).

23 Connect the brake hose to the caliper, using new sealing washers on each side of the banjo fitting **(see illustration 3.17)**. Align the hose as noted on removal. Tighten the banjo bolt to the torque setting specified at the beginning of the Chapter.

24 Refer to Section 11 to fill and bleed the system.

25 Operate the brake pedal until the pads contacts the disc. Check the level of fluid in the reservoir and top-up if necessary (see *Pre-ride checks*).

26 Check that there are no fluid leaks and test the brake before riding the motorcycle.

8 Rear brake disc

Inspection

1 Refer to Section 4, noting that the dial gauge should be attached to the swingarm.

Removal

Note: *Honda recommend using new disc mounting bolts. This is because the bolts are pre-treated with a locking compound. It is possible, however, to clean up the old bolts and reinstall them using a suitable non-permanent thread locking compound that is commercially available.*

2 Remove the rear wheel (see Section 18).

3 On CBR250RA models remove the pulse ring from the wheel (see Section 14).

4 If you are not replacing the disc with a new one, mark the relationship of the disc to the wheel or stub axle so it can be installed in the same position. Unscrew the disc bolts, loosening them evenly and a little at a time in a criss-cross pattern to avoid distorting the disc, then remove the disc **(see illustration)**.

Installation

5 Before fitting the disc, make sure there is no dirt or corrosion where the disc seats on the hub. If the disc does not sit flat when it is bolted down, it will appear to be warped when checked or when the rear brake is used.

6 Fit the disc on the wheel with its marked side facing out, aligning the previously applied matchmarks (if you're reinstalling the original disc).

7 Either fit the new bolts, or clean the threads of the original bolts and apply fresh thread locking compound. Tighten the bolts evenly and a little at a time in a criss-cross pattern to the torque setting specified at the beginning of this Chapter. Clean the disc using acetone or brake system cleaner. If a new disc has been installed, remove any protective coating from its working surfaces and fit new brake pads.

8 On CBR250RA models fit the pulse ring (see Section 14).

9 Install the rear wheel (see Section 18).

10 Operate the brake pedal several times to bring the pads into contact with the disc. Check the operation of the brakes before riding the motorcycle.

7.18a Fit the piston...

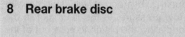

7.18b ...and push it all the way in

8.4 Rear brake disc bolts (arrowed)

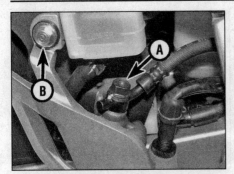

9.2 Brake hose banjo bolt (A), reservoir bolt (B)

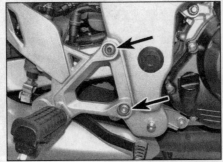

9.4 Footrest bracket bolts (arrowed)

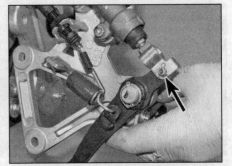

9.5 Remove the split pin (arrowed) and withdraw the clevis pin

9 Rear brake master cylinder

Warning: Overhaul must be done in a spotlessly clean work area to avoid contamination and possible failure of the brake hydraulic system components. Do not, under any circumstances, use petroleum-based solvents to clean brake parts. Use clean DOT 4 brake fluid, dedicated brake cleaner or denatured alcohol only, as described. To prevent damage from spilled brake fluid, always cover paintwork when working on the braking system, and have plenty of absorbent rag to hand to catch and wipe off any spilled fluid.

Removal

CBR125 models

1 Drain the brake fluid from the system (see Section 11).

2 Unscrew the brake hose banjo bolt and detach the banjo union, noting its alignment with the master cylinder **(see illustration)**. Seal the banjo union to prevent any dirt getting in **(see illustration 3.2b)**. Note that new sealing washers will be required later.

3 Unscrew the reservoir bolt and displace the reservoir **(see illustration 9.2)**.

4 Unscrew the footrest bracket bolts and displace the bracket so you can access the back **(see illustration)**.

9.6 Master cylinder bolts (arrowed)

9.8 Brake hose banjo bolt (arrowed)

5 Straighten the ends of the split pin and withdraw it from the master cylinder pushrod clevis pin, then withdraw the clevis pin **(see illustration)**.

6 Unscrew the master cylinder bolts and remove the master cylinder along with the reservoir **(see illustration)**.

CBR250R/RA models

7 Drain the brake fluid from the system (see Section 11).

8 Unscrew the brake hose banjo bolt and detach the banjo union, noting its alignment with the master cylinder **(see illustration)**. Seal the banjo union to prevent any dirt getting in **(see illustration 3.2b)**. Note that new sealing washers will be required later.

9 Unscrew the reservoir bolt and displace the reservoir **(see illustration)**.

10 Straighten the ends of the split pin and

withdraw it from the master cylinder pushrod clevis pin, then withdraw the clevis pin **(see illustration)**.

11 Unscrew the master cylinder bolts and remove the master cylinder along with the reservoir **(see illustration)**.

CRF250 models

Note: Honda recommend using new master cylinder mounting bolts. This is because the bolts are pre-treated with a locking compound. If they are not available it is possible, however, to clean up the old bolts and reinstall them using a suitable non-permanent thread locking compound that is commercially available.

12 Drain the brake fluid from the system (see Section 11).

13 Unscrew the brake hose banjo bolt and detach the banjo union, noting its alignment

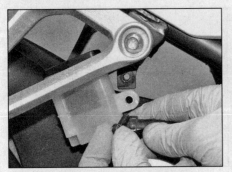

9.9 Unscrew the reservoir bolt

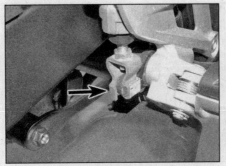

9.10 Remove the split pin (arrowed) and withdraw the clevis pin

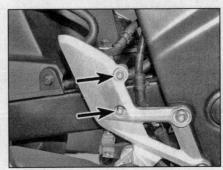

9.11 Master cylinder bolts (arrowed)

9.13 Brake hose banjo bolt (arrowed)

9.14 Release the hose (arrowed)

9.15 Remove the split pin (arrowed) and withdraw the clevis pin

9.16 Master cylinder bolts (arrowed)

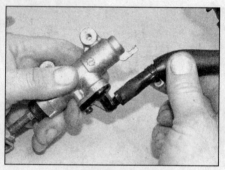

9.18a Detach the hose...

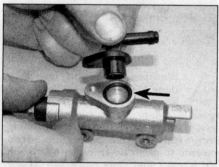

9.18b ...and remove the union if required, in which case replace the O-ring (arrowed)

with the master cylinder (see illustration). Seal the banjo union to prevent any dirt getting in (see illustration 3.2b). Note that new sealing washers will be required later.

14 Release the reservoir hose from its guide (see illustration).

15 Straighten the ends of the split pin and withdraw it from the master cylinder pushrod clevis pin, then withdraw the clevis pin (see illustration).

16 Unscrew the master cylinder bolts (see illustration).

17 Displace the master cylinder, then release the reservoir hose clamp and detach the hose. Cover the bottom of the hose in rag to catch residual fluid.

Overhaul

18 On CBR models release the clip securing the reservoir hose to the union on the master

cylinder and detach the hose, being prepared to catch any residual fluid (see illustration). If required, undo the reservoir hose union screw and remove the union (see illustration). Remove the O-ring – a new one must be used. Check the reservoir hose for cracks or splits and replace it with a new one if necessary.

19 On CRF models, if required, release the reservoir hose union circlip and remove the union. If the circlip deformed replace it with a new one. Remove the O-ring – a new one must be used. Check the reservoir hose for cracks or splits and replace it with a new one if necessary.

20 Dislodge the rubber dust boot from the base of the master cylinder and from around the pushrod, noting how it locates (see illustration). Push the pushrod in and, using circlip pliers, remove the circlip from its groove in the master cylinder and slide out the

pushrod, piston and spring noting how they fit (see illustrations). Lay the parts out in order as you remove them to prevent confusion during reassembly.

21 Clean the master cylinder with clean brake fluid. If compressed air is available, blow it through the fluid galleries to ensure they are clear (make sure the air is filtered and unlubricated).

Caution: Do not, under any circumstances, use a petroleum-based solvent to clean brake parts.

22 Check the master cylinder bore for corrosion, scratches, nicks and score marks. If damage or wear is evident, the master cylinder must be replaced with a new one. If the master cylinder is in poor condition, then the caliper should be checked as well.

23 The dust boot, circlip, piston, seal, cup and spring are all included in the master

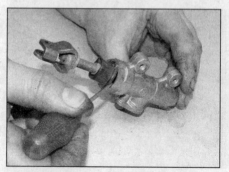

9.20a Remove the rubber boot...

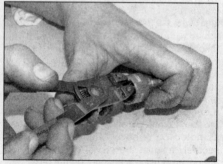

9.20b ...then release the circlip...

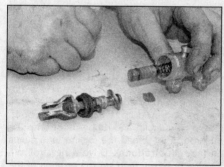

9.20c ...and remove the pushrod, piston and spring

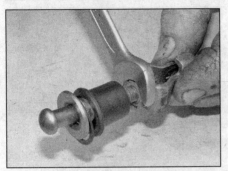

9.24a Slacken the locknut...

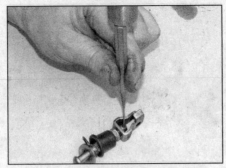

9.24b ...then remove the roll pin

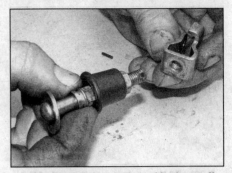

9.24c Thread the clevis and locknut off
then remove the boot and circlip

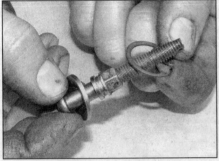

9.24d Fit the circlip...

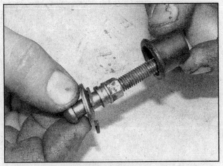

9.24e ...boot...

9.24f ... locknut...

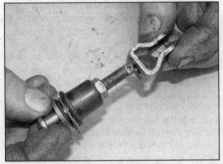

9.24g ...and clevis...

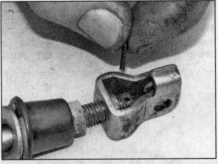

9.24h ...then drive the roll pin into the hole

9.24i Set the clevis position then tighten
the locknut against it

cylinder rebuild kit. Use all of the new parts, regardless of the apparent condition of the old ones.

24 On CBR125 models counter-hold the pushrod using a spanner on the hex and slacken the locknut holding the clevis on the bottom of the pushrod, then dislodge and remove the roll pin from under the clevis using a suitable drift **(see illustrations)**. Note how far the clevis is threaded up the pushrod, then thread it off, followed by the locknut, **(see illustration)**. Remove the rubber boot and the circlip. Smear some silicone grease onto the lips and inside of the new rubber boot. Fit the new circlip and rubber boot onto the pushrod, then thread the locknut and clevis on **(see illustrations)**. Drive a new roll pin into the pushrod, then set the position of the clevis as noted on removal **(see illustration)**. Tighten the locknut securely against the clevis,

counter-holding the pushrod using a spanner on the hex **(see illustration)**.

25 On CBR250R/RA and CRF250 models counter-hold the pushrod using a spanner on the hex and slacken the locknut holding the clevis on the bottom of the pushrod **(see illustration 9.24i)**. Note how far the clevis is threaded up the pushrod, then thread it off, followed by the locknut **(see illustrations 9.24g and f)**. Remove the rubber boot and the circlip **(see illustrations 9.24e and d)**. Smear some silicone grease onto the lips and inside of the new rubber boot. Fit the new circlip and rubber boot onto the pushrod, then thread the locknut and clevis on, setting the position as noted on removal. Tighten the locknut securely against the clevis, counter-holding the pushrod using a spanner on the hex.

26 On CBR125 models smear the cup and seal with new brake fluid and if not already in

place fit them into their grooves in the piston so their wider ends will fit into the master cylinder first **(see illustration)**. Fit the spring

9.26a Correct fitting of cup and seal on
piston

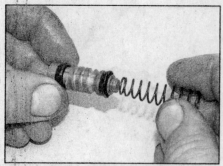

9.26b Fit the spring onto the end of the piston...

9.26c ...then fit them into the cylinder

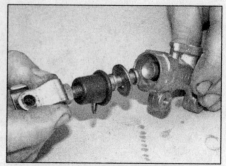

9.26d Locate the pushrod against the piston and push them in...

9.26e ...then fit the circlip into the groove

9.26f Fit the new boot into the cylinder...

9.26g ...and locate it in its groove

onto the piston **(see illustration)**. Lubricate the master cylinder bore with new brake fluid. Slide the spring and piston assembly into the master cylinder **(see illustration)**. Make sure the lips on the cup and seal do not turn

inside out. Smear some silicone grease onto the rounded end of the pushrod and around the lips of the boot. Push the piston in using the pushrod until the washer is beyond the circlip groove, then locate the circlip in the

groove **(see illustration)**. Fit the rubber boot, making sure the lips are seated correctly in the master cylinder and around the pushrod **(see illustrations)**.
27 On CBR250R/RA and CRF250 models smear the cup and seal with new brake fluid. If the seal is not already on the piston, fit it into its groove so the wider end will fit into the master cylinder first **(see illustration)**. Fit the cup onto the narrow end of the spring, locating the peg in the hole **(see illustration)**. Lubricate the master cylinder bore with new brake fluid. Fit the spring wide-end first into the master cylinder and push the cup in, making sure its lips do not turn inside out **(see illustration)**. Slide the piston into the master cylinder and up against the cup and spring **(see illustration)**. Make sure the lips on the seal do not turn inside out. Smear some silicone grease onto the rounded end of the pushrod and around the lips of the boot. Push the piston in using

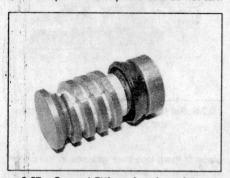

9.27a Correct fitting of seal on piston

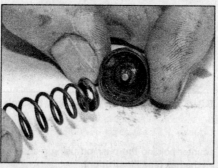

9.27b Fit the cup onto the end of the spring, locating the peg in the hole

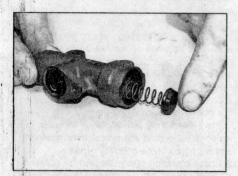

9.27c Fit the spring making sure the cup locates correctly in the bore...

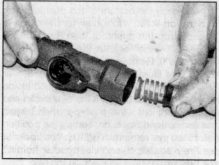

9.27d ...then push the piston in

9.27e Position the circlip on the washer...

9.27f ...then depress the pushrod and fit the circlip into the groove

9.27g Fit the new boot...

9.27h ...then press it into the cylinder...

9.27i ...and make sure it is correctly located around the pushrod

the pushrod until the washer is beyond the circlip groove, then locate the circlip in the groove **(see illustrations)**. Fit the rubber boot, making sure the lips are seated correctly in the master cylinder and around the pushrod **(see illustrations)**.

28 On CBR models, if removed fit a new fluid reservoir hose union O-ring smeared with brake fluid, then press the union into the master cylinder and secure it with the screw **(see illustration 9.18b)**. Connect the hose to the union, making sure it is correctly aligned, and secure it with the clip **(see illustration 9.18a)**. Check that the hose is secured with a clip at the reservoir end as well. If the clips have weakened, use new ones.

29 On CRF models, if removed fit a new fluid reservoir hose union O-ring smeared with brake fluid, then press the union into the master cylinder and secure it with the circlip.

Installation

30 Installation is the reverse of removal, noting the following:

● Use a new split pin to secure the clevis and bend the ends round to lock it.
● Tighten the master cylinder and footrest bracket bolts to the torque settings specified at the beginning of the Chapter as required according to model.
● Use new sealing washers on each side of the brake hose banjo fitting. Align the hose as noted on removal. Tighten the banjo bolt to the specified torque setting.
● Refer to Section 11 to fill and bleed the system.
● Check that there are no fluid leaks and test brake before riding the motorcycle.

10 Brake hoses and fittings

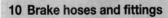

Inspection

1 To fully inspect all the brake hoses and pipes on CBR250RA models remove the right-hand fairing side panel (see Chapter 7), the fuel tank (see Chapter 4) and the modulator cover (see Section 14).

2 Check brake hose condition regularly (see Chapter 1). Twist and flex the hoses while looking for cracks, bulges and seeping hydraulic fluid. Check extra carefully around the areas where the hoses connect with the banjo fittings, as these are common areas for hose failure.

3 On CBR250RA models also check the brake pipes, the hose and pipe joints, the proportional control valve and delay valve, and the modulator, referring to the relevant Sections of this Chapter, for signs of fluid leakage and for any dents or cracks in the pipes.

Removal and installation

4 Drain all old brake fluid from the system (see Section 11).

5 The brake hoses have banjo fittings on each end. Cover the surrounding area with plenty of rags and unscrew the banjo bolt at each end of the hose, noting the alignment of the fitting with the master cylinder or brake caliper **(see illustrations 3.2a, 5.5, 7.2, 9.8, and 9.13)**. Free the hose from any clips or guides and remove it, noting its routing. Discard the sealing washers. **Note:** *Do not operate the brake lever or pedal while a brake hose is disconnected.*

6 Position the new hose, making sure it isn't twisted or otherwise strained, and ensure that it is correctly routed through any clips or guides and is clear of all moving components.

7 Check that the fittings align correctly, then fit the banjo bolts, using a new sealing washer on each side of each fitting **(see illustration 3.17)**. Tighten the banjo bolts to the torque setting specified at the beginning of this Chapter.

8 On CBR250RA models the brake pipes are held by nuts. There are no sealing washers. Unscrew the nuts and detach the pipes. Make sure the pipe is correctly positioned, fitted into any clips, and with any joint blocks secured, before tightening the nuts. If the correct tools are available tighten the nuts to the torque setting specified at the beginning of this Chapter for your model.

9 Refill the system with new DOT 4 brake fluid (see *Pre-ride checks*) and bleed the air from it (see Section 11).

10 Check the operation of the brakes before riding the motorcycle.

11 Brake system bleeding and fluid change

Special tool: *Honda recommend using a vacuum-type brake bleeding tool* **(see illustration 11.23)**. *If bleeding the system using the conventional method does not work sufficiently well, it is advisable to obtain this tool and repeat the procedure detailed below, following the manufacturer's instructions for using the tool.*

Bleeding principles

1 Bleeding a brake is the process of removing aerated brake fluid from the master cylinder, the hose and the caliper. Bleeding is necessary whenever a brake system hydraulic connection is loosened, after a component or hose is replaced with a new one, when a master cylinder or a caliper is overhauled, or when there is a spongy feel to the lever or pedal and it travels all the way to its stop, and where braking force is less than it should be, and it is not due to any mechanical fault in the system (i.e. a sticking piston in the caliper, or a pad that is not moving as it should due to corrosion, for example on the pad pin). Leaks in the system may also allow air to enter, but leaking brake fluid will reveal their presence and warn you of the need for repair.

2 Brake bleeding is considered by some as a bit of a black art – seasoned professionals sometimes have trouble getting a good firm feel in the brake lever, while a first timer may

11.5a Undo the screws...

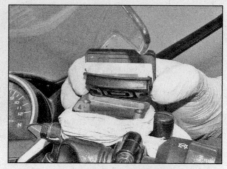

11.5b ...and remove the cap, diaphragm plate and diaphragm

11.6a Bleed valve (arrowed)

11.6b Fit the ring spanner over the valve then connect the hose

11.6c One-man bleeding kit connected to front caliper

have no trouble at all. One of the problems, particularly with the front brake system, is that you are working against natural principles – science dictates that air bubbles in a liquid will rise to the top, but the process entails pumping the brake fluid and any air bubbles it contains down, from the master cylinder at the top to the bleed valve in the caliper at the bottom, so while the fluid is moving down the air bubbles will try to rise. Air bubbles can also get trapped, particularly where there are high points in its path.

3 To bleed the brakes using the conventional method, you will need some new DOT 4 brake fluid, a length of clear flexible hose, a small container partially filled with clean brake fluid, some rags, and a spanner to fit the brake

caliper bleed valve. Bleeding kits that include the hose, a one-way valve and a container are available relatively cheaply from a good auto store, and simplify the task.

4 Cover painted components to prevent damage in the event that brake fluid is spilled. *Caution: Brake fluid attacks painted finishes and some plastics – to prevent damage from spilled fluid, always cover paintwork when working on the braking system, and clean up any spills immediately using brake cleaner.*

Bleeding the front brake system

5 Turn the handlebars so the brake fluid reservoir is level. Remove the reservoir cover, diaphragm plate and diaphragm **(see**

illustrations)**. Slowly pump the brake lever a few times to dislodge any air bubbles from the holes in the bottom of the reservoir.

6 Pull the dust cap off the bleed valve on the caliper **(see illustration)** – on CBR250RA models remove the cap from the upper of the two bleed valves. If using a ring spanner (which is preferable to an open-ended one) fit it onto the valve **(see illustration)**. Attach one end of the bleed hose to the bleed valve and, if not using a kit, submerge the other end in the clean brake fluid in the container **(see illustration)**.

7 Check the fluid level in the reservoir – keep it topped up and do not allow the level to drop below the bottom of the window during the procedure **(see illustration)**.

8 Slowly pump the brake lever three or four times, then hold it in and open the bleed valve a quarter turn **(see illustration)**. When the valve is opened, brake fluid will flow out into the clear tubing, and the lever will move toward the handlebar. Tighten the bleed valve, then release the brake lever gradually.

9 If there is air in the system there will be air bubbles visible in the brake fluid, but not necessarily on the first pump. Repeat the process until no air bubbles have been seen for a few pumps, and the lever is firm when applied, topping the reservoir up when necessary.

10 When the system has been successfully bled there should be a good and progressively

11.7 Keep the reservoir topped up

11.8 Bleeding the front brake

firm feel as the lever is applied, and the lever should not be able to travel all the way back to the handlebar.

11 On completion remove the equipment and make sure the bleed valve is tight (but do not overtighten it as the threads in the caliper are easily stripped), then fit the dust cap. Top-up the reservoir, then fit the diaphragm, diaphragm plate and cover **(see illustrations 11.5b and a)**. Check for spilled brake fluid and clean up as required. Check that there are no fluid leaks from the system and check the operation of the brake before riding the motorcycle.

Bleeding the rear brake system

12 Undo the reservoir bolt and position the reservoir for access to the cover screws **(see illustration 9.2, 9.9 or 11.12a)**. Undo the screws and remove the cover, diaphragm plate and diaphragm **(see illustrations)**. During the bleeding procedure the reservoir will require repeated topping up, so it must be supported to allow this without any danger of it tipping and spilling fluid. It is best to remount the reservoir with the cover off, and if it is difficult to tip the fluid straight from the bottle to top it up using a small funnel or a syringe. Make sure anything used is spotlessly clean.

13 Slowly pump the brake pedal a few times to dislodge any air bubbles from the holes in the bottom of the reservoir.

14 On CBR250RA bleed the front portion of the system first using the lower bleed valve on the front caliper, then bleed the rear portion using the bleed valve on the rear caliper. Note that the rear brake pedal may have some resistance to it as you push it down – this is due to the proportional control valve and is normal, but make sure you push the pedal all the way down

15 Pull the dust cap off the bleed valve on the caliper **(see illustration)**. If using a ring spanner (which is preferable to an open-ended one) fit it onto the valve **(see illustration)**. Attach one end of the bleed hose to the bleed valve and, if not using a kit, submerge the other end in the clean brake fluid in the container **(see illustration)**.

16 Check the fluid level in the reservoir –

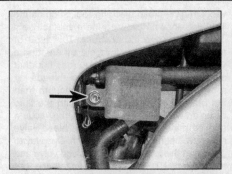
11.12a Reservoir bolt (arrowed) – CRF250

11.12b Undo the screws...

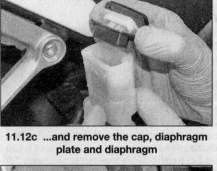
11.12c ...and remove the cap, diaphragm plate and diaphragm

11.15a Rear caliper bleed valve (arrowed)

11.15b Fit the ring spanner over the valve then connect the hose

11.15c One-man bleeding kit connected to rear caliper

keep it topped up and do not allow the level to drop below the bottom of the window during the procedure **(see illustration)**.

17 Slowly pump the brake pedal three or four times, then hold it down and open the bleed valve a quarter turn **(see illustration)**. When

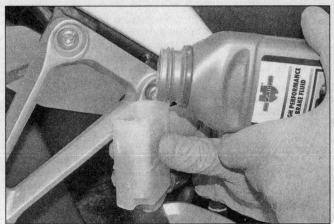
11.16 Keep the reservoir topped up

11.17 Bleeding the rear brake

the valve is opened, brake fluid will flow out into the clear tubing, and the pedal will move down. Tighten the bleed valve, then release the brake pedal gradually.

18 If there is air in the system there will be air bubbles visible in the brake fluid, but not necessarily on the first pump. Repeat the process until no air bubbles have been seen for a few pumps, and the pedal is firm when applied, topping the reservoir up when necessary.

19 When the system has been successfully bled there should be a good and progressively firm feel as the pedal is applied.

20 On completion remove the equipment used and make sure the bleed valve is tight (but do not overtighten it as the threads in the caliper are easily stripped), then fit the dust cap. Top-up the reservoir, then fit the diaphragm, diaphragm plate and cover **(see illustration 11.12c)**. Displace the reservoir to tighten the cover screws, then refit it and tighten the bolt. Check for spilled brake fluid and clean up as required. Check that there are no fluid leaks from the system and check the operation of the brake before riding the motorcycle.

Bleeding problems

21 If it is not possible to produce a firm feel to the lever or pedal look for any high point in the system in which a pocket of air may become trapped. Displace and move the hose so the bubble can be dislodged – tapping it may help. If necessary displace the master cylinder and/or the caliper, and free the brake hose from its guides and move the parts around to dislodge the air and encourage it towards the bleed valve – refer to the relevant Sections as required to displace components.

22 If you are still having trouble the fluid may be full of many tiny air bubbles rather than a few big ones. To remedy this apply some pressure to the system, for the front brake by tying the front brake lever lightly back to the handlebar, and for the rear by tying a weight to the brake pedal – do not apply too much pressure or the cup and seals in the master cylinder and caliper may fail. Let the fluid stabilise for a few hours, after which the tiny bubbles should either have risen to the top in the reservoir, or have formed into one or more big bubbles that can be more easily bled out by repeating the bleeding procedure.

23 If bleeding the system using the conventional tools and methods stated does not give satisfactory results, you can use a

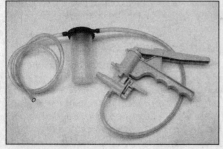

11.23 Vacuum-type brake bleeding tool

vacuum-type brake bleeding tool, such as the Mity-vac shown, following the manufacturer's instructions **(see illustration)**. This type of tool literally sucks the fluid out by creating a vacuum at the bleed valve. You may find that air is sucked past the bleed valve threads (air provides less resistance to the vacuum than the brake fluid) where it mixes with the fluid being drawn out. If this is the case the vacuum applied may be too great, or the bleed valve may have been loosened too much. One way to get round this is to remove the bleed valve and thread some PTFE tape around its threads, but note that doing so will be a bit messy, so have some rag to hand. Also make sure the hose from the brake bleeding tool forms an air-tight fit over the bleed valve head, otherwise air will be drawn in from around the valve head.

Fluid change

24 Changing the brake fluid is a similar process to bleeding the brake and requires the same materials plus a suitable tool (such as a syringe, or alternatively lots of absorbent rag or paper) for siphoning the fluid out of the reservoir.

25 Remove the reservoir cover (see Step 12 for the rear master cylinder reservoir), diaphragm plate and diaphragm and siphon the old fluid out of the reservoir **(see illustrations 11.5a and b (front) or 11.12b and c (rear))**. Wipe the reservoir clean. Fill the reservoir with new brake fluid **(see illustration 11.7 (front) or 11.16 (rear))**.

26 Connect the brake bleeding hose to the bleed valve (see Step 6 (front) and Steps 14 and 15 (rear)). Slowly pump the brake lever or pedal three or four times then hold it in and open the bleed valve. When the valve is opened, brake fluid will flow out of the valve into the clear tubing, and the lever will move toward the handlebar, or the pedal will move down.

27 Tighten the bleed valve, then release the brake lever or pedal gradually. Keep the reservoir topped-up with new fluid at all times or air may enter the system and greatly increase the length of the task. Repeat the process until new fluid can be seen emerging from the caliper bleed valve.

> **HAYNES HiNT** *Old brake fluid is invariably much darker in colour than new fluid, making it easy to see when all old fluid has been expelled from the system.*

28 Check the operation of the brakes before riding the motorcycle. If the lever or pedal action is spongy, carry out the bleeding operation as described above.

Draining the system for overhaul

29 Draining the brake fluid is again a similar process to bleeding the brakes. The quickest and easiest way is to use a vacuum-type brake bleeding tool (see Step 23). Otherwise follow the procedure described above for changing the fluid, but quite simply do not put any new

fluid into the reservoir – the system fills itself with air instead.

30 When it comes to refilling the system start by adding new fluid from a sealed container to the reservoir, then perform the bleeding procedure as described above until the fluid comes out of the bleed valve, and keep at it until you are certain there is no more air left in the system. When doing the linked circuit via the rear brake pedal on CBR250RA models, start with the lower bleed valve on the front caliper, and transfer to the rear when it is obvious that there is mostly fluid coming out, even though there may still be some air – this is normal as the rear portion of the circuit is still full of air and some may be working its way to the front. When the rear portion is mostly filled with fluid bleed the system as described above, front portion first.

12 ABS operation – CBR250RA

1 The anti-lock brake system (ABS) on CBR250RA models prevents the wheels from locking up under hard braking or on uneven road surfaces, and links the rear brake with part of the front, actuating the centre piston in the front caliper via a proportional control valve and a delay valve, whenever the pedal is depressed. A sensor on each wheel transmits information about the speed of rotation to the control unit in the ABS modulator; if the unit senses that a wheel is about to lock, it releases brake pressure to that wheel momentarily, preventing a skid.

2 The anti-lock system is self-checking and is activated when the ignition switch is turned on – the ABS indicator light in the instrument cluster will come on and will remain on until road speed increases above 6 mph (10 kmh) at which point, if the ABS is normal, the light will go off. **Note:** *If the ABS indicator light does not come on initially there is a fault in the system – see Section 13.*

3 If the indicator light remains on, flashes, or starts flashing while the machine is being ridden, there is a fault in the system and the ABS function will be switched off – the brakes will still function but in normal mode. If you turn the ignition OFF while the light is flashing, the fault code will not be displayed again if the ignition is switched on again, but will be stored in the system's memory.

4 The warning light emits long (1.3 second) and short (0.3 second) flashes to give out the fault code. A long flash is used to indicate the first digit of the double-digit fault code. For example, two long (1.3 sec) flashes followed by three short (0.3 sec) flashes indicates the fault code number 23. If there is more than one fault code, there will be a 3.6 sec gap before the next code is revealed (the codes are revealed in ascending numerical order). Once all codes have been revealed, the display will continuously run through the code(s) stored in its memory, revealing each one in turn with a short gap between them. The fault codes are shown in the table in Section 13. To check the ABS components see Section 14.

5 To retrieve any stored fault codes, remove the rider's seat (see Chapter 7) to access the service check connector, which is a 3-pin connector fitted into a blanked socket on a bracket on the frame. Ensure the ignition is switched OFF. Release the connector. Using a short jumper wire, connect between the grey/red and green wire terminals in the connector. Turn the ignition ON with the kill switch set to run and observe the ABS warning light. If there are stored fault codes, the light will come on for 2 seconds, then go out for 3.6 seconds, then start to flash the fault code. If the light comes on and stays on without flashing after the 3.6 second gap no fault codes are stored. Do not apply the brake lever or pedal during code retrieval.

6 Turn the ignition switch OFF and remove the jumper wire when the code or codes have been recorded.

7 Once the fault has been corrected, erase the fault code(s) as follows. Follow Step 5 to connect the terminals in the service check connector. Hold the front brake lever on and with the kill switch set to run turn the ignition switch on – the ABS light should come on for two seconds, then go out. When the light goes out immediately release the brake lever – the light should come on. When the light comes on immediately apply the brake lever – the light should go out. When the light goes out immediately release the brake lever. The code(s) should now be erased, in which case the light will flash twice, then come on and stay on. If the light continues to flash check again for any fault codes, then repeat the erasure procedure.

8 Turn the ignition switch OFF and remove the jumper wire when the code or codes have been erased. Check that the ABS is operating normally (see Step 2).

9 If necessary, repeat the reset procedure.

Note: *The ABS indicator may diagnose a fault if tyre sizes other than those specified by Honda are fitted, if the tyre pressures are incorrect, if the machine has been run continuously over bumpy roads, if the front wheel comes off the ground whilst riding (wheelie) or if the machine is on an auxiliary stand with the engine running and the rear wheel turning.*

13 ABS fault diagnosis – CBR250RA

1 If a fault is indicated in the ABS, first check that the battery is fully charged, then check the ABS fuses (see Chapter 8).

2 Unless specified otherwise, carry out all checks with the ignition switch OFF.

3 Refer to Chapter 8, Section 2, for general electrical fault finding procedures and equipment.

4 If after a thorough check, the source of a fault has not been identified, have the system tested by a Honda dealer.

Fault codes	Faulty component or system	Possible causes
11, 12, 21	Front wheel speed sensor circuit Front wheel speed sensor Front wheel pulse ring	Faulty wiring or wiring connector Faulty sensor Damaged pulse ring
13, 14, 23	Rear wheel speed sensor circuit Rear wheel speed sensor Rear wheel pulse ring	Faulty wiring or wiring connector Faulty sensor Damaged pulse ring
31, 32, 33, 34, 37 and 38	Modulator solenoid valve	Faulty modulator
41 and 42	Front wheel lock – riding conditions Front wheel speed sensor circuit Front wheel speed sensor Front wheel pulse ring	Faulty sensor Faulty wiring or wiring connector Damaged pulse ring
43	Rear wheel lock – riding conditions Rear wheel speed sensor circuit Rear wheel speed sensor Rear wheel pulse ring	Faulty wiring or wiring connector Faulty sensor Damaged pulse ring
51	Modulator motor lock	Faulty modulator or wiring ABS motor (30A) fuse
52	Modulator motor stuck OFF	Faulty modulator or wiring ABS motor (30A fuse
53	Modulator motor stuck ON	Faulty modulator or wiring ABS motor (30A) fuse
54	Fail-safe relay circuit	ABS fail-safe (30A) fuse Faulty relay circuit Faulty modulator
61	Power supply voltage low	ABS ECU (10A) fuse Faulty wiring or wiring connector Faulty modulator
62	Power supply voltage high	Faulty wiring or wiring connector Faulty modulator
71	Incorrect tyre size	Incorrect tyre
81	CPU in modulator control unit	Faulty modulator

Fault codes 11, 12, 21, 41 and 42

Note: *Before carrying out any of the checks, follow the procedure in Section 12 to reset the control unit memory, then activate the self-checking procedure. If the fault code is the result of unusual riding or conditions and the ABS is normal, the indicator light will go off. Otherwise perform the following checks.*

5 Measure the air gap between the front wheel speed sensor and the pulse ring with a feeler gauge, then compare the result with the Specification at the beginning of this Chapter. The gap is not adjustable – if it is outside the specification, check that the sensor and pulse ring fixings are tight. Also check that the components are not damaged and that there is no dirt or anything else on the sensor tip or between the slots in the pulse ring. If any of the components are damaged they must be replaced with new ones.

6 Remove the fairing left-hand side panel (see Chapter 7). Remove the modulator cover. Disconnect the modulator wiring connector. Trace the wheel sensor wiring to the 2-pin blue connector and disconnect it. Check for continuity first in the pink wire between the control unit wiring connector and the sensor wiring connector and then in the green/blue

wire – there should be continuity in each wire between the connectors, and no continuity to earth. If not locate and repair the break.

7 If there is continuity in the wiring next check for continuity between each terminal in the sensor side of the sensor connector and earth (ground). If there is continuity in either of the wires the sensor is faulty and must be replaced with a new one.

8 If all the checks have failed to identify the fault, replace the wheel sensor with a known good one. Connect all wiring connectors then follow the procedure in Section 12 to reset the control unit memory, then activate the self-checking procedure. If the indicator light is no longer flashing, the original sensor was faulty. If the fault code reappears have the modulator checked by a Honda dealer.

Fault codes 13, 14, 23 and 43

Note: *Before carrying out any of the checks, follow the procedure in Section 12 to reset the control unit memory, then activate the self-checking procedure. If the fault code is the result of unusual riding or conditions and the ABS is normal, the indicator light will go off. Otherwise perform the following checks.*

9 Measure the air gap between the rear wheel speed sensor and the pulse ring with a feeler gauge, then compare the result with the Specification at the beginning of this Chapter. The gap is not adjustable – if it is outside the specification, check that the sensor and pulse ring fixings are tight. Also check that the components are not damaged and that there is no dirt or anything else on the sensor tip or between the slots in the pulse ring. If any of the components are damaged they must be replaced with new ones.

10 Remove the right-hand side cover (see Chapter 7). Remove the modulator cover. Disconnect the modulator wiring connector. Trace the wheel sensor wiring to the 2-pin orange connector and disconnect it. Check for continuity first in the pink/white wire between the control unit wiring connector and the sensor wiring connector and then in the green/red wire – there should be continuity in each wire between the connectors, and no continuity to earth. If not locate and repair the break.

11 If there is continuity in the wiring next check for continuity between each terminal in the sensor side of the sensor connector and earth (ground). If there is continuity in either of the wires the sensor is faulty and must be replaced with a new one.

12 If all the checks have failed to identify the fault, replace the wheel sensor with a known good one. Connect all wiring connectors then follow the procedure in Section 12 to reset the control unit memory, then activate the self-checking procedure. If the indicator light is no longer flashing, the original sensor was faulty. If the fault code reappears have the modulator checked by a Honda dealer.

Fault codes 31, 32, 33, 34, 37 and 38

13 Erase the fault code (see Section 12). Start the engine and go for a short ride so the ABS system performs its self-diagnosis. If the ABS indicator light stays off, the fault was temporary.

14 If the ABS indicator light still flashes fault code 31, 32, 33, 34, 37 or 38 the ABS modulator is faulty.

Fault codes 51, 52 and 53

15 Check the ABS 30A motor fuse (see Chapter 8). If the fuse has blown, remove the modulator cover. Disconnect the modulator wiring connector. Check for continuity in the lower of the two red wires in the connector to earth. If there is continuity, repair the wire, then replace the blown fuse with a new one. If there is no continuity replace the blown fuse with a new one, then connect the wiring connector and follow the procedure in Section 12 to reset the control unit memory, then activate the self-checking procedure. If the fault code is no longer shown there was a temporary fault.

16 If the fuse has not blown refit it. Remove the modulator cover. Disconnect the modulator wiring connector. Check for battery voltage at the lower of the two red wires in the connector at all times (i.e. with the ignition on

or off). If there is no voltage check the wire for continuity to the battery via the fusebox, and repair the circuit as required.

17 If there is voltage erase the fault code (see Section 12). Start the engine and go for a short ride so the ABS system performs its self-diagnosis. If the ABS indicator light stays off, the fault was temporary.

18 If the ABS indicator light still flashes the same fault code, the ABS modulator is faulty.

Fault code 54

19 Check the ABS 30A fail safe relay fuse (see Chapter 8). If the fuse has blown, remove the modulator cover. Disconnect the modulator wiring connector. Check for continuity in the upper of the two red wires in the connector to earth. If there is continuity, repair the wire, then replace the blown fuse with a new one. If there is no continuity replace the blown fuse with a new one, then connect the wiring connector and follow the procedure in Section 12 to reset the control unit memory, then activate the self-checking procedure. If the fault code is no longer shown there was a temporary fault.

20 If the fuse has not blown refit it. Remove the modulator cover. Disconnect the modulator wiring connector. Check for battery voltage at the upper of the two red wires in the connector at all times (i.e. with the ignition on or off). If there is no voltage check the wire for continuity to the battery via the fusebox, and repair the circuit as required.

21 If there is voltage erase the fault code (see Section 12). Start the engine and go for a short ride so the ABS system performs its self-diagnosis. If the ABS indicator light stays off, the fault was temporary.

22 If the ABS indicator light still flashes the same fault code, the ABS modulator is faulty.

Fault codes 61 and 62

23 Check the ABS 10A ECU fuse (see Chapter 8). If the fuse has blown, remove the modulator cover. Disconnect the modulator wiring connector. Check for continuity in the red/blue wire terminal in the connector to earth. If there is continuity, repair the wire, then replace the blown fuse with a new one. If there is no continuity replace the blown fuse with a new one, then connect all wiring connectors and follow the procedure in Section 12 to reset the control unit memory, then activate the self-checking procedure. If the fault code is no longer shown there was a temporary fault.

24 If the fuse has not blown refit it. Remove the modulator cover. Disconnect the modulator wiring connector. Check for battery voltage at the red/blue wire terminal in the connector with the ignition on and the kill switch set to run. If there is no voltage check the red/blue wire from the connector to the fusebox for continuity, and if that is good check the black/red wire for continuity to the ignition switch, and repair the circuit as required.

25 If there is voltage erase the fault code

(see Section 12). Start the engine and go for a short ride so the ABS system performs its self-diagnosis. If the ABS indicator light stays off, the fault was temporary.

26 If the ABS indicator light still flashes the same fault code, the ABS modulator is faulty.

Fault code 71

27 First check the tyre pressure (see *Pre-Ride Checks*). Next make sure the correct tyres are fitted, comparing the tyre size codes on the sidewall to the Specifications at the beginning of the Chapter. Also check the tyres and wheels for deformations. Correct any problems found.

28 Erase the fault code (see Section 12). Start the engine and go for a short ride so the ABS system performs its self-diagnosis. If the ABS indicator light stays off, the fault was temporary.

29 If the ABS indicator light still flashes the same fault code, the modulator is faulty.

Fault code 81

30 Erase the fault code (see Section 12). Start the engine and go for a short ride so the ABS system performs its self-diagnosis. If the ABS indicator light stays off, the fault was temporary.

31 If the ABS indicator light still flashes the same fault code, the modulator is faulty.

14 ABS components – CBR250RA

Front wheel sensor

1 Remove the fairing left-hand side panel (see Chapter 7). Trace the wheel sensor wiring to the 2-pin blue connector and disconnect it.

2 Release the sensor wiring guides and feed the wire down to the sensor, noting its routing. Unscrew the sensor bolts and remove the sensor.

3 Make sure the tip of the sensor, its mounting surfaces, and the pulse ring are clean. Fit the sensor and tighten the bolts. Feed the wiring up to the connector, routing and securing it as noted on removal.

4 Check the air gap (see Section 13, Step 5).

Front pulse ring

5 Remove the front wheel (see Section 17).

6 Undo the screws securing the ring and lift it off.

7 Ensure there is no dirt or corrosion where the ring seats on the hub – if the ring does not sit flat when it is installed the sensor air gap will be incorrect. Clean the threads of the bolts and apply a non-permanent thread locking compound (or alternatively use new bolts from Honda which come pre-treated) and tighten them to the torque setting specified at the beginning of the Chapter.

8 Install the front wheel (see Section 17). Check the speed sensor air gap (see Section 13, Step 5).

Rear wheel sensor

9 Remove the right-hand side cover (see Chapter 7). Trace the wheel sensor wiring to the 2-pin orange connector and disconnect it.
10 Release the sensor wiring guides and feed the wire down to the sensor, noting its routing. Unscrew the sensor bolts and remove the sensor.
11 Make sure the tip of the sensor, its mounting surfaces, and the pulse ring are clean. Fit the sensor and wiring guide and tighten the bolts. Feed the wiring up to the connector, routing and securing it as noted on removal.
12 Check the air gap (see Section 13, Step 9). Install the side cover (see Chapter 7).

Rear pulse ring

13 Remove the rear wheel (see Section 18).
14 Undo the screws securing the ring and lift it off.
15 Ensure there is no dirt or corrosion where the ring seats on the hub – if the ring does not sit flat when it is installed the sensor air gap will be incorrect. Clean the threads of the bolts and apply a non-permanent thread locking compound (or alternatively use new bolts from Honda which come pre-treated) and tighten them to the torque setting specified at the beginning of the Chapter.
16 Install the rear wheel (see Section 18). Check the sensor air gap (see Section 13, Step 9).

Modulator

Note: *The modulator cannot be dismantled for overhaul, and no component parts are available. If it fails, it must be replaced with a new one.*
17 Remove the side covers (see Chapter 7). Remove the air filter housing (see Chapter 4). Remove the battery (see Chapter 8).
18 Remove the chainguard/hugger, noting the collars with the bolts.
19 Drain the brake fluid from the system (see Section 11).
20 Remove the rear wheel (see Section 18).
21 Displace the fuseboxes and the starter relay from their mounts and release the wiring from the undertray.
22 Unscrew the undertray bolts and draw the tray out.
23 Remove the modulator cover. Disconnect the modulator wiring connector.
24 Unscrew the brake pipe nuts and detach the pipes.
25 Displace the pipe/hose joint piece and sensor wire guide. Unscrew the modulator bolts and remove the modulator, taking care not to snag the brake pipes. Cover the ends of the pipes in clean rag.
26 Installation is the reverse of removal, noting the following:
● Smear the pipe nut threads with clean brake fluid, and fit them all finger-tight before finally tightening any of them. If the correct tools are available tighten

them to the torque setting specified at the beginning of the Chapter.
● Make sure the wiring connector is secure.
● Refer to Section 11 to fill and bleed the system. Check that there are no fluid leaks and test the operation of the brakes before riding the motorcycle.
Caution: Brake fluid attacks painted finishes and plastics – to prevent damage from spilled fluid, always cover paintwork when working on the braking system, and clean up any spills immediately using brake cleaner.

Proportional control valve

Note: *The valve cannot be dismantled for overhaul, and no component parts are available. If either valve fails, it must be replaced with a new one.*
27 Remove the modulator (Steps 17 to 25).
28 Unscrew the rear pipe joint nut on the PCV.
29 Unscrew the modulator bracket bolts and release the bracket grommets, then detach the rear pipe and remove the bracket/PCV assembly.
30 Unscrew the front pipe nut and remove the pipe. Unscrew the bolts and remove the valve. Cover the ends of the pipes in clean rag.
31 Installation is the reverse of removal, noting the following:
● Smear the pipe nut threads with clean brake fluid. Do not tighten the front pipe nut until the pipe is seated in the modulator to ensure correct alignment. If the correct tools are available tighten the nuts to the torque setting specified at the beginning of the Chapter.
● Refer to Section 11 to fill and bleed the system. Check that there are no fluid leaks and test the operation of the brakes before riding the motorcycle.

Delay valve

Note: *The valve cannot be dismantled for overhaul, and no component parts are available. If either valve fails, it must be replaced with a new one.*
32 Drain the brake fluid from the rear brake system (see Section 11).
33 Remove the fuel tank (see Chapter 4).
34 Unscrew the pipe joint nuts.
35 Unscrew the delay valve bolts, then detach the pipes and remove the valve. Cover the ends of the pipes in clean rag.
36 Installation is the reverse of removal, noting the following:
● Smear the pipe nut threads with clean brake fluid. If the correct tools are available tighten the nuts to the torque setting specified at the beginning of the Chapter.
● Refer to Section 11 to fill and bleed the system. Check that there are no fluid leaks and test the operation of the brakes before riding the motorcycle.

15 Wheel inspection and repair

1 Clean the wheels thoroughly to remove mud and dirt that may interfere with inspection or mask defects. Make a general check of the wheels (see Chapter 1) and tyres (see *Pre-ride checks*).
2 Inspect the wheels for cracks, flat spots on the rim and other damage. Look very closely for dents in the area where the tyre bead contacts the rim. Dents in this area may prevent complete sealing of the tyre against the rim, which leads to deflation of the tyre over a period of time. If damage is evident, or if runout in either direction is excessive, the wheel will have to be replaced with a new one. Never attempt to repair a damaged alloy wheel.
3 To check axial (side-to-side) runout of the wheel rim attach a dial gauge to the fork or the swingarm and position its tip against the side of the wheel rim. Spin the wheel slowly and check the amount of run-out, comparing it to the specification listed at the beginning of the Chapter **(see illustration)**.
4 In order to accurately check radial (out of round) runout with the dial gauge, remove the wheel from the machine, and the tyre from the wheel. With the axle clamped in a vice and the dial gauge positioned on the top of the rim, the wheel can be rotated to check the runout **(see illustration 15.3)**.
5 An easier, though slightly less accurate,

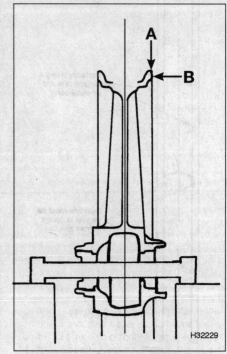

15.3 Check the wheel for radial (out-of-round) runout (A) and axial (side-to-side) runout (B)

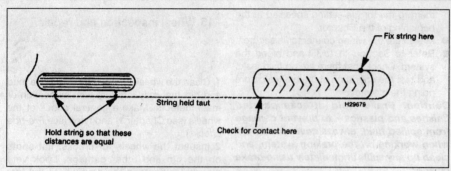

16.5 Wheel alignment check using string

method is to attach a stiff wire pointer to the fork or the swingarm and position the end a fraction of an inch from the wheel rim where the wheel and tyre join. If the wheel is true, the distance from the pointer to the rim will be constant as the wheel is rotated.

6 If wheel runout is excessive, first check the wheel bearings. If they are good, on CBR models you will have to fit a new wheel. On

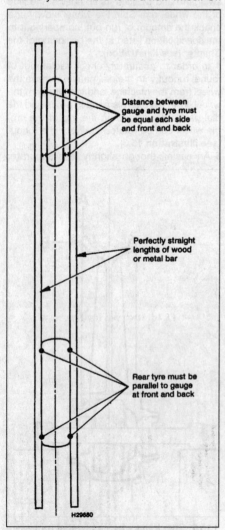

16.7 Wheel alignment check using a straight-edge

CRF models it should be possible to realign the wheel by adjusting the spokes, but to do this accurately takes some knowledge and skill, and should be left to an experienced wheel builder.

16 Wheel alignment check

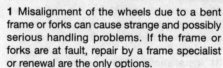

1 Misalignment of the wheels due to a bent frame or forks can cause strange and possibly serious handling problems. If the frame or forks are at fault, repair by a frame specialist or renewal are the only options.

2 To check wheel alignment you will need an assistant, a length of string or a perfectly straight piece of wood and a ruler. A plumb bob or spirit level for checking that the wheels are vertical will also be required.

3 Support the bike on an auxiliary stand. Measure the width of both tyres at their widest points. Subtract the smaller measurement from the larger measurement, then divide the difference by two. The result is the amount of offset that should exist between the front and rear tyres on both sides of the machine.

4 If the string method is used, have your assistant hold one end of it about halfway between the floor and the rear axle, with the string touching the back edge of the rear tyre sidewall.

5 Run the other end of the string forward and pull it tight so that it is roughly parallel to the floor (see illustration). Slowly bring the string

17.3a Unscrew the axle nut...

into contact with the front edge of the rear tyre sidewall, then turn the front wheel until it is parallel with the string. Measure the distance from the front tyre sidewall to the string.

6 Repeat the procedure on the other side of the motorcycle. The distance from the front tyre sidewall to the string should be equal on both sides.

7 As previously mentioned, a perfectly straight length of wood or metal bar may be substituted for the string (see illustration).

8 If the distance between the string and tyre is greater on one side, or if the rear wheel appears to be out of alignment, have your machine checked by a Honda dealer or frame specialist.

9 If the front-to-back alignment is correct, the wheels still may be out of alignment vertically.

10 Using a plumb bob or spirit level, check the rear wheel to make sure it is vertical. To do this, hold the string of the plumb bob against the tyre upper sidewall and allow the weight to settle just off the floor. If the string touches both the upper and lower tyre sidewalls and is perfectly straight, the wheel is vertical. If it is not, adjust the stand until it is.

11 Once the rear wheel is vertical, check the front wheel in the same manner. If both wheels are not perfectly vertical, the frame and/or major suspension components are bent.

17 Front wheel

Removal

1 Support the motorcycle on an auxiliary stand so the front wheel is off the ground. Always make sure the motorcycle is properly supported.

2 On CBR250RA models unscrew the speed sensor bolts and displace the sensor.

3 On CBR125 models unscrew the nut from the left-hand end of the axle (see illustration). Take the weight of the wheel, then push the axle through from the left and withdraw it from the right, and lower the wheel (see illustration). Displace the speed sensor from the left-hand side of the wheel, and if necessary remove the driveplate (see illustrations). Remove the

17.3b ...then withdraw the axle and remove the wheel

17.3c Displace the sensor...

17.3d ...and if required remove the driveplate from the left side...

17.3e ...and remove the spacer from the right

spacer from the right-hand side of the wheel **(see illustration)**. Remove the wheel, taking care not to knock the caliper against the rim.

4 On CBR250 models unscrew the nut from the right-hand end of the axle **(see illustration)**. Slacken the axle clamp bolt on the bottom of the left-hand fork **(see illustration)**. Take the weight of the wheel, then push the axle through from the right and withdraw it from the left, and lower the wheel **(see illustration)**. Remove the spacer from each side of the wheel **(see illustration)**. Remove the wheel, taking care not to knock the caliper against the rim.

5 On CRF250 models slacken the axle clamp bolts on the bottom of the right-hand fork **(see illustration)**. Unscrew the axle. Take the weight of the wheel, then withdraw the axle and lower the wheel **(see illustration)**. Remove the bearing cap/spacer from each side of the wheel **(see illustration)**. Remove the wheel, taking care not to knock the caliper against the rim.

Caution: Don't lay the wheel down and allow it to rest on the disc – it could become warped. Keep it upright, or set the wheel on wood blocks so the disc doesn't support the weight. Do not operate the brake lever with the wheel removed.

Installation

6 Manoeuvre the wheel into position between the forks with the brake disc on the right on CBR models, and on the left on CRF models.

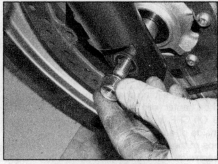

17.4a Unscrew the nut

17.4b Slacken the clamp bolt (arrowed)...

17.4c ...then withdraw the axle

17.4d Remove the spacers

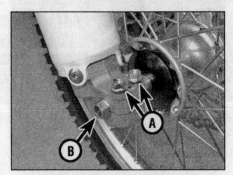

17.5a Slacken the clamp bolts (A), then unscrew the axle (B)...

17.5b ...and draw it out

17.5c Remove the cap from each side

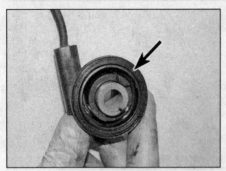

17.7a Grease the seal (arrowed)

17.7b Seat the lug (arrowed) in the groove between the ribs

7 On CBR125 models smear some grease to the inside of the wheel spacer and to the lips of the bearing seal. Fit the spacer into the right-hand side of the wheel **(see illustration 17.3e)**. Smear grease onto the speed sensor seal and around the driveplate **(see illustration)**. If removed fit the driveplate into the hub, locating the tabs in the slots **(see illustration 17.3d)**. Fit the sensor, locating the driveplate tabs in the slots **(see illustration 17.3c)**. Apply a thin coat of grease to the axle. Lift the wheel into place, making sure the spacer and speed sensor stay in place and the disc fits between the brake pads, and that the sensor is correctly positioned so the lug on the fork sits in the groove in the sensor **(see illustration)**, and slide the axle through from the right **(see illustration 17.3b)**. Fit the nut and tighten it to the torque setting specified at the beginning of the Chapter **(see illustration 17.3a)**.

8 On CBR250 models smear some grease to the inside of each wheel spacer and to the lips of the bearing seals. Fit a spacer into each side of the wheel **(see illustration 17.4d)**. Apply a thin coat of grease to the axle. Lift the wheel into place, making sure the spacers stay in place and the disc fits between the brake pads, and slide the axle through from the left **(see illustration 17.4c)**. Fit the nut and tighten it to the torque setting specified at the beginning of the Chapter **(see illustration 17.4a)**.

9 On CRF models smear some grease to the inside of each bearing cap/spacer and to the lips of the bearing seals. Fit a cap/spacer into each side of the wheel **(see illustration 17.5c)**. Apply a thin coat of grease to the axle. Lift the wheel into place, making sure the caps/spacers stay in place and the disc fits between the brake pads, and slide the axle through from the right **(see illustration 17.5b)**. Tighten

the axle to the torque setting specified at the beginning of the Chapter.
10 Pump the front brake, and on CBR250RA models the rear brake pedal, a few times to bring the pads back into contact with the disc. Remove the stand.
11 On CBR250 models apply the brake lever and pump the front forks a few times to settle all components in position. Tighten the axle clamp bolt on the bottom of the left-hand fork to the specified torque **(see illustration 17.4b)**.
12 On CRF models apply the brake lever and pump the front forks a few times to settle all components in position. Tighten the axle clamp bolts on the bottom of the right-hand fork to the specified torque **(see illustration 17.5a)**.
13 On CBR250RA fit the speed sensor and check the air gap (see Section 13).
14 Clean the disc using brake system cleaner. Pump the brake lever to bring the pads into contact with the disc. Test the brakes before riding the motorcycle.

18 Rear wheel

Removal

1 Position the bike on an auxiliary stand so that the rear wheel is off the ground. Tie the front brake lever to the handlebar. Always make sure the motorcycle is properly supported.
2 On CBR250RA models unscrew the speed sensor bolts and displace the sensor.
3 Create some slack in the chain (see Chapter 1, Section 1).
4 Unscrew the axle nut and remove the adjustment marker **(see illustrations)**.
5 Take the weight of the wheel, then withdraw the axle, bringing the adjustment marker with it, and lower the wheel to the ground **(see illustration)**. If the axle is difficult to withdraw, drive it out using a soft mallet to prevent damage to the threads. On CBR models remove the chain adjuster from each side of the swingarm if required **(see illustration)**.
6 Disengage the chain from the sprocket **(see illustration)**. Displace the caliper bracket from

18.4a Remove the axle nut and adjustment marker (arrowed) – CBR250 models

18.4b Remove the axle nut and adjustment marker (arrowed) – CRF250

18.5a Withdraw the axle and lower the wheel – CBR shown, CRF axle comes out the other side

18.5b Remove the adjusters if required

18.6a Slip the chain off the sprocket

18.6b Draw the wheel back and displace the caliper bracket when clear

18.11a Fit the right-hand spacer...

18.11b ...and the left-hand spacer

18.11c On CRF models the spacers are the same for each side

18.14 Make sure the adjustment marker seats correctly under the swingarm

19.3 Lever out the bearing seal(s)

its guide on the swingarm, then lift it out and support it clear **(see illustration)**. Remove the wheel. Fit the caliper bracket back onto the swingarm if required, and secure it using a cable-tie.

7 Remove the spacer from each side of the wheel, on CBR models noting which fits where **(see illustration 18.11a)**.

8 Clean all dirt and old grease off all components. Remove any corrosion from the axle using wire wool or a suitable alternative.

9 Check the axle is straight by rolling it on a flat surface. If the equipment is available, place the axle in V-blocks and measure the runout using a dial gauge. If the axle is bent, replace it with a new one.

Caution: Don't lay the wheel down and allow it to rest on the disc or sprocket – they could become warped. Keep it upright, or set the wheel on wood blocks so the disc doesn't support the weight. Do not operate the brake pedal with the wheel removed.

10 Check the condition of the grease seals and wheel bearings (see Section 19).

Installation

11 Apply a smear of grease to the inside of the wheel spacers, and to the lips of the grease seals. On CBR125 models fit the long spacer into the left-hand side of the wheel and the short spacer into the right-hand side. On CBR250 models fit the long spacer into the right-hand side of the wheel and the short spacer into the left-hand side **(see illustrations)**. On CRF models fit the spacer

into each side of the wheel **(see illustration)**. Apply a thin coat of grease to the axle. If the caliper bracket is located on the swingarm displace it and support it clear.

12 Fit the adjustment marker onto the axle, on CBR models with the angled section facing away from the head, and on CRF models with the index lines facing the axle head and on the bottom.

13 Manoeuvre the wheel into position between the ends of the swingarm. Locate the brake caliper bracket between the wheel and the swingarm and locate it on its guide **(see illustration 18.6b)**. Engage the drive chain with the sprocket **(see illustration 18.6a)**. On CBR models slide the chain adjusters into the swingarm with the index lines facing the outer wall **(see illustration 18.5b)**.

14 Lift the wheel into position, seating the brake disc between the pads, and slide the axle in from the left on CBR125 and CRF250 models, and from the right on CBR250 models **(see illustration 18.5a)**, making sure the spacers and caliper bracket remain correctly installed. On CBR models locate the bottom edge of the adjustment marker under the swingarm **(see illustration)**. Check that everything is correctly aligned. Fit the adjustment marker onto the end of the axle, then fit the axle nut but leave it loose **(see illustration 18.4a or b)**.

15 Check and adjust the drive chain slack (see Chapter 1). On completion tighten the axle nut to the torque setting specified at the beginning of the Chapter.

16 On CBR250RA fit the speed sensor and check the air gap (see Section 13).

17 Clean the disc using brake system cleaner. Pump the brake pedal to bring the pads into contact with the disc. Test the brake before riding the bike.

19 Wheel bearings

Note: *Always renew the wheel bearings in sets, never individually. Avoid using a high pressure cleaner on the wheel bearing area.*

Front wheel bearings

1 Remove the wheel (see Section 17). Support the wheel rim on wood blocks.

2 Inspect the seal(s) and bearings – check that the bearing inner race turns smoothly and that the outer race is a tight fit in the hub (see *Tools and Workshop Tips* (Section 5) in the Reference Section). **Note:** *Do not remove the bearings unless they are going to be replaced with new ones.*

3 If new components are needed lever out the bearing seal, from the right-hand side of the hub on 125 models and from each side on 250 models, using a flat-bladed screwdriver or a seal hook **(see illustration)**. Take care not to damage the hub. New seals must be fitted on reassembly.

4 Move the centre spacer to one side to expose the inner race of the lower bearing,

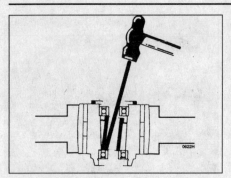

19.4a Move the spacer aside and drive the bearing out using a drift as shown

19.4b Fit the attachment behind the bearing...

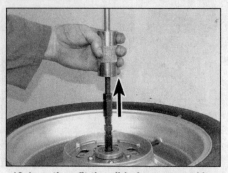

19.4c ...then fit the slide-hammer and jar the bearing out

then locate a drift on it and drive the bearing out **(see illustration)**. If you can't move the spacer, or if you can't get sufficient purchase with the drift, remove the bearings using an internal expanding puller with slide-hammer attachment, which can be obtained commercially – select the correct attachment and locate it between the inner race of the upper bearing and the spacer, then tighten the inner bolt to expand and lock the puller **(see illustration)**. Attach the slide-hammer, hold the wheel firmly down and jar the bearing out **(see illustration)**. Remove the spacer that fits between the bearings.

5 Drive the other bearing out using a suitable drift (such as a socket on an extension) inserted from the opposite side and located on the inner race of the bearing.

6 Thoroughly clean the hub area of the wheel with a suitable solvent and inspect the bearing housing for scoring and wear.

7 Fit the new bearings with the marked side facing out. Fit the right-hand bearing first on CBR models and the left-hand bearing first on CRF models. Drive the bearing in using a bearing driver or suitable socket that bears only on the outer race, and make sure the bearing fits squarely and all the way onto its seat **(see illustration 19.18)**.

8 Turn the wheel over and fit the bearing spacer. Fit the second bearing in the same way as the first until its inner race seats on the spacer.

9 Fit the new seal(s) into the hub using finger pressure or a suitable driver that bears on the outer rim, setting them flush with the hub **(see illustration)**. Smear the seal lips with grease.

10 Clean the disc using brake system cleaner. Install the wheel (see Section 17).

Rear wheel bearings

11 Remove the wheel (see Section 18). Support the wheel rim on wood blocks.

12 On CBR models lift the sprocket coupling out of the hub **(see illustration)**.

13 Inspect the seal(s) and bearings – check that the bearing inner race turns smoothly and that the outer race is a tight fit in the hub (see *Tools and Workshop Tips* (Section 5) in the Reference section). **Note:** *Do not remove the bearings unless they are going to be replaced with new ones.*

14 If new components are needed lever out the bearing seal from the right-hand side of the hub on CBR models and from each side on CRF models, using a flat-bladed screwdriver or a seal hook **(see illustration 19.3)**. Take care not to damage the hub. New seals must be fitted on reassembly.

15 Move the centre spacer to one side to expose the inner race of the lower bearing, then locate a drift on it and drive the bearing out **(see illustration 19.4a)**. If you can't move the spacer or if you can't get sufficient purchase with the drift, remove the bearings using an internal expanding puller with slide-hammer attachment, which can be obtained commercially – select the correct

attachment and locate it between the inner race of the upper bearing and the spacer, then tighten the inner bolt to expand and lock the puller **(see illustration 19.4b)**. Attach the slide-hammer, hold the wheel firmly down and jar the bearing out **(see illustration 19.4c)**. Remove the spacer that fits between the bearings.

16 Drive the other bearing out using a suitable drift (such as a socket on an extension) inserted from the opposite side and located on the inner race of the bearing.

17 Thoroughly clean the hub area of the wheel with a suitable solvent and inspect the bearing housing for scoring and wear.

18 If the new bearings are not sealed pack them with grease. Fit the new bearings with the marked side facing out. Fit the right-hand bearing first. Drive the bearing in using a bearing driver or suitable socket that bears only on the outer race, and make sure the bearing fits squarely and all the way onto its seat **(see illustration)**.

19 Turn the wheel over and fit the bearing spacer. Fit the second bearing in the same way as the first.

20 Fit the new seal(s) into the hub using finger pressure or a suitable driver that bears on the outer rim, setting it flush with the hub **(see illustration 19.9)**. Smear the seal lips with grease.

21 On CBR models check the sprocket coupling/rubber dampers (see Section 23). Check the condition of the hub O-ring

19.9 Fit the seal, setting it flush with the rim

19.12 Lift the sprocket coupling off the wheel

19.18 Using a socket to drive the bearing in

19.21 Fit a new O-ring (arrowed) if
necessary

19.26 Lever out the bearing seal

19.27 Drive the spacer out of the bearing
from the outside

and clean it or replace it with a new one
if necessary (see illustration). Smear the
O-ring and the mating surface of the hub and
sprocket coupling with grease. Fit the coupling
(see illustration 19.12).

22 Clean the brake disc using acetone or
brake system cleaner.

23 Install the wheel (see Section 18).

Sprocket coupling bearing (CBR models)

24 Remove the wheel (see Section 18). Lift
the sprocket coupling out of the hub (see
illustration 19.12).

25 Inspect the seal and bearing – check that
the bearing inner races turn smoothly and that
the outer race is a tight fit in the coupling (see
Tools and Workshop Tips (Section 5) in the
Reference Section). Note: *Do not remove the
bearing unless it is being replaced with a new
one.*

26 If new components are needed lever
out the bearing seal using a flat-bladed
screwdriver or a seal hook (see illustration).
Take care not to damage the rim of the
coupling. Discard the seal – a new one must be
fitted.

27 Remove the bearing spacer from inside
the coupling – if it is tight place the coupling
on the work surface, sprocket side up, and
drive it out using a suitably sized socket (see
illustration).

28 Support the coupling on blocks of wood,

19.28 Drive the bearing out from the inside

sprocket side down, and drive the bearing
out from the inside using a bearing driver or
socket (see illustration).

29 Thoroughly clean the coupling with a
suitable solvent and inspect the bearing
housing for scoring and wear.

30 If the new bearing is not sealed pack
it with grease. Fit the new bearing with the
marked side facing out. Drive the bearing in
using a bearing driver or suitable socket that
bears only on the outer race, and make sure
the bearing fits squarely and all the way onto
its seat (see illustration).

31 Fit the spacer – if it is tight support the
inner race of the bearing on a socket as
shown and tap the spacer into the bearing
(see illustration).

32 Fit the new seal into the coupling

19.30 Drive the bearing in from the outside

finger pressure or a suitable driver that bears
on the outer rim, setting it flush with the hub
(see illustration). Smear the seal lips with
grease.

33 Check the sprocket coupling/rubber
dampers (see Section 23). Check the condition
of the hub O-ring and clean it or replace
it with a new one if necessary (see illustration 19.21). Smear the O-ring and the
mating surface of the hub and sprocket
coupling with grease.

34 Fit the coupling (see illustration 19.12).
Install the wheel (see Section 18).

20 Tyres

General information

1 The wheels on CBR models are designed to
take tubeless tyres only. The wheels on CRF
models are designed to take tubed tyres only.
Tyre sizes are given in the Specifications at
the beginning of this chapter.

2 Refer to the *Pre-ride checks* listed
at the beginning of this manual for tyre
maintenance.

3 When selecting new tyres, refer to the
tyre information in the Owner's Handbook.
Ensure that front and rear tyre types are
compatible, the correct size and correct
speed rating; if necessary seek advice from

19.31 Support the bearing and fit the
spacer into it

19.32 Press the new seal into the hub

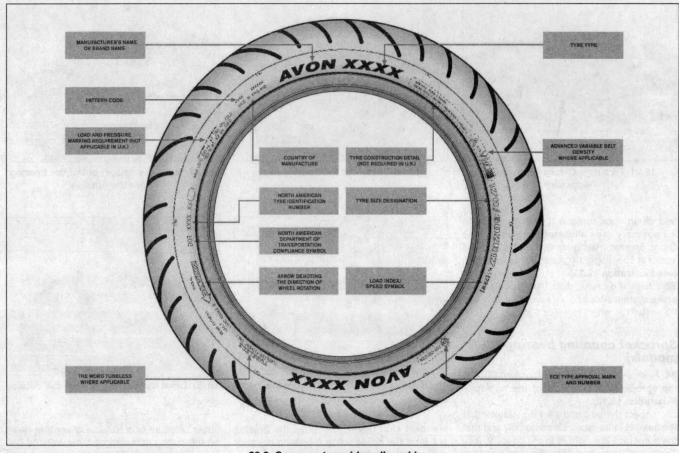

20.3 Common tyre sidewall markings

a Honda dealer or tyre fitting specialist **(see illustration).**

Fitting new tubeless tyres (CBR models)

4 Tubeless tyres are best fitted by a motorcycle tyre specialist rather than attempting to do it yourself. The force required to break the seal between the wheel rim and tyre bead is substantial, and is usually beyond the capabilities of an individual working with normal tyre levers. Additionally, the specialist will be able to balance the wheels after tyre fitting.

5 Note that punctured tubeless tyres can in some cases be repaired. External repairs made using a repair kit should only ever be considered as a temporary measure to get you to a dealer for a new tyre, and riding at speed or with any extra load should be avoided. Internal repairs carried out by a motorcycle tyre fitting specialist are better. Make sure a wheel with a repaired tyre is balanced before it is fitted back on the bike. Honda advise that a repaired tyre should not be used at speeds above 50 mph (80 kmh) for the first 24 hours, and not above 80 mph (130 kmh) thereafter, and carrying heavy loads should be avoided.

6 Punctured inner tubes can be repaired using a patch or sealant, but any such repairs should be considered temporary. It is far better to replace the inner tube with a new one.

Fitting new tubed tyres and inner tubes (CRF models)

7 Tyre changing is a specialist task. If you attempt it at home you'll need at least two motorcycle tyre levers and some rim protectors (as shown in the accompanying series of photographs). The rim protectors will prevent damage to the rims by the tyre levers and also protect their finish. Following tyre renewal, the wheel should be balanced by a tyre specialist.

Removal

8 Begin by removing the wheel from the motorcycle. If the tyre is going to be re-used, mark it next to the valve stem with chalk.

9 Deflate the tyre by removing the valve stem core. When it is fully deflated, push the bead of the tyre away from the rim on both sides. In some extreme cases, this can only be accomplished with a bead breaking tool, but most often it can be carried out with tyre levers. Riding on a deflated tyre to break the bead is not recommended, as damage to the rim and tyre will occur.

10 Dismounting a tyre is easier when the tyre is warm, so an indoor tyre change is recommended in cold climates. The rubber gets very stiff and is difficult to manipulate when cold.

11 Place the wheel on a thick pad or old blanket. This will help keep the wheel and tyre from slipping around. Take care to protect the disc/sprocket from damage – if necessary, remove it.

12 Once the bead is completely free of the rim, lubricate the inside edge of the rim and the tyre bead with soap and water or rubber lubricant (do not use any type of petroleum-based lubricant, as it will cause the tyre to deteriorate). Remove the locknut and push the tyre valve through the rim.

13 Insert one of the tyre levers under the bead of the tyre at the valve stem and lift the bead up over the rim. This should be fairly easy. Take care not to pinch the inner tube as this is done. If it is difficult to pry the bead up, make sure that the rest of the bead opposite the valve stem is in the dropped centre section of the rim.

14 Hold the tyre lever down with the bead over the rim, then move about 1 or 2 inches to either side and insert the second tyre lever. Be careful not to cut or slice the bead or the tyre may split when inflated. Also, take care not to catch or pinch the inner tube as the second tyre lever is levered over. For this reason, tyre levers are recommended over screwdrivers or other implements.

TYRE CHANGING SEQUENCE - TUBED TYRES

1 Deflate tyre. After pushing tyre beads away from rim flanges push tyre bead into well of rim at point opposite valve. Insert tyre lever adjacent to valve and work bead over edge of rim.

2 Use two levers to work bead over edge of rim. Note use of rim protectors.

3 Remove inner tube from tyre

4 When first bead is clear, remove tyre as shown.

5 When fitting, partially inflate inner tube and insert in tyre

6 Work first bead over rim and feed valve through hole in rim. Partially screw on retaining nut to hold valve in place.

7 Check that inner tube is positioned correctly and work second bead over rim using tyre levers. Start at a point opposite valve.

8 Work final area of bead over rim while pushing valve inwards to ensure that inner tube is not trapped.

15 With a small section of the bead up over the rim, one of the levers can be removed and reinserted 1 or 2 inches farther around the rim until about 1/4 of the tyre bead is above the rim edge. Make sure that the rest of the bead is in the dropped centre of the rim. At this point, the bead can usually be pulled up over the rim by hand.

16 Once all of the first bead is over the rim, the inner tube can be withdrawn from the tyre and rim. Push in on the valve stem, lift up on the tyre next to the stem, reach inside the tyre and carefully pull out the inner tube. It is usually not necessary to completely remove the tyre from the rim to fit a new inner tube, however it is recommended because checking for foreign objects in the tyre is difficult while it is still mounted on the rim.

17 To remove the tyre completely, make sure the bead is broken all the way around on the remaining edge, then stand the tyre and wheel up on the tread and grab the wheel with one hand. Push the tyre down over the same edge of the rim while pulling the rim away from the tyre. If the bead is correctly positioned in the dropped centre of the rim, the tyre should roll off and separate from the rim very easily. If tyre levers are used to work this last bead over the rim, the outer edge of the rim may be marred. If a tyre lever is necessary, be sure to protect the rim as described earlier.

Inspection

18 Fitting a new inner tube is advised when fitting a new tyre and also if the existing inner tube is punctured. Puncture repair kits are available, but the expense of a new inner tube is minimal.

19 Check the rim for sharp edges or damage. Make sure the rubber trim band is in good condition and properly installed before inserting the inner tube.

20 Check the inside of the tyre to make sure the object that caused the puncture is not still inside. Also check the outside of the tyre, particularly the tread area, to make sure nothing is projecting through the tyre that may cause another puncture.

Installation

21 Some tyres have a balance mark and/or directional arrows molded into the tyre sidewall. Look for these marks so that the tyre can be installed properly. The dot should be aligned with the valve stem.

22 If the tyre was not removed completely to fit the inner tube, the inner tube should be inflated just enough to make it round. Sprinkle it with talcum powder, which acts as a dry lubricant, then carefully lift up the tyre edge and install the inner tube with the valve stem next to the hole in the rim. Once the inner tube is in place, push the valve stem through the rim and start the locknut on the stem.

23 Lubricate the tyre bead, then push it over the rim edge and into the dropped centre section opposite the inner tube valve stem. Work around each side of the rim, carefully pushing the bead over the rim. The last section may have to be levered on with tyre levers. If so, take care not to pinch the inner tube as this is done.

24 Once the bead is over the rim edge, check to see that the inner tube valve stem is pointing to the centre of the hub. If it's angled slightly in either direction, rotate the tyre on the rim to straighten it out. Thread the locknut the rest of the way onto the stem but don't tighten it completely.

25 Inflate the inner tube to approximately 40 psi (2.7 Bar) and check to make sure the guidelines on the tyre sidewalls are the same distance from the rim around the circumference of the tyre.

 Warning: Do not overinflate the inner tube or the tyre may burst, causing serious injury.

26 After the tyre bead is correctly seated on the rim, adjust the tyre pressure to 22 psi (1.5 Bar) for CRF250L models or 29 psi (2.0 Bar) for CRF250M models, then tighten the valve stem locknut securely and tighten the cap.

27 It is recommended that a motorcycle tyre specialist balances the wheel.

21 Drive chain

Note: *The original equipment drive chain fitted to these models has a staked-type master (joining) link which can be disassembled using either the Honda service tool, Pt. No. 07HMH-MR10103, or one of several commercially-available drive chain cutting/staking tools (but the cheap ones are best avoided). Such chains can be recognised by the master joining link side plate's identification marks (and usually its different colour), as well as by the staked ends of the link's two pins which look as if they have been deeply centre-punched, instead of peened over as with all the other pins.*

Removal

1 If possible support the bike on an auxiliary stand so that the rear wheel is off the ground. Locate the joining link in a suitable position to work on by rotating the back wheel. Slacken the drive chain as described in Chapter 1.

2 Remove the front sprocket cover **(see illustrations)**.

3 Split the chain at the joining link using the chain tool, following carefully the manufacturer's operating instructions (see also Section 8 in *Tools and Workshop Tips* in the Reference Section). Remove the chain from the bike, noting its routing around the swingarm.

Cleaning

4 Refer to Chapter 1, Section 1, for details of routine cleaning with the chain installed on the sprockets.

5 If the chain is extremely dirty remove it from the motorcycle and soak it in paraffin (kerosene) for approximately five or six minutes, then clean it using a soft brush.

Caution: Don't use gasoline (petrol), solvent or other cleaning fluids that might damage its internal sealing properties. Don't use high-pressure water. Remove

21.2a Front sprocket cover bolts (arrowed) – 125 models

21.2b Front sprocket cover bolts (arrowed) – 250 models

22.5 Unscrew the bolts (arrowed)

22.7a Remove the retainer plate as described

the chain, wipe it off, then blow dry it with compressed air immediately. The entire process shouldn't take longer than ten minutes – if it does, the O-rings in the chain rollers could be damaged.

Installation

⚠️ *Warning: NEVER fit a drive chain which uses a clip-type master (split) link. Use ONLY the correct service tools to secure the staked-type of master link – if you do not have access to such tools, have the chain replaced by a Honda dealer.*

Note: *The specifications referred to in Steps 8 and 9 only apply to the drive chain types fitted as original equipment (see Specifications).*

6 Route the drive chain around the sprockets leaving the two ends mid-way between the sprockets along the bottom run.

7 Referring to Section 8 in *Tools and Workshop Tips* in the Reference Section, fit the new joining link from the inside using new O-rings. Fit the new sideplate using new O-rings and with its identification marks facing out. Use the chain tool to press the sideplate onto the joining link. Measure the amount that the joining link pins project from the sideplate and check they are within the measurements specified at the beginning of the Chapter for the chain type fitted. Stake the new link using the chain tool, following carefully the instructions of both the chain manufacturer and the tool manufacturer. DO NOT re-use old joining link components.

8 After staking, check the joining link and staking for any signs of cracking. If there is any evidence of cracking, the joining link, O-rings and side plate must be replaced. Measure the diameter of the staked ends in two directions and check that it is evenly staked and within the measurements specified at the beginning of the Chapter. Check that the link pivots freely.

9 Fit the sprocket cover (see illustration 21.2a or b).

10 On completion, adjust and lubricate the chain following the procedures described in Chapter 1.

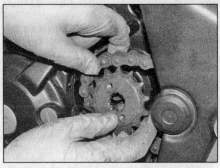

22.7b Draw the sprocket off the shaft and disengage the chain

22 Sprockets

Sprocket check

1 Remove the front sprocket cover (see illustration 21.2a or b).

2 Check the wear pattern on both sprockets (see Chapter 1, Section 1). If the sprocket teeth are worn excessively, replace the chain and both sprockets as a set. Whenever the sprockets are inspected, the drive chain should be inspected also (see Chapter 1). Always renew the chain and sprockets as a set – worn sprockets can ruin a new drive chain and *vice versa*.

3 Adjust and lubricate the chain following the procedures described in Chapter 1.

Sprocket removal and installation

Front sprocket

4 Remove the front sprocket cover (see illustration 21.2a or b).

5 Have an assistant apply the rear brake and unscrew the sprocket retainer bolts (see illustration).

6 Fully slacken the drive chain as described in Chapter 1. If the rear sprocket is being removed as well, remove the rear wheel now to give full slack (see Section 18). Otherwise disengage the chain from the rear sprocket if required to provide more slack.

22.13 Rear sprocket nuts/bolts

7 Turn the retainer to offset the splines and slide it off the shaft (see illustration). Slide the chain and sprocket off the shaft, then slip the sprocket out of the chain (see illustration).

8 Engage the new sprocket with the chain, making sure the marked side is facing out, and slide it on the shaft (see illustration 22.7b). Slide the retainer on until it aligns with the groove, then turn it to align the bolt holes (see illustration 22.7a). Fit the bolts and tighten them finger-tight (see illustration 22.5).

9 If removed, fit the rear sprocket now, and install the wheel (see Section 18). If the chain was merely disengaged, fit it back onto the rear sprocket. Take up the slack in the chain.

10 Tighten the bolts to the torque setting specified at the beginning of the Chapter, holding the rear brake on to prevent the sprocket turning.

11 Fit the sprocket cover (see illustration 21.2a or b). Adjust and lubricate the chain following the procedures described in Chapter 1.

Rear sprocket

12 Remove the rear wheel (see Section 18). Rest it sprocket side up on some blocks of wood.

13 On 125 models unscrew the sprocket nuts. On 250 models counter-hold the sprocket bolts and unscrew the nuts, on CRF models remove the washers, withdraw the bolts, and lift the sprocket off, noting which way round it fits (see illustration).

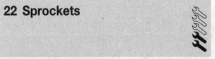

23.3 Check the rubber dampers as described

14 On 125 models check the studs are tight – if any are loose or are in poor condition remove them, and if necessary fit new ones. If the original ones are being reused clean the threads and apply some fresh threadlock. Thread the studs in until they seat so they project 20 to 21 mm from the coupling. Use two nuts locked together on the exposed threads to unscrew and tighten the studs.

15 Fit the sprocket onto the hub with the marked side facing out. On 250 models fit the bolts, with the washers on CRF models. On all models fit the nuts, and tighten them evenly and in a criss-cross sequence to the torque setting specified at the beginning of the Chapter, on 250 models counter-holding the bolts.

16 Install the rear wheel (see Section 18).

23 Rear sprocket coupling/ rubber dampers (CBR models)

1 Remove the rear wheel (see Section 18). Check for play between the sprocket coupling and the wheel hub by turning the sprocket. Any play indicates worn rubber damper segments.

Caution: Do not lay the wheel down on the disc as it could become warped. Lay the wheel on wooden blocks so that the disc is off the ground.

2 Lift the sprocket coupling off the wheel leaving the rubber dampers in position **(see illustration 19.12)**. Note the spacer inside the coupling – it should be a tight fit. Check the coupling for cracks or any obvious signs of damage.

3 Lift the rubber damper segments from the wheel and check them for cracks, hardening and general deterioration **(see illustration)**. Replace them with a new set if necessary.

4 Check the condition of the hub O-ring and clean it or replace it with a new one if necessary **(see illustration 19.21)**. Smear the O-ring and the mating surface of the hub and coupling with grease.

5 Checking and replacement procedures for the sprocket coupling bearing are in Section 19.

6 Installation is the reverse of removal. Make sure the spacer is correctly fitted in the coupling (see Section 19). Align the coupling correctly with the rubber dampers and press it fully into the hub **(see illustration 19.12)**.

7 Install the rear wheel (see Section 18).

Chapter 7
Bodywork

Contents

Degrees of difficulty

Easy, suitable for novice with little experience	Fairly easy, suitable for beginner with some experience	Fairly difficult, suitable for competent DIY mechanic	Difficult, suitable for experienced DIY mechanic	Very difficult, suitable for expert DIY or professional

1 General information

This Chapter covers the procedures necessary to remove and install the bodywork.

In the case of damage to the bodywork, it is usually necessary to remove the broken component and replace it with a new (or used) one. The material that the body panels are composed of doesn't lend itself to conventional repair techniques, but there are some companies that specialize in 'plastic welding' and there are a number of bodywork repair kits now available for motorcycles.

When attempting to remove any body panel, first study it closely, noting any fasteners and associated fittings, to be sure of returning everything to its correct place on installation. Refer to Section 2 for more information on the types of trim clip used and how to release and refit them. In some cases the aid of an assistant may be useful when removing panels, to help avoid the risk of damage to paintwork. Once the evident fasteners have been removed, try to remove the panel as described but DO NOT FORCE IT – if it will not release the chances are a locating tab is stuck, but first check that all fasteners have been removed before trying again.

When installing a body panel, be sure of returning every fastener to its correct place along with any washer or collar fitted with it. Check that all fasteners are in good condition, including the trim clips and rubber grommets; replace any faulty fasteners with new ones before the panel is reassembled. Check also that all mounting brackets are straight and repair them or replace them with new ones if necessary before attempting to install the panel.

Make sure all locating tabs engage correctly with their related panel. Tighten the fasteners securely, but be careful not to overtighten any of them or the panel may break (not always immediately) due to the uneven stress.

2 Trim clips

1 Three types of plastic trim clip are used across the range of models covered, so carefully note which fits where when removing the fairing panels.
2 The first type has a centre pin with a round head. To release them push the head of the pin into the body of the clip then draw the clip out of the panel (see illustrations). To fit them, push the centre pin back out so its head protrudes from the body, then fit the body into its hole and push the centre pin in so that it is flush with the body (see illustration). The clip should now be locked in place.

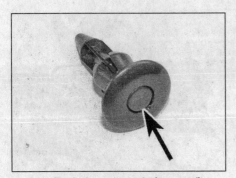

2.2a Push the centre pin (arrowed)...

2.2b ...into the body to release the clip

2.2c Push the centre pin out before installing the clip, then push it in to lock it

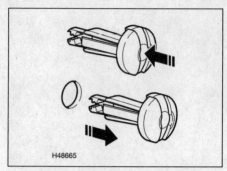

2.3a Push the oblong head into the body of the clip and withdraw the clip from the panel

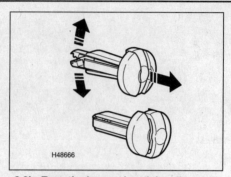

2.3b Ease the inner tabs of the clip apart and push the oblong head out...

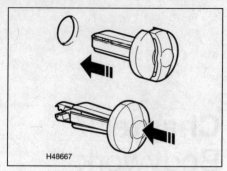

2.3c ...insert the clip and push the head in to lock it

2.4a Undo the centre screw then pull the clip out

2.4b Fit the clip in the hole then push the centre in to lock it

3.1 Unlock and lift the seat

3 The second type has a centre pin with an oblong head. To release them push the head of the pin into the body of the clip then draw the clip out of the panel **(see illustration)**. To fit them, first expand the end tabs of the pin and push it back out so its head protrudes from the body, then fit the body into its hole and push the centre pin in so that it is flush with the body **(see illustrations)**. The clip should now be locked in place.

4 The third type has a centre pin with a Phillips screw head. To release, turn the screw head ¼ turn anti-clockwise, holding the rim of the body to prevent it turning, then draw the clip out of the panel **(see illustration)**. To fit, install the body into its hole and push the centre pin in so that it is flush with the body **(see illustration)**. The clip should now be locked in place.

3 Bodywork – CBR models

Seats

Removal

1 Insert the ignition key into the seat lock and turn it clockwise to unlock the passenger seat **(see illustration)**. Lift the back of the seat and draw it back to disengage the hooks.

2 Unscrew the two bolts, noting the collars **(see illustration)**. Lift the back of the rider's seat and draw it back to disengage the hook at the front.

Installation

3 Installation is the reverse of removal. Make sure the hook on the front of the rider's seat locates correctly under the bracket **(see illustration)**.

4 Make sure the hooks at the front of the passenger seat locate correctly, and push down on the back to engage the latch **(see illustration)**.

Grab-rails

5 Remove the passenger seat.

6 Unscrew the bolts and remove the grab-rail from each side **(see illustration)**.

7 Installation is the reverse of removal.

Seat cowling

8 Remove the seats.

9 Remove the grab-rails.

10 Release the trim clips securing the access panel on the underside **(see illustration)**.

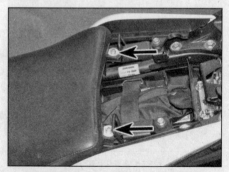

3.2 Unscrew the bolts (arrowed)

3.3 Locate the rider's seat hook under the bracket

3.4 Locate the passenger seat hooks under the brackets

3.6 Grab-rail bolts (arrowed)

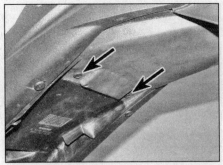

3.10a Release the trim clips (arrowed)...

3.10b ...and remove the panel

3.11 Turn the bulbholder anti-clockwise to release it

3.12a Detach the cable end...

3.12b ...and release it from the guides, noting its routing

Lower the front of the panel and draw it forwards to release the tabs along the rear edge (see illustration).

11 Release the bulbholder from the tail light (see illustration).

12 Release the seat lock cable from the lock and its guides (see illustrations).

13 Release the trim clips on the underside (see illustration).

14 Unscrew the four bolts, noting the collars (see illustration).

15 Carefully pull each side away at the front to release the pegs from the grommets, and remove the cowling (see illustrations).

16 Installation is the reverse of removal. Make sure the collars are fitted in the grommets (see illustration).

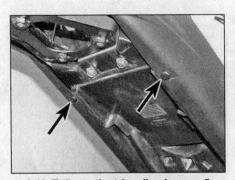

3.13 Release the trim clips (arrowed)

3.14 Unscrew the bolts (arrowed)

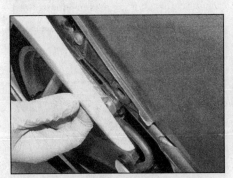

3.15a Release the pegs from the grommets at the front...

3.15b ...then draw the cowling back to release the tail light pegs from their grommets

3.16 There is a collar for each bolt mount

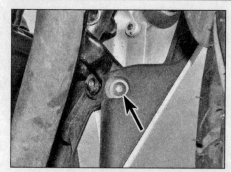

3.17a Undo the bottom front screw (arrowed)...

3.17b ...the top front screw...

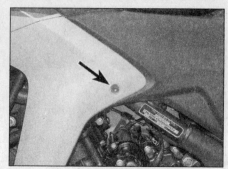

3.17c ...and the rear screw

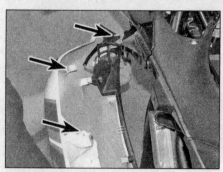

3.18 Carefully release the clips (arrowed)...

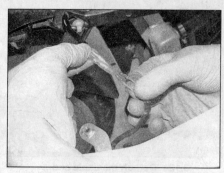

3.19 ...then disconnect the wiring

Fairing side panels

17 Undo the three screws (see illustrations).
18 Carefully pull the panel away to release the three snap-fit clips along the top (see illustration).
19 Disconnect the turn signal wiring connectors (see illustration).
20 Installation is the reverse of removal – push the snap-fit clips in until they locate, keeping them square to the sockets. The shouldered screw goes in the top front position.

Fuel tank covers

Side covers

21 Remove the fairing side panels.
22 Release the trim clips and undo the screw (see illustrations).
23 Pull the snap-fit clip at the back out then release the tabs at the front and remove the cover (see illustrations).
24 Installation is the reverse of removal – push the snap-fit clip in until it locates, keeping it square to the socket.

Top cover

25 Remove the fuel tank side covers.
26 Carefully pull the cover away from the tank to release the pegs from the grommets (see illustration).
27 Installation is the reverse of removal. Make sure the hole on each side seats over the peg on the bracket.

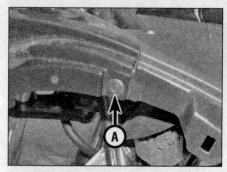

3.22a Release the trim clips (A)...

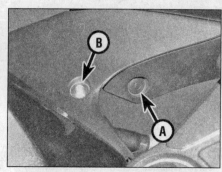

3.22b ...and undo the screw (B)

3.23a Carefully release the clip...

3.23b ...and the tabs

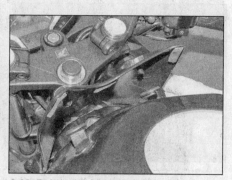

3.26 Release the pegs from the grommets

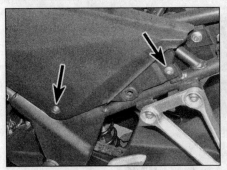

3.31 Undo the screws (arrowed)

3.32 Carefully pull the pegs out of the grommets

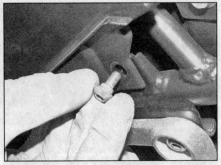

3.33 Fit the shouldered screw into the rear mount

Side panels

28 Remove the fairing side panels.
29 Remove the fuel tank side covers.
30 Remove the seat cowling.
31 Undo the two screws **(see illustration)**.
32 Carefully pull each cover away at the front to release the pegs from the grommets **(see illustration)**.
33 Installation is the reverse of removal – the shouldered screw goes at the back **(see illustration)**.

Lower fairing

34 Remove the fairing side panels.
35 Undo the four screws **(see illustration)**.
36 Release each mounting hole from its boss and remove the lower fairing.
37 Installation is the reverse of removal – make sure each mounting hole locates over its boss.

Mirrors

38 Unscrew the two bolts and remove the mirror **(see illustration)**.

39 Installation is the reverse of removal.

Fairing

40 Remove the fuel tank side covers.
41 Undo the instrument trim panel screws **(see illustration)**. Carefully pull each side of the panel up to release the snap-fit clips and so the pegs are clear of the grommets **(see illustration)**.
42 On 125 models release the wiring loom from the right-hand side of the fairing **(see illustration)**.

3.35 Undo the two screws (arrowed) on each side

3.38 Mirror bolts (arrowed)

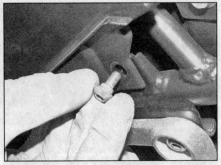

3.41a Undo the screws (arrowed)...

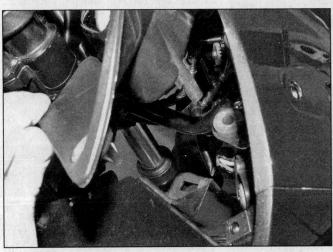

3.41b ...then release the clip and the peg on each side

3.42 Release the loom (arrowed) from the fairing

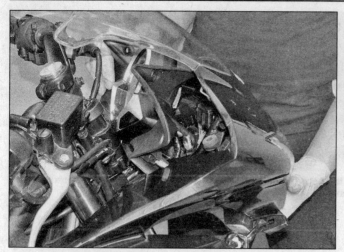

3.44a Displace the fairing forwards...

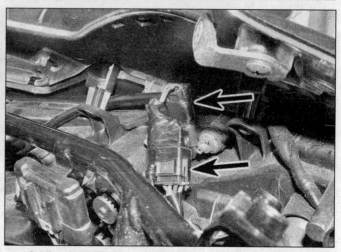

3.44b ...and disconnect the wiring connectors (arrowed)

43 Remove the mirrors.

44 Lift the fairing off the mirror mounts and draw it forwards to release the pegs from the grommets, and disconnect the headlight and lean angle sensor wiring connectors **(see illustrations)**.

45 Installation is the reverse of removal. Make sure the mirror pad is on the bracket **(see illustration)**. Lift the instrument trim panel as you fit the fairing so its front edge seats above the lean angle sensor wiring connector and

to seat the fairing on the mirror mounts **(see illustration 3.44a)**. Seat the trim panel pegs in the grommets, then push the snap-fit clips into their slots, holding the underside of the bracket as you do.

Windshield

46 Remove the fairing. Remove the headlight from the fairing (see Chapter 8).

47 Undo the windshield screws and remove the brackets, noting their alignment **(see illustration)**.

48 Release and remove the windshield.

49 Installation is the reverse of removal.

Front mudguard

CBR125

50 Unscrew the rear bolt on each side and release the brake hose and wiring **(see illustration)**. Note the collars in the grommets.

51 Undo the front bolts on each side and remove the washers **(see illustration)**. Lift the mudguard up and then draw it forwards, squeezing the sides in.

52 Remove the bracket from the underside of the mudguard if required. Note the collars in the grommets.

53 Installation is the reverse of removal. Make sure the grommets are in good condition and the collars and washers are fitted.

CBR250

54 Remove the front wheel (see Chapter 6).

55 Unscrew the rear bolt on each side, noting the washer, and release the brake hose and wiring as required according to model **(see illustration)**. Note the collars in the grommets.

3.45 Check the rubber pad (arrowed) is on the mount

3.47 Windshield screws (arrowed)

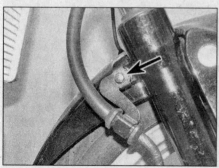

3.50 Unscrew the rear bolt (arrowed) on each side

3.51 Unscrew the bolts (arrowed) on each side and remove the mudguard

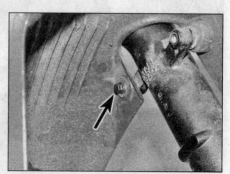

3.55 Unscrew the rear bolt (arrowed) on each side

3.56a Unscrew the bolts (arrowed) on each side and remove the mudguard

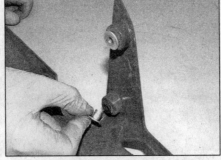
3.56b Remove the collars for safekeeping and check the grommets

4.1 Unscrew the bolt on each side to release the seat

56 Undo the front bolts on each side (see illustration). Lift the mudguard up and then draw it forwards, squeezing the sides in. Note the collars in the grommets (see illustration).
57 Installation is the reverse of removal. Make sure the grommets are in good condition and the collars and washers are fitted.

4 Bodywork – CRF models

Seat

1 Unscrew the two hook bolts at the back, noting the collars (see illustration). Lift the back of the seat and draw it back to disengage the hooks in the middle and the tab and slot at the front.

2 Installation is the reverse of removal. Make sure the slot, tab and hooks locate correctly (see illustration).

Side panels

3 Unscrew the bolt at the bottom, noting the collar with the right-hand panel (see illustration).
4 Carefully pull the panel away at the back to release the peg from the grommet, then draw it back to release it from the fuel tank cover tabs (see illustrations).
5 Installation is the reverse of removal.

Fuel tank covers

6 On the right-hand side release the trim clips and undo the screw securing the coolant reservoir cover and remove the cover, noting how the peg locates in the hole (see illustrations).

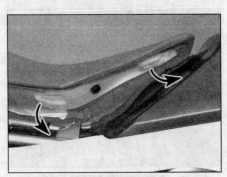
4.2 Make sure the seat hooks engage correctly

7 Remove the side panel.
8 Undo the screws and remove the cover (see illustration).
9 Installation is the reverse of removal.

4.3 Unscrew the bolt (arrowed)

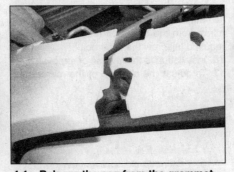
4.4a Release the peg from the grommet...

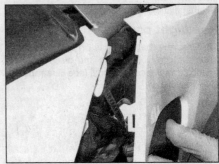
4.4b ...then disengage the tabs

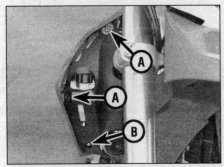
4.6a Release the trim clips (A) and undo the screw (B)...

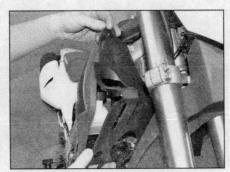
4.6b ...and remove the cover

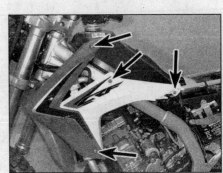
4.8 Fuel tank cover screws (arrowed)

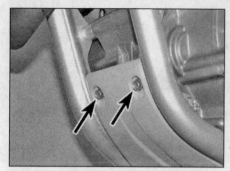

4.10a Unscrew the bolts (arrowed)...

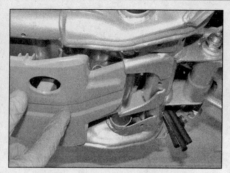

4.10b ...and remove the guard

4.12a Draw the cowl off the lug...

4.12b ...and disconnect the headlight connector (arrowed) and sidelight connector

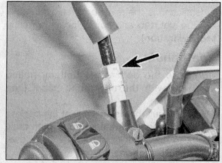

4.15 Lift the boot, slacken the nut (arrowed) and unscrew the mirror

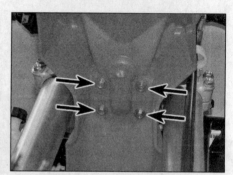

4.18 Mudguard bolts (arrowed)

Sump guard

10 Unscrew the two bolts and draw the guard forwards to release the tab at the back **(see illustrations)**.

11 Installation is the reverse of removal.

Headlight cowl

12 Unscrew the two bolts on each side, then draw the cowl off the lug and disconnect the headlight wiring connector(s) **(see illustrations)**.

13 Installation is the reverse of removal.

Mirrors

14 Pull the rubber boot up off the base of the mirror stem.

15 Slacken the top nut, then unscrew the mirror from the base bolt **(see illustration)**. If required unscrew the base bolt.

16 Installation is the reverse of removal.

17 To adjust the position of the mirror stem slacken the locknut, adjust the mirror, then tighten the locknut.

Front mudguard

18 Unscrew the four bolts and remove the mudguard **(see illustration)**. Note the collars in the top.

19 Installation is the reverse of removal. Make sure the collars are fitted.

Chapter 8
Electrical system

Contents

Degrees of difficulty

| **Easy,** suitable for novice with little experience | 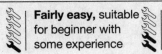 | **Fairly easy,** suitable for beginner with some experience | | **Fairly difficult,** suitable for competent DIY mechanic | | **Difficult,** suitable for experienced DIY mechanic | | **Very difficult,** suitable for expert DIY or professional | |

Specifications

Battery

Type
  CBR125 . . . . YTZ6V
  CBR250 and CRF250. . . . . YTX7L-BS
Capacity
  CBR125 . . . . 12 V, 5.0 Ah
  CBR250 and CRF250. . . . . 12 V, 6.0 Ah
Voltage
  Fully-charged . . . . 13.0 to 13.2 V
  Uncharged . . . . below 12.3 V
Charging rate
  CBR125
    Normal . . . . 0.5 A for 5 to 10 hrs
    Quick. . . . . 2.5 A for 1 hr
  CBR250 and CRF250
    Normal . . . . 0.6 A for 5 to 10 hrs
    Quick. . . . . 3.0 A for 1 hr
Current leakage
  CBR125 . . . . 0.1 mA (max)
  CBR250 and CRF250. . . . . 0.34 mA (max)

Charging system

Regulated voltage output	15.5 V max. @ 5000 rpm
Alternator stator coil resistance	0.1 to 1.0 ohms

Starter motor

Brush length
CBR125	
Standard	6.7 to 7.3 mm
Service limit (min)	3.5 mm
CBR250 and CRF250	
Standard	11.8 to 12.3 mm
Service limit (min)	6.5 mm

Fuses

See wiring diagrams for circuits covered

Main	30 A
Others	10 A x 5
ABS (CBR250RA)	30 A x 2, 10 A x 1

Bulbs

Headlight	55/60 W H4
Sidelight	5 W
Brake/tail light	21/5 W
Turn signal lights	21 W (RY on CBR models)
Licence plate light	5 W
Instrument lights	LED
Turn signal indicator light	LED
HI beam indicator light	LED
Neutral indicator light	
CBR models	1.7 W
CRF models	LED
PGM-FI malfunction indicator light	LED
ABS indicator light (CBR250RA)	LED

Torque settings

Alternator rotor nut or bolt	
125 models	64 Nm
250 models	128 Nm
Alternator stator bolts	10 Nm
CKP sensor bolts	10 Nm
Fork clamp bolts (top yoke)	
CBR125	23 Nm
CBR250	22 Nm
CRF250	32 Nm
Handlebar clamp bolts	
CBR125	26 Nm
CBR250	27 Nm
Ignition switch bolts (250 models)	24 Nm
Neutral switch (250 models)	12 Nm
Steering stem nut	
CBR125	88 Nm
CBR250 and CRF250	103 Nm

1 General information

All models have a 12 volt electrical system charged by a three-phase alternator with a separate regulator/rectifier.

The regulator maintains the charging system output within the specified range to prevent overcharging, and the rectifier converts the ac (alternating current) output of the alternator to dc (direct current) to power the lights and other components and to charge the battery. The alternator rotor is mounted on the left-hand end of the crankshaft.

The starter motor is mounted on the front of the engine on 125 models and on top of the crankcase behind the cylinder on 250 models. The starting system includes the motor, the battery, the relay and the various wires and switches. Some of the switches are part of a starter interlock system that prevents the engine from being started if the sidestand is down and the engine is in gear – see Chapter 1 for further information and checks on the system.

Note: *Keep in mind that electrical parts, once purchased, often cannot be returned. To avoid unnecessary expense, make very sure the faulty component has been positively identified before buying a replacement part.*

2 Electrical system fault finding

1 A typical electrical circuit consists of an electrical component, the switches, relays, etc, related to that component and the wiring and connectors that link the component to the battery and the frame.

2 Before tackling any troublesome electrical circuit, first study the wiring diagram thoroughly to get a complete picture of what makes up that individual circuit. Trouble spots can often be located by noting if other components related to that circuit are operating properly or not. If several components or circuits fail at one time, chances are the fault lies either in the fuse or in a common earth (ground) connection, as several circuits are often routed through the same fuse and earth (ground) connections **(see illustrations)**.

3 Electrical problems often stem from simple causes, such as loose or corroded connections or a blown fuse. Prior to any electrical fault finding, always visually check the condition of the fuse, wires and connections in the problem circuit. Intermittent failures can be especially frustrating, since you can't always duplicate the failure when it's convenient to test. In such situations, a good practice is to clean all connections in the affected circuit, whether or not they appear to be good – where possible use a dedicated electrical cleaning spray along with sandpaper, wire wool or other abrasive material to remove corrosion, and a dedicated electrical protection spray to prevent further problems. All of the connections and wires should also be wiggled to check for looseness that can cause intermittent failure.

4 If you don't have a multimeter it is highly advisable to obtain one – they are not expensive and will enable a full range of electrical tests to be made **(see illustration)**. Go for a modern digital one with an LCD display, as they are easier to use. A continuity tester and/or test light are useful for certain electrical checks as an alternative, though are limited in their usefulness compared to a multimeter **(see illustrations)**.

2.2a Common earth point (arrowed) behind right-hand side panel – CBR125

2.2c ...and earth junction box (arrowed) on fairing bracket – CBR250

2.2b Common earth point (arrowed) behind left-hand side panel...

2.2d Common earth point (arrowed) behind fuel tank right-hand cover – CRF250

Continuity checks

5 The term continuity describes the uninterrupted flow of electricity through an electrical circuit. Continuity can be checked with a multimeter set either to its continuity function (a beep is emitted when continuity is found), or to the resistance (ohms / Ω) function, or with a dedicated continuity tester. Both instruments are powered by an internal battery, therefore the checks are made with the ignition OFF. As a safety precaution, always disconnect the battery negative (-) lead before making continuity checks, particularly if ignition switch checks are being made.

6 If using a multimeter, select the continuity function if it has one, or the resistance (ohms) function. Touch the meter probes together and check that a beep is emitted or the meter reads zero, which indicates continuity. If there

is no continuity there will be no beep or the meter will show infinite resistance. After using the meter, always switch it OFF to conserve its battery.

7 A continuity tester can be used in the same way – its light should come on or it should beep to indicate continuity in the switch ON position, but should be off or silent in the OFF position.

8 Note that the polarity of the test probes doesn't matter for continuity checks, although care should be taken to follow specific test procedures if a diode or solid-state component is being checked.

Switch continuity checks

9 If a switch is at fault, trace its wiring to the wiring connectors. Separate the connectors and inspect them for security and condition. A build-up of dirt or corrosion here will most

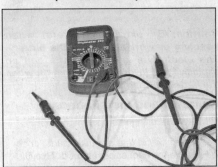

2.4a A digital multimeter can be used for all electrical tests

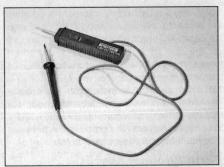

2.4b A battery-powered continuity tester

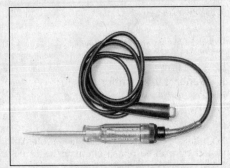

2.4c A simple test light is useful for voltage tests

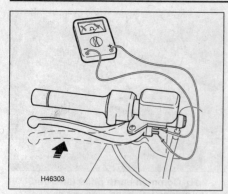

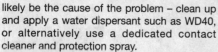

2.10 Continuity should be indicated across switch terminals when lever is operated

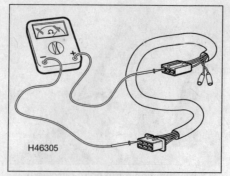

2.12 Wiring continuity check. Connect the meter probes across each end of the same wire

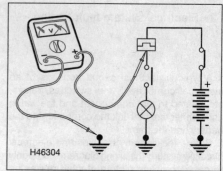

2.15 Voltage check. Connect the meter positive probe to the component and the negative probe to earth

likely be the cause of the problem – clean up and apply a water dispersant such as WD40, or alternatively use a dedicated contact cleaner and protection spray.

10 If using a multimeter, select the continuity function if it has one, or the resistance (ohms) function, and connect its probes to the terminals in the connector **(see illustration)**. Simple ON/OFF type switches, such as brake light switches, only have two wires whereas combination switches, like the handlebar switches, have many wires. Study the wiring diagram to ensure that you are connecting to the correct pair of wires. Continuity should be indicated with the switch ON and no continuity with it OFF.

Wiring continuity checks

11 Many electrical faults are caused by damaged wiring, often due to incorrect routing or chaffing on frame components. Loose, wet or corroded wire connectors can also be the cause of electrical problems.

12 A continuity check can be made on a single length of wire by disconnecting it at each end and connecting the meter or continuity tester probes to each end of the wire **(see illustration)**. Continuity (low or no resistance – 0 ohms) should be indicated if the wire is good. If no continuity (high resistance) is shown, suspect a broken wire.

13 To check for continuity to earth in any earth wire connect one probe of your meter or tester to the earth wire terminal in the connector and the other to the frame, engine,

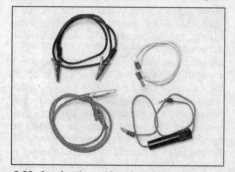

2.23 A selection of insulated jumper wires

or battery earth (-) terminal. Continuity (low or no resistance – 0 ohms) should be indicated if the wire is good. If no continuity (high resistance) is shown, suspect a broken wire or corroded or loose earth point (see below).

Voltage checks

14 A voltage check can determine whether power is reaching a component. Use a multimeter set to the dc voltage scale, or a test light. The test light is the cheaper component, but the meter has the advantage of being able to give a voltage reading.

15 Connect the meter or test light in parallel, i.e. across the load **(see illustration)**.

16 First identify the relevant wiring circuit by referring to the wiring diagram at the end of this manual. If other electrical components share the same power supply (i.e. are fed from the same fuse), take note whether they are working correctly – this is useful information in deciding where to start checking the circuit.

17 If using a meter, check first that the meter leads are plugged into the correct terminals on the meter (red to positive (+), black to negative (-). Set the meter to the dc volts function, where necessary at a range suitable for the battery voltage – 0 to 20 vdc. Connect the meter red probe (+) to the power supply wire and the black probe to a good metal earth (ground) on the bike's frame or directly to the battery negative terminal. Battery voltage should be shown on the meter with the ignition switch, and if necessary any other relevant switch, ON.

18 If using a test light, connect its positive (+) probe to the power supply terminal and its negative (-) probe to a good earth (ground) on the bike's frame. With the switch, and if necessary any other relevant switch, ON, the test light should illuminate.

19 If no voltage is indicated, work back towards the fuse continuing to check for voltage. When you reach a point where there is voltage, you know the problem lies between that point and your last check point.

Earth (ground) checks

20 Earth connections are made either directly to the engine or frame via the mounting of the

component, or by a separate wire into the earth circuit of the wiring harness. Alternatively a short earth wire is sometimes run from the component directly to the bike's frame.

21 Corrosion is a common cause of a poor earth connection, as is a loose earth terminal fastener.

22 If total or multiple component failure is experienced, check the security of the main earth lead from the negative (-) terminal of the battery, the earth lead bolted to the engine, and the main earth point(s) on the frame (see Step 2). If corroded, dismantle the connection and clean all surfaces back to bare metal. Remake the connection and prevent further corrosion from forming by smearing battery terminal grease over the connection.

23 To check the earth of a component, use an insulated jumper wire to temporarily bypass its earth connection **(see illustration)** – connect one end of the jumper wire to the earth terminal or metal body of the component and the other end to the bike's frame. If the circuit works with the jumper wire installed, the earth circuit is faulty.

24 To check an earth wire first check for corroded or loose connections, then check the wiring for continuity (Step 13) between each connector in the circuit in turn, and then to its earth point, to locate the break.

---

3 Battery removal and maintenance

Caution: Be extremely careful when handling or working around the battery. The electrolyte is very caustic and an explosive gas (hydrogen) is given off when the battery is charging.

Removal and installation

1 Make sure the ignition is switched OFF.

CBR125

2 Remove the rider's seat (see Chapter 7).

3 Release and remove the battery cover clip by unscrewing the centre of the clip then drawing the body out of the cover **(see**

3.3 Release the clip and lift the cover

3.4 Disconnect negative lead (A) first then positive lead (B) – CBR125

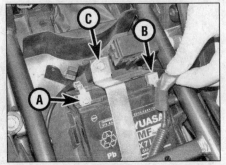

3.8 Disconnect negative lead (A) first then positive lead (B). Battery holder bolt (C) – CBR250

illustration). Lift the cover to expose the battery.

4 Unscrew the negative (–) terminal bolt first and disconnect the lead from the battery (see illustration). Lift up the red insulating cover to access the positive (+) terminal, then unscrew the bolt and disconnect the lead.

5 Lift the battery out.

6 Installation is the reverse of removal. Clean the battery terminals and lead ends with a wire brush, emery paper or steel wool. Reconnect the leads, connecting the positive (+) terminal first.

CBR250

7 Remove the rider's seat (see Chapter 7).

8 Unscrew the negative (–) terminal bolt first and disconnect the lead from the battery (see illustration). Lift up the red insulating cover to access the positive (+) terminal, then unscrew the bolt and disconnect the lead.

9 Unscrew the holder bolt, displace the holder and lift the battery out (see illustration 3.8).

10 Installation is the reverse of removal. Clean the battery terminals and lead ends with a wire brush, emery paper or steel wool. Reconnect the leads, connecting the positive (+) terminal first.

CRF250

11 Remove the left-hand side panel (see Chapter 7).

12 Unscrew the negative (–) terminal bolt first and disconnect the lead from the battery (see illustration). Lift up the red insulating cover to

access the positive (+) terminal, then unscrew the bolt and disconnect the lead.

13 Unscrew the holder bolts, remove the holder and lift the battery out (see illustration 3.12).

14 Installation is the reverse of removal. Clean the battery terminals and lead ends with a wire brush, emery paper or steel wool. Reconnect the leads, connecting the positive (+) terminal first.

> **HAYNES HiNT** *Battery corrosion can be kept to a minimum by applying a layer of battery terminal grease or petroleum jelly (Vaseline) to the terminals after the leads have been connected. DO NOT use a mineral based grease.*

Inspection and maintenance

15 The battery on all models is of the maintenance free (sealed) type, therefore requiring no regular maintenance. However, the following checks should still be performed.

16 Check the state of charge by measuring the voltage at the battery terminals (see illustration). Connect the voltmeter positive (+) probe to the battery positive (+) terminal, and the negative (–) probe to the battery negative (–) terminal. When fully-charged there should be 13.0 to 13.2 volts present. If the voltage falls below 12.3 volts remove

the battery (see above), and recharge it as described in Section 4.

17 Check the battery terminals and leads are tight and free of corrosion. If corrosion is evident, clean the terminals as described above, then protect them from further corrosion (see *Haynes Hint*).

18 Keep the battery case clean to prevent current leakage, which can discharge the battery over a period of time (especially when it sits unused). Wash the outside of the case with a solution of baking soda and water. Rinse the battery thoroughly, then dry it.

19 Look for cracks in the case and replace the battery with a new one if any are found. If acid has been spilled on the frame or battery box, neutralise it with a baking soda and water solution, then dry it thoroughly.

20 If the motorcycle sits unused for long periods of time, disconnect the leads from the battery terminals, negative (–) terminal first. Refer to Section 4 and charge the battery once every month to six weeks.

4 Battery charging

Caution: Be extremely careful when handling or working around the battery. The electrolyte is very caustic and an explosive gas (hydrogen) is given off when the battery is charging.

1 Remove the battery (see Section 3).

2 Connect the charger to the battery, making sure that the positive (+) lead on the charger is connected to the positive (+) terminal on the battery, and the negative (–) lead is connected to the negative (–) terminal.

3 Honda recommend that the battery is charged at the normal rate specified at the beginning of the Chapter. A higher 'quick charge' rate that can be used if absolutely necessary is also specified, but note that exceeding this could cause the battery to overheat, buckling the plates and rendering it useless. If a normal domestic charger is used check that after a possible initial peak, the charge rate falls to a safe level. If the battery becomes hot during charging **stop**.

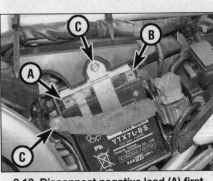

3.12 Disconnect negative lead (A) first then positive lead (B). Battery holder bolts (C) – CRF250

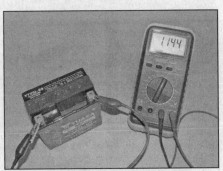

3.16 Checking battery voltage

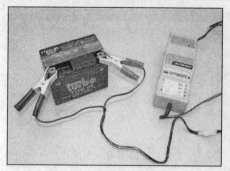

4.3 Battery connected to a charger

5.2a Disconnect the connector to access the main fuse (arrowed)

5.2b Fusebox (arrowed) – CBR125

Further charging will cause damage. Note that there are many bike-specific chargers available from good suppliers that are designed for the maintenance and recovery of motorcycle batteries, in particular catering for the requirements of heavily discharged MF batteries **(see illustration)**. They are a worthwhile investment, especially if the bike is not used over winter. Follow the manufacturer's instructions.

4 If the recharged battery discharges rapidly when left disconnected it is likely that an internal short caused by physical damage or sulphation has occurred. A new battery will be required. A sound item will tend to lose its charge at about 1% per day.

5 Install the battery (see Section 3).

6 If the motorcycle sits unused for long periods of time, charge the battery once every month to six weeks and leave it disconnected.

5 Fuses and main relay

Fuses

1 The electrical system as a whole is protected by the main fuse, and individual circuits are protected by other fuses of different ratings.

2 On CBR125 models the main fuse is housed in the starter relay – to access it remove the right-hand side panel (see Chapter 7), then unclip the relay wiring connector **(see**

illustration). All other fuses are housed in the fusebox, located under the rider's seat **(see illustration)**. The location, identity and rating of each fuse is marked on the box lid. Unclip the lid to access the fuses **(see illustration)**. A spare main fuse is housed on the battery cover, and a spare 10A fuse is housed in the fusebox **(see illustration)**.

3 On CBR250 models the main fuse is housed in the starter relay – to access it remove the rider's seat (see Chapter 7) and the air filter cover **(see illustration)**. Unclip the relay wiring connector **(see illustrations)**. All other fuses are housed in the fusebox or boxes (the ABS fuses on RA models are housed separately), also located under the rider's seat **(see illustration)**. Unclip the lid to access the

5.2c Unclip the lid to access the fuses and relays

5.2d Spare main fuse (arrowed)

5.3a Undo the screws (arrowed) and remove the cover

5.3b Disconnect the connector...

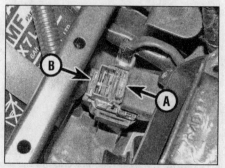

5.3c ...to access the main fuse (A) and its spare (B)

5.3d Fusebox (arrowed) – CBR250

5.3e Unclip the lid to access the fuses and relays

5.4a Disconnect the connector...

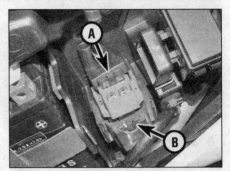

5.4b ...to access the main fuse (A) and its spare (B)

fuses (see illustration). The location, identity and rating of each fuse is marked in the box lid. A spare main fuse is housed in the relay holder, and a spare 10A fuse is housed in the fusebox.

4 On CRF250 models the main fuse is housed in the starter relay – to access it remove the left-hand side panel (see Chapter 7), then unclip the relay wiring connector (see illustrations). All other fuses are housed in the fusebox, also located behind the left-hand side panel (see illustration). Unclip the lid to access the fuses (see illustration). The location, identity and rating of each fuse is marked in the box lid. A spare main fuse is housed in the relay holder, and a spare 10A fuse is housed in the fusebox.

5 The fuses can be removed and checked visually – if you can't pull the fuse out with your fingertips, use a pair of suitable pliers. A blown fuse is easily identified by a break in the element (see illustration), but if there is any doubt check the fuse for continuity (see Section 2). Each fuse is clearly marked with its rating and must only be replaced by a fuse of the correct rating. If a spare fuse is used, always replace it with a new one so that a spare of each rating is carried on the bike at all times.

 Warning: Never put in a fuse of a higher rating or bridge the terminals with any other substitute, however temporary it may be. Serious damage may be done to the circuit, or a fire may start.

5.4c Fusebox (arrowed) – CRF250

5.4d Unclip the lid to access the fuses and relays

6 If the new fuse blows immediately check the wiring circuit very carefully for evidence of a short-circuit. Look for bare wires and chafed, melted or burned insulation.

7 Occasionally a fuse will blow or cause an open-circuit for no obvious reason. Corrosion of the fuse ends and fusebox terminals may occur and cause poor fuse contact. If this happens, remove the corrosion with a wire brush or emery paper, then spray the fuse end and terminals with electrical contact cleaner.

Main relay (CBR125 only)

8 The relay supplies power from the ignition switch to the fuses controlling all lighting and signalling and most instrumentation functions. If the relay is suspected of being faulty, remove the fuel tank left-hand cover (see Chapter 7). Carefully pull the side panel away from the

tank to release the pegs from the grommets. Remove the relay (see illustration).

9 Test the relay as follows: set a multimeter to the ohms x 1 scale and connect it across the relay's A and B terminals (see illustration). There should be no continuity (infinite resistance). Using a fully-charged 12 volt battery and two insulated jumper wires, connect the positive (+) terminal of the battery to the C terminal on the relay, and the negative (–) terminal to the D terminal. At this point the relay should be heard to click and the meter read 0 ohms (continuity). If this is the case the relay is good. If the relay does not click when battery voltage is applied and indicates no continuity (infinite resistance) across its terminals, it is faulty and must be replaced with a new one.

10 If the relay is good, check for battery

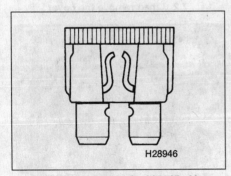

5.5 A blown fuse can be identified by a break in its element

5.8 Main relay (arrowed)

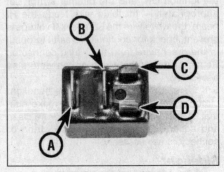

5.9 Relay test set-up

voltage at the black/white wire terminal in the connector with the ignition ON. Also check for continuity to earth in the green wire. If necessary check all the wiring in the circuit for continuity, referring to the wiring diagrams at the end of the Chapter. Also make sure that all the terminals in the connectors are clean and secure. Repair or renew the wiring or connectors as necessary.

6 Lighting system check

Note: *Refer to electrical system fault finding in Section 2 and to the wiring diagram for your model at the end of this Chapter.*

1 If a light fails first check the bulb (see relevant Section), the bulb terminals in the holder, and the wiring connector. Next check the fuse (Section 5). If none of the lights work, check battery voltage – low voltage indicates either a faulty battery or a defective charging system. Refer to Section 3 for battery checks and Section 27 for charging system tests. If there is a problem with more than one circuit at the same time, or with all circuits, it is likely to be a fault relating to a multi-function component, such as the fuse or the ignition switch. When checking for a blown filament in a bulb, it is advisable to back up a visual check with a continuity test of the filament as it is not always apparent that a bulb has blown. When testing for continuity, remember that on single terminal bulbs it is the metal body of the bulb that is the earth (ground). Refer to Section 2 for details of testing electrical circuits.

Headlight

2 All models have one twin filament bulb, one for high beam and one for low beam.
3 If a beam fails to work, first check the bulb (see Section 7). If it is good, the problem lies in the wiring or connectors, the starter button or the dimmer switch. Refer to Section 18 for the switch testing procedures, and also to the wiring diagrams at the end of this Chapter. If neither beam works, check the fuse (Section 5)
4 If a beam does not work, and the bulb is good, check for battery voltage on the loom side of the headlight wiring connector with the ignition ON, and the dimmer switch set appropriately – the blue wire feeds the HI beam, the white wire the LO beam. If voltage is present, check for continuity to earth (ground) in the green wire from the wiring connector. Repair or renew the wiring or connectors as necessary.
5 If there is no voltage check the headlight circuit wiring for continuity. Also make sure that all the terminals and connectors are clean and secure. Repair or renew the wiring or connectors as necessary.

Sidelight

6 On CBR models, if one sidelight fails to work, first check the bulb (Section 7). If both sidelights fail check for battery voltage to each bulbholder at the white/green wire with the ignition switch ON. If voltage is present, check for continuity to earth (ground) in the green wire in the loom side of the headlight wiring connector. If no voltage is indicated, check the wiring and connectors in the sidelight circuit.
7 On CRF models, if the sidelight fails to work, first check the bulb (Section 7). If the bulb is good check for battery voltage to the bulbholder at the blue/white wire with the ignition switch ON. If voltage is present, check for continuity to earth (ground) in the green wire in the loom side of the headlight wiring connector. If no voltage is indicated, check the wiring and connectors in the sidelight circuit.

Tail light

8 If the tail light fails to work, first check the bulb (Section 9). If it is good, check for battery voltage in the brown (CBR models) or black (CRF models) wire in the connector with the ignition switch ON. If voltage is present, check for continuity to earth (ground) in the green wire from the connector. If no voltage is indicated, check the wiring and connectors in the tail light circuit.

Brake light

9 If the brake light fails to work, first check the bulb (Section 9). If it is good, check for battery voltage in the green/yellow wire in the connector, first with the front brake lever pulled in, then with the rear brake pedal pressed down. If voltage is present with one brake on but not the other, then the switch or its wiring is faulty. If voltage is present in both cases, check for continuity to earth (ground) in the green wire from the connector. If no voltage

is indicated, check the wiring and connectors between the brake light and the switches, then check the switches themselves. Refer to Section 14 for the switch testing procedures.

Licence plate light (CBR models)

10 If the licence plate light fails to work, first check whether the tail light is working – they run off the same circuit. If it isn't refer to Step 8. If the tail light is working, check the licence plate light bulb (Section 9). If the bulb and tail light are both good check the brown wire between the connector on the tail light and that on the licence plate light for continuity.

Turn signals

11 See Section 11.

7 Headlight and sidelight bulbs

Note: *The headlight bulb is of the quartz-halogen type. Do not touch the bulb glass as skin acids will shorten the bulb's service life. If the bulb is accidentally touched, it should be wiped carefully when cold with a rag soaked in methylated spirit and dried before fitting.*

Headlight bulb

CBR models

1 Remove the fairing side panel from one side (see Chapter 7). Disconnect the wiring connector from the bulb **(see illustration)**.
2 Remove the rubber cover **(see illustration)**.
3 Release the bulb retaining clip noting how it fits, then remove the bulb **(see illustrations)**.

7.1 Disconnect the wiring connector...

7.2 ...then remove the cover

7.3a Release the clip...

7.3b ...and remove the bulb

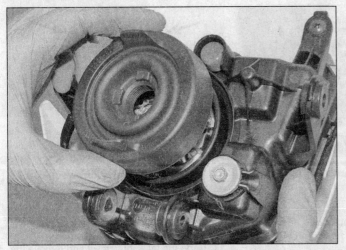

7.9 Remove the cover

7.10a Release the clip...

4 Fit the new bulb into the headlight, bearing in mind the information in the **Note** above. Make sure it locates correctly, and secure it with the retaining clip **(see illustrations 7.3b and a)**.
5 Fit the cover with the tabs at top and bottom **(see illustration 7.2)**.
6 Connect the wiring connector **(see illustrations 7.1)**.
7 Check the operation of the headlight.

 HAYNES HINT *Always use a paper towel or dry cloth when handling new bulbs to prevent injury if the bulb should break and to increase bulb life.*

7.10b ...and remove the bulb

7.15a Remove the fairing side panel to access the sidelight bulbholder (arrowed)

CRF models

8 Remove the headlight cowl (see Chapter 7).
9 Remove the rubber cover **(see illustration)**.
10 Release the bulb retaining clip noting how it fits, then remove the bulb **(see illustrations)**.
11 Fit the new bulb into the headlight, bearing in mind the information in the **Note** above. Make sure it locates correctly, and secure it with the retaining clip **(see illustrations 7.10b and a)**.
12 Fit the cover with the tabs at top and bottom **(see illustration 7.9)**.
13 Install the headlight cowl (see Chapter 7).
14 Check the operation of the headlight.

Sidelight bulb

15 On CBR models remove the fairing side panel from the relevant side (see Chapter 7) **(see illustration)**. Turn the bulbholder anti-clockwise and draw it out, then pull the bulb out of the holder **(see illustrations)**.
16 On CRF models remove the headlight cowl (see Chapter 7). Pull the bulbholder out, then pull the bulb out of the holder **(see illustrations)**.
17 Fit the new bulb into the holder and the holder into the headlight, on CBR models turning it clockwise to lock it.
18 Check the operation of the sidelight.

7.15b Release the bulbholder...

7.15c ...and pull the bulb out

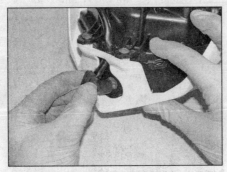

7.16a Release the bulbholder...

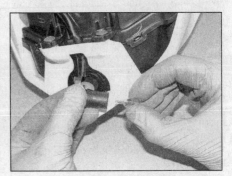

7.16b ...and pull the bulb out

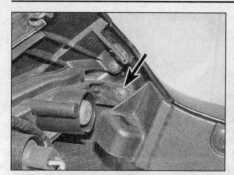

8.3a On CBR models undo the screw (arrowed) on each side…

8.3b …and the four screws (arrowed)

8.3c Headlight screws (arrowed) – CRF models

8 Headlight

1 On CBR models remove the fairing (see Chapter 7).
2 On CRF models remove the headlight cowl (see Chapter 7).
3 Undo the screws and remove the headlight (see illustrations).
4 If required remove the bulbs (see Section 7).
5 Installation is the reverse of removal. Check the operation of the headlights and sidelight(s). Check the headlight aim (see Chapter 1).

9 Brake/tail light/licence plate bulbs

Note: *It is a good idea to use a paper towel or dry cloth when handling bulbs to prevent injury if it breaks, and to increase bulb life.*

Brake/tail light bulb

CBR models

1 Remove the passenger seat (see Chapter 7). For easiest access release the trim clips securing the access panel on the underside (see illustration). Lower the front of the panel and draw it forwards to release the tabs along the rear edge (see illustration).
2 Turn the bulbholder anti-clockwise and draw it out (see illustration).
3 Carefully push the bulb in and turn it anti-clockwise to release it (see illustration).
4 Check the socket terminals for corrosion and clean them if necessary.
5 Line up the pins of the new bulb with the slots in the socket, then push the bulb in and turn it clockwise until it locks into place.
6 Fit the bulbholder and turn it clockwise.
7 Check the operation of the tail and brake lights.

CRF models

8 Remove the seat (see Chapter 7).

9 Unscrew the two hook bolts at the back, noting the collars, and remove the top cover (see illustration).

10 Unscrew the four bolts and remove the licence plate holder (see illustration).
11 Undo the tail light screws and remove the

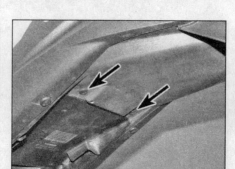

9.1a Release the trim clips (arrowed)…

9.1b …and remove the panel

9.2 Release the bulbholder…

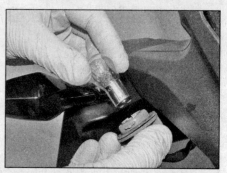

9.3 …and remove the tail light bulb

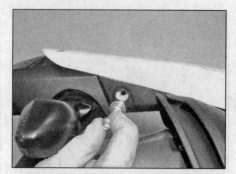

9.9 Unscrew the bolt on each side to release the top cover

9.10 Licence plate holder bolts (arrowed)

collars, then remove the tail light, and on US and Canada models disconnect the licence plate light wiring **(see illustrations)**.

12 Turn the bulbholder anti-clockwise and draw it out **(see illustration)**.

13 Carefully push the bulb in and turn it anti-clockwise to release it **(see illustration)**.

14 Check the socket terminals for corrosion and clean them if necessary.

15 Line up the pins of the new bulb with the slots in the socket, then push the bulb in and turn it clockwise until it locks into place.

16 Fit the bulbholder and turn it clockwise.

17 Fit the tail light in reverse order of removal.

18 Check the operation of the tail and brake lights.

Licence plate light bulb

19 Undo the two screws and remove the cover **(see illustration)**.

20 Carefully pull the bulb out and replace with a new one **(see illustration)**.

21 Make sure the rubber seal is in good condition and correctly in place before fitting the cover. Do not overtighten the screws.

22 Check the operation of the light.

---

10 Tail light and licence plate light

Tail light

CBR models

1 Remove the seat cowling (see Chapter 7).

2 Undo the tail light cover screws and the tail light screws **(see illustrations)**. Draw the cover back to release the tabs from the seat cowling **(see illustration)**.

3 Release the light from the cowling.

4 Installation is the reverse of removal. Check the operation of the tail and brake lights.

CRF models

5 Remove the brake/tail light bulb (see Section 9).

6 On UK and European models remove the

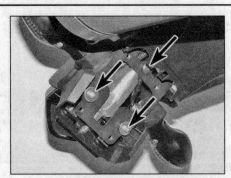

9.11a Undo the screws (arrowed)...

9.11b ...and remove the tail light

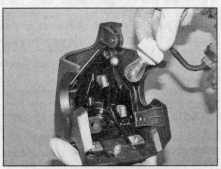

9.12 Release the bulbholder...

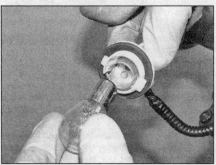

9.13 ...and remove the tail light bulb – CRF250

9.19 Undo the screws (arrowed) and remove the cover

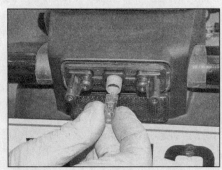

9.20 Pull the licence plate light bulb out of the socket

10.2a Undo the screw (arrowed)...

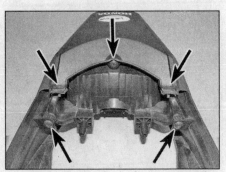

10.2b ...and the screws (arrowed)

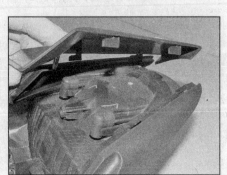

10.2c Remove the cover

10.6 Undo the nut and remove the reflector

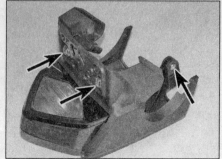

10.7 Tail light screws (arrowed)

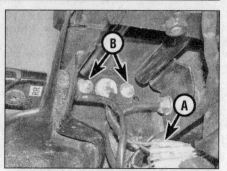

10.10 Disconnect the relevant connectors (A), then undo the nuts (B) and remove the light

rear reflector **(see illustration)**. On US and Canada models remove the licence plate light (see below).

7 Undo the tail light unit screws and detach the cover from the light **(see illustration)**.

8 Installation is the reverse of removal. Check the operation of the tail and brake lights.

Licence plate light

CBR models

9 Release the trim clips securing the access panel on the underside, then draw the panel forwards to release the tab at the back **(see illustrations 9.1a and b)**.

10 On UK and European models disconnect the licence plate light wiring connectors, then undo the nuts and remove the licence plate light **(see illustration)**. Remove the collars and rubber pad if required.

11 On US and Canada models disconnect the licence plate light wiring connectors, then undo the screws and remove the licence plate light holder. Undo the nuts and remove the licence plate light from the holder. Remove the collars and rubber pad if required.

12 Installation is the reverse of removal. Check the operation of the light.

US and Canada CRF models

13 Remove the brake/tail light bulb (see Section 9).

14 Undo the screws and remove the licence plate light holder.

15 Undo the nuts and remove the licence plate light from the holder. Remove the collars and rubber pad if required.

16 Installation is the reverse of removal. Check the operation of the light.

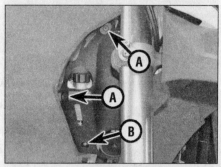

11.2a Release the trim clips (A) and undo the screw (B)...

11.2b ...and remove the cover

11.3a Turn signal relay (arrowed) – CBR models

11.3b Turn signal relay (arrowed) – CRF models

11 Turn signal circuit check

Note: *Refer to electrical system fault finding in Section 2 and to the wiring diagram for your model at the end of this Chapter.*

1 Most turn signal problems are the result of a burned out bulb or corroded socket. This is especially true when the turn signals function properly in one direction (although possibly too quickly), but fail to flash in the other direction. If this is the case, first check the bulbs, the sockets and the wiring connectors (see Sections 12 and 13). If all the turn signals fail to work, check the fuse (see Section 5), and then the relay (see Steps 2 to 4). If they are good, the problem lies in the wiring or connectors, or the switch. Refer to Section 18 for the switch testing procedures, and also to the wiring diagrams at the end of this Chapter.

2 To check the relay, on CBR models remove the fairing left-hand side panel (see Chapter 7). On CRF models release the trim clips and undo the screw securing the coolant reservoir cover and remove the cover, noting how the peg locates in the hole **(see illustrations)**.

3 Displace the relay and disconnect the wiring connector **(see illustrations)**. Short between the brown and grey (CBR125), black and grey (CBR250) or black/orange and grey (CRF250) wire terminals on the loom side of the connector using a jumper wire. Turn the ignition ON and operate the turn signal switch, first in one direction then the other. If the lights come on (they won't flash), the relay is faulty and must be replaced with a new one.

4 If the lights do not come on, check the grey wire for continuity to the left-hand switch housing and the brown, black or black/orange wire for continuity to the fusebox, and repair or renew the wiring or connectors as required. On 250 models also check the green wire for continuity to earth.

5 If all is good so far, or if the lights came on one side but not the other, check the wiring between the left-hand switch housing and the turn signals themselves. Repair or renew the wiring or connectors as necessary.

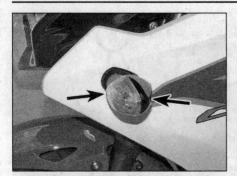

12.1a Turn signal lens screws (arrowed) – CBR models

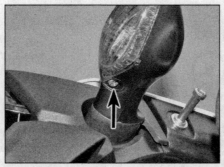

12.1b Turn signal lens screw (arrowed) – CRF models

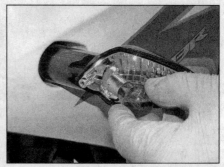

12.2 Push the bulb in and turn it anti-clockwise to release it

12 Turn signal bulbs

Note: *It is a good idea to use a paper towel or dry cloth when handling bulbs to prevent injury if the bulb should break and to increase bulb life.*

1 Undo the screw(s) and detach the lens from the housing, on CRF models noting how the tab locates **(see illustrations)**. On CBR models remove the rubber seal if it is loose, and replace it with a new one it if it is damaged, deformed or deteriorated.

2 Push the bulb in and twist it anti-clockwise to release it **(see illustration)**. Check the socket terminals for corrosion and clean them if necessary.

3 Line up the pins of the new bulb with the slots in the socket, then push the bulb in and turn it clockwise until it locks into place. Note that the bulb slots on CBR models are spaced to accept the offset pins of the RY (amber) bulbs.

4 On CBR models fit a new rubber seal if required, and make sure it is properly seated and does not get pinched **(see illustration)**. Fit the lens onto the housing, on CRF models locating the tab in the cut-out, and fit the

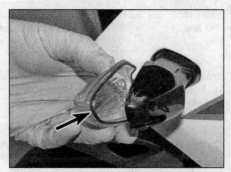

12.4a On CBR models make sure the seal (arrowed) is in place

screw(s) **(see illustration)**. Do not overtighten the screw(s) as it is easy to strip the threads or crack the lens.

13 Turn signal assemblies

Front turn signals

CBR models

1 Remove the fairing side panel (see Chapter 7).

12.4b On CRF models locate the tab (arrowed) in its cut-out

2 Unscrew the nut, remove the bracket, and withdraw the turn signal, taking care as you draw the wire through **(see illustration)**.

3 Installation is the reverse of removal. Make sure the cut-out in the bracket seats over the pin on the panel. Check the operation of the turn signals.

CRF models

4 Remove the headlight cowl (see Chapter 7).

5 Release the cable-tie around the rubber boot and disconnect the turn signal wiring connector **(see illustration)**. Release the left-hand turn signal wiring from its tie.

6 Unscrew the nut and remove the turn signal,

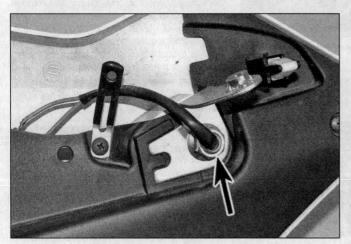

13.2 Front turn signal nut (arrowed)

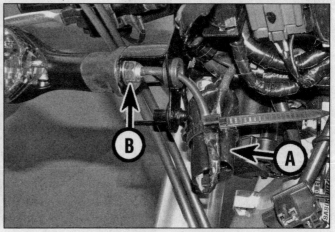

13.5 Turn signal wiring connectors (A, inside boot) and mounting nut (B) – CRF

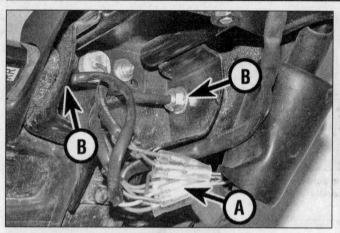

13.9 Turn signal wiring connectors (A) and mounting nut (B) – CBR

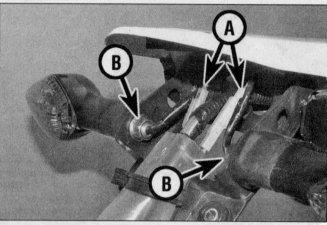

13.13 Turn signal wiring connectors (A) and mounting nut (B) – CRF

taking care as you draw the wire through **(see illustration 13.5).**

7 Installation is the reverse of removal. Align the flats on the turn signal and bracket. Check the operation of the turn signals.

Rear turn signals

CBR models

8 Release the trim clips securing the access panel on the underside, then draw the panel forwards to release the tab at the back **(see illustrations 9.1a and b).**
9 Disconnect the turn signal wiring connectors **(see illustration).**
10 Unscrew the nut and remove the turn

signal, taking care as you draw the wire through **(see illustration 13.9).**
11 Installation is the reverse of removal. Align the flats on the turn signal and bracket. Check the operation of the turn signals.

CRF models

12 Remove the brake/tail light bulb (see Section 9).
13 Disconnect the turn signal wiring connector **(see illustration).**
14 Unscrew the nut and remove the turn signal, taking care as you draw the wire through **(see illustration 13.13).**
15 Installation is the reverse of removal. Align the flats on the turn signal and bracket. Check the operation of the turn signals.

14 Brake light switches

Circuit check

Note: *Refer to electrical system fault finding in Section 2 and to the wiring diagram for your model at the end of this Chapter.*
1 Before checking the switches, and if not already done, check the brake light circuit (see Section 6).
2 The front brake light switch is mounted on the underside of the brake master cylinder. Disconnect the wiring connectors from the switch **(see illustration).** Using a continuity tester, connect the probes to the terminals of the switch. With the brake lever at rest, there should be no continuity. With the brake lever applied, there should be continuity. If the switch does not behave as described, replace it with a new one.
3 The rear brake light switch is mounted on the inside of the rider's right-hand footrest bracket **(see illustration 14.9c).** To access the wiring connector, on CBR models remove the right-hand side panel and on CRF models remove the left-hand side panel (see Chapter 7). On CBR250 models displace the ECM holder from its mounts **(see illustration).** Disconnect the wiring connector **(see illustrations).** Using

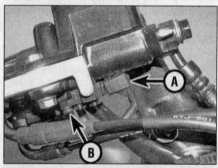

14.2 Front brake switch wiring connectors (A) and mounting screw (B)

14.3a Displace the ECM

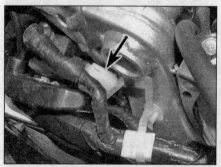

14.3b Rear brake switch wiring connector (arrowed) – CBR125

14.3c Rear brake switch wiring connectors – CBR250

14.3d Rear brake switch, sidestand switch, alternator and CKP sensor wiring connectors – CRF250

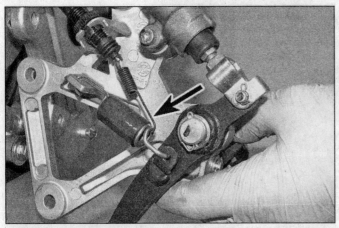

14.9a On CBR125 models unhook the spring (arrowed) from the pedal return spring

14.9b On CBR250 unhook the spring (arrowed) from the pedal

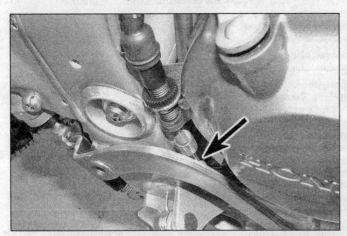

14.9c On CRF models unhook the spring (arrowed) from the pedal

14.9d Pull the switch out of its bracket

a continuity tester, connect the probes to the terminals on the switch side of the wiring connector. With the brake pedal at rest, there should be no continuity. With the brake pedal applied, there should be continuity. If the switch does not behave as described, replace it with a new one, although check first that the spring has not become detached or broken, and the switch is adjusted correctly (see Chapter 1).

4 If the switches are good, refer to electrical system fault finding in Section 2 and to the wiring diagram for your model at the end of this Chapter and check the wiring and connectors in the brake light circuit. Repair or renew the wiring as necessary.

Switch replacement

Front brake lever switch

5 The switch is mounted on the underside of the brake master cylinder. Disconnect the wiring connectors from the switch (see illustration 14.2).

6 Undo the screw and remove the switch.

7 Installation is the reverse of removal. Make sure the peg on the switch is correctly located in its hole before tightening the screw. The switch isn't adjustable.

Rear brake pedal switch

8 The rear brake light switch is mounted on the inside of the rider's right-hand footrest bracket. To access the wiring connector, on CBR models remove the right-hand side panel and on CRF models remove the left-hand side panel (see Chapter 7). On CBR250 models displace the ECM holder from its mounts (see illustration 14.3a). Disconnect the wiring connector (see illustration 14.3b, c or d). Feed the wiring down to the switch, noting its routing and releasing it from any ties.

9 Unhook the bottom end of the switch spring from the brake pedal (see illustrations). Lift the switch from its bracket (see illustration).

10 Installation is the reverse of removal. Make sure the brake light is activated just before the rear brake pedal takes effect. If adjustment is necessary, refer to Chapter 1, Section 2.

15 Instrument removal and installation

CBR models

1 Remove the fairing (see Chapter 7).

2 Disconnect the instrument wiring connector and remove the instrument/trim panel assembly (see illustration).

15.2 Disconnect the wiring and remove the panel

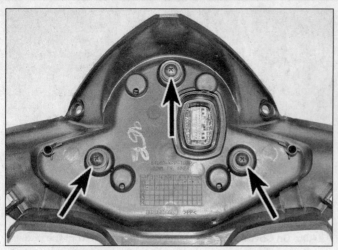

15.3 Instrument cluster screws (arrowed)

15.6 Release the connectors from the bracket

3 Undo the screws, noting the washers, and remove the instrument cluster from the trim panel **(see illustration)**.
4 Installation is the reverse of removal. Make sure the rubber grommets are in good condition.

CRF models

5 Remove the headlight cowl (see Chapter 7).
6 Release the wiring clips and connectors from the bracket **(see illustration)**.
7 Undo the screws, noting the washers, then displace the instrument cluster and disconnect the wiring **(see illustrations)**.
8 Installation is the reverse of removal. Make sure the rubber grommets are in good condition.

16 Instrument check and replacement

Check

Note: *Refer to electrical system fault finding in*

Section 2 and to the wiring diagram for your model at the end of this Chapter.

Instrument cluster power check

1 If none of the instruments or displays are working, first check the fuse (see Section 5).
2 If the fuse is good, refer to Section 15 to access the instrument wiring connector. Pull back the rubber boot and check the connector for loose or broken wires.
3 To check the power input wire, check for battery voltage between the brown (125 models) or black (250 models) wire terminal and a good earth (ground) with the ignition switch ON. There should be battery voltage. If there is no voltage, refer to the wiring diagrams and check the wire between the instrument cluster and the fusebox for loose or broken connections or a damaged wire.
4 To check the back-up power wire, check for battery voltage between the red/green (125 models) or red (250 models) wire terminal and a good earth (ground) with the ignition switch OFF. There should be battery voltage. If there is no voltage, refer to the wiring diagrams and check the wire between the instrument

cluster and the fusebox for loose or broken connections or a damaged wire.
5 If there is voltage, and to check the earth (ground) wire, check for continuity between the green wire terminal and earth (ground). If there is no continuity, check the circuit for loose or broken connections or a damaged wire and repair as necessary.
6 If all power input and earth wires are good, but there is no display or instrument function, then the printed circuit board (PCB) is faulty. On CBR models disassemble the instrument cluster and replace the PCB with a new one (Steps 18 to 20). On CRF models replace the instrument cluster with a new one – the PCB is not available separately.

Speedometer and speed sensor

7 Refer to Section 15 to access the instrument wiring connector. Pull back the rubber boot and check the connector for loose or broken wires.
8 If the wiring is good, place the bike on an auxiliary stand so the rear wheel is off the ground. Connect a voltmeter between the white/red (+) and black/green (CBR models) or

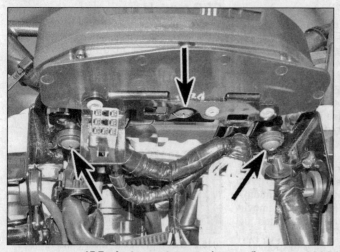

15.7a Instrument screws (arrowed)

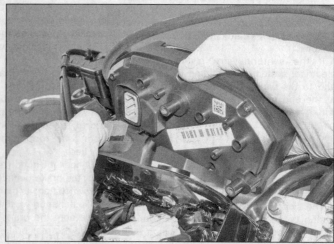

15.7b Lift the instruments off the bracket and disconnect the wiring green/black (CRF models) wire terminals in the connector – make sure the probes make good contact when inserted into the connector. With the ignition switch ON, have an assistant turn the rear wheel by hand and check that a fluctuating voltage reading between 0 and 5 volts is obtained. If the correct reading is obtained the printed circuit board (PCB) is faulty. On CBR models disassemble the instrument cluster and replace the PCB with a new one (Steps 18 to 20). On CRF models replace the instrument cluster with a new one – the PCB is not available separately. If no reading is obtained, check for continuity in each wire to the speed sensor wiring connector (see Steps 21 to 23 for access).

9 If the wiring is good check for battery voltage at the red/black (CBR models) or black/red (CRF models) wire terminal on the loom side of the connector. If there is no voltage refer to the wiring diagrams and check the wire for continuity to the instrument connector and repair any loose or broken connection or damaged wire.

10 If all is good so far, the speed sensor is faulty and must be replaced with a new one (Steps 21 to 24).

Tachometer (CBR models)

11 When the ignition is switched on the tachometer needle should swing from zero to maximum, then return to zero. If it doesn't check the power input (Steps 1 to 6).

12 If the tachometer does not work, refer to Section 15 to access the instrument wiring connector. Pull back the rubber boot and check the connector for loose or broken wires.

13 If the wiring is good, on 125 models remove the fairing left-hand side panel, and on 250 models remove the right-hand side panel (see Chapter 7). Check there is continuity in the yellow/green wire to the ECM wiring connector (refer to Chapter 4 for access). If there is no continuity there is a break in the wire or faulty connector. Refer to the wiring diagrams and trace and rectify the fault. If the wiring is good, the ECM could be faulty (see Chapter 4).

All other functions

14 If none of the functions are working, check the instrument cluster power input and earth wires (Steps 1 to 6). If all is good, on CBR models disassemble the instrument cluster (see below) and check for any obvious internal fault – if none is apparent replace the PCB with a new one. On CRF models replace the instrument cluster with a new one – the PCB is not available separately.

15 If an individual function is not working, refer to Chapter 3 for the coolant temperature and warning display, Chapter 4 for the low fuel warning and FI lights, Section 6 for the HI beam light, and Section 19 for the neutral switch (after checking the bulb (see Step 17) on CBR models). If the particular component and its circuit are good the PCB is faulty. On CBR models disassemble the instrument cluster and replace the PCB with a new one (Steps 18 to 20). On CRF models replace the instrument cluster with a new one – the PCB is not available separately.

Instrument and warning lights

16 With the exception of the neutral switch light on CBR models all instrument and warning lights are LEDs, which are part of the instrument cluster printed circuit board and are not available individually. If one of the LEDs fails, on CBR models disassemble the instrument cluster (see below) and check for any obvious internal fault – if none is apparent replace the PCB with a new one. On CRF models replace the instrument cluster with a new one – the PCB is not available separately.

17 To replace the neutral switch light on CBR models remove the instrument cluster (see Section 15). Remove the bulb cover (see illustration). Turn the bulbholder anti-clockwise to release it and replace it with a new one (see illustration) – the bulb and holder come as an assembly.

Instrument disassembly and replacement (CBR models)

18 Remove the instrument cluster (see Section 15).

19 Undo the seven screws on the back and remove the front cover (see illustrations). Lift the WARRANTY VOID IF REMOVED sticker and undo the screw under it, then remove the PCB from the rear cover (see illustration). Check the condition of the sealing ring and replace it with a new one if necessary (see illustration 16.20).

20 Installation is the reverse of removal. Make sure the sealing ring is seated in its groove (see illustration). Do not over-tighten the screws.

16.17a Remove the cover...

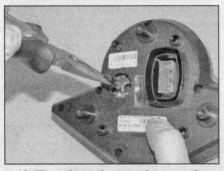
16.17b ...then release and remove the bulbholder

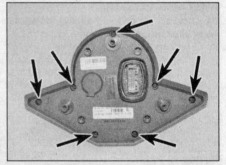
16.19a Undo the screws (arrowed)...

16.19b ...and remove the front cover

16.19c The remaining screw is under the sticker (arrowed)

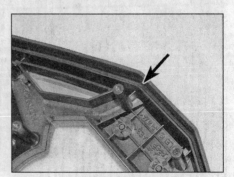
16.20 Check the sealing ring (arrowed)

16.22 Speed sensor, sidestand switch, alternator and CKP sensor wiring connectors – CBR250

16.23 Speed sensor connector (arrowed) – CRF250

16.24 Speed sensor bolt (arrowed)

Speed sensor removal and installation

21 On CBR125 models raise the fuel tank (see Chapter 4). Disconnect the speed sensor wiring connector **(see illustration 17.2a)**. Feed the wiring down to the front wheel, releasing the clamps and noting its routing. Remove the front wheel (see Chapter 6).

22 On CBR250 models remove the fuel tank (see Chapter 4). Disconnect the sensor wiring connector; use a screwdriver from above to release the catch and ease the connector apart **(see illustration)**. Release the wiring, noting its routing.

23 On CRF models remove the left-hand side panel (see Chapter 7). Remove the fuel tank (see Chapter 4). On US models remove the EVAP system purge control valve and canister (see Chapter 4). Disconnect the sensor wiring connector **(see illustration)**. Release the wiring, noting its routing.

24 Unscrew the bolt and remove the sensor **(see illustration)**. Check the condition of its O-ring and replace it with a new one if it is damaged or there is evidence of leakage around it, but note that Honda do not list it as being available separately. While the sensor is removed plug the orifice with clean rag.

25 Installation is the reverse of removal, using a new O-ring if necessary.

17 Ignition switch

⚠️ *Warning: To prevent the risk of short circuits, disconnect the battery negative (–) lead before making any ignition switch checks.*

Check

Note: *Refer to electrical system fault finding in Section 2 and to the wiring diagram for your model at the end of this Chapter.*

1 The switch can be checked for continuity using an ohmmeter or a continuity test light. Disconnect the battery negative (–) lead, which will prevent the possibility of a short circuit, before making the checks (see Section 3).

2 On CBR models raise the fuel tank (see Chapter 4). On 125 models lift the rubber cover. Disconnect the switch wiring connector **(see illustrations)**.

3 On CRF models remove the headlight cowl (see Chapter 7). Release the brown connector

from the underside of the instrument bracket and disconnect it **(see illustration 15.6)**.

4 Using an ohmmeter or a continuity tester, check for continuity between the black and red/black (125 models) or red/white and black/red (250 models) wire terminals on the switch side of the connector with the ignition key turned to the ON position. If there is no continuity replace the switch with a new one.

Removal

5 As a precaution, on CBR models remove the fuel tank cover and the fairing, and on CRF models remove the fuel tank covers (see Chapter 7). Though not actually necessary, this will prevent the possibility of damage should a tool slip.

6 Disconnect the battery negative (–) lead (see Section 3).

7 Refer to Step 2 or 3 according to model and disconnect the switch wiring connector. Feed the wiring back to the switch, noting its routing and releasing it from any clips and ties.

8 Displace the handlebars from the top yoke (see Chapter 5). On 250 models release all wiring and cables from the top yoke, and on CRF models displace and support the instrument bracket. Slacken the fork clamp

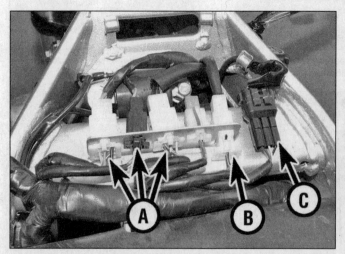

17.2a Handlebar switch connectors (A), ignition switch connector (B), speed sensor connector (C) – CBR125

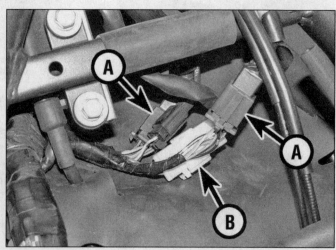

17.2b Handlebar switch connectors (A), ignition switch connector (B), speed sensor connector (C) – CBR250

bolts in the top yoke **(see illustration)**. Unscrew the steering stem nut and remove the washer **(see illustration)**. Gently ease the top yoke up off the forks and remove it.

9 On 250 models, if required detach the contact plate from the bottom of the switch **(see illustration)** – it is available separately from the main body of the switch.

10 On CBR125 models undo the two screws and remove the switch **(see illustration)**.

11 On 250 models one-way security bolts (which can be done up but not undone using conventional tools) are fitted **(see illustration 17.9)** – drive the heads around using a small cold chisel. Place the yoke in a vice with some protective card or rag to do this if required.

Installation

12 Installation is the reverse of removal. On 250 models use new ignition switch bolts if necessary, and tighten them to the torque setting specified at the beginning of the Chapter. Tighten the steering stem nut before the fork clamp bolts, and tighten them, and on CBR models the handlebar clamp bolts, to the torque settings specified at the beginning of the Chapter. Make sure the wiring connector is correctly routed and securely connected.

17.8a Slacken the clamp bolt(s) (arrowed) on each side...

17.8b ...then unscrew the nut and remove the washer

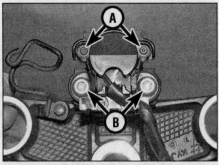

17.9 Contact plate screws (A), ignition switch bolts (B)

17.10 Ignition switch screws (arrowed)

---

18 Handlebar switches

Check

Note: *Refer to electrical system fault finding in Section 2 and to the wiring diagram for your model at the end of this Chapter.*

1 Generally speaking, the switches are reliable and trouble-free. Most troubles, when they do occur, are caused by dirty or corroded contacts, but wear and breakage of internal parts is a possibility that should not be overlooked. If breakage does occur, the entire switch and related wiring harness will have to be replaced with a new one, as individual parts are not available.

2 The switches can be checked for continuity using an ohmmeter or a continuity test light. Disconnect the battery negative (–) lead, which will prevent the possibility of a short circuit, before making the checks (see Section 3).

3 On CBR models raise the fuel tank (see Chapter 4). On 125 models lift the rubber cover. Disconnect the switch wiring connector(s) **(see illustration 17.2a or b)**.

4 On CRF models remove the headlight cowl (see Chapter 7). For the right-hand switch release the wiring clips and the ignition switch wiring clip, then disconnect the switch wiring connector **(see illustration 15.6)**. For the left-hand switch release the wiring clip, then release the connector from the bracket and disconnect it.

5 Check for continuity between the terminals of the switch connector with the switch in the various positions (i.e. switch off – no continuity, switch on – continuity – see the wiring diagram for your model at the end of this Chapter. Continuity should exist between the terminals connected by a solid line on the diagram when the switch is in the indicated position.

6 If the continuity check indicates a problem exists, displace the switch housing (Step 9), and spray the switch contacts with electrical contact cleaner (there is no need to remove the switch completely). If they are accessible, the contacts can be scraped clean with a knife or polished with crocus cloth. If switch components are damaged or broken, it will be obvious when the switch is disassembled.

Removal and installation

7 Refer to Step 3 or 4 according to model and disconnect the switch wiring connector. Feed the wiring back to the switch, freeing it from any clips and ties and noting its routing.

8 If removing the right-hand switch disconnect the wires from the brake light switch **(see illustration 14.2)**. If removing the left-hand switch disconnect the wires from the clutch switch **(see illustration 21.2a or b)**.

9 Undo the switch housing screws and separate the halves from the handlebar **(see illustrations)** – on CBR250 models refer to Chapter 4 for disconnection of the throttle cables.

10 Installation is the reverse of removal. Make sure the locating pin in the housing locates in the hole in the handlebar. Tighten the front screw first, then the rear, and do not overtighten them.

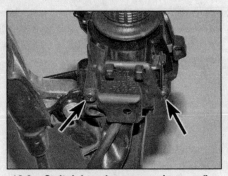

18.9a Switch housing screws (arrowed) – CBR models

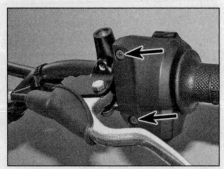

18.9b Switch housing screws (arrowed) – CRF models

19.2a Release the loom from the clips (arrowed)...

19.2b ...and displace the relays

19.2c Connectors for neutral switch, sidestand switch, alternator are inside the boot

19 Neutral switch

Note: *Refer to electrical system fault finding in Section 2 and to the wiring diagram for your model at the end of this Chapter.*

1 The neutral switch is located in the left-hand side of the engine below the front sprocket. The neutral light should come whenever the ignition switch is ON and the transmission is in neutral. The switch is part of the starter interlock safety circuit that prevents or stops the engine running if the transmission is in gear while the sidestand is down, and prevents the engine from starting if the transmission is in gear unless the sidestand is up and the clutch is pulled in.

Check

2 On 125 models remove the fuel tank (see Chapter 4), then displace the relays and release the loom clips **(see illustrations)**. Pull the rubber boot off the connectors and disconnect the neutral switch connector **(see illustration)**.
3 On 250 models pull the wiring connector off the switch **(see illustration)**.
4 Check for continuity between the terminal on the switch side of the connector and the crankcase on 125 models, and between the switch terminal and the crankcase on 250 models. With the transmission in neutral, there should be continuity. With the transmission in gear, there should be no continuity. If not, remove the switch (see below). On 125 models check the contacts on the inner face of the switch and the plunger tip for wear and damage make sure the plunger spring is not compressed

or distorted **(see illustration)**. On 250 models check whether the plunger is bent or damaged, or just stuck **(see illustration)**. Replace the switch with a new one if necessary.
5 If the switch is good check for continuity in the wire from the connector to the diode block in the fusebox. Next check the other components (clutch switch, sidestand switch, diode block) in the starter safety circuit, and check the wiring between them for continuity, and the connectors for loose or broken connections.

Removal and installation

125 models

6 Remove the front sprocket cover **(see illustration)**.
7 Refer to Step 2 and disconnect the switch wiring connector. Feed the wire down to the switch, noting its routing.
8 Clean the area around the switch. Unscrew the bolt and pull the switch from the crankcase **(see illustration)**. Note that there is a plunger with a spring behind in a bore in the end of the selector drum that bears against the switch contact – take care they do not drop out as you remove the switch, and remove them for safekeeping **(see illustration 19.10)**.
9 Check the condition of the O-ring on the switch and replace it with a new one if necessary **(see illustration 19.4a)** – Honda specify to fit a new one as a matter of course, but do not list it as a spare part, so you may have to locate an O-ring dealer.
10 Fit the spring and plunger into the offset

19.3 Pull the connector off the switch

19.4a Check the contacts and the plunger tip. Switch O-ring (arrowed)

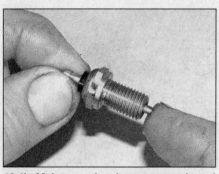

19.4b Make sure the plunger moves in and out smoothly and freely

19.6 Unscrew the bolts (arrowed) and remove the cover

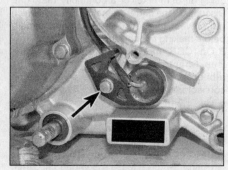

19.8 Unscrew the bolt (arrowed) and remove the switch

19.10 Fit the spring and plunger...

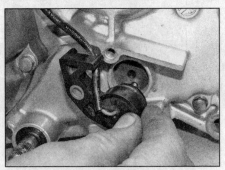

19.11 ...then fit the switch, making sure the plunger and O-ring stay in place

hole in the end of the selector drum **(see illustration)**.
11 Smear the O-ring with oil, then fit the switch and tighten the bolt **(see illustration)**.
12 Feed the wiring up to the connector, making sure it is correctly routed, and connect it. Check the operation of the neutral light.
13 Fit the front sprocket cover.

250 models

14 Drain the engine oil (see Chapter 1).
15 On CRF models remove the gearchange lever (see Chapter 5).
16 Pull the wiring connector off the switch **(see illustration 19.3)**.
17 Clean the area around the switch, then unscrew it from the crankcase. Remove the sealing washer – a new one should be used.
18 Fit the switch using a new washer and tighten it to the torque setting specified at the beginning of the Chapter.

19 Connect the wiring connector and check the operation of the neutral light.
20 On CRF models fit the gearchange lever (see Chapter 5).
21 Add the engine oil (see Chapter 1).

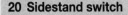

20 Sidestand switch

1 The sidestand switch is mounted on the stand pivot. The switch is part of the starter interlock safety circuit that prevents or stops the engine running if the transmission is in gear while the sidestand is down, and prevents the engine from starting if the transmission is in gear unless the sidestand is up and the clutch is pulled in.

Check

Note: Refer to electrical system fault finding in

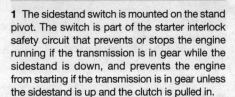

Section 2 and to the wiring diagram for your model at the end of this Chapter.
2 On CBR models remove the fuel tank (see Chapter 4), then on 125 models displace the relays and release the loom clips **(see illustrations 19.2a and b)**. Draw the rubber boot off the wiring connectors and disconnect the sidestand switch (green 2-pin) connector **(see illustration 19.2c (125) or 16.22 (250))**.
3 On CRF models remove the left-hand side panel (see Chapter 7). Draw the rubber boot off the wiring connectors and disconnect the sidestand switch (green 2-pin) connector **(see illustration 14.3d)**.
4 Check the operation of the switch using an ohmmeter or continuity tester. Connect the meter between the terminals on the switch side of the connector. With the sidestand up there should be continuity (zero resistance) between the terminals, and with the stand down there should be no continuity (infinite resistance).
5 If the switch does not perform as expected, it is faulty and must be replaced with a new one.
6 If the switch is good, check the other components (clutch switch, neutral switch, diode block) in the starter safety circuit, and check the wiring between them for continuity, and the connectors for loose or broken connections.

Removal

Note: Honda specify that the switch bolt be replaced with a new one every time it is disturbed – the new bolt has a locking compound already applied to its threads. However there is nothing to stop you cleaning up the threads on the old bolt and applying a suitable non-permanent thread locking compound on installation.
7 On CBR models remove the lower fairing (see Chapter 7). Refer to Step 2 and disconnect the sidestand switch connector. Feed the wiring back to the switch, releasing it from its clips and noting its routing.
8 On CRF models remove the left-hand side panel (see Chapter 7) and the fuel tank (see Chapter 4). Disconnect the sidestand switch connector and release the wiring clips **(see illustration 14.3d)**. Remove the silencer cover and unscrew the silencer mounting bolts **(see illustrations)**. Slacken the nuts on the

20.8a Undo the screws (arrowed) and remove the cover...

20.8b ...then unscrew the bolt (arrowed)...

20.8c ...and the bolt

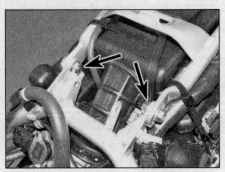

20.8d Slacken the nuts (arrowed)...

20.8e ...then unscrew the bolt (arrowed) on each side

20.8f Raise the sub-frame and pull the wiring (arrowed) out of the frame

20.9 Sidestand switch bolt (arrowed) – CBR125

20.10 Sidestand switch bolt (arrowed) – CBR250

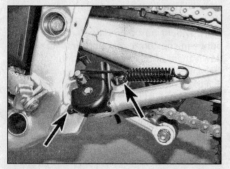

20.11a Switch cover bolts (arrowed)

20.11b Unscrew the bolt...

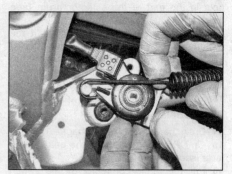

20.11c ...and remove the switch

rear sub-frame top bolts, and unscrew the bottom bolts **(see illustrations)**. Raise the rear sub-frame and free the sidestand switch wiring from the frame **(see illustration)** – either support the sub-frame in its raised position using a block of wood between the rear tyre and the undertray and tighten the nuts on the top bolts, or lower it again and refit the left-hand bottom bolt.

9 On CBR125 models unscrew the switch bolt and remove the retainer plate, washer and switch from the stand, noting how they fit **(see illustration)**.

10 On CBR250 models unscrew the switch bolt and remove the switch from the stand, noting how it fits **(see illustration)**.

11 On CRF250 models unscrew the switch cover bolts and remove the cover **(see**

illustration)**. Unscrew the switch bolt and remove the switch from the stand, noting how it fits **(see illustrations)**.

Installation

12 Installation is the reverse of removal. Secure the switch with a new bolt, or clean the threads of the original one and apply some fresh threadlock. Make sure the wiring is correctly routed. Check the operation of the sidestand switch.

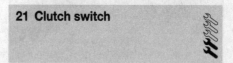

21 Clutch switch

1 The clutch switch is mounted in the clutch

lever bracket. The switch is part of the starter interlock safety circuit that prevents or stops the engine running if the transmission is in gear while the sidestand is down, and prevents the engine from starting if the transmission is in gear unless the sidestand is up and the clutch lever is pulled in. The switch isn't adjustable.

Check

Note: *Refer to electrical system fault finding in Section 2 and to the wiring diagram for your model at the end of this Chapter.*

2 To check the switch, disconnect the wiring connectors from it **(see illustrations)**. Connect the probes of an ohmmeter or a continuity tester to the two switch terminals. With the clutch lever pulled in, there should be continuity. With the clutch lever out, there should be no continuity (infinite resistance).

3 If the switch is good, check the other components (sidestand switch, neutral switch, diode block) in the starter safety circuit, and check the wiring between them for continuity, and the connectors for loose or broken connections.

Removal and installation

4 Disconnect the wiring connectors from the switch **(see illustration 22.2a or b)**.

5 On CBR models release the catch securing

21.2a Clutch switch wiring connectors (arrowed) – CBR models

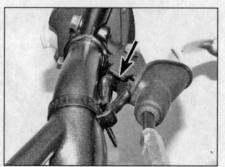

21.2b Clutch switch wiring connectors (arrowed) – CRF models

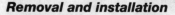

21.5 Release the switch via the hole (arrowed)

21.6 Undo the screw via the hole on the underside

the switch via the hole in the lever bracket and draw the switch out **(see illustration)**.

6 On CRF models undo the single screw securing the switch and remove it, noting how it fits **(see illustration)**.

7 Installation is the reverse of removal.

22 Diode block

Note: *Refer to electrical system fault finding in Section 2 and to the wiring diagram for your model at the end of this Chapter.*

1 On all models a diode block plugs into a connector in the fusebox, which is located under the rider's seat on CBR models (see illustrations 5.2b and c, 5.3d and e), and behind the left-hand side panel on CRF models (see illustrations 5.4c and d). The block contains two diodes, which are part of the starter interlock safety circuit that prevents or stops the engine running if the transmission is in gear whilst the sidestand is down, and prevents the engine from starting if the transmission is in gear unless the sidestand is up and the clutch lever is pulled in (see illustration 22.3). CBR250 models have another block containing a single diode that is part of the same circuit and plugs

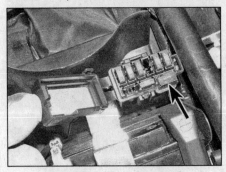

22.2 Diode block (arrowed)

directly into the wiring loom that runs along the inside of the frame above the engine on the left-hand side.

2 To check the diode block, open the fusebox lid and pull the diode block out of its socket **(see illustration)**.

3 Using an ohmmeter or continuity tester, connect the positive (+) probe to one of the outer terminals of the diode block and the negative (–) probe to the middle terminal of the block **(see illustration)**. The diode being tested should show continuity (with a small resistance). Now reverse the probes. The diode should show no continuity. Repeat the tests between the other outer terminal and the middle terminal. The same results should be achieved. If it doesn't behave as stated, replace the diode block with a new one.

4 To check the single diode block on CBR250 models remove the insulating tape and pull the diode block out of its socket. Using an ohmmeter or continuity tester, connect the positive (+) probe to the terminal parallel with the end of the diode block and the negative (–) probe to the terminal parallel with the side of the block. The diode should show continuity (with a small resistance). Now reverse the probes. The diode should show no continuity. If it doesn't behave as stated, replace the diode block with a new one.

22.3 Test the diode as described

5 If the diodes are good, check the other components (sidestand switch, neutral switch, clutch switch) in the starter safety circuit, and check the wiring between them for continuity, and the connectors for loose or broken connections.

23 Horn

Check

Note: *Refer to electrical system fault finding in Section 2 and to the wiring diagram for your model at the end of this Chapter.*

1 On CBR models the horn is below the radiator on the left-hand side. On CRF models the horn is behind the fuel tank right-hand cover. If it doesn't work first check the fuse (see Section 5).

2 If the fuse is good, on CRF models release the trim clips and undo the screw securing the coolant reservoir cover and remove the cover, noting how the peg locates in the hole **(see illustrations 11.2a and b)**.

3 Disconnect the wiring connectors and check for loose wires **(see illustration 23.3a, b or c)**. Using two jumper wires, apply voltage from a fully-charged 12V battery directly to the terminals on the horn. If the horn doesn't sound, replace it with a new one.

4 If the horn sounds, check for voltage at the black (125 models) or light/green (250 models) wire connector with the ignition ON and the horn button pressed. If voltage is present, check the other black (125 models) or green (250 models) wire for continuity to earth. On 125 models where both wires are black, there should be voltage at one of them and the other goes to earth – if you don't get voltage at the first wire tested check the other before assuming there is no voltage to the horn.

5 If no voltage was present, check the black or light green wire for continuity between

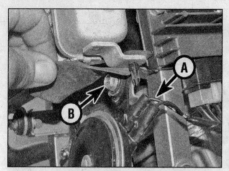

23.8a Horn wiring connectors (A) and mounting bolt (B) – CBR125

23.8b Horn wiring connectors (A) and mounting bolt (B) – CBR250

23.8c Horn wiring connectors (A) and mounting bolt (B) – CRF models

the horn and the horn button. Next, with the ignition switch ON, check that there is voltage at the supply wire to the horn button. If there is, check the button contacts in the switch housing (see Section 18).

6 If there isn't voltage at the supply wire, check the wire from the switch to the fusebox.

Replacement

7 On CRF models release the trim clips and undo the screw securing the coolant reservoir cover and remove the cover, noting how the peg locates in the hole (see illustrations 11.2a and b).

8 Disconnect the wiring connectors (see illustrations). Unscrew the bolt and remove the horn.

9 Installation is the reverse of removal. Check that the horn works.

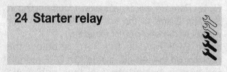

24 Starter relay

Check

1 If the starter circuit is faulty, first check the fuses (see Section 5).

2 To access the relay, on CBR125 models remove the right-hand side panel (see Chapter 7); on CBR250 models remove the rider's seat (see Chapter 7), then remove the air filter cover (see illustration 5.3a); on CRF models remove the left-hand side panel (see Chapter 7).

3 Make sure the transmission is in neutral. Lift the rubber cover and unscrew the bolt securing the starter motor lead (the red lead on the terminal marked M – the other lead is the battery lead on the terminal marked B) (see illustrations) – be careful not to touch the battery lead with the tool while unscrewing the starter motor lead, and then position the lead away from the relay.

4 With the ignition switch ON, the engine kill switch in the RUN position, and the transmission in neutral, press the starter switch. The relay should be heard to click.

5 If the relay doesn't click, switch off the ignition, remove the relay as described below, and test it as follows:

6 Set a multimeter to the ohms x 1 scale and connect it across the relay's starter motor and battery lead terminals. There should be no continuity. Using a fully-charged 12 volt battery and two insulated jumper wires, connect the positive (+) terminal of the battery to the yellow/red wire terminal of the relay, and the negative (−) terminal to the green/red wire terminal of the relay. At this point the relay should be heard to click and the multimeter read 0 ohms (continuity). If this is the case the relay is proved good. If the relay does not click when battery voltage is applied and indicates no continuity (infinite resistance) across its terminals, it is faulty and must be replaced with a new one.

7 If the relay is good, check for continuity in the main power lead from the battery to the relay. Also check that the terminals and connectors at each end of the lead are tight and corrosion-free.

8 Next check for battery voltage at the yellow/red wire terminal in the relay wiring connector with the transmission in neutral, the kill switch in the RUN position, the ignition ON, and the starter button pressed. If there is no voltage, check the wiring between the relay wiring connector and the starter button.

9 If voltage is present, check that there is continuity to earth in the green/red wire with the transmission in neutral (note that there will be a very slight resistance due to the diodes in the starter interlock circuit). If not check the wiring and connectors between the relay, the fusebox and the neutral switch, then if that is good check the switch itself and the diode block.

10 Now shift the transmission into gear, raise the sidestand and pull the clutch lever in and check for continuity to earth again. If there is no continuity, check the clutch switch and sidestand switch as described in the relevant sections of this Chapter. If all components are good, check the wiring between the various components (see the wiring diagrams at the end of this Chapter).

Replacement

11 To access the relay, on CBR125 models remove the right-hand side panel, on CBR250 models remove the rider's seat, and on CRF models remove the left-hand side panel (see Chapter 7).

12 Disconnect the battery (see Section 3).

13 Disconnect the relay wiring connector (see illustration 24.3a, b or c). Lift the rubber cover and unscrew the bolts securing the

24.3a Starter relay – CBR125

24.3b Starter relay – CBR250

24.3c Starter relay (arrowed) – CRF models

starter motor and battery leads to the relay. If the relay is being replaced with a new one, remove the fuse(s) and fit it/them into the new relay.

14 Installation is the reverse of removal. Connect the lead from the battery to the terminal marked B and the lead from the starter motor to the terminal marked M, and make sure the terminal bolts are securely tightened. Do not forget to fit the fuse(s) into the relay, if removed. Connect the negative (–) lead last when reconnecting the battery.

25 Starter motor removal and installation

Removal

125 models

1 The starter motor is mounted on the front of the engine. Disconnect the battery negative (–) lead. Remove the lower fairing (see Chapter 7).
2 Peel back the rubber terminal cover on the starter motor **(see illustration)**. Unscrew the nut and detach the lead.
3 Unscrew the two bolts securing the starter motor to the crankcase, noting the earth lead **(see illustration)**. Slide the starter motor out – if it is tight use a screwdriver to lever it out.
4 Remove the O-ring on the end of the starter motor – a new one must be used **(see illustration)**.

25.2 Pull back the terminal cover then unscrew the nut (arrowed) and detach the lead

250 models

5 The starter motor is mounted on the top of the crankcase. Disconnect the battery negative (–) lead.
6 On CBR models remove the fairing right-hand side panel (see Chapter 7).
7 On US CRF models remove the EVAP control valve and canister (see Chapter 4).
8 Unscrew the clutch cable bracket bolts and detach the cable end from the release arm **(see illustrations)**.
9 Peel back the rubber terminal cover on the starter motor **(see illustration)**. Unscrew the nut and detach the lead.
10 Unscrew the two bolts securing the starter motor to the crankcase, noting the earth lead **(see illustration)**. Slide the starter motor out. If it is tight use a screwdriver to lever it out.
11 Remove the O-ring on the end of the

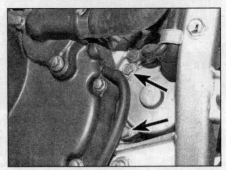

25.3 Starter motor bolts (arrowed) – note the earth lead

starter motor and discard it as a new one must be used **(see illustration)**.

Installation

12 Fit a new O-ring onto the end of the starter motor, making sure it is seated in its groove **(see illustration 25.4 or 25.11)**. Apply a smear of engine oil to the O-ring.
13 Manoeuvre the motor into position and slide it into the crankcase, meshing starter motor teeth with those of the starter idle/reduction gear. Fit the mounting bolts, securing the earth lead, and tighten them **(see illustration 25.3 or 25.10)**.
14 Connect the starter lead to the motor and secure it with the nut **(see illustration 25.2 or 25.9)**. Fit the rubber cover over the terminal.
15 Install the remaining components in reverse order of removal.

25.4 Remove the O-ring

25.8a Unscrew the bolts (arrowed)...

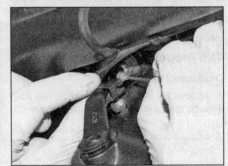

25.8b ...and detach the cable

25.9 Pull back the terminal cover then unscrew the nut (arrowed) and detach the lead

25.10 Starter motor bolts (arrowed) – note the earth lead

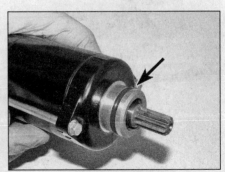

25.11 Remove the O-ring

26.4 Note the alignment marks between the housing and the covers

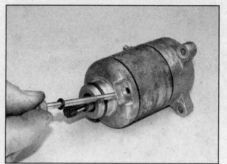

26.5a Unscrew and remove the two bolts...

26.5b ...then remove the front cover and sealing ring (arrowed)

26 Starter motor overhaul

Check

1 Remove the starter motor (see Section 25).
2 Using a fully-charged 12 volt battery and two insulated jumper wires, connect the lead from the positive (+) terminal of the battery to the protruding terminal on the starter motor, then hold the motor down on a bench, keeping your fingers clear of the shaft, and touch the lead from the negative (–) jumper terminal to one of the motor's mounting lugs. At this point the starter motor should spin. If this is the case the motor is proved good, though it is worth disassembling it and checking it if you suspect it of not working properly under load. If the motor does not spin, disassemble it for inspection.

125 models

Disassembly

3 Remove the starter motor (see Section 25).
4 Note any alignment marks between the

26.5c Remove the tabbed washer...

26.5d ...and the insulating washer and shim(s)

main housing and the front and rear covers, or make your own if they aren't clear **(see illustration)**.
5 Unscrew the two long bolts, noting the O-rings, then remove the front cover from the motor along with its sealing ring **(see illustrations)**. Remove the tabbed washer from the cover and slide the insulating washer and shim(s) from the front end of the armature, noting their correct fitted order **(see illustrations)**.
6 Hold the rear cover and armature and draw

the main housing off **(see illustration)** – it is held in by the attraction of the magnets, so take care not to lose your grip before the magnets lose theirs. Remove the sealing ring.
7 Withdraw the armature from the rear cover **(see illustration)**. Remove the shim(s) from the rear end of the armature or from in the rear cover **(see illustration 26.21a)**.
8 At this stage check for continuity between the terminal bolt and its brush – there should be continuity (zero resistance). Check for continuity between the terminal bolt and the

26.6 Remove the housing and the sealing ring

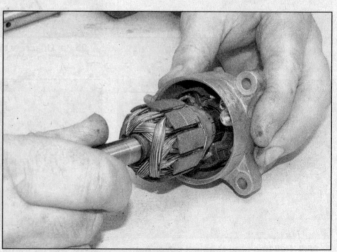

26.7 Draw the armature out of the rear cover

26.9a Slide the brushes out and remove the springs, then undo the screws (arrowed)...

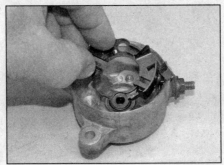

26.9b ...and remove the brushplate...

26.9c ...and the insulators

cover – there should be no continuity (infinite resistance). Also check for continuity between the other brush and the rear cover – there should be continuity (zero resistance). If there is no continuity when there should be or *vice versa*, identify the faulty component and replace it with a new one.

9 Slide the brushes out of their housings and remove the springs **(see illustration)**. Undo the two screws securing the brushplate, noting how one secures a brush, and remove the washers. Lift the brushplate out of the cover **(see illustration)**. Remove the two insulators **(see illustration)**.

10 Noting the correct fitted location of each component, unscrew the nut from the terminal bolt and remove the plain washer, the one large and two small insulating washers **(see illustration)**. Withdraw the terminal bolt from the cover, noting how it locates **(see illustration)**. Remove the O-ring from the bolt and the insulator piece from the cover.

Inspection

11 The parts of the starter motor that are most likely to require attention are the brushes. Measure the length of each brush and compare to the length listed in this Chapter's Specifications **(see illustration)**. If either of the brushes are worn beyond the service limit, fit a new set. If the brushes are not worn, cracked, chipped, or otherwise damaged, they may be reused. Check the brush springs for

26.10a Unscrew the nut (arrowed) and remove the plain washer and the large and small insulating washers

26.10b Remove the terminal bolt and its O-ring, and the insulator (arrowed)

distortion and fatigue. Check the brushplate and insulators for damage.

12 Inspect the commutator bars on the armature for scoring, scratches and discoloration. The commutator can be cleaned and polished with crocus cloth, but do not use sandpaper or emery paper. After cleaning, wipe away any residue with a cloth soaked in electrical system cleaner or denatured alcohol.

13 Using an ohmmeter or a continuity test light, check for continuity between the commutator bars **(see illustration)**. Continuity should exist between each bar and all of the others. Also, check for continuity between the commutator bars and the armature shaft **(see

illustration)**. There should be no continuity (infinite resistance) between the commutator and the shaft. If the checks indicate otherwise, the armature is defective and a new starter motor bust be obtained – the armature is not available separately.

14 Check the front end of the armature shaft for worn, cracked, chipped and broken teeth. If the shaft is damaged or worn, a new starter motor must be obtained – the armature is not available separately.

15 Inspect the front and rear covers for signs of cracks or wear. Check the oil seal and the needle bearing in the front cover and the bush in the rear cover for wear and damage – the seal, bearing, bush and covers are not listed as

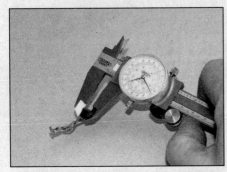

26.11 Measure the length of each brush

26.13a There should be continuity between the bars...

26.13b ...and no continuity between the bars and the shaft

26.15a Check the bearing and seal in the front cover...

26.15b ...and the bush (arrowed) in the rear cover

26.18a Fit the insulator piece into its cut-out

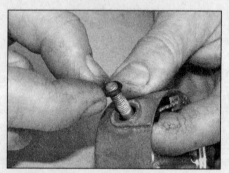

26.18b Fit the O-ring over the bolt...

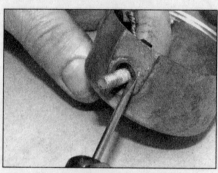

26.18c ...then slide it down and press it into place

26.19a Locate the brushplate...

26.19b ...then fit the washers...

being available separately so if necessary a new starter motor must be fitted (see illustrations).

16 Inspect the magnets in the main housing and the housing itself for cracks.

17 Inspect the insulating washers, O-ring, and sealing rings for signs of damage, deformation and deterioration and replace them with new ones if necessary.

Reassembly

18 Fit the insulator piece into the rear cover (see illustration). Insert the terminal bolt through its hole (see illustration 26.10b). Fit the O-ring down over the bolt and press it into place between the bolt and the cover (see illustrations). Slide the small insulating washers onto the terminal bolt, followed by the large insulating washer and the plain washer (see illustration 26.10a). Fit the nut onto the terminal bolt and tighten it securely.

19 Fit the brush insulators into the rear cover (see illustration 26.9c). Fit the brushplate, making sure it locates correctly, then fit the washers and the screws, not forgetting to secure the brush (see illustrations). Slide the springs and brushes back into position in their housings (see illustrations).

20 At this stage check for continuity between the terminal bolt and the cover – there should be no continuity (infinite resistance). Also check for continuity between the uninsulated brush and the rear cover – there should be continuity (zero resistance). If there is no continuity when there should be or vice versa, identify the faulty component and replace it with a new one.

26.19c ...and the screws, not forgetting the brush

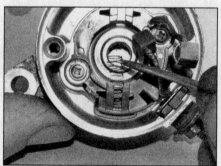

26.19d Fit the springs...

26.19e ...then slide each brush into its housing

26.21a Fit the shim(s) onto the shaft...

26.21b ...then push the brushes back as shown...

26.21c ...and fit the armature into the rear cover making sure the brushes locate correctly onto the commutator

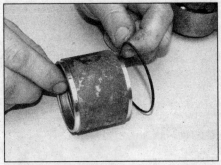

26.22a Fit a new sealing ring onto the rear of the housing...

26.22b ...then fit the housing onto the armature...

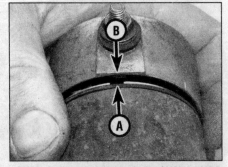

26.22c ...locating the cut-out (A) over the tab (B)

21 Fit the shim(s) onto the rear of the armature shaft (see illustration). Apply a smear of grease to the end of the shaft. Using a pair of external circlip pliers or similar, push the brushes into the housing and hold them there (see illustration). Insert the armature into the

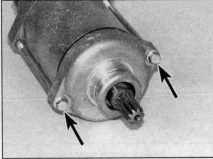

26.24 Fit a new sealing ring onto the front of the housing

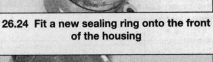

26.28 Note the alignment marks (highlighted) between the housing and the covers

rear cover so that the shaft end locates in its bush, then release the brushes so they locate against the commutator (see illustration).
22 Fit the sealing ring onto the rear of the main housing, which has a cut-out in its rim (see illustration). Grasp both the armature

and the rear cover in one hand and hold them together – this will prevent the armature being drawn out by the magnets in the housing. Note however that you should take care not to let the housing be drawn forcibly onto the armature by the magnets. Carefully allow the housing to be drawn onto the armature, making sure the end with the cut-out faces the rear cover, that the cut-out locates over the tab on the insulator piece, and the marks between the cover and housing align (Step 4) (see illustrations).
23 Apply a smear of grease to the front cover oil seal lip. Fit the tabbed washer into the cover so that its teeth are correctly located with the cover ribs (see illustration 26.5c).
24 Fit the sealing ring onto the front of the housing (see illustration). Slide the shim(s) onto the front end of the armature shaft then fit the insulating washer (see illustration 26.5d). Slide the front cover into position, aligning the marks (see illustration 26.5b).
25 Check the marks made on removal are correctly aligned then fit the long bolts with their O-rings and tighten them (see illustration 26.5a).
26 Install the starter motor (see Section 25).

250 models

Disassembly

27 Remove the starter motor (see Section 25).
28 Note any alignment marks between the main housing and the front and rear covers, or make your own if they aren't clear (see illustration).
29 Unscrew the two long bolts and remove the front cover from the motor (see illustrations).

26.29a Unscrew the bolts (arrowed)...

26.29b ...and remove the front cover...

26.30 ...and the rear cover

26.31 Withdraw the armature

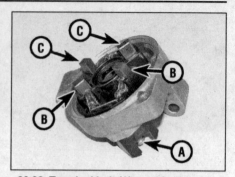

26.32 Terminal bolt (A), positive brushes (B), negative brushes (C)

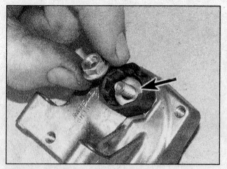

26.33a Undo the nut and remove the plain washer (arrowed)...

26.33b ...the insulator...

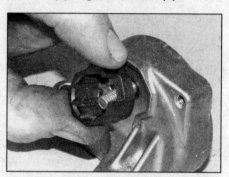

26.33c ...the shield...

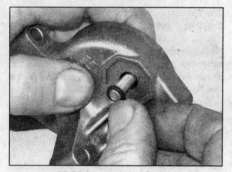

26.33d ...and the O-ring

26.33e Withdraw the terminal bolt and brush assembly (arrowed)...

26.33f ...and remove the brush springs

30 Remove the rear cover **(see illustration)**.
31 Withdraw the armature from the main housing **(see illustration)** – it is held in by the attraction of the magnets, so take care not to lose your grip on the armature before the magnets lose theirs.
32 At this stage check for continuity between the terminal bolt and the positive brushes **(see illustration)** – there should be continuity (zero resistance). Check for continuity between the terminal bolt and the cover – there should be no continuity (infinite resistance). Also check for continuity between the negative and positive brushes – there should be no continuity (infinite resistance). If there is no continuity when there should be or *vice versa*, identify the faulty component and replace it with a new one.
33 Noting the correct fitted location of each component, unscrew the nut from the terminal bolt and remove the plain washer, the

insulator, the terminal shield and the O-ring **(see illustrations)**. Remove the positive brush and terminal bolt assembly, then remove the positive brush springs **(see illustrations)**.

34 Undo the screw and remove the negative brush assembly **(see illustration)**. Remove the brush springs, then remove the holder **(see illustrations)**.

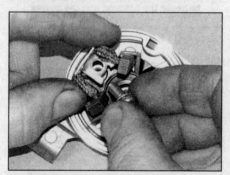

26.34a Undo the screw and remove the negative brush assembly...

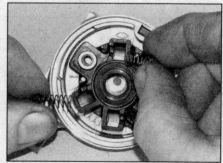

26.34b ...and springs...

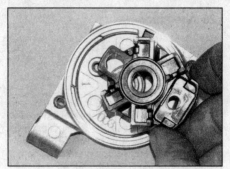

26.34c ...then remove the brushholder

26.35 Measure the length of each brush

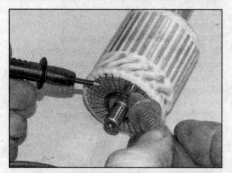

26.37a There should be continuity between the bars...

Inspection

35 The parts of the starter motor that are most likely to require attention are the brushes. Measure the length of each brush and compare the results to the length listed in this Chapter's Specifications **(see illustration)**. If worn replace the brushes with new ones. If the brushes are not worn excessively, nor cracked, chipped, or otherwise damaged, they can be re-used.

36 Inspect the commutator bars on the armature for scoring, scratches and discoloration. The commutator can be cleaned and polished with crocus cloth, but do not use sandpaper or emery paper. After cleaning, wipe away any residue with a cloth soaked in electrical system cleaner or denatured alcohol.

37 Using an ohmmeter or a continuity test light, check for continuity between the commutator bars **(see illustration)**. Continuity should exist between each bar and all of the others. Also, check for continuity between the commutator bars and the armature shaft **(see illustration)**. There should be no continuity (infinite resistance) between the commutator and the shaft. If the checks indicate otherwise, the armature is defective and a new starter motor must be obtained – the armature is not available separately.

38 Check the front end of the armature shaft for worn, cracked, chipped and broken teeth. If the shaft is damaged or worn, a new starter motor must be obtained – the armature is not available separately.

39 Inspect the front and rear covers for signs of cracks or wear. Check the oil seal and the

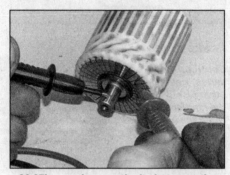

26.37b ...and no continuity between the bars and the shaft

needle bearing in the front cover and the bush in the rear cover for wear and damage **(see illustration)** – the seal, bearing, bush and covers are not listed as being available separately so if necessary a new starter motor must be fitted.

40 Inspect the magnets in the main housing and the housing itself for cracks.

41 Inspect the terminal bolt shield, insulator, and O-ring, and the sealing rings on the housing, for signs of damage, deformation and deterioration and replace them with new ones if necessary.

Reassembly

42 Locate the brush holder on the rear cover **(see illustration 26.34c)**. Fit the negative brush springs and brush assembly and secure it and the holder with the screw **(see illustrations 26.34b and a)**.

43 Fit the positive brush springs into their housings **(see illustration 26.33f)**. Fit the

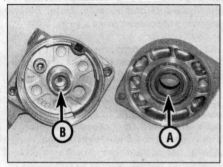

26.39 Check the bearing and seal (A) and the bush (B)

terminal bolt through the holder and rear cover **(see illustration 26.33e)**. Roll the O-ring down the bolt and press it into the gap between the bolt and the cover **(see illustration)**. Fit the shield, aligning it as shown **(see illustration 26.33c)**. Fit the insulator and the washer, then tighten the nut **(see illustrations 26.33b and a)**. Locate the brushes in their housings against the springs, with the wires in the slots.

44 To check for correct installation do the continuity checks described in Step 32.

45 If removed fit the sealing rings onto the main housing **(see illustration)**.

46 Grasp the housing and carefully allow the armature to be drawn in, making sure the cut-out in the housing is at the same end as the commutator bars **(see illustration 26.31)**.

47 Apply a smear of grease to the short end of the shaft. Fit the rear cover, aligning the marks, and making sure the brushes remain square and seat against the commutator **(see illustration)**.

26.43 Fit the O-ring between the bolt and the cover

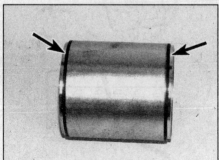

26.45 Main housing sealing rings (arrowed)

26.47 Align the marks when fitting the cover

48 Apply a smear of grease to the front cover oil seal lip. Slide the front cover on, aligning the marks **(see illustration 26.29b)**.
49 Check the marks made on removal are correctly aligned then fit the long bolts and tighten them **(see illustration 26.29a)**.
50 Install the starter motor (see Section 25).

27 Charging system testing

1 If the performance of the charging system is suspect, the system as a whole should be checked first, followed by testing of the individual components. **Note:** *Before beginning the checks, make sure the battery is in good condition and fully charged, and that all system connections are clean and tight.*
2 Checking the output of the charging system and the performance of the various components within the charging system requires the use of a multimeter (with voltage, current and resistance checking facilities). If a multimeter is not available, the job of checking the charging system should be left to a Honda dealer.
3 When making the checks, follow the procedures carefully to prevent incorrect connections or short circuits resulting in irreparable damage to electrical system components.
4 On CBR models remove the rider's seat (see Chapter 7). On CRF models remove the left-hand side panel (see Chapter 7).
5 On CBR125 models release and remove the battery cover clip by unscrewing the centre of the clip then drawing the body out of the cover **(see illustration 3.3)**. Lift the cover to expose the battery.

Regulated voltage output test

6 Start the engine, warm it up and allow the engine to idle with the headlight on main beam. Connect a multimeter set to the 0-20 volts DC scale across the terminals of the battery with the positive (+) meter probe to battery positive (+) terminal and the negative

(-) meter probe to battery negative (-) terminal (see Section 3) **(see illustration)**.
7 Slowly increase the engine speed to 5000 rpm and note the reading obtained. Compare the result with the Specification at the beginning of this Chapter. If the regulated voltage output is outside the specification, check the alternator and the regulator/rectifier (Sections 28 and 29).

 Clues to a faulty regulator are constantly blowing bulbs, with brightness varying considerably with engine speed, and battery overheating.

Leakage test

Caution: Always connect an ammeter in series, never in parallel with the battery, otherwise it will be damaged. Do not turn the ignition ON or operate the starter motor when the ammeter is connected – a sudden surge in current will blow the meter's fuse.
8 Make sure the ignition is OFF. Set the multimeter to the Amps function and connect its negative (-) probe to the battery negative (-) terminal, and positive (+) probe to the disconnected negative (-) lead **(see illustration)**. Always set the meter to a high amps range initially and then bring it down to the mA (milli Amps) range; if there is a high current flow in the circuit it may blow the meter's fuse.
9 Battery current leakage should not exceed the maximum limit (see Specifications). If a higher leakage rate is shown there is a short circuit in the wiring, although if an after-market immobiliser or alarm is fitted, its current draw should be taken into account. Disconnect the meter and reconnect the battery negative (-) lead.
10 If leakage is indicated, refer to the Wiring Diagrams at the end of this Chapter to systematically disconnect individual electrical components and repeat the test until the source is identified.

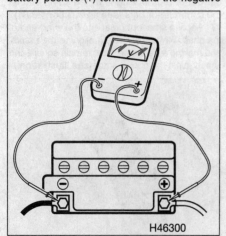

27.6 Checking the voltage output – connect the meter as shown

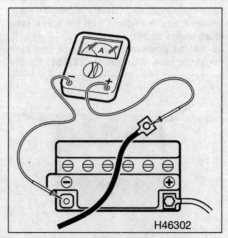

27.8 Checking for current leakage – connect the meter as shown

28 Alternator

Stator coil check

1 On CBR models remove the fuel tank (see Chapter 4), then on 125 models displace the relays and release the loom clips **(see illustrations 19.2a and b)**. On CRF models remove the left-hand side panel (see Chapter 7) and the fuel tank (see Chapter 4).
2 Draw the rubber boot off the wiring connectors and disconnect the alternator wiring connector (with three yellow wires on CBR125 and CRF models, and three black wires on CBR250 models) **(see illustration 19.2c (CBR125), 16.22 (CBR250) or 14.3d CRF models))**. Check the connector terminals for corrosion and security.
3 Using a multimeter set to the ohms x 1 (ohmmeter) scale measure the resistance between each of the yellow or black wire pairs on the alternator side of the connector, taking a total of three readings, then check for continuity between each terminal and ground (earth). If the stator coil windings are in good condition the three readings should be within the range shown in the Specifications at the start of this Chapter, and there should be no continuity (infinite resistance) between any of the terminals and ground (earth). If not, the alternator stator coil assembly is at fault and should be replaced with a new one. **Note:** *Before condemning the stator coils, check the fault is not due to damaged wiring between the connector and the coils.*

Removal

Special tools: *A rotor holding strap and rotor puller are needed (see Steps 8 and 9 or 10, according to model).*
4 On CBR models remove the lower fairing (see Chapter 7). On CRF models remove the left-hand side panel (see Chapter 7) and the gearchange lever (see Chapter 5). On all models remove the front sprocket cover.
5 Refer to Steps 1 and 2 and access the wiring connector(s). On 125 models disconnect the alternator/CKP sensor wiring connector. On 250 models disconnect the alternator and CKP sensor wiring connectors, and pull the wiring connector off the neutral switch **(see illustration 19.3)**. Feed the wiring down to the alternator cover, releasing it from any ties and noting its routing.
6 If you have an auxiliary stand place the bike on it so that it is level – this minimises oil loss. If you do not have an auxiliary stand it is best to drain the oil (see Chapter 1). Alternatively place a container under the engine to catch the oil that will come out when the alternator cover is removed.
7 Working in a criss-cross pattern, evenly slacken then remove the alternator cover bolts **(see illustration)**. Draw the cover off the engine, noting that it will be restrained by the force of the rotor magnets, and be prepared to

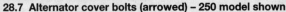

28.7 Alternator cover bolts (arrowed) – 250 model shown

28.8 Using a rotor strap to hold the rotor while unscrewing the bolt

catch the residual oil. Remove the dowels from either the cover or the crankcase if they are loose. Remove the gasket – a new one must be used. On 125 models a sealing washer is fitted with the centre top bolt **(see illustration 28.18d)** – a new one must be used.

8 To remove the rotor nut or bolt it is necessary to stop the rotor from turning using a commercially available rotor strap **(see illustration)**. Unscrew the nut or bolt, noting the washer.

9 On 125 models, to remove the rotor from the shaft it is necessary to use a rotor puller (Honda part No. 07KMC-HE00100, or its commercially available equivalent). Thread the rotor puller onto the centre of the rotor, then counter-hold it using a spanner on the flats and tighten the bolt in its centre until the rotor is displaced from the shaft **(see illustrations)**. If the rotor doesn't come off easily tap the end of the bolt when it is tight, and if necessary heat the rotor hub using a hot air gun.

10 On 250 models, withdraw the idle/reduction gear shaft and remove the gear **(see illustration)**. To remove the rotor from the shaft it is necessary to use a rotor puller – use either the Honda tool (part No. 07733-0020001 in Europe and 07933-3950000 in the US) or a commercially available equivalent. Thread the rotor puller into the centre of the rotor and turn it until the rotor is displaced from the shaft, holding the rotor to prevent the engine turning **(see illustrations)**. If the rotor doesn't come

28.9a Thread the puller onto the rotor...

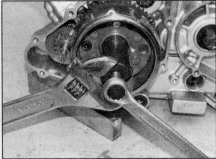

28.9b ...then hold the puller and turn the bolt

28.10a Withdraw the shaft and remove the gear

28.10b Thread the puller into the rotor...

28.10c ...then hold the rotor and turn the puller, using extra leverage if required

28.11 Remove the Woodruff key (arrowed) if loose – 250 shown

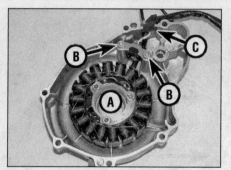

28.12 Stator bolts (A), CKP sensor bolts (B), grommet (C)

28.16 Slide the rotor onto the shaft

28.17a Lubricate the nut or bolt then fit it with its washer...

28.17b ...and tighten it to the specified torque

off easily use some extra leverage on the tool, and/or tap the end of the tool when it is tight, and if necessary heat the rotor hub using a hot air gun.

11 Remove the Woodruff key from its slot in the crankshaft for safekeeping if loose **(see illustration)**. If required detach the starter clutch from the rotor (see Chapter 2A or 2B).

12 To remove the stator from the cover, unscrew its bolts and the CKP sensor bolts, and on 125 models the wiring clamp bolt, then remove the assembly, noting how the rubber wiring grommet fits **(see illustration)**.

Installation

13 Fit the stator and CKP sensor into the cover, aligning the rubber wiring grommet with the groove **(see illustration 28.12)**. Fit the stator bolts and tighten them to the torque setting specified at the beginning of the Chapter. Clean the threads of the CKP sensor bolts and apply some fresh threadlock, and tighten them to the specified torque. Apply a suitable sealant to the wiring grommet, then press it into the cut-out in the cover. On 125 models secure the wiring with its clamp and tighten the bolt.

14 If removed the install the starter clutch components (see Chapter 2A or 2B).

15 Clean all old gasket off the cover and crankcase mating surfaces and wipe them with a suitable solvent. Clean the tapered end of the crankshaft and the corresponding mating surface on the inside of the rotor with the solvent.

16 Fit the Woodruff key into its slot in the crankshaft if removed **(see illustration 28.11)**. Make sure that no metal objects have attached themselves to the magnet on the

inside of the rotor. Slide the rotor onto the shaft, locating the slot in its centre over the key **(see illustration)**.

17 Apply some clean oil to the rotor nut or bolt threads and the underside of the head. Fit the nut or bolt with its washer and tighten it to the torque setting specified at the beginning of the Chapter for your model, holding the rotor as on removal **(see illustrations)**.

18 Fit the dowels into the cover or crankcase if removed **(see illustrations)**. Fit a new gasket onto the dowels. Apply a smear of

28.18a Alternator cover dowels (arrowed) – 125 models

28.18b Alternator cover dowels (arrowed) – 250 models

28.18c Apply sealant to the wiring grommet

28.18d Use a new sealing washer

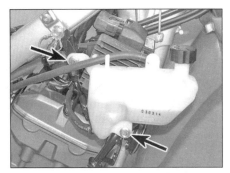

29.1 Unscrew the bolts (arrowed) and move the reservoir aside

suitable sealant to the mating surface of the wiring grommet **(see illustration)**. Fit the alternator cover, noting that the rotor magnets will forcibly draw the cover/stator on, making sure the gasket remains in place and the dowels locate. Fit the cover bolts and tighten them evenly in a criss-cross sequence – use a new sealing washer on the centre top bolt on 125 models **(see illustration)**.

19 On 250 models lubricate the idle/reduction gear shaft, then position the gear, engaging the teeth, and insert the shaft **(see illustration 28.10a)**.

20 Route and secure the wiring and connect the connectors (see Step 5).

21 Fill the engine with the correct quantity of oil, or top it up to the correct level, as required according to your removal method (see Chapter 1). Install all remaining components (see Step 4).

29 Regulator/rectifier

Check

1 On CBR125 models remove the fairing left-hand side panel (see Chapter 7). On

CBR250 models remove the left-hand side panel (see Chapter 7). On CRF models remove the fuel tank right-hand cover (see Chapter 7), then displace the coolant reservoir and support it clear of the regulator/rectifier **(see illustration)**.

2 Disconnect the regulator/rectifier wiring connector **(see illustrations)**. Check the connector terminals for corrosion and security.

3 Set the multimeter to the 0 to 20 dc volts setting. Connect the meter positive (+) probe to the red wire terminal in the loom side of the connector and the negative (–) probe to a suitable ground (earth) and check for voltage. Full battery voltage should be present at all times.

4 Switch the multimeter to the resistance (ohms) scale. Check for continuity between the green wire terminal in the connector and ground (earth). There should be continuity to earth.

5 Set the multimeter to the ohms x 1 (ohmmeter) scale and measure the resistance between each of the black or yellow wires (according to model) in the connector, taking a total of three readings, then check for continuity between each terminal and ground (earth). The three readings should be within the range shown in the Specifications for the

alternator stator coil at the start of this Chapter, and there should be no continuity (infinite resistance) between any of the terminals and ground (earth).

6 If the above checks do not provide the expected results check the wiring and connectors between the battery, regulator/rectifier and alternator for shorts, breaks, and loose or corroded terminals (see the wiring diagrams at the end of this chapter).

7 If the wiring checks out, the regulator/rectifier unit is probably faulty. Honda provide no test data for the unit itself. Take it to a Honda dealer for confirmation of its condition before replacing it with a new one.

> **HAYNES HiNT**
> *Clues to a faulty regulator are constantly blowing bulbs, with brightness varying considerably with engine speed, and battery overheating.*

Removal and installation

8 Follow Steps 1 and 2.

9 Unscrew the two bolts and remove the regulator/rectifier.

10 Installation is the reverse of removal.

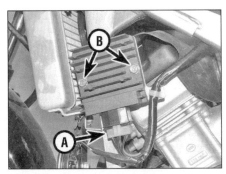

29.2a Regulator/rectifier wiring connector (A) and mounting bolts (B) – CBR125

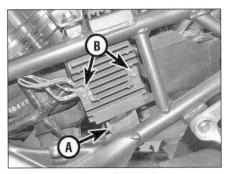

29.2b Regulator/rectifier wiring connector (A) and mounting bolts (B) – CBR250

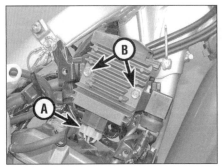

29.2c Regulator/rectifier wiring connector (A) and mounting bolts (B) – CRF250

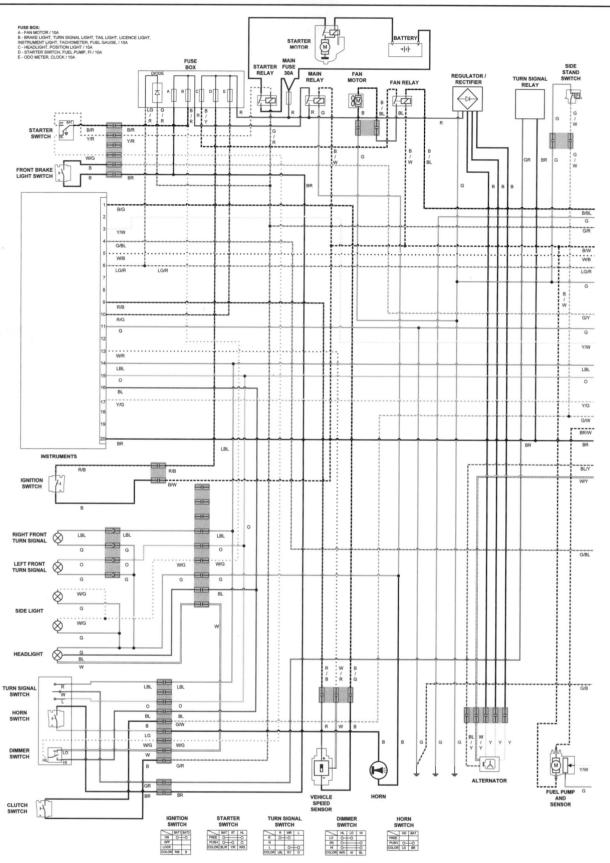

CBR125R - EUROPE

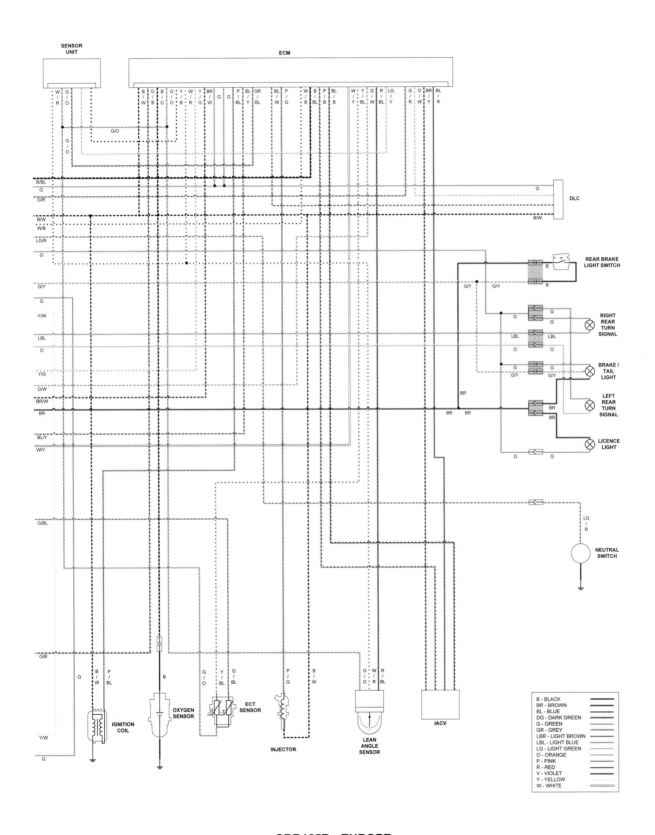

CBR125R - EUROPE

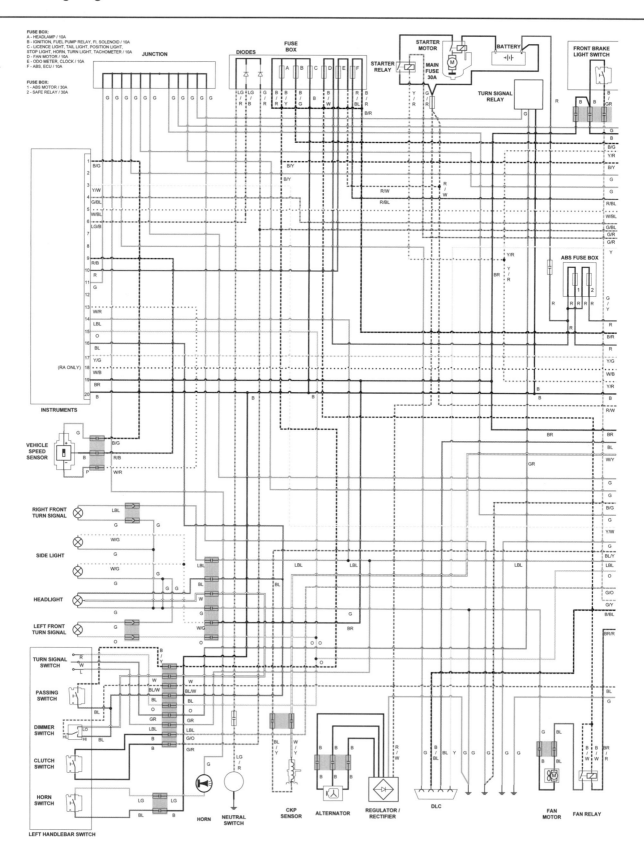

CBR250 R AND RA - EUROPE   (ABS components – RA only)

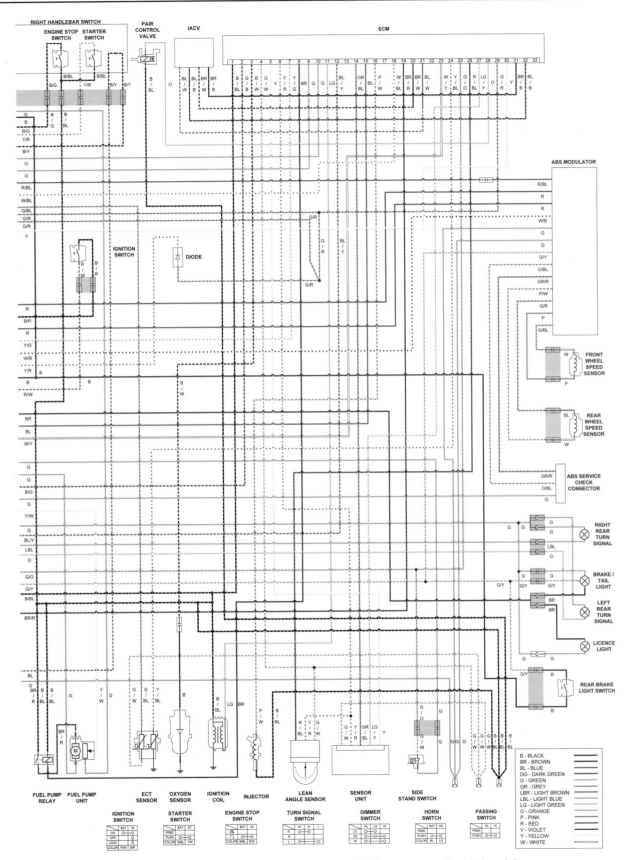

CBR250 R AND RA - EUROPE   (ABS components – RA only)

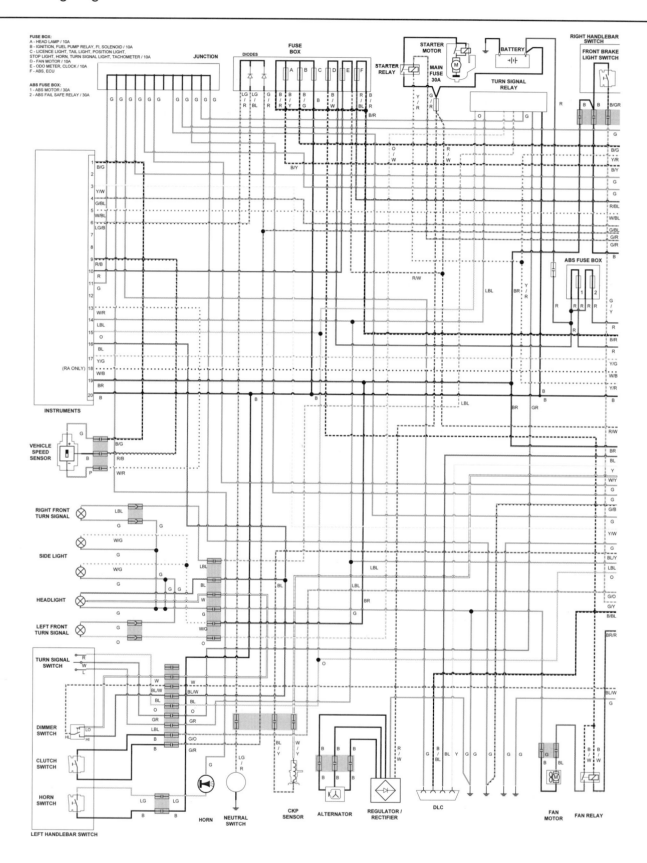

CBR250 R AND RA - US   **(ABS components – RA only)**

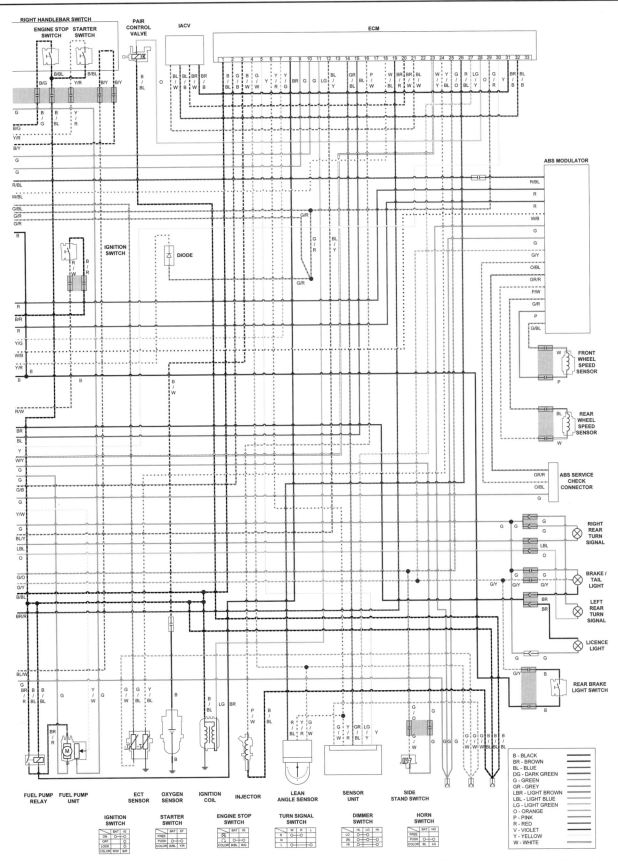

CBR250 R AND RA - US　　(ABS components – RA only)

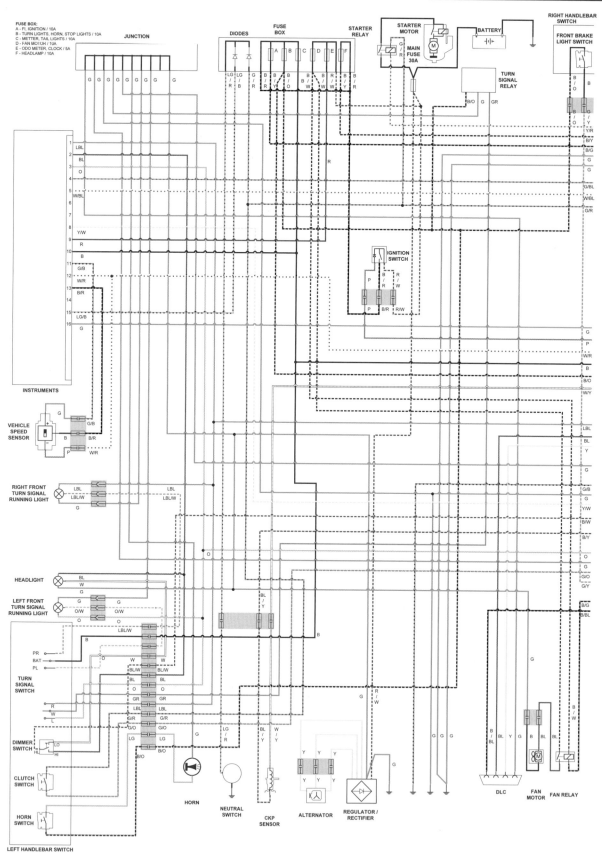

CRF250 L AND M - US

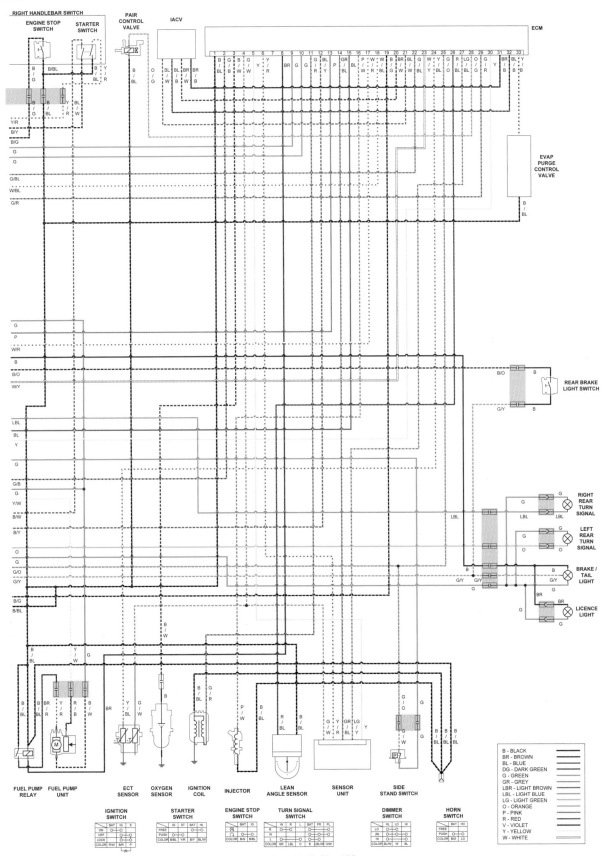

CRF250 L AND M - US

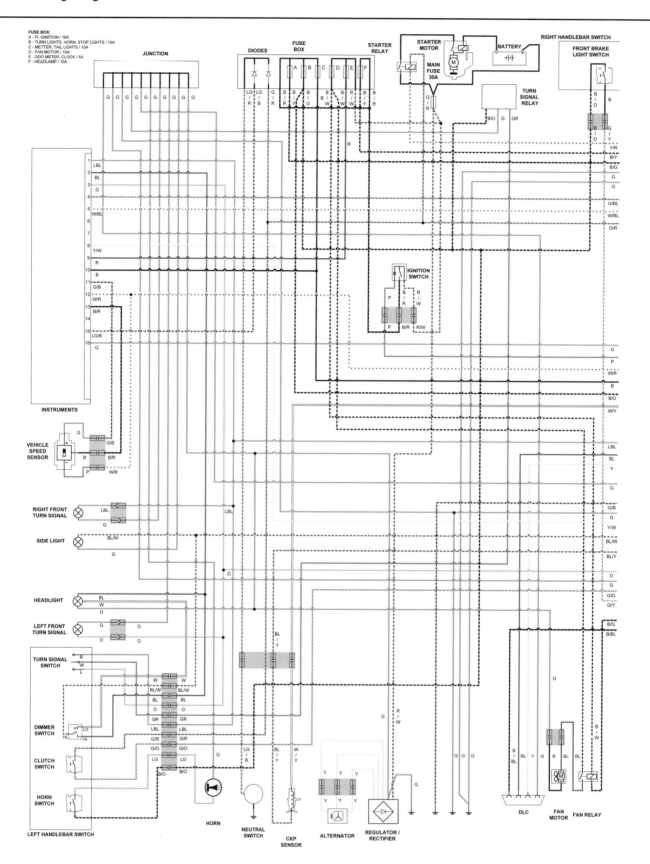

CRF250 L AND M - EUROPE

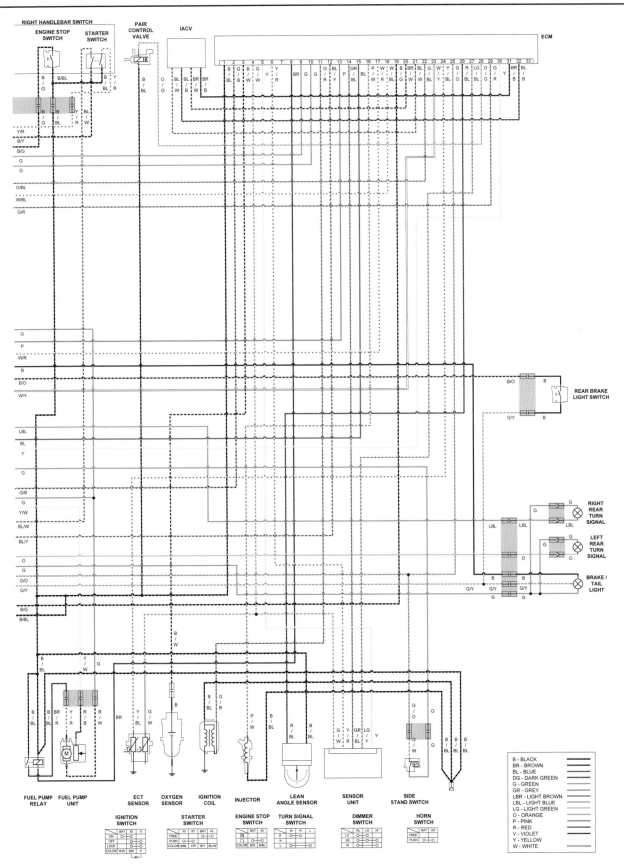

CRF250 L AND M - EUROPE

Notes

Reference

Tools and Workshop Tips

● Building up a tool kit and equipping your workshop ● Using tools ● Understanding bearing, seal, fastener and chain sizes and markings ● Repair techniques

Security

● Locks and chains ● U-locks ● Disc locks ● Alarms and immobilisers ● Security marking systems ● Tips on how to prevent bike theft

Lubricants and fluids

● Engine oils ● Transmission (gear) oils ● Coolant/anti-freeze ● Fork oils and suspension fluids ● Brake/clutch fluids ● Spray lubes, degreasers and solvents

MOT Test Checks

● A guide to the UK MOT test ● Which items are tested ● How to prepare your motorcycle for the test and perform a pre-test check

Storage

● How to prepare your motorcycle for going into storage and protect essential systems ● How to get the motorcycle back on the road

Conversion Factors

34 Nm x 0.738 = 25 lbf ft

● Formulae for conversion of the metric (SI) units used throughout the manual into Imperial measures

Fault Finding

● Common faults and their likely causes ● Links to main chapters for testing and repair procedures

Technical Terms Explained

● Component names, technical terms and common abbreviations explained

Index

Buying tools

A toolkit is a fundamental requirement for servicing and repairing a motorcycle. Although there will be an initial expense in building up enough tools for servicing, this will soon be offset by the savings made by doing the job yourself. As experience and confidence grow, additional tools can be added to enable the repair and overhaul of the motorcycle. Many of the specialist tools are expensive and not often used so it may be preferable to hire them, or for a group of friends or motorcycle club to join in the purchase.

As a rule, it is better to buy more expensive, good quality tools. Cheaper tools are likely to wear out faster and need to be renewed more often, nullifying the original saving.

> ⚠️ **Warning: To avoid the risk of a poor quality tool breaking in use, causing injury or damage to the component being worked on, always aim to purchase tools which meet the relevant national safety standards.**

The following lists of tools do not represent the manufacturer's service tools, but serve as a guide to help the owner decide which tools are needed for this level of work. In addition, items such as an electric drill, hacksaw, files, soldering iron and a workbench equipped with a vice, may be needed. Although not classed as tools, a selection of bolts, screws, nuts, washers and pieces of tubing always come in useful.

For more information about tools, refer to the Haynes *Motorcycle Workshop Practice Techbook* (Bk. No. 3470).

Manufacturer's service tools

Inevitably certain tasks require the use of a service tool. Where possible an alternative tool or method of approach is recommended, but sometimes there is no option if personal injury or damage to the component is to be avoided. Where required, service tools are referred to in the relevant procedure.

Service tools can usually only be purchased from a motorcycle dealer and are identified by a part number. Some of the commonly-used tools, such as rotor pullers, are available in aftermarket form from mail-order motorcycle tool and accessory suppliers.

Maintenance and minor repair tools

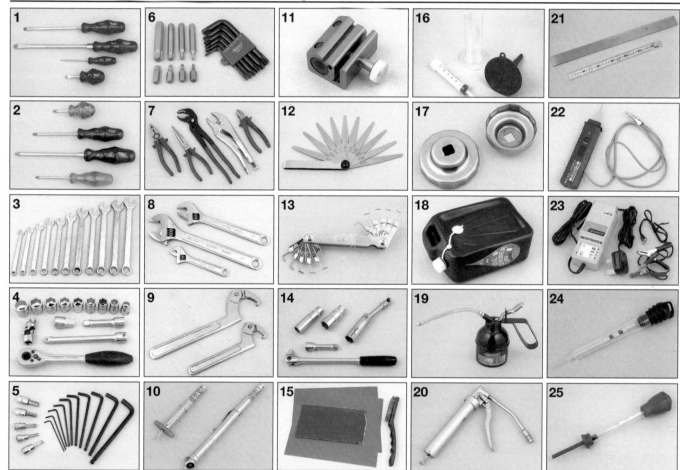

1 Set of flat-bladed screwdrivers
2 Set of Phillips head screwdrivers
3 Combination open-end and ring spanners
4 Socket set (3/8 inch or 1/2 inch drive)
5 Set of Allen keys or bits
6 Set of Torx keys or bits
7 Pliers, cutters and self-locking grips (Mole grips)
8 Adjustable spanners
9 C-spanners
10 Tread depth gauge and tyre pressure gauge
11 Cable oiler clamp
12 Feeler gauges
13 Spark plug gap measuring tool
14 Spark plug spanner or deep plug sockets
15 Wire brush and emery paper
16 Calibrated syringe, measuring vessel and funnel
17 Oil filter adapters
18 Oil drainer can or tray
19 Pump type oil can
20 Grease gun
21 Straight-edge and steel rule
22 Continuity tester
23 Battery charger
24 Hydrometer (for battery specific gravity check)
25 Anti-freeze tester (for liquid-cooled engines)

Repair and overhaul tools

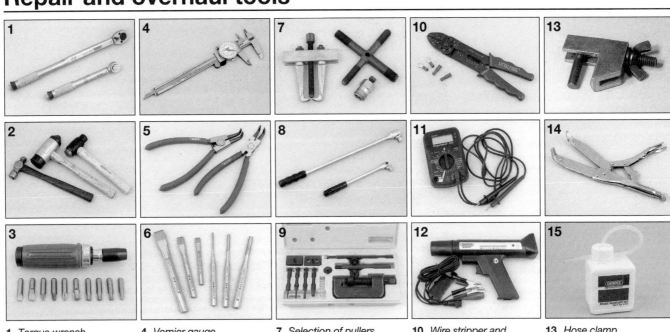

1 Torque wrench
  (small and mid-ranges)
2 Conventional, plastic or
  soft-faced hammers
3 Impact driver set
4 Vernier gauge
5 Circlip pliers (internal and
  external, or combination)
6 Set of cold chisels
  and punches
7 Selection of pullers
8 Breaker bars
9 Chain breaking/
  riveting tool set
10 Wire stripper and
   crimper tool
11 Multimeter (measures
   amps, volts and ohms)
12 Stroboscope (for
   dynamic timing checks)
13 Hose clamp
   (wingnut type shown)
14 Clutch holding tool
15 One-man brake/clutch
   bleeder kit

Specialist tools

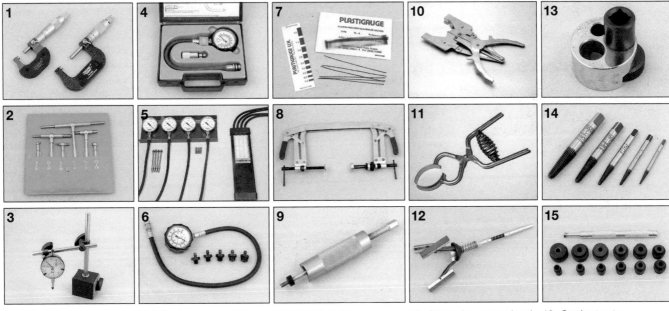

1 Micrometers
  (external type)
2 Telescoping gauges
3 Dial gauge
4 Cylinder
  compression gauge
5 Vacuum gauges (left) or
  manometer (right)
6 Oil pressure gauge
7 Plastigauge kit
8 Valve spring compressor
  (4-stroke engines)
9 Piston pin drawbolt tool
10 Piston ring removal and
   installation tool
11 Piston ring clamp
12 Cylinder bore hone
   (stone type shown)
13 Stud extractor
14 Screw extractor set
15 Bearing driver set

1 Workshop equipment and facilities

The workbench

● Work is made much easier by raising the bike up on a ramp - components are much more accessible if raised to waist level. The hydraulic or pneumatic types seen in the dealer's workshop are a sound investment if you undertake a lot of repairs or overhauls (see illustration 1.1).

1.1 Hydraulic motorcycle ramp

● If raised off ground level, the bike must be supported on the ramp to avoid it falling. Most ramps incorporate a front wheel locating clamp which can be adjusted to suit different diameter wheels. When tightening the clamp, take care not to mark the wheel rim or damage the tyre - use wood blocks on each side to prevent this.

● Secure the bike to the ramp using tie-downs (see illustration 1.2). If the bike has only a sidestand, and hence leans at a dangerous angle when raised, support the bike on an auxiliary stand.

1.2 Tie-downs are used around the passenger footrests to secure the bike

● Auxiliary (paddock) stands are widely available from mail order companies or motorcycle dealers and attach either to the wheel axle or swingarm pivot (see illustration 1.3). If the motorcycle has a centrestand, you can support it under the crankcase to prevent it toppling whilst either wheel is removed (see illustration 1.4).

1.3 This auxiliary stand attaches to the swingarm pivot

1.4 Always use a block of wood between the engine and jack head when supporting the engine in this way

Fumes and fire

● Refer to the Safety first! page at the beginning of the manual for full details. Make sure your workshop is equipped with a fire extinguisher suitable for fuel-related fires (Class B fire - flammable liquids) - it is not sufficient to have a water-filled extinguisher.

● Always ensure adequate ventilation is available. Unless an exhaust gas extraction system is available for use, ensure that the engine is run outside of the workshop.

● If working on the fuel system, make sure the workshop is ventilated to avoid a build-up of fumes. This applies equally to fume build-up when charging a battery. Do not smoke or allow anyone else to smoke in the workshop.

Fluids

● If you need to drain fuel from the tank, store it in an approved container marked as suitable for the storage of petrol (gasoline) (see illustration 1.5). Do not store fuel in glass jars or bottles.

1.5 Use an approved can only for storing petrol (gasoline)

● Use proprietary engine degreasers or solvents which have a high flash-point, such as paraffin (kerosene), for cleaning off oil, grease and dirt - never use petrol (gasoline) for cleaning. Wear rubber gloves when handling solvent and engine degreaser. The fumes from certain solvents can be dangerous - always work in a well-ventilated area.

Dust, eye and hand protection

● Protect your lungs from inhalation of dust particles by wearing a filtering mask over the nose and mouth. Many frictional materials still contain asbestos which is dangerous to your health. Protect your eyes from spouts of liquid and sprung components by wearing a pair of protective goggles (see illustration 1.6).

1.6 A fire extinguisher, goggles, mask and protective gloves should be at hand in the workshop

● Protect your hands from contact with solvents, fuel and oils by wearing rubber gloves. Alternatively apply a barrier cream to your hands before starting work. If handling hot components or fluids, wear suitable gloves to protect your hands from scalding and burns.

What to do with old fluids

● Old cleaning solvent, fuel, coolant and oils should not be poured down domestic drains or onto the ground. Package the fluid up in old oil containers, label it accordingly, and take it to a garage or disposal facility. Contact your local authority for location of such sites or ring the oil care hotline.

OIL CARE

Note: It is antisocial and illegal to dump oil down the drain. To find the location of your local oil recycling bank in the UK, call 08708 506 506 or visit www.oilbankline.org.uk

In the USA, note that any oil supplier must accept used oil for recycling.

2 Fasteners - screws, bolts and nuts

Fastener types and applications

Bolts and screws

● Fastener head types are either of hexagonal, Torx or splined design, with internal and external versions of each type **(see illustrations 2.1 and 2.2)**; splined head fasteners are not in common use on motorcycles. The conventional slotted or Phillips head design is used for certain screws. Bolt or screw length is always measured from the underside of the head to the end of the item **(see illustration 2.11)**.

2.1 Internal hexagon/Allen (A), Torx (B) and splined (C) fasteners, with corresponding bits

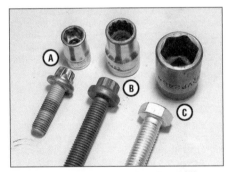

2.2 External Torx (A), splined (B) and hexagon (C) fasteners, with corresponding sockets

● Certain fasteners on the motorcycle have a tensile marking on their heads, the higher the marking the stronger the fastener. High tensile fasteners generally carry a 10 or higher marking. Never replace a high tensile fastener with one of a lower tensile strength.

Washers (see illustration 2.3)

● Plain washers are used between a fastener head and a component to prevent damage to the component or to spread the load when torque is applied. Plain washers can also be used as spacers or shims in certain assemblies. Copper or aluminium plain washers are often used as sealing washers on drain plugs.

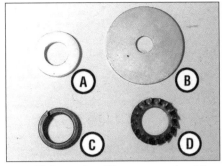

2.3 Plain washer (A), penny washer (B), spring washer (C) and serrated washer (D)

● The split-ring spring washer works by applying axial tension between the fastener head and component. If flattened, it is fatigued and must be renewed. If a plain (flat) washer is used on the fastener, position the spring washer between the fastener and the plain washer.
● Serrated star type washers dig into the fastener and component faces, preventing loosening. They are often used on electrical earth (ground) connections to the frame.
● Cone type washers (sometimes called Belleville) are conical and when tightened apply axial tension between the fastener head and component. They must be installed with the dished side against the component and often carry an OUTSIDE marking on their outer face. If flattened, they are fatigued and must be renewed.
● Tab washers are used to lock plain nuts or bolts on a shaft. A portion of the tab washer is bent up hard against one flat of the nut or bolt to prevent it loosening. Due to the tab washer being deformed in use, a new tab washer should be used every time it is disturbed.
● Wave washers are used to take up endfloat on a shaft. They provide light springing and prevent excessive side-to-side play of a component. Can be found on rocker arm shafts.

Nuts and split pins

● Conventional plain nuts are usually six-sided **(see illustration 2.4)**. They are sized by thread diameter and pitch. High tensile nuts carry a number on one end to denote their tensile strength.

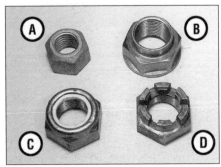

2.4 Plain nut (A), shouldered locknut (B), nylon insert nut (C) and castellated nut (D)

● Self-locking nuts either have a nylon insert, or two spring metal tabs, or a shoulder which is staked into a groove in the shaft - their advantage over conventional plain nuts is a resistance to loosening due to vibration. The nylon insert type can be used a number of times, but must be renewed when the friction of the nylon insert is reduced, ie when the nut spins freely on the shaft. The spring tab type can be reused unless the tabs are damaged. The shouldered type must be renewed every time it is disturbed.
● Split pins (cotter pins) are used to lock a castellated nut to a shaft or to prevent slackening of a plain nut. Common applications are wheel axles and brake torque arms. Because the split pin arms are deformed to lock around the nut a new split pin must always be used on installation - always fit the correct size split pin which will fit snugly in the shaft hole. Make sure the split pin arms are correctly located around the nut **(see illustrations 2.5 and 2.6)**.

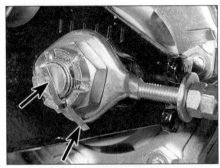

2.5 Bend split pin (cotter pin) arms as shown (arrows) to secure a castellated nut

2.6 Bend split pin (cotter pin) arms as shown to secure a plain nut

Caution: If the castellated nut slots do not align with the shaft hole after tightening to the torque setting, tighten the nut until the next slot aligns with the hole - never slacken the nut to align its slot.

● R-pins (shaped like the letter R), or slip pins as they are sometimes called, are sprung and can be reused if they are otherwise in good condition. Always install R-pins with their closed end facing forwards **(see illustration 2.7)**.

2.7 Correct fitting of R-pin. Arrow indicates forward direction

Circlips (see illustration 2.8)

● Circlips (sometimes called snap-rings) are used to retain components on a shaft or in a housing and have corresponding external or internal ears to permit removal. Parallel-sided (machined) circlips can be installed either way round in their groove, whereas stamped circlips (which have a chamfered edge on one face) must be installed with the chamfer facing away from the direction of thrust load **(see illustration 2.9)**.

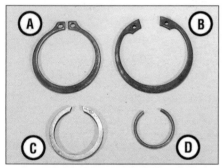

2.8 External stamped circlip (A), internal stamped circlip (B), machined circlip (C) and wire circlip (D)

● Always use circlip pliers to remove and install circlips; expand or compress them just enough to remove them. After installation, rotate the circlip in its groove to ensure it is securely seated. If installing a circlip on a splined shaft, always align its opening with a shaft channel to ensure the circlip ends are well supported and unlikely to catch **(see illustration 2.10)**.

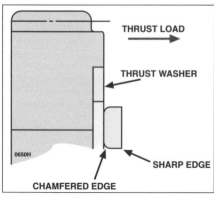

2.9 Correct fitting of a stamped circlip

THRUST LOAD

THRUST WASHER

SHARP EDGE

CHAMFERED EDGE

0650H

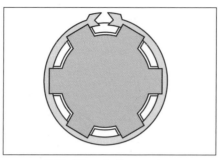

2.10 Align circlip opening with shaft channel

● Circlips can wear due to the thrust of components and become loose in their grooves, with the subsequent danger of becoming dislodged in operation. For this reason, renewal is advised every time a circlip is disturbed.
● Wire circlips are commonly used as piston pin retaining clips. If a removal tang is provided, long-nosed pliers can be used to dislodge them, otherwise careful use of a small flat-bladed screwdriver is necessary. Wire circlips should be renewed every time they are disturbed.

Thread diameter and pitch

● Diameter of a male thread (screw, bolt or stud) is the outside diameter of the threaded portion **(see illustration 2.11)**. Most motorcycle manufacturers use the ISO (International Standards Organisation) metric system expressed in millimetres, eg M6 refers to a 6 mm diameter thread. Sizing is the same for nuts, except that the thread diameter is measured across the valleys of the nut.
● Pitch is the distance between the peaks of the thread **(see illustration 2.11)**. It is expressed in millimetres, thus a common bolt size may be expressed as 6.0 x 1.0 mm (6 mm thread diameter and 1 mm pitch). Generally pitch increases in proportion to thread diameter, although there are always exceptions.
● Thread diameter and pitch are related for conventional fastener applications and the accompanying table can be used as a guide. Additionally, the AF (Across Flats), spanner or socket size dimension of the bolt or nut **(see illustration 2.11)** is linked to thread and pitch specification. Thread pitch can be measured with a thread gauge **(see illustration 2.12)**.

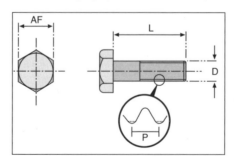

2.11 Fastener length (L), thread diameter (D), thread pitch (P) and head size (AF)

AF

L

D

P

2.12 Using a thread gauge to measure pitch

AF size	Thread diameter x pitch (mm)
8 mm	M5 x 0.8
8 mm	M6 x 1.0
10 mm	M6 x 1.0
12 mm	M8 x 1.25
14 mm	M10 x 1.25
17 mm	M12 x 1.25

● The threads of most fasteners are of the right-hand type, ie they are turned clockwise to tighten and anti-clockwise to loosen. The reverse situation applies to left-hand thread fasteners, which are turned anti-clockwise to tighten and clockwise to loosen. Left-hand threads are used where rotation of a component might loosen a conventional right-hand thread fastener.

Seized fasteners

● Corrosion of external fasteners due to water or reaction between two dissimilar metals can occur over a period of time. It will build up sooner in wet conditions or in countries where salt is used on the roads during the winter. If a fastener is severely corroded it is likely that normal methods of removal will fail and result in its head being ruined. When you attempt removal, the fastener thread should be heard to crack free and unscrew easily - if it doesn't, stop there before damaging something.
● A smart tap on the head of the fastener will often succeed in breaking free corrosion which has occurred in the threads **(see illustration 2.13)**.
● An aerosol penetrating fluid (such as WD-40) applied the night beforehand may work its way down into the thread and ease removal. Depending on the location, you may be able to make up a Plasticine well around the fastener head and fill it with penetrating fluid.

2.13 A sharp tap on the head of a fastener will often break free a corroded thread

● If you are working on an engine internal component, corrosion will most likely not be a problem due to the well lubricated environment. However, components can be very tight and an impact driver is a useful tool in freeing them **(see illustration 2.14)**.

2.14 Using an impact driver to free a fastener

● Where corrosion has occurred between dissimilar metals (eg steel and aluminium alloy), the application of heat to the fastener head will create a disproportionate expansion rate between the two metals and break the seizure caused by the corrosion. Whether heat can be applied depends on the location of the fastener - any surrounding components likely to be damaged must first be removed **(see illustration 2.15)**. Heat can be applied using a paint stripper heat gun or clothes iron, or by immersing the component in boiling water - wear protective gloves to prevent scalding or burns to the hands.

2.15 Using heat to free a seized fastener

● As a last resort, it is possible to use a hammer and cold chisel to work the fastener head unscrewed **(see illustration 2.16)**. This will damage the fastener, but more importantly extreme care must be taken not to damage the surrounding component.

Caution: Remember that the component being secured is generally of more value than the bolt, nut or screw - when the fastener is freed, do not unscrew it with force, instead work the fastener back and forth when resistance is felt to prevent thread damage.

2.16 Using a hammer and chisel to free a seized fastener

Broken fasteners and damaged heads

● If the shank of a broken bolt or screw is accessible you can grip it with self-locking grips. The knurled wheel type stud extractor tool or self-gripping stud puller tool is particularly useful for removing the long studs which screw into the cylinder mouth surface of the crankcase or bolts and screws from which the head has broken off **(see illustration 2.17)**. Studs can also be removed by locking two nuts together on the threaded end of the stud and using a spanner on the lower nut **(see illustration 2.18)**.

2.17 Using a stud extractor tool to remove a broken crankcase stud

2.18 Two nuts can be locked together to unscrew a stud from a component

● A bolt or screw which has broken off below or level with the casing must be extracted using a screw extractor set. Centre punch the fastener to centralise the drill bit, then drill a hole in the fastener **(see illustration 2.19)**. Select a drill bit which is approximately half to three-quarters the diameter of the fastener

2.19 When using a screw extractor, first drill a hole in the fastener . . .

and drill to a depth which will accommodate the extractor. Use the largest size extractor possible, but avoid leaving too small a wall thickness otherwise the extractor will merely force the fastener walls outwards wedging it in the casing thread.

● If a spiral type extractor is used, thread it anti-clockwise into the fastener. As it is screwed in, it will grip the fastener and unscrew it from the casing **(see illustration 2.20)**.

2.20 . . . then thread the extractor anti-clockwise into the fastener

● If a taper type extractor is used, tap it into the fastener so that it is firmly wedged in place. Unscrew the extractor (anti-clockwise) to draw the fastener out.

> ⚠ *Warning: Stud extractors are very hard and may break off in the fastener if care is not taken - ask an engineer about spark erosion if this happens.*

● Alternatively, the broken bolt/screw can be drilled out and the hole retapped for an oversize bolt/screw or a diamond-section thread insert. It is essential that the drilling is carried out squarely and to the correct depth, otherwise the casing may be ruined - if in doubt, entrust the work to an engineer.

● Bolts and nuts with rounded corners cause the correct size spanner or socket to slip when force is applied. Of the types of spanner/socket available always use a six-point type rather than an eight or twelve-point type - better grip

2.21 Comparison of surface drive ring spanner (left) with 12-point type (right)

is obtained. Surface drive spanners grip the middle of the hex flats, rather than the corners, and are thus good in cases of damaged heads **(see illustration 2.21)**.

● Slotted-head or Phillips-head screws are often damaged by the use of the wrong size screwdriver. Allen-head and Torx-head screws are much less likely to sustain damage. If enough of the screw head is exposed you can use a hacksaw to cut a slot in its head and then use a conventional flat-bladed screwdriver to remove it. Alternatively use a hammer and cold chisel to tap the head of the fastener around to slacken it. Always replace damaged fasteners with new ones, preferably Torx or Allen-head type.

HAYNES
HiNT

A dab of valve grinding compound between the screw head and screwdriver tip will often give a good grip.

Thread repair

● Threads (particularly those in aluminium alloy components) can be damaged by overtightening, being assembled with dirt in the threads, or from a component working loose and vibrating. Eventually the thread will fail completely, and it will be impossible to tighten the fastener.

● If a thread is damaged or clogged with old locking compound it can be renovated with a thread repair tool (thread chaser) **(see illustrations 2.22 and 2.23)**; special thread

2.22 A thread repair tool being used to correct an internal thread

2.23 A thread repair tool being used to correct an external thread

chasers are available for spark plug hole threads. The tool will not cut a new thread, but clean and true the original thread. Make sure that you use the correct diameter and pitch tool. Similarly, external threads can be cleaned up with a die or a thread restorer file **(see illustration 2.24)**.

2.24 Using a thread restorer file

● It is possible to drill out the old thread and retap the component to the next thread size. This will work where there is enough surrounding material and a new bolt or screw can be obtained. Sometimes, however, this is not possible - such as where the bolt/screw passes through another component which must also be suitably modified, also in cases where a spark plug or oil drain plug cannot be obtained in a larger diameter thread size.

● The diamond-section thread insert (often known by its popular trade name of Heli-Coil) is a simple and effective method of renewing the thread and retaining the original size. A kit can be purchased which contains the tap, insert and installing tool **(see illustration 2.25)**. Drill out the damaged thread with the size drill specified **(see illustration 2.26)**. Carefully retap the thread **(see illustration 2.27)**. Install the

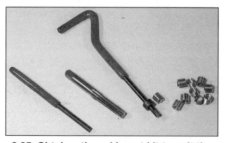

2.25 Obtain a thread insert kit to suit the thread diameter and pitch required

2.26 To install a thread insert, first drill out the original thread . . .

2.27 . . . tap a new thread . . .

2.28 . . . fit insert on the installing tool . . .

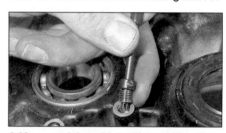

2.29 . . . and thread into the component . . .

2.30 . . . break off the tang when complete

insert on the installing tool and thread it slowly into place using a light downward pressure **(see illustrations 2.28 and 2.29)**. When positioned between a 1/4 and 1/2 turn below the surface withdraw the installing tool and use the break-off tool to press down on the tang, breaking it off **(see illustration 2.30)**.

● There are epoxy thread repair kits on the market which can rebuild stripped internal threads, although this repair should not be used on high load-bearing components.

Thread locking and sealing compounds

● Locking compounds are used in locations where the fastener is prone to loosening due to vibration or on important safety-related items which might cause loss of control of the motorcycle if they fail. It is also used where important fasteners cannot be secured by other means such as lockwashers or split pins.

● Before applying locking compound, make sure that the threads (internal and external) are clean and dry with all old compound removed. Select a compound to suit the component being secured - a non-permanent general locking and sealing type is suitable for most applications, but a high strength type is needed for permanent fixing of studs in castings. Apply a drop or two of the compound to the first few threads of the fastener, then thread it into place and tighten to the specified torque. Do not apply excessive thread locking compound otherwise the thread may be damaged on subsequent removal.

● Certain fasteners are impregnated with a dry film type coating of locking compound on their threads. Always renew this type of fastener if disturbed.

● Anti-seize compounds, such as copper-based greases, can be applied to protect threads from seizure due to extreme heat and corrosion. A common instance is spark plug threads and exhaust system fasteners.

3 Measuring tools and gauges

Feeler gauges

● Feeler gauges (or blades) are used for measuring small gaps and clearances (see illustration 3.1). They can also be used to measure endfloat (sideplay) of a component on a shaft where access is not possible with a dial gauge.

● Feeler gauge sets should be treated with care and not be bent or damaged. They are etched with their size on one face. Keep them clean and very lightly oiled to prevent corrosion build-up.

3.1 Feeler gauges are used for measuring small gaps and clearances - thickness is marked on one face of gauge

● When measuring a clearance, select a gauge which is a light sliding fit between the two components. You may need to use two gauges together to measure the clearance accurately.

Micrometers

● A micrometer is a precision tool capable of measuring to 0.01 or 0.001 of a millimetre. It should always be stored in its case and not in the general toolbox. It must be kept clean and never dropped, otherwise its frame or measuring anvils could be distorted resulting in inaccurate readings.

● External micrometers are used for measuring outside diameters of components and have many more applications than internal micrometers. Micrometers are available in different size ranges, eg 0 to 25 mm, 25 to 50 mm, and upwards in 25 mm steps; some large micrometers have interchangeable anvils to allow a range of measurements to be taken. Generally the largest precision measurement you are likely to take on a motorcycle is the piston diameter.

● Internal micrometers (or bore micrometers) are used for measuring inside diameters, such as valve guides and cylinder bores. Telescoping gauges and small hole gauges are used in conjunction with an external micrometer, whereas the more expensive internal micrometers have their own measuring device.

External micrometer

Note: *The conventional analogue type instrument is described. Although much easier to read, digital micrometers are considerably more expensive.*

● Always check the calibration of the micrometer before use. With the anvils closed (0 to 25 mm type) or set over a test gauge

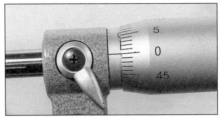

3.2 Check micrometer calibration before use

(for the larger types) the scale should read zero **(see illustration 3.2)**; make sure that the anvils (and test piece) are clean first. Any discrepancy can be adjusted by referring to the instructions supplied with the tool. Remember that the micrometer is a precision measuring tool - don't force the anvils closed, use the ratchet (4) on the end of the micrometer to close it. In this way, a measured force is always applied.

● To use, first make sure that the item being measured is clean. Place the anvil of the micrometer (1) against the item and use the thimble (2) to bring the spindle (3) lightly into contact with the other side of the item **(see illustration 3.3)**. Don't tighten the thimble down because this will damage the micrometer - instead use the ratchet (4) on the end of the micrometer. The ratchet mechanism applies a measured force preventing damage to the instrument.

● The micrometer is read by referring to the linear scale on the sleeve and the annular scale on the thimble. Read off the sleeve first to obtain the base measurement, then add the fine measurement from the thimble to obtain the overall reading. The linear scale on the sleeve represents the measuring range of the micrometer (eg 0 to 25 mm). The annular scale

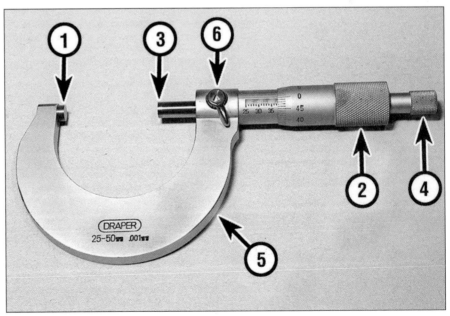

3.3 Micrometer component parts

1 Anvil	3 Spindle	5 Frame
2 Thimble	4 Ratchet	6 Locking lever

on the thimble will be in graduations of 0.01 mm (or as marked on the frame) - one full revolution of the thimble will move 0.5 mm on the linear scale. Take the reading where the datum line on the sleeve intersects the thimble's scale. Always position the eye directly above the scale otherwise an inaccurate reading will result.

In the example shown the item measures 2.95 mm **(see illustration 3.4)**:

Linear scale	2.00 mm
Linear scale	0.50 mm
Annular scale	0.45 mm
Total figure	2.95 mm

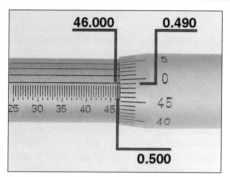

3.5 Micrometer reading of 46.99 mm on linear and annular scales . . .

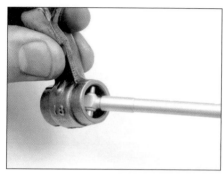

3.7 Expand the telescoping gauge in the bore, lock its position . . .

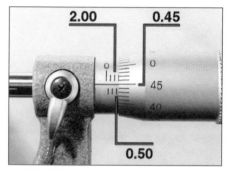

3.4 Micrometer reading of 2.95 mm

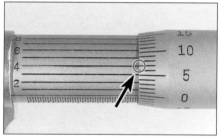

3.6 . . . and 0.004 mm on vernier scale

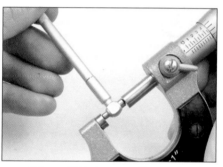

3.8 . . . then measure the gauge with a micrometer

Most micrometers have a locking lever (6) on the frame to hold the setting in place, allowing the item to be removed from the micrometer.
● Some micrometers have a vernier scale on their sleeve, providing an even finer measurement to be taken, in 0.001 increments of a millimetre. Take the sleeve and thimble measurement as described above, then check which graduation on the vernier scale aligns with that of the annular scale on the thimble **Note:** *The eye must be perpendicular to the scale when taking the vernier reading - if necessary rotate the body of the micrometer to ensure this.* Multiply the vernier scale figure by 0.001 and add it to the base and fine measurement figures.

In the example shown the item measures 46.994 mm **(see illustrations 3.5 and 3.6)**:

Linear scale (base)	46.000 mm
Linear scale (base)	00.500 mm
Annular scale (fine)	00.490 mm
Vernier scale	00.004 mm
Total figure	46.994 mm

Internal micrometer

● Internal micrometers are available for measuring bore diameters, but are expensive and unlikely to be available for home use. It is suggested that a set of telescoping gauges and small hole gauges, both of which must be used with an external micrometer, will suffice for taking internal measurements on a motorcycle.
● Telescoping gauges can be used to

measure internal diameters of components. Select a gauge with the correct size range, make sure its ends are clean and insert it into the bore. Expand the gauge, then lock its position and withdraw it from the bore **(see illustration 3.7)**. Measure across the gauge ends with a micrometer **(see illustration 3.8)**.
● Very small diameter bores (such as valve guides) are measured with a small hole gauge. Once adjusted to a slip-fit inside the component, its position is locked and the gauge withdrawn for measurement with a micrometer **(see illustrations 3.9 and 3.10)**.

Vernier caliper

Note: *The conventional linear and dial gauge type instruments are described. Digital types are easier to read, but are far more expensive.*
● The vernier caliper does not provide the precision of a micrometer, but is versatile in being able to measure internal and external diameters. Some types also incorporate a depth gauge. It is ideal for measuring clutch plate friction material and spring free lengths.
● To use the conventional linear scale vernier, slacken off the vernier clamp screws (1) and set its jaws over (2), or inside (3), the item to be measured **(see illustration 3.11)**. Slide the jaw into contact, using the thumb-wheel (4) for fine movement of the sliding scale (5) then tighten the clamp screws (1). Read off the main scale (6) where the zero on the sliding scale (5) intersects it, taking the whole number to the left of the zero; this provides the base measurement. View along the sliding scale and select the division which

3.9 Expand the small hole gauge in the bore, lock its position . . .

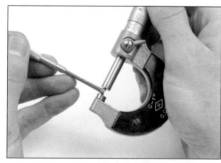

3.10 . . . then measure the gauge with a micrometer

lines up exactly with any of the divisions on the main scale, noting that the divisions usually represents 0.02 of a millimetre. Add this fine measurement to the base measurement to obtain the total reading.

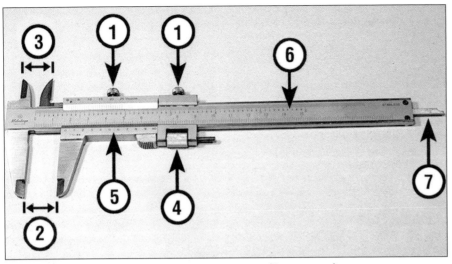

3.11 Vernier component parts (linear gauge)

1 Clamp screws	3 Internal jaws	5 Sliding scale	7 Depth gauge
2 External jaws	4 Thumbwheel	6 Main scale	

In the example shown the item measures 55.92 mm **(see illustration 3.12)**:

Base measurement	55.00 mm
Fine measurement	00.92 mm
Total figure	55.92 mm

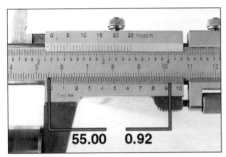

3.12 Vernier gauge reading of 55.92 mm

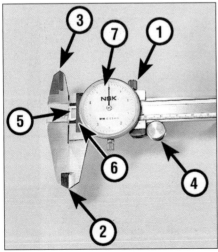

3.13 Vernier component parts (dial gauge)

1 Clamp screw	5 Main scale
2 External jaws	6 Sliding scale
3 Internal jaws	7 Dial gauge
4 Thumbwheel	

● Some vernier calipers are equipped with a dial gauge for fine measurement. Before use, check that the jaws are clean, then close them fully and check that the dial gauge reads zero. If necessary adjust the gauge ring accordingly. Slacken the vernier clamp screw (1) and set its jaws over (2), or inside (3), the item to be measured **(see illustration 3.13)**. Slide the jaws into contact, using the thumbwheel (4) for fine movement. Read off the main scale (5) where the edge of the sliding scale (6) intersects it, taking the whole number to the left of the zero; this provides the base measurement. Read off the needle position on the dial gauge (7) scale to provide the fine measurement; each division represents 0.05 of a millimetre. Add this fine measurement to the base measurement to obtain the total reading.

In the example shown the item measures 55.95 mm **(see illustration 3.14)**:

Base measurement	55.00 mm
Fine measurement	00.95 mm
Total figure	55.95 mm

3.14 Vernier gauge reading of 55.95 mm

Plastigauge

● Plastigauge is a plastic material which can be compressed between two surfaces to measure the oil clearance between them. The width of the compressed Plastigauge is measured against a calibrated scale to determine the clearance.

● Common uses of Plastigauge are for measuring the clearance between crankshaft journal and main bearing inserts, between crankshaft journal and big-end bearing inserts, and between camshaft and bearing surfaces. The following example describes big-end oil clearance measurement.

● Handle the Plastigauge material carefully to prevent distortion. Using a sharp knife, cut a length which corresponds with the width of the bearing being measured and place it carefully across the journal so that it is parallel with the shaft **(see illustration 3.15)**. Carefully install both bearing shells and the connecting rod. Without rotating the rod on the journal tighten its bolts or nuts (as applicable) to the specified torque. The connecting rod and bearings are then disassembled and the crushed Plastigauge examined.

3.15 Plastigauge placed across shaft journal

● Using the scale provided in the Plastigauge kit, measure the width of the material to determine the oil clearance **(see illustration 3.16)**. Always remove all traces of Plastigauge after use using your fingernails.

Caution: Arriving at the correct clearance demands that the assembly is torqued correctly, according to the settings and sequence (where applicable) provided by the motorcycle manufacturer.

3.16 Measuring the width of the crushed Plastigauge

Dial gauge or DTI (Dial Test Indicator)

● A dial gauge can be used to accurately measure small amounts of movement. Typical uses are measuring shaft runout or shaft endfloat (sideplay) and setting piston position for ignition timing on two-strokes. A dial gauge set usually comes with a range of different probes and adapters and mounting equipment.

● The gauge needle must point to zero when at rest. Rotate the ring around its periphery to zero the gauge.

● Check that the gauge is capable of reading the extent of movement in the work. Most gauges have a small dial set in the face which records whole millimetres of movement as well as the fine scale around the face periphery which is calibrated in 0.01 mm divisions. Read off the small dial first to obtain the base measurement, then add the measurement from the fine scale to obtain the total reading.

In the example shown the gauge reads 1.48 mm (see illustration 3.17):

Base measurement	1.00 mm
Fine measurement	0.48 mm
Total figure	1.48 mm

3.17 Dial gauge reading of 1.48 mm

● If measuring shaft runout, the shaft must be supported in vee-blocks and the gauge mounted on a stand perpendicular to the shaft. Rest the tip of the gauge against the centre of the shaft and rotate the shaft slowly whilst watching the gauge reading (see illustration 3.18). Take several measurements along the length of the shaft and record the

3.18 Using a dial gauge to measure shaft runout

maximum gauge reading as the amount of runout in the shaft. **Note:** *The reading obtained will be total runout at that point - some manufacturers specify that the runout figure is halved to compare with their specified runout limit.*

● Endfloat (sideplay) measurement requires that the gauge is mounted securely to the surrounding component with its probe touching the end of the shaft. Using hand pressure, push and pull on the shaft noting the maximum endfloat recorded on the gauge (see illustration 3.19).

3.19 Using a dial gauge to measure shaft endfloat

● A dial gauge with suitable adapters can be used to determine piston position BTDC on two-stroke engines for the purposes of ignition timing. The gauge, adapter and suitable length probe are installed in the place of the spark plug and the gauge zeroed at TDC. If the piston position is specified as 1.14 mm BTDC, rotate the engine back to 2.00 mm BTDC, then slowly forwards to 1.14 mm BTDC.

Cylinder compression gauges

● A compression gauge is used for measuring cylinder compression. Either the rubber-cone type or the threaded adapter type can be used. The latter is preferred to ensure a perfect seal against the cylinder head. A 0 to 300 psi (0 to 20 Bar) type gauge (for petrol/gasoline engines) will be suitable for motorcycles.

● The spark plug is removed and the gauge either held hard against the cylinder head (cone type) or the gauge adapter screwed into the cylinder head (threaded type) (see illustration 3.20). Cylinder compression is measured with the engine turning over, but not running. The

3.20 Using a rubber-cone type cylinder compression gauge

gauge will hold the reading until manually released.

Oil pressure gauge

● An oil pressure gauge is used for measuring engine oil pressure. Most gauges come with a set of adapters to fit the thread of the take-off point (see illustration 3.21). If the take-off point specified by the motorcycle manufacturer is an external oil pipe union, make sure that the specified replacement union is used to prevent oil starvation.

3.21 Oil pressure gauge and take-off point adapter (arrow)

● Oil pressure is measured with the engine running (at a specific rpm) and often the manufacturer will specify pressure limits for a cold and hot engine.

Straight-edge and surface plate

● If checking the gasket face of a component for warpage, place a steel rule or precision straight-edge across the gasket face and measure any gap between the straight-edge and component with feeler gauges (see illustration 3.22). Check diagonally across the component and between mounting holes (see illustration 3.23).

3.22 Use a straight-edge and feeler gauges to check for warpage

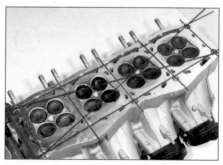

3.23 Check for warpage in these directions

● Checking individual components for warpage, such as clutch plain (metal) plates, requires a perfectly flat plate or piece or plate glass and feeler gauges.

4 Torque and leverage

What is torque?

● Torque describes the twisting force about a shaft. The amount of torque applied is determined by the distance from the centre of the shaft to the end of the lever and the amount of force being applied to the end of the lever; distance multiplied by force equals torque.

● The manufacturer applies a measured torque to a bolt or nut to ensure that it will not slacken in use and to hold two components securely together without movement in the joint. The actual torque setting depends on the thread size, bolt or nut material and the composition of the components being held.

● Too little torque may cause the fastener to loosen due to vibration, whereas too much torque will distort the joint faces of the component or cause the fastener to shear off. Always stick to the specified torque setting.

Using a torque wrench

● Check the calibration of the torque wrench and make sure it has a suitable range for the job. Torque wrenches are available in Nm (Newton-metres), kgf m (kilograms-force metre), lbf ft (pounds-feet), lbf in (inch-pounds). Do not confuse lbf ft with lbf in.

● Adjust the tool to the desired torque on the scale (see illustration 4.1). If your torque wrench is not calibrated in the units specified, carefully convert the figure (see Conversion Factors). A manufacturer sometimes gives a torque setting as a range (8 to 10 Nm) rather than a single figure - in this case set the tool midway between the two settings. The same torque may be expressed as 9 Nm ± 1 Nm. Some torque wrenches have a method of locking the setting so that it isn't inadvertently altered during use.

4.1 Set the torque wrench index mark to the setting required, in this case 12 Nm

● Install the bolts/nuts in their correct location and secure them lightly. Their threads must be clean and free of any old locking compound. Unless specified the threads and flange should be dry - oiled threads are necessary in certain circumstances and the manufacturer will take this into account in the specified torque figure. Similarly, the manufacturer may also specify the application of thread-locking compound.

● Tighten the fasteners in the specified sequence until the torque wrench clicks, indicating that the torque setting has been reached. Apply the torque again to double-check the setting. Where different thread diameter fasteners secure the component, as a rule tighten the larger diameter ones first.

● When the torque wrench has been finished with, release the lock (where applicable) and fully back off its setting to zero - do not leave the torque wrench tensioned. Also, do not use a torque wrench for slackening a fastener.

Angle-tightening

● Manufacturers often specify a figure in degrees for final tightening of a fastener. This usually follows tightening to a specific torque setting.

● A degree disc can be set and attached to the socket (see illustration 4.2) or a protractor can be used to mark the angle of movement on the bolt/nut head and the surrounding casting (see illustration 4.3).

4.2 Angle tightening can be accomplished with a torque-angle gauge . . .

4.3 . . . or by marking the angle on the surrounding component

Loosening sequences

● Where more than one bolt/nut secures a component, loosen each fastener evenly a little at a time. In this way, not all the stress of the joint is held by one fastener and the components are not likely to distort.

● If a tightening sequence is provided, work in the REVERSE of this, but if not, work from the outside in, in a criss-cross sequence (see illustration 4.4).

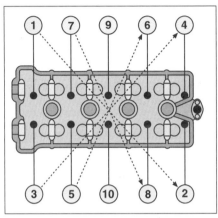

4.4 When slackening, work from the outside inwards

Tightening sequences

● If a component is held by more than one fastener it is important that the retaining bolts/nuts are tightened evenly to prevent uneven stress build-up and distortion of sealing faces. This is especially important on high-compression joints such as the cylinder head.

● A sequence is usually provided by the manufacturer, either in a diagram or actually marked in the casting. If not, always start in the centre and work outwards in a criss-cross pattern (see illustration 4.5). Start off by securing all bolts/nuts finger-tight, then set the torque wrench and tighten each fastener by a small amount in sequence until the final torque is reached. By following this practice,

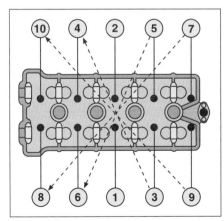

4.5 When tightening, work from the inside outwards

the joint will be held evenly and will not be distorted. Important joints, such as the cylinder head and big-end fasteners often have two- or three-stage torque settings.

Applying leverage

● Use tools at the correct angle. Position a socket wrench or spanner on the bolt/nut so that you pull it towards you when loosening. If this can't be done, push the spanner without curling your fingers around it **(see illustration 4.6)** - the spanner may slip or the fastener loosen suddenly, resulting in your fingers being crushed against a component.

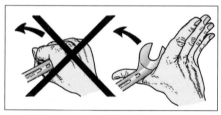

4.6 If you can't pull on the spanner to loosen a fastener, push with your hand open

● Additional leverage is gained by extending the length of the lever. The best way to do this is to use a breaker bar instead of the regular length tool, or to slip a length of tubing over the end of the spanner or socket wrench.
● If additional leverage will not work, the fastener head is either damaged or firmly corroded in place (see Fasteners).

5 Bearings

Bearing removal and installation

Drivers and sockets

● Before removing a bearing, always inspect the casing to see which way it must be driven out - some casings will have retaining plates or a cast step. Also check for any identifying markings on the bearing and if installed to a certain depth, measure this at this stage. Some roller bearings are sealed on one side - take note of the original fitted position.
● Bearings can be driven out of a casing using a bearing driver tool (with the correct size head) or a socket of the correct diameter. Select the driver head or socket so that it contacts the outer race of the bearing, not the balls/rollers or inner race. Always support the casing around the bearing housing with wood blocks, otherwise there is a risk of fracture. The bearing is driven out with a few blows on the driver or socket from a heavy mallet. Unless access is severely restricted (as with wheel bearings), a pin-punch is not recommended unless it is moved around the bearing to keep it square in its housing.

● The same equipment can be used to install bearings. Make sure the bearing housing is supported on wood blocks and line up the bearing in its housing. Fit the bearing as noted on removal - generally they are installed with their marked side facing outwards. Tap the bearing squarely into its housing using a driver or socket which bears only on the bearing's outer race - contact with the bearing balls/rollers or inner race will destroy it **(see illustrations 5.1 and 5.2)**.
● Check that the bearing inner race and balls/rollers rotate freely.

5.1 Using a bearing driver against the bearing's outer race

5.2 Using a large socket against the bearing's outer race

Pullers and slide-hammers

● Where a bearing is pressed on a shaft a puller will be required to extract it **(see illustration 5.3)**. Make sure that the puller clamp or legs fit securely behind the bearing and are unlikely to slip out. If pulling a bearing

5.3 This bearing puller clamps behind the bearing and pressure is applied to the shaft end to draw the bearing off

off a gear shaft for example, you may have to locate the puller behind a gear pinion if there is no access to the race and draw the gear pinion off the shaft as well **(see illustration 5.4)**.

> **Caution: Ensure that the puller's centre bolt locates securely against the end of the shaft and will not slip when pressure is applied. Also ensure that puller does not damage the shaft end.**

5.4 Where no access is available to the rear of the bearing, it is sometimes possible to draw off the adjacent component

● Operate the puller so that its centre bolt exerts pressure on the shaft end and draws the bearing off the shaft.
● When installing the bearing on the shaft, tap only on the bearing's inner race - contact with the balls/rollers or outer race with destroy the bearing. Use a socket or length of tubing as a drift which fits over the shaft end **(see illustration 5.5)**.

5.5 When installing a bearing on a shaft use a piece of tubing which bears only on the bearing's inner race

● Where a bearing locates in a blind hole in a casing, it cannot be driven or pulled out as described above. A slide-hammer with knife-edged bearing puller attachment will be required. The puller attachment passes through the bearing and when tightened expands to fit firmly behind the bearing **(see illustration 5.6)**. By operating the slide-hammer part of the tool the bearing is jarred out of its housing **(see illustration 5.7)**.
● It is possible, if the bearing is of reasonable weight, for it to drop out of its housing if the casing is heated as described opposite.

5.6 Expand the bearing puller so that it locks behind the bearing . . .

5.7 . . . attach the slide hammer to the bearing puller

If this method is attempted, first prepare a work surface which will enable the casing to be tapped face down to help dislodge the bearing - a wood surface is ideal since it will not damage the casing's gasket surface. Wearing protective gloves, tap the heated casing several times against the work surface to dislodge the bearing under its own weight **(see illustration 5.8)**.

5.8 Tapping a casing face down on wood blocks can often dislodge a bearing

● Bearings can be installed in blind holes using the driver or socket method described above.

Drawbolts

● Where a bearing or bush is set in the eye of a component, such as a suspension linkage arm or connecting rod small-end, removal by drift may damage the component. Furthermore, a rubber bushing in a shock absorber eye cannot successfully be driven out of position. If access is available to a engineering press, the task is straightforward. If not, a drawbolt can be fabricated to extract the bearing or bush.

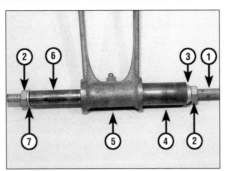

5.9 Drawbolt component parts assembled on a suspension arm

1. *Bolt or length of threaded bar*
2. *Nuts*
3. *Washer (external diameter greater than tubing internal diameter)*
4. *Tubing (internal diameter sufficient to accommodate bearing)*
5. *Suspension arm with bearing*
6. *Tubing (external diameter slightly smaller than bearing)*
7. *Washer (external diameter slightly smaller than bearing)*

5.10 Drawing the bearing out of the suspension arm

● To extract the bearing/bush you will need a long bolt with nut (or piece of threaded bar with two nuts), a piece of tubing which has an internal diameter larger than the bearing/bush, another piece of tubing which has an external diameter slightly smaller than the bearing/bush, and a selection of washers **(see illustrations 5.9 and 5.10)**. Note that the pieces of tubing must be of the same length, or longer, than the bearing/bush.

● The same kit (without the pieces of tubing) can be used to draw the new bearing/bush back into place **(see illustration 5.11)**.

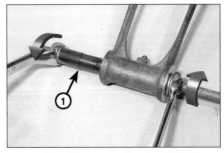

5.11 Installing a new bearing (1) in the suspension arm

Temperature change

● If the bearing's outer race is a tight fit in the casing, the aluminium casing can be heated to release its grip on the bearing. Aluminium will expand at a greater rate than the steel bearing outer race. There are several ways to do this, but avoid any localised extreme heat (such as a blow torch) - aluminium alloy has a low melting point.

● Approved methods of heating a casing are using a domestic oven (heated to 100°C) or immersing the casing in boiling water **(see illustration 5.12)**. Low temperature range localised heat sources such as a paint stripper heat gun or clothes iron can also be used **(see illustration 5.13)**. Alternatively, soak a rag in boiling water, wring it out and wrap it around the bearing housing.

> ⚠ **Warning: All of these methods require care in use to prevent scalding and burns to the hands. Wear protective gloves when handling hot components.**

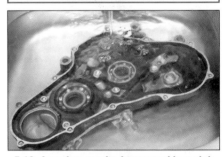

5.12 A casing can be immersed in a sink of boiling water to aid bearing removal

5.13 Using a localised heat source to aid bearing removal

● If heating the whole casing note that plastic components, such as the neutral switch, may suffer - remove them beforehand.

● After heating, remove the bearing as described above. You may find that the expansion is sufficient for the bearing to fall out of the casing under its own weight or with a light tap on the driver or socket.

● If necessary, the casing can be heated to aid bearing installation, and this is sometimes the recommended procedure if the motorcycle manufacturer has designed the housing and bearing fit with this intention.

● Installation of bearings can be eased by placing them in a freezer the night before installation. The steel bearing will contract slightly, allowing easy insertion in its housing. This is often useful when installing steering head outer races in the frame.

Bearing types and markings

● Plain shell bearings, ball bearings, needle roller bearings and tapered roller bearings will all be found on motorcycles (see illustrations 5.14 and 5.15). The ball and roller types are usually caged between an inner and outer race, but uncaged variations may be found.

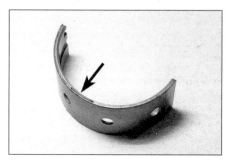

5.14 Shell bearings are either plain or grooved. They are usually identified by colour code (arrow)

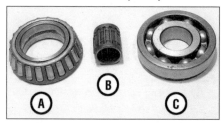

5.15 Tapered roller bearing (A), needle roller bearing (B) and ball journal bearing (C)

● Shell bearings (often called inserts) are usually found at the crankshaft main and connecting rod big-end where they are good at coping with high loads. They are made of a phosphor-bronze material and are impregnated with self-lubricating properties.
● Ball bearings and needle roller bearings consist of a steel inner and outer race with the balls or rollers between the races. They require constant lubrication by oil or grease and are good at coping with axial loads. Taper roller bearings consist of rollers set in a tapered cage set on the inner race; the outer race is separate. They are good at coping with axial loads and prevent movement along the shaft - a typical application is in the steering head.
● Bearing manufacturers produce bearings to ISO size standards and stamp one face of the bearing to indicate its internal and external diameter, load capacity and type (see illustration 5.16).
● Metal bushes are usually of phosphor-bronze material. Rubber bushes are used in suspension mounting eyes. Fibre bushes have also been used in suspension pivots.

5.16 Typical bearing marking

Bearing fault finding

● If a bearing outer race has spun in its housing, the housing material will be damaged. You can use a bearing locking compound to bond the outer race in place if damage is not too severe.
● Shell bearings will fail due to damage of their working surface, as a result of lack of lubrication, corrosion or abrasive particles in the oil (see illustration 5.17). Small particles of dirt in the oil may embed in the bearing material whereas larger particles will score the bearing and shaft journal. If a number of short journeys are made, insufficient heat will be generated to drive off condensation which has built up on the bearings.

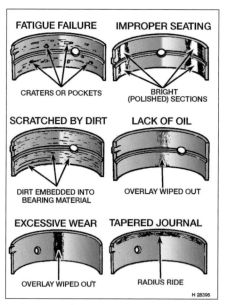

5.17 Typical bearing failures

● Ball and roller bearings will fail due to lack of lubrication or damage to the balls or rollers. Tapered-roller bearings can be damaged by overloading them. Unless the bearing is sealed on both sides, wash it in paraffin (kerosene) to remove all old grease then allow it to dry. Make a visual inspection looking to dented balls or rollers, damaged cages and worn or pitted races (see illustration 5.18).
● A ball bearing can be checked for wear by listening to it when spun. Apply a film of light oil to the bearing and hold it close to the ear - hold the outer race with one hand and spin the

5.18 Example of ball journal bearing with damaged balls and cages

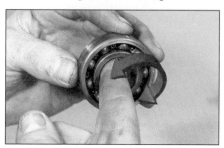

5.19 Hold outer race and listen to inner race when spun

inner race with the other hand (see illustration 5.19). The bearing should be almost silent when spun; if it grates or rattles it is worn.

6 Oil seals

Oil seal removal and installation

● Oil seals should be renewed every time a component is dismantled. This is because the seal lips will become set to the sealing surface and will not necessarily reseal.
● Oil seals can be prised out of position using a large flat-bladed screwdriver (see illustration 6.1). In the case of crankcase seals, check first that the seal is not lipped on the inside, preventing its removal with the crankcases joined.

6.1 Prise out oil seals with a large flat-bladed screwdriver

● New seals are usually installed with their marked face (containing the seal reference code) outwards and the spring side towards the fluid being retained. In certain cases, such as a two-stroke engine crankshaft seal, a double lipped seal may be used due to there being fluid or gas on each side of the joint.

● Use a bearing driver or socket which bears only on the outer hard edge of the seal to install it in the casing - tapping on the inner edge will damage the sealing lip.

Oil seal types and markings

● Oil seals are usually of the single-lipped type. Double-lipped seals are found where a liquid or gas is on both sides of the joint.
● Oil seals can harden and lose their sealing ability if the motorcycle has been in storage for a long period - renewal is the only solution.
● Oil seal manufacturers also conform to the ISO markings for seal size - these are moulded into the outer face of the seal (see illustration 6.2).

6.2 These oil seal markings indicate inside diameter, outside diameter and seal thickness

7 Gaskets and sealants

Types of gasket and sealant

● Gaskets are used to seal the mating surfaces between components and keep lubricants, fluids, vacuum or pressure contained within the assembly. Aluminium gaskets are sometimes found at the cylinder joints, but most gaskets are paper-based. If the mating surfaces of the components being joined are undamaged the gasket can be installed dry, although a dab of sealant or grease will be useful to hold it in place during assembly.
● RTV (Room Temperature Vulcanising) silicone rubber sealants cure when exposed to moisture in the atmosphere. These sealants are good at filling pits or irregular gasket faces, but will tend to be forced out of the joint under very high torque. They can be used to replace a paper gasket, but first make sure that the width of the paper gasket is not essential to the shimming of internal components. RTV sealants should not be used on components containing petrol (gasoline).
● Non-hardening, semi-hardening and hard setting liquid gasket compounds can be used with a gasket or between a metal-to-metal joint. Select the sealant to suit the application: universal non-hardening sealant can be used on virtually all joints; semi-hardening on joint faces which are rough or damaged; hard setting sealant on joints which require a permanent bond and are subjected to high temperature and pressure. **Note:** *Check first if the paper gasket has a bead of sealant*

impregnated in its surface before applying additional sealant.
● When choosing a sealant, make sure it is suitable for the application, particularly if being applied in a high-temperature area or in the vicinity of fuel. Certain manufacturers produce sealants in either clear, silver or black colours to match the finish of the engine. This has a particular application on motorcycles where much of the engine is exposed.
● Do not over-apply sealant. That which is squeezed out on the outside of the joint can be wiped off, whereas an excess of sealant on the inside can break off and clog oilways.

Breaking a sealed joint

● Age, heat, pressure and the use of hard setting sealant can cause two components to stick together so tightly that they are difficult to separate using finger pressure alone. Do not resort to using levers unless there is a pry point provided for this purpose (see illustration 7.1) or else the gasket surfaces will be damaged.
● Use a soft-faced hammer (see illustration 7.2) or a wood block and conventional hammer to strike the component near the mating surface. Avoid hammering against cast extremities since they may break off. If this method fails, try using a wood wedge between the two components.

> Caution: If the joint will not separate, double-check that you have removed all the fasteners.

7.1 If a pry point is provided, apply gently pressure with a flat-bladed screwdriver

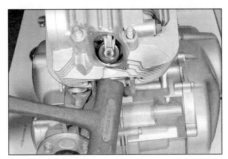

7.2 Tap around the joint with a soft-faced mallet if necessary - don't strike cooling fins

Removal of old gasket and sealant

● Paper gaskets will most likely come away complete, leaving only a few traces stuck

HAYNES HiNT

Most components have one or two hollow locating dowels between the two gasket faces. If a dowel cannot be removed, do not resort to gripping it with pliers - it will almost certainly be distorted. Install a close-fitting socket or Phillips screwdriver into the dowel and then grip the outer edge of the dowel to free it.

on the sealing faces of the components. It is imperative that all traces are removed to ensure correct sealing of the new gasket.
● Very carefully scrape all traces of gasket away making sure that the sealing surfaces are not gouged or scored by the scraper (see illustrations 7.3, 7.4 and 7.5). Stubborn deposits can be removed by spraying with an aerosol gasket remover. Final preparation of

7.3 Paper gaskets can be scraped off with a gasket scraper tool . . .

7.4 . . . a knife blade . . .

7.5 . . . or a household scraper

7.6 Fine abrasive paper is wrapped around a flat file to clean up the gasket face

7.7 A kitchen scourer can be used on stubborn deposits

the gasket surface can be made with very fine abrasive paper or a plastic kitchen scourer (see illustrations 7.6 and 7.7).

● Old sealant can be scraped or peeled off components, depending on the type originally used. Note that gasket removal compounds are available to avoid scraping the components clean; make sure the gasket remover suits the type of sealant used.

8 Chains

Breaking and joining final drive chains

● Drive chains for all but small bikes are continuous and do not have a clip-type connecting link. The chain must be broken using a chain breaker tool and the new chain securely riveted together using a new soft rivet-type link. Never use a clip-type connecting link instead of a rivet-type link, except in an emergency. Various chain breaking and riveting tools are available, either as separate tools or combined as illustrated in the accompanying photographs - read the instructions supplied with the tool carefully.

> ⚠️ **Warning: The need to rivet the new link pins correctly cannot be overstressed - loss of control of the motorcycle is very likely to result if the chain breaks in use.**

● Rotate the chain and look for the soft link. The soft link pins look like they have been

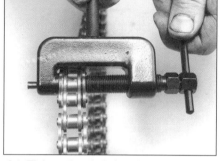

8.1 Tighten the chain breaker to push the pin out of the link . . .

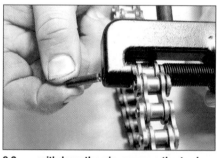

8.2 . . . withdraw the pin, remove the tool . . .

8.3 . . . and separate the chain link

deeply centre-punched instead of peened over like all the other pins (see illustration 8.9) and its sideplate may be a different colour. Position the soft link midway between the sprockets and assemble the chain breaker tool over one of the soft link pins (see illustration 8.1). Operate the tool to push the pin out through the chain (see illustration 8.2). On an O-ring chain, remove the O-rings (see illustration 8.3). Carry out the same procedure on the other soft link pin.

> **Caution: Certain soft link pins (particularly on the larger chains) may require their ends to be filed or ground off before they can be pressed out using the tool.**

● Check that you have the correct size and strength (standard or heavy duty) new soft link - do not reuse the old link. Look for the size marking on the chain sideplates (see illustration 8.10).

● Position the chain ends so that they are engaged over the rear sprocket. On an O-ring

8.4 Insert the new soft link, with O-rings, through the chain ends . . .

8.5 . . . install the O-rings over the pin ends . . .

8.6 . . . followed by the sideplate

chain, install a new O-ring over each pin of the link and insert the link through the two chain ends (see illustration 8.4). Install a new O-ring over the end of each pin, followed by the sideplate (with the chain manufacturer's marking facing outwards) (see illustrations 8.5 and 8.6). On an unsealed chain, insert the link through the two chain ends, then install the sideplate with the chain manufacturer's marking facing outwards.

● Note that it may not be possible to install the sideplate using finger pressure alone. If using a joining tool, assemble it so that the plates of the tool clamp the link and press the sideplate over the pins (see illustration 8.7). Otherwise, use two small sockets placed over

8.7 Push the sideplate into position using a clamp

8.8 Assemble the chain riveting tool over one pin at a time and tighten it fully

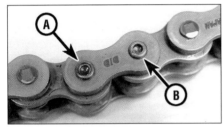

8.9 Pin end correctly riveted (A), pin end unriveted (B)

the rivet ends and two pieces of the wood between a G-clamp. Operate the clamp to press the sideplate over the pins.

● Assemble the joining tool over one pin (following the maker's instructions) and tighten the tool down to spread the pin end securely **(see illustrations 8.8 and 8.9)**. Do the same on the other pin.

 Warning: Check that the pin ends are secure and that there is no danger of the sideplate coming loose. If the pin ends are cracked the soft link must be renewed.

Final drive chain sizing

● Chains are sized using a three digit number, followed by a suffix to denote the chain type **(see illustration 8.10)**. Chain type is either standard or heavy duty (thicker sideplates), and also unsealed or O-ring/X-ring type.

● The first digit of the number relates to the pitch of the chain, ie the distance from the centre of one pin to the centre of the next pin **(see illustration 8.11)**. Pitch is expressed in eighths of an inch, as follows:

8.10 Typical chain size and type marking

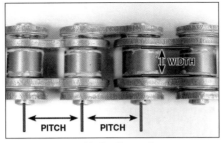

8.11 Chain dimensions

| Sizes commencing with a 4 (eg 428) have a pitch of 1/2 inch (12.7 mm) |
| Sizes commencing with a 5 (eg 520) have a pitch of 5/8 inch (15.9 mm) |
| Sizes commencing with a 6 (eg 630) have a pitch of 3/4 inch (19.1 mm) |

● The second and third digits of the chain size relate to the width of the rollers, again in imperial units, eg the 525 shown has 5/16 inch (7.94 mm) rollers **(see illustration 8.11)**.

9 Hoses

Clamping to prevent flow

● Small-bore flexible hoses can be clamped to prevent fluid flow whilst a component is worked on. Whichever method is used, ensure that the hose material is not permanently distorted or damaged by the clamp.

a) A brake hose clamp available from auto accessory shops **(see illustration 9.1)**.
b) A wingnut type hose clamp **(see illustration 9.2)**.

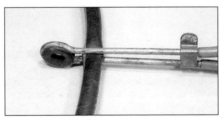

9.1 Hoses can be clamped with an automotive brake hose clamp . . .

9.2 . . . a wingnut type hose clamp . . .

c) Two sockets placed each side of the hose and held with straight-jawed self-locking grips **(see illustration 9.3)**.
d) Thick card each side of the hose held between straight-jawed self-locking grips **(see illustration 9.4)**.

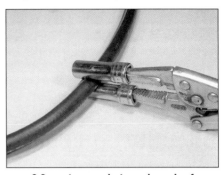

9.3 . . . two sockets and a pair of self-locking grips . . .

9.4 . . . or thick card and self-locking grips

Freeing and fitting hoses

● Always make sure the hose clamp is moved well clear of the hose end. Grip the hose with your hand and rotate it whilst pulling it off the union. If the hose has hardened due to age and will not move, slit it with a sharp knife and peel its ends off the union **(see illustration 9.5)**.

● Resist the temptation to use grease or soap on the unions to aid installation; although it helps the hose slip over the union it will equally aid the escape of fluid from the joint. It is preferable to soften the hose ends in hot water and wet the inside surface of the hose with water or a fluid which will evaporate.

9.5 Cutting a coolant hose free with a sharp knife

Introduction

In less time than it takes to read this introduction, a thief could steal your motorcycle. Returning only to find your bike has gone is one of the worst feelings in the world. Even if the motorcycle is insured against theft, once you've got over the initial shock, you will have the inconvenience of dealing with the police and your insurance company.

The motorcycle is an easy target for the professional thief and the joyrider alike and the official figures on motorcycle theft make for depressing reading; on average a motor-cycle is stolen every 16 minutes in the UK!

Motorcycle thefts fall into two categories, those stolen 'to order' and those taken by opportunists. The thief stealing to order will be on the look out for a specific make and model and will go to extraordinary lengths to obtain that motorcycle. The opportunist thief on the other hand will look for easy targets which can be stolen with the minimum of effort and risk.

Whilst it is never going to be possible to make your machine 100% secure, it is estimated that around half of all stolen motorcycles are taken by opportunist thieves. Remember that the opportunist thief is always on the look out for the easy option: if there are two similar motorcycles parked side-by-side, they will target the one with the lowest level of security. By taking a few precautions, you can reduce the chances of your motorcycle being stolen.

Security equipment

There are many specialised motorcycle security devices available and the following text summarises their applications and their good and bad points.

Once you have decided on the type of security equipment which best suits your needs, we recommended that you read one of the many equipment tests regularly carried out by the motorcycle press. These tests

Ensure the lock and chain you buy is of good quality and long enough to shackle your bike to a solid object

compare the products from all the major manufacturers and give impartial ratings on their effectiveness, value-for-money and ease of use.

No one item of security equipment can provide complete protection. It is highly recommended that two or more of the items described below are combined to increase the security of your motorcycle (a lock and chain plus an alarm system is just about ideal). The more security measures fitted to the bike, the less likely it is to be stolen.

Lock and chain

Pros: *Very flexible to use; can be used to secure the motorcycle to almost any immovable object. On some locks and chains, the lock can be used on its own as a disc lock (see below).*

Cons: *Can be very heavy and awkward to carry on the motorcycle, although some types*

will be supplied with a carry bag which can be strapped to the pillion seat.

● Heavy-duty chains and locks are an excellent security measure **(see illustration 1).** Whenever the motorcycle is parked, use the lock and chain to secure the machine to a solid, immovable object such as a post or railings. This will prevent the machine from being ridden away or being lifted into the back of a van.

● When fitting the chain, always ensure the chain is routed around the motorcycle frame or swingarm **(see illustrations 2 and 3).** Never merely pass the chain around one of the wheel rims; a thief may unbolt the wheel and lift the rest of the machine into a van, leaving you with just the wheel! Try to avoid having excess chain free, thus making it difficult to use cutting tools, and keep the chain and lock off the ground to prevent thieves attacking it with a cold chisel. Position the lock so that its lock barrel is facing downwards; this will make it harder for the thief to attack the lock mechanism.

Pass the chain through the bike's frame, rather than just through a wheel . . .

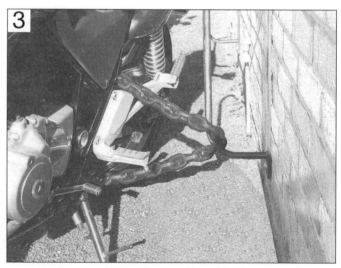

. . . and loop it around a solid object

U-locks

Pros: *Highly effective deterrent which can be used to secure the bike to a post or railings. Most U-locks come with a carrier which allows the lock to be easily carried on the bike.*

Cons: *Not as flexible to use as a lock and chain.*

● These are solid locks which are similar in use to a lock and chain. U-locks are lighter than a lock and chain but not so flexible to use. The length and shape of the lock shackle limit the objects to which the bike can be secured **(see illustration 4)**.

Disc locks

Pros: *Small, light and very easy to carry; most can be stored underneath the seat.*

Cons: *Does not prevent the motorcycle being lifted into a van. Can be very embarrassing if*

U-locks can be used to secure the bike to a solid object – ensure you purchase one which is long enough

you forget to remove the lock before attempting to ride off!

● Disc locks are designed to be attached to the front brake disc. The lock passes through one of the holes in the disc and prevents the wheel rotating by jamming against the fork/brake caliper **(see illustration 5)**. Some are equipped with an alarm siren which sounds if the disc lock is moved; this not only acts as a theft deterrent but also as a handy reminder if you try to move the bike with the lock still fitted.

● Combining the disc lock with a length of cable which can be looped around a post or railings provides an additional measure of security **(see illustration 6)**.

Alarms and immobilisers

Pros: *Once installed it is completely hassle-free to use. If the system is 'Thatcham' or 'Sold Secure-approved', insurance companies may give you a discount.*

A typical disc lock attached through one of the holes in the disc

Cons: *Can be expensive to buy and complex to install. No system will prevent the motorcycle from being lifted into a van and taken away.*

● Electronic alarms and immobilisers are available to suit a variety of budgets. There are three different types of system available: pure alarms, pure immobilisers, and the more expensive systems which are combined alarm/immobilisers **(see illustration 7)**.
● An alarm system is designed to emit an audible warning if the motorcycle is being tampered with.
● An immobiliser prevents the motorcycle being started and ridden away by disabling its electrical systems.
● When purchasing an alarm/immobiliser system, check the cost of installing the system unless you are able to do it yourself. If the motorcycle is not used regularly, another consideration is the current drain of the system. All alarm/immobiliser systems are powered by the motorcycle's battery; purchasing a system with a very low current drain could prevent the battery losing its charge whilst the motorcycle is not being used.

A disc lock combined with a security cable provides additional protection

A typical alarm/immobiliser system

Indelible markings can be applied to most areas of the bike – always apply the manufacturer's sticker to warn off thieves

Chemically-etched code numbers can be applied to main body panels . . .

. . . again, always ensure that the kit manufacturer's sticker is applied in a prominent position

Security marking kits

Pros: *Very cheap and effective deterrent. Many insurance companies will give you a discount on your insurance premium if a recognised security marking kit is used on your motorcycle.*

Cons: *Does not prevent the motorcycle being stolen by joyriders.*

● There are many different types of security marking kits available. The idea is to mark as many parts of the motorcycle as possible with a unique security number **(see illustrations 8, 9 and 10)**. A form will be included with the kit to register your personal details and those of the motorcycle with the kit manufacturer. This register is made available to the police to help them trace the rightful owner of any motorcycle or components which they recover should all other forms of identification have been removed. Always apply the warning stickers provided with the kit to deter thieves.

Ground anchors, wheel clamps and security posts

Pros: *An excellent form of security which will deter all but the most determined of thieves.*

Cons: *Awkward to install and can be expensive.*

● Whilst the motorcycle is at home, it is a good idea to attach it securely to the floor or a solid wall, even if it is kept in a securely locked garage. Various types of ground anchors, security posts and wheel clamps are available for this purpose **(see illustration 11)**. These security devices are either bolted to a solid concrete or brick structure or can be cemented into the ground.

Permanent ground anchors provide an excellent level of security when the bike is at home

Security at home

A high percentage of motorcycle thefts are from the owner's home. Here are some things to consider whenever your motorcycle is at home:
● Where possible, always keep the motorcycle in a securely locked garage. Never rely solely on the standard lock on the garage door, these are usual hopelessly inadequate. Fit an additional locking mechanism to the door and consider having the garage alarmed. A security light, activated by a movement sensor, is also a good investment.

● Always secure the motorcycle to the ground or a wall, even if it is inside a securely locked garage.
● Do not regularly leave the motorcycle outside your home, try to keep it out of sight wherever possible. If a garage is not available, fit a motorcycle cover over the bike to disguise its true identity.
● It is not uncommon for thieves to follow a motorcyclist home to find out where the bike is kept. They will then return at a later date. Be aware of this whenever you are returning

home on your motorcycle. If you suspect you are being followed, do not return home, instead ride to a garage or shop and stop as a precaution.
● When selling a motorcycle, do not provide your home address or the location where the bike is normally kept. Arrange to meet the buyer at a location away from your home. Thieves have been known to pose as potential buyers to find out where motorcycles are kept and then return later to steal them.

Security away from the home

As well as fitting security equipment to your motorcycle here are a few general rules to follow whenever you park your motorcycle.
● Park in a busy, public place.
● Use car parks which incorporate security features, such as CCTV.

● At night, park in a well-lit area, preferably directly underneath a street light.
● Engage the steering lock.
● Secure the motorcycle to a solid, immovable object such as a post or railings with an additional lock. If this is not possible,

secure the bike to a friend's motorcycle. Some public parking places provide security loops for motorcycles.
● Never leave your helmet or luggage attached to the motorcycle. Take them with you at all times.

Lubricants and fluids

A wide range of lubricants, fluids and cleaning agents is available for motor-cycles. This is a guide as to what is available, its applications and properties.

Four-stroke engine oil

● Engine oil is without doubt the most important component of any four-stroke engine. Modern motorcycle engines place a lot of demands on their oil and choosing the right type is essential. Using an unsuitable oil will lead to an increased rate of engine wear and could result in serious engine damage. Before purchasing oil, always check the recommended oil specification given by the manufacturer. The manufacturer will state a recommended 'type or classification' and also a specific 'viscosity' range for engine oil.

● The oil 'type or classification' is identified by its API (American Petroleum Institute) rating. The API rating will be in the form of two letters, e.g. SG. The S identifies the oil as being suitable for use in a petrol (gasoline) engine (S stands for spark ignition) and the second letter, ranging from A to J, identifies the oil's performance rating. The later this letter, the higher the specification of the oil; for example API SG oil exceeds the requirements of API SF oil. **Note:** *On some oils there may also be a second rating consisting of another two letters, the first letter being C, e.g. API SF/CD. This rating indicates the oil is also suitable for use in a diesel engines (the C stands for compression ignition) and is thus of no relevance for motorcycle use.*

● The 'viscosity' of the oil is identified by its SAE (Society of Automotive Engineers) rating. All modern engines require multigrade oils and the SAE rating will consist of two numbers, the first followed by a W, e.g. 10W/40. The first number indicates the viscosity rating of the oil at low temperatures (W stands for winter – tested at –20°C) and the second number represents the viscosity of the oil at high temperatures (tested at 100°C). The lower the number, the thinner the oil. For example an oil with an SAE 10W/40 rating will give better cold starting and running than an SAE 15W/40 oil.

● As well as ensuring the 'type' and 'viscosity' of the oil match the recommendations, another consideration to make when buying engine oil is whether to purchase a standard mineral-based oil, a semi-synthetic oil (also known as a synthetic blend or synthetic-based oil) or a fully-synthetic oil. Although all oils will have a similar rating and viscosity, their cost will vary considerably; mineral-based oils are the cheapest, the fully-synthetic oils the most expensive with the semi-synthetic oils falling somewhere in-between. This decision is very much up to the owner, but it should be noted that modern synthetic oils have far better lubricating and cleaning qualities than traditional mineral-based oils and tend to retain these properties for far longer. Bearing in mind the operating conditions inside a modern, high-revving motorcycle engine it is highly recommended that a fully synthetic oil is used. The extra expense at each service could save you money in the long term by preventing premature engine wear.

● As a final note always ensure that the oil is specifically designed for use in motorcycle engines. Engine oils designed primarily for use in car engines sometimes contain additives or friction modifiers which could cause clutch slip on a motorcycle fitted with a wet-clutch.

Two-stroke engine oil

● Modern two-stroke engines, with their high power outputs, place high demands on their oil. If engine seizure is to be avoided it is essential that a high-quality oil is used. Two-stroke oils differ hugely from four-stroke oils. The oil lubricates only the crankshaft and piston(s) (the transmission has its own lubricating oil) and is used on a total-loss basis where it is burnt completely during the combustion process.

● The Japanese have recently introduced a classification system for two-stroke oils, the JASO rating. This rating is in the form of two letters, either FA, FB or FC – FA is the lowest classification and FC the highest. Ensure the oil being used meets or exceeds the recommended rating specified by the manufacturer.

● As well as ensuring the oil rating matches the recommendation, another consideration to make when buying engine oil is whether to purchase a standard mineral-based oil, a semi-synthetic oil (also known as a synthetic blend or synthetic-based oil) or a fully-synthetic oil. The cost of each type of oil varies considerably; mineral-based oils are the cheapest, the fully-synthetic oils the most expensive with the semi-synthetic oils falling somewhere in-between. This decision is very much up to the owner, but it should be noted that modern synthetic oils have far better lubricating properties and burn cleaner than traditional mineral-based oils. It is therefore recommended that a fully synthetic oil is used. The extra expense could save you money in the long term by preventing premature engine wear, engine performance will be improved, carbon deposits and exhaust smoke will be reduced.

● Always ensure that the oil is specifically designed for use in an injector system. Many high quality two-stroke oils are designed for competition use and need to be pre-mixed with fuel. These oils are of a much higher viscosity and are not designed to flow through the injector pumps used on road-going two-stroke motorcycles.

Transmission (gear) oil

● On a two-stroke engine, the transmission and clutch are lubricated by their own separate oil bath which must be changed in accordance with the Maintenance Schedule.
● Although the engine and transmission units of most four-strokes use a common lubrication supply, there are some exceptions where the engine and gearbox have separate oil reservoirs and a dry clutch is used.
● Motorcycle manufacturers will either recommend a monograde transmission oil or a four-stroke multigrade engine oil to lubricate the transmission.
● Transmission oils, or gear oils as they are often called, are designed specifically for use in transmission systems. The viscosity of these oils is represented by an SAE number, but the scale of measurement applied is different to that used to grade engine oils. As a rough guide a SAE90 gear oil will be of the same viscosity as an SAE50 engine oil.

Shaft drive oil

● On models equipped with shaft final drive, the shaft drive gears are will have their own oil supply. The manufacturer will state a recommended 'type or classification' and also a specific 'viscosity' range in the same manner as for four-stroke engine oil.
● Gear oil classification is given by the number which follows the API GL (GL standing for gear lubricant) rating, the higher the number, the higher the specification of the oil, e.g. API GL5 oil is a higher specification than API GL4 oil. Ensure the oil meets or

exceeds the classification specified and is of the correct viscosity. The viscosity of gear oils is also represented by an SAE number but the scale of measurement used is different to that used to grade engine oils. As a rough guide an SAE90 gear oil will be of the same viscosity as an SAE50 engine oil.
● If the use of an EP (Extreme Pressure) gear oil is specified, ensure the oil purchased is suitable.

Fork oil and suspension fluid

● Conventional telescopic front forks are hydraulic and require fork oil to work. To ensure the forks function correctly, the fork oil must be changed in accordance with the Maintenance Schedule.
● Fork oil is available in a variety of viscosities, identified by their SAE rating; fork oil ratings vary from light (SAE 5) to heavy (SAE 30). When purchasing fork oil, ensure the viscosity rating matches that specified by the manufacturer.
● Some lubricant manufacturers also produce a range of high-quality suspension fluids which are very similar to fork oil but are designed mainly for competition use. These fluids may have a different viscosity rating system which is not to be confused with the SAE rating of normal fork oil. Refer to the manufacturer's instructions if in any doubt.

Brake and clutch fluid

● All disc brake systems and some clutch systems are hydraulically operated. To ensure correct operation, the hydraulic fluid must be changed in accordance with the Maintenance Schedule.
● Brake and clutch fluid is classified by its DOT rating with most motorcycle manufacturers specifying DOT 3 or 4 fluid. Both fluid types are glycol-based and can be mixed together without adverse effect; DOT 4 fluid exceeds the requirements of DOT 3

fluid. Although it is safe to use DOT 4 fluid in a system designed for use with DOT 3 fluid, never use DOT 3 fluid in a system which specifies the use of DOT 4 as this will adversely affect the system's performance. The type required for the system will be marked on the fluid reservoir cap.
● Some manufacturers also produce a DOT 5 hydraulic fluid. DOT 5 hydraulic fluid is silicone-based and is not compatible with the glycol-based DOT 3 and 4 fluids. Never mix DOT 5 fluid with DOT 3 or 4 fluid as this will seriously affect the performance of the hydraulic system.

Coolant/antifreeze

● When purchasing coolant/antifreeze, always ensure it is suitable for use in an aluminium engine and contains corrosion inhibitors to prevent possible blockages of the internal coolant passages of the system. As a general rule, most coolants are designed to be used neat and should not be diluted whereas antifreeze can be mixed with distilled water to provide a coolant solution of the required strength. Refer to the manufacturer's instructions on the bottle.
● Ensure the coolant is changed in accordance with the Maintenance Schedule.

Chain lube

● Chain lube is an aerosol-type spray lubricant specifically designed for use on motorcycle final drive chains. Chain lube has two functions, to minimise friction between the final drive chain and sprockets and to prevent corrosion of the chain. Regular use of a good-quality chain lube will extend the life of the drive chain and sprockets and thus maximise the power being transmitted from the transmission to the rear wheel.
● When using chain lube, always allow some time for the solvents in the lube to evaporate before riding the motorcycle. This will minimise the amount of lube which will

'fling' off from the chain when the motorcycle is used. If the motorcycle is equipped with an 'O-ring' chain, ensure the chain lube is labelled as being suitable for use on 'O-ring' chains.

Degreasers and solvents

● There are many different types of solvents and degreasers available to remove the grime and grease which accumulate around the motorcycle during normal use. Degreasers and solvents are usually available as an aerosol-type spray or as a liquid which you apply with a brush. Always closely follow the manufacturer's instructions and wear eye protection during use. Be aware that many solvents are flammable and may give off noxious fumes; take adequate precautions when using them (see Safety First!).
● For general cleaning, use one of the many solvents or degreasers available from most motorcycle accessory shops. These solvents are usually applied then left for a certain time before being washed off with water.

Brake cleaner is a solvent specifically designed to remove all traces of oil, grease and dust from braking system components. Brake cleaner is designed to evaporate quickly and leaves behind no residue.

Carburettor cleaner is an aerosol-type solvent specifically designed to clear carburettor blockages and break down the hard deposits and gum often found inside carburettors during overhaul.

Contact cleaner is an aerosol-type solvent designed for cleaning electrical components. The cleaner will remove all traces of oil and dirt from components such as switch contacts or fouled spark plugs and then dry, leaving behind no residue.

Gasket remover is an aerosol-type solvent designed for removing stubborn gaskets from engine components during overhaul. Gasket remover will minimise the amount of scraping required to remove the gasket and therefore reduce the risk of damage to the mating surface.

Spray lubricants

● Aerosol-based spray lubricants are widely available and are excellent for lubricating lever pivots and exposed cables and switches. Try to use a lubricant which is of the dry-film type as the fluid evaporates, leaving behind a dry-film of lubricant. Lubricants which leave behind an oily residue will attract dust and dirt which will increase the rate of wear of the cable/ lever.

● Most lubricants also act as a moisture dispersant and a penetrating fluid. This means they can also be used to 'dry out' electrical components such as wiring connectors or switches as well as helping to free seized fasteners.

Greases

● Grease is used to lubricate many of the pivot-points. A good-quality multi-purpose grease is suitable for most applications but some manufacturers will specify the use of specialist greases for use on components such as swingarm and suspension linkage bushes. These specialist greases can be purchased from most motorcycle (or car) accessory shops; commonly specified types include molybdenum disulphide grease, lithium-based grease, graphite-based grease, silicone-based grease and high-temperature copper-based grease.

Gasket sealing compounds

● Gasket sealing compounds can be used in conjunction with gaskets, to improve their sealing capabilities, or on their own to seal metal-to-metal joints. Depending on their type, sealing compounds either set hard or stay relatively soft and pliable.

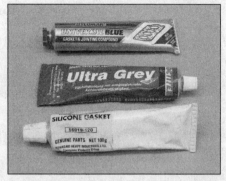

● When purchasing a gasket sealing compound, ensure that it is designed specifically for use on an internal combustion engine. General multi-purpose sealants available from DIY stores may appear visibly similar but they are not designed to withstand the extreme heat or contact with fuel and oil encountered when used on an engine (see 'Tools and Workshop Tips' for further information).

Thread locking compound

● Thread locking compounds are used to secure certain threaded fasteners in position to prevent them from loosening due to vibration. Thread locking compounds can be purchased from most motorcycle (and car) accessory shops. Ensure the threads of the both components are completely clean and dry before sparingly applying the locking compound (see 'Tools and Workshop Tips' for further information).

Fuel additives

● Fuel additives which protect and clean the fuel system components are widely available. These additives are designed to remove all traces of deposits that build up on the carburettors/injectors and prevent wear, helping the fuel system to operate more efficiently. If a fuel additive is being used, check that it is suitable for use with your motorcycle, especially if your motorcycle is equipped with a catalytic converter.

● Octane boosters are also available. These additives are designed to improve the performance of highly-tuned engines being run on normal pump-fuel and are of no real use on standard motorcycles.

About the MOT Test

In the UK, all vehicles more than three years old are subject to an annual test to ensure that they meet minimum safety requirements. A current test certificate must be issued before a machine can be used on public roads, and is required before a road fund licence can be issued. Riding without a current test certificate will also invalidate your insurance.

For most owners, the MOT test is an annual cause for anxiety, and this is largely due to owners not being sure what needs to be checked prior to submitting the motorcycle for testing. The simple answer is that a fully roadworthy motorcycle will have no difficulty in passing the test.

This is a guide to getting your motorcycle through the MOT test. Obviously it will not be possible to examine the motorcycle to the same standard as the professional MOT tester, particularly in view of the equipment required for some of the checks. However, working through the following procedures will enable you to identify any problem areas before submitting the motorcycle for the test.

It has only been possible to summarise the test requirements here, based on the regulations in force at the time of printing. Test standards are becoming increasingly stringent, although there are some exemptions for older vehicles. More information about the MOT test can be obtained from the TSO publications, *How Safe is your Motorcycle* and *The MOT Inspection Manual for Motorcycle Testing*.

Many of the checks require that one of the wheels is raised off the ground. If the motorcycle doesn't have a centre stand, note that an auxiliary stand will be required. Additionally, the help of an assistant may prove useful.

Certain exceptions apply to machines under 50 cc, machines without a lighting system, and Classic bikes - if in doubt about any of the requirements listed below seek confirmation from an MOT tester prior to submitting the motorcycle for the test.

Check that the frame number is clearly visible.

Electrical System

Lights, turn signals, horn and reflector

● With the ignition on, check the operation of the following electrical components. **Note:** *The electrical components on certain small-capacity machines are powered by the generator, requiring that the engine is run for this check.*

a) *Headlight and tail light. Check that both illuminate in the low and high beam switch positions.*

b) *Position lights. Check that the front position (or sidelight) and tail light illuminate in this switch position.*

c) *Turn signals. Check that all flash at the correct rate, and that the warning light(s) function correctly. Check that the turn signal switch works correctly.*

d) *Hazard warning system (where fitted). Check that all four turn signals flash in this switch position.*

e) *Brake stop light. Check that the light comes on when the front and rear brakes are independently applied. Models first used on or after 1st April 1986 must have a brake light switch on each brake.*

f) *Horn. Check that the sound is continuous and of reasonable volume.*

● Check that there is a red reflector on the rear of the machine, either mounted separately or as part of the tail light lens.

● Check the condition of the headlight, tail light and turn signal lenses.

Headlight beam height

● The MOT tester will perform a headlight beam height check using specialised beam setting equipment **(see illustration 1)**. This equipment will not be available to the home mechanic, but if you suspect that the headlight is incorrectly set or may have been maladjusted in the past, you can perform a rough test as follows.

● Position the bike in a straight line facing a brick wall. The bike must be off its stand, upright and with a rider seated. Measure the height from the ground to the centre of the headlight and mark a horizontal line on the wall at this height. Position the motorcycle 3.8 metres from the wall and draw a vertical

Headlight beam height checking equipment

line up the wall central to the centreline of the motorcycle. Switch to dipped beam and check that the beam pattern falls slightly lower than the horizontal line and to the left of the vertical line **(see illustration 2)**.

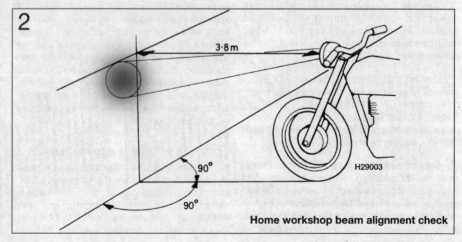

Home workshop beam alignment check

Exhaust System and Final Drive

Exhaust

● Check that the exhaust mountings are secure and that the system does not foul any of the rear suspension components.
● Start the motorcycle. When the revs are increased, check that the exhaust is neither holed nor leaking from any of its joints. On a linked system, check that the collector box is not leaking due to corrosion.

● Note that the exhaust decibel level ("loudness" of the exhaust) is assessed at the discretion of the tester. If the motorcycle was first used on or after 1st January 1985 the silencer must carry the BSAU 193 stamp, or a marking relating to its make and model, or be of OE (original equipment) manufacture. If the silencer is marked NOT FOR ROAD USE, RACING USE ONLY or similar, it will fail the MOT.

Final drive

● On chain or belt drive machines, check that the chain/belt is in good condition and does not have excessive slack. Also check that the sprocket is securely mounted on the rear wheel hub. Check that the chain/belt guard is in place.
● On shaft drive bikes, check for oil leaking from the drive unit and fouling the rear tyre.

Steering and Suspension

Steering

● With the front wheel raised off the ground, rotate the steering from lock to lock. The handlebar or switches must not contact the fuel tank or be close enough to trap the rider's hand. Problems can be caused by damaged lock stops on the lower yoke and frame, or by the fitting of non-standard handlebars.
● When performing the lock to lock check, also ensure that the steering moves freely without drag or notchiness. Steering movement can be impaired by poorly routed cables, or by overtight head bearings or worn bvearings. The tester will perform a check of the steering head bearing lower race by mounting the front wheel on a surface plate, then performing a lock to

lock check with the weight of the machine on the lower bearing (see illustration 3).
● Grasp the fork sliders (lower legs) and attempt to push and pull on the forks

Front wheel mounted on a surface plate for steering head bearing lower race check

(see illustration 4). Any play in the steering head bearings will be felt. Note that in extreme cases, wear of the front fork bushes can be misinterpreted for head bearing play.
● Check that the handlebars are securely mounted.
● Check that the handlebar grip rubbers are secure. They should by bonded to the bar left end and to the throttle cable pulley on the right end.

Front suspension

● With the motorcycle off the stand, hold the front brake on and pump the front forks up and down (see illustration 5). Check that they are adequately damped.

Checking the steering head bearings for freeplay

Hold the front brake on and pump the front forks up and down to check operation

Inspect the area around the fork dust seal for oil leakage (arrow)

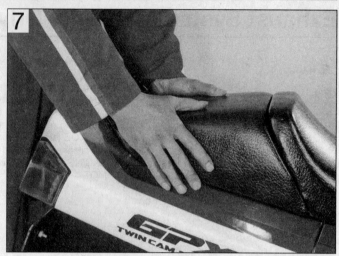

Bounce the rear of the motorcycle to check rear suspension operation

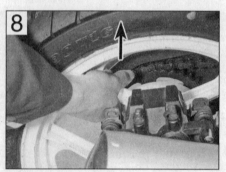

Checking for rear suspension linkage play

● Inspect the area above and around the front fork oil seals (see illustration 6). There should be no sign of oil on the fork tube (stanchion) nor leaking down the slider (lower leg). On models so equipped, check that there is no oil leaking from the anti-dive units.

● On models with swingarm front suspension, check that there is no freeplay in the linkage when moved from side to side.

Rear suspension

● With the motorcycle off the stand and an assistant supporting the motorcycle by its handlebars, bounce the rear suspension (see illustration 7). Check that the suspension components do not foul on any of the cycle parts and check that the shock absorber(s) provide adequate damping.

● Visually inspect the shock absorber(s) and check that there is no sign of oil leakage from its damper. This is somewhat restricted on certain single shock models due to the location of the shock absorber.

● With the rear wheel raised off the ground, grasp the wheel at the highest point and attempt to pull it up (see illustration 8). Any play in the swingarm pivot or suspension linkage bearings will be felt as movement. Note: Do not confuse play with actual suspension movement. Failure to lubricate suspension linkage bearings can lead to bearing failure (see illustration 9).

● With the rear wheel raised off the ground, grasp the swingarm ends and attempt to move the swingarm from side to side and forwards and backwards - any play indicates wear of the swingarm pivot bearings (see illustration 10).

Worn suspension linkage pivots (arrows) are usually the cause of play in the rear suspension

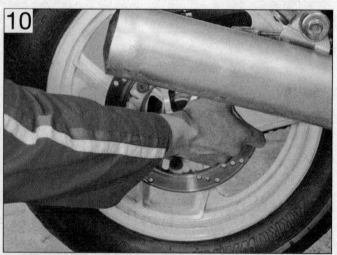

Grasp the swingarm at the ends to check for play in its pivot bearings

Brake pad wear can usually be viewed without removing the caliper. Most pads have wear indicator grooves (arrowed) and some also have indicator tangs or cut-outs.

On drum brakes, check the angle of the operating lever with the brake fully applied. Most drum brakes have a wear indicator pointer or scale.

Brakes, Wheels and Tyres

Brakes

● With the wheel raised off the ground, apply the brake then free it off, and check that the wheel is about to revolve freely without brake drag.
● On disc brakes, examine the disc itself. Check that it is securely mounted and not cracked.
● On disc brakes, view the pad material through the caliper mouth and check that the pads are not worn down beyond the limit **(see illustration 11)**.
● On drum brakes, check that when the brake is applied the angle between the operating lever and cable or rod is not too great **(see illustration 12)**. Check also that the operating lever doesn't foul any other components.
● On disc brakes, examine the flexible hoses from top to bottom. Have an assistant hold the brake on so that the fluid in the hose is under pressure, and check that there is no sign of fluid leakage, bulges or cracking. If there are any metal brake pipes or unions, check that these are free from corrosion and damage. Where a brake-linked anti-dive system is fitted, check the hoses to the anti-dive in a similar manner.
● Check that the rear brake torque arm is secure and that its fasteners are secured by self-locking nuts or castellated nuts with split-pins or R-pins **(see illustration 13)**.
● On models with ABS, check that the self-check warning light in the instrument panel works.
● The MOT tester will perform a test of the motorcycle's braking efficiency based on a calculation of rider and motorcycle weight. Although this cannot be carried out at home, you can at least ensure that the braking systems are properly maintained. For hydraulic disc brakes, check the fluid level, lever/pedal feel (bleed of air if its spongy) and pad material. For drum brakes, check adjustment, cable or rod operation and shoe lining thickness.

Wheels and tyres

● Check the wheel condition. Cast wheels should be free from cracks and if of the built-up design, all fasteners should be secure. Spoked wheels should be checked for broken, corroded, loose or bent spokes.
● With the wheel raised off the ground, spin the wheel and visually check that the tyre and wheel run true. Check that the tyre does not foul the suspension or mudguards.
● With the wheel raised off the ground, grasp the wheel and attempt to move it about the axle (spindle) **(see illustration 14)**. Any play felt here indicates wheel bearing failure.

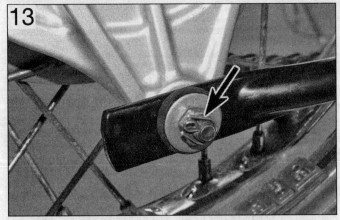

Brake torque arm must be properly secured at both ends

Check for wheel bearing play by trying to move the wheel about the axle (spindle)

Checking the tyre tread depth

Tyre direction of rotation arrow can be found on tyre sidewall

Castellated type wheel axle (spindle) nut must be secured by a split pin or R-pin

Two straightedges are used to check wheel alignment

● Check the tyre tread depth, tread condition and sidewall condition **(see illustration 15)**.
● Check the tyre type. Front and rear tyre types must be compatible and be suitable for road use. Tyres marked NOT FOR ROAD USE, COMPETITION USE ONLY or similar, will fail the MOT.

● If the tyre sidewall carries a direction of rotation arrow, this must be pointing in the direction of normal wheel rotation **(see illustration 16)**.
● Check that the wheel axle (spindle) nuts (where applicable) are properly secured. A self-locking nut or castellated nut with a split-pin or R-pin can be used **(see illustration 17)**.
● Wheel alignment is checked with the motorcycle off the stand and a rider seated. With the front wheel pointing straight ahead, two perfectly straight lengths of metal or wood and placed against the sidewalls of both tyres **(see illustration 18)**. The gap each side of the front tyre must be equidistant on both sides. Incorrect wheel alignment may be due to a cocked rear wheel (often as the result of poor chain adjustment) or in extreme cases, a bent frame.

General checks and condition

● Check the security of all major fasteners, bodypanels, seat, fairings (where fitted) and mudguards.

● Check that the rider and pillion footrests, handlebar levers and brake pedal are securely mounted.

● Check for corrosion on the frame or any load-bearing components. If severe, this may affect the structure, particularly under stress.

Sidecars

A motorcycle fitted with a sidecar requires additional checks relating to the stability of the machine and security of attachment and swivel joints, plus specific wheel alignment (toe-in) requirements. Additionally, tyre and lighting requirements differ from conventional motorcycle use. Owners are advised to check MOT test requirements with an official test centre.

Preparing for storage

Before you start

If repairs or an overhaul is needed, see that this is carried out now rather than left until you want to ride the bike again.

Give the bike a good wash and scrub all dirt from its underside. Make sure the bike dries completely before preparing for storage.

Engine

● Remove the spark plug(s) and lubricate the cylinder bores with approximately a teaspoon of motor oil using a spout-type oil can (see illustration 1). Reinstall the spark plug(s). Crank the engine over a couple of times to coat the piston rings and bores with oil. If the bike has a kickstart, use this to turn the engine over. If not, flick the kill switch to the OFF position and crank the engine over on the starter (see illustration 2). If the nature on the ignition system prevents the starter operating with the kill switch in the OFF position, remove

the spark plugs and fit them back in their caps; ensure that the plugs are earthed (grounded) against the cylinder head when the starter is operated (see illustration 3).

⚠️ *Warning: It is important that the plugs are earthed (grounded) away from the spark plug holes otherwise there is a risk of atomised fuel from the cylinders igniting.*

> **HAYNES HINT**
> *On a single cylinder four-stroke engine, you can seal the combustion chamber completely by positioning the piston at TDC on the compression stroke.*

● Drain the carburettor(s) otherwise there is a risk of jets becoming blocked by gum deposits from the fuel (see illustration 4).

● If the bike is going into long-term storage, consider adding a fuel stabiliser to the fuel in the tank. If the tank is drained completely, corrosion of its internal surfaces may occur if left unprotected for a long period. The tank can be treated with a rust preventative especially for this purpose. Alternatively, remove the tank and pour half a litre of motor oil into it, install the filler cap and shake the tank to coat its internals with oil before draining off the excess. The same effect can also be achieved by spraying WD40 or a similar water-dispersant around the inside of the tank via its flexible nozzle.

● Make sure the cooling system contains the correct mix of antifreeze. Antifreeze also contains important corrosion inhibitors.

● The air intakes and exhaust can be sealed off by covering or plugging the openings. Ensure that you do not seal in any condensation; run the engine until it is hot,

Squirt a drop of motor oil into each cylinder

Flick the kill switch to OFF . . .

. . . and ensure that the metal bodies of the plugs (arrows) are earthed against the cylinder head

Connect a hose to the carburettor float chamber drain stub (arrow) and unscrew the drain screw

Exhausts can be sealed off with a plastic bag

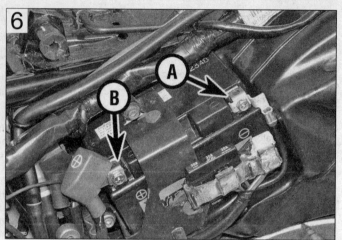

Disconnect the negative lead (A) first, followed by the positive lead (B)

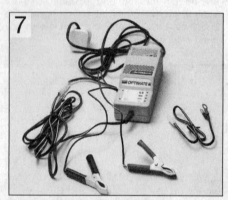

Use a suitable battery charger - this kit also assess battery condition

then switch off and allow to cool. Tape a piece of thick plastic over the silencer end(s) (see illustration 5). Note that some advocate pouring a tablespoon of motor oil into the silencer(s) before sealing them off.

Battery

● Remove it from the bike - in extreme cases of cold the battery may freeze and crack its case (see illustration 6).

● Check the electrolyte level and top up if necessary (conventional refillable batteries). Clean the terminals.
● Store the battery off the motorcycle and away from any sources of fire. Position a wooden block under the battery if it is to sit on the ground.
● Give the battery a trickle charge for a few hours every month (see illustration 7).

Tyres

● Place the bike on its centrestand or an auxiliary stand which will support the motorcycle in an upright position. Position wood blocks under the tyres to keep them off the ground and to provide insulation from damp. If the bike is being put into long-term storage, ideally both tyres should be off the ground; not only will this protect the tyres, but will also ensure that no load is placed on the steering head or wheel bearings.
● Deflate each tyre by 5 to 10 psi, no more or the beads may unseat from the rim, making subsequent inflation difficult on tubeless tyres.

Pivots and controls

● Lubricate all lever, pedal, stand and footrest

pivot points. If grease nipples are fitted to the rear suspension components, apply lubricant to the pivots.
● Lubricate all control cables.

Cycle components

● Apply a wax protectant to all painted and plastic components. Wipe off any excess, but don't polish to a shine. Where fitted, clean the screen with soap and water.
● Coat metal parts with Vaseline (petroleum jelly). When applying this to the fork tubes, do not compress the forks otherwise the seals will rot from contact with the Vaseline.
● Apply a vinyl cleaner to the seat.

Storage conditions

● Aim to store the bike in a shed or garage which does not leak and is free from damp.
● Drape an old blanket or bedspread over the bike to protect it from dust and direct contact with sunlight (which will fade paint). This also hides the bike from prying eyes. Beware of tight-fitting plastic covers which may allow condensation to form and settle on the bike.

Getting back on the road

Engine and transmission

● Change the oil and replace the oil filter. If this was done prior to storage, check that the oil hasn't emulsified - a thick whitish substance which occurs through condensation.
● Remove the spark plugs. Using a spout-type oil can, squirt a few drops of oil into the cylinder(s). This will provide initial lubrication as the piston rings and bores comes back into contact. Service the spark plugs, or fit new ones, and install them in the engine.

● Check that the clutch isn't stuck on. The plates can stick together if left standing for some time, preventing clutch operation. Engage a gear and try rocking the bike back and forth with the clutch lever held against the handlebar. If this doesn't work on cable-operated clutches, hold the clutch lever back against the handlebar with a strong elastic band or cable tie for a couple of hours (see illustration 8).
● If the air intakes or silencer end(s) were blocked off, remove the bung or cover used.
● If the fuel tank was coated with a rust

Hold clutch lever back against the handlebar with elastic bands or a cable tie

preventative, oil or a stabiliser added to the fuel, drain and flush the tank and dispose of the fuel sensibly. If no action was taken with the fuel tank prior to storage, it is advised that the old fuel is disposed of since it will go off over a period of time. Refill the fuel tank with fresh fuel.

Frame and running gear

● Oil all pivot points and cables.
● Check the tyre pressures. They will definitely need inflating if pressures were reduced for storage.
● Lubricate the final drive chain (where applicable).
● Remove any protective coating applied to the fork tubes (stanchions) since this may well destroy the fork seals. If the fork tubes weren't protected and have picked up rust spots, remove them with very fine abrasive paper and refinish with metal polish.
● Check that both brakes operate correctly. Apply each brake hard and check that it's not possible to move the motorcycle forwards, then check that the brake frees off again once released. Brake caliper pistons can stick due to corrosion around the piston head, or on the sliding caliper types, due to corrosion of the slider pins. If the brake doesn't free after repeated operation, take the caliper off for examination. Similarly drum brakes can stick

due to a seized operating cam, cable or rod linkage.
● If the motorcycle has been in long-term storage, renew the brake fluid and clutch fluid (where applicable).
● Depending on where the bike has been stored, the wiring, cables and hoses may have been nibbled by rodents. Make a visual check and investigate disturbed wiring loom tape.

Battery

● If the battery has been previously removal and given top up charges it can simply be reconnected. Remember to connect the positive cable first and the negative cable last.
● On conventional refillable batteries, if the battery has not received any attention, remove it from the motorcycle and check its electrolyte level. Top up if necessary then charge the battery. If the battery fails to hold a charge and a visual checks show heavy white sulphation of the plates, the battery is probably defective and must be renewed. This is particularly likely if the battery is old. Confirm battery condition with a specific gravity check.
● On sealed (MF) batteries, if the battery has not received any attention, remove it from the motorcycle and charge it according to the information on the battery case - if the battery fails to hold a charge it must be renewed.

Starting procedure

● If a kickstart is fitted, turn the engine over a couple of times with the ignition OFF to distribute oil around the engine. If no kickstart is fitted, flick the engine kill switch OFF and the ignition ON and crank the engine over a couple of times to work oil around the upper cylinder components. If the nature of the ignition system is such that the starter won't work with the kill switch OFF, remove the spark plugs, fit them back into their caps and earth (ground) their bodies on the cylinder head. Reinstall the spark plugs afterwards.
● Switch the kill switch to RUN, operate the choke and start the engine. If the engine won't start don't continue cranking the engine - not only will this flatten the battery, but the starter motor will overheat. Switch the ignition off and try again later. If the engine refuses to start, go through the fault finding procedures in this manual. **Note:** *If the bike has been in storage for a long time, old fuel or a carburettor blockage may be the problem. Gum deposits in carburettors can block jets - if a carburettor cleaner doesn't prove successful the carburettors must be dismantled for cleaning.*
● Once the engine has started, check that the lights, turn signals and horn work properly.
● Treat the bike gently for the first ride and check all fluid levels on completion. Settle the bike back into the maintenance schedule.

Conversion factors

Length (distance)

Inches (in)	x 25.4	= Millimetres (mm)	x 0.0394	=	Inches (in)
Feet (ft)	x 0.305	= Metres (m)	x 3.281	=	Feet (ft)
Miles	x 1.609	= Kilometres (km)	x 0.621	=	Miles

Volume (capacity)

Cubic inches (cu in; in³)	x 16.387	= Cubic centimetres (cc; cm³)	x 0.061	=	Cubic inches (cu in; in³)
Imperial pints (Imp pt)	x 0.568	= Litres (l)	x 1.76	=	Imperial pints (Imp pt)
Imperial quarts (Imp qt)	x 1.137	= Litres (l)	x 0.88	=	Imperial quarts (Imp qt)
Imperial quarts (Imp qt)	x 1.201	= US quarts (US qt)	x 0.833	=	Imperial quarts (Imp qt)
US quarts (US qt)	x 0.946	= Litres (l)	x 1.057	=	US quarts (US qt)
Imperial gallons (Imp gal)	x 4.546	= Litres (l)	x 0.22	=	Imperial gallons (Imp gal)
Imperial gallons (Imp gal)	x 1.201	= US gallons (US gal)	x 0.833	=	Imperial gallons (Imp gal)
US gallons (US gal)	x 3.785	= Litres (l)	x 0.264	=	US gallons (US gal)

Mass (weight)

Ounces (oz)	x 28.35	= Grams (g)	x 0.035	=	Ounces (oz)
Pounds (lb)	x 0.454	= Kilograms (kg)	x 2.205	=	Pounds (lb)

Force

Ounces-force (ozf; oz)	x 0.278	= Newtons (N)	x 3.6	=	Ounces-force (ozf; oz)
Pounds-force (lbf; lb)	x 4.448	= Newtons (N)	x 0.225	=	Pounds-force (lbf; lb)
Newtons (N)	x 0.1	= Kilograms-force (kgf; kg)	x 9.81	=	Newtons (N)

Pressure

Pounds-force per square inch (psi; lbf/in²; lb/in²)	x 0.070	= Kilograms-force per square centimetre (kgf/cm²; kg/cm²)	x 14.223	=	Pounds-force per square inch (psi; lbf/in²; lb/in²)
Pounds-force per square inch (psi; lbf/in²; lb/in²)	x 0.068	= Atmospheres (atm)	x 14.696	=	Pounds-force per square inch (psi; lbf/in²; lb/in²)
Pounds-force per square inch (psi; lbf/in²; lb/in²)	x 0.069	= Bars	x 14.5	=	Pounds-force per square inch (psi; lbf/in²; lb/in²)
Pounds-force per square inch (psi; lbf/in²; lb/in²)	x 6.895	= Kilopascals (kPa)	x 0.145	=	Pounds-force per square inch (psi; lbf/in²; lb/in²)
Kilopascals (kPa)	x 0.01	= Kilograms-force per square centimetre (kgf/cm²; kg/cm²)	x 98.1	=	Kilopascals (kPa)
Millibar (mbar)	x 100	= Pascals (Pa)	x 0.01	=	Millibar (mbar)
Millibar (mbar)	x 0.0145	= Pounds-force per square inch (psi; lbf/in²; lb/in²)	x 68.947	=	Millibar (mbar)
Millibar (mbar)	x 0.75	= Millimetres of mercury (mmHg)	x 1.333	=	Millibar (mbar)
Millibar (mbar)	x 0.401	= Inches of water (inH₂O)	x 2.491	=	Millibar (mbar)
Millimetres of mercury (mmHg)	x 0.535	= Inches of water (inH₂O)	x 1.868	=	Millimetres of mercury (mmHg)
Inches of water (inH₂O)	x 0.036	= Pounds-force per square inch (psi; lbf/in²; lb/in²)	x 27.68	=	Inches of water (inH₂O)

Torque (moment of force)

Pounds-force inches (lbf in; lb in)	x 1.152	= Kilograms-force centimetre (kgf cm; kg cm)	x 0.868	=	Pounds-force inches (lbf in; lb in)
Pounds-force inches (lbf in; lb in)	x 0.113	= Newton metres (Nm)	x 8.85	=	Pounds-force inches (lbf in; lb in)
Pounds-force inches (lbf in; lb in)	x 0.083	= Pounds-force feet (lbf ft; lb ft)	x 12	=	Pounds-force inches (lbf in; lb in)
Pounds-force feet (lbf ft; lb ft)	x 0.138	= Kilograms-force metres (kgf m; kg m)	x 7.233	=	Pounds-force feet (lbf ft; lb ft)
Pounds-force feet (lbf ft; lb ft)	x 1.356	= Newton metres (Nm)	x 0.738	=	Pounds-force feet (lbf ft; lb ft)
Newton metres (Nm)	x 0.102	= Kilograms-force metres (kgf m; kg m)	x 9.804	=	Newton metres (Nm)

Power

Horsepower (hp)	x 745.7	= Watts (W)	x 0.0013	=	Horsepower (hp)

Velocity (speed)

Miles per hour (miles/hr; mph)	x 1.609	= Kilometres per hour (km/hr; kph)	x 0.621	=	Miles per hour (miles/hr; mph)

Fuel consumption*

Miles per gallon, Imperial (mpg)	x 0.354	= Kilometres per litre (km/l)	x 2.825	=	Miles per gallon, Imperial (mpg)
Miles per gallon, US (mpg)	x 0.425	= Kilometres per litre (km/l)	x 2.352	=	Miles per gallon, US (mpg)

Temperature

Degrees Fahrenheit = (°C x 1.8) + 32   Degrees Celsius (Degrees Centigrade; °C) = (°F - 32) x 0.56

It is common practice to convert from miles per gallon (mpg) to litres/100 kilometres (l/100km), where mpg x l/100 km = 282

This Section provides an easy reference-guide to the more common faults that are likely to afflict your machine. Obviously, the opportunities are almost limitless for faults to occur as a result of obscure failures, and to try and cover all eventualities would require a book. Indeed, a number have been written on the subject.

Successful troubleshooting is not a mysterious 'black art' but the application of a bit of knowledge combined with a systematic and logical approach to the problem. Approach any troubleshooting by first accurately identifying the symptom and then checking through the list of possible causes, starting with the simplest or most obvious and progressing in stages to the most complex.

Take nothing for granted, but above all apply liberal quantities of common sense.

The main symptom of a fault is given in the text as a major heading below which are listed the various systems or areas which may contain the fault. Details of each possible cause for a fault and the remedial action to be taken are given, in brief, in the paragraphs below each heading. Further information should be sought in the relevant Chapter.

1 Engine doesn't start or is difficult to start

- ☐ Starter motor doesn't rotate
- ☐ Starter motor rotates but engine does not turn over
- ☐ Starter works but engine won't turn over (seized)
- ☐ No fuel flow
- ☐ Engine flooded
- ☐ No spark or weak spark
- ☐ Compression low
- ☐ Stalls after starting
- ☐ Rough idle

2 Poor running at low speed

- ☐ Spark weak
- ☐ Fuel/air mixture incorrect
- ☐ Compression low
- ☐ Poor acceleration

3 Poor running or no power at high speed

- ☐ Firing incorrect
- ☐ Fuel/air mixture incorrect
- ☐ Compression low
- ☐ Knocking or pinking
- ☐ Miscellaneous causes

4 Overheating

- ☐ Engine overheats
- ☐ Firing incorrect
- ☐ Fuel/air mixture incorrect
- ☐ Compression too high
- ☐ Engine load excessive
- ☐ Lubrication inadequate
- ☐ Miscellaneous causes

5 Clutch problems

- ☐ Clutch slipping
- ☐ Clutch not disengaging completely

6 Gearchanging problems

- ☐ Doesn't go into gear, or lever doesn't return
- ☐ Jumps out of gear
- ☐ Overselects

7 Abnormal engine noise

- ☐ Knocking or pinking
- ☐ Piston slap or rattling
- ☐ Valve noise
- ☐ Other noise

8 Abnormal driveline noise

- ☐ Clutch noise
- ☐ Transmission noise
- ☐ Final drive noise

9 Abnormal frame and suspension noise

- ☐ Front end noise
- ☐ Shock absorber noise
- ☐ Brake noise

10 Oil pressure warning light comes on

11 Excessive exhaust smoke

- ☐ White smoke
- ☐ Black smoke
- ☐ Brown smoke

12 Poor handling or stability

- ☐ Handlebar hard to turn
- ☐ Handlebar shakes or vibrates excessively
- ☐ Handlebar pulls to one side
- ☐ Poor shock absorbing qualities

13 Braking problems

- ☐ Brakes are spongy, don't hold
- ☐ Brake lever or pedal pulsates
- ☐ Brakes drag

14 Electrical problems

- ☐ Battery dead or weak
- ☐ Battery overcharged

1 Engine doesn't start or is difficult to start

Starter motor doesn't rotate

- [ ] Engine kill switch OFF.
- [ ] Fuse blown (Chapter 8).
- [ ] Battery voltage low. Check battery condition and recharge or replace battery (Chapter 8).
- [ ] Loose or corroded battery connections/terminals. Tighten or clean connections.
- [ ] Starter motor defective. Make sure the wiring to the starter is secure and free of corrosion. Replace or repair the motor if defective (Chapter 8).
- [ ] Starter relay defective. Make sure the wiring to relay is secure and free of corrosion. Test the operation of the relay, internal corrosion or arcing can cause the relay to not pass sufficient current to the starter motor even if it clicks when the start button is operated (Chapter 8).
- [ ] Starter switch not contacting. The contacts could be wet, corroded or dirty. Disassemble and clean the switch (Chapter 8).
- [ ] Wiring open or shorted. Check all wiring connections and harnesses to make sure that they are dry, tight and not corroded. Also check for broken or frayed wires that can cause a short to ground (earth) (see Wiring diagrams, Chapter 8).
- [ ] Ignition or kill switch defective. This is usually caused by water, corrosion, damage or excessive wear. The switches can be disassembled and cleaned with electrical contact cleaner. If cleaning does not help, replace the switches (Chapter 8).
- [ ] Faulty neutral switch, sidestand switch or clutch switch. Check the wiring to each switch and the switch itself (see Chapter 8).
- [ ] Faulty starter circuit diode (Chapter 8).
- [ ] Fuel injection system shutdown due to system fault (Chapter 4).

Starter motor rotates but engine does not turn over

- [ ] Starter clutch defective. Inspect and repair or replace with a new one (see Chapter 2A or 2B).
- [ ] Damaged idler or starter gears. Inspect and replace the damaged parts (see Chapter 2A or 2B).

Starter works but engine won't turn over (seized)

- [ ] Seized engine caused by one or more internally damaged components. Failure due to wear, abuse or lack of lubrication. Damage can include seized valves, rockers, camshaft, piston, crankshaft, connecting rod bearings, or transmission gears or bearings. Refer to Chapter 2A or 2BA or 2B for engine disassembly.

No fuel flow

- [ ] No fuel in tank.
- [ ] Fuel tank breather hose obstructed.
- [ ] Fuel pump faulty (see Chapter 4).
- [ ] Faulty fuel pump relay (250 models). Check the relay (see Chapter 4).
- [ ] Fuel filter blocked (see Chapter 4).
- [ ] Fuel hose kinked. Fit a new hose.
- [ ] Fuel injector clogged. If a machine has been unused for several months, the fuel turns to a varnish-like liquid, which can cause the injector needle to stick to its seat. Drain the tank and fuel system, ultrasonically clean or replace fuel injector (Chapter 4).

Engine flooded

- [ ] Injector needle valve worn or stuck open. A piece of dirt, rust or other debris can cause the needle to seat improperly, causing excess fuel to be admitted to the throttle body. In this case, the injector should be cleaned and the needle and seat inspected (see Chapter 4). If the needle and seat are worn, then the leaking will persist and the parts should be replaced with new ones.
- [ ] Starting technique incorrect. Under normal circumstances (i.e. if all the components of the fuel injection system are good) the machine should start with the throttle closed.

No spark or weak spark

- [ ] Ignition switch OFF.
- [ ] Engine kill switch turned to the OFF position.
- [ ] Ignition or kill switch shorted. This is usually caused by water, corrosion, damage or excessive wear. The switches can be disassembled and cleaned with electrical contact cleaner. If cleaning does not help, replace the switches (see Chapter 8).
- [ ] Battery voltage low. Check battery condition and recharge or replace battery (Chapter 8).
- [ ] Spark plug cap not making good contact. Make sure that the cap fits snugly over the plug.
- [ ] Spark plug dirty, defective or worn out. Identify reason for fouled plug using spark plug condition chart on the inside back cover and follow the plug maintenance procedures (see Chapter 1).
- [ ] Incorrect spark plug. Wrong type or heat range. Check and install correct plug (see Chapter 1).
- [ ] Ignition coil defective. Test and replace with new one if necessary (Chapter 4).
- [ ] Fuel injection system shutdown due to system fault (Chapter 4).
- [ ] Crankshaft position (CKP) sensor defective (see Chapter 4).
- [ ] Faulty sidestand switch (Chapter 8).
- [ ] Engine control module (ECM) defective (see Chapter 4).
- [ ] Wiring shorted or broken between:
  - a) Ignition switch and engine kill switch (or blown fuse)
  - b) ECM and engine kill switch
  - c) ECM and ignition coils
  - d) ECM and CKP sensor
- [ ] Make sure that all wiring connections are clean, dry and tight. Look for chafed and broken wires (see Chapters 4 and 8).

Compression low

- [ ] Spark plug loose. Remove the plug and inspect the threads. Reinstall and tighten securely (see Chapter 1).
- [ ] Cylinder head not sufficiently tightened down. If the cylinder head is suspected of being loose, then there's a chance that the gasket or head is damaged if the problem has persisted for any length of time. The camshaft holder nuts (125 engine) or cylinder head nuts (250 engine) should be tightened to the proper torque and in the correct sequence (Chapter 2A or 2B).
- [ ] Improper valve clearance. This means that the valve is not closing completely and compression pressure is leaking past the valve. Check and adjust the valve clearances (Chapter 1).
- [ ] Cylinder and/or piston worn. Excessive wear will cause compression pressure to leak past the rings. This is usually accompanied by worn rings as well. A top-end overhaul is necessary (Chapter 2A or 2B).
- [ ] Piston rings worn, weak, broken, or sticking. Broken or sticking piston rings usually indicate a lubrication or fuelling problem that causes excess carbon deposits to form on the piston and rings. Top-end overhaul is necessary (Chapter 2A or 2B).
- [ ] Piston ring-to-groove clearance excessive. This is caused by excessive wear of the piston ring lands. Piston renewal is necessary (Chapter 2A or 2B).
- [ ] Cylinder head gasket damaged. If the head is allowed to become loose, or if excessive carbon build-up on the piston crown and combustion chamber causes extremely high compression, the head gasket may leak. Retorquing the head is not always sufficient to restore the seal, so a new gasket is necessary (Chapter 2A or 2B).
- [ ] Cylinder head warped. This is caused by overheating or improperly tightened camshaft holder nuts (125 engine) or cylinder head nuts (250 engine). Machine shop resurfacing or head renewal is necessary (Chapter 2A or 2B).
- [ ] Valve spring broken or weak. Caused by component failure or wear; the springs must be renewed (Chapter 2A or 2B).

1 Engine doesn't start or is difficult to start (continued)

Compression low (continued)

☐ Valve not seating properly. This is caused by a bent valve (from over-revving or improper valve adjustment), burned valve or seat (incorrect air/fuel mixture) or an accumulation of carbon deposits on the seat. The valves must be cleaned and/or renewed and the seats serviced (Chapter 2A or 2B).

Stalls after starting

☐ Faulty fast idle system. Check the operation of the idle air control valve (IACV) (see Chapter 4).
☐ Engine idle speed incorrect. Turn idle adjusting screw until the engine idles at the specified rpm (Chapter 1).
☐ Ignition malfunction (see Chapter 4).
☐ Fuel injection system malfunction (see Chapter 4).
☐ Fuel contaminated. The fuel can be contaminated with either dirt or water, or can change chemically if the machine has been unused for several months. Drain the tank and fuel system (Chapter 4).
☐ Intake air leak. Check for loose throttle body-to-intake duct clamp (Chapter 4).

Rough idle

☐ Idle speed incorrect (see Chapter 1).
☐ Ignition fault (see Chapter 4).
☐ Fuel injection system malfunction (see Chapter 4).
☐ Fuel contaminated. The fuel can be contaminated with either dirt or water, or can change chemically if the machine has been unused for several months. Drain the tank and the fuel system (Chapter 4).
☐ Intake air leak. Check for loose throttle body-to-intake duct clamp (Chapter 4).
☐ Air filter clogged. Clean the air filter element or replace it with a new one (Chapter 1).

2 Poor running at low speeds

Spark weak

☐ Battery voltage low. Check battery condition and recharge or replace battery (Chapter 8).
☐ Spark plug cap not making good contact. Make sure that the cap is pushed fully onto the spark plug.
☐ Spark plug dirty, defective or worn out. Locate reason for fouled plug using spark plug condition chart on the inside back cover and follow the plug maintenance procedures (see Chapter 1).
☐ Incorrect spark plug. Wrong type or heat range. Check and install correct plug (see Chapter 1).
☐ Ignition coil defective. Test and replace with new one if necessary (see Chapter 4).
☐ Loose or corroded connections on low tension side of coil. Check security and clean connections.

Fuel/air mixture incorrect

☐ Fuel tank breather hose obstructed.
☐ Fuel pump faulty (see Chapter 4).
☐ Fuel filter blocked (see Chapter 4).
☐ Fuel hose kinked. Fit a new the fuel hose.
☐ Fuel injector clogged. In some cases, if a machine has been unused for several months, the fuel turns to a varnish-like liquid, which can cause the injector needle to stick to its seat. Drain the tank and fuel system, ultrasonically clean or replace fuel injector (Chapter 4).
☐ Intake air leak. Check for loose throttle body-to-intake duct clamp (Chapter 4).
☐ Air filter clogged. Clean the air filter element or replace it with a new one (Chapter 1).

Compression low

Check by performing a compression test (see Chapter 2A or 2B).
☐ Spark plug loose. Remove the plug and inspect the threads. Reinstall and tighten securely (see Chapter 1).
☐ Cylinder head not sufficiently tightened down. If the cylinder head is suspected of being loose, then there's a chance that the gasket or head is damaged if the problem has persisted for any length of time. The camshaft holder nuts (125 engine) or cylinder head nuts (250 engine) should be tightened to the proper torque and in the correct sequence (Chapter 2A or 2B).

☐ Improper valve clearance. This means that the valve is not closing completely and compression pressure is leaking past the valve. Check and adjust the valve clearances (Chapter 1).
☐ Cylinder and/or piston worn. Excessive wear will cause compression pressure to leak past the rings. This is usually accompanied by worn rings as well. A top-end overhaul is necessary (Chapter 2A or 2B).
☐ Piston rings worn, weak, broken, or sticking. Broken or sticking piston rings usually indicate a lubrication or fuelling problem that causes excess carbon deposits to form on the piston and rings. Top-end overhaul is necessary (Chapter 2A or 2B).
☐ Piston ring-to-groove clearance excessive. This is caused by excessive wear of the piston ring lands. Piston renewal is necessary (Chapter 2A or 2B).
☐ Cylinder head gasket damaged. If the head is allowed to become loose, or if excessive carbon build-up on the piston crown and combustion chamber causes extremely high compression, the head gasket may leak. Retorquing the head is not always sufficient to restore the seal, so a new gasket is necessary (Chapter 2A or 2B).
☐ Cylinder head warped. This is caused by overheating or improperly tightened camshaft holder nuts (125 engine) or cylinder head nuts (250 engine). Machine shop resurfacing or head renewal is necessary (Chapter 2A or 2B).
☐ Valve spring broken or weak. Caused by component failure or wear; the springs must be renewed (Chapter 2A or 2B).
☐ Valve not seating properly. This is caused by a bent valve (from over-revving or improper valve adjustment), burned valve or seat (improper fuelling) or an accumulation of carbon deposits on the seat (from fuelling or lubrication problems). The valves must be cleaned and/or renewed and the seats serviced (Chapter 2A or 2B).

Poor acceleration

☐ Timing not advancing. The crankshaft position sensor (CKP) or the engine control module (ECM) may be defective (see Chapter 4).
☐ Engine oil viscosity too high. Using a heavier oil than that recommended in Chapter 1 can damage the oil pump or lubrication system and cause drag on the engine.
☐ Brakes dragging. Usually caused by corrosion behind dust seals, ingestion of dirt past a deteriorated seal or from a warped disc or bent axle (Chapter 6).

3 Poor running or no power at high speed

Firing incorrect

☐ Spark plug cap not making good contact. Make sure that the cap is pushed fully onto the spark plug.

☐ Spark plug dirty, defective or worn out. Identify reason for fouled plug using spark plug condition chart on the inside back cover and follow the plug maintenance procedures (see Chapter 1).

☐ Incorrect spark plug. Wrong type or heat range. Check and install correct plug (see Chapter 1).

☐ Ignition coil defective. Test and replace with new one if necessary (see Chapter 4).

☐ Faulty ECM (engine control module) (see Chapter 4).

Fuel/air mixture incorrect

☐ Fuel tank breather hose obstructed.

☐ Fuel pump faulty (see Chapter 4).

☐ Fuel filter blocked (see Chapter 4).

☐ Fuel hose kinked. Fit a new fuel hose.

☐ Fuel injector clogged. In some cases, if a machine has been unused for several months, the fuel turns to a varnish-like liquid, which can cause the injector needle to stick to its seat. Drain the tank and fuel system, ultrasonically clean or replace fuel injector (Chapter 4).

☐ Intake air leak. Check for loose throttle body-to-intake duct clamp (Chapter 4).

☐ Air filter clogged. Clean the air filter element or replace it with a new one (Chapter 1).

Compression low

Check by performing a compression test (see Chapter 2A or 2B).

☐ Spark plug loose. Remove the plug and inspect the threads. Reinstall and tighten securely (see Chapter 1).

☐ Cylinder head not sufficiently tightened down. If the cylinder head is suspected of being loose, then there's a chance that the gasket or head is damaged if the problem has persisted for any length of time. The camshaft holder nuts (125 engine) or cylinder head nuts (250 engine) should be tightened to the proper torque and in the correct sequence (Chapter 2A or 2B).

☐ Improper valve clearance. This means that the valve is not closing completely and compression pressure is leaking past the valve. Check and adjust the valve clearances (Chapter 1).

☐ Cylinder and/or piston worn. Excessive wear will cause compression pressure to leak past the rings. This is usually accompanied by worn rings as well. A top-end overhaul is necessary (Chapter 2A or 2B).

☐ Piston rings worn, weak, broken, or sticking. Broken or sticking piston rings usually indicate a lubrication or fuelling problem that causes excess carbon deposits to form on the piston and rings. Top-end overhaul is necessary (Chapter 2A or 2B).

☐ Piston ring-to-groove clearance excessive. This is caused by excessive wear of the piston ring lands. Piston renewal is necessary (Chapter 2A or 2B).

☐ Cylinder head gasket damaged. If a head is allowed to become loose, or if excessive carbon build-up on the piston crown and combustion chamber causes extremely high compression, the head gasket may leak. Retorquing the head is not always sufficient to restore the seal, so a new gasket is necessary (Chapter 2A or 2B).

☐ Cylinder head warped. This is caused by overheating or improperly tightened camshaft holder nuts (125 engine) or cylinder head nuts (250 engine). Machine shop resurfacing or head renewal is necessary (Chapter 2A or 2B).

☐ Valve spring broken or weak. Caused by component failure or wear; the springs must be replaced with new ones (Chapter 2A or 2B).

☐ Valve not seating properly. This is caused by a bent valve (from over-revving or improper valve adjustment), burned valve or seat (improper fuelling) or an accumulation of carbon deposits on the seat (from fuelling or lubrication problems). The valves must be cleaned and/or renewed and the seats serviced (Chapter 2A or 2B).

Knocking or pinking

☐ Carbon build-up in combustion chamber. Use of a fuel additive that will dissolve the adhesive bonding the carbon particles to the piston crown and chamber is the easiest way to remove the build-up. Otherwise, the cylinder head will have to be removed and decarbonised (Chapter 2A or 2B).

☐ Incorrect or poor quality fuel. Old or improper grades of fuel can cause detonation. This causes the piston to rattle, thus the knocking or pinking sound. Drain old fuel and always use the recommended fuel grade.

☐ Spark plug heat range incorrect. Uncontrolled detonation indicates the plug heat range is too hot. The plug in effect becomes a glow plug, raising cylinder temperatures. Install the proper heat range plug (Chapter 1).

☐ Improper air/fuel mixture. This will cause the cylinder to run hot, which leads to detonation. A blockage in the fuel system or an air leak can cause this imbalance (see Chapter 4).

Miscellaneous causes

☐ Throttle valve doesn't open fully. Adjust the throttle twistgrip freeplay (see Chapter 1).

☐ Clutch slipping due loose or worn clutch components (see Chapter 2A or 2B).

☐ Timing not advancing. The crankshaft position sensor (CKP) or the engine control unit (ECM) may be defective (see Chapter 4).

☐ Engine oil viscosity too high. Using a heavier oil than the one recommended in Chapter 1 can damage the oil pump or lubrication system and cause drag on the engine.

☐ Brakes dragging. Usually caused by corrosion behind dust seals, ingestion of dirt past a deteriorated seal or from a warped disc or bent axle (Chapter 6).

4 Overheating

Engine overheats

- [ ] Coolant level low. Check and add coolant (see *Pre-ride checks*).
- [ ] Leak in cooling system. Check cooling system hoses and radiator for leaks and other damage. Repair or renew parts as necessary (see Chapter 3).
- [ ] Faulty thermostat. Check and renew as described in Chapter 3.
- [ ] Faulty radiator cap. Remove the cap and have it pressure tested.
- [ ] Coolant passages clogged. Drain, flush and refill with fresh coolant (Chapter 1).
- [ ] Water pump defective. Remove the pump and check the components (see Chapter 3).
- [ ] Clogged or damaged radiator fins (see Chapter 3).
- [ ] Faulty cooling fan, fan relay or ECT sensor (see Chapter 3).

Firing incorrect

- [ ] Spark plug dirty, defective or worn out. Identify reason for fouled plug using spark plug condition chart on the inside back cover and follow the plug maintenance procedures (see Chapter 1).
- [ ] Incorrect spark plug. Wrong type or heat range. Check and install correct plug (see Chapter 1).
- [ ] Ignition coil defective. Test and replace with a new one if necessary (see Chapter 4).
- [ ] Faulty ECM (engine control module) (see Chapter 4).

Fuel/air mixture incorrect

- [ ] Fuel tank breather hose obstructed.
- [ ] Fuel pump faulty (see Chapter 4).
- [ ] Fuel filter blocked (see Chapter 4).
- [ ] Fuel hose kinked. Fit a new fuel hose.
- [ ] Fuel injector clogged. In some cases, if a machine has been unused for several months, the fuel turns to a varnish-like liquid, which can cause the injector needle to stick to its seat. Drain the tank and fuel system, ultrasonically clean or replace fuel injector (Chapter 4).
- [ ] Intake air leak. Check for loose throttle body-to-intake duct clamp (Chapter 4).
- [ ] Air filter clogged. Clean the air filter element or replace it with a new one (Chapter 1).

Compression too high

Check by performing a compression test (see Chapter 2A or 2B).

- [ ] Carbon build-up in combustion chamber. Use of a fuel additive that will dissolve the adhesive bonding the carbon particles to the piston crown and chamber is the easiest way to remove the build-up. Otherwise, the cylinder head will have to be removed and decarbonised (Chapter 2A or 2B).
- [ ] Improperly machined head surface or installation of incorrect gasket during engine assembly.

Engine load excessive

- [ ] Clutch slipping due to loose or worn clutch components (see Chapter 2A or 2B).
- [ ] Engine oil level too high. Too much oil will cause pressurisation of the crankcase and inefficient engine operation. Check Specifications and drain to proper level (Chapter 1 and *Pre-ride checks*).
- [ ] Engine oil viscosity too high. Using a heavier oil than the one recommended in Chapter 1 can damage the oil pump or lubrication system as well as cause drag on the engine.
- [ ] Brakes dragging. Usually caused by corrosion behind dust seals, ingestion of dirt past deteriorated seal or from a warped disc or bent axle (Chapter 6).

Lubrication inadequate

- [ ] Engine oil level too low. Friction caused by intermittent lack of lubrication or from oil that is overworked can cause overheating. The oil provides a definite cooling function in the engine. Check the oil level (see *Pre-ride checks*).
- [ ] Low engine oil pressure. Check the pressure (see Chapter 2A or 2B).
- [ ] Blocked oil filter or strainer (see Chapters 1 and 2A or 2B).

Miscellaneous causes

- [ ] Modification to exhaust system. Most aftermarket exhaust systems cause the engine to run leaner, which make them run hotter. When installing an accessory exhaust system, always check with the manufacturer/supplier as to whether the fuel system requires re-mapping.

5 Clutch problems

Clutch slipping

- [ ] Clutch wrongly adjusted or clutch release mechanism fault (see Chapters 1 and 2A or 2B).
- [ ] Clutch plates worn or warped. Overhaul the clutch assembly (see Chapter 2A or 2B).
- [ ] Clutch springs broken or weak. Old or heat-damaged (from slipping clutch) springs should be renewed (Chapter 2A or 2B).
- [ ] Faulty clutch release mechanism. Replace any defective parts with new ones (see Chapter 2A or 2B).
- [ ] Clutch centre or housing unevenly worn. This causes improper engagement of the plates. Replace the damaged or worn parts (see Chapter 2A or 2B).
- [ ] Incorrect oil used in engine. Oils designed for car engines often contain friction modifiers, which if used in an engine with a wet clutch can promote clutch slip. Always use an oil designed for motorcycle engines (see *Pre-ride checks*).

Clutch not disengaging completely

- [ ] Clutch wrongly adjusted or clutch release mechanism fault (see Chapters 1 and 2A or 2B).

- [ ] Clutch plates warped or damaged. This will cause clutch drag, which in turn will cause the machine to creep. Overhaul the clutch assembly (see Chapter 2A or 2B).
- [ ] Clutch springs fatigued or broken. Check and renew the springs (see Chapter 2A or 2B).
- [ ] Engine oil deteriorated. Old, thin oil will not provide proper lubrication for the plates, causing the clutch to drag. Renew the oil and filter (see Chapter 1).
- [ ] Engine oil viscosity too high. Using a heavier oil than recommended in Chapter 1 can cause the plates to stick together. Change to the correct weight oil.
- [ ] Clutch housing bearing seized on the transmission input shaft. Lack of lubrication, severe wear or damage can cause the bearing to seize. Overhaul of the clutch, and perhaps transmission, may be necessary to repair the damage (see Chapter 2A or 2B).
- [ ] Faulty clutch release mechanism. Renew any defective parts (see Chapter 2A or 2B).
- [ ] Loose clutch nut. Causes housing and centre misalignment putting a drag on the engine. Engagement adjustment continually varies. Overhaul the clutch assembly (see Chapter 2A or 2B).

6 Gearchanging problems

Doesn't go into gear or lever doesn't return

- ☐ Clutch not disengaging (see above).
- ☐ Gearchange mechanism stopper arm spring weak or broken, or arm roller broken or worn. Replace the spring or arm with a new one (see Chapter 2A or 2B).
- ☐ Selector fork(s) bent, worn or seized. Overhaul the transmission (see Chapter 2A or 2B).
- ☐ Gear(s) stuck on shaft. Most often caused by a lack of lubrication or excessive wear in transmission bearings and bushes. Overhaul the transmission (see Chapter 2A or 2B).
- ☐ Selector drum binding. Caused by lubrication failure or excessive wear. Replace the drum and/or its bearing with a new one (see Chapter 2A or 2B).
- ☐ Gearchange mechanism return spring weak or broken (see Chapter 2A or 2B).
- ☐ Gearchange linkage arm broken. Splines stripped out of arm or shaft, caused by a loose linkage arm pinch bolt or from dropping the machine (see Chapter 2A or 2B).

Jumps out of gear

- ☐ Selector fork(s) worn (see Chapter 2A or 2B).
- ☐ Selector fork groove(s) in selector drum worn (see Chapter 2A or 2B).
- ☐ Gear pinion dogs or dog slots worn or damaged. The gear pinions should be inspected and renewed. No attempt should be made to repair the worn parts.

Overselects

- ☐ Gearchange mechanism stopper arm spring weak or broken, or arm roller broken or worn. Renew the spring or arm (see Chapter 2A or 2B).
- ☐ Gearchange mechanism return spring weak or broken (see Chapter 2A or 2B).

7 Abnormal engine noise

Knocking or pinking

- ☐ Carbon build-up in combustion chamber. Use of a fuel additive that will dissolve the adhesive bonding the carbon particles to the piston crown and chamber is the easiest way to remove the build-up. Otherwise, the cylinder head will have to be removed and decarbonised (Chapter 2A or 2B).
- ☐ Incorrect or poor quality fuel. Old or improper grades of fuel can cause detonation. This causes the piston to rattle, thus the knocking or pinking sound. Drain old fuel and always use the recommended fuel grade.
- ☐ Spark plug heat range incorrect. Uncontrolled detonation indicates the plug heat range is too hot. The plug in effect becomes a glow plug, raising cylinder temperatures. Install the proper heat range plug (Chapter 1).
- ☐ Improper air/fuel mixture. This will cause the cylinder to run hot, which leads to detonation. A blockage in the fuel system or an air leak can cause this imbalance (see Chapter 4).

Piston slap or rattling

- ☐ Cylinder-to-piston clearance excessive. Cylinder and/or piston worn, usually accompanied by worn rings as well. A top-end overhaul is necessary (see Chapter 2A or 2B).
- ☐ Piston ring(s) worn, broken or sticking. Overhaul the top-end (see Chapter 2A or 2B).
- ☐ Piston pin, piston pin bore or connecting rod small-end worn from high mileage or seized due to lack of lubrication (see Chapter 2A or 2B).
- ☐ Piston seizure damage. Usually from lack of lubrication or overheating. Rebore the cylinder and fit an oversize piston and rings on 125 models (see Chapter 2A). Replace the piston and cylinder on 250 models (see Chapter 2B).
- ☐ Connecting rod big-end clearance excessive. Caused by excessive wear or lack of lubrication. Replace worn parts.
- ☐ Connecting rod bent. Caused by over-revving, trying to start a badly flooded engine or from ingesting a foreign object into the combustion chamber. Replace the damaged parts (Chapter 2A or 2B).

Valve noise

- ☐ Incorrect valve clearances – check and adjust (see Chapter 1).
- ☐ Valve spring broken or weak. Check and replace weak valve springs with new ones (see Chapter 2A or 2B).
- ☐ Camshaft, camshaft bearings or rockers worn or damaged. Lubrication failure at high rpm is usually the cause of damage due to insufficient oil or failure to change the oil at the recommended intervals. Since there are no replaceable bearings in the head, the head itself will have to be replaced with a new one (see Chapter 2A or 2B).

Other noise

- ☐ Cylinder head gasket leaking. Check around the joint for blowing with the engine running.
- ☐ Exhaust pipe leaking at cylinder head connection. Caused by incorrect fit of pipe(s), loose exhaust flange or damaged gasket. All exhaust system fasteners should be tightened evenly and carefully to avoid leaks (see Chapter 4).
- ☐ Crankshaft runout excessive. Caused by a bent crankshaft (from over-revving) or damage from an upper cylinder component failure.
- ☐ Engine mounting bolts loose – ensure all the bolts are tightened to the specified torque settings (see Chapter 2A or 2B).
- ☐ Crankshaft bearings worn (see Chapter 2A or 2B).
- ☐ Cam chain rattle, due to worn chain or defective tensioner. Also worn chain tensioner/guide blades (see Chapter 2A or 2B).

8 Abnormal driveline noise

Clutch noise

☐ Clutch housing/friction plate clearance excessive (Chapter 2A or 2B).
☐ Wear between the clutch housing splines and input shaft splines (Chapter 2A or 2B).
☐ Worn release bearing (Chapter 2A or 2B).

Transmission noise

☐ Bearings worn. Also includes the possibility that the shafts are worn. Overhaul the transmission (Chapter 2A or 2B).
☐ Gears worn or chipped (Chapter 2A or 2B).
☐ Metal chips jammed in gear teeth. Probably pieces from a broken clutch, gear or selector mechanism that were picked up by the gears. This will cause early bearing failure (Chapter 2A or 2B).

☐ Engine oil level too low. Causes a howl from transmission. Also affects engine power and clutch operation (*Pre-ride checks*).

Final drive noise

☐ Chain not adjusted properly (Chapter 1).
☐ Front or rear sprocket loose. Tighten fasteners (Chapter 6).
☐ Sprockets and/or chain worn. Fit new sprockets and chain (Chapter 6).
☐ Rear sprocket warped. Fit a new sprocket (Chapter 6).
☐ Rubber dampers in rear sprocket coupling worn (CBR models) (Chapter 6).

9 Abnormal frame and suspension noise

Front end noise

☐ Low fluid level or improper viscosity oil in forks. This can sound like spurting and is usually accompanied by irregular fork action (Chapter 5).
☐ Spring weak or broken. Makes a clicking or scraping sound. Fork oil, when drained, will have a lot of metal particles in it (Chapter 5).
☐ Steering head bearings loose or damaged. Clicks when braking. Check and adjust or replace with new ones as necessary (Chapters 1 and 5).
☐ Fork yoke clamp bolts loose – ensure all the bolts are tightened to the specified torque (Chapter 5).
☐ Forks bent. Good possibility if machine has been dropped. Replace the tubes with new ones as required (Chapter 5).
☐ Front axle nut or axle pinch bolt (where fitted) loose. Tighten them to the specified torque (Chapter 6).
☐ Loose or worn wheel bearings. Check and replace with new ones as needed (Chapters 1 and 6).

Rear end noise

☐ Fluid level incorrect. Indicates a leak caused by defective seal. Shock will be covered with oil. Replace shock with a new one or seek advice on repair from a suspension specialist (Chapter 5).
☐ Defective shock absorber with internal damage. This is in the body of the shock and can't be remedied. The shock must be replaced with a new one or rebuilt (Chapter 5).
☐ Bent or damaged shock body or mounts. Check the mounts. If the shock absorber itself is damaged replace it with a new one (Chapter 5).

☐ Loose or worn suspension linkage components (250 models). Check and replace with new ones as necessary (Chapter 5).
☐ Loose or worn wheel bearings/sprocket bearing. Check and replace with new ones as needed (Chapters 1 and 6).

Brake noise

☐ Squeal caused by pad shim not installed or positioned correctly (where fitted) (Chapter 6).
☐ Squeal caused by dust on brake pads. Usually found in combination with glazed pads. Clean using brake cleaning solvent (Chapter 6).
☐ Pads glazed. Caused by excessive heat from prolonged hard use or from contamination. DO NOT use sandpaper, emery cloth, carborundum cloth or any other abrasive to roughen the pad surfaces as abrasives will stay in the pad material and damage the disc. A very fine flat file can be used, but new pads is the best remedy (Chapter 6).
☐ Contamination of brake pads. Oil or brake fluid can cause the brake pads to chatter or squeal. Fit new pads. Identify the cause of the contamination, especially check the caliper piston seals for leaking fluid. Clean disc thoroughly with brake system cleaner (Chapter 6).
☐ Disc warped. Can cause a chattering, clicking or intermittent squeal. Usually accompanied by a pulsating lever and uneven braking. Replace the disc with new one (Chapter 6).
☐ Loose or worn wheel bearings. Check and replace with new ones as needed (Chapters 1 and 6).

10 Oil pressure warning light comes on

☐ Engine oil level low. Inspect for leak or other problem causing low oil level and add recommended oil (see *Pre-ride checks*).

☐ Engine oil pump defective, blocked oil strainer gauze or failed pressure regulator. Carry out an oil pressure check (Chapter 2A or 2B).

☐ Engine oil viscosity too low. Very old, thin oil or an improper weight of oil used in the engine. Change to correct oil (Chapter 1).

☐ Excessive wear causing drop in oil pressure. Abnormal wear could be caused by oil starvation at high rpm from low oil level or improper weight or type of oil (Chapter 1).

11 Excessive exhaust smoke

White smoke

☐ Piston rings worn or broken, causing oil from the crankcase to be pulled past the piston into the combustion chamber. Replace the rings with new ones (Chapter 2A or 2B).

☐ Cylinder worn or scored. Caused by overheating or oil starvation. On 125 models have the cylinder rebored and fit an oversize piston and rings (see Chapter 2A). On 250 models install a new cylinder barrel, piston and rings (Chapter 2B).

☐ Valve stem oil seal damaged or worn. Replace the oil seals with new ones (Chapter 2A or 2B).

☐ Valve guide worn. Perform a complete valve job (Chapter 2A or 2B).

☐ Engine oil level too high, which causes the oil to be forced past the rings. Drain oil to the proper level (see Chapter 1 and *Pre-ride checks*).

☐ Head gasket broken between oil return and cylinder. Causes oil to be pulled into the combustion chamber. Replace the head gasket with a new one and check the head for warpage (Chapter 2A or 2B).

☐ Abnormal crankcase pressurisation which forces oil past the rings, usually caused by a clogged breather.

Black smoke

☐ Air filter clogged. Clean the air filter element or replace it with a new one (Chapter 1).

☐ Fuel injection system malfunction (Chapter 4).

Brown smoke

☐ Air filter poorly sealed or not installed (Chapter 1).

☐ Fuel injection system malfunction (Chapter 4).

12 Poor handling or stability

Handlebars hard to turn

☐ Steering head bearing adjuster nut too tight. Check adjustment as described in Chapter 1.

☐ Bearings damaged. Roughness can be felt as the bars are turned from side-to-side. Replace the bearings with new ones (Chapter 5).

☐ Races dented or worn. Denting results from wear in only one position (e.g., straight ahead), from a collision or hitting a pothole or from dropping the machine. Replace the bearings with new ones (Chapter 5).

☐ Steering stem lubrication inadequate. Causes are grease getting hard from age or being washed out by pressure washers. Disassemble steering head and repack bearings (Chapter 5).

☐ Steering stem bent. Caused by a collision, hitting a pothole or by dropping the machine. Replace damaged part. Don't try to straighten the steering stem (Chapter 5).

☐ Front tyre air pressure too low (*Pre-ride checks*).

Handlebar shakes or vibrates excessively

☐ Tyres worn or out of balance (Chapter 6).

☐ Swingarm bearings worn. Replace the bearings with new ones (Chapter 5).

☐ Wheel rim(s) warped or damaged. Inspect wheels for runout (Chapter 6).

☐ Wheel bearings worn. Worn front or rear wheel bearings can cause poor tracking. Worn front bearings will cause wobble (Chapters 1 and 6).

☐ Fork yoke clamp bolts or handlebar clamp bolts loose. Tighten them to the specified torque (Chapter 5).

☐ Engine mounting bolts loose. Will cause excessive vibration with increased engine rpm – ensure all the bolts are tightened to the specified torque settings (see Chapter 2A or 2B).

Machine pulls to one side

☐ Frame bent. Definitely suspect this if the machine has been dropped. May or may not be accompanied by cracking near the steering head, swingarm mountings or engine mountings. Replace the frame with a new one (Chapter 5).

☐ Wheels out of alignment. Caused by improper location of axle spacers or from bent steering stem or frame (Chapter 5).

☐ Forks bent. Disassemble the forks and replace the damaged parts (Chapter 5).

☐ Swingarm bent or twisted. Replace the arm with a new one (Chapter 5).

☐ Fork oil level uneven. Check and add or drain as necessary (Chapter 5).

Poor shock absorbing qualities

☐ Too hard:
   a) Fork oil level excessive (Chapter 5).
   b) Fork oil viscosity too high. Use a lighter oil (see the Specifications in Chapter 5).
   c) Fork tube bent. Causes a harsh, sticking feeling (Chapter 5).
   d) Fork internal damage (Chapter 5).
   e) Rear shock absorber pre-load too high (250 models).
   f) Shock shaft or body bent or damaged (Chapter 5).
   g) Shock internal damage.
   h) Tyre pressure too high (*Pre-ride checks*).

☐ Too soft:
   a) Fork oil level too low (Chapter 5).
   b) Fork oil viscosity too light (Chapter 5).
   c) Fork springs weak or broken (Chapter 5).
   d) Fork or shock oil leaking (Chapter 5).
   e) Rear shock absorber pre-load too low (250 models).
   f) Shock internal damage (Chapter 5).

13 Braking problems

Brakes are spongy, don't hold

- [ ] Low brake fluid level (see *Pre-ride checks*).
- [ ] Air in hydraulic system. Caused by inattention to master cylinder fluid level or by leakage. Locate problem and bleed brakes (Chapter 6).
- [ ] Pad or disc worn (Chapters 1 and 6).
- [ ] Contaminated pads. Caused by contamination with oil, grease, brake fluid, etc. Fit new pads. Identify the cause of the contamination, especially check the caliper piston seals for leaking fluid. Clean disc thoroughly with brake system cleaner (Chapter 6).
- [ ] Brake fluid deteriorated. Fluid is old or contaminated. Drain system, replenish with new fluid and bleed the system (Chapter 6).
- [ ] Master cylinder internal seals worn or damaged causing fluid to bypass (Chapter 6).
- [ ] Master cylinder bore scratched by foreign material or broken spring. Fit a new master cylinder (Chapter 6).
- [ ] Disc warped. Replace disc with new one (Chapter 6).

Brake lever or pedal pulsates

- [ ] Disc warped. Replace disc with new one (Chapter 6).
- [ ] Axle bent. Replace axle with new one (Chapter 6).
- [ ] Brake caliper bolts loose – tighten the bolts to the specified torque (Chapter 6).
- [ ] Wheel warped or otherwise damaged (Chapter 6).
- [ ] Wheel bearings damaged or worn (Chapters 1 and 6).

Brakes drag

- [ ] Master cylinder piston seized. Caused by wear or damage to piston or cylinder bore (Chapter 6).
- [ ] Lever balky or stuck. Check pivot and lubricate (Chapter 6).
- [ ] Brake caliper piston seized in bore. Caused by corrosion behind dust seals or ingestion of dirt past deteriorated seal (Chapter 6).
- [ ] Caliper sticking on slider pins due to corrosion. Clean and lubricate pins and check dust boots (Chapter 6).
- [ ] Brake pad damaged. Pad material separated from backing plate. Usually caused by faulty manufacturing process or from contact with chemicals. Fit new pads (Chapter 6).
- [ ] Pads improperly installed (Chapter 6).
- [ ] Brake caliper incorrectly installed (Chapter 6).

14 Electrical problems

Battery dead or weak

- [ ] Battery faulty. Caused by sulphated plates which are shorted through sedimentation. Confirm by terminal voltage check (Chapter 8).
- [ ] Broken battery terminal making only occasional contact.
- [ ] Battery leads making poor contact (Chapter 8).
- [ ] Load excessive. Caused by addition of high wattage lights or other electrical accessories.
- [ ] Ignition switch defective. Switch either grounds (earths) internally or fails to shut off system. Renew the switch (Chapter 8).
- [ ] Regulator/rectifier defective (Chapter 8).
- [ ] Alternator stator coil open or shorted (Chapter 8).
- [ ] Charging system fault. Check for excessive current leakage (Chapter 8).
- [ ] Wiring faulty. Wiring grounded (earthed) or connections loose in ignition, charging or lighting circuits (Chapter 8).

Battery overcharged

- [ ] Regulator/rectifier defective. Overcharging is noticed when battery gets excessively warm (Chapter 8).
- [ ] Battery faulty. Confirm with battery terminal voltage check (Chapter 8).
- [ ] Battery amperage too low, wrong type or size of battery. Install manufacturer's specified amp-hour battery to handle charging load (Chapter 8).

A

ABS (Anti-lock braking system) A system, usually electronically controlled, that senses incipient wheel lockup during braking and relieves hydraulic pressure at wheel which is about to skid.

Aftermarket Components suitable for the motorcycle, but not produced by the motorcycle manufacturer.

Allen key A hexagonal wrench which fits into a recessed hexagonal hole.

Alternating current (ac) Current produced by an alternator. Requires converting to direct current by a rectifier for charging purposes.

Alternator Converts mechanical energy from the engine into electrical energy to charge the battery and power the electrical system.

Ampere (amp) A unit of measurement for the flow of electrical current. Current = Volts ÷ Ohms.

Ampere-hour (Ah) Measure of battery capacity.

Angle-tightening A torque expressed in degrees. Often follows a conventional tightening torque for cylinder head or main bearing fasteners **(see illustration)**.

Angle-tightening con-rod bolts

Antifreeze A substance (usually ethylene glycol) mixed with water, and added to the cooling system, to prevent freezing of the coolant in winter. Antifreeze also contains chemicals to inhibit corrosion and the formation of rust and other deposits that would tend to clog the radiator and coolant passages and reduce cooling efficiency.

Anti-dive System attached to the fork lower leg (slider) to prevent fork dive when braking hard.

Anti-seize compound A coating that reduces the risk of seizing on fasteners that are subjected to high temperatures, such as exhaust clamp bolts and nuts.

API American Petroleum Institute. A quality standard for 4-stroke motor oils.

Asbestos A natural fibrous mineral with great heat resistance, commonly used in the composition of brake friction materials. Asbestos is a health hazard and the dust created by brake systems should never be inhaled or ingested.

ATF Automatic Transmission Fluid. Often used in front forks.

ATU Automatic Timing Unit. Mechanical device for advancing the ignition timing on early engines.

ATV All Terrain Vehicle. Often called a Quad.

Axial play Side-to-side movement.

Axle A shaft on which a wheel revolves. Also known as a spindle.

B

Backlash The amount of movement between meshed components when one component is held still. Usually applies to gear teeth.

Ball bearing A bearing consisting of a hardened inner and outer race with hardened steel balls between the two races.

Bearings Used between two working surfaces to prevent wear of the components and a build-up of heat. Four types of bearing are commonly used on motorcycles: plain shell bearings, ball bearings, tapered roller bearings and needle roller bearings.

Bevel gears Used to turn the drive through 90°. Typical applications are shaft final drive and camshaft drive **(see illustration)**.

Bevel gears are used to turn the drive through 90°

BHP Brake Horsepower. The British measurement for engine power output. Power output is now usually expressed in kilowatts (kW).

Bias-belted tyre Similar construction to radial tyre, but with outer belt running at an angle to the wheel rim.

Big-end bearing The bearing in the end of the connecting rod that's attached to the crankshaft.

Bleeding The process of removing air from an hydraulic system via a bleed nipple or bleed screw.

Bottom-end A description of an engine's crankcase components and all components contained there-in.

BTDC Before Top Dead Centre in terms of piston position. Ignition timing is often expressed in terms of degrees or millimetres BTDC.

Bush A cylindrical metal or rubber component used between two moving parts.

Burr Rough edge left on a component after machining or as a result of excessive wear.

C

Cam chain The chain which takes drive from the crankshaft to the camshaft(s).

Canister The main component in an evaporative emission control system (California market only); contains activated charcoal granules to trap vapours from the fuel system rather than allowing them to vent to the atmosphere.

Castellated Resembling the parapets along the top of a castle wall. For example, a castellated wheel axle or spindle nut.

Catalytic converter A device in the exhaust system of some machines which converts certain pollutants in the exhaust gases into less harmful substances.

Charging system Description of the components which charge the battery, ie the alternator, rectifier and regulator.

Circlip A ring-shaped clip used to prevent endwise movement of cylindrical parts and shafts. An internal circlip is installed in a groove in a housing; an external circlip fits into a groove on the outside of a cylindrical piece such as a shaft. Also known as a snap-ring.

Clearance The amount of space between two parts. For example, between a piston and a cylinder, between a bearing and a journal, etc.

Coil spring A spiral of elastic steel found in various sizes throughout a vehicle, for example as a springing medium in the suspension and in the valve train.

Compression Reduction in volume, and increase in pressure and temperature, of a gas, caused by squeezing it into a smaller space.

Compression damping Controls the speed the suspension compresses when hitting a bump.

Compression ratio The relationship between cylinder volume when the piston is at top dead centre and cylinder volume when the piston is at bottom dead centre.

Continuity The uninterrupted path in the flow of electricity. Little or no measurable resistance.

Continuity tester Self-powered bleeper or test light which indicates continuity.

Cp Candlepower. Bulb rating commonly found on US motorcycles.

Crossply tyre Tyre plies arranged in a criss-cross pattern. Usually four or six plies used, hence 4PR or 6PR in tyre size codes.

Cush drive Rubber damper segments fitted between the rear wheel and final drive sprocket to absorb transmission shocks **(see illustration)**.

Cush drive rubbers dampen out transmission shocks

D

Decarbonisation The process of removing carbon deposits - typically from the combustion chamber, valves and exhaust port/system.

Degree disc Calibrated disc for measuring piston position. Expressed in degrees.

Detonation Destructive and damaging explosion of fuel/air mixture in combustion chamber instead of controlled burning.

Dial gauge Clock-type gauge with adapters for measuring runout and piston position. Expressed in mm or inches.

Diaphragm The rubber membrane in a master cylinder or carburettor which seals the upper chamber.

Diaphragm spring A single sprung plate often used in clutches.

Direct current (dc) Current produced by a dc generator.

Diode An electrical valve which only allows current to flow in one direction. Commonly used in rectifiers and starter interlock systems.

Disc valve (or rotary valve) A induction system used on some two-stroke engines.

Double-overhead camshaft (DOHC) An engine that uses two overhead camshafts, one for the intake valves and one for the exhaust valves.

Drivebelt A toothed belt used to transmit drive to the rear wheel on some motorcycles. A drivebelt has also been used to drive the camshafts. Drivebelts are usually made of Kevlar.

Driveshaft Any shaft used to transmit motion. Commonly used when referring to the final driveshaft on shaft drive motorcycles.

E

Earth return The return path of an electrical circuit, utilising the motorcycle's frame.

ECU (Electronic Control Unit) A computer which controls (for instance) an ignition system, or an anti-lock braking system.

EGO Exhaust Gas Oxygen sensor. Sometimes called a Lambda sensor.

Electrolyte The fluid in a lead-acid battery.

EMS (Engine Management System) A computer controlled system which manages the fuel injection and the ignition systems in an integrated fashion.

Endfloat The amount of lengthways movement between two parts. As applied to a crankshaft, the distance that the crankshaft can move side-to-side in the crankcase.

Endless chain A chain having no joining link. Common use for cam chains and final drive chains.

EP (Extreme Pressure) Oil type used in locations where high loads are applied, such as between gear teeth.

Evaporative emission control system Describes a charcoal filled canister which stores fuel vapours from the tank rather than allowing them to vent to the atmosphere. Usually only fitted to California models and referred to as an EVAP system.

Expansion chamber Section of two-stroke engine exhaust system so designed to improve engine efficiency and boost power.

F

Feeler blade or gauge A thin strip or blade of hardened steel, ground to an exact thickness, used to check or measure clearances between parts.

Final drive Description of the drive from the transmission to the rear wheel. Usually by chain or shaft, but sometimes by belt.

Firing order The order in which the engine cylinders fire, or deliver their power strokes, beginning with the number one cylinder.

Flooding Term used to describe a high fuel level in the carburettor float chambers, leading to fuel overflow. Also refers to excess fuel in the combustion chamber due to incorrect starting technique.

Free length The no-load state of a component when measured. Clutch, valve and fork spring lengths are measured at rest, without any preload.

Freeplay The amount of travel before any action takes place. The looseness in a linkage, or an assembly of parts, between the initial application of force and actual movement. For example, the distance the rear brake pedal moves before the rear brake is actuated.

Fuel injection The fuel/air mixture is metered electronically and directed into the engine intake ports (indirect injection) or into the cylinders (direct injection). Sensors supply information on engine speed and conditions.

Fuel/air mixture The charge of fuel and air going into the engine. See Stoichiometric ratio.

Fuse An electrical device which protects a circuit against accidental overload. The typical fuse contains a soft piece of metal which is calibrated to melt at a predetermined current flow (expressed as amps) and break the circuit.

G

Gap The distance the spark must travel in jumping from the centre electrode to the side electrode in a spark plug. Also refers to the distance between the ignition rotor and the pickup coil in an electronic ignition system.

Gasket Any thin, soft material - usually cork, cardboard, asbestos or soft metal - installed between two metal surfaces to ensure a good seal. For instance, the cylinder head gasket seals the joint between the block and the cylinder head.

Gauge An instrument panel display used to monitor engine conditions. A gauge with a movable pointer on a dial or a fixed scale is an analogue gauge. A gauge with a numerical readout is called a digital gauge.

Gear ratios The drive ratio of a pair of gears in a gearbox, calculated on their number of teeth.

Glaze-busting see **Honing**

Grinding Process for renovating the valve face and valve seat contact area in the cylinder head.

Gudgeon pin The shaft which connects the connecting rod small-end with the piston. Often called a piston pin or wrist pin.

H

Helical gears Gear teeth are slightly curved and produce less gear noise that straight-cut gears. Often used for primary drives.

Helicoil A thread insert repair system. Commonly used as a repair for stripped spark plug threads **(see illustration)**.

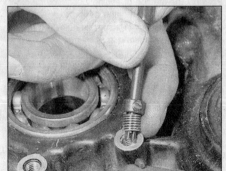

Installing a Helicoil thread insert

Honing A process used to break down the glaze on a cylinder bore (also called glaze-busting). Can also be carried out to roughen a rebored cylinder to aid ring bedding-in.

HT (High Tension) Description of the electrical circuit from the secondary winding of the ignition coil to the spark plug.

Hydraulic A liquid filled system used to transmit pressure from one component to another. Common uses on motorcycles are brakes and clutches.

Hydrometer An instrument for measuring the specific gravity of a lead-acid battery.

Hygroscopic Water absorbing. In motorcycle applications, braking efficiency will be reduced if DOT 3 or 4 hydraulic fluid absorbs water from the air - care must be taken to keep new brake fluid in tightly sealed containers.

I

lbf ft Pounds-force feet. An imperial unit of torque. Sometimes written as ft-lbs.

lbf in Pound-force inch. An imperial unit of torque, applied to components where a very low torque is required. Sometimes written as in-lbs.

IC Abbreviation for Integrated Circuit.

Ignition advance Means of increasing the timing of the spark at higher engine speeds. Done by mechanical means (ATU) on early engines or electronically by the ignition control unit on later engines.

Ignition timing The moment at which the spark plug fires, expressed in the number of crankshaft degrees before the piston reaches the top of its stroke, or in the number of millimetres before the piston reaches the top of its stroke.

Infinity (∞) Description of an open-circuit electrical state, where no continuity exists.

Inverted forks (upside down forks) The sliders or lower legs are held in the yokes and the fork tubes or stanchions are connected to the wheel axle (spindle). Less unsprung weight and stiffer construction than conventional forks.

J

JASO Quality standard for 2-stroke oils.

Joule The unit of electrical energy.

Journal The bearing surface of a shaft.

K

Kickstart Mechanical means of turning the engine over for starting purposes. Only usually fitted to mopeds, small capacity motorcycles and off-road motorcycles.

Kill switch Handebar-mounted switch for emergency ignition cut-out. Cuts the ignition circuit on all models, and additionally prevent starter motor operation on others.

km Symbol for kilometre.

kmh Abbreviation for kilometres per hour.

L

Lambda (λ) sensor A sensor fitted in the exhaust system to measure the exhaust gas oxygen content (excess air factor).

Lapping see Grinding.
LCD Abbreviation for Liquid Crystal Display.
LED Abbreviation for Light Emitting Diode.
Liner A steel cylinder liner inserted in a aluminium alloy cylinder block.
Locknut A nut used to lock an adjustment nut, or other threaded component, in place.
Lockstops The lugs on the lower triple clamp (yoke) which abut those on the frame, preventing handlebar-to-fuel tank contact.
Lockwasher A form of washer designed to prevent an attaching nut from working loose.
LT Low Tension Description of the electrical circuit from the power supply to the primary winding of the ignition coil.

M

Main bearings The bearings between the crankshaft and crankcase.
Maintenance-free (MF) battery A sealed battery which cannot be topped up.
Manometer Mercury-filled calibrated tubes used to measure intake tract vacuum. Used to synchronise carburettors on multi-cylinder engines.
Micrometer A precision measuring instrument that measures component outside diameters **(see illustration)**.

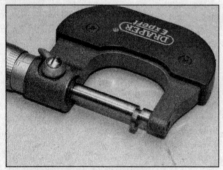

Tappet shims are measured with a micrometer

MON (Motor Octane Number) A measure of a fuel's resistance to knock.
Monograde oil An oil with a single viscosity, eg SAE80W.
Monoshock A single suspension unit linking the swingarm or suspension linkage to the frame.
mph Abbreviation for miles per hour.
Multigrade oil Having a wide viscosity range (eg 10W40). The W stands for Winter, thus the viscosity ranges from SAE10 when cold to SAE40 when hot.
Multimeter An electrical test instrument with the capability to measure voltage, current and resistance. Some meters also incorporate a continuity tester and buzzer.

N

Needle roller bearing Inner race of caged needle rollers and hardened outer race. Examples of uncaged needle rollers can be found on some engines. Commonly used in rear suspension applications and in two-stroke engines.
Nm Newton metres.
NOx Oxides of Nitrogen. A common toxic pollutant emitted by petrol engines at higher temperatures.

O

Octane The measure of a fuel's resistance to knock.
OE (Original Equipment) Relates to components fitted to a motorcycle as standard or replacement parts supplied by the motorcycle manufacturer.
Ohm The unit of electrical resistance. Ohms = Volts ÷ Current.
Ohmmeter An instrument for measuring electrical resistance.
Oil cooler System for diverting engine oil outside of the engine to a radiator for cooling purposes.
Oil injection A system of two-stroke engine lubrication where oil is pump-fed to the engine in accordance with throttle position.
Open-circuit An electrical condition where there is a break in the flow of electricity - no continuity (high resistance).
O-ring A type of sealing ring made of a special rubber-like material; in use, the O-ring is compressed into a groove to provide the sealing action.
Oversize (OS) Term used for piston and ring size options fitted to a rebored cylinder.
Overhead cam (sohc) engine An engine with single camshaft located on top of the cylinder head.
Overhead valve (ohv) engine An engine with the valves located in the cylinder head, but with the camshaft located in the engine block or crankcase.
Oxygen sensor A device installed in the exhaust system which senses the oxygen content in the exhaust and converts this information into an electric current. Also called a Lambda sensor.

P

Plastigauge A thin strip of plastic thread, available in different sizes, used for measuring clearances. For example, a strip of Plastigauge is laid across a bearing journal. The parts are assembled and dismantled; the width of the crushed strip indicates the clearance between journal and bearing.
Polarity Either negative or positive earth (ground), determined by which battery lead is connected to the frame (earth return). Modern motorcycles are usually negative earth.
Pre-ignition A situation where the fuel/air mixture ignites before the spark plug fires. Often due to a hot spot in the combustion chamber caused by carbon build-up. Engine has a tendency to 'run-on'.
Pre-load (suspension) The amount a spring is compressed when in the unloaded state. Preload can be applied by gas, spacer or mechanical adjuster.
Premix The method of engine lubrication on older two-stroke engines. Engine oil is mixed with the petrol in the fuel tank in a specific ratio. The fuel/oil mix is sometimes referred to as "petroil".
Primary drive Description of the drive from the crankshaft to the clutch. Usually by gear or chain.
PS Pfedestärke - a German interpretation of BHP.
PSI Pounds-force per square inch. Imperial measurement of tyre pressure and cylinder pressure measurement.
PTFE Polytetrafluroethylene. A low friction substance.
Pulse secondary air injection system A process of promoting the burning of excess fuel present in the exhaust gases by routing fresh air into the exhaust ports.

Q

Quartz halogen bulb Tungsten filament surrounded by a halogen gas. Typically used for the headlight **(see illustration)**.

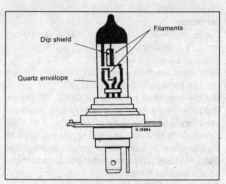

Quartz halogen headlight bulb construction

R

Rack-and-pinion A pinion gear on the end of a shaft that mates with a rack (think of a geared wheel opened up and laid flat). Sometimes used in clutch operating systems.
Radial play Up and down movement about a shaft.
Radial ply tyres Tyre plies run across the tyre (from bead to bead) and around the circumference of the tyre. Less resistant to tread distortion than other tyre types.
Radiator A liquid-to-air heat transfer device designed to reduce the temperature of the coolant in a liquid cooled engine.
Rake A feature of steering geometry - the angle of the steering head in relation to the vertical **(see illustration)**.

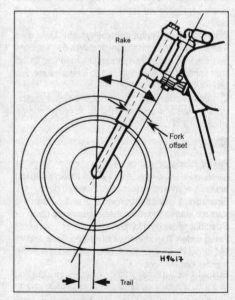

Steering geometry

Rebore Providing a new working surface to the cylinder bore by boring out the old surface. Necessitates the use of oversize piston and rings.

Rebound damping A means of controlling the oscillation of a suspension unit spring after it has been compressed. Resists the spring's natural tendency to bounce back after being compressed.

Rectifier Device for converting the ac output of an alternator into dc for battery charging.

Reed valve An induction system commonly used on two-stroke engines.

Regulator Device for maintaining the charging voltage from the generator or alternator within a specified range.

Relay A electrical device used to switch heavy current on and off by using a low current auxiliary circuit.

Resistance Measured in ohms. An electrical component's ability to pass electrical current.

RON (Research Octane Number) A measure of a fuel's resistance to knock.

rpm revolutions per minute.

Runout The amount of wobble (in-and-out movement) of a wheel or shaft as it's rotated. The amount a shaft rotates 'out-of-true'. The out-of-round condition of a rotating part.

S

SAE (Society of Automotive Engineers) A standard for the viscosity of a fluid.

Sealant A liquid or paste used to prevent leakage at a joint. Sometimes used in conjunction with a gasket.

Service limit Term for the point where a component is no longer useable and must be renewed.

Shaft drive A method of transmitting drive from the transmission to the rear wheel.

Shell bearings Plain bearings consisting of two shell halves. Most often used as big-end and main bearings in a four-stroke engine. Often called bearing inserts.

Shim Thin spacer, commonly used to adjust the clearance or relative positions between two parts. For example, shims inserted into or under tappets or followers to control valve clearances. Clearance is adjusted by changing the thickness of the shim.

Short-circuit An electrical condition where current shorts to earth (ground) bypassing the circuit components.

Skimming Process to correct warpage or repair a damaged surface, eg on brake discs or drums.

Slide-hammer A special puller that screws into or hooks onto a component such as a shaft or bearing; a heavy sliding handle on the shaft bottoms against the end of the shaft to knock the component free.

Small-end bearing The bearing in the upper end of the connecting rod at its joint with the gudgeon pin.

Spalling Damage to camshaft lobes or bearing journals shown as pitting of the working surface.

Specific gravity (SG) The state of charge of the electrolyte in a lead-acid battery. A measure of the electrolyte's density compared with water.

Straight-cut gears Common type gear used on gearbox shafts and for oil pump and water pump drives.

Stanchion The inner sliding part of the front forks, held by the yokes. Often called a fork tube.

Stoichiometric ratio The optimum chemical air/fuel ratio for a petrol engine, said to be 14.7 parts of air to 1 part of fuel.

Sulphuric acid The liquid (electrolyte) used in a lead-acid battery. Poisonous and extremely corrosive.

Surface grinding (lapping) Process to correct a warped gasket face, commonly used on cylinder heads.

T

Tapered-roller bearing Tapered inner race of caged needle rollers and separate tapered outer race. Examples of taper roller bearings can be found on steering heads.

Tappet A cylindrical component which transmits motion from the cam to the valve stem, either directly or via a pushrod and rocker arm. Also called a cam follower.

TCS Traction Control System. An electronically-controlled system which senses wheel spin and reduces engine speed accordingly.

TDC Top Dead Centre denotes that the piston is at its highest point in the cylinder.

Thread-locking compound Solution applied to fastener threads to prevent slackening. Select type to suit application.

Thrust washer A washer positioned between two moving components on a shaft. For example, between gear pinions on gearshaft.

Timing chain See **Cam Chain**.

Timing light Stroboscopic lamp for carrying out ignition timing checks with the engine running.

Top-end A description of an engine's cylinder block, head and valve gear components.

Torque Turning or twisting force about a shaft.

Torque setting A prescribed tightness specified by the motorcycle manufacturer to ensure that the bolt or nut is secured correctly. Undertightening can result in the bolt or nut coming loose or a surface not being sealed. Overtightening can result in stripped threads, distortion or damage to the component being retained.

Torx key A six-point wrench.

Tracer A stripe of a second colour applied to a wire insulator to distinguish that wire from another one with the same colour insulator. For example, Br/W is often used to denote a brown insulator with a white tracer.

Trail A feature of steering geometry. Distance from the steering head axis to the tyre's central contact point.

Triple clamps The cast components which extend from the steering head and support the fork stanchions or tubes. Often called fork yokes.

Turbocharger A centrifugal device, driven by exhaust gases, that pressurises the intake air. Normally used to increase the power output from a given engine displacement.

TWI Abbreviation for Tyre Wear Indicator. Indicates the location of the tread depth indicator bars on tyres.

U

Universal joint or U-joint (UJ) A double-pivoted connection for transmitting power from a driving to a driven shaft through an angle. Typically found in shaft drive assemblies.

Unsprung weight Anything not supported by the bike's suspension (ie the wheel, tyres, brakes, final drive and bottom (moving) part of the suspension).

V

Vacuum gauges Clock-type gauges for measuring intake tract vacuum. Used for carburettor synchronisation on multi-cylinder engines.

Valve A device through which the flow of liquid, gas or vacuum may be stopped, started or regulated by a moveable part that opens, shuts or partially obstructs one or more ports or passageways. The intake and exhaust valves in the cylinder head are of the poppet type.

Valve clearance The clearance between the valve tip (the end of the valve stem) and the rocker arm or tappet/follower. The valve clearance is measured when the valve is closed. The correct clearance is important - if too small the valve won't close fully and will burn out, whereas if too large noisy operation will result.

Valve lift The amount a valve is lifted off its seat by the camshaft lobe.

Valve timing The exact setting for the opening and closing of the valves in relation to piston position.

Vernier caliper A precision measuring instrument that measures inside and outside dimensions. Not quite as accurate as a micrometer, but more convenient.

Wet liner arrangement

VIN Vehicle Identification Number. Term for the bike's engine and frame numbers.

Viscosity The thickness of a liquid or its resistance to flow.

Volt A unit for expressing electrical "pressure" in a circuit. Volts = current x ohms.

W

Water pump A mechanically-driven device for moving coolant around the engine.

Watt A unit for expressing electrical power. Watts = volts x current.

Wear limit see **Service limit**

Wet liner A liquid-cooled engine design where the pistons run in liners which are directly surrounded by coolant (see illustration).

Wheelbase Distance from the centre of the front wheel to the centre of the rear wheel.

Wiring harness or loom Describes the electrical wires running the length of the motorcycle and enclosed in tape or plastic sheathing. Wiring coming off the main harness is usually referred to as a sub harness.

Woodruff key A key of semi-circular or square section used to locate a gear to a shaft. Often used to locate the alternator rotor on the crankshaft.

Wrist pin Another name for gudgeon or piston pin.

Note: *References throughout this index are in the form - "Chapter number" • "Page number"*

Note: *References throughout this index are in the form - "Chapter number" • "Page number"*

Note: *References throughout this index are in the form - "Chapter number" • "Page number"*

Haynes Motorcycle Manuals – The Complete List

Title		Book No
APRILIA RS50 (99 – 06) & RS125 (93 – 06)		4298
Aprilia RSV1000 Mille (98 – 03)	♦	4255
Aprilia SR50		4755
BMW 2-valve Twins (70 -96)	♦	0249
BMW F650	♦	4761
BMW K100 & 75 2-valve models (83 - 96)	♦	1373
BMW F800 (F650) Twins (06 – 10)	♦	4872
BMW R850, 1100 & 1150 4-valve Twins (93 – 06)	♦	3466
BMW R1200 (04 – 09)	♦	4598
BMW R1200 dohc Twins (10 – 12)	♦	4925
BSA Bantam (48 – 71)		0117
BSA Unit Singles (58 – 72)		0127
BSA Pre-unit Singles (54 – 61)		0326
BSA A7 & A10 Twins (47 – 62)		0121
BSA A50 & A65 Twins (62 – 73)		0155
CHINESE, Taiwanese & Korean Scooters		4768
Chinese, Taiwanese & Korean 125cc motorcyles		4781
DUCATI 600, 620, 750 & 900 2-valve V-twins (91 – 05)	♦	3290
Ducati Mk III & Desmo singles (69 – 76)	◇	0445
Ducati 748, 916 & 996 4-valve V-twins (94 – 01)	♦	3756
GILERA Runner, DNA, Ice & SKP/Stalker (97 – 11)		4163
HARLEY-DAVIDSON Sportsters (70 – 10)	♦	2534
Harley-Davidson Shovelhead & Evolution Big Twins (70 -99)	♦	2536
Harley-Davidson Twin Cam 88, 96 & 103 models (99 – 10)	♦	2478
HONDA NB, ND, NP & NS50 Melody (81 -85)	◇	0622
Honda NE/NB50 Vision & SA50 Vision Met-in (85-95)	◇	1278
Honda MB, MBX, MT & MTX50 (80 – 93)		0731
Honda C50, C70 & C90 (67 – 03)		0324
Honda XR50/70/80/100R & CRF50/70/80/100F (85 – 07)		2218
Honda XL/XR 80, 100, 125, 185 & 200 2-valve models (78 – 87)		0566
Honda H100 & H100S Singles (80 – 92)	◇	0734
Honda 125 Scooters (00 – 09)		4873
Honda ANF125 Innova Scooters (03 -12)	♦	4926
Honda CB/CD125T & CM125C Twins (77 – 88)	◇	0571
Honda CBF125 (09 – 12)	♦	5540
Honda CG125 (76 – 07)	◇	0433
Honda NS125 (86 – 93)	◇	3056
Honda CBR125R (04 – 10)		4620
Honda MBX/MTX125 & MTX200 (83 – 93)	◇	1132
Honda XL125V & VT125C (99 – 11)		4899
Honda CD/CM185 200T & CM250C 2-valve Twins (77 – 85)		0572
Honda CMX250 Rebel & CB250 Nighthawk Twins (85 – 09)	◇	2756
Honda XL/XR 250 & 500 (78 – 84)		0567
Honda XR250L, XR250R & XR400R (86 – 03)		2219
Honda CB250 & CB400N Super Dreams (78 – 84)	◇	0540
Honda CR Motocross Bikes (86 – 07)		2222
Honda CRF250 & CRF450 (02 – 06)		2630
Honda CBR400RR Fours (88 – 99)	◇♦	3552
Honda VFR400 (NC30) & RVF400 (NC35) V-Fours (89 – 98)	◇♦	3496
Honda CB500 (93 – 02) & CBF500 (03 – 08)	◇	3753
Honda CB400 & CB550 Fours (73 – 77)		0262
Honda CX/GL500 & 650 V-Twins (78 – 86)		0442
Honda CBX550 Four (82 – 86)	◇	0940
Honda XL600R & XR600R (83 – 08)	♦	2183
Honda XL600/650V Transalp & XRV750 Africa Twin (87 – 07)	♦	3919
Honda CB600 Hornet, CBF600 & CBR600F (07 – 12)	♦	5572
Honda CBR600F1 & 1000F Fours (87 – 96)	♦	1730
Honda CBR600F2 & F3 Fours (91 – 98)	♦	2070
Honda CBR600F4 (99 – 06)	♦	3911
Honda CB600F Hornet & CBF600 (98 – 06)	◇♦	3915
Honda CBR600RR (03 – 06)	♦	4590
Honda CBR600RR (07 -12)	♦	4795
Honda CB650 sohc Fours (78 – 84)		0665
Honda NTV600 Revere, NTV650 & NT650V Deauville (88 – 05)	◇♦	3243
Honda Shadow VT600 & 750 (USA) (88 – 09)		2312
Honda NT700V Deauville & XL700V Transalp (06 -13)	♦	5541
Honda CB750 sohc Four (69 – 79)		0131
Honda V45/65 Sabre & Magna (82 – 88)		0820
Honda VFR750 & 700 V-Fours (86 – 97)	♦	2101
Honda VFR800 V-Fours (97 – 01)	♦	3703
Honda VFR800 V-Tec V-Fours (02 – 09)	♦	4196
Honda CB750 & CB900 dohc Fours (78 – 84)		0535
Honda CBF1000 (06 -10) & CB1000R (08 – 11)	♦	4927
Honda VTR1000 Firestorm, Super Hawk & XL1000V Varadero (97 – 08)	♦	3744
Honda CBR900RR Fireblade (92 – 99)	♦	2161
Honda CBR900RR Fireblade (00 – 03)	♦	4060
Honda CBR1000RR Fireblade (04 – 07)	♦	4604
Honda CBR1100XX Super Blackbird (97 – 07)	♦	3901
Honda ST1100 Pan European V-Fours (90 – 02)	♦	3384
Honda ST1300 Pan European (02 -11)	♦	4908
Honda Shadow VT1100 (USA) (85 – 07)		2313
Honda GL1000 Gold Wing (75 – 79)		0309
Honda GL1100 Gold Wing (79 – 81)		0669
Honda Gold Wing 1200 (USA) (84 - 87)		2199
Honda Gold Wing 1500 (USA) (88 – 00)		2225
Honda Goldwing GL1800	♦	2787
KAWASAKI AE/AR 50 & 80 (81 – 95)		1007
Kawasaki KC, KE & KH100 (75 – 99)		1371
Kawasaki KMX125 & 200 (86 – 02)	◇	3046
Kawasaki 250, 350 & 400 Triples (72 – 79)		0134
Kawasaki 400 & 440 Twins (74 – 81)		0281
Kawasaki 400, 500 & 550 Fours (79 – 91)		0910
Kawasaki EN450 & 500 Twins (Ltd/Vulcan) (85 – 07)		2053
Kawasaki ER-6F & ER-6N (06 -10)	♦	4874
Kawasaki EX500 (GPZ500S) & ER500 (ER-5) (87 – 08)	♦	2052
Kawasaki ZX600 (ZZ-R600 & Ninja ZX-6) (90 – 06)	♦	2146
Kawasaki ZX-6R Ninja Fours (95 – 02)	♦	3451
Kawasaki ZX-6R (03 – 06)	♦	4742
Kawasaki ZX600 (GPZ600R, GPX600R, Ninja 600R & RX) & ZX750 (GPX750R, Ninja 750R) (85 – 97)	♦	1780
Kawasaki 650 Four (76 – 78)		0373
Kawasaki Vulcan 700/750 & 800 (85 – 04)	♦	2457
Kawasaki Vulcan 1500 & 1600 (87 – 08)	♦	4913
Kawasaki 750 Air-cooled Fours		0574
Kawasaki ZR550 & 750 Zephyr Fours (90 – 97)	♦	3382
Kawasaki Z750 & Z1000 (03 – 08)	♦	4762
Kawasaki ZX750 (Ninja ZX-7 & ZXR750) Fours (89 – 96)	♦	2054
Kawasaki Ninja ZX-7R & ZX-9R (94 – 04)	♦	3721
Kawasaki 900 & 1000 Fours (73 – 77)		0222
Kawasaki ZX900, 1000 & 1100 Liquid-cooled Fours (83 – 97)	♦	1681
KTM EXC Enduro & SX Motocross (00 – 07)	♦	4629
LAMBRETTA Scooters (58 – 00)	♦	5573
MOTO GUZZI 750, 850 & 1000 V-Twins (74 – 78)		0339
MZ ETZ models (81 – 95)	◇	1680
NORTON 500, 600, 650 & 750 Twins (57 – 70)		0187
Norton Commando (68 – 77)		0125
PEUGEOT Speedfight, Trekker & Vivacity Scooters (96 – 08)	◇	3920
PIAGGIO (Vespa) Scooters (91 – 09)	◇	3492
SUZUKI GT, ZR & TS50 (77 – 90)	◇	0799
Suzuki TS50X (84 – 00)	◇	1599
Suzuki 100, 125, 185 & 250 Air-cooled Trail bikes (79 – 89)		0797
Suzuki GP100 & 125 Singles (78 – 93)	◇	0576
Suzuki GS, GN, GZ & DR125 Singles (82 – 05)	◇	0888
Suzuki Burgman 250 & 400 (98 – 11)	♦	4909
Suzuki GSX-R600/750 (06 – 09)	♦	4790
Suzuki 250 & 350 Twins (68 – 78)		0120
Suzuki GT250X7, GT200X5 & SB200 Twins (78 – 83)	◇	0469
Suzuki DR-Z400 (00 – 10)	◇	2933
Suzuki GS/GSX250, 400 & 450 Twins (79 – 85)		0736
Suzuki GS500 Twin (89 – 08)	♦	3238
Suzuki GS550 (77 – 82) & GS750 Fours (76 – 79)		0363
Suzuki GS/GSX550 4-valve Fours (83 – 88)		1133
Suzuki SV650 & SV650S (99 – 08)	♦	3912
Suzuki GSX-R600 & 750 (96 – 00)	♦	3553
Suzuki GSX-R600 (01 – 03), GSX-R750 (00 – 03) & GSX-R1000 (01 – 02)	♦	3986
Suzuki GSX-R600/750 (04 – 05) & GSX-R1000 (03 – 06)	♦	4382
Suzuki GSF600, 650 & 1200 Bandit Fours (95 – 06)	♦	3367
Suzuki Intruder, Marauder, Volusia & Boulevard (85 – 09)	♦	2618
Suzuki GS850 Fours (78 – 88)		0536
Suzuki GS1000 Four (77 – 79)		0484
Suzuki GSX-R750, GSX-R1100 (85 – 92) GSX600F, GSX750F, GSX1100F (Katana) Fours (88 – 96)	♦	2055
Suzuki GSX600/750F & GSX750 (98 – 02)	♦	3987
Suzuki GS/GSX1000, 1100 & 1150 4-valve Fours (79 – 88)		0737
Suzuki TL1000S/R & DL V-Strom (97 – 04)	♦	4083
Suzuki GSF650/1250 (07 – 09)	♦	4798
Suzuki GSX1300R Hayabusa (99 – 04)	♦	4184
Suzuki GSX1400 (02 – 08)	♦	4758
TRIUMPH Tiger Cub & Terrier (52 – 68)		0414
Triumph 350 & 500 Unit Twins (58 – 73)		0137
Triumph Pre-Unit Twins (47 – 62)		0251
Triumph 650 & 750 2-valve Unit Twins (63 – 83)		0122
Triumph 675 (06 – 10)	♦	4876
Triumph 1050 Sprint, Speed Triple & Tiger (05 -13)	♦	4796
Triumph Trident & BSA Rocket 3 (69 – 75)		0136
Triumph Bonneville (01 – 12)	♦	4364
Triumph Daytona, Speed Triple, Sprint & Tiger (97 – 05)	♦	3755
Triumph Triples & Fours (carburetor engines) (91 – 04)	♦	2162
VESPA P/PX125, 150 & 200 Scooters (78 – 12)		0707
Vespa GTS125, 250 & 300 (05 – 10)		4898
Vespa Scooters (59 – 78)		0126
YAMAHA DT50 & 80 Trail Bikes (78 – 95)	◇	0800
Yamaha T50 & 80 Townmate (83 – 95)	◇	1247
Yamaha YB100 Singles (73 – 91)	◇	0474
Yamaha RS/RXS 100 & 125 Singles (74 – 95)		0331
Yamaha RD & DT125LC (82 – 87)	◇	0887
Yamaha TZR125 (87 – 93) & DT125R (88 – 07)	◇	1655
Yamaha TY50, 80, 125 & 175 (74 – 84)	◇	0464
Yamaha XT & SR125 (82 – 03)	◇	1021
Yamaha YBR125 & XT125R/X (05 – 13)		4797
Yamaha YZF-R125 (08 – 11)	♦	5543
Yamaha Trail Bikes (81 – 00)		2350
Yamaha 2-stroke Motocross Bikes (86 – 06)		2662
Yamaha YZ & WR 4-stroke Motorcross Bikes (98 – 08)		2689
Yamaha 250 & 350 Twins (70 – 79)		0040
Yamaha XS250, 360 & 400 sohc Twins (75 – 84)		0378
Yamaha RD250 & 350LC Twins (80 – 82)		0803
Yamaha RD350 YPVS Twins (83 – 95)		1158
Yamaha RD400 Twin (75 – 79)		0333
Yamaha XT, TT & SR500 Singles (75 – 83)		0342
Yamaha XZ550 Vision V-Twins (82 – 85)		0821
Yamaha FJ, FX, XY & YX600 Radian (84 – 92)		2100
Yamaha XT660 & MT-03 (04 – 11)	♦	4910
Yamaha XJ600S (Diversion, Seca II) & XJ600N Fours (92 – 03)	♦	2145
Yamaha YZF600R Thundercat & FZS600 Fazer (96 – 03)	♦	3702
Yamaha FZ-6 Fazer (04 – 08)	♦	4751
Yamaha YZF-R6 (99 – 02)	♦	3900
Yamaha YZF-R6 (03 – 05)	♦	4601
Yamaha YZF-R6 (06 – 13)	♦	5544
Yamaha 650 Twins (70 – 83)		0341
Yamaha XJ650 & 750 Fours (80 – 84)		0738
Yamaha XS750 & 850 Triples (76 – 85)		0340
Yamaha TDM850, TRX850 & XTZ750 (89 – 99)	◇♦	3450
Yamaha YZF750R & YZF1000R Thunderace (93 – 00)	♦	3720
Yamaha FZR600, 750 & 1000 Fours (87 – 96)	♦	2056
Yamaha XV (Virago) V-Twins (81 – 03)	♦	0802
Yamaha XVS650 & 1100 Drag Star/V-Star (97 – 05)	♦	4195
Yamaha XJ900F Fours (83 – 94)	♦	3239
Yamaha XJ900S Diversion (94 – 01)	♦	3739
Yamaha YZF-R1 (98 – 03)	♦	3754
Yamaha YZF-R1 (04 – 06)	♦	4605
Yamaha FZS1000 Fazer (01 – 05)	♦	4287
Yamaha FJ1100 & 1200 Fours (84 – 96)	♦	2057
Yamaha XJR1200 & 1300 (95 – 06)	♦	3981
Yamaha V-Max (85 – 03)	♦	4072
ATV's		
Honda ATC 70, 90, 110, 185 & 200 (71 – on)		0565
Honda Rancher, Recon & TRX250EX ATVs		2553
Honda TRX300 Shaft Drive ATVs (88 – 00)		2125
Honda Foreman (95 – 11)		2465
Honda TRX300EX, TRX400EX & TRX450R/ER ATVs (93 – 06)		2318
Kawasaki Bayou 220/250/300 & Prairie 300 ATVs (86 – 03)		2351
Polaris ATVs (85 – 97)		2302
Polaris ATVs (98 – 07)		2508
Suzuki/Kawasaki/Artic Cat ATVs (03 – 09)		2910
Yamaha YFS200 Blaster ATV (88 – 06)		2317
Yamaha YFM350 & YFM400 (ER & Big Bear) ATVs (87 – 09)		2126
Yamaha YFZ450 & YFZ450R (04 – 10)		2899
Yamaha Banshee and Warrior ATVs (87 – 10)		2314
Yamaha Kodiak and Grizzly ATVs (93 – 05)		2567
ATV Basics		10450
TECHBOOK SERIES		
Twist and Go (automatic transmission) Scooters Service and Repair Manual		4082
Motorcycle Basics Techbook (2nd edition)		3515
Motorcycle Electrical Techbook (3rd edition)		3471
Motorcycle Fuel Systems Techbook		3514
Motorcycle Maintenance Techbook		4071
Motorcycle Modifying		4272
Motorcycle Workshop Practice Techbook (2nd edition)		3470

◇ = not available in the USA ♦ = Superbike

The manuals on this page are available through good motorcycle dealers and accessory shops.
In case of difficulty, contact: **Haynes Publishing**
(UK) **+44 1963 442030** (USA) **+1 805 498 6703**
(SV) **+46 18 124016**
(Australia/New Zealand) **+61 2 8713 1400**

Preserving Our Motoring Heritage

< The Model J Duesenberg Derham Tourster. Only eight of these magnificent cars were ever built – this is the only example to be found outside the United States of America

Almost every car you've ever loved, loathed or desired is gathered under one roof at the Haynes Motor Museum. Over 300 immaculately presented cars and motorbikes represent every aspect of our motoring heritage, from elegant reminders of bygone days, such as the superb Model J Duesenberg to curiosities like the bug-eyed BMW Isetta. There are also many old friends and flames. Perhaps you remember the 1959 Ford Popular that you did your courting in? The magnificent 'Red Collection' is a spectacle of classic sports cars including AC, Alfa Romeo, Austin Healey, Ferrari, Lamborghini, Maserati, MG, Riley, Porsche and Triumph.

A Perfect Day Out

Each and every vehicle at the Haynes Motor Museum has played its part in the history and culture of Motoring. Today, they make a wonderful spectacle and a great day out for all the family. Bring the kids, bring Mum and Dad, but above all bring your camera to capture those golden memories for ever. You will also find an impressive array of motoring memorabilia, a comfortable 70 seat video cinema and one of the most extensive transport book shops in Britain. The Pit Stop Cafe serves everything from a cup of tea to wholesome, home-made meals or, if you prefer, you can enjoy the large picnic area nestled in the beautiful rural surroundings of Somerset.

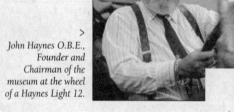

John Haynes O.B.E., Founder and Chairman of the museum at the wheel of a Haynes Light 12. >

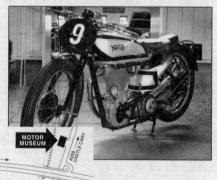

< The 1936 490cc sohc-engined International Norton – well known for its racing success

The Museum is situated on the A359 Yeovil to Frome road at Sparkford, just off the A303 in Somerset. It is about 40 miles south of Bristol, and 25 minutes drive from the M5 intersection at Taunton.
Open 9.30am - 5.30pm (10.00am - 4.00pm Winter) 7 days a week, *except Christmas Day, Boxing Day and New Years Day*
Special rates available for schools, coach parties and outings Charitable Trust No. 292048